Y0-DJO-675

THE INSIDERS' GUIDE® TO

Virginia's Blue Ridge

INCLUDING THE SHENANDOAH VALLEY

by
Margaret Camlin
and
Lin Chaff

Richmond Times-Dispatch

9 780912 367460

Co-published and marketed by:
Richmond Newspapers, Inc.
333 East Grace St.
Richmond, VA 23219
(804) 649-6000

•

Co-published and distributed by:
The Insiders' Guides®, Inc.
P.O. Box 2057 • Highway 64
Manteo, NC 27954
(919) 473-6100

•

SECOND EDITION
1st printing

•

Copyright ©1993
by Richmond Newspapers, Inc.

•

Printed in the United States
of America

•

All rights reserved. No part of this
book may be reproduced in any
form without permission, in writing,
from the publisher, except by a
reviewer who wishes to quote brief
passages in connection with a review
in a magazine or newspaper.

•

ISBN 0-912367-49-0

Richmond Newspapers, Inc.
Supplemental Publications

Director, Marketing Development
Robert J Bowerman

Manager
Ernie Chenault

Account Executives
**Heidi Crandall, Peg Lewis, Adair
Frayser Roper, John Wade**

Project Coordination
Bonnie Widener

Artists
**Susan Doyle, Nerina Lakenda
North, Ronnie Johnson, Sean
Contreras, Chris Novelli**

The Insiders' Guides®, Inc.

Publisher/Managing Editor
Beth P Storie

President/General Manager
Michael McOwen

Project Manager
Sue Maloney

Manager/Creative Services
David Haynes

Manager/Distribution
Giles Bissonnette

Editorial Assistant
Georgia Beach

Fulfillment Coordination
Gina Twiford

Controller
Claudette Forney

Preface

Welcome to our favorite place.

Many Americans still long for a simpler way of life in smaller towns. This is where they find it, trading in business suits for blue jeans. It's a privilege to live in the Blue Ridge of Virginia, pure and simple. Every day is a feast for the senses. And at night, you can drift off to sleep knowing that if your environment can impact upon your sense of well-being, you are one of the luckiest - - and happiest – people around.

This is the nostalgic land of Earl Hamner's John-Boy and the Walton family. You can still find lots of general stores like Uncle Ike's. You can still find clucking, blue-haired ladies preparing banana pudding and fried chicken for Sunday School picnics in the country, and small congregations worshipping in white, clapboard chapels. You can still find the strong family values that compel generations of extended families to all live down the same country lane. You'll find neighbors who mind their own business but are ever willing to lend a helping hand.

Welcome to a place where people still wave to strangers on back country roads; where our children and the family dog still swim with patched innertubes in pristine creeks under covered bridges. Welcome to life in the slow lane, with the same benefits, but few of the hassles, as life in the fast lane.

For sheer beauty and tranquility, nothing equals the Blue Ridge of Virginia's mountains, flora, fauna, rivers and lakes. We're a rhapsody of riotous bursts of yellow fuchsia and redbuds in the spring. We're a sonnet of sunny meadows with hovering hummingbirds and singing songbirds in the summer. We're a painter's palette of colors in the autumn. We're an aria to the simple setting of the first Christmas as we celebrate with hand-picked wreaths and the tree we just cut out back, on the snow-covered mountain.

We revere our environment, realizing a covenant with the land. We pull our cars off our highways to watch as the sun goes down and are filled with a sense of awe that a pinpoint of light bursting through a cloud can make a mountain appear to be wrapped in red velvet.

Ours is a land of great dynamics. We are inventors, like Cyrus McCormick, whose Shenandoah Valley mechanical reaper revolutionized the world. We are the land of Thomas Jefferson, the quintessential Renaissance man, who invented not only the concept of democracy in America, but also the dumb waiter, the original mimeograph and the brave art of eating the "love tomatoe." We are the land of robots and fiber optics in Roanoke, smart road technology in the New River Valley and solar-powered Sirius Earthship homes in Floyd County.

We are a land of great leaders. On our Natural Bridge, George Washington left his initials and then stayed to later bail Washington & Lee University out of impending bankruptcy. Our's is a land where Robert E. Lee led our troops to great valor and honor during a four-year Civil War that was supposed to last just a few weeks. Our Shenandoah Valley is where Stonewall Jackson exasperated his students at the Virginia Military Institute with his toughness and humorlessness then went on to create a legend in military strategy that is still taught by U.S. military leaders today.

We are a land that reveres its history and honors its dead. We preserve our crumbling cemeteries and battlefields as hallowed ground. We build museums in the tiniest of communities as we welcome at least half a million people a year to Monticello and Montpelier in Charlottesville. We build monuments to every Civil War battle ever fought, and museums to honor our fallen soldiers.

We are a land of great scholarship and creativity, where the slave Booker T. Washington grew up in Franklin County to become one of the great African American thinkers and leaders of all time. Here the great Harlem Renaissance poet, Anne Spencer, entertained Martin Luther King, Congressman Adam Clayton Powell, Justice Thurgood Marshall and singers Paul Robeson and Marion Anderson at her Lynchburg garden home.

This is also a land of enormous, diverse culture. We flat-foot on Friday nights in the Alleghany Highlands. We go to car drive-in movies and eat buttered popcorn in Rockbridge County while celebrities fly in from around the world to see our American Film Festival in nearby Charlottesville. We provide one of the largest residential colonies in the world for international artists and writers to stir their creative juices in Amherst County, near Lynchburg. At our colleges and cities, we display works of art and crafts equal to any.

We're a big playground where you can camp, hike, bike, canoe, golf, boat, swim, horseback ride, hunt, fish, hang-glide and soar until you drop!

We're a land of festivity, looking for excuses to celebrate. We stage festivals to honor everything from apples, strawberries, garlic, dogwoods, ramps, wine and maple sugar to folklife and railroads.

This is also a land of superlatives. No matter which region of the Blue Ridge you visit, you'll find "the biggest," "the oldest," "the most important," or "nationally-known," and "internationally-acclaimed." Every region is a gem of multi-faceted culture, like precious stones on a necklace, the common thread being the beauty of the Blue Ridge and our vast quality of life.

We are Charlottesville, land of Jeffersonian mystique and international chic. We are Staunton, heart of the Blue Ridge with our famous July Fourth picnics in Gypsy Hill, where your hosts, the world-famous Statler Brothers, come home every summer to celebrate with their friends. We are Harrisonburg, with fields of golden, waving grain and hills white with turkeys, and Roanoke, Capital of the Blue Ridge, the largest metropolitan area off the Blue Ridge Parkway, voted by travel writers as the most beautiful road in the world. We are the intellectually stimulating New River Valley, home to gigantic Virginia Tech, as well as a tie-dyed counterculture that came to Floyd County and never left the 60s. We're the staid German Baptists at Smith Mountain Lake, the playground of western Virginia, and we still hunt for the cryptic, elusive Beale Treasure in nearby Bedford County. We're Jerry Falwell and the Moral Majority in Lynchburg, the home of one of the largest churches in America. We're the residents of the pastoral Alleghany Highlands, where the sheep outnumber the human population and life is as slow and sweet as the maple sugar that trickles down the trees in the

spring.

Welcome to our favorite place. Everywhere you travel, you'll find beauty that stops you in your tracks, people who are courteous, trusting and kind and the opportunity to be transformed by the goodness of your environment.

Visit with us awhile. Rock on our wide front porches and sit a spell. Join us in our favorite pastime of watching the setting sun go down over the Blue Ridge of Virginia. Have some peach cobbler and Virginia-made wine to settle you for the night. And when the stars blanket the Blue Ridge of Virginia, pack away your worries and tough times and mount a carousel horse (you can buy one in Newbern!) to ride through your dreams. Now, say good night to John-Boy Walton and the rest of the family. Dream of waking up to the warmth and promise of Blue Ridge sunshine and the goodness it will bring.

Good night, John-Boy.
Good night.

Acknowledgements

Margaret wishes to thank Andy Dawson, Executive Director of the Shenandoah Valley Travel Association; Ruth Deskins, Manager of the Harrisonburg Convention and Visitors Bureau; Kitty Zuckerman, director of the Winchester Visitors Center; Terri Higgins and Susan Abramson at the *Winchester Star*; Gary Rutherford, manager of Hotel Strasburg; Eleanor Schwartz, co-owner of Edgewood Farm Bed and Breakfast; Steve Walker, past president of the Virginia Foothills Association; Pete Holladay, president of the Bed and Breakfast Association of Virginia and owner of Holladay House in Orange; Bruce Herndon of Herndon Real Estate in Orange; Art Pierson, president of the Charlottesville Area Association of Realtors; Daphne Hutchinson, a Rappahannock County writer; Susan DeAlba, a Charlottesville writer and historian; Barbara Cochran, director of the Charlottesville/Albemarle Convention and Visitors Bureau; Candace Wilson of the 1817 Antique Inn in Charlottesville; Ida Lee Wooten of the University of Virginia News Office; Kate Andrews, deputy director of the Piedmont Council on the Arts; Pam Humbert, head of the Orange County Visitors Center; Martha Doss and her staff at the Lexington Visitors Bureau, and last, but certainly not least, Lin Chaff Public Relations and Advertising.

Lin wishes to acknowledge Chuck Crow, Smith Mountain Lake

Partnership; Andy Dawson, Shenandoah Valley Travel Association; Martha Doss, Lexington Visitors Center; Sergei Troubetzkoy, City of Staunton Department of Economic Development and Tourism; Stevie Dovel, Lynchburg Convention & Visitors Bureau; Nita Echols, the *Vinton Messenger*; Kitty Ward Grady, Town of Wytheville; Larry Hincker, Virginia Tech University Relations; Helen Looney, Craig County Historical Society; Martha Mackey, Catherine Fox and the entire staff, Roanoke Valley Convention and Visitors Bureau; Ned McElwaine and Donna Johnson, Botetourt County; Russ Merritt, Franklin County Chamber of Commerce; Franklyn Moreno, New River Valley Economic Development Alliance; Anne Piedmont, Roanoke Valley of Virginia Economic Development Partnership; Barbara Ring, Bedford County Chamber of Commerce; Tracy Roberts, Lin Chaff Public Relations and Advertising; Prof. James Robertson, Virginia Tech; John Strutner and Martha Steger, Department of Economic Development, State of Virginia; Gary G. Walker, Civil War expert on Southwestern Virginia; Michelle Wright, Alleghany Highlands Chamber of Commerce; the New River Valley Hosts; the directors of the 14 Southwestern Virginia counties' Chambers and Economic Development groups; and a host of others who firmly believe the Blue Ridge of Virginia is the most beautiful, special place on earth.

This book is dedicated to the all-encompassing beauty of both the land and the spirit of the people who are fortunate enough to live and work in the Blue Ridge of Virginia.

About The Authors

Margaret Camlin, a native of South Carolina, came to the Blue Ridge region in early 1988 to work for *The Winchester Star* after earning a master's degree in journalism from the University of Wisconsin at Madison.

The next year she married and became an education writer for the *Roanoke Times & World-News* ' New River Valley Bureau.

She is currently a free lance writer. During the period of writing this book, she lived near Lexington with her husband, Fritz Ritsch, and her baby girl, Sara Caitlin, and enjoyed a magnificent view of the Blue Ridge mountains from their front porch.

Camlin received her undergraduate degree from the College of William & Mary in 1980. She won a first-place award from the Virginia Press Association for in-depth/investigative reporting in 1989. Her articles have appeared in *Mid-Atlantic Country, Virginia, Episcopal Life, Iris-A Journal About Women* and several newspapers.

She thanks her husband for his patience and support during the many months of this project and her baby for keeping her laughing.

Lin D. Chaff arrived in Blacksburg, fresh out of West Virginia University in 1972, as the editor of the *Blacksburg Sun*. While there, she fell in love with the Blue Ridge of Virginia and ever since has made it her life's mission to live and work there, taking time out to earn a graduate journalism degree at Northwestern University.

Before moving back in 1978, to join the staff of the *Roanoke Times* as a reporter in the New River Valley Bureau, she worked for the Gannett newspapers, Associated Press, and on Capitol Hill and received a string of journalism awards.

After the birth of her first daughter, she became manager of publicity for Dominion Bankshares Corp. (now First Union) in Roanoke. After the birth of her second daughter, she started her own public relations, marketing and advertising firm, in part, to promote tourism in western Virginia. The firm's work has been honored by Virginia's premier Public Relations Society of America competition.

Chaff belongs to numerous tourism marketing groups including the Blue Ridge Commission's Marketing Committee, and is accredited by PRSA. She thanks her husband, John Wade, and her daughters, Elizabeth and Priscilla, for their patience, support and shared enthusiasm for this labor of love.

Table of Contents

PREFACE ·· v
ACKNOWLEDGEMENTS ·· VIII
ABOUT THE AUTHORS ·· X
TABLE OF CONTENTS ·· XI
HOW TO USE THIS BOOK ·· 1
CITIES AND TOWNS OVERVIEWS ··· 9
THE CIVIL WAR ·· 85
THE BLUE RIDGE PARKWAY AND SKYLINE DRIVE ·· 101
RECREATION ·· 111
SKIING ·· 141
WINERIES ··· 149
OTHER ATTRACTIONS ·· 161
ANNUAL EVENTS ·· 177
ARTS AND CULTURE ·· 199
SHOPPING ··· 261
RESORTS ·· 297
BED AND BREAKFASTS ··· 313
OTHER ACCOMMODATIONS ·· 361
RESTAURANTS ·· 385
NIGHT LIFE ·· 431
REAL ESTATE ·· 437
RETIREMENT ··· 453
AIRPORTS AND BUS LINES ·· 469
HOSPITALS ·· 476
EDUCATION ··· 483
SOUTHWESTERN VIRGINIA ··· 495
INSIDERS' GUIDES® ORDER FORM ··· 526
INDEX OF ADVERTISERS ·· 527
INDEX ··· 529

Directory of Maps

OVERVIEW ·· 3
SHENANDOAH VALLEY ··· 4
EAST OF THE BLUE RIDGE ·· 5
NEW RIVER VALLEY ·· 6
ALLEGHANY HIGHLANDS ··· 7
SOUTHWESTERN VIRGINIA ··· 497

How to Use This Book

When we decided to produce an Insiders' Guide® to the Blue Ridge, the most time-consuming discussions went into figuring out just how to present the material on such a large geographic area in a sensible and accessible way. It wasn't easy! If you are already familiar with this region, you'll sympathize with us... from, roughly, Winchester down through the New River Valley then over to the Alleghany Highlands and far Southwest areas of Virginia, a lot of ground is covered, with so much to do and see in between that we hardly knew where to start recommending! But, we think we've produced a guide that will make you feel like a true "insider" and one that is organized in such a way that you can easily find what you're looking for.

The basic organizing principle in this guide is that each chapter is presented geographically, in regional segments, from north to south and east to west. The regional segments we've defined are the Shenandoah Valley, East of the Blue Ridge (also sometimes referred to as "the foothills"), the New River Valley and the Alleghany Highlands. So, each chapter starts with a regional header to orient you, then information about towns and cities in that region, with the overall geographic "traffic pattern" starting from the top of the Blue Ridge area

then flowing south, zigzagging back and forth from east to west.

We begin the book by introducing, in a general way, the four main regions of the Blue Ridge, as noted above, and their cities and towns. Then, sections on such topics as Civil War sites, restaurants and accommodations follow, using the same geographical framework. In other words, if you're interested in visiting a winery that's located in the Shenandoah Valley, you look under the Valley heading in the Wineries chapter. The same rule applies with health care, retirement, night spots, shopping, annual events and most all the other topics we cover.

One exception to this organization is the chapter on the Shenandoah National Park's Skyline Drive and the Blue Ridge Parkway. Here, we let you know where you can eat and spend the night without departing from the two connecting mountaintop highways.

Some special chapters like restaurants or arts and culture will describe all the best restaurants or museums, galleries, dance groups, etc. in a given city in alphabetical order, but again the city falls under its region. In other chapters, such as shopping, we let you know about all the good stores in a given neighborhood or shopping center in every major city or town. But you still need to look first for the major region, i.e., the Shenandoah Valley. Then, under the Shenandoah Valley headline, you look under Lexington for a description of all the neat little boutiques and shops in its historic downtown district.

At the end of the book, we provide you with a comprehensive look at the area known as the Far Southwest. This huge region, falling to the south and west of the New River Valley and including towns such as Marion, Wytheville and the vast Jefferson National Forest, is made up of 14 counties, all unique and interesting in their own right.

We've included maps to help you and it's a good idea if you aren't already familiar with this area to spend some time studying them before you dive into the book, just so you'll be better oriented. They will help you understand, visually,

how the regions are divided and what towns and cities belong in each one.

This is not meant to be the kind of guide that you must read from beginning to end to reap the benefit of buying it. But we do recommend that you start out by reading our introductions to each region of the Blue Ridge; these will give you a flavor for what the areas have to offer, what makes our cities, towns and little hamlets unique and worth visiting.

We hope you have a good time exploring both this guide and the beautiful Blue Ridge area. Let us know what you think of the book, its organization and helpfulness. We really want your input. Write us at:

The Insiders' Guides®, Inc.
P.O. Box 2057
Manteo, NC 27954

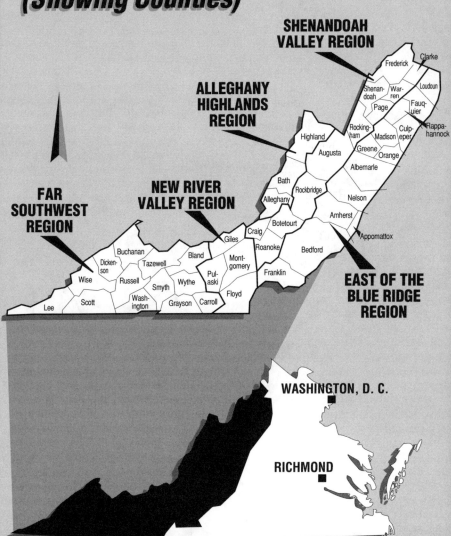

Virginia's Blue Ridge

(Showing Counties)

SHENANDOAH VALLEY REGION

ALLEGHANY HIGHLANDS REGION

NEW RIVER VALLEY REGION

FAR SOUTHWEST REGION

EAST OF THE BLUE RIDGE REGION

Clarke
Frederick
Loudoun
Shenandoah
Warren
Page
Fauquier
Rockingham
Rappahannock
Highland
Madison
Culpeper
Augusta
Greene
Orange
Albemarle
Bath
Rockbridge
Nelson
Alleghany
Amherst
Botetourt
Appomattox
Giles
Craig
Bedford
Roanoke
Buchanan
Bland
Montgomery
Dickenson
Tazewell
Franklin
Wise
Russell
Pulaski
Wythe
Smyth
Floyd
Scott
Washington
Grayson
Carroll
Lee

WASHINGTON, D. C.

RICHMOND

New River Valley Region

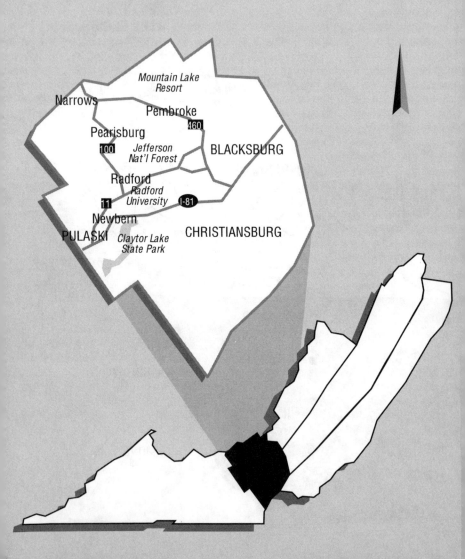

Mountain Lake
Resort

Narrows

Pembroke

460

Pearisburg

100

Jefferson
Nat'l Forest

BLACKSBURG

Radford
Radford
University

I-81

Newbern

11

PULASKI

Claytor Lake
State Park

CHRISTIANSBURG

Alleghany Highlands Region

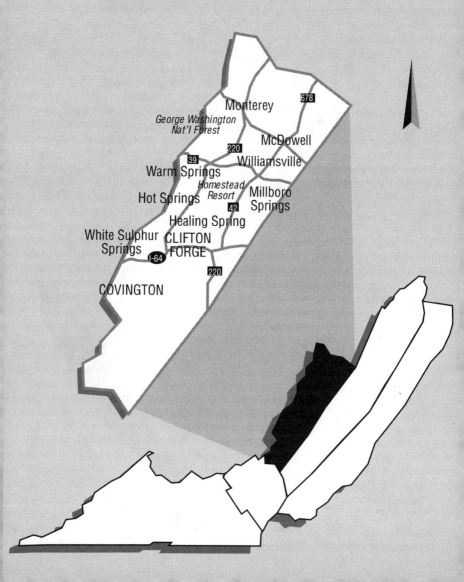

Shenandoah Valley Region

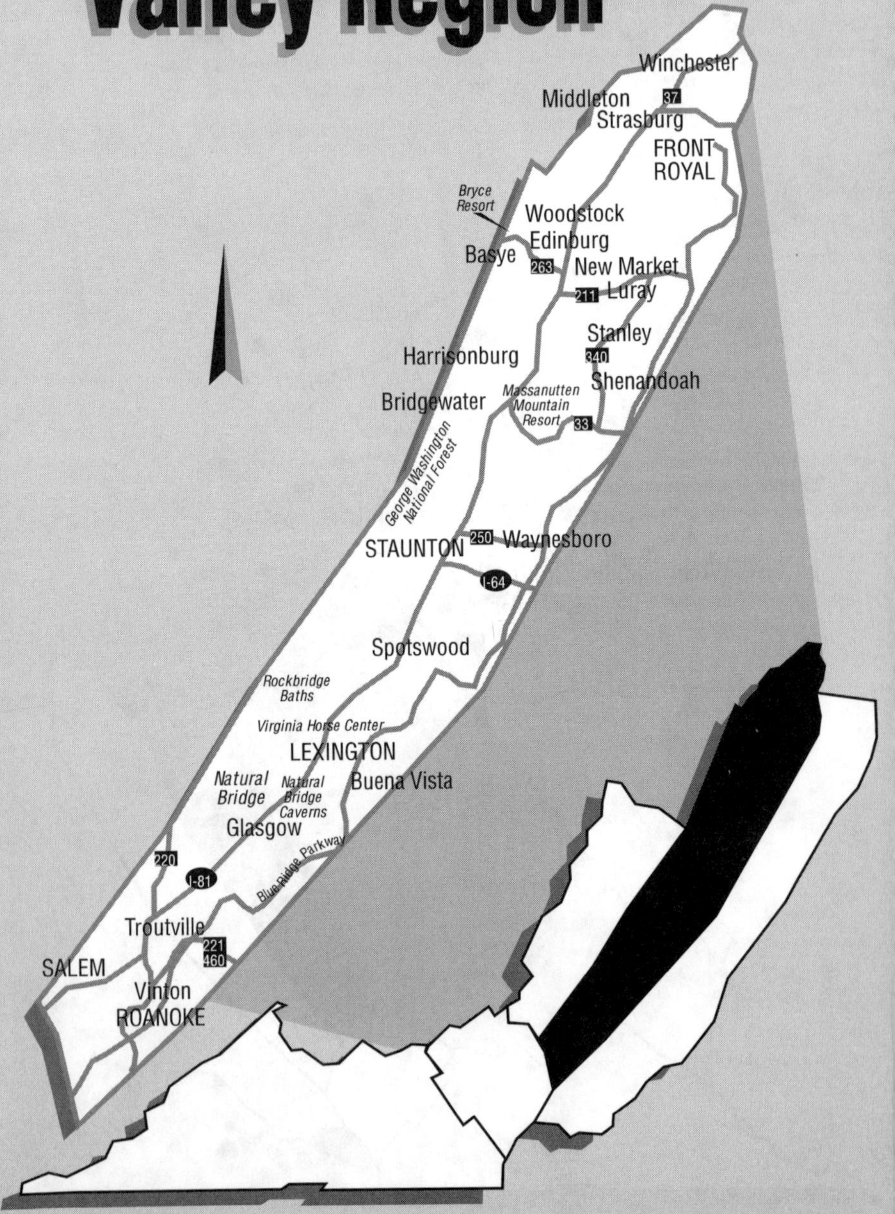

Winchester

Middleton 37

Strasburg

FRONT ROYAL

Bryce Resort

Woodstock

Edinburg

Basye 263

New Market

211 Luray

Stanley

340

Shenandoah

Harrisonburg

Bridgewater

Massanutten Mountain Resort 33

George Washington National Forest

STAUNTON 250 Waynesboro

I-64

Spotswood

Rockbridge Baths

Virginia Horse Center

LEXINGTON

Natural Bridge

Natural Bridge Caverns

Buena Vista

Glasgow

Blue Ridge Parkway

220

I-81

Troutville

221 460

SALEM

Vinton

ROANOKE

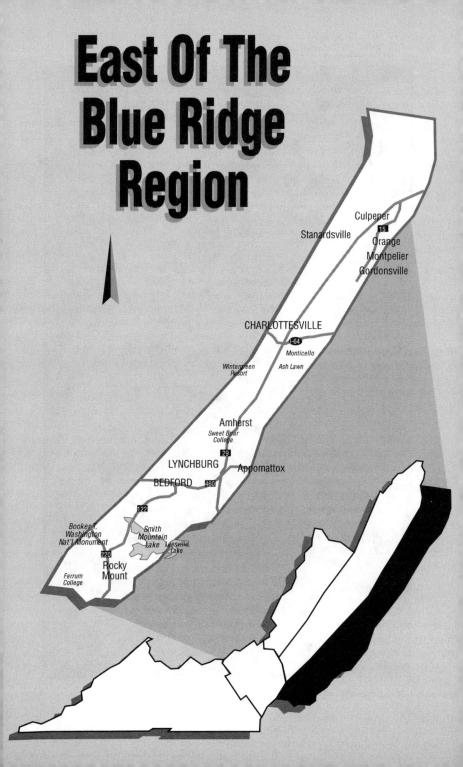

East Of The Blue Ridge Region

Culpeper
Stanardsville
15
Orange
Montpelier
Gordonsville

CHARLOTTESVILLE
I-64
Monticello
Wintergreen
Resort
Ash Lawn

Amherst
Sweet Briar
College
29
LYNCHBURG
Appomattox
BEDFORD
460

122
Booker T.
Washington
Nat'l Monument
Smith
Mountain
Lake
Leesville
Lake
220
Rocky
Ferrum
Mount
College

Cascading waterfalls can be found just off Skyline Drive in Shenandoah National Park.

Cities and Towns
Overviews

The Shenandoah Valley Region

Shenandoah—the name conjures up images of rolling green farmland, beautiful old barns and the legendary Shenandoah River that winds its way to Harper's Ferry, West Virginia.

Shenandoah means "Daughter of the Stars," a name Native Americans gave this 200-mile-long valley of breathtaking beauty hundreds of years ago. White explorers traveled through the valley as early as the mid-1600s, but it wasn't until the early 1700s that the first German and Scotch-Irish families began to put down roots here. They had migrated south in most part from Maryland and Pennsylvania, seeking rich, cheap land and greater freedom for themselves and their children.

The German families settled mainly along the land extending from Winchester to Staunton; the Scotch-Irish, on the other hand, chose Staunton and the valley south for their homesites. This is only a general pattern of settlement; to some extent both groups were interspersed along the entire length of the valley.

Original barns and homesteads dot the landscape up and down the valley, and many museums along I-81 give visitors a closer look of the daily lives of these rugged pioneers.

From the Woodstock Museum in Shenandoah County and the Tuttle and Spice General Store and the Battlefield Military Museum in New Market, to the Cyrus McCormick Farm near Steele's Tavern and the lively Museum of American Frontier Culture in Staunton, all offer a glimpse into the valley's past. You can see early American farm equipment, pottery, furniture, Indian artifacts and Civil War exhibits, and watch costumed interpreters perform such pioneer chores as churning butter and shearing sheep.

The fertile, wheat-producing Shenandoah Valley was known as the "Breadbasket of the Confederacy" — that is until Union Gen. Philip Sheridan began torching nearly all the barns and mills in the valley. Crops were destroyed, and livestock and horses confiscated to the extent that "a crow flying across the Valley would have to pack its lunch."

Some of the heaviest fighting during the four-year conflict took place in the valley, and many of the war's hardiest soldiers hailed from here. According to Lt. Col. C.F.R. Henderson, author of the two-volume *Stonewall Jackson and the Civil War*, "...no better material for soldiers ever existed than the men of the valley....All classes mingled in the ranks, and all ages....They were a mountain people, nurtured in a wholesome climate bred to manly sports, and hardened by the free life of the field and forest. To social distinctions they gave little heed. They were united for a common purpose ... and their patriotism was proved by the sacrifice of all personal consideration and individual interest."

The valley is the burial place of many heroes of that terrible war. Both Robert E. Lee and Stonewall Jackson's resting places are in Lexington; Lee was president of the city's Washington College (now Washington and Lee) after the war, and Jackson had taught at the Virginia Military Institute for years. Jackson's horse, Little Sorrell, remains close to his master in Lexington. Still standing in the VMI Museum, the preserved horse is a little mangy — but you would be too if you had to keep standing more than 100 years after you died. (Actually, it is the real hide, stretched over a plastic form!...)

Jackson is memorialized in a rollicking musical called "Stonewall Country," performed under the stars every summer at Lexington's Lime Kiln Theater.

The Shenandoah Valley was also home to other great leaders of our nation; Woodrow Wilson was born in Staunton, and a new fascinating museum next to his birth place tells all about his life and his vision for world peace. Also in Lexington is a museum honoring George C. Marshall, a VMI graduate who went on to lead the U.S. Army during WWII and later devise a plan to rebuild Europe after the war.

Visitors to the valley need not have a strong interest in history to enjoy themselves. There are great caverns offering cool tours among rooms filled with ancient and colorful calcite formations. There's the magnificence of Natural Bridge, once owned by Thomas Jefferson. There are rivers running through the valley where you can take a quiet, lazy canoe trip or an action-packed whitewater run.

Antique lovers will be wowed by the shops in charming small towns and out in the "middle of nowhere." And if you time your visit right, you can catch some of the East's finest fairs and festivals: Virginia's number one Agricultural Fair at Harrisonburg, the Maple Festival in Highland County, and the wildly popular Apple Blossom Festival in Winchester.

There are downtown districts that are great to explore on foot in the valley, offering a concentration of beautiful architecture, fine restaurants, boutiques and galleries. You can spend hours exploring Roanoke's city market area, or historic downtown Lexington or Staunton.

All kinds of modern accommodations can be found throughout the valley, and there are also dozens of inns and bed and breakfasts in beautifully restored old

Safe Drivers React Quickly To Our Low Car Insurance Rates.

1-800-841-3000

GEICO
AUTO INSURANCE

homes. The Virginia Division of Tourism will recommend B&Bs and make reservations (804/786-4484), and there are also other reservation services (see our Bed and Breakfasts chapter).

The Shenandoah Valley has many more villages and towns worth exploring than we were able to highlight in this book because of its large scope.

But we hope the following introductions will give you a taste of what each area has to offer. For more detailed information on restaurants, museums, accommodations, antiquing, etc., read on!

WINCHESTER

Once called Frederick Town after Frederick, father of King George III, Winchester is full of reminders of our nation's early history. The city and surrounding area was first settled by Pennsylvania Quakers in 1732; soon after, Germans, Scotch, Irish, English, Welsh and French Huguenots also followed the great wagon road from Pennsylvania and put down roots here. Winchester was a thriving center of commerce during the settlement of our nation; pioneers obtained their wagons and provisions here for trips further west and south.

The city saw much action during the Civil War. Five battles and many skirmishes were fought within or near Winchester, which changed hands more than 70 times. Stonewall Jackson used a home on Braddock St. for his headquarters during the war, and today his office remains much the way it was during his stay. The new Kurtz Cultural Center downtown opened a permanent exhibit this year called "Shenandoah — Crossroads of the Civil War." All kinds of displays provide details on the major battles here.

The father of our country started his career in Winchester when he was 16, as a surveyor for Lord Thomas Fairfax (owner of a 5-million-acre royal grant who lived in nearby White Post). George Washington later held great responsibility for protecting Virginia's frontier as a colonel. He oversaw the construction of Fort Loudoun, today a museum in Winchester. He also was elected to his first political office — as a member of the House of Burgesses — in Winchester.

Country music fans know Winchester as the birthplace of Patsy Cline, that spunky, honey-voiced singer made famous by her renditions of "I Fall to Pieces, "After Midnight," and "Sweet Dreams" in the early 60s. In 1963 Cline was killed in an airplane crash when she was 30; she was buried at the Shenandoah Memorial Cemetery on 522 south, also known as the Patsy Cline Memorial Highway. The singer's mother and sister still live in town.

On a literary note, the Winchester area was also the birthplace of another pioneering woman — the novelist Willa Cather. Cather's family moved from Frederick County to Nebraska when she was 10.

Winchester is probably best known for its annual Shenandoah Apple Blossom Festival. Every spring, Winchester plays host for four days to more than 250,000 visitors who

ENJOY A NUTTY LEGEND
ON YOUR WAY TO THE BLUE RIDGE!

*Since 1929 Our "Railroad Car Diner" On Hwy. 460 In Wakefield
Has Been A Favorite Stopping-Off Point For Weary Travelers
From The World Over Wanting To Enjoy Fresh Roasted Peanuts,
Down Home Cookin' & Real Southern Hospitality!
Stop In...Enjoy Our Delicious Dishes & Irresistible Peanut Confections.
Take Time To Browse Through Our Gift Shop & Be Sure To Take
Along Some World Famous Kettle Cooked Virginia Diner Peanuts
With You On Your Travels Through The Blue Ridge!
See For Yourself Why We Have Come To Be Known As*
"A Legend In A Nutshell...Since 1929!"

For More Information & A Free Virginia Diner Gift Catalog

CALL TOLL·FREE
1·800·868·6887

DON'T FORGET
TO FIND OUR
VALUABLE COUPON
IN THE COUPON
SECTION OF
THIS GUIDE!

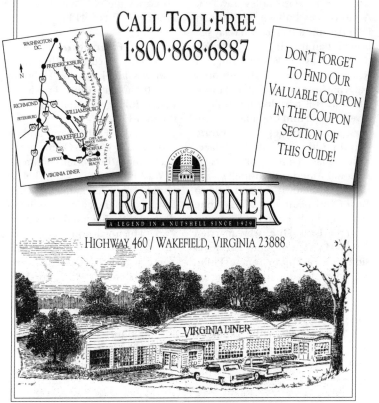

VIRGINIA DINER
A LEGEND IN A NUTSHELL SINCE 1929

HIGHWAY 460 / WAKEFIELD, VIRGINIA 23888

converge to enjoy the Grand Feature Parade, the Queen's coronation, arts and crafts festivals, races, dances and a circus.

For more information about attractions, events and tours of the Winchester area, contact the Chamber of Commerce and Visitor Center, 1360 S. Pleasant Valley Rd., Winchester, VA 22601. (703) 662-4135

MIDDLETOWN

This quaint little town in southern Frederick County lies along U.S. 11, once the Great Wagon Road — the most important frontier highway in colonial America.

It has always been a favorite stopping place for valley travelers. A tavern was built in 1797 which later became a stagecoach relay station and an inn. It is still in operation today as the Wayside Inn and Restaurant, a beautifully restored watering hole in the center of town. The inn is a paradise for antique lovers. You'll find Colonial furnishings, rare antiques, and historic paintings throughout the place, which is also famous for its hearty regional American cuisine.

Middletown is also home to Belle Grove plantation, a large stone mansion built between 1794 and 1797 by Isaac Hite, who married James Madison's sister. The mansion served as Union General Philip Sheridan's headquarters during the decisive 1864 Battle of Cedar Creek, which occurred two miles south of town.

Every October, the plantation grounds attract huge crowds for a major Civil War reenactment, hosted by the Cedar Creek Battlefield Foundation, Inc. The foundation is raising money to secure complete ownership of the 158-acre Cedar Battlefield which lies adjacent to the plantation.

Wayside Theatre in downtown Middletown is the second oldest theatre in the state, performing dramas, comedies and mysteries from May through December. Some famous faces got their start here, including Susan Sarandon, Jill Eikenberry of "L.A. Law," and Peter Boyle.

For more information about Middletown attractions, contact the Winchester-Frederick County Chamber of Commerce at 1360 S. Pleasant Valley Rd., Winchester, VA 22601, (703) 662-4135

FRONT ROYAL

This northern Blue Ridge town was once known as "Helltown" for all the shootings, brawls and hard drinking that went on here in the mid-1700s.

Today Front Royal and the surrounding Warren County are fast becoming a bedroom community of Washington, D.C., whose beltway is only 57 miles away. But Front Royal is also the gateway to the wilderness of the Shenandoah National Park. The north and south forks of the majestic Shenandoah River come together here, and campgrounds and canoe outfitters abound.

Front Royal has a revitalized downtown district, full of interesting boutiques and antique shops. An old fashioned town clock sits in the Village Common, where a gazebo and picnic tables welcome tourists and downtown workers to sit for a spell.

The town has a Confederate Museum, which documents how this important rail and river junction witnessed numerous clashes during the Civil War. Belle Boyd, the beautiful aristocratic Confederate spy, stayed for a while in Front Royal during the war, and one night was upstairs in the same home where a Union general and his officers stopped to make plans for further maneuvers.

Belle watched and listened through a small hole in the closet floor, and heard every word of their plans. She wrote down in cipher each plan, stole down the back steps, and rode horseback for 15 miles in the middle of the night to carry the message to Confederate troops.

Abundant attractions in the Front Royal area include Skyline Caverns, the Skyline Drive, and two wineries offering tours and tastings: Oasis Vineyard and Linden Vineyards and Orchards, both about eight miles south of town.

Front Royal pulls out the stops every May for the Virginia Mushroom Festival. Virginia Shiitake mushrooms, which are cultivated in the Warren County area, are featured, along with wine tastings, arts and crafts exhibits and cooking demonstrations.

For more information, contact the Chamber of Commerce of Front Royal and Warren County, 414 East Main St., P.O. Box 568, Front Royal, VA 22630, (703) 635-3185.

STRASBURG

Staufferstadt was the original name of Strasburg, a busy little town just south of Middletown. German Mennonites and Dunkards who had migrated from York County, Pennsylvania settled the village, and Peter Stover petitioned for a charter for the town in 1761. He then changed the name to Strasburg, in honor of its home city in Germany.

Later, the town was nicknamed "Pottown" for the high quality pottery produced here during the antebellum period. The first potter came in 1761, and since then at least 17 potters have produced earthen and stoneware in Strasburg.

You can see some of this pottery in the Strasburg Museum and Gift Shop, which was originally a steam pottery built in 1891. Also in the museum are Civil War relics, Indian artifacts, blacksmith collections and displays from Colonial farms and businesses.

Antique lovers will have a heyday in Strasburg. Nearly 100 dealers of high quality antiques are housed under one roof in the downtown Strasburg Emporium. You'll find not just furniture representing every American era, but also carriages, chandeliers, rugs, quilts, lace, old carousel horses and pottery.

The place to stay overnight in town is the Hotel Strasburg, a renovated Victorian hotel whose rooms are decorated with antiques that are also for sale. The hotel's restaurant has a popular following among folks from nearby valley towns, and is by far the best place to dine for miles around. For more information on Strasburg, Woodstock, New Market, and other Shenandoah County towns such as Edinburg, Mt. Jackson, Basye and Orkney Springs, call the Shenandoah County Travel Council, Woodstock, VA 22664 at (703) 459-5522.

WOODSTOCK

This charming valley town was originally called Muellerstadt after its founder Jacob Mueller, who arrived from Germany in 1749. In 1761 the frontier settlement was chartered by an act of the Virginia Assembly, an act sponsored by George Washington, a representative from Frederick County. Its name was then changed to Woodstock. Artifacts recalling the valley's early settlement can be seen at the Woodstock Museum on West Court Street. These include Native American tools, maps, ledgers, portraits, furniture, quilts, a moonshine still and Civil War memorabilia.

The museum sponsors a walking tour through town, where you can see examples of Federal, Greek Revival and Classic Revival architecture. The courthouse, whose original part was built in 1795, is the oldest courthouse west of the Blue Ridge in continuous use as a court building.

Nearby Orkney Springs hosts the Shenandoah Valley Music Festival every spring and summer. Concerts are held in a covered, open-air pavilion and on the grounds of the historic Orkney Springs Hotel, a 19th century mineral springs spa and resort.

NEW MARKET

Here you will find caverns, museums, golf, a battlefield historical park and an excellent tourist information center for the whole Shenandoah Valley.

New Market was a little later in becoming settled than other valley towns. English settlers from the north and east settled here and named their village after a horse racing town in England named New Market. In the early days, there was a racetrack near New Market about a mile long.

New Market is famous for the 1864 battle that drew in 247 eager cadets fresh from the classrooms of the Virginia Military Institute. A stirring account of the battle can be seen on film at the Hall of Valor Museum at the New Market Battlefield Historical Park. The museum also presents a non-partisan view of major Civil War events with its artifacts, murals and life size models. Also on the 220-acre battlefield is the restored farm of Jacob and Sarah Bushong, whose home became one of the hospitals and whose orchards became the killing fields of war. Equipped wheelwright and blacksmith shops, loom house and a summer kitchen have the workings of a 19th-century typical valley farm.

New Market is a center of caverns in the valley: Shenandoah Caverns are to the north and Endless Caverns to the south, and within a short drive you can also reach Luray and Grand Caverns.

Many historic buildings continue to stand in the downtown and can be seen along a walking tour. While it may sound like a sleeper of an attraction, you shouldn't miss

Shop Downtown New Market, Va.

Exit 264 off I-81

BLUE RIDGE MOTOR LODGE

A MOUNTAIN VIEW FROM EVERY ROOM

- Cable TV
- Direct Dial Phones
- Refrigerators
- Playgrounds/Basketball
- Free Coffee
- BBQ/Picnic Area
- Children Under 12 Free

RESV. 1-800-545-8776 ROOMS 703-740-8088 + EXT

I-81-Exit 264-1 Mile N. On US 11

New Market CAFE'

Lunch & Dinner
Starting at
$3.95
Everything is Homemade!
Even The Cheesecake!
Open Tues.-Sat. 11-8
Sunday 11-6
9478 Congress St.,
New Market
740-3211

New Market Battlefield Military Museum

Visit a one of a kind museum which focuses on the personal aspect of America's Military History from the American Revolution to the Gulf War. Particular emphasis is placed on the Civil War as the museum sits on the New Market Battlefield. Over 2500 items on display in 108 exhibits. Historically based film and troop positions markers are also offered. Extensive selection of military books (over 800 titles) Original artifacts/ relics/ memorabilia for sale.

9 to 5 daily March 15-December 1
Rt 305 (Collins Dr) P O Box 1131   New Market, VA 22844 **703/740-8065**

Quarter Creek

Custom-built
Upholstered
18th Century Furniture

European Lace Curtains
Table Lace

Elegant Gifts

Sat. & Mon. 10-5, Sun. 12-5
9408 Congress Street,
New Market, VA
(703) 740-4431

Shenandoah Valley Travel Association Tourist Information Center

OPEN DAILY 9am-5pm
Call or write for FREE 72 page
TRAVEL GUIDE & CALENDAR OF
EVENTS listing attractions, lodging,
campgrounds & restaurants

SVTA
PO Box 1040, Depts. IG   New Market, VA 22844
703/740-3132

MING DYNASTY RESTAURANT

fine Chinese **740-4321**
cuisine & drink

Daily Lunch Buffet
Mon-Fri
11am-2:30pm
OPEN:
Mon-Thurs
11am-9pm
Fri-Sat
11am-10pm
Sun 12noon-9pm

185 E. Lee Hwy (Rt. 211
East toward Luray)
NEW MARKET VA 22844

The JOHN SEVIER GALLERY

9391 Congress St.
New Market, VA
22844
703/740-3911

ORIGINAL ART BY LOCAL ARTISTS

watercolors, oils,
pastels, pen & ink

Open daily 10-4

the Bedrooms of America Museum on Congress Street (U.S. 11). There are 11 different rooms of authentic furniture showing every period of America's bedrooms, from William and Mary (circa 1650) through Art Deco (circa 1930). The museum is housed in the same 18th century building used by General Jubal Early as his headquarters during the Civil War.

For shopping, don't miss Paper Treasures also on the main drag of Congress Street . The store has an extraordinary collection of old books, maps and magazines, such as *Ebony, Collier's Weekly* and the *Saturday Evening Post.* The store also sells framed hand-tinted illustrations from some of these old magazines.

The River Farm is a working sheep farm near town that offers weekend workshops in spinning, weaving and dying, and lodging for students. A shop sells fleece, fibers, spinning wheels and looms.

You can also see a marvelous old covered bridge north of town, about two miles south of Mount Jackson. Meem's Bottom Bridge stretches 191 feet across the North Fork of the Shenandoah River. Built in 1892-93, it is the longest covered bridge of the nine remaining in Virginia and the last crossing the Shenandoah.

LURAY

There is no agreement as to how this town got its name. Some insist that the Huguenots who escaped from France and migrated to the valley named the new settlement Lorraine, and that Luray is a

corruption of the former name.

Luray is a central gateway to the 105-mile-long Skyline Drive. The Shenandoah National Park borders Page County on the east, and the George Washington National Forest on the west.

As the county seat of Page, Luray is the home of the internationally famed Luray Caverns, which are open every day, all year round. The magical underground world of stalactites, stalagmites and crystal-clear pools can be explored in an hour-long guided tour. Housed in the same complex is the Historic Car and Carriage Caravan, an exhibit of antique cars, carriages, coaches and costumes dating back to 1625. Rudolph Valentino's 1925 Rolls Royce is here!

Shenandoah River Outfitters in Luray and the Down River Canoe Company in nearby Bentonville both offer canoe trips on the south fork of the Shenandoah River, which travels the entire length of Page County. Guilford Ridge Vineyard is just a few miles out of town, and offers tours and tastings of its wines by appointment. And would you believe one of the state's largest reptile collections is in Luray? The Luray Reptile Center and Dinosaur Park on Rt. 211 will keep your kids squealing for hours. Its petting zoo has tame deer and llamas.

A good time to visit the area is on Columbus Day weekend in October, when Page County throws its annual Heritage Festival. First held in 1969, it is one of the oldest arts and crafts shows in Virginia. Craft demonstrations range from quilt making, woodworking, wheel spinning and soap making to apple butter boiling and apple cider pressings. The festival offers an antique tractor steam and gas engine show, mule train rides, country bands and clogging demonstrations.

For more information about attractions and events in Page County, contact the Chamber of Commerce, 46 E. Main St., Luray, VA 22835, (703) 743-3915.

HARRISONBURG

Harrisonburg is a thriving city and the seat of one of the nation's leading agricultural counties. In fact, so valuable is poultry to Rockingham County's economy that a proud statue of a turkey stands alongside U.S. 11 south of town. And every May Harrisonburg hosts the week-long Poultry Festival, which includes a "Friends of Feathers" banquet.

There are more than 2,000 farms in the county, and nearly half the land is classified as agricultural. The county is the state's leading producer of dairy, poultry and beef products. The city also is home to 20 major industries and serves as the major financial and retail center for eight counties, including three in neighboring West Virginia.

Opportunities for higher education abound in the area. Bridgewater College, Eastern Mennonite College and Seminary, and James Madison University are all here, so students and professors comprise a large part of the population.

In 1778, Virginia Governor Patrick Henry named Rockingham County for the Marquis of Rockingham, one of the few friends Virginia had at the Court of London. The following year, a prominent farmer named Thomas Harrison donated two and one-half acres for a courthouse, and the city of Harrisonburg was born.

During the Civil War, productive farms in the area helped feed the Confederate army. Stonewall Jackson used Harrisonburg as one of his headquarters, and today, his military strategies that so confounded Union officers are described by way of an electric, wall-sized map at the Shenandoah Valley Heritage Museum in nearby Dayton.

Testimony to other battles can also be seen at Dayton's Daniel Harrison House, also known as Fort Harrison. This beautiful stone house was built in the mid 1750s, when bands of Native Americans frequently roamed the area threatening the settlers. The house served as a fort, and had a stockade and underground passage to a nearby spring.

Dayton is also home to a wonderful indoor Farmer's Market, where you will find fresh cheeses, baked goods, antiques, bulk grains and spices, and a fantastic country restaurant run by a former Mennonite missionary.

It's not unusual to see a black carriage or two with horses parked out front; about 1,000 Old Order Mennonites live in the greater area and are easily identified by their simple style of dress, including white hats for women. Their horse-drawn buggies and immaculate farms are a common sight in the southwestern region of the county.

More than 139,000 acres of George Washington National Forest lie in western Rockingham County. On the east, the county is bordered by the Shenandoah National Park. The Massanutten Mountain range is just east of town and is home to Massanutten Resort, a year round residential community that is know for its ski slopes, golf courses and impressive indoor sports complex. Here visitors can also fish swim, hike and ride horses.

Another recreational attraction near Harrisonburg (but in Augusta County) is Natural Chimneys, a place where huge rocks tower to heights of 120 feet. From one perspective, these rocks resemble a foreboding medieval castle with turrets and towers, and this may have inspired the creation of the Natural Chimneys Jousting Tournament more than 150 years ago. The tournament is the oldest continuously held sporting event in America, having begun in 1821. Modern-day knights still match their skills in the ancient art of jousting here on the third Saturday in August every year.

The Natural Chimneys Regional Park has 120 campsites, a swimming pool, picnic area, camp store, nature and bike trails and more.

For more information about attractions in the Harrisonburg and Rockingham County area, contact the Chamber of Commerce at 191 S. Main St., P.O. Box 1, Harrisonburg, VA 22801, (703) 434-3862.

STAUNTON

Staunton is a great city to explore on foot — full of Victorian era architecture and unique shops, one-of-a-kind eateries and important historical sites. The city is the birthplace of President Woodrow Wilson, who was born in 1856 to a Presbyterian minister and his wife in a Greek Revival manse on Coalter Street. Today the manse is open for tours, and sits next door to a fascinating museum where you can learn all about Wilson's life, his political views and his vision for world peace. The new Woodrow Wilson Museum also houses the president's 1919 Pierce Arrow limousine.

Another major attraction in Staunton is the Museum of American Frontier Culture, an indoor-outdoor living museum that features four authentic working farms from Germany, England, Northern Ireland and early America. Children love this place, where lambs and chickens, cats and all kinds of farm critters animate the landscape. In 1993, it received the Phoenix Award of excellence from the National Association of Travel writers.

Staunton is an appropriate place for a museum that documents life in frontier America. It is the seat of Augusta County, which once stretched all the way to Mississippi. Most early settlers in the area were Scotch-Irish, including John Lewis, the first white man to build a homestead here in 1732. In 1749, Lewis' son Thomas laid out lots and streets for the new town of Staunton, named in honor of Lady Rebecca Staunton, Gov. William Gooch's wife.

Staunton became Virginia's

capital for 17 days in June, 1781, as Gov. Thomas Jefferson and the General Assembly fled advancing British troops led by Tarleton. Those redcoats had already captured seven Virginia delegates in nearby downtown Charlottesville, including Daniel Boone.

Nineteenth century Staunton grew by leaps and bounds following incorporation as a town in 1801. Education became a priority, with the establishment of the Virginia Institute for the Deaf and the Blind in 1839, Augusta Female Seminary in 1842 (now Mary Baldwin College), Virginia Female Institute in 1844 (now Stuart Hall School) and Staunton Military Academy in 1884.

The railroad came to Staunton in 1854, and this stimulated the city's growth as a center of commerce for the region. Today, Amtrak continues to serve the city, and the old C&O train station is a showcase of meticulous restoration work. There, you'll find an authentic 1880s Victorian Ice Cream Parlor, serving dense, Italian style ice cream in a room with antique parlor and drug store furnishings from ceiling to floor. Next door the Depot Grille boasts a gorgeous, hand-carved antique walnut bar, and in the same building Depot Antiques sells fine collectibles, Victorian and country furniture.

The wharf area is undergoing much restoration work; the old mill buildings and warehouses already house antique shops, a pottery workshop and studio, and a marvelous antique car dealership, but you can expect much more in the future. The Historic Staunton Foundation has produced a detailed brochure to guide visitors on a walking tour of the city, as well as a new guide to antique shops.

Other attractions in Staunton include the beautiful Gypsy Hill Park, which has tennis courts, softball fields, a lake and a duck pond. Right across the street is the Statler Brothers museum and office complex. Yes, these famous down-home country music stars actually live and work in Staunton and their children go to school here. For 25 years the Statler Brothers have thrown a huge "Happy Birthday U.S.A." celebration in Gypsy Hill Park, complete with concerts, firework displays, free tours of their museum, and patriotic speeches. Their sponsorship of the event will finally end in 1994, so take advantage of this popular event next July!

For additional information about Staunton, contact the Office of Tourism, P.O. Box 58, Staunton, VA 24401, (703) 885-2839.

WAYNESBORO-STUARTS DRAFT-FISHERSVILLE

Named in honor of Revolutionary War hero General Anthony Wayne, Waynesboro thrived as an industrial community during the late 1800s and the trend continues today. Thanks in part to its convenient location just eight miles east of the intersection of I-81 and I-64, DuPont, Genicom and Hershey are a few of the plants located here.

Waynesboro is also known for being a friendly town and a wonderful place to raise children. Nearby Stuarts Draft and Fishersville are also attractive communities for fami-

Photo: Richmond Newspapers

Bluegrass music is popular in the Blue Ridge Mountains.

lies.

Waynesboro extends to Afton Mountain, from which you can see clear to Charlottesville and further east. The Shenandoah National Park's southern tip ends on that mountain, and the Blue Ridge Parkway begins its southern trek there. One note of caution: It's not a fun mountain to cross during foggy weather; many fatal accidents have occurred here due to fog so thick you can barely see car lights in front of you. So, park yourself in pleasant Waynesboro if such conditions exist.

In Waynesboro, the P. Buckley Moss Museum, named for "The People's Artist," is located in a tall brick house surrounded by trees—a scene reminiscent of one of her watercolors. Since the early 1960s, the world-renowned, multimillionaire artist and philanthropist has found her inspiration and much of her subject matter in valley scenery and in the Amish and Mennonite peoples of the area. The museum is within easy walking distance to the Waynesboro Outlet Village, a fantastic place to find bargains in designer clothing, leather goods, imported china and much more.

While in Waynesboro, you can also watch age-old techniques of brass molding at the Virginia Metalcrafters factory showroom. The Shenandoah Valley Art Center in downtown Waynesboro offers residents and visitors a place to enjoy the arts through exhibits, workshops, classes and performances.

Mennonites who live in the area have established some businesses that provide a refreshing alternative to standard grocery stores. Kinsinger's Kountry Kitchen, on Rt. 651 off Rt. 608, sells yummy homemade pies, cinnamon rolls, cakes, cookies and jams — all made from scratch by Mennonites. The Cheese Shop up the road on 608 sells fresh cheeses at great prices, along with bulk nuts and seeds, dried fruits and baking ingredients. Milmont Greenhouses on Rt. 340 started as a Mennonite housewife's hobby nearly 20 years ago, and today offers a large selection of house plants, perennials, annuals and vegetables — depending on the season.

Speaking of green things, one of the leading perennial nurseries in the nation is based in Fishersville and is definitely worth visiting. Andre Viette Farm and Nursery has beautiful gardens which feature more than 1,000 varieties of day lilies, hosta, oriental poppies, peonies and iris — as well as many rare species of other flowers and plants. Garden tours, lectures and free garden design assistance are all offered here. The nursery is on Rt. 608, 2.5 miles north of Rt. 250 in Fishersville.

Recreational opportunities abound in the area. The Sherando Lake State Park is just outside Waynesboro, and Shenandoah Acres Resort is in Stuarts Draft. At the latter, you can swim, ride horses, play badminton, mini golf, croquet and volley ball and camp or stay in cottages that are available year round.

For more information about attractions in the Waynesboro-East Augusta County area, contact the Chamber of Commerce, 301 W.

Main St., Waynesboro, VA 22980-0339, (703) 949-8203.

LEXINGTON

Perhaps more than any other place in the valley, downtown Lexington has retained the graceful beauty and genteel character of its prosperous past.

And no other city or town in the Blue Ridge has a history that is so well preserved and honored by its citizens, a town whose heritage that includes four of the greatest American generals.

It seems that everywhere you go, you are walking on historic, hallowed ground.

Film-makers agree. Last summer, tons of dirt were dumped on downtown streets along an unusual number of 19th Century buildings for scenes in the Civil War-era movie, "Sommersby," starring Richard Gere and Jodie Foster.

Throughout Lexington's history, the presence of its great military leaders has inspired its preservation efforts. They are George Washington, the father of our country, the great Confederate generals Robert E. Lee and Thomas J. "Stonewall" Jackson, and World War II hero Gen. George C. Marshall, the Nobel Peace Prize-winning creator of the Marshall Plan that rebuilt war-torn Europe.

Lexington is the historic and cultural heart of Rockbridge County (population 32,000), whose most prosperous residents enjoy a genteel country-estate way of life. Many are early retirees from New York, New Jersey, Connecticut and elsewhere, who devote their consider-able knowledge and energy to the community as volunteers and activists. Others are college professors at nearby Virginia Military Institute and Washington and Lee University.

The county boasts the breathtaking three-mile-long Goshen Pass, a journey along the Maury River through rhododendron, laurel, ferns, mosses, magnificent pines, hemlocks, maples, dogwood and mountain ash.

Goshen Pass, a popular place for swimming, tubing, canoeing and picnicking, is so beautiful that one prominent Lexington citizen, Matthew Fontaine Maury, asked his body be carried through the pass when the rhododendron was in bloom after he died. Complying with his request in 1873, Virginia Military Institute cadets formed an honor guard and gave their professor his last wish.

The roles that Lexington's world-famous universities, VMI and Washington & Lee University, have played in the area's historic culture cannot be underestimated. In 1796, George Washington saved W&L from bankruptcy with a gift of $50,000 that still receives dividends. VMI cadets are immortalized forever both on campus, with the statue of "Virginia Mourning Her Dead," and at the New Market Battlefield Museum and Hall of Valor, (an hour north of the city), for their role in the Civil War.

The Civil War Battle of New Market in 1864 was the first and only time in American history that an entire student body was recruited to fight a war. When the smoke cleared, 10 cadets lay dead, including Cadet Thomas G. Jefferson, 17, progeny of our nation's third president.

As a city which has had more than its share of encounters with famous presidents, one came in an unlikely way. Visitors can see the National Historic Landmark cadet barracks where actor Ronald Reagan's movie, "Brother Rat," was filmed. The movie's premier was held at Lexington's State Theatre.

VMI is now facing one of its toughest battles ever, this time with the Virginia Court system, which is challenging why the state-funded college should not become coed. Round one was awarded to VMI by a sympathetic judge, but the fight reached the state Supreme Court this past spring. The court refused to consider the case, returning it to a federal judge for resolution. It is expected that the Supreme Court will hear again from VMI on this contentious issue.. In the meantime, you can still see the all-male cadets and marvel at their precision during one of their formal dress parades.

Many of Lexington's attractions focus on its famous former citizens. There's the Stonewall Jackson House, where the tough general lived while teaching natural philosophy at VMI, and the Stonewall Jackson Cemetery, his final resting place after he was mistakenly killed by his own soldiers. You can see his bullet-pierced raincoat at the VMI Museum, along with the curious taxidermy display of his favorite war horse, Little Sorrel. His birthday is celebrated in Lexington every Jan. 21 with a ceremony, cake and a free tour of the only home he ever owned.

Lee Chapel, still in use by W&L students, is another famous site, where the famous Edward Valentine's striking white statue of the recumbent Lee is alone worth a visit to Lexington. The chapel also is the site of the famous Peale portrait of George Washington. You can see Lee's office as he left it in 1870 after assuming the presidency of W&L after his Civil War defeat. Lee's favorite mount, Traveller, also is buried on campus.

The third famous military landmark to see is the George C. Marshall Museum, where Marshall, VMI Class of 1901, began a remarkable military career that led to U.S. Army Chief of Staff and later the Nobel Prize in 1953. An electric map detailing the military march of World War II shows you the breadth of what this military genius accomplished and why the U.S. earned a reputation world-wide as a country with a heart in the aftermath of the war.

Lexington's historic sites are well documented by its history-loving populace. You can even see the troughs where its famous equestrian residents, Little Sorell and Traveller, refreshed themselves. A complete map and guide, called "One Hundred Historic Sites and Structures in Rockbridge County" will keep you exploring enough bridges and locks, churches, cemeteries, houses, mills, baths and springs that will quench even the most avid history buff's thirst for knowledge. It is available at the Visitors Center at

102 East Washington St. or by calling (703) 463-3777.

The Center, run by an extremely able director and an enthusiastic staff and volunteers, can tell you everything you want to know about the historic downtown and its surrounding area, from a walking map of historic sites to historic homes. They'll also let you know there's much more than history to keep you busy here, and ply you with pamphlets on shopping, restaurants, bed and breakfasts, hotels, and Lexington's many other attractions, including a nearby museum dedicated to Cyrus McCormick (inventor of the mechanized reaper).

Every day, the Lexington Carriage Company leaves its hitching post at the Visitors Center and carries passengers from 9:30 AM to 5:30 PM. You can ride the same streets as Jackson and Lee did on their famous horses.

Since the memory of two famous horses are awarded such places of honor in Lexington, it stands to reason that the Commonwealth of Virginia saw fit to award Lexington its $12 million Horse Center, situated on 400 rolling acres. It is one of the top equine facilities in the U.S. with 4,000 spectator seats, 610 permanent stalls and a gigantic show arena. Its schedule of events includes everything from the Bonnie Blue Nationals to the Northeast Peruvian Horse Club Show. Last year it hosted the return of the Rockbridge Regional Fair after 50 years' absence following WWII. This year the fair will be held again July 20 through 24 and is expected to be a regular event.

Also bringing fame and visitors to the area is Lime Kiln Theatre, named by *Theatre Journal* magazine as "the most unusual theater setting in the United States" because of its location in an abandoned kiln beside a craggy hillside overgrown with wildflowers. Lime Kiln puts on an array of plays and musicals every summer that highlights the history and culture of the Southern mountains. The theater also offers a Sunday night concert series with an eclectic slate of musicians from across the country and around the world. Every year, Robin and Linda Williams of National Public Radio's "Prairie Home Companion" fame also perform at one of the concerts. They make their home in nearby Staunton.

Going out into the countryside, there's the beautiful Chessie Nature Trail along the Maury River and numerous hiking paths in nearby mountains — among them the Appalachian Trail. If you'd like to see 100 years of nostalgia, stop by Maury River Mercantile on the way to Goshen Pass, in Rockbridge Baths. If you're into horseback riding, Virginia Mountain Outfitters will put together half-day or overnight trips that will take you along forest trails and trout-filled rivers to the tops of mountains (the phone number is (703) 261-1910).

If canoeing is your passion, the James River Basin Canoe Livery will outfit you with boats, supplies, maps and a shuttle service for a trip along with the mighty James River and the rushing Maury ((703) 261-7334).

The great outdoors should also include a visit to Hull's Drive-In, one of the premier mom-and-pop operations anywhere and one of the few surviving drive-in theaters in Virginia. It's open weekends mid-March through November.

In Buena Vista, the only other city in the county which is six miles east of Lexington, you will find much of the county's manufacturing industry. You'll also find The General Store, a trip back in time for an unusual shopping experience. Every Labor Day, Buena Vista attracts huge crowds and state political leaders to a popular festival in Glen Maury Park.

Do not leave Rockbridge County without visiting Natural Bridge, one of the seven wonders of the natural world. The awesome limestone bridge is 23 stories high and 90 feet long. A beautiful walking trail allows you to hike along a wide stream until you are directly beneath the bridge (and beyond). You may strain your neck when you look up and try to take in the entire view of the awesome structure. It is easy to see why the Monocan Indians considered it such a sacred place.

One of the most spiritually moving Easter Sunrise Services in the world is conducted there annually to a hushed crowd of several thousand. The Natural Bridge Wax Museum and gift shop are also loads of fun, especially for children, who will love to fool their friends with candy that looks like real rocks.

Whether visiting the Lexington area for its history, beauty or attractions, you'll be impressed with its sense of historical importance, its gracious old homes, and its vibrant downtown district with fine restaurants and one-of-a-kind shops.

The Roanoke Valley

God lives here. You can tell from the scenery. So does Elvis, at least in miniature, at Miniature Graceland in Roanoke. The Roanoke Valley of Virginia, including the bedroom communities of Botetourt and Craig counties, is home to about a quarter million people who work and play in a cultured, historical place of incredible beauty.

Even the Interstate, (I-81) that connects the Roanoke Valley is beautiful. One of the first things visitors usually say is that they can't get over the absence of potholes and rough pavement. Then they marvel at all the wildflowers, redbud and yellow forsythia, and the flowering orchards along western Virginia's main thoroughfare.

People usually don't set out to move to the Roanoke Valley. Instead, they are converted into relocating here. When you talk to people about how they came to live here, so many times the story starts out, "We were driving down the (fill in the blank with either A. Interstate or B. Blue Ridge Parkway), when we were so smitten that we moved here without even having jobs." Or else, they discovered the Roanoke Valley while hiking on the Appalachian Trail, taking the Bikecentennial path coast to coast, or vacationing at nearby Smith Mountain Lake. Inevitably, the conversation ends with, "...and we'd never go back home. We'll never leave this place."

Consider this: the Roanoke Valley of Virginia was the first in the state to have curbside recycling, mandatory comprehensive recycling and a downtown recycling program that also was a first on the North American continent. This should tell you something about Valley citizens' overwhelming sensitivity to their environment.

Parenting magazine calls the Roanoke Valley one of the 10 best places to raise a family in the U.S. The U.S. Department of Education has recognized Roanoke Valley schools for being among the nation's best. *Inc.* magazine named the Roanoke Valley one of the country's top 100 hot spots for business development.

Whether they live in Historic Botetourt County, the lush, forested Catawba Valley of Craig County, the energetic cities of Roanoke or Salem, suburban Roanoke County or the quaint town of Vinton, Roanoke Valley residents are always glad to come home...and most of them never leave.

BOTETOURT COUNTY

If Virginia can be referred to as the "Mother of States," then Botetourt could be called the "Mother of Counties." With a population of 25,000, the residents are an independent, history-loving lot who are smug in the fact that their county, a land grant to Lord Botetourt, once stretched the whole way to the Mississippi River. His-

toric Fincastle has been the county seat since 1770. This vast tract of land once included the entirety of the present state of Kentucky and much of what is now West Virginia, Ohio, Indiana and Illinois.

George Washington, Patrick Henry and Thomas Jefferson either appeared in Fincastle or sent their agents to lay claim to tracts of wilderness lands. Jefferson designed a county courthouse. After the Lewis and Clark expedition west, William Clark returned to Fincastle to marry resident Judith Hancock.

Thousands of English, German and Scotch-Irish pioneers passed through on their way down the great Valley Road which traversed the famed Shenandoah Valley to settle the western frontier country.

Combining the talents of German craftsmen and Scotch-Irish merchants and lawyers, Fincastle built a town of well proportioned houses and public buildings, a substantial number of which still survive. These include the Old Jail Building, the Court House Complex, the Presbyterian Church, the Botetourt Museum Building and the Botetourt County Courthouse. Newer buildings, such as the historic Bank of Fincastle, a major force in the community, are centrally located to carefully blend into the historic environment. Guided tours, by appointment, are happily arranged by Historic Fincastle, Inc. Write them at P.O. Box 19, Fincastle, VA 24090.

On your tour, you will see beautiful wrought iron fences, balconies and gates, flagstone walks from the early 19th century, horse mounting stones in front of the Presbyterian Church and early gravestones in church cemeteries with the oldest dating to 1795. Steeples contain bells, the focal point of a much publicized and honored tradition, ringing out the old and ringing in the New Year.

It stands to reason that Botetourt County residents love antiques. The Chamber of Commerce will send you a brochure listing 25 different shops, most of them clustered in Troutville and Fincastle. The Troutville Antique Mart has a plethora of these shops. Located across the street is Goodwill Tinker Mountain Industries, a sheltered workshop for Roanoke Valley's handicapped where you can donate second-hand items to its retail stores in Hollins and Salem, named the nation's best Goodwill retail store in 1993.

People love to come to Botetourt County in the spring. For a breathtaking view of orchards in bloom, take Laymantown Rd., left past Troutville Baptist, a cut-through road to U.S. 220. The mounds of blooming apple trees in the setting sun are indeed a sight to behold. In the fall, the fruit of the harvest is available for the picking at seven different orchards, most of them huge operations that also offer seasonal items such as acres of pumpkins for Halloween. Agriculture is still a big industry but farmland is at a premium. There are bounties on Botetourt County real estate, with people desperate to buy the scenic farmland. Farmers have lived there for generations and people with an independent streak are attracted to the county.

There is even a farm for emus and ostriches off T-652 (Blue Ridge Rd.), between Troutville and Blue Ridge. Residents on the road love to exchange stories about the time an ostrich got loose, blocked the road, and caused drivers to think they were losing their minds. It took a rodeo cowboy with a lasso to catch the errant fowl, truss it up and carry it home in a flatbed truck.

Two scenic landmarks tourists especially enjoy are the unusual, huge, jutting Eagle Rock boulders off U.S. 220, which appear as if they'll fall off any moment into the gorge below. Beyond on 220 is Eagle Rock's Roaring Run Furnace, part of the Jefferson National Forest and typical of the scores of iron furnaces that were scattered throughout the hills and mountains of western Virginia. The single-stack, hot-blast charcoal furnace built of large, squared stones was constructed in 1832, rebuilt in 1845 and rebuilt again early in the Civil War. Most of the pig iron produced was shipped to Richmond for the war effort.

A third landmark on the National Register of Historic Places is Wilson Warehouse, built in 1839, and now Buchanan's Community House. Located at Washington and Lowe Streets, it is a relic of western Virginia antebellum prosperity.

It stands to reason that Botetourt County's largest and most popular festival is Historic Fincastle Days in the autumn. Sponsored by Historic Fincastle, Inc., and held in the charming, historic downtown, attending is serendipity to lovers of fine art and crafts, since Fincastle is home to several well-known Virginia artists including Mark Woody and Harold Little. The show is hung in the historic town square.

Recreational opportunities abound, including hiking the Appalachian and Bikecentennial Trials, which go by T-652 (Blue Ridge Road) in Troutville. Other major activities are canoeing or floating the James River and Craig's Creek and hunting, camping and fishing.

Although Botetourt County is a county with a past, it is definitely a county with a bright future, trying to hang on to its pastoral environment. A major grassroots organization is working hard to keep a hazardous waste-burning operation from starting up there. For more information, contact the Botetourt County Chamber of Commerce at P.O. Box 92, Fincastle, VA 24090, (703) 473-8280.

CRAIG COUNTY

Just as Botetourt residents are trying to protect their pristine environment, the rural residents of pastoral Craig (population 4,500) fiercely guard their stake in God's country. Tourism is a major industry in this county, which is more than half covered by the Jefferson National Forest.

The county got its name from Robert Craig, delegate to the General Assembly from Roanoke County, instrumental in legislation to form Craig County in 1851. New Castle was designated the county seat and the historic courthouse was erected the same year by slave labor. Its bell was cast at the same

foundry as the Liberty Bell.

Early settlers probably first traveled up Craig's Creek, the county's major waterway, in the 1730s. By the end of the Indian Wars of 1756-1762, 45 families lived along the creek. George Washington reportedly passed through the junction of Craig's Creek and Meadow Creek, the site of New Castle.

The county seat contains several charming old buildings that have been designated historical landmarks including the courthouse, (which was miraculously spared during the Civil War), a jail, Central Hotel and Star Saloon (now official headquarters of the Craig County Historical Society), First National Bank and the G.W. Layman office building. You'll see several lovely old homes in the area, including the frame house on the corner of routes 311 and 42 (the Layman house), built in 1901, and the big, brick "castle" at the top of the hill going out of town on Route 42 (the Todd house).

Also worth a visit is Tingler's Mill at Paint Bank. While this particular mill was built in 1873, grinding had been going on at the site since 1783. Henry Tingler was excused from military service for the Confederate Army because grinding meal was a higher war need. After 182 years of daily operation, the mill closed in 1965 but is now being restored.

One interesting, little-known fact that would stump any game show contestant is that, because of Civil War geographical boundary changes, the mill has been in two different states and five different counties without ever having been moved! In 1783, the land was part of Botetourt County, until 1792, when Monroe County, VA, was created. In 1851, Craig County was carved from parts of Botetourt, Monroe, Roanoke and Giles counties. In 1863, that portion of the county joined Monroe County when West Virginia was formed during the Civil War, but was returned to Craig County after the war. The route of General David Hunter's retreat in the summer of 1864 still has natives talking. The soldiers burned marriage records and Deed Book 1 and spilled ink on all the others. Then they chopped up parts of the courthouse for kindling. However, an order to burn the courthouse was somehow overlooked.

This gentle beauty of a county, rich in history, is noted as one of the most popular playgrounds in western Virginia. The scenery is spectacular! If you want to see the epitome of a quaint country road, travel Route 42 from New Castle to Giles County. This delightful road, which crosses the eastern Continental Divide, passes old farms with rail fences, graveyards of Civil War veterans and late 19th-century houses.

Route 658 in the John's Creek area takes you to the sites of two now defunct summer resorts where people would come to "take the cure" of the orange sulphur mineral waters. The 1987 movie, "In a Shallow Grave," used the site of Blue Healing Springs resorts' crumbling dance hall.

Another site to see is Hebron Church, built in 1830, complete with its own slave balcony. Locked during the week, arrangements may be made to visit through the Craig County Historical Society (see the Arts & Culture chapter).

The Appalachian Trail is one of the county's major attractions with 30 miles of the Maine-to-Georgia footpath available with several shelters and camping facilities along the way. The Trout Branch to Dragon's Tooth section is seven rugged miles, but the views are spectacular. There's a parking lot off Route 311 in Roanoke County.

For mountain bike enthusiasts, hikers and horseback riders, Craig County is full of trails that range from the easy to challenging and all with scenic value. Some local favorites include Route 179, the road over Bald Mountain, and Route 177 over Potts Mountain. Route 188, the road across the top of Brush Mountain, will take you past the monument where World War II hero Audie Murphy's plane crashed.

Camping enthusiasts will enjoy Craig Creek Recreation area, Steel Bridge and the Pines. Some of the best information on Craig County can be obtained from the New Castle Ranger Office by calling (703) 868-5196 weekdays. It is located on Route 615, three miles east of New Castle.

If you're looking for adventure, wildlife and blessed isolation and meditation, Craig County is the place to live or visit. For more information, contact the County of Craig, Corner of Court & Main St., New Castle, VA 24127, (703) 864-5010.

ROANOKE

Capital of the Blue Ridge, Roanoke (population 96,400) has it all — history, culture, close-knit neighborhoods and a heady sense of environment. Its downtown was the first in North America to offer recycling, thanks to Downtown Roanoke, Inc.

These happy environmental facts are due to a cutting-edge grassroots environmental group, Clean Valley Council, gutsy government officials willing to take a stand and Cycle Systems, a 75-year-old, fourth-generation recycling firm that has led Virginia in the recycling effort. Just like at Disneyland, you can count the moments before a piece of dropped litter is whisked out of sight...that is, if anybody has the gall to drop a piece in this earth-conscious area.

And, also like at brightly lit Disneyland, you'll probably do a double-take the first time you see Roanoke's landmark Mill Mountain Star, seen nightly glowing for a radius of 60 miles. The 43-year-old, 100-foot-high star is a popular landmark for airplane pilots who frequently feel compelled to explain to passengers that what they think they're seeing below really is a gigantic, manmade star. The star has lured many people, including Elvis Presley, who donned a disguise to see it, following a concert after his curiosity got the best of him. Beside the star, there are scores of happy, well-illuminated animals at Mill Mountain Zoological Park.

And, just in case you think that Roanokers are the only ones who brag about their community, let's talk about awards. A University of Kentucky study calls Roanoke one of the nation's top 20 cities for quality of life. Zero Population Growth says Roanoke is one of the 10 least stressful cities for quality of life. Downtown Roanoke's revitalization has been touted as one of America's 10 best by the National Trust for Historic Preservation. And

We Are Proud To Be Your "Community Neighbor."

SIGNET®
One day we'll be your bank.

7 Convenient Locations In The Roanoke Area.

Signet Bank/Virginia. Member FDIC. Signet® is a registered service mark of Signet Banking Corporation.

A double-decker bus in Abingdon.

Photo: Virginia Division of Tourism

Goshen Pass, a breathtaking gorge formed by the Maury River, is near Lexington.

twice in the past decade, Roanoke has received the "All-America City" designation.

A crossroads for commerce, Roanoke's history began in the early 17th century. Indian resistance to settlers was fierce. The city, formerly called Big Lick (for its salt marshes), was later named Roanoke. "Rawrenock," meaning white beads — shells with holes, worn on strings around the neck and arms and passed as currency among Native Americans — was described early on by Captain John White, who attempted to settle Roanoke Island in North Carolina.

Little towns first formed what is now the city of Roanoke. New Antwerp appeared in 1802 followed by Gainesborough in 1825 and Old Lick in 1834. In 1874, the town of Big Lick, population 500, was chartered. It became a railroad crossroads, eventually home to the Norfolk and Western Railroad in 1882. This marked the start of Roanoke's rapid growth. Its historic city market, also begun in the early years, still functions and is the anchor of the revitalized City Market square downtown.

Today, Roanoke is the largest metropolitan city in Virginia west of Richmond and off the widely traveled Blue Ridge Parkway. It is the major center for transportation, ranging from the Norfolk Southern Railway to its Valley Metro bus system, which energetically and conveniently serves city residents. The city sports a new $25 million airport terminal and is also the medical center of western Virginia, with more than 2,400 hospital beds and a gigantic medical center, Roanoke Memorial Hospitals.

The Roanoke Valley has a culture all its own. The Roanoke Symphony and its darling of the media, conductor Victoria Bond, have been featured on the "Today Show" and in the *New York Times* and *Wall Street Journal*. There's Opera Roanoke, a popular cultural complement, and Center in the Square, a unique, multi-cultural institution that is home to five resident organizations of art, history, theatre and science.

A new national exhibition, "To the Rescue," puts Roanoke on the map as the birthplace of the volunteer rescue squad movement. On the drawing boards is the Explore Project, currently under construction. Open now by appointment only, the state park re-creation of an 18th-century pioneer village will be built on nearly 1,500 acres.

Perhaps the most curious of Roanoke's attractions is Miniature Graceland, a private collection of miniature buildings built by Kim Epperly, the editor of the international Elvis newsletter and the Ultimate Elvis Fan. Elvis lovers are invited to stroll through the Miniature Graceland grounds beside Epperly's house on Riverland Blvd. and hear an Elvis song anytime of the day or night as a revolving Elvis doll sings to an audience of adoring Barbies. A "world first" exhibition of Epperly's private Elvis memorabilia will be displayed at the history museum at Center in the Square beginning in January of 1994. A large Elvis gala also is planned.

An innovative Roanoke landmark was added during the summer of 1993. Cycle Systems, a leading East Coast recycling firm, presented a 75th Anniversary gift to the City of Roanoke. It is a lighted fountain of recycled metal which can be seen off I-581 beside the Cycle Systems scrap yard.

There's family entertainment aplenty in Roanoke. Striving to live up to its name as "Festival City of Virginia," Roanoke hosts the block-buster, 2-weekend-long Festival in the Park each May. Festival is a massive celebration of art, music and the human spirit and nearly 400,000 people who agree show up to enjoy it. It's Roanoke's signal that summer is ready to begin! There are other festivals ranging from a celebration of African American culture on Henry Street in the fall to the Chili Cook-off and Community School Strawberry Festival, held on the first May weekend, when palates burning from flaming chili can get cooling ice cream and berries just down the block.

Roanoke is a great center for jumping off to other trips nearby. The number of attractions within an hour's radius is unbelievable, and you'd need a good week's stay at a great place such as the Roanoke Marriott or the historic Patrick Henry Hotel downtown just to have time to see and do even half of what's available. Be sure to stop by the Roanoke Valley Convention & Visitors Bureau on the City Market. An enthusiastic staff and dynamic director will guide you to the many local attractions. You can contact them at 1-800-635-5535.

ROANOKE COUNTY

Roanoke County (population 80,000) is the mostly affluent suburban area surrounding the city of Roanoke. It includes the placid, comfortable town of Vinton as well. The county is noted for its superior school system, network of top-notch recreational centers and willingness to pay to support a superior quality of life.

Roanoke County celebrated its 150th birthday in 1988. In 1838, it was carved out of the huge county of Botetourt. The mountainous county has many areas named for its peaks. One of the most unique may be Twelve O'Clock Knob, so named because slaves west of Salem could look at the mountain and tell it was time for lunch when the sun was at a point just over the 2,707-foot peak.

Another of its natural resources, underground springs, sparked names for many areas ranging from Virginia Etna Springs, site of a former water bottling plant, and Big Cook Spring in Bonsack, an area heavily touched by the Civil War due to several blanket factories located there. Legend has it that one was burned to the ground by the Yankees but the other was spared because its owner, with fingers crossed, promised not to sell blankets to the Confederate merchants down the road in Roanoke City. Another spring, Botetourt Springs, became the site of Hollins College, one of the most prestigious undergraduate women's colleges in America. Graduate programs are co-educational.

Bonsack, east of Vinton, also was the home of Jim Bonsack, who quit Roanoke College to work on a competition for the first cigarette-rolling machine. Young Bonsack won the $75,000 competition, patented it in 1880 at the age of 22, made a fortune and spawned a national industry.

Roanoke County's pioneering spirit has extended to modern times. The county was the Roanoke Valley's pioneer in curbside recycling and has led the rest of the Valley in environmental concerns and issues. It also has been nationally recognized for governmental cooperation in a joint industrial park and library built with Botetourt County. In 1987, community leaders began the Blue Ridge Region economic marketing group, a legislative group targeting General Assembly action to improve the area's quality of life. In 1989, Roanoke County was named an All-America City for its governmental cooperation, quality of life and support of the Explore Project.

Explore, a unique recreational and educational experience, is the county's tourism focus. It is expected to be open to the public in 1994, after the National Park Service completes a road to the area. Nevertheless, many events are being held there now including astronomy field trips, bird-watching, Sierra Club hikes and Scout projects. The restored Hofauger Farmhouse, the focus of the park, is complete and available for use with advance reservations.

Explore's three main parts include a frontier settlement, a North American wilderness zoological park, and an environmental education center. The park will be completed in various phases, with a major emphasis on environmental preservation.

Recreation and historical preservation have been a focus for Roanoke Countians. Green Hill Equestrian Park is the site of the annual autumn polo match benefiting the Roanoke Symphony. This year, again, the Park hosts a Civil War battle recreation, Gen. David Hunter's Retreat. It is one of 44 parks and recreational facilities.

Roanoke County is known for its family-oriented neighborhoods with a wide range of styles and prices. Available are urban townhouses, bucolic farmhouses and suburban subdivisions. The average price of a Roanoke County home is $80,000.

Many move to the county for its superior school system. Both remedial education as well as classes for the gifted are available.

Roanoke County also is a popular industrial site. Major employers include ITT, manufacturer of night vision goggles, Ingersoll Rand and Allstate Insurance.

For shopping, Tanglewood Mall is a popular place visited regionally by many looking for a wide variety of speciality shops. In the same area are numerous family restaurants that serve as a magnet for the whole valley.

Most of all, however, Roanoke County is known as a desirable place to live because of the high quality and variety of suburban services it offers residents. For more information, contact the Roanoke County -

Salem Chamber of Commerce at 7 S. College Ave., Salem, VA 24153, (703) 387-0267.

SALEM

There's an old story in the *Roanoke Times* newspaper office about a young cub reporter who had just moved to Salem. Feeling a sense of isolation, she asked a Salem native reporter, ready to retire, about just how long it would take to get "accepted" by her neighbors. "Oh, about three," the Salem native replied. "Three years?" responded the incredulous cub. "No, three generations, my dear!" was the reply.

To say that the city of Salem (population 25,000) has a sense of its own history and self-sufficiency is an understatement. Salem, its name derived from "shalom," meaning peace, is the oldest and southernmost community in the Roanoke Valley. That historical fact pervades Salem's quaint, charming culture. Many of its historic downtown Victorian homes with stained glass windows, tin roofs and pointed towers are on the National Historic Register.

General Andrew Lewis started the settlement in 1768 when he acquired his estate named "Richfield." In 1806, a charter to James Simpson created the town of Salem out of the Lewis estate, bounded by Union Street, Church Alley, Clay and Calhoun streets. Salem was chartered as a city in 1968. The local historical society recently opened a museum downtown.

Salem also has an excellent sense of community, especially when it comes to sports. The Salem Civic Center is the site of the fabulous Salem Fair and Exposition, an event that is a real coup for Salem and the largest of its kind in Virginia. You can do everything there from bungee jump to watch pigs race. The Civic Center seats 7,500 and offers a wide and varied program of community events. For example, it's home to the Roanoke Valley Horse Show, one of the 10 largest in the country. Salemites' love for athletics borders on the fanatic and considerable emphasis is placed on recreation, with more opportunities available than in most other areas of similar size. Facilities recently were expanded to include an 8,000-seat football stadium for the beloved Salem High Spartans.

Salem also provides exciting Class A professional baseball through the Salem Buccaneers, a Pittsburgh Pirate farm team who play at Salem Municipal Field. There are also three golf courses in Salem. In 1993, Salem will be the site of the national Alonzo Stagg Bowl.

Salemites also have a heart that never stops beating for their own. When high school football star, Chance Crawford, was paralyzed by a spinal injury during a football game in the early '80s, the townspeople rallied to pay his medical expenses. Beyond that, an annual ball tournament was arranged to assure the Crawfords would have no financial worries. As a final tribute, last year, Crawford was overwhelmingly elected to public office.

Festivals are especially popular. Old Salem Days in September features one of the largest antique car shows on the East Coast, as well as fine Salem art. One of the Roanoke Valley's best-known artists, Walter Biggs, lived here, and his legacy is carried on by Salem artists such as Harriet Stokes.

Salem is also a town full of strong, large industries such as General Electric and the regional VA Hospital. It is home to Roanoke College, a Lutheran-affiliated private liberal arts school that lends enormous culture to the area's charm. Salem's shopping district downtown is full of antique stores and "Mom and Pop" operations and Roanoke College students enjoy the local hang-outs, Mac & Bob's and Macados.

Many of Salem's citizens work, live and play within its boundaries and never feel the need to leave their beloved city, regardless of how long it really takes to become an "insider." For more information, contact the Roanoke Co.-Salem Chamber of Commerce at 7 S. College Ave., Salem, VA 24153, (703) 387-0267.

VINTON

Vinton, a small, unpretentious town (population 7,665) east of Roanoke, must be doing something right. Over the past several decades, in the midst of its homespun lifestyle, it has spawned and nurtured some of Virginia's most important modern leaders.

On any given day, Virginia House Majority Leader C. Richard Cranwell, called "the most powerful man in the Blue Ridge of Vir-

ginia," can be found having lunch downtown with his constituency who call him "Dicky" and tell him how to run Virginia's Legislature. Fortune 500 Norfolk and Southern CEO David Goode still visits his wise dad, Ott, founder of Vinton's famous Dogwood Festival, at Ott's 50-year-old downtown real estate business to get advice.

Vinton also is an important leader in its own right. In 1990, it set other Virginia municipalities on notice when its forward-looking town council began the first mandatory comprehensive recycling program in the state, effectively reducing landfilled solid waste by 25 percent. Vinton is also proud of a school system ranked among the state's top 10 and its populace comes out in droves for the William Byrd High Terriors. Its school system has the highest average achievement scores in the Valley and teachers' salaries rank 9th in the state.

From what beginnings did such an important town spring? Gish's Mill, built prior to 1838, provided a start for the town. David Gish sold his mill to Isaac White Vinyard in 1867 and, by this time, enough people had settled around the mill to form the basis of the town of Vinton. Although the mill burned, some of the brick walls still are standing. The town was chartered in 1884 and relied on the railroad for employment. Moving into the future, the N&W Railway continued to be Vinton's most important industry. Today, Precision Weaving is Vinton's largest employer.

Vinton residents play as hard

as they work. The town is strategically located beside the Blue Ridge Parkway, providing easy recreational access. Vinton's Folklife Festival and Farmer's Market are annual excuses to have a good time. And the oldest festival in the Roanoke Valley, the Dogwood Festival is held in Vinton and has hosted a number of celebrities during the past 38 years. It is always a pageantry of queens, bands, floats and politicians. The first-class, All-American parade always ends at the Vinton War Memorial, Vinton's landmark building and cultural center.

An incredibly moving parade followed the Persian Gulf War, when the slain former William Byrd High School star athlete and straight-A student, VMI cadet Terry Plunk, was honored with a dogwood tree planted at the War Memorial by the Kuwaitian ambassador. Vinton also received national recognition for its downtown Persian Gulf War information and support center, in the true spirit of Small Town, USA.

Vinton serves its citizens well with wonderful recreational and spectator sports activities. Its municipal pool is beautiful and its recreation department program and special events are second to none.

Vinton's untapped tourism potential is enormous. It is the center of the politically-designated Blue Ridge Region of Virginia. In addition to its proximity to the well-traveled Parkway (9 million annual visitors through the Virginia section), Vinton is the last commercial center before Smith Mountain Lake, the state's largest lake. It also is the gateway to the Explore Project.

In the meantime, it's the epitome of the best of small town living. The best is yet to come. For more information, contact the town of Vinton at 311 S. Pollard St., Vinton, VA 24179, (703) 983-0613.

East of the Blue Ridge Region

This gorgeous stretch of land begins in Warren County, east of Front Royal, and sweeps southward along the mountains all the way through Charlottesville and Lynchburg to Franklin County south of Roanoke.

For the most part, we are talking about rural territory with few blaring billboards, convenience stores and shopping malls. It's an area rich in history that has little in common with the Shenandoah Valley across the mountains.

Whereas the Valley was settled primarily by Scotch-Irish and Germans who migrated south from Pennsylvania and Maryland, the foothills east of the Blue Ridge — especially Charlottesville and to the north — became home to families moving west from Richmond and the Tidewater.

No super highway cuts through the region, as does I-81 in the Valley. Route 29 is the major highway from Culpeper to Lynchburg, where you will find wineries, splendid antique shops and quaint country stores right off the road. The secondary roads winding through the region will also carry you to gorgeous country inns and bed and breakfasts, vineyards, pick-your-own apple orchards and historic mansions open for tours.

It takes a little more effort to tour this region and do it right. But it is well worth it.

In the north, Rappahannock County is home to one of the most charming, even utopic, towns in America — "Little" Washington. It is the oldest of the 28 towns in the United States named for the Father of Our Country, who surveyed and laid out the town around 1749. Washington has its own internationally known five-star restaurant and inn, a performing arts center, an artists' cooperative and several classy galleries, boutiques and antique shops.

Just to the south, historic Sperryville sits below the entrance to Skyline Drive. It's a great little town to explore on foot, with antique stores, galleries, arts and crafts studios and a shop where you can buy Native American weavings, jewelry, quilts and crafts.

In the northern foothills region are two entry ways into Shenandoah National Park: Thornton Gap at Rt. 211 near Sperryville and Swift Run Gap at Rt. 33 through Greene County.

There is no road into the park from Madison County — a source of longstanding frustration among many residents. Madison County lost more land to the national park than any other county, and was reportedly promised an entryway. But for some reason, national leaders reneged. This history explains in large part the level of outrage local residents felt when park officials proposed expanding the national

park's boundaries into the county. The officials eventually dropped the idea, realizing how ugly a battle it would have become.

Madison County's earliest settlers were German iron workers. When they had completed the terms of their indentured servitude at Lord Spotswood's Germanna mines in Orange County, the Germans set out to build new lives for themselves as craftsmen and farmers. That tradition continues in Madison County. Many craftspeople — furniture makers, potters, wood carvers, quilters and jewelry artisans, make this area their home.

The same can be said for Greene County, where you can drop by the Blue Ridge Pottery on Rt. 33 to Skyline Drive and chat with local potter Alan Ward as he works at his wheel. The store is kind of a headquarters for arts and crafts made especially in Greene County. Situated in the former Golden Horseshoe Inn built in 1827, Blue Ridge Pottery sells beautiful religious pewter jewelry made in nearby Stanardsville, pottery, weavings, Virginia wine and much more.

To the east, the rolling hills of Orange County hold many historical attractions, foremost being Montpelier, a 2,700-acre estate that was the life-long home of James Madison and his equally famous, and more popular wife, Dolley.

Orange County is also home to the prestigious Barboursville Vineyards, situated on the bucolic grounds of what was once an imposing brick mansion designed by Thomas Jefferson. The ruins and surrounding towering boxwoods form the backdrop for summer Shakespeare productions by the Four County Players of Barboursville.

This Italian-owned winery is one of many in the foothills region, which is truly the heart of Virginia wine country. Within a couple of miles is the family-owned Burnley Vineyards. Linden, Oasis and Farfelu vineyards lie in the northern foothills near Front Royal. Further south in Madison County, Rose River Vineyards hugs the mountains near Syria. The award-winning Misty Mountain Vineyards lies farther south in Madison, and Virginia's largest and most successful winery, Prince Michel Vineyards, is located off Va. 29 near Culpeper.

Charlottesville and Albemarle County boast six wineries — including one located on the same property where Thomas Jefferson hired an Italian viticulturalist to grow grapes more than two centuries ago.

Nelson County, southeast of Charlottesville, is home to two wineries, several bed and breakfasts and the spectacular four-season Wintergreen Resort. It is also where Earl Hamner—a.k.a. "John Boy" Walton, spent his youth. A museum dedicated to the heart-warming television series opened last fall in the same school where "John Boy" and his siblings learned their ABCs.

Another budding attraction in Nelson County is Oak Ridge, a fabulous, early 19th-century estate situated on 4,800 acres. Oak Ridge once belonged to Thomas Fortune Ryan, a local boy who became one of nation's 10 wealthiest men at the turn of the century. The mansion,

Italian gardens and grounds are being restored and are open to the public (please refer to our arts and culture chapter for more details about the Waltons Museum and Oak Ridge).

Major urban centers in the foothills region are Charlottesville and Lynchburg, both thriving university cities that are rich in history, culture and natural beauty. We'll tell you more about these cities in separate introductions farther ahead.

When Thomas Jefferson needed to escape the pressures of domestic life in Monticello he would head south to Poplar Forest, his retreat in Bedford County near Lynchburg. There, Jefferson designed what became the first octagonal home built in America. The beautiful residence still stands and today houses the Poplar Forest Foundation.

Most of Smith Mountain Lake lies in Bedford and Franklin counties. This is Virginia's largest lake, with 500 miles of shoreline. It is truly a recreation paradise, offering endless opportunities for swimming, sailing, water-skiing and camping, and sophisticated restaurants, inns and bed and breakfasts.

The southernmost county that we consider part of the foothills — or east of the Blue Ridge region, is Franklin (neighboring Floyd County is part of the New River Valley). The ethnic diversity of Franklin County makes it unusual for Southwest Virginia. There's a sizeable German Baptist population, a people whose habits and beliefs are somewhat similar to the

Amish. They operate some of the county's most impeccable farms and bake some of the most delicious sticky buns you'll find this side of heaven. Boone's Country Store in Burnt Chimney, run entirely by German Baptists, is one place to buy these treats.

Booker T. Washington was born in Franklin County, and a strong and vibrant African American community resides there. The county's Ferrum College is home to the National Blue Ridge Folk Life Institute, which preserves and documents the culture of the region and every October throws a huge folk life festival.

The following introductions will give you more of an in-depth look at the major cities and some of the counties in the area east of the Blue Ridge.

ORANGE COUNTY

Northeast of Charlottesville lies Orange County, a beautiful hilly land with a fascinating history. Lt. Gov. Alexander Spotswood used Germanna in Orange County as a base for exploring the Shenandoah Valley in the early 1700s. He and his fellow English explorers scaled what is now called Swift Run Gap to see the fertile valley for the first time, and many suffered fevers and chills and no doubt a few hangovers on the trip (one of the explorers wrote about drinking to the Royal family's health in brandy, shrub, rum, champagne, canary and burgundy and many more spirits). In jest, the group decided to call themselves the "Knights of the Golden Horseshoe."

Historians relate that when Spotswood returned to Williamsburg he promptly wrote a letter to His Majesty King George and told him of the wonderful country beyond the Blue Ridge. He also asked for a grant for the Order of the Knights of the Golden Horseshoe.

In time, a proclamation arrived from English creating such an Order, and included were 50 tiny golden horseshoes inscribed in Latin. King George must have had quite a sense of humor, because along with granting Spotswood the title of Knight, he sent him a bill for the golden horseshoes. Reportedly, Spotswood paid for them out of his own pocket without a complaint.

Today, visitors can see the "Enchanted Castle" at the Germanna Archeological Site, where Spotswood built an elegant brick mansion in the early 1720s. The house burned around 1750, and the site is undergoing extensive archeological research. It's under shelter and open to visitors, and an exhibit tells the story of Germanna and the life and contributions of Gov. Spotswood.

Orange County later became home to James Madison, the 4th U.S. President and the Father of the Constitution. Madison's own grandparents first settled Montpelier, a 2,700-acre estate that is now owned by the National Trust for Historic Preservation and open for tours. This is a fascinating place to watch the restoration process unfold, as staff archeologists and architectural historians work on-site to discover more about the vast property dur-

Visit Historic Orange County

" Montpelier "

History

Lodging

Attractions

Wineries

TOURS
→

Recreation

For more information, contact the Orange County Visitor Center IGBR 154 Madison Rd. Orange, Va 22960 (703) 672 - 1653

ing Madison's time there.

The James Madison Museum is located in nearby downtown Orange, where you can also visit the only surviving example of Thomas Jefferson's design for church architecture, St. Thomas Episcopal Church.

Also located in Orange County are reminders of the terrible war that nearly split our country in two. The Wilderness Battlefields in the eastern end of the county were the scene of the first clash between Robert E. Lee and Ulysses S. Grant in May, 1864. The battle resulted in 26,000 casualties. The battlefields are open for self-guided tours.

Nearby Gordonsville is home to the Exchange Hotel, a restored railroad hotel that served as a military hospital during the war. It now houses an excellent Civil War Museum.

Closer to Charlottesville are the Barboursville Ruins—what's left of a mansion designed by Jefferson for James Barbour, Governor of Virginia, U.S. Senator, Secretary of War and Minister to England.

Orange County boasts the most acres of grape production of any county in the Commonwealth. Along with the Barboursville Winery, which has been praised by *Wine Spectator* magazine, the county is home to the smaller Burnley Vineyards, one of the oldest vineyards in the region.

The Montpelier estate hosts a wine festival every May, featuring live music, crafts, food and local wines. Montpelier is also the scene of steeplechase and flat track races

on the first Saturday every November. This is a hallowed tradition in its 51st year that draws huge crowds of horse-lovers.

For more information about these and other attractions and fine bed and breakfasts in Orange County, contact the Visitors Bureau, P.O. Box 133, Orange, VA 22960, (703) 672-1653. A Visitor's Center is also located in the James Madison Museum at 129 Caroline Street in Orange (703) 672-1776.

NELSON COUNTY

Roughly a quarter of this rural, agricultural county lies in the George Washington National Forest. Wintergreen Resort, a four-season vacation paradise with a year round residential community, hugs the mountains in the western part of the county. Crabtree Falls, a spectacular series of cascades, is one of the highlights of the forest along Rt. 56, the scenic road that crosses the mountains and enters the Shenandoah Valley at Vesuvius. Wintergreen has led the way for tourism to become the focus for economic development in Nelson County.

But, it's probably fair to say that local leaders want the county to remain clean, beautiful and rural. Apples are the chief crop of the area's agricultural economy, and beef cattle is the second leading industry.

Earl Hamner, a.k.a. "John Boy" Walton, grew up in the tiny town of Schuyler, a mecca for fans of the popular, heart-warming television series of the 70s. For years, fans have flocked to Schuyler to track down the old home place and other reminders of the TV show. Now they can go straight to the fascinating new Waltons Mountain Museum. Thanks to support from Hamner and a $30,000 state grant, the museum opened last fall in the same school attended by Hamner and his siblings. Don't miss the regularly-shown video documentary with interviews with Hamner and the actors and screenwriters.

Another attraction under development in Nelson County is Oak Ridge, a fabulous 4,800-acre estate that belonged to Thomas Fortune Ryan, a leading financier and Democrat at the turn of the century. The mansion, formal Italian gardens, greenhouse and other buildings are being renovated by its new owners, a Tidewater couple who plan to build a horse racing track on the estate. They host all kinds of community and cultural events on the magnificent grounds, from Easter egg hunts to regional wine and harvest festivals.

Nelson County is also home to Afton Mountain Vineyards and Mountain Cove Vineyards in Lovingston. The owner of the latter, Al Weed, is a leader in the county's tourism efforts and is a great person to chat with about the area and what it has to offer.

Accommodations in the county include luxury condominiums and suites at Wintergreen Resort and several bed and breakfasts, including the Meander Inn and the Acorn Inn, a popular place with skiers.

One of the best places to eat — and eat hearty — is the Rodes Farm Inn on Rt. 613 near Nellysford. Owned by Wintergreen, Rodes Farm Inn is an unpretentious country-style restaurant in a renovated barn that serves home-cooked Southern fare.

For more information about Nelson County, contact the Nelson County Community Development Office at (800) 282-8223.

CHARLOTTESVILLE

Charlottesville is a crown jewel of a city, with so much beauty, history, culture and lively commerce that it's no wonder it is growing by leaps and bounds.

If he were alive, Thomas Jefferson, native of the territory, would probably roll his eyes and sigh at the traffic congestion that now clogs such major arteries as 250 and 29 at times. Such is the cost of the city's allure.

Fortunately, Albemarle County, which surrounds Charlottesville on all sides, remains largely rural, with rolling pastures, elegant horse farms and lush forests that lead up to the wilderness of the Shenandoah National Park. And the city itself contains many enclaves of natural beauty — from the lovely gardens along the colonnade at the University of Virginia to the fine old homes surrounded by mounds of azaleas, rhododendrons and camellias.

Reminders of the nation's early history abound in the Charlottesville area. The city took its name from the popular Queen Charlotte, wife of King George III. Albemarle County dates back to 1744, when it was named in honor

Come to Charlottesville to savor the region's rich history and pristine beauty.

For All Four Seasons:

- Points-of-Interest • Bed & Breakfasts • Country Inns
- Hotels/Resorts • Restaurants • Antiques & Galleries
- Shopping • Vineyards • Ballooning • Steeplechase Races
- Flight-Seeing • Skiing • Fishing • Tennis • Canoeing
- Hiking • Camping • Cycling • Golfing • Arts &
Entertainment • Events & Activities • Real Estate • Schools
- Retirement • Newcomer Services

Charlottesville, Virginia: The Heart of Central Virginia.

For a free Guide call or write to:
Charlottesville Guide
853 West Main St.
Charlottesville, VA 22903
(804) 979-4913

Photo: Richmond Newspapers

Mabry Mill, located on the picturesque Blue Ridge Parkway, still grinds flour for buckwheat cakes made fresh at the mill.

of William Ann Keppel, second Earl of Albemarle, who was governor general of the colony of Virginia. The Earl never laid foot in the county, but two U.S. presidents, Jefferson and James Monroe, made it their home.

Monticello, the architectural wonder that Jefferson designed and never stopped tinkering with, remains the area's leading attraction. The mountaintop estate opens its doors to visitors seven days a week, inviting all to glimpse Jefferson's genius through his architecture, gardens and innovations. Another fascinating exhibit about Jefferson's domestic life at Monticello lies down the hill and next to I-64 at the Thomas Jefferson Visitors Center.

Thanks to Jefferson's architectural abilities, the campus of the University of Virginia is considered one of the most beautiful in the nation. Jefferson designed the Rotunda of his "academic village" after the Roman Pantheon. The graceful Rotunda, the pavilions and their gardens and the whitewashed colonnade comprise the original University buildings. The American Institute of Architects voted the original campus as the most outstanding achievement in American architecture in 1976.

Not far from Monticello on another mountain slope is Ash Lawn-Highland, home of James Monroe, Jefferson's friend and America's fifth president. Strutting, showy peacocks grace the lawn at Ash Lawn-Highland, where visitors can witness Monroe's cultured lifestyle and learn about a working farm of the 19th century. The box-wood-covered grounds at Ash Lawn come to life in the summer, when light opera performances entertain guests under the stars.

There are reminders of history also in the streets of downtown Charlottesville, especially around Court Square—where Jefferson and Monroe spent much of their leisure time. Here every building bears a plaque dating it to the early days of the city, making it easy to imagine what the city must have looked like when Jefferson practiced law here.

The Albemarle County Courthouse, built in 1762, served as the meeting place of the Virginia Legislature as they fled Cornwallis's approaching army in 1781. State Legislator Daniel Boone was one of the seven men who was captured in a surprise raid on Charlottesville led by British Cavalry General Banastre Tarleton during that campaign. Tarleton failed at capturing then Gov. Jefferson, but nabbed Boone at the corner of Jefferson and Park streets.

The downtown historic district is not only of interest to history buffs. Folks of all ages enjoy strolling along the pedestrian-only downtown mall, lined on both sides with specialty boutiques, antique stores, outdoor cafes, ice-cream shops and great book stores.

Also within easy walking distance are galleries, including an elementary school that has been transformed into the lively McGuffey Art Center. Here you can observe artists at work in their studios, buy fine handcrafts, pottery, paintings, photos and prints, and visit the Second Street Gallery inside. Adjacent to the McGuffey Art Center and across the street is Vinegar Hill Theater, a place to see foreign films, documentaries and movies not usually shown in standard theaters. Within walking distance are also museums, libraries and more than 25 restaurants to choose from.

Speaking of food, the culinary scene in Charlottesville has become rather lively and diverse. If you want hot and spicy Southern barbecue or country ham and biscuits, you'll find it here. But you may also be tempted by the Indian, Vietnamese, French, German, Italian, Brazilian and American "nouvelle" cuisine in the area.

At the risk of sounding trite, we must not forget the famous figures of the film world who make Charlottesville their home. Charlottesvilleans are reportedly known for their ability to fake nonchalance at the sight of such figures as Sam Shepard, Jessica Lange and Sissy Spacek. It is considered gauche to gawk or ask for an autograph, and this must be one reason why these famous folks and their families seem to have found such a comfortable life here.

Of course, Charlottesville's association with the rich and famous is nothing new. The area was the setting for part of "Giant," the western starring Elizabeth Taylor, Rock Hudson and James Dean. Randolph Scott, a leading star in "Ride the High Country," one of the greatest westerns ever made, lived at Montpelier for a couple of years when he was married to Marion Dupont.

Land has become very expensive in the Charlottesville area, such that it is nearly impossible for people of moderate means to purchase their own place. The gulf between the "haves" and "have-nots" in Charlottesville is widening so much that even the local association of Realtors is disturbed, making the issue of affordable housing their highest priority this year.

For instance, several new developments are selling homes on lots no larger than three acres for between $300,000 and $800,000; homes that cost around $130,000 are considered low-end.

One new development east of town called Keswick is being sponsored by Sir Bernard Ashley of the Laura Ashley group. The club will cost $25,000 per person to join, and the golf course is being designed by Arnold Palmer himself. An overnight stay at the posh hotel at Keswick, scheduled to open this fall, will cost between $200 and $600 a night — expensive even by Charlottesville's standards.

The new affluence of Charlottesville has its positive side: the backing of such cultural resources as the Virginia Festival of American Film. Patricia Kluge, ex-wife of the richest man in America, provided the primary means to establish the festival, which is held at UVA every fall. Illustrious special guests have included Jimmy Stewart, Gregory Peck, Ann Margret and Charlton Heston, and a host of screenwriters, critics and academics.

More than 2,000 accommodations are available in the

Charlottesville area, ranging from economy motels to some of the most elegant inns and bed and breakfasts imaginable.

A trip to Charlottesville isn't complete without at least one stop at a local winery for a sample, a bottle, or a tour to learn how wine is made. There are ten wineries within easy driving distance of Charlottesville, the wine capital of Virginia. Jefferson would be proud to know this; he often dreamed of producing fine Virginia wines and experimented with grape growing for more than 30 years.

One of the region's finest wineries, Simeon Vineyards, is situated on the same property near Monticello that Thomas Jefferson donated to an Italian winegrower in 1773. The Italian, Philip Mazzei, had early success at making wine, but his efforts were interrupted by the Revolutionary War and his grapes were trampled to death by the horses of a Hessian general who had rented the property.

For more information about wineries, accommodations, restaurants, night life, shopping, real estate, retirement and cultural life in the Charlottesville area, please refer to the specific chapters farther on in this guide. The complimentary Charlottesville guide, which can be found in hotels and all over the city, also tells visitors what to do, where to go, and how to get there. The guide also provides information about Orange and Madison counties, Waynesboro and Staunton.

In addition, much helpful information can be obtained by writing or calling the Charlottesville/Albemarle Convention & Visitors Bureau, P.O. Box 161, Rt. 20 South, Charlottesville, VA 22902, (804) 977-1783).

LYNCHBURG

"I consider it (Lynchburg) one of the most interesting spots in the state...." Thomas Jefferson.

Democracy's founding father, who scandalized Lynchburg society by eating a "love apple," (tomatoes were thought to be poisonous) summed up best how Lynchburg's citizens feel about their city and its vast array of cultural, educational and recreational opportunities.

For the past decade, the national spotlight has shone on Lynchburg's politically active pastor of the internationally-known Thomas Roads Baptist Church here, the Rev. Jerry Falwell. Known as the "City of Churches," Lynchburg (population 70,000) has 129 other houses of worship in addition to the church that launched the Moral Majority. Although the Quakers were the first religious group to settle here and strongly influenced Lynchburg's history, their opposition to slavery caused them to migrate to Ohio and Indiana.

Long before Falwell built his national church from a small Lynchburg congregation, Lynchburg's central location and role in transporting goods by river and railroad had already made it famous.

Lynchburg was named for its founder, John Lynch, the son of Charles Lynch. A 15-year-old Irish runaway, Charles Lynch decided to learn a trade and apprenticed himself to a wealthy Quaker tobacco planter. The relationship worked out so well that the Roman Catholic Lynch married the planter's daughter. Also an enterprising young man, their son John Lynch, reared as a Quaker, started a ferry service when he was 17 across the James River in 1757. In 1786, the Virginia General Assembly granted him a charter for a town, 45 acres of his own land. Lynchburg was incorporated as a town in 1805 and a city in 1852. Lynch also built the city's first bridge, replacing his ferry in 1812.

Historically known as the "Hill City," Lynchburg attracted industrial magnates who dealt in tobacco and iron, the chief products of early Lynchburg. Their ornate, luxurious homes, bordered by enormous decorative wrought iron fences, are alone worth a visit. Three of them have been made into sumptuous bed and breakfasts, Madison House, The Mansion and Langhorne Manor. All of their proprietors will make every effort to pamper you just like the original inhabitants. They are located in Lynchburg's seven original neighborhoods, its "hills." By name, they are College Hill, Daniel's Hill, Diamond Hill, Federal Hill, Franklin Hill, Garland Hill and White Rock Hill. Walking tour maps of the area are available from Lynchburg's dynamic tourism marketing team at its Convention & Visitors Bureau. You can call them at (804) 847-1732 for a run-down on so many attractions that it will take you a good week to see them all. There are many fine restaurants and great shopping here as well.

In the decade before the Civil War, Lynchburg was one of the two wealthiest cities per capita in the U.S. As you would expect, its moneyed citizenry spawned a rich culture. Sarah Bernhardt and Anna Pavlova appeared at The Academy of Music, which opened in 1905. The old music hall has been purchased by Liberty University, which plans to restore it. Jones Memorial Library was completed in 1908 and is one of America's foremost genealogical research libraries. Lynchburg's Fine Arts Center, the city's cultural nucleus, houses two art galleries, a theatre, two dance studios and the oldest continuous theatre group in the country. Each year, 100,000 people (more than the city's population) take classes, hear concerts and see plays, ballet and art exhibits at the center.

Scores of famous authors sprang from Lynchburg's culture. Two of its most famous, curiously enough, gained their fame for their books on the opposite sides of democratic and racial issues.

The great historian Dr. Douglas Southall Freeman, born in Lynchburg in 1886, received 24 honorary degrees and two Pulitzer Prizes. One was in 1936 for his four-volume work on *The Life of Robert E. Lee*, the great Confederate general who fought to preserve slavery. (The other, in 1948, was for a series on George Washington.)

Anne Spencer, an African American poet born in 1882, is the only Virginian whose works are included in the *Norton Anthology of*

LYNCHBURG
VIRGINIA

"The most interesting spot in the state."

- Thomas Jefferson, 1817

The **Lynchburg Museum** invites you to experience the wealth of our history. From the prehistoric Monocan tribes and early Quaker settlers, artifacts and displays recall the days of King Tobacco, the Civil War, New South industrialization, and eventually the arrival of high technology. *Open daily from 1 to 4 pm. Small admission fee required*

Point of Honor was built on Daniel's Hill high above the James River around 1815. Carefully restored, this striking mansion was home to some of Lynchburg's most prominent citizens. This is a perfect tour for those who appreciate 19th century architecture and furnishings. *Open daily 1 to 4 pm. Small admission fee required.*

But perhaps Lynchburg's most time-honored tradition is the **Community Market.** For the past two centuries, local folks have come here to exchange goods, visit with friends or just pass the time away. And not only will you find fresh produce, handmade crafts and baked goods here, but this has become the city's favorite place for outdoor events. *Open Mon-Sat until 2 pm*

For more information call or write:
Greater Lynchburg Chamber Of Commerce Visitor Center
12th and Church Streets, Lynchburg, VA 24504
(804) 847-1811

Modern American and British Poetry. She helped establish Lynchburg's first lending library for African Americans and started Lynchburg's first NAACP chapter.

Frequent visitors to Spencer's restored home, garden and studio, "Edankraal," (open by appointment to visitors at 1313 Pierce St.), included Dr. Martin Luther King, Dr. George Washington Carver, Jackie Robinson and Marion Anderson, the African American singing star who was denied entrance to perform in Washington's DAR concert hall in Washington because of her race. Interestingly enough, one of the founders of the DAR, Ellet Cabell, was born at Point of Honor, a beautifully restored Lynchburg mansion, now a museum, in the same area as Spencer's house.

Point of Honor, so named for the gun duels fought there, was built by Dr. George Cabell, Sr., whose most famous patient was Patrick Henry. East of Lynchburg, at Brookneal, is Red Hill Shrine, the last home and burial place of the great patriot and orator. Point of Honor is part of Lynchburg's city museum system — one which other cities would do well to emulate.

Any discussion of Lynchburg's history must also mention the influence of Carter Glass, born in Lynchburg in 1858 and Secretary of the Treasury under President Woodrow Wilson. Glass served as Virginia State Senator from 1899-1902, in the U.S. House of Representatives from 1902-1918, and represented Virginia in the U.S. Senate from 1920-1946. He was the first living person to appear alone on a regular U.S. coin. Glass contributed greatly to Lynchburg's civic life.

Lynchburg's quality of life is also greatly enhanced by its bustling community market at Bateau Landing, where shoppers can choose fresh produce and homemade goods. The annual Festival on the James and The Bateau Festival held in June celebrate the historic James River's contributions with entertainment, historic crafts exhibits and the start of the bateau race to Richmond. Kaleidoscope is an annual fall festival celebrating life in Central Virginia with an arts festival, bands, Riverfront Jamboree, craft show, pops picnic and the Lynchburg Symphony.

Lynchburg has long been a leading industrial city. It has the highest per capita manufacturing employment in Virginia. Today, is also home to 3,000 businesses and led the way in developing one of the state's first small business incubators.

It is extraordinary how many early industries are still in business. The second-oldest funeral home in America, Diuguid's, has been comforting the bereaved since 1817. Lynchburg Gas Co., founded in 1851, was one of the first in the country to shed light on operating a gas utility. Wiley & Wilcox Engineering, started in 1901, is one of the oldest engineering firms in the U.S. In 1901, John Craddock tried the first shoe company in the South on for size in Lynchburg, founding Craddock-Terry. It was a perfect fit. Today, Craddock-Terry's downtown outlet store offers a dazzling array of 300,000 pairs of shoes, including many odd sizes. In 1889, the young pharmacist, Charles Brown, began selling his Chap-Stick lip balm. Since, his C.B. Fleet Company's product line has expanded to other national lines, including the first disposable enema and Summer's Eve douche. Babcock & Wilcox Co. and General Electric are other major employers.

As an important manufacturing center, Lynchburg played an important role in the Civil War. Perhaps none was more important than the advance of medicine for Civil War soldiers brought to the "Pest House" by Dr. John Jay Terrell. Located in the historic Lynchburg Confederate Cemetery, within the City Cemetery, the Pest House is open to visitors with displays of Dr. Terrell's pace-setting work in setting sanitary standards, including his 19th-century medical kit.

As a major educational center, Lynchburg is home to nine diverse colleges. Randolph-Macon Woman's College was the first woman's college in the South to be accredited and the first to receive a Phi Beta Kappa chapter. The Maier Museum, an outstanding collection of American art, is also at the college. Sweet Briar is another famous woman's college and is affiliated with the Virginia Center for the Creative Arts, an internationally-recognized working retreat for writers, artists and composers in Amherst County. Other colleges are Jerry Falwell's Liberty University, Lynchburg College, a liberal arts school, and a community college,

seminary and two business colleges.

Lynchburg's public schools also are outstanding. Both of its high schools and one of its middle schools have been designated model schools by the Commonwealth of Virginia. The city also has 10 private schools. The most famous is The Virginia School of the Arts, a private boarding school for students grades 7-12. Talented young people from around the nation compete to enter the school, which encourages them to achieve the highest standards for performance in dance, drama, music or the visual arts.

High school sports also are popular. Lynchburg is home to the Virginia High School Coaches Association All-Star Games, bringing the best in high school sports to the area. Colleges offer spectator sports and when springtime comes, fans head for the diamond to see the area's only Double A professional sports team, the Lynchburg Red Sox.

Golf, tennis and swimming are popular past-times. The city operates 10 parks, 24 playgrounds, 34 tennis courts, 26 baseball diamonds and eight community centers. Miller Park is home to an Olympic size pool. In the heart of Lynchburg is Blackwater Creek Natural Area with the Ruskin Freer Preserve, a 155-acre animal sanctuary.

A major medical center, Lynchburg's two hospitals, Virginia Baptist and Lynchburg General, have gained national attention by sharing staff and services to avoid duplication and keep down expenses.

Lynchburg is served by a new $8 million airport terminal. A hub for daytrips, tourists can go north to Schuyler, (pronounced Sky-ler), the restored home of Earl "John-Boy" Hamner, author of the book on which "The Waltons" TV series was based. Just west of the city is Poplar Forest, Jefferson's summer retreat under restoration and open to the public. Twenty miles east is Appomattox, the site where our nation reunited after the Civil War. Monument Terrace, in the center of Lynchburg's downtown, honors the heroes of all wars.

Whatever you decide to see and do while in Lynchburg, you'll probably echo the words of Thomas Jefferson, in deciding that it is one of the most interesting spots in the state. For more information, contact the Greater Lynchburg Chamber of Commerce at P.O. Box 2027, 2015 Memorial Ave., Lynchburg, VA 24501, (804) 845-5966.

AMHERST COUNTY

North of Lynchburg is Amherst County, (population 29,000). The Monocan Indians were the first humans to populate the area. It is named for Sir Jeffrey Amherst, the British commander of all forces in America from 1758-1763. Amherst led the British armies that successfully drove France from Canada and was the British hero of the Revolutionary War battle of Ticonderoga against the upstart Americans.

In 1761, Amherst County was created from a section of Albemarle County. In 1807, Amherst was divided and the northern part became Nelson County. Tobacco was an early cash crop, as were apples.

Three-fourths of the county's rolling terrain is forests. The Blue Ridge Parkway offers dramatic views while providing the perfect spot for an afternoon picnic. It is a popular recreational area with magnificent mountain views, clean air and thousands of acres of unspoiled forests, rivers and lakes. Numerous leisure and recreational activities can be found in the George Washington National Forest. The Appalachian Trail bisects Amherst County and affords the serious hiker the ultimate challenge.

Winton Country Club, the 18th-century manor that was the former home of Patrick Henry's sister, opens its 18-hole championship golf course to the public here.

Twenty industries also are tucked away in the hills, including a German cuckoo clock-maker, Hermle-Black Forest Clocks.

Sweet Briar College, a private woman's college built on the grounds of an old plantation near the town of Amherst, contributes to the arts experience and educational quality of life. Recently it has hosted anthropologist Jane Goodall, the Glenn Miller Orchestra and Isaac B. Singer, winner of the Nobel Prize in Literature.

The most famous Sweet Briar affiliation is The Virginia Center for the Creative Arts, an artists-in-residency program that brings in the world's most talented writers, visual artists and composers and gives them a place where they can have peace and quiet for their creativity.

Visitors will enjoy the Amherst County Historical Museum, located in the German Revival-style Kearfott-Wood House, built in 1907 by Dr. Kearfott. When renovations are completed, the museum will house four exhibit rooms and a gift shop. The upstairs is used for storing the museum's collection and office space. A reference library located there is available to the public.

Amherst County serves as a springboard into many other daytrips. It is close to Charlottesville and Wintergreen Resort.

SMITH MOUNTAIN LAKE

How do you spell relief?

L-A-K-E, Smith Mountain, that is, western Virginia's biggest playground and Virginia's largest lake. Smith Mountain Lake is 20,000 acres of placid waters, 40 miles long and surrounded by 500 miles of shoreline.

It touches Franklin, Bedford and Pittsylvania counties (combined population 142,000). The lake is a colorful place where people love to go and hate to leave. The sunsets are streaked with purple. The water is a stunning blue. Wildlife, like glossy green-headed mallard ducks and chubby, gray-striped bass, add to the local color.

Until recently, Smith Mountain Lake was a place for people who owned their own vacation home or knew somebody who owned a boat. Thanks to the state finally opening a public beach at Smith Mountain Lake State Park three years ago, the lake is now for everyone to enjoy.

As lakes go, Smith Mountain

is relatively new. Like its older sister to the south, Claytor Lake in Pulaski, the lake was formed to dam a river and generate electrical power for Appalachian Power Company. It took six years and a crew of 200 to move 300,000 cubic yards of earth to make way for the 175,000 cubic feet of concrete used to build the Smith Mountain Dam, where full pond is 613 feet above sea level. The Roanoke River started filling Smith Mountain Lake on Sept. 24, 1963, and reached capacity on March 7, 1966.

Archeologists examining the excavation necessary to build the Dam determined that the Algonquin Indians fished and hunted here long before anybody else did.

While Smith Mountain was a popular spot from day one, a real breakthrough for the lake was when developer Dave Wilson started Bernard's Landing Resort in the early 80s. Wilson, who later ran into financial problems, is widely credited with being the moving force behind opening the lake to everyone and making it a major western Virginia tourism attraction.

Since, Bernard's Landing Resort and its gourmet restaurant have become the most important tourist attraction at the lake, bringing in people from around the country as condominium owners, many of whom offer public rentals. For people who enjoy bed and breakfasts, the historic Manor at Taylor's Store on Route 122 was recently featured in *Southern Living* magazine.

A second important addition

to the lake's culture was the building of Bridgewater Plaza at Hales Ford Bridge on Rt. 122. The center of Smith Mountain's social and night life, it offers restaurants, a marina, small shops and Harbortown Miniature Golf Course, which is built out over the water. The Bluewater Cruise Company's Virginia Dare, a 19th-century side wheeler that offers lunch and dinner cruises, also calls the Plaza home port. Bands play here weekends during the summer. It's a really fun place to take the kids to ride the carousel or just pick up an ice cream cone while listening to the band.

The year round lake community itself is comprised of about 5,000 residents. Some of them you will never have the opportunity to associate with. Throughout the area, its significant staid German Baptist population rarely mingles socially with outsiders. They dress similarly to Mennnonites and can be identified by the women's mesh bonnets and the men's long beards. Widely known for their agricultural prowess, they live on some of the most beautiful farms you've ever seen and make or grow virtually everything they need.

The anchor of community events is the Smith Mountain Lake Chamber of Commerce/Partnership, whose members support the lake's goals and run a Welcome Center staffed entirely by volunteers. Many of them are retirees from the North. At the Partnership, (703) 721-1203, you can pick up lots of brochures and material about marinas, jet ski and boat rentals, lake homes for rent, campgrounds, fishing guides and anything else you need to have a good time during your stay.

Annual events include the Partnership's Fall Festival, the Wine Festival held at Bernard's Landing, various golf tournaments and dances and the Smith Mountain Tour of Homes to benefit the National Multiple Sclerosis Society. Last year's event was one of the most successful fund-raisers in the nation as people from all over came to see lake living at its best. The 1993 event will be held in October.

There are plenty of things to do at the lake weekdays and weekends. The major attraction is Booker T. Washington National Monument, the former home of the famous African American statesman. It is six miles south of Hales Ford Bridge on Rt. 122. Also stop by APCO's Visitor Center at the Dam off Va. 40 on Rt. 908. It's full of hands-on exhibits for the kids and interesting AVs about how the lake was formed. Smith Mountain Lake State Park has a full calendar of summertime activities including swimming, fishing and canoeing. Call them at (703) 297-6066. The park is open from 8 AM until dusk and is located off VA 626 near Huddleston. There's a snack bar, pavilion and information center.

Golf is a major attraction for residents. However, unless you're a member of the Waterfront or Water's Edge residential communities, your game will be at Chestnut Creek, 18 holes of beauty. Chestnut Creek's restaurant is also open to the public. As with the other planned communities, it sells villa homesites for those who want to live and play by a golf course.

Other past-times are balloon flights, offered by Blue Ridge Balloons of Vinton (703) 890-3029; Parasailing, offered by Bridgewater Marina (703) 721-1203; and jet-skiing. There are plenty of places that rent the controversial water motorcycles (jet skis). Just call the Partnership for a list. The same goes for a host of boat rental locations.

For the serious boater, of which there are many, there is the Smith Mountain Yacht Club and at least several dozen marinas offering services ranging from restaurants to drydock. Again, the Partnership will give you a complete list. A word of caution...if you are interested in a quiet day on the water, Saturday probably is not the day to be out and about. That seems to be when weekenders, intent on an extra good time, and sometimes bolstered by too much drink, take to the water. Sundays and weekdays, however, are relatively calm.

Now, let's talk about fishing, the original reason many people came to the lake. Smith Mountain has a well-deserved reputation as an angler's paradise, especially for striped bass. Some coves literally churn with stripers, especially in the autumn. Getting them to bite your bait is another matter.

The state's largest striper, 44 pounds, 14 ounces, was caught here in 1992. The rate these whoppers are growing, that record will probably soon be surpassed. If you're serious about getting one of the big ones, a professional guide is a great idea. Some good ones are R.M. King

(703) 721-4444, Dave Sines (703) 721-5007 or Spike Franceschini at (703) 297-5611. They'll try to ensure you don't go home only with tales about the one that got away.

Now that you've hooked your fish and are also hooked on the lake, let's talk about buying your own vacation home here. Many a millionaire was made from lake real estate. People all over western Virginia are kicking themselves that they didn't buy when land was cheap. There are many tales of people recouping their original investment 10 times over within a decade. Those days, however, are long gone. A prime waterfront lot can easily sell at a starting point of $100,000. However, lake property is still inexpensive to Northerners used to New Jersey-type real estate prices.

Real estate costs range from the older neighborhoods, like Isle of Pines in Bedford County, in the $165,000 beginning range, to a $300,000 average at Mountain View Shores, also in Bedford County. Many people buy condos or mobile homes for their weekend retreats. A condo at Bernard's starts at $80,000, for example, still a bargain if you're from Manhattan.

Regardless of whether you're just visiting or planning to buy real estate and stay, Smith Mountain will win your heart while you're here. There's nothing more spectacular than a Smith Mountain sunset or more beautiful than the early morning mist that blankets the lake. You'll return many times to enjoy the view and have some fun. That's no fish tale!

BEDFORD CITY & COUNTY

It's here that Thomas Jefferson came to get away from it all at his summer home in Poplar Forest. That alone should tell you something about the quality of life in Bedford County. And some things never change. Even if nobody ever finds the famous Beale Treasure here, you can easily make a case that Bedford County and its charming county seat are a real "find" in themselves. More about the tantalizing treasure later... let's talk history.

The fastest-growing county outside Virginia's Urban Crescent of Northern Virginia, Bedford County (population 45,349) borders Smith Mountain Lake and is home to Smith Mountain Lake State Park. Bedford also is off the Blue Ridge Parkway, close to one of the Parkway's main attractions, the Peaks of Otter Lodge and Restaurant at Milepost 86, located on a spectacularly beautiful twin-peaked mountain that can be seen for miles.

Bedford city is a Main Street Downtown Revitalization City with organizations devoted to its historic past. A wonderful museum is located downtown, as is the Bedford County Public Library.

Bedford County was named for John Russell, fourth Duke of Bedford who, as Secretary of State for the Southern Department of Great Britain, had supervision of Colonial affairs. It was formed in 1754 from Lunenburg County and part of Albemarle County. The city of Bedford was chartered in 1968 and in the early 80s renovated its historic downtown area.

Today, you will see many interesting downtown shops and restaurants. There are two quaint bed and breakfasts, Bedford House, and Otters Den. The most intriguing place to eat is Bedford's old train station, which has been restored to its former glory and named, aptly, Bedford Station Restaurant. If you're into natural organic food, however, try the Gunstock Creek Cooperative, a quaint 19th-century store on Rt. 640 in Wheats Valley at the foot of the Blue Ridge.

Recreation abounds in Bedford County, with the Jefferson National Forest on the north offering the many diversions of the Blue Ridge, including hunting, fishing, camping, picnicking and trails for both horseback riding and biking. Part of the Appalachian Trail passes through the area, with this section especially full of wildflowers and wildlife. The James River flows through in the northeast. City residents enjoy 59-acre Liberty Lake Park, the heart of recreation. Bedford Lake and Park, 35 acres with a white sand beach off Rt. 639, offers swimming, boating, fishing and camping.

The county is largely rural, with half of its land devoted to farming, dairy and beef cattle, and orchards. One of the oldest trees on record, definitely the oldest in Virginia, stands at Poplar Park in Bedford County.

Bedford also is a manufacturing base of many different industries that make everything from pottery to clocks and golf carts, food flavoring to stew.

Bedford citizens have a rich small-town culture. There's The Little Town Players, a community theatre organization in its 15th season. The county's Sedalia Center offers classes in everything from classical music to "back to the land" survival skills and is a tremendous asset to the community.

Every Christmas, an estimated 100,000 visitors come to see the lighting display erected by the 200 retired Benevolent and Protective Order of Elks at that fraternal organization's national home.

Poplar Forest, just outside of Lynchburg, is one of the area's most popular destinations as history-lovers flock to see the ongoing excavation and renovation of Thomas Jefferson's beloved octagonal vacation home.

The devout Christian with an imagination will enjoy seeing Holy Land USA, a 400-acre nature sanctuary whose aim is to be a replica of the Holy Land in Israel. Its owners invite study groups and individuals for a free walking tour. Primitive camping is allowed.

Since you're still reading this, you're probably wanting to know more about Bedford's world-famous hidden treasure. It's the last part of this Bedford section, to make sure you read the rest and make the super people at the Bedford Chamber of Commerce happy. Ok, are you ready? Thousands of others with shovels and backhoes over the past century have been ready, too, and have come up empty-handed, but that's not to say YOU will! But beware...100 members of the Beale Cypher Association, comprised of

the country's most renowned computer experts, are still trying to crack the last two treasure codes.

This is how the story goes...The legend of the Beale Treasure began in 1885 with the publication of the *Beale Papers* in Lynchburg. The author told how the *Beale Papers* came into his possession through Robert Morris, a well-respected Lynchburg hotel owner. It seems that on several occasions, Morris gave room and board to Thomas Beale. On his last visit in 1822, he entrusted Morris with a metal box and asked him to keep it for him.

A few months later, Beale wrote a letter explaining that if he did not return within 10 years, the important papers inside should be read. He explained, however, that without a "key," that a St. Louis friend would be mailing, the three papers would be unintelligible.

Beale never returned and no key ever arrived. After 23 years, Morris finally opened the box and tried to read its incomprehensible contents. One letter he could read, however, stated that Beale and his party of 29 friends had come to Bedford County several times to bury a treasure they found out west. It would be worth $23 million today. The other two documents, written in cryptic ciphers, told where it was.

After 20 years of trying, Morris was only able to break the ciphers (what cryptanalysts call multiple substitution ciphers) on one document which outlined the content of the treasure—2,981 pounds of gold and 5,092 pounds of silver, plus

Youngsters cool off after a hike at the falls in George Washington National Forest.

jewels. This key was based on the Declaration of Independence.

Since 1885, all attempts to break the two remaining ciphers have been unsuccessful. Over the years, many treasure-hunters have bypassed the ciphers and just started digging. Both the town's librarian and postmistress say they regularly receive correspondence and inquiries from around the world regarding the treasure. Recently, one woman, her dog, and the man whose backhoe she hired, were arrested for digging up a corpse in a cemetery. The two humans were jailed and fined and poor Fido was incarcerated in the county pound.

The most recent hunter was Mel Fisher, the famous searcher who has recovered millions of dollars from wrecked Spanish galleons. After the local newspaper offered a blow-by-blow account of his daily diggings, he abandoned his search in 1989 but vowed to return. So the question remains — is there really a Beale Treasure or is the whole incredible story just a ruse?

Nobody knows for sure. But most people figure that if Thomas Jefferson himself kept returning to Bedford County, there must be treasure enough that is much easier to find. For more information, contact the Bedford area Chamber of Commerce at 305 East Main St., Bedford, VA 24523, (703) 586-9401.

FRANKLIN COUNTY

Franklin County calls itself the "Land Between the Lakes," Smith Mountain and Philpott. More miles of shoreline touch Franklin County than either of the other two counties, Bedford or Pittsylvania. Without part-time residents who own lake vacation homes, Franklin County's population is 39,549.

For such a small, rural area, Franklin County has several important national claims to fame. It has one of the proudest African American cultures of any place in the Blue Ridge. That's because of the Booker T. Washington National Monument, home of the famous slave who became one of America's most important scholars and educators. The park, on Rt. 122, six miles south of Hales Ford Bridge, is operated as a working farm. Visitors may view a slide presentation on the life of Booker T. then tour the historic area and the reconstructions of the cabins and structures of the Burroughs Tobacco Plantation in the post Civil War era. Summers offer continuing education programs such as "Black Women - Achievement Against the Odds," and "The Black Experience in Virginia."

Franklin County's other national claim to fame is a Blue Ridge researcher's dream, the acclaimed Blue Ridge Institute at Ferrum College, whose Folklife Festival each October is a tribute to the treasured, yet nearly forgotten, skills of its Blue Ridge culture.

The Blue Ridge Institute is a great national treasure whose outreach in promoting its culture greatly transcends what many Franklin Countians take for granted as everyday life. The Institute offers a museum, archives and records division and a recreated 1800s German-American farmstead to preserve the best of Blue Ridge culture. One of is finest creations, produced for Franklin County's Bicentennial in 1986, is a pictorial record of Franklin County Life and Culture.

Visitors to the farmstead will see the architecture, gardens, livestock, furnishings, tools and housewares of the farm. The tours are led by costumed interpreters who work at appropriate chores such as baking, cooking and gardening. The farm museum also offers a Day on the Farm with hands-on experiences incorporating the tastes, smells and activities of the era. Other activities may include spinning, broom making and livestock care.

The Blue Ridge Institute's Fall Festival brings many skilled, working craftspeople in for the delight of visitors. You will see demonstrations of spinning, quilt-making, shingle-chopping and other homespun crafts. The Festival also offers unique spectator sports such as Coon Dog Trials. For more information on the Institute and the Festival, see our Arts and Culture chapter.

Another popular festival is the Boones Mill Apple Festival held each fall. Boones Mill is a great place for antiquing on the Route 220 corridor connecting with Roanoke. One word of caution, however, when driving through — Slow Down! The speed limit changes abruptly when you enter the town and Boones Mill's town officer has had national write-ups for his official police car, a white Camero, that sets on the curb and catches lots of out-of-state speedsters. It might be an important source of revenue to the town, but

you'll probably want to make your donations to the county in another manner!

Ferrum College greatly enriches the quality of life for Franklin Countians. Its Fine Arts Program supports the Jack Tale Players, whose song and drama touring company brings to life the legends of the Upland South. Its Poetic Arts Company demonstrates through performance how poetry plays a vital role in everyday life. Both students and residents enjoy participating in the Blue Ridge Summer Dinner Theatre.

The county is also known for something most Franklin County residents would prefer to put behind them — a long history of "moonshining," the illegal manufacture of whiskey. The reason they can't put it behind them is that it still goes on in the mountainous, rural county. There's rarely a month that goes by without a story in the local newspaper about someone being arrested for moonshining, often for the second or third time.

Some people admit to subscribing to the *Franklin County Post* just to read the excuses given by those who get caught with their hands on the still. At one recent hearing, one moonshiner solemnly pleaded "Not Guilty." When the judge asked him just what he had intended to do with the train-load full of sugar on the track by his backyard, he replied that his wife "is fond of putting up preserves."

Some residents hold in awe the folklore of independent, enterprising mountain men doing what it took to survive while others pretend moonshining never existed and still doesn't. Although the county's underground industry has been to some the source of amusement and the butt of jokes, a new breed of moonshiner — one selling illegal drugs as well — is causing fewer people to be amused.

The culture of the lake is vastly different, from the early settlers in the county seat of Rocky Mount, to the transplanted Northerners at Smith Mountain Lake. There is yet a third culture, the German Baptist population, which mostly keeps to itself. One exception is Boone's Country Store in Burnt Chimney. The best sticky buns on earth and other tempting edibles are prepared daily at this German Baptist store. They are truly addictive and people who live an hour's drive away admit to negotiating the winding road up Windy Gap Mountain just to stock their freezer with their "fix" of the sweet pastry.

Franklin County's history is as rich and varied as its people. Its first residents were German, French, English and Scotch-Irish settlers who moved from Pennsylvania in 1750. The county was formed in 1786 by the General Assembly. Munitions for Revolutionary War patriots were made from locally mined iron ore at an iron works on Furnace Creek, which is the county's oldest landmark.

One of the Civil War's most respected Confederate leaders, Lt. Gen. Jubal Early, was born here, second in command only to Gen. Stonewall Jackson. Rocky Mount is full of many interesting historical buildings. One, the Claiborne

House bed and breakfast, is open to the public. The Chamber of Commerce, in the courthouse downtown, can give you other pamphlets on historical tours and antique shopping opportunities.

Franklin County is also an outdoor paradise for hunting and fishing. Both Smith Mountain and Philpott lakes offer wonderful fishing if you have the patience and the right bait. Philpott, a 3,000-acre lake built by the U.S. Army Corps of Engineers, is more rustic than Smith Mountain and also offers boating, a beach and camping. Smith Mountain Lake has been called the best bass fishing lake in the country. For hunting, wild turkey proves to be the most popular game in the area.

The county's Recreation Department also offers a host of leisure-time sports and a county recreation program including the largest volleyball league in the state. Ferrum College also gives you a chance to root for championship teams in both men's and women's sports.

Another popular site in Franklin County is Whitey Taylor's Franklin County Speedway, with one of the best payoffs for a short track 75-lap race in the country, a $5,000 fund. Lots of race car fans travel to the Speedway to "go racin'."

Of all the counties surrounding the lake, Franklin's housing costs and taxes are generally the lowest, excluding its lakefront property. Farm land, scarce is so many areas of the Blue Ridge, is plentiful here. You're within easy commuting distance of either the Roanoke Valley or Martinsville, a furniture and knitting mill area with great furniture outlets (Stanleytown and Bassett) and the Tultex (sweatsuit) outlet stores. Franklin County's low taxes attract a lot of manufacturing industry. Cabinet makers, such as the 50-year-old MW Company, and Cooper Wood Products call the county home.

When you're between stops, visit the land between the lakes. Whether you play, shop or visit one of its national attractions, you'll find plenty to fill up your time. For more information, contact the Franklin County Chamber of Commerce at 124 East Court St., P.O. Box 158, Rocky Mount, VA 24151, (703)

New River Valley Region

The academically stimulating, scenic and mountainous New River Valley of Virginia is one of the most steadily growing areas of the Blue Ridge. It includes Montgomery County and its towns of Blacksburg and Christiansburg, the city of Radford, and Floyd, Giles and Pulaski counties. Although all are situated in the same area, you couldn't find a more diverse cultural group. The common thread, again, is the sheer beauty of their environment.

In the 70s decade, the New River Valley's population grew by nearly a fourth, to 152,720 by 1990. Its people just keep on staying, rather than actually coming. That's due to the presence of Virginia Tech, Virginia's largest university with 22,000 students, as well as Radford University's 8,000 students.

Every year, scores of mountain-struck students are smitten by the New River Valley Flu, a curious mental illness that causes them to turn down lucrative jobs in the big city and vow to flip hamburgers, or do whatever they have to, in order to stay.

The quality of life here is so high that the town of Blacksburg, home to Virginia Tech, a cutting-edge research institution, has been named by Rand McNally as one of the top 20 places to live in the United States. A publication for mature adults names it as one of the best retirement spots in the country. The reasons why are diverse, but mostly due to the winning combination of the Valley being a scenic mountain vacation land as well as a place of extraordinary cultural enrichment because of its university population from around the world.

An interesting historical fact is that the New River is actually old — really old! Legend has it that it's the second oldest river in the world; only the historic Nile, in Egypt, is older. The 300 million-year-old river is an anomaly because first, it flows from south to north and, next, cuts through the Alleghenies from east to west. The New River is 320 miles long from its headwaters near Blowing Rock, N.C., to the point in West Virginia where it tumultuously joins the Gauley River to form some of the best white-water rafting in the East. Outfitters at the Gauley River Gorge regularly host celebrities and nearby Washington politicians, such as Ted Kennedy, who are looking for a refreshing crash of water instead of a staggering crush of paper.

Unlike the populous Nile River area, when the first white explorers saw the area in 1654, the New River Valley was a vast, empty land with no permanent inhabitants. Drapers Meadow, near Blacksburg, is regarded as the first New River settlement. Germans in Prices Fork and Dunkards in Radford established themselves about the same time. Indians ventured in only to hunt.

For the first settlers, Indians were a threat greater than cold or starvation. Bands of Shawnees periodically would sweep in to kill settlers and destroy their homes. In 1755, they massacred many Drapers Meadow residents. Mary Draper Ingles and Betty Robinson Draper were taken hostage. Mary escaped and found her way home by following the New River. Her riveting saga is re-created each summer on an outdoor stage at the play, "The Long Way Home," in Radford. It is acted out at the homestead where Ingles and her husband eventually lived. Until her death in 1988, Ingles' great, great, great granddaughter, Mary Louise Jeffries, who lived on the homestead, played the part of Ingles' mother, Elenor Draper.

Although the New River Valley has an exciting textbook history, its research and development history has been equally exciting. Virginia Tech's IBM 3090 supercomputer was the first in the nation to be fully integrated with a university's computing network and made generally available to faculty and students. It's a fact that there are more computers than telephones on campus!

Virginia Tech's Corporate Research Center has 500 employees looking into everything from why illnesses can affect the immune system, very important to AIDS virus research, to robotics and fiber optics, all on the same 120-acre site. All total, $100 million is spent each year by Virginia Tech researchers, many of whom enjoy a national reputation. Business and industry are the largest users of the Center and often bring their problems for analyzation by some of the nation's greatest minds.

Here is a brief overview of the New River Valley's communities, with a short history and current attractions, many of which can be found outlined in detail in other chapters.

BLACKSBURG

The largest town in Virginia, Blacksburg (population 35,000) sits majestically on a mountain plateau between two of nature's masterpieces, the Blue Ridge Mountains of Virginia and the great Alleghenies.

The growing town has a na-

When pondering where to go in the vast wilderness of the Blue Ridge, it's smart to call ahead and get information from the Ranger Station for maps, brochures and general information. This way, you can better manage your time and you won't get lost, which does happen to visitors from time to time.

Insiders' Tip

tional recognition as an ideal community, charming, but with a constant flow of professors and students who lend to it most of its culture. Rand McNally has it rated in the top 20 places for both quality of life and retirement. Newcomers, students and others, are easily and quickly assimilated into the town's uniquely wonderful, abundant social life.

Touring Broadway shows, well-known speakers and popular musicians appear regularly on campus. Several university performing arts groups, the Audubon Quartet and Theatre Arts Program, are recognized nationally. Tech's NCAA Division I basketball and football teams often appear in post-game contests and tailgating is THE event every autumn. You've never seen anything until you see the enthusiasm (and the traffic!) when the Tech Hokies meet the University of Virginia Cavaliers!

These glowing quality of life reports can be attributed to the sprawling presence of Virginia Tech, its students and 5,000 employees, and its innumerable cultural offerings, many of which are free to the Blacksburg community. It would be difficult to find another community in Virginia with as many professionals of every type, from educators to seafood industry experts. One of its most famous, Prof. James Robertson (see the Civil War chapter) was named "the foremost Civil War historian in America" by the United Daughters of the Confederacy.

Tech's outreach into the community, through its Extension Service and other programs, affects the quality of life across Virginia. While businesses are sending their problems to researchers, local veterinarians, for example, routinely send their toughest cases to Tech's Veterinary School.

However, Tech wasn't always the town's main focal point. Blacksburg's name comes from the William Black family, which contributed acreage after Blacksburg was granted a town charter in 1798. For 75 years, it was known as a quiet and pleasant place to live. Then, in 1872, Dr. Henry Black petitioned the General Assembly to establish a land-grant university in his town. The university opened with one building and 43 students.

Since, the town-gown relationship has made for an ideal community that combines a small-town atmosphere with big city sophistication. Shopping malls and Blacksburg's active downtown offer many things you usually see only in places like Washington, D.C. Its restaurants are the same, from student hang-outs like Buddy's, to age-old traditions like the Greeks, to the Marriott.

The pace of life is relaxed. You won't see any smog to speak of, smell many fumes or be bothered by excessive noise. Blacksburg takes its quality of life very seriously. Its Town Council is mostly made up, traditionally, of Tech educators who put their theories into practice.

Amidst all this heady academia, there's a universal love for recreation. Virtually any can be found within minutes. Floating down the New River with an innertube and cooler is a popular past-time. There's swimming in Blacksburg's municipal pool, which sits on a ledge overlooking the spectacular mountain range, hiking in the Jefferson National Forest and sightseeing along the Blue Ridge Parkway.

Transportation is efficient, with a terrific bicycle path reminiscent of big city parks. Its municipal bus system has been recognized as the best in the nation for its size, according to the National Association of Public Transit authorities. The heavily-used Virginia Tech Airport sees many corporate jets.

As one of the fastest-growing, progressive, communities in Virginia, many more people come to Blacksburg than leave. And, with all the area has to offer, that's liable to remain the trend for a long, long time. For more information, contact the Blacksburg Chamber of Commerce at 141 Jackson St., Blacksburg, VA 24060, (703) 552-4061.

CHRISTIANSBURG

Montgomery County's seat, Christiansburg, the fourth largest town in Virginia, is a charming, historic town anchoring a county population of 73,913. The county's rural villages of Shawsville and Riner are equally quaint. Route 8 West connects the county to the 469-mile-long Blue Ridge Parkway.

A quiet river that flows under Main Street, the old Wilderness Trail, marks the continental divide. That's where flowing groundwater changes its course toward the Ohio-Mississippi river system.

The last legal gun duel in this country, the Lewis-McHenry, was fought in Christiansburg's renovated Cambria historic district. Depot Street, location of the Christiansburg Depot Museum, was the site of the depot burned in 1864 by the Union Army. The Cambria Emporium, built in 1908, is now the site of a fabulous antique mall with its own antique General Store.

The town's skyline is dotted with history including the steeples of Old Methodist Church, built sometime in the early 19th century, Christiansburg Presbyterian, circa 1853, and Schaeffer Memorial Baptist, erected in 1884.

Christiansburg's founder was Col. William Christian, an Irish Colonial settler. It served as an outpost on the Wilderness Trail, opened by Daniel Boone as the gateway to the west for settlers such as Davy Crockett.

In 1866, the legendary Booker T. Washington, of nearby Franklin County, supervised the Christiansburg Industrial School for black children.

The northern portion of Montgomery County contains nearly 20,000 acres of the Jefferson National Forest. The Bikecentennial and Appalachian Trails pass through the county. Between Blacksburg and Christiansburg, on US 460, is the 90-acre Montgomery County Park, one of the area's many recreational facilities, which includes a swimming pool, bathhouse, fitness trail and picnic area. In all, the county contains four 18-hole golf courses, 68 outdoor and five indoor tennis courts, 18 swimming pools, 37

Photo: Virginia Dept. of Economic Development

Swimmers enjoy the 108-acre lake at Hungry Mother State Park in Marion.

ballfields and numerous playgrounds.

An added plus for the area is that real estate, both land and houses, are significantly less than in Blacksburg. For the same money, you can get so much more, with a fantastic quality of life as well.

FLOYD COUNTY

Follow Route 8 south from Christiansburg and you'll find yourself in Floyd County (population 12,005). Just as movie stars are attracted to Charlottesville, 60s-era hold-outs have been migrating to Floyd for the past 30 years. Their tie-dyed counterculture communes nestle quietly along with small farms in a county whose promotional material lists an employer of six (Chateau Morrisette Winery) as one of its major industries. Many residents live quietly off the land.

Another employer makes gasohol, promoted by some since the 70s gas crisis as the only way to fuel autos. Other promotional county material outlines SIRUS (Solar Innovative Republic for Independent United Survival) in Earthships, a planned counterculture community in Riner with restrictional living. SIRUS accepts you only after you've been interviewed and analyzed according to what you can offer the community and humanity. They'll send you a video showing the property and discussing the concept (703-763-2651), which is based on homes with 3.5' thick rammed earth walls and inspiration. The latter is furnished by author Mike Reynolds' books *Earthship*, Vol. I & II, and *A Coming of Wizards*.

Just don't go to Floyd actively looking for the counterculture. They have ingratiated themselves to the local farmers with their true sense of community spirit and are safely tucked away, bothering no one and expecting the same treatment, in the hills of Floyd.

They are most visible elsewhere, actually, at regional arts and crafts shows where they sell their wares ranging from twisted grapevine baskets to tie-dyed and batik clothing and pottery. However, you don't have to leave Floyd to buy their wares.

One of the most prolific and amazing arts and crafts stores in the Blue Ridge, New Mountain Mercantile, six miles off the Blue Ridge Parkway on Locust St., is the central location for area craftspeople to display and sell. You can spend hours investigating the building, art gallery and upstairs Byrd's Walden Pond Products, which offer self-help tapes and herbal body care, among other back-to-the earth products.

Locals also can be found hanging out at the Blue Ridge Restaurant, located in an early 1900 bank building, and Pine Tavern Restaurant and Lodge, a comfortable country inn where fine food includes vegetarian fare.

The most famous regional landmark for both locals and tourists is the inimitable Cockram's General Store, where every Friday is a hoedown! During the day, the store sells the likes of corn cob jelly and local crafts. There's no admission for the Friday Night Jamboree with pure mountain music and dancing and a fun, friendly family atmosphere. Next door is the largest distributor of bluegrass and old-time music in the world. Browsers are welcome to look through more than 5,000 tapes, records, books and videos. If you like sewing, there's Schoolhouse Fabrics, housed in what was once an 1846 school, with rooms of bargain fabric and quilts. Brookfield Christmas Tree Plantation, a national shipper of holiday trees, and Chateau Morrisette Winery and Le Chien Noir Restaurant in Meadows of Dan are other places that endear Floyd County to shoppers seeking the wild and wonderful. (See Shopping and Arts and Crafts chapters for the whole scoop.)

The most famous national landmark is the picturesque Mabry Mill Blue Ridge Parkway visitors center, campground and recreation area. The restaurant here is quite good. The real feast, however, is one for the senses at the old-time water-powered grist mill and interpretive historical buildings. This is usually the first place western Virginians take internationals for a true taste of American history and beauty.

The history of Floyd is actually rather sketchy, according to its Chamber of Commerce. Early land surveys showed an attempt to settle the area in 1740. The county was officially formed from Montgomery County in 1831. Floyd's original name was Jacksonville, named for Andrew Jackson, our nation's seventh president. Incorporated in 1858, the town changed its name to Floyd in 1896, although there's no official reason why.

When you visit the New River

Valley, take a day to check out Floyd County, mingle with the locals, see some terrific arts and crafts and listen to some of the best bluegrass and gospel you'll ever hear. Floyd County truly is a sightseer's delight and photographer's paradise with the Blue Ridge Parkway's misty mountain views and miles of split-log fences. A map is smart when traveling Floyd's miles of rural, obscure back roads. You can receive this map, and other information at the Floyd County Chamber of Commerce, P.O. Box 510, Floyd, VA 24091, (703) 745-4407.

GILES COUNTY

If you love dramatic mountain scenery, don't miss Giles County, especially the autumn vista from U.S. 460 traveling south from Blacksburg. Giles County (population 16,366) is a mountain haven of forests, cliffs, cascading waterfalls, fast-flowing creeks and streams and, of course, the scenic New River. Its county seat of Pearisburg is one of only two towns located on the Maine to Georgia Appalachian Trail. Of the four covered bridges left in the Blue Ridge, two are in Giles County (see the Other Attractions chapter) at Sinking Creek.

Giles County is a paradise for the lover of the outdoors. Whether your preference is for golfing a challenging emerald green course, fly-casting in an ice-cold mountain stream for trout, canoeing the New River's white water, or hiking, Giles has it all.

Giles' most scenic attraction, one of the most photographed in the Blue Ridge, is the Cascades waterfall which follows a rigorous, three-mile hiking trail in Pembroke (see the Hiking chapter), not recommended for small children. After your uphill pull, which seems to last forever, your excellent reward for this adventure is bathing at the foot of the tumbling, 60-foot-high waterfall.

A tamer destination, just as much fun for kids, is Castle Rock Recreation Area, which offers an 18-hole golf course, tennis and swimming. Canoe and kayak rentals are available in Pembroke at the New River Canoe Livery (703) 626-7189).

Giles County's most famous attraction is the fabulous Mountain Lake Hotel and Resort, set atop the second highest mountain in Virginia, overlooking the town of Blacksburg, miles away. There's more information about this spot in our Resorts and Restaurants chapters. For years, it has been known for the beauty of its stone lodge and its gourmet cuisine. Of late, it is best known for the classic, "Dirty Dancing," which was filmed here as the epitome of early 60s-era great resorts. Mountain Lake is ageless and timeless and is not to be missed while in Giles County.

Another popular scenic destination is the attractive village of Newport, with its country store and steepled church. The quaint hamlet nestles at the foot of Gap Mountain at Sinking Creek.

Formed in 1806, the county was named for Gov. William Giles. In addition to tourism, Giles County's biggest employer is the Hoechst-Celanese Plant in Narrows. A bedroom community to many

professionals, Giles' school system has one of the lowest student to teacher rations in the state, 16-1, emphasizing a personal approach to instruction.

In addition to far-flung outdoor recreation, Giles also offers the culture of its historic Andrew Johnston House, Giles Little Theatre and great antique shopping. Lots of Virginia Tech educators and professionals have discovered Giles, so you may have trouble finding available farmland. However, there are many gorgeous, mountaintop chalets and homes on the market at any given time. Contact the New River Board of Realtors. For more information on Giles County, contact the Chamber of Commerce at P.O. Box 666, Pearisburg, VA 24134, (703) 921-5000.

RADFORD

For quality of life, Radford City (population 15,940) has the whole country beat — that is, if you want to stake it on longevity. As of this writing, the oldest person in the U.S., Margaret Skeete, at age 113, is listed in the *Guinness Book of Records*. She's in good health, goes about her daily business and shrugs off the attention, adding that she "never expected to get old."

Maybe living beside one of the oldest rivers in the World, the New River, has something to do with Skeete's remarkable life. The river, which flows through this university city, adds something truly special to its quality of life.

Radford, the region's only independent city, was incorporated in 1892 and grew to be an important rail division point. It also became the home of Radford University, enrollment 8,000, and is the site of Virginia's only outdoor historical drama, "The Long Way Home," depicting the famous story of Mary Draper Ingles' escape from the Shawnees.

Another of Radford's major attractions is 58-acre Bisset Park, with a walking trail beside nearly a mile of the tree-lined New River. This perfect park is capped off with a gazebo, swimming pool, several playgrounds and a tennis court. Colorful hot-air balloons also take off from the park. If you were to design the most charming, perfect recreational area of your dreams, this would probably be it!

Radford's energetic downtown is a Main Street community and has seen numerous unique small businesses start up, many serving the student population. To encourage small business development, Radford even publishes a *New Business Start-up Guide.*

The impact of Radford University on the city is comparable to its neighbor's, Virginia Tech, on the nearby town of Blacksburg. The Dedmon Center, a $13 million athletic facility, is an unbelievable community gem featuring an air-supported fabric roof atop a gymnasium and natorium. The adjacent grounds have several softball, soccer, field hockey and flag football fields. Radford is also fanatic about its high school Bobcats' sports teams.

Other noted Radford facilities include 2,000-square-foot Flossie Martin Art Gallery, one of the Blue Ridge region's finest. A

guest professor program has brought in entertainer Steve Allen, civil rights activist Jesse Jackson, Nobel Prize winner Elie Wiesel, Egypt's widowed Jihan Sadat (who displayed her own personal Egyptian art collection) and columnist Jack Anderson.

The city also has an outstanding academic tradition with its primary and secondary schools. Its school system, heavily influenced by college educated parents, has been nominated by the Commonwealth of Virginia as one of the nation's best. Last year, the highest passing percentage on national standardized tests in Virginia (90.4) was achieved by Radford's sixth-graders.

So, if you're looking for a casual, but academically stimulating small city, look no farther than Radford. Its environment beside the sometimes placid, sometimes raging New River is symbolic of Radford's placid, yet dynamic, quality of life. For more information, contact the Radford Chamber of Commerce at 1126 Norwood St., Radford, VA 24141, (703) 639-2202.

PULASKI

The town of Pulaski and Pulaski County (population 34,496), named for Count Pulaski of Poland, a Revolutionary War hero, is a special place with attractions ranging from the historic to vast water recreation and sports including a speedway and farm baseball team. No matter what your taste, you'll find entertainment here.

Most special is the town of Old Newbern, Pulaski's first county

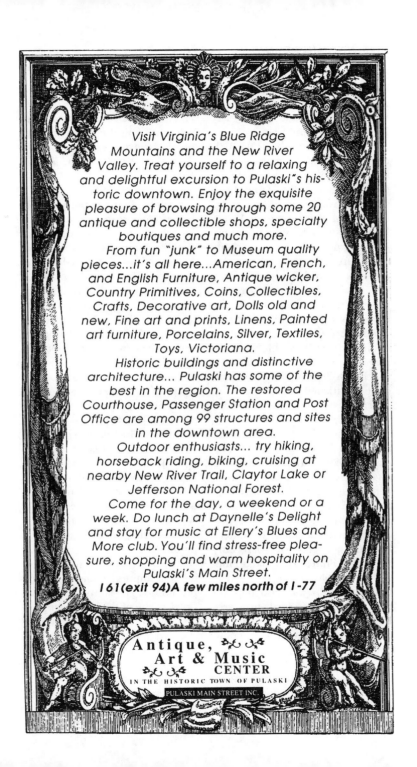

Visit Virginia's Blue Ridge
Mountains and the New River
Valley. Treat yourself to a relaxing
and delightful excursion to Pulaski's historic downtown. Enjoy the exquisite
pleasure of browsing through some 20
antique and collectible shops, specialty
boutiques and much more.

From fun "junk" to Museum quality
pieces...it's all here...American, French,
and English Furniture, Antique wicker,
Country Primitives, Coins, Collectibles,
Crafts, Decorative art, Dolls old and
new, Fine art and prints, Linens, Painted
art furniture, Porcelains, Silver, Textiles,
Toys, Victoriana.

Historic buildings and distinctive
architecture... Pulaski has some of the
best in the region. The restored
Courthouse, Passenger Station and Post
Office are among 99 structures and sites
in the downtown area.

Outdoor enthusiasts... try hiking,
horseback riding, biking, cruising at
nearby New River Trail, Claytor Lake or
Jefferson National Forest.

Come for the day, a weekend or a
week. Do lunch at Daynelle's Delight
and stay for music at Ellery's Blues and
More club. You'll find stress-free pleasure, shopping and warm hospitality on
Pulaski's Main Street.

I61(exit 94)A few miles north of I-77

Antique,
Art & Music
CENTER
IN THE HISTORIC TOWN OF PULASKI

PULASKI MAIN STREET INC.

seat and the only town in Virginia that is totally an historic district, recognized by both the National Historic Register and the Virginia Landmarks Commission.

Here, you can tour the Wilderness Road Museum, treat yourself to ice cream at the old-timey soda fountain at PJ's Carousel gift shop and village and then stop by the local historic restaurant, Valley Pike Inn, for a family meal. This family tour can be easily taken in two hours, unless someone in the crowd is an avid shopper. In that case, avoid PJ's, one of a trio of shops that manufactures and sells hand-carved, full-size and miniature wooden carousel horses and other gift items. Be sure and let the kids ride the 1923 Carousel from the Cincinnati Zoo, one of 3,000 that once flourished at the peak of America's fascination with the art form!

Pulaski's newly renovated historic Main Street is also a fun stroll, featuring 20 charming shops and quaint restaurants, arts and crafts and examples of Victorian architecture. Pulaski's downtown also is blessed with the New River Valley's cultural gem, its Fine Arts Center. Located in an 1898 Victorian commercial building, the Pulaski Fine Arts Center has a full agenda and is well utilized by the local population. There are performances, exhibits, classes, the Art Mart Gift Shop, a school outreach program and art library.

Outdoor enthusiasts will adore Claytor Lake. Like its younger counterpart, Smith Mountain, it was formed by Appalachian Power Com-

pany in 1939 for the generation of electricity. Since, it has become a haven for boaters, anglers, campers and swimmers. Its white sand beach will make you think you're at the ocean. Nearby is a spectacular condominium development, Mallard Point.

Claytor Lake State Park's 472-acres offer four campgrounds, 12 housekeeping cabins, tent spots and horseback riding. The park's visitor center is located in the 1879 Howe House and has educational displays.

Another nice park is Gatewood Reservoir Park, off Route 99. You can camp on 42 sites or park your RV along the shores of Gatewood Reservoir and fish or boat surrounded by the Jefferson National Forest.

Sports fans will appreciate the Pulaski County Speedway, located on Route 11. Open early April through late September, it is a NASCAR-Winston racing series track which seats 10,000.

Pulaski County also is home to the highly respected New River Community College in Dublin. The New River Valley Fair also is held in Dublin each summer and offers such charming events as a children's pet show.

Pulaski County workers also have an impressive mix of job opportunities. The Volvo White Truck Corp. is one of the largest employers, as well as Burlington Industries, Western Electric and the Pulaski Furniture Company.

Whether you're a nature, water, fine arts or history-lover, you'll find plenty to do in Pulaski County. For more information, contact the

Pulaski County Chamber of Commerce at P.O. Box 169, Pulaski, VA 24301-0169, (703) 480-1991.

Alleghany Highlands Region

ALLEGHANY COUNTY

Alleghany County, (population 27,820) situated on the Alleghany mountain range, is the western gateway to Virginia. Half of the county is within the George Washington National Forest. The county is a mountain playground for a multitude of fabulous vacations in gorgeous scenery. It's also next door to wild, wonderful West Virginia's Greenbrier County, home of the world-famous Greenbrier Resort.

Outdoor lovers, sportspeople, antique aficionados, railroad buffs, history lovers and gourmets all will find something to get really excited about here.

Before the formation of Alleghany County, property records were provided from Fincastle in Botetourt County, a two-day trip. So, in 1822, the County of Alleghany was formed, named after the mountains in which they lie, although the mountains are spelled differently than the county.

Its county seat, Covington, was named in honor of Gen. Leonard Covington, hero of the War of 1812 and confidante to James Madison and Thomas Jefferson. Clifton Forge, the county's other populous area, was named for its iron production and contributed cannons and cannonballs to the Civil War effort. During the Civil War, Alleghany County furnished more soldiers to the Confederacy than it had voters. The county suffered greatly in the war, since it was located next to West Virginia, which joined the Union. It took years to recover from the losses sustained.

After the war, Clifton Forge was selected by the Chesapeake and Ohio Railway as the site of its new depot. The coming of the railroad signaled important growth and in 1906, Clifton Forge received its city charter.

Hemp, used in rope production, was another important early product. Natural resources have always been Alleghany County's main industry. The biggest boost to industrial progress in the area was the decision in 1899 by the West Virginia Pulp and Paper Co. to locate a mill at Covington. The coming of the pulp mill stimulated the development of growth of other industrial and commercial interests.

Both the railroad and Westvaco Paper Mill continue to play important roles in the county's culture and economy. As expected, many of its attractions are tied to its history.

In the charming historical city of Clifton Forge, the C&O Historical Society Archives preserves artifacts and equipment of the C&O Railroad. It is one of the largest railroad historical societies in the U.S. Also worth a visit is the Alleghany Highlands Arts and Crafts Center, displaying fine regional arts and crafts. (See our Arts and Culture chapter.)

Lucy Selina Furnace stacks, more than 100 feet tall, are reminders of the area's 19th century iron industry. A stunning Victorian mansion built by the owner of the rich iron mines has been turned into the charming Firmstone Manor Bed &Breakfast. Local lore says a staff of eight was required just to maintain its gardens alone! Nearby is the Longdale Recreation Area, which features miles of mountain trails, camping and sand beach swimming. All are located off I-64's exit 10, on Rt. 269 in Longdale.

Roaring Run Recreation Area, the site of the ruins of an 1838 iron furnace, is another wonderful place to hike and picnic. It's located off Rt. 220 S. Follow the signs to Rt. 615 and then Rt. 621.

Other historic points of interest are Fort Young, a reconstruction of the original French and Indian War fort on I-64, exit 4, near Covington. Lovers of architecture will enjoy seeing Oakland Grove Presbyterian Church, which served as a hospital during the Civil War. It can be seen in Selma, on I-64 off I-64's exit 7.

Water has also played a large role in the history and life of the county. The unassuming, unmarked site of the source of Quibell Water, rivaling Perrier nationally, is located by a cattle grate crossing close to Sweet Chalybeate Springs, where trucks transport it daily for bottling in Roanoke.

Sweet Chalybeate (pronounced Ka-lee-bee) Pools and gazebo, off Route 311 near the West Virginia border, dates back 150 years as a great pre-Civil War resort. Recently renovated after laying in waste following the demise of the Civil War aristocracy, the pools now offer

bathers the most highly carbonated mineral water in the world. Locals swear by the water's healing powers and many either take a dip or drink its water daily. For more information, write them at Rt. 3, Sweet Chalybeate, Covington, VA 24426.

Twelve miles of water bring in visitors to Lake Moomaw, a relatively new lake formed for power generation 19 miles from Covington. Signs point the way. Residents and visitors have taken advantage of water skiing, boating, fishing and swimming.

Douthat State Park's 50-acre lake also offers a beach, bathhouse, boating and excellent trout fishing. Other facilities include a Visitor's Center, restaurant and lodge as well as cabins, campgrounds and miles of hiking trails.

The world's largest pump storage facility in the world, Virginia Power's Back Creek Pump Storage Station, is also worth seeing. It's located on a 325-acre recreation area with a Visitor's Center on Rt. 600. Call (703) 279-2389.

For obvious reasons, anglers find Paint Bank State Trout Hatchery on Rt. 311 an interesting place to visit. It is open daily from 7:30 AM until 4 PM. Rock-lovers will want to visit Rainbow Gap or Iron Gate Gorge, which create a geologist's paradise a mile south of Clifton Forge on Rt. 220. For 12 million years, the Jackson River has been working on this masterpiece.

Across the border, in West Virginia, the attractions also are overwhelming. The big one, of course, is the world-famous Greenbrier Resort. Take a look around its magnificent grounds while you're in the area. The resort welcomes visitors, even if you don't spend the night. Several nice restaurants are open. If you're just in the area for the day, you and the kids may enjoy just having dessert in the ice cream parlor with its pink and green striped awnings and pink crystal glasses. It's a really special experience that even those on a tight budget can afford.

Also close to the West Virginia border, but still in Virginia, is a great dining experience in a place called Crows. If you blink your eyes, you'll miss it, so keep a look out for the rustic sign with the Eagle, indicating Eagle's Nest Restaurant. Built beside a rolling waterfall, the gourmet food is so good that corporate officials flying into the area from around the world are some of its most loyal customers.

Several other West Virginia attractions within an hour's drive are north up Rt. 92. Blue Bend swimming hole in Alvon, one of the best in the Blue Ridge, is one of them. Lake Sherwood, farther up Rt 92, is nice too, and rents paddleboats. The Cass Scenic Railroad is close to Marlinton, as is Snowshoe Ski Resort. The town of Lewisburg, cultured and sophisticated, is also worth a visit for its charming downtown shops and Carnegie Hall, built by the same industrialist tycoon as its more famous counterpart.

Another aspect that makes Alleghany County so popular with visitors is that the locals really want you to visit and stay while! The people are country, friendly and downright glad to see you. Brochures of all the area's attractions can be picked up at the Jerry's Run Virginia Visitor's Center at I-64's Exit 1. Better yet, contact the Alleghany Highlands Chamber of Commerce at 403 E. Ridgeway St., Clifton Forge, VA 24422, (703) 962-2178.

BATH COUNTY

Nestled between Alleghany and Highland counties and bordering West Virginia, Bath County (population 4,799) doesn't even have a stop light. Nearly 90 percent of Bath County is forest. What it does have is pleasures of every kind for its visitors, whether they're on a budget or staying at the world-famous Homestead Resort.

The pleasures of Bath County's bubbly mineral springs, or "baths," is from whence the county got its name. Bath County was founded in 1745 by pioneers of mostly Scotch-Irish descent, most notably John Lewis, who settled at Fort Lewis. One son, Charles, died in the historic Battle of Point Pleasant in 1774. The other son, John, built the first hotel on the site of the present Homestead Resort in 1766. His structure was destroyed by fire in 1901. In the meantime, M. E. Ingalls, president of the Chesapeake and Ohio Railroad, bought the site and the modern era of the resort was launched.

Some historic sites in the county are the Warwickton Mansion at Hidden Valley, site of the movie, "Sommersby;" the Anderson Cottage in Warm Springs, and Windy Cove Presbyterian Church at

Millboro.

The real history of the county, however, lies in its springs, which have been drawing people for more than 200 years. Wrote one visitor in 1750, "The spring water is very clear and warmer than new milk." Thermal springs are found at Warm Springs, Hot Springs and Bolar Springs at temperatures ranging from 77 degrees F to 106 degrees F. They flow at rates ranging from 2,500 to 5,000 gallons a minute. The water has a soft fizz of tickling bubbles and taking of the baths is like lowering yourself into a warm vat of Perrier (or Quibell, whose source springs are in Alleghany County).

Public pools have been open at Warm Springs since 1761 and look today much as they did then. The covered pools were the cultural center of the rich and famous. Thomas Jefferson "took the waters" here for his health, as did the frail Mrs. Robert E. Lee, (she had crippling arthritis) whose chair, used to lower her into the pool, is still on display at the ladies' pool.

Thus, the stage was set for the aristocracy to visit this scenic land. That's how the internationally-known Homestead Resort, detailed in our Resorts chapter, came into being. As Bath County celebrated its Bicentennial in 1991, the Ingalls family celebrated its 100th year of running the famous Homestead Resort. At the Homestead, you will see a place of style and grandeur equalled only by its neighbor, the Greenbrier Resort, in nearby White Sulphur Springs, W.Va.

The Homestead offers the superlative of everything — recreation, shopping and gourmet restaurants. Its sporting activities attract enthusiasts from around the world. You can ski, ride horseback on hundreds of miles of trails, play tennis on 21 professional courts, fly-fish at an Orvis Fishing School, shoot skeets and golf on three championship courses including the nationally-known Cascades.

The same crowd that goes to the Homestead are regulars at an absolutely serendipitous place, Garth Newel Music Center. The sound of critically-acclaimed chamber music wafts through the mountains throughout the year with summer picnics and holiday events. Garth Newel attracts cultured people from around the world and you never know who you'll see there taking in a concert while staying at the Homestead or with friends at a country estate. Jackie Kennedy has been spotted, according to locals...who leave the celebrities alone.

You don't need to be rich, however, to really enjoy your stay in Bath County. There are many nice bed and breakfasts and one really outstanding one, Meadow Lane Lodge, a farm setting offering gourmet food and many miles to roam. Your hosts, the Hirsh family, are one of Bath County's most loved and respected philanthropic families.

Another great place to stay is scenic Fort Lewis Lodge, where hunting is the autumn and winter mainstay and spring and summer offers lazy tubing down the placid Cowpasture River, hiking and camping and Caryn Cowden's wonderful cooking. It's a wholesome, airy retreat the whole family will enjoy.

There are very nice places to eat downtown as well. The Inn at Gristmill Square, restored by the Hirsh family, is the center of Warm Springs with its dining and interesting shops. Lodging also is available there.

Quaint shopping offers interesting opportunities, especially at the Bacova Outlet in Warm Springs. Its silk-screened gifts and household goods are made at the Bacova Guild Factory, located in an old 1920s lumber mill town restored in 1965 by the Hirsh family.

There are many outdoor adventures waiting for you in Bath County. Burnsville's large caverns and sunken caves are open for the pleasure of spelunkers.

You can hike, hunt, fish or ride on some of the most beautiful forests and mountains you'll find. The George Washington National Forest, Gathright Game Management Area and Douthat State Park are in the county. The Homestead also offers any type of arranged sporting event imaginable.

Although the Homestead is Bath County's crowning jewel, there are countless other gems in this pastoral, genteel land of sophistication. The Bath County Chamber of Commerce has a wonderful Visitors Guide that will tell you everything you need to know. Contact them at P.O. Box 718, Hot Springs, VA 24445, 1-800 628-8092 for the entire story of the county known for pleasure and relaxation. Then, go

and take advantage of it!

HIGHLAND COUNTY

Nicknamed the "Switzerland of Virginia," scenic Highland County (population 2,800) has more sheep than people on land with a higher mean elevation than any county east of the Mississippi River.

Environment is everything to county residents who live in the rarefied air. Even Highland County's official brochure invites businesses to locate, providing their "environment won't be endangered." Few places have preserved their surroundings and privacy so well. One of the most influential conservation groups in America, The Ruffled Grouse Society, was founded here in 1961.

Highland County was established in 1847 from the counties of Bath and Pendleton, in what is now West Virginia. Its county seat, Monterey, sits 3,000 feet above sea level, while its western border on the Allegheny Mountains reaches elevations of 4,500.

Once the hunting grounds for Shawnee Indians, Highland's borders were first crossed by European settlers in the 1700s, when it was still a part of Augusta County, which it remained until 1787.

In the Indian War of 1754-64, the county was on the frontier. Highland men also made up the company that fought the Battle of Point Pleasant under the command of Col. Andrew Lewis.

Highland also lists German General Rommel, the "Desert Fox," who visited prior to World War I to study Jackson's military tactics at McDowell. Talk about biting the hand that feeds you! Later, Rommel used the same tactics against the United States and its allies.

To the visitor, Highland County is both beautiful and spectacular as well as stark and severe. The natural setting is augmented by pleasant activities and facilities. Every March, this small population rallies to put on an event ranked among the top 20 festivals in America, the Highland County Maple Festival, which draws 70,000 over a two-weekend span. The festival takes you back to the time when "tree sugar" and "tree lasses" were found on every table, when "opening" the trees and "boiling down the sugar water" were highland spring rituals. The tours and exhibits are both educational and enjoyable. The pancake (with maple syrup, of course) and trout suppers centered around the county seat of Monterey are unforgettable.

A Sugar Tour winds through some of the loveliest spots in Virginia, Routes 637 and 640, renowned for their unusual beauty. Maple sugar "camps" throughout the county welcome visitors to view the actual process of syrup-making, from "tapping" the trees to collecting the colorless, almost tasteless "sugar water." Gathered in plastic buckets or by plastic tubing, the water is then boiled in kettles, pans or evaporators, until a barrel is finally reduced to a gallon of pure maple syrup. The camp sites are Rexrode's Sugar Orchard, Puffenbarger's Sugar Orchard, Sugar Tree Country Store & Sugar House and Eagle's Sugar Camp. Tour maps are provided at the festival.

One of the best things about the festival is tasting and shopping for all the pure maple syrup goodies, available at a cost vastly below retail. There's sugar candy, donuts glazed with maple syrup and funnelcakes. Highland's downtown antique stores also open for the occasion. Most are clustered around the classic Victorian Highland Inn. This downtown landmark, circa 1904, has been restored and is now on the National Register of Historic Places. Its 20 rooms are furnished with antiques.

Be sure and see the Maple Museum on U.S. 220, one mile south of Monterey. This replica of an old-time "sugar house" features exhibits showing the making of maple syrup and sugar from the earliest known methods used by Native Americans to modern techniques. Tools and equipment are on display. Admission is free and the museum is always open.

Summers are as cool here as any in the East. One word of warning — if you're driving in from another part of the Blue Ridge, expect to find snow on the ground as late as April, since Highland County gets about 65 inches of the white stuff a year. Bring a jacket for the kids, since the temperature will probably be at least 10 degrees colder than where you came from.

Outside of the maple culture, there are other interesting places to visit. If you want to see where many of those mouth-watering trout come from — and part of the reason behind this area's distinction as "Trout Capital of the Eastern United States," visit the Virginia Trout Company, on Rt. 220 north of Monterey. In business for 30 years, the Virginia Trout Company hatches rainbow trout from eggs and raises them to adulthood. You can fish for your own here, buy them frozen or just watch them swim in the cold mountain water. The hatchery is open seven days a week, weekdays from 8 AM to 4 PM and weekends from 9 AM to 4 PM.

While you're in Highland County, you also can see the Confederate Breastworks (breast-high trenches) built in 1862 by 4,000 Confederate troops as a defense against Union soldiers. They are located at the top of Shenandoah Mountain on U.S. 250 at the Highland-Augusta County line.

Also on U.S. 250 east of McDowell is the McDowell Battlefield, where 4,500 Confederate troops under Gen. Stonewall Jackson defeated 2,268 Union soldiers

in a bloody conflict in 1862. This engagement was the first victory in Jackson's famous Valley Campaign. Nearby McDowell Presbyterian Church was used as a hospital and soldiers are buried there. The battlefield recently was purchased by the Association for the Preservation of Civil War sites.

Highland County is one of the few places where time seems to stand still. People enjoy Highland as much for what is missing — traffic, pollution, nose and crowds — as for what is there. The pace is slow and the scenery is beautiful. It's considered the best place in Virginia to birdwatch and fans say species that have flown the coop from other parts of the state can still be found here. If you feel like flying the coop yourself, come to Highland and slow down like the maple sugar in January. Contact the Highland County Chamber of Commerce at P.O. Box 250, Monterey, VA 24465, (703) 468-2550.

Photo: Virginia Div. of Tourism

A section of the Confederate line masses for attack during the reenactment of the 1864 Battle of New Market. Each May at New Market, the annual reenactment traces the story of the youthful courage of Virginia Military Institute's cadets who halted Union troops there despite being greatly outnumbered.

Inside
The Civil War

*I*t was, as the poet Walt Whitman described, "A strange, sad war." More Americans lost their lives in the Civil War of 1861-65 than in World Wars I and II combined. No state contributed more to the Southern Confederacy, or suffered more from the Civil War, than did Virginia. Beginning with the war's first major battle at Bull Run (First Manassas) and ending with the surrender in the tiny, peaceful village of Appomattox Court House, 60 percent of the Civil War's battles were fought in Virginia.

The Old Dominion was one of the last states to leave the Union. But because it was the most exposed geographically of the seceding states, Virginia became the major battleground of the Civil war. One borderline Shenandoah Valley city, Winchester, changed hands from Confederate to Yankee no fewer than 72 times. Thousands of men, out of a strong sense of duty and honor, heeded the call to arms and never returned. Is it any wonder that nearly 130 years later, the War Between the States is not forgotten? Certainly not in the Blue Ridge, where generations of family farms and history were laid waste, sometimes out of spite, rather than necessity.

It is not unusual to find senior citizens who fondly remember former slaves called "Auntie and Uncle," revered as family and given plots of land on the family farm after they refused to leave their masters when they were freed. On the flip side, you can see some of the earliest tintype photos ever taken showing slaves whose backs were ribbons of scars from the beatings they endured at the hands of their taskmasters. Who was in the right, and just what was the Civil War all about? Slavery alone?

The answer to those questions can be found in the Blue Ridge, the site not only of some of the bloodiest battles in the Civil War, but also home to the country's most noted Civil War scholar and author.

History Professor James I. Robertson of Virginia Tech is past executive director of the U.S. Civil War Centennial Commission. His most recent book, *Civil War! America Becomes one Nation*, an illustrated history for young readers, probably best answers those questions in a way that young and old can clearly understand. Robertson, whose books have been nominated for the Pulitzer Prize, teaches a Civil War class that is one of the hottest tickets on campus. His enthusiasm for Civil

War history comes as no surprise, since his great-grandfather was the great Confederate General Robert E. Lee's cook.

Robertson's latest book takes into account the political and socio-economic mood of the 1860s and the events that set off a movement that the South anticipated would be over within weeks, but which, in fact, lasted four years and destroyed a way of life.

The fact that the Confederacy even survived for the duration of the war was the result, in large measure, of the excellent military leadership furnished by the Blue Ridge of Virginia's Gen. Robert E. Lee and Gen. Thomas J. "Stonewall" Jackson. Jackson's nickname came, so the story goes, out of the battle of First Manassas. Gen. Barnard Bee of South Carolina pointed to Jackson's troops and shouted, "There is Jackson standing like a stone wall." In addition to his legendary nickname, Jackson's Rebel yell became his battle signature. To this day, the U.S. Army regularly conducts "staff rides" into the Shenandoah Valley for its officers, following the course of Jackson's famed Foot Cavalry.

Tragically, according to Robertson, Northerners and Southerners were both fighting for the same thing: America, as each side interpreted what America should be.

On the other hand, within time, the Civil War formed a strong union of the United States of America, withstanding foreign leaders bent on conquering the world just 50 years later, during World War I, with World War II to follow. If the South had won the war, would the history of the 20th Century have been drastically rewritten? Would we be speaking German today instead of English?

When discussing the role the Blue Ridge played in the Civil War, Robertson emphasizes the Shenandoah Valley's geographical position as a spear pointing into the North, and as the "Breadbasket of the Confederacy." The number of major battles in the site attests to the constant wrenching for control of the Valley, which prompted Jackson, the "pious blue-eyed killer" to push his men so hard in the spring of 1862 that their shoes fell apart in the fields.

And who can ever forget the heart-breaking Battle of New Market, when the fateful day, May 15, 1864, is retraced and its startling events reenacted? On that rainy Sunday afternoon, 247 Virginia Military Institute cadets advanced side by side with veteran Civil War infantrymen into a hellish cannon and rifle fire. The soldiers forged onward with parade ground precision, using each step to free the other from the furrows of mud caused by the heavy rainstorm.

The Confederate commander of Western Virginia, Major Gen. John C. Breckinridge, had enlisted the cadets to join his ragtag force of 4,500. The cadets marched forward, their muzzle-loading muskets slung over their shoulders that were destined to bear a far heavier load, their VMI flag leading the way. Coming was a battle that would go down in American history as one of the most valorous and one of the last Confederate victories in the Shenandoah Valley. As the smoke of the battle cleared, 10 cadets lay dead, including Cadet Thomas G. Jefferson, 17, descendant of our nation's third president. Another 47 cadets were wounded.

Visitors can relive this segment in American history by touring the New Market Battlefield Park and its museum, the Hall of Valor. Together, they honor these 247 brave, young cadets. In the Hall of Valor are displays of Civil War muskets, uniforms, tintype photos, day-to-day accessories, and a replica of the type cannon captured by the cadets. It is one of the most stirring of all the Blue Ridge Civil War sites. Young and old alike are fascinated by its sense of history and urgency.

Beyond the Shenandoah Valley, Southwestern Virginia was also a region of vital importance to the Confederacy, points out Robertson. Through it ran the Virginia and Tennessee Railroad, the only lifeline between Richmond and the West. The lead mines at Austinville, the salt works at Saltville and the coal mines throughout the region provided the embattled South with essential natural resources. The May, 1864, Battle of Cloyd's Mountain near Dublin in Pulaski County remains the largest engagement ever fought in Southwestern Virginia. A future president, Col. Rutherford B. Hayes, was a hero of the battle. Today, only a marker commemorates the site.

Roanoker Gary C. Walker, author of *The War in Southwest Vir-*

ginia and *Hunter's Fiery Raid Through Virginia's Valleys*," outlines in great detail the way the war was fought in the Southwestern part of Virginia. He captures the mood of the area, geographically a third of Virginia, which broke away to join the Yankees and form its own state, West Virginia.

Walker's book on Maj. Gen. David Hunter, known for his unquenchable hatred of slavery, shows how Hunter reaped his vengeance upon Southwestern Virginia before its secession. States Walker, "Civilian property became an official military target. Both men and women were arrested without charge. Routinely, Southern ladies and their crying babies were forced from their homes with nothing but the clothes on their bodies. Their manor houses were plundered and burned before their horrified eyes." In Hunter's books, one can almost smell the smoke, feel the perspiration drip from the brow and hear the heart pound as the lines clashed and the men fell with hideous and gaping wounds.

Walker also is a consultant to the growing hobby of Civil War battle reenactments, held throughout the East Coast. The most recent Blue Ridge addition is Roanoke County's reenactment of Hunter's Raid at Green Hill Park in July, 1993 and is scheduled for the first weekend in August in 1994. Also during 1993, Oct. 16-17, Civil War buffs can see a reenactment at Cedar Creek in Middletown.

The Battle of Cedar Creek, 1864, marked the end of Confederate dominion over the Shenandoah

Valley and its essential food supplies. It also marked the end of famed Gen. Jubal Early's career and of the war-weariness that had plagued the North. And, it marked the end of Confederate hopes for a negotiated peace with the Union. The victory freed Gen. Philip Sheridan and his men, including Gen. George Custer, (who had the misfortune of tangling with Chief Sitting Bull at the Battle of Little Big Horn), to play crucial roles in the final battles of the Civil War the following spring.

The Cedar Creek Battlefield Foundation is fighting to save the battlefield's 158 acres from development. So far, $125,000 of the $450,000 needed has been raised. If the rest is not forthcoming, the land will be developed. In the meantime, the history preservationists are hoping their museum, relic shop and annual battle reenactments will help stave off the bulldozers. Their October event includes open camps, drills, dress parades and demonstrations of military and civilian life. For more information, call (703) 869-2064, or write: PO Box 229, Middletown, VA 22645.

For schedules of battle reenactments throughout the country, write the Camp Chase Gazette, PO Box 707, Marietta, Ohio 45750. If you've never seen one of these events, you're in for a real experience. The men who do this take it very seriously, as does Vinton attorney Bruce Mayer. Since taking up his hobby six years ago, Mayer has appeared in the movies, "Glory" and "Lincoln," in a National Geographic TV special and in the TV film, "North South." His 15-man unit performed at a birthday party for actor and Civil War buff Richard Dreyfuss at Smith Mountain Lake during the filming of "What about Bob?" He also is scheduled to appear in "Killer Angels," based on the Battle of Gettysburg.

Mayer says authenticity is a "must." Sack cloth, shell jacket and frock coat are required of all participants on the field. Eyeglasses must be of period construction. Only period footwear is allowed, preferably mule hide with square toes and wooden pegs. Uniforms must be woolen. Many of the soldiers carry their own original binoculars, pistols and bayonet rifles. No, they don't use real bullets, but they do use real gunpowder.

Regardless of whose side, if any, you believe was right in the War Between the States, there are hundreds of monuments, museums and battle re-enactments which await you in the Blue Ridge of Virginia. There are also more than 250 historic markers that are on-the-spot history lessons. We list below only actual sites where you can see or do something. For a complete list of Virginia Civil War battlefields and markers, write the state of Virginia at: 1021 East Cary St., Richmond, VA 23219 or call (804) 786-2051. A great guide available is Robertson's book, *Civil War Sites in Virginia, a Tour Guide*, published by The University Press of Virginia.

Historic Lexington

STONEWALL JACKSON HOUSE

Guided tours on the hour and half hour

HISTORIC HOUSE, GARDEN AND MUSEUM SHOP
8 E. Washington St. • Lexington, VA 24450
703-463-2552

™

Exciting horse events twelve months a year. Truly one of the top equine facilities in the United States.

For additional information call or write the
Virginia Horse Center, P.O. Box 1051, Lexington, VA 24450, **703/463-2194**.

★ ★ ★ ★ ★
GEORGE C.
MARSHALL
MUSEUM
LEXINGTON, VIRGINIA
Open Mon. — Sun.: 9:00 A.M. - 5:00 P.M.

FANTASIES

More Than Just A Gift Shop
The Subtle • The Dazzling
21 Nelson St., West
(703) 463-7222

THE
SECOND STORY
New & Used Books
Unusual Gifts
7 E. Washington St.
(703) 463-6264

Uncommon Gifts
From The Commonwealth
16W. Washington St.
(800) 437-2452

Pappagallo
Ladies' Clothing
& Accessories
23 N. Main St.
(703) 463-5988

LEXINGTON HISTORICAL SHOP
Rare & Used Books, Prints
9 E. Washington St.
(703) 463-2615

The
WILLSON-
WALKER
HOUSE
Restaurant
Fine Dining
30 N. Main St.
(703) 463-3020

Artists in Cahoots
A dazzling display of
beautiful things made by
local artists and crafters.

1 West
Washington St.
(703) 464-1147

★ ★ ★ FOR MORE INFORMATION, CALL OR STOP BY ★ ★ ★
Historic Lexington Visitor Center   102 E. Washington Street • (703) 463-3777

Sites with Something to See or Do

Unless otherwise noted, sites are free of charge.

Shenandoah Valley Region

Winchester

GEN. STONEWALL JACKSON'S HEADQUARTERS
515 N. Braddock Street   (703) 667-3242
Open 9 AM - 5 PM daily April - Oct.
Weekends in Nov. & Dec.
Adults $3.50 $1.75 Children

From this brick house, Jackson commanded his forces in defense of the strategic Shenandoah Valley. The French-style house contains artifacts of Jackson, Gen. Turner Ashby, Jackson's calvary chief, and others.

STONEWALL AND NATIONAL CEMETERIES
In two cemeteries a few blocks east of the business district are buried 3,000 Confederate and 4,500 Union soldiers killed in nearby battles. National is one of the largest national cemeteries in Virginia.

Middletown

BELLE GROVE PLANTATION
Cedar Creek Battlefield   (703) 869-2028
Open daily 10 AM - 4 PM Mon. - Sat.,
1 - 5 Sun. March - Nov.
Adults $3.50 $2 Ages 6-12

Spared during the Civil War even though it served as Gen. Philip Sheridan's headquarters during the decisive 1864 Battle of Cedar Creek, Belle Grove was built between 1794 and 1797 with the design assistance of Thomas Jefferson. James and Dolley Madison honeymooned there. Today, the house and grounds exemplify the home and working farm of a wealthy Federalist planter.

CEDAR CREEK BATTLEFIELD FOUNDATION REENACTMENT
Cedar Creek Battlefield   (703) 869-2064
$5 Adults. Children under six free.

October 16-17, 1993, the Cedar Creek Battlefield Foundation, which is striving to save the 154-acre historic battlefield from development, will stage a Civil War Living History Weekend. Reenactment of the battle will take place at 4 PM Saturday and 2 PM Sunday. Various drills, dress parades and military and civilian demonstrations will be presented throughout the weekend. Sutlers (vendors) Row will be a living history in Belle Grove presented by the Frederick Ladies Relief Society. All proceeds go to the preservation of the battlefield.

CEDAR CREEK RELIC SHOP
7841 Main St.   (703) 869-5207
Open Fri.-Mon. 10 AM - 6:30 PM

Cedar Creek Relics has the largest collection of authentic Civil

War relics for sale in the Shenandoah Valley. This includes swords, bayonets, carbines, muskets, buttons, plates, artillery shells, tintypes, documents and other relics. The store also sells tapes and books. Civil War and antique weapons are bought and sold.

Strasburg

HUPP'S HILL BATTLEFIELD PARK & STUDY CENTER

Route 11 South   (703) 465-5884
Open 10 AM - 4 PM Mon., Wed., Thurs., Fri.,
11 AM - 5 PM Sat. & Sun.
$3.50 Adults $2.50 Ages 7-16

A living history learning experience, Hupp's Hill features the third largest collection of Confederate currency in the world, a 100-foot hand-painted mural depicting the history of the Civil War and the world's largest map on the Battle of Cedar Creek. The museum is dedicated to teaching visitors, especially children. They can try on costumes and uniforms, among other "hands on" experiences.

STRASBURG MUSEUM

East King Street   (703) 465-3175
Open 10 AM - 4 PM, May - Oct.
$2 Adults $1 Children

There are many quality Civil War and railroad relics to see here. You'll enjoy the Blacksmith, Cooper and Potter's shop collections.

Photo: Virginia Dept. of Tourism

A young participant in a Civil War battle reenactment.

Front Royal

BELLE BOYD COTTAGE

101 Chester St.   (703) 636-1446
Open 10 AM - 4 PM Mon - Fri. Nov. - April;
10 AM - 4 PM Mon. - Sat.,
Noon - 4 PM Sunday May - Oct.
Adults $1, 50 cents Ages 12-16

This cottage museum, dedicated to the famed Confederate spy, teenager Belle Boyd, depicts life in Warren County and Front Royal during the Civil War. Belle was famous for the information she gathered which helped Jackson win the Battle of Front Royal on May 23, 1862.

WARREN RIFLES CONFEDERATE MUSEUM

95 Chester St.   (703) 636-6982
Open 9 AM - 5 PM Weekdays, Noon - 5 PM
Weekends April 15 - Nov. 1

Included in this museum is memorabilia from generals Lee, Jackson, Early, Ashby and Boyd. Other artifacts of the war in the Shenandoah are abundant.

PROSPECT HILL CEMETERY

Within the cemetery, you will find a memorial, Soldier's Circle Monument, over the graves of 276 Confederate dead. Also there is Mosby Monument, flanked by two Parrott rifled cannon. The marker remembers seven members of a Confederate group named Mosby's Rangers, illegally executed as spies in 1864.

Edinburg

EDINBURG MILL

Route 11

In 1864, Union soldiers began a systematic destruction of the Shenandoah, known as "The Burning." Open as a restaurant until last year, and noted for its child ghost, "Frankie," Edinburg Mill was miraculously spared when two young women tearfully begged Gen. Sheridan to spare it since it was Edinburg's only livelihood. Sheridan ordered his soldiers to extinguish the flames. There are

New Market Battlefield Historical Park

▶ *Civil War Museum*
▶ *19th Century Farm*
▶ *Scenic Overlook*
▶ *280 Acre Park*
▶ *Picnic Facilities*

Exit 264, I-81

Hall of Valor Civil War Museum   *703-740-3101*

several stories about just who the child ghost is, but the most noted is that "Frankie" was a slave who was caught in the mill wheel. Waitresses over the years have claimed he plaintively appears and reappears at unusual times.

New Market

New Market Battlefield Historical Park

I-81, Exit 264   (703) 740-3101
Open daily 9 AM - 5 PM except holidays
Adults $5 $2 Ages 7-15

New Market Battlefield Historical Park, owned and operated by Virginia Military Institute, offers a family adventure into one of America's most dramatic eras and is one of the finest Civil War museums in Virginia. Children can climb on cannons where, in 1864, 6,000 Federals clashed with 4,500 Confederates, including the famous VMI cadets desperately recruited from college to help the South's cause. It was the first and only time in American history that an entire student body was recruited to fight a war.

The Hall of Valor, focal point of the 260-acre battlefield park, presents a concise, graphic survey of the entire war. Exhibits highlight the war chronologically. There are two films including a stirring account of the cadets' baptism by fire, and one about Stonewall Jackson, a former VMI professor. You will see a life-size artillery unit, a model railroad, exquisitely sculp-

Photo: Lexington Visitors Center

Robert E. Lee (1870) and Stonewall Jackson (1851).

tured soldiers and four battle scenes among the three-dimensional exhibits in the Virginia Room.

The circa 1825 Bushong farmhouse around which part of the battle swirled still stands, with its reconstructed blacksmith shop, meat and loom house, wheelwright shop, oven, hen house and other artifacts of life in the 1860s. It served as a hospital after the battle. Scenic pathways lead to the "Field of Lost Shoes," where the mud was so thick that soldiers' mulehide shoes were often irretrievable. The celebrated Shenandoah River flows nearby.

New Market Battlefield Military Museum

Collins Drive   (703) 740-8065
Open 9 AM - 5 PM Daily, March 15 - Dec.,
and by appointment.
Adults $5 $2.50 Ages 7-14

Modeled after Gen. Robert E. Lee's Arlington House, the museum stands where the battle of New Market began in the spring of 1864. The museum houses a fine collection of more than 2,500 artifacts focusing on the Civil War and other American wars from 1775 to the present. A film shown regularly gives patrons an overview of the Civil War in the museum's 54-seat theatre.

Harrisonburg

Warren-Sipe Museum

Harrisonburg Rockingham Historical Society
301 S. Main St.   (703) 434-4762
Open 10 AM - 4 PM April - Oct. Call ahead
since hours fluctuate due to volunteers.

The highlight of this museum is its huge electrified relief map with accompanying audio cassette outlining Stonewall Jackson's Valley Campaign of 1862 for control of the Shenandoah Valley. There are many interesting artifacts, photos and paintings which help illustrate what happened in Rockingham County. Don't miss it for a blow-by-blow scenario of the great Jackson.

Fort Harrison

Off Rt. 42 South, Dayton   (703) 879-9965
Open 1 PM - 5 PM Weekends May 31 - Oct.

Guided tours are available for the home of Daniel Harrison, brother of Harrisonburg founder Thomas Harrison. The stone house was a natural fort used by local citizens when tribes of Indians terrorized the area during the 18th century and later, during the Civil War.

Lexington

Stonewall Jackson Cemetery
300 Block, S. Main St.

Marked by Edward Valentine's bronze statue of the General, which faces South, Stone-

Insiders' Tip

Go to your local library or video store and check out PBS's "Civil War" documentary. This acclaimed series will give you a real feeling for what the Civil War meant to the Blue Ridge area and to the country.

wall Jackson Memorial Cemetery contains the remains of the 39-year-old leader of battle, who died May 10, 1863, from wounds received at the Battle of Chancellorsville. The statue is probably the only time Jackson ever turned his back on his enemy. Some 400 other Confederate soldiers also are buried there. John Mercer Brooke, the inventor of the iron-clad ship, the *Merrimac*, is at final rest here. So is William Washington (1834-70), well-known artist of the Civil War period. He is especially known for his Battle of Lantane painting.

STONEWALL JACKSON HOUSE
8 E. Washington St.   (703) 463-2552
Open Daily Mon.-Sat. 9 AM - 5 PM,
Sun. 1 - 5 PM, until 6 PM June, July & Aug.
Closed holidays.
Adults $4 $2 Ages 6-12.

Built in 1801, the only home Jackson ever owned is furnished with his personal possessions. A brief slide show and guided tours interpret Jackson's life as a citizen, soldier, VMI professor of natural philosophy, church leader and family man. Guided tours are given every half hour of the home, restored garden and museum shop which specializes in books, prints and Victoriana.

WASHINGTON & LEE UNIVERSITY
Main St.   (703) 463-8400

W&L's beautiful front campus includes Lee Chapel, the focal point of the campus. Robert E. Lee served as president in the five years after the Civil War. The remains of Lee and most of his family are entombed here. Edward Valentine,

who also did the statue of Stonewall Jackson in the cemetery, sculpted the famous pose of the recumbent Lee. In the basement is a museum emphasizing Lee. His office is preserved as he left it.

VIRGINIA MILITARY INSTITUTE AND MUSEUM
VMI Parade Grounds,
N. Main St.   (703) 464-7000
Open Daily 9 AM - 5 PM Mon. - Sat.,
Sun 2 - 5 PM. Closed holidays

Since its establishment in 1839, VMI has been known for the officers and men it contributed to the Confederacy. In the center of campus is a statue of Jackson standing in the wind. Nearby are cannon from the Rockbridge Artillery. The famous statue, "Virginia Mourning Her Dead," a monument to the VMI cadets who fell at New Market, stands on the Parade Ground. In Jackson Memorial Hall is a mural of the famous cadet charge during the battle. The VMI Museum includes Jackson's beloved war horse, Little Sorrel (yes, the *real* hide, stretched over a plastic form...considered state-of-the-art taxidermy in those times), among many other Civil War exhibits.

East of the Blue Ridge Region

Charlottesville

JACKSON STATUE
4th Street

Charles Keck created a bareheaded Jackson galloping forward on his favorite mount, Little Sorrel.

Photo: New Market Battlefield

A young soldier in the Civil War, Thomas Garland Jefferson, was mortally wounded in the Battle of New Market at age 17. He was a descendant of President Thomas Jefferson.

LEE STATUE
Park between 1st and 2nd Streets

The work of sculptors H. M. Shrady and Leo Lentelli, this is an equestrian statue of Lee.

UNIVERSITY CEMETERY
Alderman & McCormick Rd.
North of UVA Football Stadium

Charlottesville, even during the Civil War, was known for its health care facilities. The remains of 1,200 Confederate soldiers lie in University Cemetery, most the victims of disease. A bronze statue of a bareheaded Confederate soldier is at the center.

Lynchburg

APPOMATTOX COURT HOUSE NATIONAL HISTORICAL PARK
Village 20 minutes
east of Lynchburg   (804) 352-2621

This site is not to be missed! If you're going to Lynchburg to see Civil War history, just 20 minutes further, you will be at Appomattox, where our nation reunited on April 9, 1865. Living history exhibits are held during the summer and the park is open daily except holidays from November through February. In the park, you will find a totally restored village as it was during the day when generals Grant and Lee ended the war on a handshake. There's Meeks Store, Woodson Law Office, Clover Hill Tavern and Surrender Triangle, to name a few. You will find the Appomattox County Museum located in Court House Square. Every Autumn, Appomattox is the site of its famous Railroad

Festival.

DANIEL MONUMENT
Intersection of Park Ave., 9th & Floyd St.

John Warwick Daniel was a member of Gen. Jubal Early's staff who went on to become a distinguished orator and U.S. senator. This monument to the "Lame Lion of Lynchburg," so named for Daniel's wound at the battle of the Wilderness, was created by Sir Moses Ezekiel, a famous postwar sculptor.

LYNCHBURG MUSEUM AT OLD COURT HOUSE
5th St.   (804) 847-1459
Open Daily 1 - 4 PM. Closed holidays
Adults $1   Students 50 cents

The tragedy of the Civil War is one of many facts gleaned from the exhibits seen in this historical representation of Lynchburg's history. The city was at the center of Confederate supply lines, making it a frequent target. Housed in Lynchburg's Old Court House built in 1855, it is one of Virginia's outstanding Greek Revival civil buildings.

PEST HOUSE MEDICAL MUSEUM AND CONFEDERATE CEMETERY
Old City Cemetery, 4th and
Taylor Streets   (804) 847-1811
Open sunrise to sunset
Self-guided tours or by appointment

Founded 1806, Old City Cemetery contains graves of 2,701 Confederate soldiers from 14 states. The Pest House Medical Museum is a restored white frame building which was built in the 1840s and was the medical office of Dr. John Jay Terrell. By 1861, Lynchburg was a major Civil War hospital center, and the Pest House was used as the quarantine hospital for Confederate soldiers. The dead were buried a few yards away. Dr. Terrell discovered the wretched conditions of the Pest House and assumed responsibility for the soldiers. The reforms enacted by Dr. Terrell reduced the Pest House mortality rate from 50 percent to five percent. On display are medical instruments from the 1860s including a surgical amputation kit used on many soldiers. Dr. Terrell died at age 93, leaving a heroic medical legacy to Lynchburg.

SPRING HILL CEMETERY
Fort Ave.

Buried here is Gen. Jubal Early, who saved the City of Lynchburg from destruction during 1864, when he ran empty railroad cars up and down the tracks to convince the Yankees that Confederate reinforcements were arriving for a major battle. The Union forces retreated and Lynchburg was saved from the destruction of Gen. David Hunter.

SOUTHERN SOLDIER STATUE
Monument Terrace
Center of Downtown

Honoring heroes of all wars, a statue of a Southern infantryman stands at the top of Monument Terrace. It was designed by James O. Scott and erected in 1898.

RIVERSIDE PARK
2240 Rivermont Ave.

Here you will find a fragment of the hull of the canalboat *Marshall*, which transported the body of Jackson from Lynchburg to Lexington for burial in 1863.

Bedford

BEDFORD CITY/COUNTY MUSEUM
201 E. Main St.,
Bedford, VA 24523   (703) 586-4520
Open 10 AM - 5 PM Tues. - Sat.
Adults $1 Children 50 cents

This interesting local collection includes a number of artifacts from the Civil War including weapons, flags, photos and personal effects.

LONGWOOD CEMETERY
Bridge St.

A Civil War monument of valor marks the final resting place of soldiers who died at one of five Confederate hospitals located in and around Bedford. A tall obelisk is over the single grave of 192 soldiers and a nurse.

New River Valley Region

Pulaski County

THE WILDERNESS ROAD MUSEUM
Newbern   (703) 674-4835
Open 10:30 AM - 4:30 PM Weekdays and
Sat., 1:30 -4:30 PM Sunday.

Operated by the New River Historical Society, there are three historic structures on this six-acre tract. There are various Civil War displays, including a drum, since the area is close to Cloyd's Mountain, the major Civil War battle (May 9, 1864) site for Southwestern Virginia.

Alleghany Highlands Region

Highland County

Bath County

WARM SPRINGS SPA
Warm Springs

In the Ladies Bath House of the spa is a chair made especially for the arthritically crippled Mrs. Robert E. Lee, who came often while her husband undertook his duties as a professor at Washington & Lee University after the Civil War.

McDOWELL PRESBYTERIAN CHURCH
US 250 West, McDowell

The site of the second major battle of Jackson's Valley campaign, McDowell, is marked by the roadside. Inside the village is McDowell Presbyterian Church, used as a hospital during and after the fighting.

Photo: Richmond Newspapers

Driving on Skyline Drive, motorists can enjoy the grandeur of mountain vistas and valley overlooks.

Inside
The Blue Ridge Parkway and Skyline Drive

*I*t seems almost a miracle that in the late 20th century you can drive from practically one end of an East Coast state to another and see no fast-food restaurants, trucks or blaring billboards.

This miracle in Virginia is a scenic stretch of highway that begins in Front Royal as Skyline Drive, running the entire length of Shenandoah National Park, and becoming the Blue Ridge Parkway at Waynesboro. From Waynesboro, the Blue Ridge Parkway meanders 469 miles all the way to the Great Smoky Mountains in North Carolina, offering magnificent views of valleys, forests, and mountain ranges.

In 1931 construction of Skyline Drive began, spurred on by President Herbert Hoover who spent many a weekend at his fishing camp in the area. Reportedly Hoover was riding his horse along the crest of the Blue Ridge Mountains one day in 1930 when he said: "These mountains are made for a road, and everybody ought to have a chance to get the views from here. I think they're the greatest in the world, and I've been nearly everywhere in the world."

A year later, construction began. Mountaineer farmers provided the labor with help from the Civilian Conservation Corps, and finished the 105-mile long Skyline Drive on August 29, 1939 during the administration of Franklin D. Roosevelt.

Today it costs $5 per vehicle to enter Skyline Drive at any point. That fee and the 35 mile-per-hour speed limit helps keep the road free of commuters and speedsters.

Most visitors traveling Skyline Drive expect to see clear, sublime views of the Shenandoah Valley and distant mountain ranges. Unfortunately, this is not always possible. Visibility in the Shenandoah National Park has dropped 50 percent over the past 40 years, and is at its worst during summer months. In fact, visibility has declined by 80 percent during the summer over the past four decades.

At least 75 percent of the haze seen on hot summer days is pollution — much of it caused by coal-burning power plants. And unless the trend is reversed, the problem is likely to worsen.

In 1992, a third of the days from May to October were classified by the National Park Service as having visibility of zero to 10 miles. Only 16 percent of the days had good visibility, and July had very few good days at all.

In the last six years, the Virginia Air Pollution Control Board has approved permits to build at least 23 coal-fired power plants in the state and is considering another five applications (as of summer, 1993). Two other coal-fired power plants are planned for Pennsylvania and Maryland; these would be close enough to affect visibility.

Park officials say the Virginia Air Pollution Control Board has never denied a permit to a power plant. The proposed plants would emit many more tons of sulfur dioxide, further reducing visibility in the park and the Shenandoah Valley. If this makes you mad, then write to your congressional representative or the White House, Park officials suggest.

Meanwhile, if you're planning a trip to Shenandoah National Park and want to know what the visibility is like, you can call the dispatch office at (703) 999-3644 or (703) 999-2243. Every day park officials do a visibility check at 1 PM and post the results at 2 PM. around the park.

Now, on to information about the beauty of Skyline Drive and the Parkway — of which there is still much to say. This chapter will tell you all about where you can eat and stay overnight without departing from either Skyline Drive or the Blue Ridge Parkway. Because once you enter these pristine mountains you may not want to leave.

Along the road you'll find lodges, cabins and camp-sites where you can spot deer and raccoons from your doorstep. You'll find

plenty of way-stations with souvenirs, fudge and ice-cream, and restaurants offering Southern specialties like Virginia ham, blackberry cobbler and buckwheat pancakes.

Of course there are hundreds of restaurants, motels, hotels and bed and breakfasts a short drive from Skyline Drive and the Blue Ridge Parkway. But this chapter includes only places situated along the scenic highways. The facilities in Shenandoah National Park are operated by concessionaires for the National Park Service. By contrast, some of the restaurants and accommodations along the Blue Ridge Parkway are privately owned and operated. This is because the parkway's boundaries are quite narrow in places, bordering private property where people live or make a living.

Accommodations, restaurants and snack bars described below are organized from north to south. Along Skyline Drive and the Blue Ridge Parkway you will see numbered mileposts, starting at 0.6 at the Front Royal Entrance Station. The listings in this chapter indicate the milepost where the facility is located. To make matters somewhat confusing, however, the numbering system starts again at zero when Skyline Drive becomes the Blue Ridge Parkway at Rockfish Gap. But, so long as you know to look out for it, it's not too confusing. By the way, you'll find a Howard Johnson's restaurant and a Holiday Inn where the two highways come together at Rockfish Gap.

Accommodations along Skyline Drive in the Shenandoah National Park

SKYLAND LODGE
Mile 41.7   *(800) 999-4714*
                          or (703) 999-2211

This is the first lodging facility you come to when driving south on Skyline Drive, after entering at Front Royal. Once a private resort, the lodge was built in 1894 by George Freeman Pollock, one of the people instrumental in establishing the Shenandoah National Park.

It occupies the highest elevation along Skyline Drive, and most of its 186 guest rooms overlook the Shenandoah Valley. The facilities include the lodge, some quaint rustic cabins, a glass-walled dining room, tap room, and entertainment most weekend nights in the summer. There are no phones in the guest rooms, but most have televisions. Service shelters have pay phones, ice and soda machines.

Skyland is a lively place for a family vacation. There are guided horseback trips for adults and pony rides for children. There's a playground with swings, bars, seesaws and plenty of grass and dirt, and an amphitheater where the National Park Service conducts educational programs. Naturalists lead hikes along numerous trails near the lodge in spring and summer and offer evening programs on such topics as bird-watching, wildflowers, and acid rain. You can also gaze through a telescope at the brilliant stars. Skyland also has a shop stocked with beautiful mountain crafts, photo supplies, and a newsstand

with daily papers and magazines.

Rates range from $70 per night for a single unit on weekdays to $130 per night for a suite with living room on weekends. Rustic cabins cost anywhere from $41 to $70 per night on weekdays and from $43 to $72 per night on weekends. The lodge is usually open from late March to the end of November.

The most popular month is October, that magical time of brilliant color in the Blue Ridge. Room rates are slightly higher this month. Reservations are often made a year in advance for these autumn nights. It's not a bad idea to make reservations well in advance for summer nights, too.

Skyland Lodge also has meeting rooms and audio-visual equipment to accommodate conferences.

BIG MEADOWS LODGE
Mile 51.3   *(800) 999-4714*
                          or (703) 999-2221

Nine miles south of Skyland Lodge you come to a clearing, the only large treeless area in the Shenandoah National Park. Big Meadows was probably created by fire, either accidentally by lightning or on purpose by Native Indians to encourage the growth of wild berries. The Park Service keeps the area clear to this day, and it's an excellent place for visitors to see a diversity of wildlife, including berries and wildflowers.

The resort is situated on the meadow and includes a big lodge built in 1939 by mountaineers. The mountaineer builders used native chestnut for the lodge's paneling; this wood is nearly extinct today due to the chestnut blight in the early 1930s. The resort includes several rustic cabins and some smaller, more modern lodges with suites. The main lodge's 21 rooms offer spectacular views of the valley, while the cabins with fireplaces sit among the trees. The most modern units feature king-sized beds, a fireplace, and sitting area with TV.

The main lodge has an outdoor deck where guests can lounge by day and star-gaze by night. For a quarter you can look more closely at the stars through a telescope.

The main lodge's lofty central room is a relaxing, casual place to hang out day or night. Several board games are available, and there are lots of comfortable old sofas and chairs and two fireplaces. The lodge also has a dining room with huge windows and a tap room open from 4 to 11 PM. Big Meadows Lodge offers naturalist activities and a children's playground.

One plus of staying at Big Meadows is the Byrd Visitor Center within walking distance. Here you will find fascinating exhibits about the park's history and the folkways of its former inhabitants. There is also an exhibit about the growing threat of air pollution and decreasing visibility in and near the park. Dozens of books for children and adults are for sale, from wildflower coloring books to histories of the region.

The resort is open from early May through October. Rates range from $60 per night in the main lodge on weekdays to $102 per night for a suite with a living room on weekends. Rates are slightly higher in October.

LEWIS MOUNTAIN CABINS

Mile 57.5   (800) 999-4714
                          or (703) 999-2255

For an even more tranquil experience, you can spend the night in one of the cabins on Lewis Mountain. There are no room phones or televisions to disturb your peace and quiet. The cabins have furnished bedrooms and private baths, heat, towels and linens. Cooking is done in the connecting outdoor area where there is a fireplace, grill and picnic table.

The cabins are open from mid May through October. Rates range from $50 per night on weekdays for a single room cabin to $77 per night on the weekends for a two-room cabin. Rates are slightly higher in October.

CABINS

The Potomac Appalachian Trail Club also operates six cabins in the back country of the Shenandoah National Park.

This can be a gritty or sublime experience, depending upon your perspective. You've got to hike in, chop your own firewood and draw your own water from a nearby spring. Each cabin has a table and fireplace, bunks for up to 12 people, and a pit toilet. There's no electricity, so you must also bring your own source of light.

But at just a few dollars a night per person, it's no wonder these cabins are so popular. Friday and Saturday nights are usually taken by Trail Club members. Non-members may reserve a cabin no more than three weeks in advance.

The cabins are Range View (mile 22.1), Corbin (mile 37.9), Rock Spring (mile 81.1), Pocosin (mile 59.5), Doyles River (mile 81.1), and Jones Mountain (accessible from Criglersville but not from Skyline Drive).

The cabins are locked, so a key must be obtained from the PATC, by mail, prior to your visit. For reservations, call (202) 638-5306 or write PATC, 1718 N St., NW, Washington, D.C. 20036.

CAMPING

Most years Shenandoah National Park operates three campgrounds on a first-come, first-served basis: at Mathews Arm (mile 22), Lewis Mountain (mile 57.5) and Loft Mountain (mile 80). However, because of budgetary constraints on the Park Service Mathews Arm is closed this year. At Big Meadows Campground, reservations are recommended from late May through October and can be made by calling (800) 365-2267 no more than eight weeks in advance.

All campgrounds have a 14-day limit, allow pets, and do not accept credit cards. The campgrounds accommodate tent campers, recreational vehicles (Rvs) and tent trailers. Water and electric hook-ups are not available for Rvs, however.

For further information, call Park Headquarters at (703) 999-2229 or refer to the Recreation chapter of this book.

Photo: Richmond Newspapers

Bikers ride through an underpass of the Blue Ridge Parkway near Roanoke.

Places to eat along Skyline Drive

ELKWALLOW WAYSIDE
Mile 24.1

From May to late October this stop along the drive offers groceries, camping supplies, wood, ice and gasoline. Sandwiches, burgers, fries and ice-cream are sold for carry-out.

PANORAMA RESTAURANT
Mile 31.5 at U.S. 211

This restaurant is situated in a complex with two interesting gift shops and an information station for the Shenandoah National Park.

The restaurant serves breakfast, lunch and dinner seven days a week from April to mid November. You'll find soups, salads, fried catfish, lasagna and Virginia ham for lunch or dinner. Breakfasts are also hearty.

SKYLAND LODGE
Mile 41.7

The glass-walled dining room here serves breakfast, lunch and dinner every day from late March through November. For breakfast you can have Virginia-style eggs Benedict, biscuits and gravy or plainer offerings. Dinner selections include prime rib, trout with pecan butter, and barbecued ribs. A tap room serves beer, wine and spirits from 3 to 11 PM daily.

BIG MEADOWS
Mile 51.2

The menus at this restaurant sound equally yummy: for breakfast there's the Skyline Egg Bake — an open-faced omelette with ham, scallions, potatoes and apples, and topped with herbed cream cheese. For lunch there are sandwiches, soups, quiche, steak and more. The dinner menu includes pizza, Shepherd's pie, catfish and fried chicken. The restaurant serves three meals a day from May through October. There's also a pub open from 4 to 11 PM. The Big Meadows Wayside closer to milepost 51 has a coffee shop and counter service.

Accommodations along the Blue Ridge Parkway

PEAKS OF OTTER LODGE
Mile 86   (800) 542-5927 (in Virginia) or (703) 586-1081

Unlike the lodges in Shenandoah National Park, Peaks of Otter is open year round. The lodge is nestled in a valley in Bedford County, surrounded by gentle mountains and facing a beautiful lake. Each room has two double beds, a private bath and a private balcony or terrace that overlooks the lake. There are no televisions or telephones in the guest rooms.

The lodge's restaurant serves hearty Southern fare and has an unusually large salad bar. A gift shop features very fine Virginia crafts, stationery, books, jellies and more.

Camping is also available at Peaks of Otter. Park rangers give talks on nature topics during peak season, and hikers can enjoy miles of well-marked trails near the lodge.

Rates for the lodge are $45 for one person or $65 for two people per room, plus tax. Each additional

Photo: Richmond Newspapers

White slashes mark the way on the Appalachian Trail for these hikers.

guest older than 16 pays an extra $4 per night.

Between the Sunday after Thanksgiving and the Thursday before Easter the lodge has a special deal, offering both breakfast and supper for an additional $10 per night Sunday through Thursday. On Friday and Saturday nights, however, the special offers only supper for the extra $10 per person per night.

ROCKY KNOB CABINS
Mile 174   *(703) 593-3503*

These cabins were built in the 1930s for the Civilian Conservation Corps workers who constructed much of the Blue Ridge Parkway. They have no fireplaces and no other source of heat, so it's understandable that they are only open from late May through Labor Day. The cabins have completely furnished electric kitchens but no bathrooms. There's a bathhouse with private shower stalls within 50 feet of each cabin and a washer and dryer. Rates are $41 for two and $5 for each extra person. Children 12 and under stay for free.

DOE RUN LODGE RESORT AND CONFERENCE CENTER
Mile 189   *(703) 398-2212*

This family-oriented resort sits on beautiful Groundhog Mountain and offers tennis, swimming, saunas and golf. There are poolside chalets, townhouse villas, tennis center chalets and single-family residences. Natural stone, wooden beams and floor-to-ceiling windows make this resort a tribute to the environment. All of the accommo-

dations are large suites which have a fireplace, two bedrooms, two full baths and a living/dining area. Many have complete kitchens. The High Country restaurant offers seafood, steak and Southern specialties. Doe Run also offers a honeymoon package at its "Millpond Hideaway" and a range of golf packages.

Families can especially benefit from the good deals here. The $89 weekday rate can accommodate two parents and up to four children; remember, we're talking about two bedrooms, two baths and a living room. Weekend rates range from $109 per night for a chalet to $119 per night for a two-story villa. But there is a $15 charge for each additional person over 12. These rates are true from May 1 to Nov. 1. During the winter season rates are lower. The resort is open year round.

Places to eat along the Blue Ridge Parkway

WHETSTONE RIDGE
Mile .29   *(703) 377-6397*

This restaurant near Montebello is open from early May through October. It shares the same menu as the Otter Creek Restaurant listed below, offering such breakfast specialties as buckwheat pancakes and sandwiches and burgers for lunch. The simple dinner menu lists fried chicken, hamburger steak, flounder or country ham. Don't miss the warm apple dumpling for desert.

OTTER CREEK RESTAURANT

Mile 60.8   *(804) 299-5862*

This restaurant is located next to a year round campground and small gift shop. Open from mid April through mid November, the restaurant has the same menu as Whetstone Ridge, listed above.

PEAKS OF OTTER LODGE

Mile 86   *(800) 542-5927*

This restaurant is popular among locals and known for its friendly service and hearty portions. Both the lodge and restaurant are open year round. Breakfasts are hearty, and lunches include big salads, burgers and ham steak with buttered apples. The dinner menu offers Southern dishes like barbecued ribs and salty country ham, as well as prime rib and tenderloin steak. The coffee shop sells picnic lunches to guests wanting to eat outdoors.

HIGH COUNTRY RESTAURANT AT DOE RUN LODGE

Mile 189   *(703) 398-2212*

Open year round, this restaurant serves breakfast, lunch and dinner seven days a week. The menu is seasonal and offers such gourmet selections as she-crab soup, venison, fresh rainbow trout from Doe Run's stocked pond, lamb, duck, steaks, country ham and more. The restaurant also offers picnic lunches "to go."

MABRY MILL COFFEE SHOP

Mile 176

Located at Mabry Mill, a famous pioneer attraction along the parkway, the coffee shop offers a single menu all day. Country ham, barbecue, and corn and buckwheat cakes are specialties. Mabry Mill is open from late April through October. The coffee shop serves guests from 8 AM to 7 PM during summer months and from 8 AM to 6 PM during May, September and October.

ORCHARD GAP DELI

Between mileposts 193 and 194

This private establishment about 50 yards off the parkway in Fancy Gap serves big deli sandwiches, homemade sourdough and raisin bread, Moravian sugar cake and imported and domestic beer and wine. It's open seven days a week. The deli also offers a full line of groceries, fresh produce and gasoline.

For more information about accommodations, restaurants and attractions along and near to Skyline Drive and the Blue Ridge Parkway, write to:

The Blue Ridge Parkway Association, P.O. Box 453, Asheville, NC 28802

The Parkway Association will send you a complete directory and a four-foot strip map of the parkway that you can't find at many of the information centers that are privately operated.

Photo: Richmond Newspapers

The New River in Southwest Virginia is a popular place for boating, tubing and canoeing.

Inside
Recreation

*R*ecreation: It's a concept we learn from our kindergarten days that never leaves us. The whole world loves to play. That's the major reason why visitors come to the Blue Ridge Mountains. Historically, visitors flocked to this region to partake of its pristine waters and gaze on its lofty mountains as a tonic for both body and soul. That's still true today.

The name, "Blue Ridge," is synonymous with the word "recreation" to many visitors and residents. There are so many leisure activities here that the wise visitor will plan an itinerary well in advance. However, getting sidetracked is a regional past-time in the Blue Ridge, hazardous only to a tight vacation schedule, certainly not to the spirit or health.

People come to play. And many of them stay, or return. There is a common bond among residents of the Blue Ridge. A smug feeling that only they have the privilege of living every day in a lush area which has brought Virginia international recognition in the realm of outdoor recreation. A reverence that they, the Blue Ridge citizen, can live each day in an area that others travel hundreds, even thousands of miles to visit.

The big draw, of course, is the scenery. Mother Nature blessed Virginia's Blue Ridge with lush greenery, bands of misty purple haze surrounding jutting mountain peaks and cool mountain streams. She blessed us with waving grain in golden fields, populated by languid dairy cattle meandering at dusk through meadow wildflowers to quaint country barns.

The Blue Ridge's recreational wonders vary widely. One, Natural Bridge, actually has been called one of the seven wonders of the modern world. And the good news is that the offerings are aplenty whether you're on a shoestring budget or have saved all year to play golf and stay at the Homestead or the Greenbrier, two of our nation's Mobil Four and Five-star resorts.

Many believe that the Blue Ridge's greatest strengths are its camping opportunities and national forest recreation. Two national parks, legends for their wilderness recreational opportunities, have been preserved here—the Jefferson and George Washington. The Shenandoah National Park, Virginia's mountain playground, is here. State parks including Claytor, Douthat, Sky Meadows and Smith Mountain Lake offer recreational opportunities galore, from horse-back riding trails to cross-country skiing.

Two outdoor mega-attractions are here also. The fabled Bikecentennial Trail that stretches from Williamsburg, Virginia, to the West Coast, and the Appalachian Trail, stretching from Maine to Georgia. Natives in towns such as Troutville take for granted a continuing stream of blaze orange-clad backpackers and bikers enjoying country byways.

The forest preserves naturally offer some of the finest fishing and hunting in the Southeast. Hunters and anglers appreciate both primitive sporting opportunities as well as those that are well planned, with guides who will do their best to ensure a trophy goes home with each sportsman. Licenses can be obtained at a variety of stores.

Visitors with picnic gear wishing to look, instead of stalk, will appreciate outdoor sports with a wide variety of wildlife including black bear, deer, wild turkeys and a great mixture of song birds.

A bounty of fresh mountain streams and rivers and the largest lake in Virginia, Smith Mountain, bordering Franklin, Bedford and Pittsylvania counties, is here. They offer the popular sports of boating, canoeing, swimming and tubing, a past-time especially enjoyed by college students who like to carry a drink and snack-stocked cooler on an extra inner tube as they float through the water on a hot, lazy afternoon.

A subterranean underground noted for its commercial caverns also offers plenty of action for spelunkers and rock climbing enthusiasts.

Or, if you prefer that your most rugged outing be on a sandtrap, there is a nationally-known offering of public, semi-private and resort courses. Many family attractions are within minutes of the 18th hole almost anywhere in the Blue Ridge.

As you're probably beginning to suspect, looking for recreation in the Blue Ridge Mountains is like trying to select a buffet meal from a mile-long Virginia groaning board. With so much to do and so many of our offerings in primitive wilderness areas, information in advance is a must.

There are far too many recreational opportunities to list completely in these pages. We highly recommend that you send for brochures and guides offered by the Commonwealth of Virginia and tourism and recreational associations. This is especially important to avoid disappointment for many camping reservations. Look for information contacts listed within the various recreation categories in the following pages. Then, go out there and have fun! You'll be in good company.

Hiking

It almost goes without saying that Virginia is a hiker's nirvana. There are so many hundreds of trails over such diverse terrain, from rhododendron-covered meadows to mountain peaks and rushing cascades, that it is not possible to describe them all in a book of this scope. Many good reference books have already been written on the subject of hiking in Virginia's mountains. Among them, we highly recommend: *Hiking the Old Dominion* by Allen de Hart (a Sierra Club Totebook), *Walking the Blue Ridge* by Leonard M. Adkins, and *Backpacker Magazine's Guide* to the Appalachian Trail by Jim Chase.

But before you go rushing to your local library, let us introduce you to the major areas for hiking in the Blue Ridge region.

Hiking the Appalachian Trail

First you have the famous Appalachian Trail, which zig-zags along the crest of the Appalachian Mountains from Georgia to Maine. More than 500 miles of the "AT" — about a quarter of its total distance — wind through Virginia. The portion of the trail that runs through the Shenandoah National Park — starting in Front Royal and ending at Rockfish Gap at I-64 — is considered one of the most beautiful parts of the Appalachian Trail by veteran hikers.

The trail continues south through the George Washington National Forest, the Jefferson Na-

PRIMLAND
HUNTING RESERVE
Quality hunting in the Blue Ridge Mountains

Pheasant • Quail • Ducks • Whitetail Deer
• Sporting Clay Course • Fishing

European Style Driven Shoots
and Walk Up Hunts

**Rt. 1 Box 265-C
Claudeville, VA 24076
(703) 251-8012
(703) 952-2825**

tional Forest, and then winds through the Mount Rogers National Recreation Area, a spectacular stretch of land in far southwest Virginia that includes the state's two highest peaks.

Hiking in the Shenandoah National Park Region

Back to the Shenandoah National Park. Its 194,327 acres contain not just the AT, but also 421 miles of other hiking paths. These range from rugged climbs up steep, rocky terrain to lazy nature trails with interpretive guideposts. Some of the best day hikes on the AT in the park include:

*A cascade hike along White Oak Run. You'll see a half-dozen falls ranging in height from 35 to 86 feet over a distance of about a mile. This trail can be reached from Skyland Lodge (mile 41.7 on Skyline Drive) on the White Oak Canyon Trail.

*The Ridge Trail to Old Rag Mountain, the park's most celebrated peak. On this route the AT travels through narrow rock-walled corridors that are the remains of the dikes through which lava flowed 700 million years ago. This is a challenging hike. But the rewards are great when you reach the top, catch your breath and stretch out on a boulder to gaze at the view over the vast, rolling mountains.

*A hike through Big Meadows, the only large treeless area in the park. Depending upon the season, you'll find wildflowers, strawberries and blueberries along the

path. This is also an excellent place to see a diversity of wildlife, since many animals depend on this grassy area for sustenance. Big Meadows is at the lodge that goes by the same name at mile 51.3 on Skyline Drive.

Excellent hiking maps and trail guides to the Shenandoah National Park are available at both visitor centers, entrance stations, and by mail from the Shenandoah Natural History Association, Rt. 4, Box 348, Luray, VA 22835 (703) 999-3581.

The Shenandoah National Park and Skyline Drive end at Rockfish Gap just east of Waynesboro. Here is the gateway to the Blue Ridge Parkway, the 469-mile-long scenic route that travels all the way past the Cherokee Indian Reservation in North Carolina.

Hiking along the Blue Ridge Parkway

Along the parkway are dozens of trails that are managed by the National Park Service. These trails are highly accessible, even for the laziest of walkers. But if you've got the energy, you can hike through tunnels of rhododendron that lead you to rushing waterfalls, or out to soaring mountain peaks covered with mountain laurel and spruce.

Hiking in these mountains also provides a glimpse of what life was like for its early settlers. It's not uncommon to stumble upon the crumbling rock foundation of a cabin no longer in existence, or a stone wall that used to keep in the livestock. The ridges and valleys were inhabited when the Park Service began to obtain land for the Parkway decades ago.

Many trails lead to farms and communities that have been reconstructed by the Park Service. For instance, at the Mountain Farm Trail near Humpback Rocks (close to Charlottesville) you might see a ranger posing as grandma churning butter on the front porch of an old cabin and brother John plucking on a hand-made dulcimer nearby.

Many interpretive programs are offered by the Park Service along the Blue Ridge Parkway trails. Rangers conduct guided walks during the heaviest tourist months, talking about everything from endangered plants to old-time farming methods.

Most Blue Ridge Parkway trails are so short and well marked that you don't need a map to walk them. But it would be helpful to have a national forest map or two when driving along the Parkway, because they can lead you to additional trails, campsites and campgrounds. Also, if you are going to hike any of the other trails in either the George Washington or Jefferson National Forest you ought to have a map, since these trails are used less than the Parkway trails and are not as well maintained.

For a map of the George Washington National Forest (which covers the Blue Ridge Parkway from mile 0 to 63.7) write to: Forest Supervisor, G.W. National Forest, P.O. Box 233, Harrisonburg, VA 22801. For a map of the Jefferson National Forest, Glenwood Ranger District Map (which covers the Parkway from mile 63.9 to 104.3) write to the U.S. Forest Service, Jefferson National Forest, 3517 Brandon Ave. Roanoke, VA 24108.

Some of the best day hikes along the Blue Ridge Parkway include:

*Mountain Farm Trail. This quarter-mile trail at mile 5.9 along the Parkway is an easy, self-guiding route that begins at the Humpback Rocks Visitor Center, not too far from Charlottesville. It travels along beside log cabins, chicken houses and a mountaineer's garden, and presents a good introduction to the everyday life of the Blue Ridge's former inhabitants.

*Humpback Rocks. This is a steep and rocky section of the Appalachian Trail that you can easily hike to from the Mountain Farm trail described above. Then it is a strenuous hike for nearly four miles to the summit of Humpback Mountain, from which you can see Rockfish Gap and the Shenandoah National Park to the north, the Shenandoah Valley to the west and the Rockfish River Valley to the east. In late spring, mountain laurel and azaleas are blooming all along the path and make for a colorful, fragrant hike.

*Crabtree Falls Trail. This 3-mile hike in Nelson County passes along what are the highest cascading falls in Virginia. Its trailhead is a parking lot on VA Rt. 56, a few miles east of Montebello. Five major cascades tumble down the mountain, and beautiful, well-worn trails make is possible to enjoy it all without getting dangerously close to the falls. Hikers are advised to stay on the trails and off the slippery rocks — too many careless individuals have met their maker or, at least, suffered injuries from a fall.

*Rock Castle Gorge Trail. This 10-mile, round-trip hike in northern Patrick County is one you shouldn't miss. You'll see high open meadows, panoramic views, tumbling cascades and historical sites on the way to the summit of Rocky Knob, at 3,572 feet. Until the 1920s a mountain community lived in this rugged area, where the rushing waters of Rock Castle Creek fueled a thriving industry of sawmills and gristmills. You'll see many reminders of these days along the trails. This hike is merely one of hundreds in the 4,500-acre Rocky Knob Recreation Area, which has a Park Service visitor center, campground, rustic cabins for rent and picnic grounds.

*Farther west than the Blue Ridge Parkway lies the Mount Rogers National Recreation Area, an enormous stretch of land 55 miles long and nearly 10 miles wide. This spectacular area, part of the Jefferson National Forest, is often said to resemble the Swiss Alps because of its high plateau and wide, open Alpine meadows.

The area has 300 miles of trails, many of which climb to the crest zone — where three mountains reach to nearly 6,000 feet. At Mount Rogers you will find dazzling displays of purple rhododendron, dense red spruce and Fraser fir, wild horses and vast, panoramic views. For more information, contact the area's headquarters at Rt. 1,

Box 303, Marion, VA 24354 (703) 783-5196.

*The Virginia Creeper Trail is the former railroad grade between Damascus at the southern-most tip of the Mount Rogers area and Abingdon. The entire trail is 34 miles, but there are many starting and stopping points. This is a wonderful, easy trail — great for enjoying fall foliage without working up too much of a sweat.

*In Giles County, west of Blacksburg, there are wonderful hikes along the Appalachian Trail and other recreation areas. One excellent two-mile day hike is alongside Little Stoney Creek, which takes you to the 60-foot Cascades waterfall. The Civilian Conservation Corps constructed this beautiful trail in the 1930s. It is well-maintained, with benches along the creek and pretty wooden bridges. In the summer, the pathway is lush and heavily shaded — the perfect place to cool off. You can also take a dip in the clear mountain pool at the base of the falls. To get there, go to Pembroke then take the road marked Cascades Recreation Area just east of the Dairy Queen on Rt. 460.

Hiking in the Blue Ridge Region's State Parks and Recreation Areas

There are also countless possibilities for hiking in the Blue Ridge region's state parks and in its city and county recreational areas. Between Lexington and Staunton, for instance, the state runs a 34,000-acre wildlife management area.

Here, alluring trails offer solitude and scenic views of the Maury River, the gorge at Goshen Pass and all manner of flora and fauna.

One moderately easy trail in this area starts near the wayside picnic area at Goshen Pass on VA 39. Called the Laurel Run Trail, the two-mile uphill path travels along a tumbling creek that pours into the Maury River. Rosebay rhododendron, oaks, maples and hemlock abound.

Nearby, the seven-mile Old Chessie Trail links historic Lexington with Buena Vista. This is an easy, flat pathway that provides glimpses of the Maury River and its gorgeous rocky banks. Wildflowers are abundant in the spring. It follows the old railroad grade of the Chesapeake and Ohio, and is owned and maintained by the Virginia Military Institute Foundation. In Lexington, you can get to the trail from North Main Street at VMI by taking a side street down to Woods Creek and a parking area on VMI Island. Follow trail signs, cross a pedestrian bridge over the Maury River, and pass under the US 11 bridge.

Douthat State Park in Bath and Alleghany counties has 4,493 acres of scenic high ridges and more miles of hiking trails than almost any other state park. The trails are color-coded and generally in good condition. A hiking map from the visitor center is recommended for long hikes. Don't miss the easy Buck Lick Trail, constructed by the Civilian Conservation Corps in the '30s, that has 17 interpretive signs about geological features, trees, wild ani-

Photo: Wintergreen Resort

An afternoon ride through the mountains.

mals, lichens, forest succession and more.

In Highland County, best known for its annual Maple Festival, there are also endless possibilities for hiking in a 13,978-acre wilderness area operated by the state. One option is a strenuous five-mile hike up an old fire road to Sounding Knob, at 4,400-feet, the best-known landmark in the county. The mountain top includes a grazed open area, and the views are splendid. The trail begins at the junction of Rt. 615 and the Fire Trail Road established by the Civilian Conservation Corps.

There are also nature trails in municipal parks throughout the region. In Charlottesville, for instance, the 215 Ivy Creek Natural Area is an unspoiled stretch of forest, streams and fields traversed only by footpaths. A network of six miles of trails includes self-guided trails. This area is on Hydraulic Road two miles north of the city.

Several miles away at Ash Lawn, a 535-acre estate that was once home to President James Monroe, a historical trail leads you through pastures and woods to the top of Carter's Mountain. Ecology markers are posted along the 3-mile trail, which begins at the museum shop. Ash Lawn is just off I-64, two and a half miles beyond Thomas Jefferson's Monticello (see the Arts and Culture chapter for more information about Ash Lawn and other historical sites).

Boating

Canoe Outfitters

You can find many reputable canoe outfitters in the Blue Ridge region. Several are located along the South Fork of the Shenandoah River, which meanders between the Massanutten and Blue Ridge mountain ranges. These outfitters also rent rubber rafts and inner tubes, if you prefer the kind of trip that allows you to turn off your brain and relax.

Other outfitters are located near the James River, the longest and largest river in Virginia. Only Lexington's James River Basin Canoe Livery leads canoe trips down both the Maury and the James rivers.

Further southwest in Giles County, the New River Canoe Livery in Pembroke runs trips down the magnificent New River, which many claim is the second oldest river on earth.

Most canoe outfitters will only allow you to travel down familiar waters, unless you're an expert and willing to assume the risks (financial and otherwise) of canoeing a lesser-traveled tributary. Generally speaking, a single fee includes the canoe rental, paddles, life-jackets, maps, shuttle service and an orientation. The shortest trips cost anywhere from $22 to $28 per canoe, while longer all-day trips run anywhere from $40 to $50. Tubing costs much less.

Here are some good places

24

to rent boats and equipment in the Blue Ridge region, from north to south:

FRONT ROYAL CANOE CO.
P.O. Box 473, Front Royal, VA 22630
(703) 635-5440
Open March 15 - November 15

Located three miles south of the entrance to Skyline Drive, this outfit rents canoes, tubes and flatbottom boats. It offers trips on the Shenandoah River that range from leisure fishing to whitewater adventures. Multi-day canoe trips can also be arranged. Reservations are recommended. The Front Royal Canoe Co. will also provide a shuttle service for people with private canoes.

DOWNRIVER CANOE COMPANY
P.O. Box 10, Bentonville, VA 22610
(703) 635-5526
Open April 1 - October 31

This outfit leads canoe trips along the South Fork of the Shenandoah River for novices and moderately experienced canoeists. Detailed maps describing the river course and the best way to negotiate it are provided. The maps also point out the best camping areas, picnic sites, swimming holes and fishing spots.

Multiple day trips can also be arranged. Reservations are recommended, but last-minute canoe trips are often possible. This company also offers a shuttle service for people with their own canoes.

RIVER RENTAL & CAMPSTORE
P.O. Box 145, Bentonville, VA 22610
(703) 635-5050
March 15 - November 1; Also open weekends in November by reservation.

"Bring us your weekend ... and we'll do the rest!" is this business's motto. It offers canoe and tube trips down the Shenandoah River, and organizes fishing, camping, hiking and biking trips. The outfit will custom-design a weekend vacation for the entire family, and offers packages with the nearby Skyline Bend Farm, Warren County's oldest licensed bed and breakfast.

Reservations are strongly recommended for weekends and holidays.

The business also rents kayaks, 10-speed bicycles, fishing equipment and camping gear, and sells fishing tackle and all kinds of supplies.

SHENANDOAH RIVER OUTFITTERS, INC.
Rt. 3, Box 144, Luray, VA 22835
(703) 743-4159
Open all year

This outfit offers canoe and tube rentals and canoe sales, and organizes overnight trips complete with tents, sleeping bags and even music. It is situated on the Shenandoah River between the Massanutten Mountain Trails and the Appalachian Trail in the George Washington National Forest. All-you-can-eat steak dinners can even be arranged in advance. Reservations are recommended.

JAMES RIVER RUNNERS INC.
Rt. 4 Box 106, Scottsville, VA 24590
(804) 286-2338
Open March-October

This place 35 minutes south

of Charlottesville offers canoe and rafting trips down the James River. Families are the business's specialty. Owners Christie and Jeff Schmick will arrange a variety of outings suitable for families (children over 6), as well as challenging whitewater runs.

They also arrange day and overnight trips for larger groups — even conventions. A special two-day package features canoeing for nine miles the first day, camping overnight by the river, and tubing the next day.

Tubing trips for up to 600 people can be arranged and groups of 25 or more get a discount. Recommendations are recommended.

JAMES RIVER REELING AND RAFTING
P.O. Box 757, Scottsville, VA 24590
(804) 286-4FUN
March 1 - Oct. 31

This business offers canoe, rafting and tubing trips for people at all levels of experience. It specializes in customizing overnight trips to suit the customer's fancy. "Describe what you want and let us design a trip for you," reads its brochure. Trips can be organized for convention groups, which get a 10 percent discount when five or more boats are rented. The company also rents fishing equipment.

It is located at the corner of Main and Ferry streets in downtown Scottsville at the James River Trading Post. Here you will find fishing and camping supplies and anything else you may have left behind.

JAMES RIVER BASIN CANOE LIVERY LTD.
RFD 4 Box 125, Lexington, VA 24450
(703) 261-7334
Open year round, depending upon river conditions

This outfit arranges day and overnight trips down both the Maury and James rivers. You can take an adventurous run down Balcony Falls, the mighty rapids where the James breaks through the Blue Ridge Mountains. Or you can spend a couple of hours paddling down a slow stretch of the breathtakingly beautiful Maury.

Owner Glenn Rose gives a solid orientation with instructions on safety and basic canoeing strokes. A video program also familiarizes canoeists with the stretch of river about to be boated.

NEW RIVER CANOE LIVERY
P.O. Box 100, Pembroke, VA 24136
(703) 626-7189
Open April - October

Owner Dave Vicenzi rents canoes and tubes for trips along the vast New River in Giles County. Vicenzi takes a laid-back approach to orienting his customers to the river: "They give me five minutes to tell 'em what to do." The easiest trip is a 7-mile run from Eggleston to Pembroke. The most popular trip is an 11-mile run from Pembroke to Pearisburg, with a number of Class II (intermediate) whitewater drops.

In the spring when the water is high Vicenzi allows customers to canoe down Walker and Wolf creeks, both tributaries of the New River. Multiple-day trips can also be arranged, but customers must supply their own camping gear.

Other boating possibilities in the Blue Ridge

Let's not forget boating on Virginia's beautiful lakes. There are three state parks in the heart of the mountains where boats can be rented.

At Douthat State Park near Clifton Forge, you can rent rowboats and paddle boats on a 50-acre lake. You can also rent rowboats and paddle boats on a 108-acre lake at Hungry Mother State Park in far southwest Virginia, near Marion. In Pulaski County — about an hour south of Roanoke, the 4,500-acre Claytor Lake in Pulaski County also rents rowboats.

Generally boats are available on weekends beginning in mid-May and daily from Memorial Day through Labor Day weekend. Smith Mountain Lake's 500 miles of winding shoreline and 20,600 acres of sparkling waters also offer countless possibilities for boating. There are about a dozen places where various types of boats can be rented, from yachts and pontoons to motor boats, sailboats and house boats. For information and brochures, contact the Smith Mountain Lake Welcome Center at (703) 721-1203.

Photo: Wintergreen Resort

A breathtaking Blue Ridge vista.

Swimming

Swimmers who enjoy the outdoors can count on the Blue Ridge of Virginia's cool mountain streams, lakes and even waterfalls for the most refreshing dip they'll ever take.

Municipal pools, such as the Town of Blacksburg's, perched atop a mountain vista, or the City of Radford's, beside the ancient New River, are a panacea to the eye and spirit by virtue of their environmentally beautiful settings.

Some of the best swimming can be found in the area's state parks and national forests. Picture yourself swimming at the bottom of a sparkling waterfall after a two-mile hike at the Cascades in Pembroke in Giles County. Or how about lying on Claytor Lake's white sand beach in Pulaski County while horseback riders amble by! For the strong in spirit, there's icy cold Cave Mountain Lake near Glasgow. All have sparse, but clean and accommodating changing and shower facilities.

Primitive swimming fans will find the 10-mile venture across the West Virginia border near Covington worthwhile to delight in the coldest water in the Blue Ridge — Blue Bend, a flat rock-lined "swimming hole" in the truest sense, in Alvon, W. Va. Built in the Monongahela National Forest during the Depression by CCC workers, Blue Bend is said to earn its name from the color of swimmers' lips after they emerge. For added charm, there's even a swinging foot bridge adjacent to picnic tables and a primitive campground.

Families with small children will be interested in an abundance of private campgrounds with lovely swimming areas overseen by lifeguards. One of the best-known is Shenandoah Acres Resort at Stuart's Draft near the Waynesboro intersection of Skyline Drive and the Blue Ridge Parkway.

Following is an "Insiders' List" of swimming lovers' sites definitely worth the drive from anywhere:

Municipal Pools

City of Waynesboro
(703) 949-7665

War Memorial Pool is located in the center of lovely Ridgeview Park. Surrounded by a playground, tennis courts, a baseball diamond and an open field, the managers of this Olympic-size pool pride themselves on its cleanliness and pleasing view. Open from Memorial Day to Labor Day, the pool's general admission hours are from noon to 6 PM Monday through Saturday and 1 to 6 PM on Sunday. Family Swim, when parents only must pay, is offered from 10 AM to noon Monday through Saturday. Fees: $1 for ages 15 and under, $2 for ages 16 and up.

City of Staunton
(703) 886-7946

Gypsy Hill Park Pool is a fairly new L-shaped pool, having opened just five years ago. The pool is Olympic-size and has a wading pool. The facility opens for the season around Memorial Day and closes Labor Day. Open from 11 AM to 6 PM Monday through Saturday and from 1 to 6

PM on Sunday. The fee is $3 for all day, all ages.

CITY OF CHARLOTTESVILLE

Washington Park Pool, 14th Street and
Preston Avenue   (804) 977-2607
Onesty Pool, Meade Avenue
                        (804) 295-7532
Crow Pool, Rosehill Drive
                        (804) 977-1362
Smith Pool, Cherry Avenue
                        (804) 977-1960
McIntire Pool, 250 Bypass
                        (804) 295-9072
Forest Hills Pool, Forest Hills Avenue
                        (804) 296-1444

The city of Charlottesville boasts six municipal pools: two outdoor — Washington Park Pool and Onesty Pool; two indoor — Crow and Smith pools; and two wading pools — McIntire and Forest Hills pools. The outdoor and indoor pools are all 75 feet long and the facilities feature showers, hair dryers and lockers. The indoor pools are heated. The wading pools are small and shallow, designed for children 12 and under. The outdoor and wading pools are open from Memorial Day to Labor Day. The hours for the outdoor pools are noon to 6 PM Monday through Friday and noon to 5 PM Saturday and Sunday. The wading pools are open 10:30 AM to 4:30 PM Monday through Friday and noon to 5 PM Saturday and Sunday. The indoor pools are open year round, but hours are widely varied, so call ahead of time. Admission for non-city residents for the outdoor and indoor facilities is $1.25 for children and $2.75 for adults. There is no charge for the wading pools.

CITY OF LYNCHBURG
(804) 528-9794

Two play areas and a place for picnics surround this pool, located in Miller Park. The Olympic-size pool features a high dive and a kiddie pool. Lessons are offered each morning. Miller Park Pool is open from Memorial Day through Labor Day. On Monday, Wednesday, Friday and Saturday the hours are noon to 6 PM; Tuesday and Thursday from noon to 5:30 PM and again from 6:30 to 9 PM; Sunday from 1 to 7 PM. Admission is $1.50 for ages two and up. The charge for the evening swims is $1. Pass books of ten tickets can be purchased for $10. These can be used for afternoon or evening swim sessions.

TOWN OF BLACKSBURG
(703) 961-1103

Mountain scenery lovers will gasp at the view from this mountain-top panorama. You'll bathe in mountain beauty as you swim.

The facility is open June through August 15, 1 to 5:30 PM seven days a week. The fee is 75 cents for ages 3 - 14, $1 for ages 15 and up. The pool is located on Graves Avenue, off South Main Street, past Blacksburg Middle School. And better still, on August 30, 1992, the grand opening was held for Blacksburg's new 25-yard indoor swimming facility sporting six lanes, sauna, spa and diving area. It is located on Patrick Henry Drive across from Blacksburg High.

CITY OF RADFORD
(703) 731-3633

Radford's city pool is an Olympic-size swimming pool located in Bisset Park, just off Norwood Street in Radford, bordering nearly a mile of the scenic New River. Its setting on a 58-acre municipal park makes this pool unique. It is surrounded by six lighted tennis courts, lighted picnic shelters, playgrounds, a gazebo and fitness station. The facility is open May 23 through Labor Day. Hours are Monday - Thursday, 1 to 5 PM and 7 to 8:30 PM; Friday, 1 to 5 PM and weekends 1 to 8:30 PM. Admission is 50 cents for ages 7 to 15 and 75 cents ages 16 and older. Children under six are free with a paying adult.

State Parks

CASCADES
(703) 921-5000

From Pembroke in Giles County, return to U.S. 460 and head north and west about a mile, turning right onto Virginia 623 to Cascades State Park, featuring a three-mile hike to a 60-foot waterfall. Picture yourself hiking and then jumping into a cool, placid pool of water right under a thundering waterfall. This is one of the most photogenic sites in the New River Valley. Warning: Don't try jumping into the water from off the cliffs of the waterfall. There have been at least three deaths in recent memory from careless youth who did! This swimming area is not recommended for small children. Call the Giles County Chamber of Commerce for more information (above) or write: PO Box 666, Pearisburg, VA 24134.

CLAYTOR LAKE
(703) 674-5492

This beautiful park area is located near Dublin in Pulaski County, off Exit 33, I-81. You'll think you're on an ocean beach with the ample white sand surrounded by a full-service boat marina beside the sparkling water. Camping, horseback riding rentals and sports fishing are also popular at this 4,500-acre lake. Its historic Howe House (circa 1879) features exhibits about the life of early settlers in the region. June kicks off with a family fishing tournament and Labor Day weekend brings the annual Appalachian Arts and Crafts Festival.

SMITH MOUNTAIN LAKE
(703) 297-4062

To reach Smith Mountain Lake, from U.S. 460, take Virginia 43 to Route 626 South. This lakefront beach nestled in the tall blue mountains of Bedford County offers a never-ending show of gliding sailboats in the distance. It's a paradise for water enthusiasts and has a visitor center with really special nature programs for the whole family during the summer. Special events include the Ruritans Bass Fishing Tournament in March, an Arts in the Park in June and Ruritan Supper and Festival in September.

National Forests

GEORGE WASHINGTON NATIONAL FOREST

Sherando Lake   *(703) 433-2491*

Off I-64, near Waynesboro, Sherando Lake offers a pristine beach within a natural paradise of camping, boating and fishing. Daily swimming fee is $4 per vehicle or $1 per person.

JEFFERSON NATIONAL FOREST

Cave Mountain Lake   *(703) 291-2189*

To reach this popular recreation area off of I-81, take Natural Bridge Exit 49 or 50 and turn onto Virginia 130 at Natural Bridge. Follow it 3.2 miles and turn onto paved VA 759. Follow 759 for 3.2 miles and turn right onto paved VA 781. Follow 781 1.6 miles to the recreation area entrance road, which is paved. The long trip to isolation is worth it. Cave Mountain Lake Campground is nearby with its unusual picnic tables and sites often surrounded by stone, set amidst large pines and hardwoods. There is a large open field with plenty of sunshine and the lake is cool and refreshing. It's a real getaway.

MONONGAHELA NATIONAL FOREST (WEST VIRGINIA)

Blue Bend Recreation Area   *(304) 536-1440*

Off the White Sulphur Springs, W.Va., exit on I-64, then take Route 92 10 miles north to Alvon. Turn left at the Blue Bend sign and proceed several miles to the Blue Bend Recreation Area. A true "swimming hole," Blue Bend is known for its chilling mountain stream waters surrounded by huge, flat rocks for sunbathers. Built by the CCC camp workers during the Depression, the rock craftsmanship makes this place unusual. After emerging, there is no more invigorating feeling in the world than baptism by Blue Bend's waters. Swimming is within view of an authentic swinging foot bridge. Primitive camping and picnic tables are nearby in this deeply wooded out-of-the way area populated mostly by locals. Don't miss this place!

Private Swimming Areas

SHENANDOAH ACRES RESORT

(703) 337-1911

Follow the signs from the Waynesboro exit of the Skyline Drive and the Blue Ridge Parkway to reach what some call "America's finest Inland Beach." It's reminiscent of the 1930s with its boardwalk-enclosed pavilion. Swimming is superb with a sand-bottomed lake of pure, soft, water — 500,000 gallons a day.

Children are giggly and ecstatic playing with the bubbling water emerging from pipes. There are slides, merry-go-rounds, a drop cable and even water volleyball. Life guards are on duty at all times, May through September. The recreational area includes camping, cottages, picnic tables and fireplaces. This is a wonderful family retreat for all ages! Write: Shenandoah Acres Resort, PO Box 300, Stuarts Draft, VA 24477.

Fishing

Naturalist Henry David Thoreau of Walden Pond, said, "In the night, I dream of trout-fishing." In Virginia's Blue Ridge, anglers see their dreams become reality in clear, cold mountain streams, rivers and lakes. Visiting fishermen can rest easy at night knowing that, at any given moment, millions of fish are surging upstream or lying tantalizingly in wait in stone river recesses.

An aggressive conservation effort by the state is part of the fishing charm of the Blue Ridge. For example, the mountain streams found in Shenandoah National Park are one of the last completely protected strongholds of the native eastern brook trout. Savvy Virginia tourism experts report that since Robert Redford's naturalistic film on fly-fishing, based on the book, *A River Runs Through*, hit the screens last year, the numbers of fly fishermen in Virginia were thicker than the black flies they're trying to imitate. But don't worry. The out-of-the-way waters far outnumber those that aren't.

Outstanding waters by species include: Brown trout: Lake Moomaw, Mossy Creek and Smith River; Largemouth bass: James River; Smallmouth bass: James River, Smith Mountain Lake, Claytor Lake and Lake Philpott; Striped bass: Claytor Lake, Smith Mountain Lake; Walleye: Smith Mountain Lake, Philpott Lake, Claytor Lake, Carvins Cove, Roanoke River.

And now for bragging rights!

To name a few records: Smallmouth bass - 7 lbs. 7 oz, New River; Roanoke bass - 2 lbs., 6 oz., Smith Mountain Lake; Striped bass - 44 lbs., 14 oz., Smith Mountain Lake; Walleye - 12 lbs., 2 oz., New River; Northern pike -27 lbs., 12 oz., Hungry Mother State Park.

Figures for fish citations are equally impressive. For 1990, the James River set the record with 549 citations of 16 species, followed by Smith Mountain Lake with 442 citations of 14 species; the New River with 174 of 14: Lake Moomaw with 114 of 8; Claytor Lake with 89 of 11; and Philpott Reservoir with 46 of 7 species.

The primary objective of this chapter is to give directions for finding some of the Blue Ridge's classic streams, rivers and lakes — the ones where there aren't other fishermen falling over each other. After you get to your spot, you may want to rough it on your own. Or, you can hire your own guide.

Otherwise, there are literally hundreds of fishing places recommended by the Virginia Department of Game and Inland Fisheries. You can find out about real gem daytrips. An especially fun one for lovers of both fishing and horseback riding is the package offered by Virginia Mountain Outfitters in Buena Vista, near Lexington. Trips range from one day to five and include a clinic. Call Deborah Sensabaugh at (703) 261-1910 at Outfitters to find out more.

Farther north, at the charming tin-roofed town of Edinburg, Murrray's Fly Shop is the place to find out where you can fish in the

Shenandoah Valley for the really big ones. Harry Murray is the author of several books including *Trout Fishing in the Shenandoah National Park* and promises to help you catch "Valley" fish. Murray offers numerous clinics and can be reached at (703) 984-4212 for a complete list.

Wintergreen Resort in Wintergreen offered its first Fly Fisher's Symposium last year. Call Chuck Furimsky at (800) 325-2200 for more information and lodging at a first-class resort which also offers great golfing and skiing. Also for fly fishing supreme, westward in Bath County, there's Meadow Lane Lodge, site of a former Orvis Fishing School on the Jackson River. Call (703) 839-5959.

For details, and the widest array of locations, the Department of Game & Inland Fisheries' Virginia Fishing Guide is a must. Traditionally, topographic maps published by the U.S. Geological Survey have been the most useful sources of information for anglers. These maps can tell you whether streams flow through open or forested land, how steep the land is and where tributaries enter. Directions on how to get both guides are listed at this fishing section's end.

So, now you're excited about all the fishing possibilities, we hope! But, don't forget your license. They may be obtained from county circuit court clerks, city corporation court clerks and authorized agents, usually small retail stores which are numerous in fishing country. License requirements and fees for both residents and non-residents are as follows:

RESIDENT

County or city resident to fish in county or city of residence - $5.

State resident to fish only - $12.

Resident to fish statewide for five consecutive days in private waters or public waters not stocked with trout - $5.

State and county resident to trout fish in designated waters stocked with trout, in addition to regular fishing license - $6.50.

65 and over state resident license to fish - $1.

Virginia resident special lifetime to fish - $250.

NON-RESIDENT

Non-resident to fish only - $30

Non-resident to fish for five consecutive days statewide in private waters or public waters not stocked with trout - $6.

Non-resident to fish in designated waters stocked with trout in addition to regular fishing license - $30.

Virginia non-resident special lifetime to fish - $500.

Regardless of whether you're testing the waters of the Blue Ridge as an experienced fisherman or a novice, it doesn't hurt to remember safety at all times, especially cold weather hazards. Although getting away from it all is most of the fun, don't forget to let somebody know where you are. Despite the best of precautions, you'll probably fall in at some point. In hot weather, it's an inconvenience. In cold weather, which is most of the year, it can be fatal. Many anglers do not realize that hypothermia can strike when the temperature is in the 40s. Prevention is always best, including waders with rough soles in our streams and life preservers in our rivers and lakes. And don't forget snakes (timber rattlers and copperheads are the two poisonous species) and ticks, the latter of which are "fishing" for you!

Listed below are some favorite fishing areas of the Blue Ridge. Source material for complete listings are at the end of this fishing section.

RIVIANNA RESERVOIR

Located just outside Charlottesville, this is often called the best bet for fishing in the area surrounding this historic city. It supports good populations of bass, crappie, bream and channel cats with occasional walleye and muskie. There is a public boat ramp near the filtration plant of the Charlottesville water supply reservoir, which may be reached from U.S. 29 north of Charlottesville by taking routes 631 (Rio Road) or 743 to routes 659 or 676. The ramp is at the end of Route 659.

LAKE MOOMAW
(703) 962-2214

This flood control reservoir was completed in 1981 with the closing of the Gathright Dam on the Jackson River. Ever since, its 43 miles of shoreline has proven to be a popular playground for residents of Alleghany, Bath and Highland counties. Much of the shoreline is adjacent to the Gathright Wildlife Management Area. Crappie fishing is outstanding, with 1.5-pounders

common. There is an equal compliment of large-mouth and small-mouth bass. Thirty-seven citation rainbows were also pulled from the lake. For more information, call the James River Ranger District in Covington at the number above.

SMITH MOUNTAIN LAKE
(703) 297-4062

The striper population is the most noticed at Smith Mountain, bordering Bedford, Pittsylvania and Franklin counties. It ranked second in citations in state waters with 442 of 14 species! Anglers appear to be going over to fishing live bait more than artificials. A real pro who has been fishing the lake since its beginnings with Appalachian Power Company in the 60s says the secret for big stripers is live shad, which can be caught at dockside in casting nets. For a great fishing guide, call Bob King at (703) 721-4444. The lake provides lot of camping and recreational opportunities, including a swimming beach, through Smith Mountain Lake State Park.

CLAYTOR LAKE
(703) 961-1103

This lake, also impounded by Appalachian Power, on the New River near Dublin, is known as a fantastic white bass fishery, producing many citations annually. Claytor has traditionally also been a good flathead catfish lake with fish going up to 25 pounds or more. Crappie also have shown good growth rates. Claytor Lake State Park provides fine marinas, camping, cottages and a swimming beach.

Hungry Mother Lake
(703) 783-3422
Located in the rustic high-lands of its namesake state park near Marion, this lake provides good largemouth fishing, quality bluegill and good crappie (up to 13 inches). Camping is available and boats can be rented.

References for the total scoop on fishing:
Available from the Virginia Department of Games and Inland Fisheries, 4010 Broad Street, PO Box 11104, Richmond, VA 23230-1104, (804) 367-1000:
Sportsman Calendar
Virginia Fishing Regulations
Virginia Fishing Guide
Fishing with Nets
National Forest Maps
Virginia Freshwater Fish Identification Booklet
Fishing the Water James
Trout Fishing Guide
References for Fresh Water Fishing Guides

For individual US Geological Survey maps:
Distribution branch, US Geological Survey, Box 25286, Federal Center, Denver, Colorado 80225

For an outstanding collection of Virginia topographic maps:
Virginia Atlas & Gazetteer, The DeLorme Mapping Company, PO Box 298, Freeport, Maine 04032

For lake and river maps:
Alexandria Drafting Co., 6440 General Green Way, Alexandria, VA 22312

For a great trout stream book:
Virginia Trout Streams, by

Whitewater "Katayaking" (a Russian-made boat) on the Russell Fork River in Dickenson County.

Harry Slone, published by Backcountry Publications

A Fly Fisherman's Blue Ridge, by Christopher Camuto, published by Henry Holt & Company.

Golf

The Blue Ridge of Virginia is for golf lovers. Many golfers and their families keep coming back year after year since the Blue Ridge offers golfers an entertaining and challenging mix of courses. The quality of golf in the foothills of the Blue Ridge Mountains, like its quality of life, has always been nothing short of outstanding.

An area rich in history, golfers will find the nation's oldest first tee still in use at the Homestead, a Four-star Mobil Award, Gold Medal Golf Resort in Hot Springs, where golf legend Sam Snead's estate is close by. Its top-rated course, Cascades, has been the site of numerous USGA championships and the 1988 US Amateur. Special treats await golfers there. One example is just behind the Cascades' 13th green, where a clear mountain stream cascades down the gorge — an idyllic picnic site! Just 30 scenic miles away is yet another ultimate in golfing at another Five-Star Mobil resort, the Greenbrier, at nearby White Sulphur Springs, West Virginia.

The Shenandoah Valley sports multi-recreational playgrounds at Wintergreen and Massanutten resorts, where you can actually play golf and ski on the same day. Nearby Shenvalee's 18-hole PGA course has been entertaining New Market visitors for years. Chestnut Creek at Bernard's Landing, at Smith Mountain Lake, is one of the area's newest and has been winning fast and true fans since the day it opened.

Other challenging new courses such as Hanging Rock in Salem, in the Roanoke Valley, are adding to Virginia's growing reputation as a top-notch state with more than 135 public, semi-private and resort courses available. The best are here in the Blue Ridge.

With far too many courses to list, we at the Insiders' Guide recommend three sources for a complete listing of public, semi-private and military courses with including the number of holes, par length, description, location and phone number of each course.

Virginia Golf Association, (804) 378-2300

Tee Time Magazine

Mid-Atlantic Golf Magazine, 12407 New Point Drive, Richmond, VA 23233, (804) 360-3336 or (301) 913-0061

Virginia Division of Tourism, 1021 East Cary Street, Richmond, VA 23219, (800) 93-BACK 9

Camping

From primitive campsites to modern RV campgrounds with all the amenities, camping in the Blue Ridge Mountains is a four-season activity.

Forests cover two-thirds of Virginia's total acreage, with most of it in Virginia's Blue Ridge Mountains and national forest regions. Camping here is a huge, inexpensive, family-oriented recreational past-time, whether you like KOA Kamping Kabins with all the comforts of home, or just a rustic plot of beautiful land. At Blue Ridge of Virginia campgrounds, you'll usually find swimming in cool mountain streams or lakes and the hiking experience of a lifetime. Some even have boat rental and horseback riding.

NATIONAL FOREST CAMPGROUNDS

National forest areas accept no reservations. Family campgrounds are on a first-come, first-served basis. The only exception is group camping, which requires reservations which may be made up to 120 days in advance, and must be made 10 days in advance. No rental cabins or other lodging facilities are available in the national forest campgrounds. But, if you want to bring along your pets for protection or company, that's just fine.

VIRGINIA STATE PARK CAMPGROUNDS

Virginia state parks do accept and highly recommend reservations up to 364 days in advance. The maximum camping period is 14 days and, again, pets are permitted.

DEVELOPED CAMPSITES

Developed campsites can accommodate one piece of camping equipment and/or one motor vehicle and a maximum of six people. Expect a grill, picnic table and access to bathhouses.

ELECTRICAL/WATER HOOKUP

Electrical/water hookup sites are generally larger sites that can accommodate recreational vehicles and campers. They are available at Claytor Lake and Fairy Stone parks.

CABINS

Cabins are located in Claytor, Douthat and Fairy Stone state parks and are available the end of May through Labor Day. There is a $4.50 fee for advance registration. Reservations begin on Monday at 3 PM and end on the following Monday at 10 AM. Any cabins not reserved become available on a first-come, first-served basis for a minimum of two nights.

GROUP CAMPING

Group camping is available with a minimum of three sites.

Camping Fees (Nightly Rates)
Primitive sites, $6
Developed sites, $8.50
Group sites, $8.50
Electricity & water, $12.00
Pet fee, $1.00
Advance reservation, $4.50/site
Cancellation fee, $5.00/ticket
Off-season primitive, $4 - $6

Cabin Fees (Nightly)
1 Room, $168
1 Bedroom, $198
2 Bedroom, $282
Lodge (Douthat Only), $550
Extra Bed, $21
Pet fee, $3

Virginia Campground Association (private campgrounds)
9415 Hull Street Road, Suite B, Richmond, VA 23236, (804) 276-8614

George Washington National Forest, Harrison Plaza, 101 North Main Street, Harrisonburg, VA 22801, (703) 433-2491

Jefferson National Forest, 210 Franklin Road, SW, Caller Service 2900, Roanoke, VA 24001, (703) 982-6270

Shenandoah National Park, Route 4, Box 348, Luray, VA 22835, (703) 999-2243

Virginia State Parks, Department of Conservation & Recreation, Division of State Parks, 203 Governor Street, Suite 306, Richmond, VA 23219, (804) 786-1712

General Information:
(804) 490-3939
Reservations by Phone:
(804) 371-9502
(TDD number)
State Forest Superintendent:
Route 1, Box 250,
Cumberland, VA 23040-9515,
(804) 492-4121
Blue Ridge
Parkway Camping:
200 BB&T Building,
One Pack Square,
Asheville, NC 28801
US Army Corps of
Engineers: (Philpott
Lake, Bassett, ONLY)
Wilmington District,
Philpott Lake, Route 6,
Box 140, Bassett, VA 24055

Virginia Division of Tourism, Telephone Requests Only (804) 786-4484

Mail Requests Only, Bell Tower on Capitol Square, Richmond, VA 23219

Campgrounds in Virginia, Virginia Travel Council, PO Box 15067, Richmond, VA 23227, (804) 266-0444

Shenandoah Valley Travel Association, PO Box 1040, Dept. TG92, New Market, VA 22844, (703) 740-3132

To get information, on private campgrounds, call or write the Virginia Travel Council or Virginia Campgrounds Association.

Horseback Riding

Virginia's Blue Ridge should not only be explored by automobile or by foot. There is a wealth of horseback riding outfitters up and down the Shenandoah Valley, offering one-hour trips for beginners, half or full-day explorations for those with tougher hides, and all kinds of overnight trips.

You can rough it and camp beside a trout stream with Deborah Sensabaugh's Virginia Mountain Outfitters, grilling fresh trout over a campfire and listening to the whippoorwills at sunset. Or you can sit back and be served dinner by candlelight with Overnight Wilderness Camping, which offers the thrill of the wild without the sweat. There are country inns that specialize in guided trail riding, and horse outfitters that offer packages with nearby bed and breakfasts so that you can soak in a hot tub after a long day's ride.

If you yearn to travel the mountains in October to see the brilliant foliage, consider going by horseback. "It's the best way to see the leaves rather than bumper-to-bumper on the parkway," says Tom Seay of Overnight Wilderness Camping.

In this section, we only list places that rent horses to the public and lead guided trips. In Virginia's Blue Ridge there are also many private liveries, horse clubs and an endless number of trails, both public and private.

MOUNTAIN SPRINGS STABLES
P.O. Box 169, Sperryville, VA 22740
(703) 987-9545

Owners and operators Heather Marsh and Daphne Lowrie offer private trail rides seven days a week that give visitors an up-close look at the Blue Ridge foothills. They lead journeys through open fields and forests and along streams and rivers, with unspoiled views of rolling mountains. They offer catered picnics and romantic moonlit rides, and can arrange either English or Western riding styles. Marsh, also an experienced professional photographer, takes her camera along so clients can take the view and their memories back home with them. The facilities also include indoor and outdoor riding arenas, private riding lessons and video instructions. Please call for reservations, but don't hesitate to call on short notice in case Marsh and Lowrie have an opening.

OVERNIGHT WILDERNESS CAMPING
P.O. Box 832, Locust Grove, VA 22508
(703) 786-7329

This sophisticated operation leads cushy, overnight trail rides in the Shenandoah National Park, serving up everything from a candlelight dinner on china to well-cushioned sleeping bags and spare toothbrushes. "We just wait on 'em hand and foot," says Tom Seay, a former TV producer of outdoor sporting shows. "The only rule we have is, 'Take your watch off when you show up.'"

Seay and his partners will meet riders in Washington, Richmond or on Skyline Drive — wherever clients want to be picked up — then head for the hills with their horses.

Amazingly, it only costs $99 a day per person, and that includes the use of a horse, a minimum of three guides, meals, a sleeping bag, tent and other equipment desired including fishing or hunting gear. Trips are offered year round, depending upon the weather. Small children — even toddlers — are welcome.

SHENANDOAH NATIONAL PARK
ARA Skyline, P.O. Box 727
Luray, VA 22835   *(703) 999-2210*

Guided trail rides leave from the National Park's Skyland Lodge several times daily. The horses follow a trail called the White Oak Canyon, with several waterfalls along the way. Rides cost $16 per person, per hour, and must be booked one day in advance. There's also a more advanced, two and one-half-hour ride leaving early in the morning on weekdays in the summer.

MARRIOTT RANCH
Rt. I, Box 133, Hume, VA 22639
(703) 364-2627

This 4,200-acre beef cattle ranch, owned and operated by Marriott Corporation, is home to one of the largest Western trail ride operations in the northern Virginia piedmont. Rides are usually 1/2 hours long and are available every day of the week, except Mondays. On weekdays, rides go out at 10 AM., noon and 2 PM, and on weekends an additional 4 PM ride is offered. On weekdays, rides cost $20 per person; on weekends, $25 per person, with group rates available. The minimum riding age is 10. The trails run through winding streams, open valleys and wooded hills on the ranch. Horse drawn buggy, stage coach and haywagon rides are also offered. Reservations are required for all types of rides.

Marriott Ranch also specializes in corporate Western special events like barbecues and country/western dances, as well as formal affairs such as wedding receptions and garden parties.

In the fall of 1993 they are throwing a series of Saturday night parties called "Steak Bake and Boot Scoot" that include haywagon rides, Western-style steak cook-outs, country/western dance instructions and Western comedy entertainment. The price is $55 per person and reservations are required.

JORDAN HOLLOW FARM INN
Rt. 2, Box 375, Stanley, VA 22851
(703) 778-2285

This is a wonderful vacation spot for horse lovers. The 145-acre farm is nestled in a secluded "hollow" between the Massanutten and Blue Ridge mountains range, six miles south of Luray.

You can spend the night at the 200-year-old restored country inn or one of the two lodges, dine on "country cosmopolitan" cuisine, and ride horses through lovely meadows or woods. The facilities also include a pub, recreation room with a pool table and fully equipped meeting rooms.

The inn offers three beginner trail rides a day, Western style, for $20 per person per hour. A more advanced, two-hour ride is also offered daily, on either English or Western saddle. Pony rides are available for children under eight.

All-day rides for experienced riders must be arranged in advance; they cost $10 per person for a minimum of six hours and there must be at least two riders. There's also a flat fee of $80 for the guide and horse transportation, to be divided among the participants. The all-day rides travel exciting trails in the Blue Ridge and Massanutten mountains.

Jordan Hollow Farm also claims to be the only country inn in Virginia with a full program for carriage driving.

WOODSTONE MEADOWS STABLE
Rt. I, Box 110-L, McGaheysville, VA 22840
(703) 289-6152

Located in the Shenandoah Valley across from Massanutten

Resort, this outfit offers leisurely trail rides in the rugged Massanutten Mountains. They match horse and rider according to the rider's ability, and give everyone instructions before taking off. Trail rides cost $18 per person if you pay at least an hour in advance. Otherwise, they cost $20. The rides last an hour.

MOUNTAINTOP RANCH
Rt. 1, Box 402, Elkton, VA 22827
(703) 298-9542

Between Shenandoah and Elkton, this mountaintop ranch leads trail rides throughout its 3,000 acres. It is surrounded on three sides by the Shenandoah National Park. Rides last anywhere from one hour to four days, costing $18 per person for the shortest trip. Half-day rides cost $50, and full-day rides cost $75, and this includes lunch. Groups of 10 or more receive a discount. The wilderness trails pass through meadows, forests, along waterfalls and babbling brooks.

The ranch also has a fully-furnished cabin that sleeps eight. It can be rented for $70 a night on weekdays and $100 on Friday or Saturday night.

OAK MANOR FARMS
(703) 234-8101
(please call for details and directions)

Located halfway between Harrisonburg and Staunton, this outfit leads guided trail rides up and down a small beautiful mountain in the Blue Ridge. The thoroughbred horses are reportedly very gentle. Trips last about an hour and cost $20 per person. Appointments are necessary.

MONTFAIR STABLES
Rt. 2, Box 383, Crozet, VA 22932
(804) 823-6961

Fifteen miles west of Charlottesville, this ranch offers half-hour, one-hour, half-day and all-day rides for the beginner or expert, on Western or English saddle. The stables are located at the foot of Pasture Fence Mountain in the Blue Ridge and are open year round, weather permitting.

Owners Julie and Sam Strong also lead overnight trail rides once a month from May through September. On the overnighter, an afternoon ride up Pasture Fence Mountain is followed by dinner around the campfire. Riders sleep outdoors in a tent and have breakfast the next morning before heading back down the mountain. These overnight trips are for experienced riders and cost $125 per person. Reservations fill up quickly!

General fees range from $12 for a 1/2 hour ride to $60 for a 1/2 day ride. Discounts are offered for groups of eight or more. Rides are scheduled by reservation.

WINTERGREEN RESORT - RODES FARM STABLES
Wintergreen, VA 22958
(804) 325-2200 x819

Guided trail rides in the mountains and Rockfish Valley are offered daily, from mid-March through December except Wednesdays. There are pony rides for kids, sunset trail rides through Rockfish Valley, riding lessons, horsemanship classes and private rides for advanced riders.

Trail rides last one hour and

15 minutes, and they are all English saddle. Trail rides cost $25 for resort guests and $30 for the public during the week. On the weekend rides cost $3 more. Pony rides are $10 for guests and $12 for other children. Reservations are required. (For more information on Wintergreen, see our Resorts chapter.)

RIVER RIDGE RANCH
Rt. 1, Box 119-1, Millboro, VA 24460
(703) 996-4148

This 377-acre ranch, located about 10 miles from The Homestead in Bath County, has about 15 horses for guided trail rides through unspoiled forests and fields. There are breathtaking mountain top views of the Cowpasture River Valley and an abundance of wildlife that roam the vast ranch. Riders can use English or Western tack. It costs $25 for an hour ride or $70 for a half-day ride plus $5 for lunch. A 10 percent discount is offered to groups of four or more for half-day rides.

Highly popular are the Saturday night haywagon rides and cookouts at the top of River Ridge Mountain. We're not talking hotdogs on a clothes hanger, but New York strip, barbecued chicken or fresh mountain trout grilled over a campfire.

River Ridge Ranch has a honeymoon cabin, lodge, and another family unit for overnight accommodations. The ranch, which also offers fishing, swimming in the Cowpasture River, and hiking, can accommodate 12 guests, and a full country breakfast is always provided. The ranch is open year round.

THE HOMESTEAD
Hot Springs, VA 24445
(703) 839-5500

Guided trail rides are among the multitude of activities offered at this five-star resort in Bath County. There are more than 100 miles of trails, and you can ride either Western or Hunter (English) style. The escorted trail rides are private – in other words, you need not bear the company of strangers while getting to know your horse and the terrain. Reservations should be made as far in advance as possible. The rides last between 45 minutes and one hour and cost $42 per person. Children who are at least 4-feet-tall are welcome.

VIRGINIA MOUNTAIN OUTFITTERS
Rt. 1, Box 244, Buena Vista, VA 24416
(703) 261-1910

Deborah Sensabaugh runs a year round horseback outfitter service, offering a variety of trips in both the Blue Ridge and Alleghany mountains. Half-day trail rides from Buena Vista up to the Parkway and back last about four hours and provide majestic views of the Shenandoah Valley. Half-day rides cost $45 per person, and a hearty picnic lunch is included.

Full-day rides travel along the Pedlar River, through farms and foothill country and into the mountains. The price is $80 per person and the trip lasts nearly seven hours. You can fish for trout on the return trip if you like — there's no hurry.

Sensabaugh also organizes overnight rides and furnishes her riders everything except for sleeping bags and personal items. Riders usually camp beside a mountain river or stream and cook dinner over a campfire. This costs $150 per person, which also includes all meals, from lunch on the arrival day to lunch and an afternoon snack the following day.

She also offers three- to five-night pack trips for die-hard riders. "You'll ride in all kinds of weather, all kinds of terrain, with a generous dose of history and trail lore along the way," Sensabaugh says. Camping is primitive. The trips cost $80 per person per day – a price that includes all meals, tents and camping gear other than sleeping bags.

Sensabaugh's most popular package, called "Horse Lovers Holiday," combines two all-day horseback trips with overnight stays at a nearby bed and breakfast, Lavender Hill Farm. You can work up quite an appetite riding in these mountains, a hunger that Lavender Hill's hearty European cuisine will more than satisfy. The cost is $225 per person, which includes two nights at Lavender Hill, all meals and the horseback trips and equipment.

An even more deluxe bed and breakfast package is offered with Irish Gap Inns, which is located high in the mountains and just off the Blue Ridge Parkway. Innkeeper Dillard Saunders charges between $98 and $118 night for a stay at her luxurious B&B, and Sensabaugh leads horseback trips from the inns.

DUN ROAMING STABLES
Smith Mountain Lake
P.O. Box 471, Moneta, VA 24121
(703) 297-6844

Danny Wagner came up with this unusual name for his stables after reflecting on his years of roaming as a horseman. "I'm 30, so I reckon it's time to settle down," Danny says. He and his wife, Cindy, lead guided horse rides along Smith Mountain Lake, through woods, along creeks and through fields. Fees are $15 an hour per person. Dinner rides cost $36, and include dinner over a campfire and a two to three hour trip. Overnight trips cost $48 per person a night, including dinner and breakfast. You must bring your own camping equipment. Reservations are required for all trail rides.

Southwest Virginia has two state parks with horse rentals and guided trail rides:

HUNGRY MOTHER STATE PARK
Rt. 5, Box 109, Marion, VA 23454
(703) 783-3422

A few miles north of Marion is a state park known for its beautiful woodlands and placid 108-acre lake in the heart of the mountains. It's also home to a newly renovated conference center called Hemlock Haven.

At Hungry Mother, guided trail rides lasting 1/2 hour cost $6 per person. If you have small children, just sit 'em right behind you on the park's gentle horses.

Claytor Lake State Park

Rt. 1, Box 267, Dublin, VA 24084
(703) 674-5492

Horseback riding is a popular sport at this beautiful state park with a 4,500-acre lake in the New River Valley. As of our print deadline, guided trail rides were expected to cost around $6 per person this year and last about 40 minutes.

Hunting

A fellow once commented that he hunted to feed his body and his soul. In the Blue Ridge of Virginia, no hunter goes hungry.

As expected, wildlife is concentrated around farmland or other areas where there is food. With much of the Blue Ridge lying in the 1.5 million acres of the George Washington and Jefferson national forests and state lands, food for wildlife is in abundant quantity. An annual $3 stamp is required to hunt in the National Forest and can be purchased at most outlets that sell hunting licenses. Maps of the forests are available for purchase through their regional offices listed below. Also ask about hunting regulations, license outlets and seasons and bag limits for the particular county you plan to visit.

Hunting is allowed in designated areas of five Virginia State Parks including Fairy Stone in nearby Patrick County, Cumberland State Forest and Grayson Highlands State Park in Grayson County. A $5 hunting fee applies. Also in Patrick County, Primland Hunting Reserve in Claudville, half an hour south of the Blue Ridge Parkway, is a well known hunting preserve of 10,000 acres specializing in birds, deer and even sporting clays. Call Rick Hill at (703) 251-8012. Guides and dogs are available.

Westvaco Corporation, a huge paper and bleached board milling concern, also offers hunting/fishing permits on vast holdings of company land in Virginia and West Virginia. Westvaco's office is listed below.

The most popular game are squirrel, grouse, bear, deer, bobcat, fox, duck, rabbit, pheasant and quail. For truly adventurous pioneers, muzzle-loading rifles, bow hunting and other primitive weapons are allowed at various times.

The Blue Ridge holds most of the record-setting areas for hunting in Virginia. Latest statistics single out Bedford County for having the highest turkey harvest, with 595 birds harvested. Bedford also came in second highest for deer, with 4,686. In 1990, the five North Central Mountain counties (Alleghany, Augusta, Bath, Highland and Rockbridge) harvested a record 17,466 whitetail deer, up 13 percent from the year before.

Whether you're going on your own or signing up with a hunting lodge (a superb one is Fort Lewis Lodge in Millboro in Bath County, a mountain paradise; call John Cowden there at (703) 925-2314), you're going to need a valid license, which can be obtained by clerks of circuit courts and other authorized agents (see below). Licenses and permits are good from July 1 through June 30. Hunting seasons and bag limits are set by the Virginia Department of Game and Inland Fisheries and vary according to county. Some counties are off-limits to hunters of certain species while others have liberalized hunting rules.

The best suggestion to assure you are hunting within the bounds of the rules and regulations is to send for the latest pamphlet from the Department of Game and Inland Fisheries, "Hunting in Virginia Regulations." The brochure lists everything you need to know about how and where to hunt in the Blue Ridge, or where to find specific game information. To obtain the brochure, write or call:

Department of Games and Inland Fisheries, PO Box 11104, Richmond, VA 23230-1104, (804) 367-1000

For other information about where to hunt in the Blue Ridge, write or call:

Virginia State Parks, 203 Governor Street, Suite 306, Richmond, VA 23219, (804) 786-1712

Jefferson National Forest, 210 Franklin Rd., SW, Roanoke, VA 24001, (703) 982-6270

George Washington National Forest, Harrison Plaza, 101 North Main Street, Harrisonburg, VA 22801, (703) 433-2491

Westvaco Corporation, Appalachian Woodlands, PO Box 577, Rupert, W.Va. 25984

Blue Ridge skiing can challenge any skier, from beginner to expert.

Inside
Skiing

*H*eavy snow only rarely blankets Virginia's Blue Ridge, but this hardly stands in the way of a good time at the region's four ski resorts. Some of the best snow-making systems in the country can be found in Virginia, making it possible to ski even after the first crocuses break ground in early March. "We don't need natural snow—we like to think we can make it better and put it where we want it," quips Mark Glickman, president of the Virginia Ski Association.

All the state's ski resorts offer such a dizzying array of activities that there is no reason not to bring your in-laws along, even if they don't cotton to the sport. Swimming, golfing, hiking, horseback riding, aerobics, snowboarding, sleigh-riding, dancing, dining and movie-going — the list goes on of things to do besides skiing at many of the resorts.

Wintergreen, The Homestead, Bryce Resort and Massanutten are all true year round vacation spots. To learn more about their services and activities other than skiing, please refer to our Resorts chapter.

There are so many variables affecting the cost of a ski vacation that detailed price information is not provided by this book. Whether

you ski during the day or after dark, rent or bring your own skis, stay overnight or spend the night, take a private or group lesson — all are factors affecting the price. A range of cost-saving packages is available at every resort.

Of the four resorts, only the Homestead rents cross-country skis and has trails for the sport. But if you own your own, there's no place better for cross-country skiing than along the Blue Ridge Parkway or Skyline Drive after a heavy snow. In addition, the Mount Rogers National Recreation Area in southwest Virginia is a breathtaking place for cross-country skiing during much of the winter, thanks to its high altitudes. The Recreation Area does not rent skis or have ski trails per se, but there are miles of pathways on hiking trails and primitive roads where the adventurous can glide to their heart's content.

Shenandoah Valley Region

Bryce Resort

P.O. Box 3
Basye, VA 22810

(703) 856-2121
Hours: 9 AM - 10 PM

This intimate, family-oriented ski resort is a little more than an hour from the Washington Beltway or Richmond, and just a few miles off I-81. Tucked within the Allegheny Mountains, Bryce is owned by the 400-odd families who live on Bryce Mountain and utilize the facilities, which include a 45-acre lake, an 18-hole golf course, nine tennis courts, a swimming pool and a small airport for private planes.

Although most skiers at Bryce drive in from the Northern Virginia, Washington, D.C. area, the resort has become a favorite spot for Valley residents, particularly on weekday evenings.

There's nothing quite like twilight skiing under the lights and afterwards warming up with a hot-buttered rum inside the glass-walled Copper Kettle Lounge. Manfred Locher manages the resort, and his brother, Horst, directs the ski school, the ski area, and an extensive racing program. Both have been at Bryce since the resort opened in 1965.

Bryce's most notable feature is its racing program. The resort is known for being one of the best places in the South for skiers of any age to improve their ski techniques in ways that are only possible through participation in a racing program. For 20 years Bryce has sponsored NASTAR races, starting a trend among Southern ski resorts. Every Saturday, Sunday and holiday at 3:30 PM the NASTAR races begin, offering skiers the chance to test their abilities against the pros. The race is handicapped according to age and gender.

The Virginia Governor's Cup and the Jeep National Ski Club Challenge were just two of the many races held at Bryce in 1992.

Bryce has seven slopes covering 20 acres, two double chair lifts and two rope tows. The resort gets about 40 inches of snow annually, but produces enough snow to cover all its slopes.

A broad beginners area is easily seen from the deck and huge picture windows of the two lodges at the ski slopes' base. One lodge houses the Copper Kettle Lounge and a restaurant that serves hearty breakfasts, lunches, and dinner. The second lodge houses a cafeteria, ski rental and repair facility, and a shop that sells everything from goggles and ski boots to flashy, fashionable ski-wear.

The Horst Locher Ski School offers private and group lessons. On weekends and holidays children between the ages of 4 and 7 can attend the SKIwee Children's School, where games are used as a teaching tool to hold children's attention.

Many ski vacation packages are available at Bryce. Cheaper group rates for 20 or more people include lift tickets, equipment and lessons but are not offered on weekends or holidays.

In the summer, grass skiing at Bryce is the popular sport for local adventurers. Invented in Europe as a summer training method for skiers, grass skiing mimics snow skiing but substitutes short tread-like skates for skis. Rentals and lessons in grass skiing are offered in the summer and fall.

A variety of accommodations is available in condos, chalets and townhouses near the slopes for weekend rentals or longer-term stays. For lodging information and reservations, call (800) 296-2121.

The ski resort accepts MasterCard and Visa.

Directions: Bryce is only 11 miles from I-81. Take exit 69 at Mt. Jackson. Follow to Rt. 11. Turn right on Rt. 263 follow straight to Bayse.

MASSANUTTEN RESORT

P.O. Box 1227
Harrisonburg, VA 22801
(703) 289-9441
Hours: 9 AM - 10 PM

This ski resort is an easy two-hour drive from Richmond, Washington, D.C. or Roanoke. In the heart of the Shenandoah Valley, it sits atop Massanutten mountain — once upon a time a haven for moonshiners.

The resort's 14 trails and 68 acres of skiing tower above an attractive, airy lodge at the base. Inside is a cafeteria, convenience store and a glass-walled nightclub with a big dance floor. This place gets real lively on Saturday nights. Another feature of the enormous lodge, which sets it apart from most other ski facilities in the state, is a large windowed room with tables and chairs where guests can bring their own food, "camp out" during the day and watch the skiing without spending a dime.

The resort only gets about 34 inches of snowfall a year, but it has greatly expanded its snow making operations to bring about quicker recovery to the slopes when conditions are less than favorable. Massanutten was the first ski resort to open and the last to close last season. Diamond Jim, a 3,400-foot run with a vertical drop of 1,110 feet, brings a greater challenge for expert skiers at Massanutten. The resort's highest point is 2,880 feet, where the expert slopes Diamond Jim and Paradice start downhill. Both are lit for night skiing and are served by Virginia's first quad chairlift.

Like other resorts, Massanutten is open for skiing night and day. No half-day tickets are sold on weekends or holidays. Children 5 and younger receive free lift tickets. For children 5 and older, the Ski Wee ski school provides lessons, rentals, lift tickets and lunch for $40 on weekdays and $45 on weekends and holidays. On Saturdays and Sundays, one trail is open exclusively for NASTAR racing.

An extensive program for the disabled is a special feature at Massanutten; instruction is offered for people with special needs on Tuesdays, Thursdays, Sundays, and by appointment.

Plenty of special rates are offered, from coupon books that give you eight lift tickets for the price of five, to ski passes if you plan to ski for at least five consecutive days. Special rates are also offered to groups of 20 or more.

Group lessons cost $15 a person for one and one-half hours for all ability levels; private, one-hour lessons are $30 for the first person and $20 for each additional skier. A weekday "Learn to Ski Guarantee" for beginners costs $30 and includes rentals, a lesson and beginner lifts.

Overnight lodging and ski

packages are offered at Massanutten's chalets, villas, and hotel rooms, and at hotels in nearby Harrisonburg. The resort's supply of overnight accommodations is limited. Reservations should be made far in advance. For those who are lucky enough to stay "on mountain," as the locals say, a sports complex called "Le Club" offers indoor swimming, sauna, outdoor hot tubs, an extensive exercise gym, children's movies, ping-pong and more. Call Massanutten for information on all accommodations and ski packages.

MasterCard, Visa and American Express are accepted, as well as most skier discount cards.

Directions: To get to Massanutten, take Rt. 33 east off I-81 in Harrisonburg. Go 10 miles to Rt. 644, where you'll see signs to the resort. ast

East of the Blue Ridge Region

WINTERGREEN

P.O. Box 706
Wintergreen, VA 22958

(800) 325-2200
Hours: 9 AM - 4:30 PM daily, 7-11 PM nightly. After Jan. 1: 12:30 PM - 11 PM Sunday-Friday

Skiing magazine called Wintergreen "the South's single best ski resort" in 1991. Just 43 miles from Charlottesville, Wintergreen's accommodations, restaurants, shops and other amenities bring to mind some of the poshest ski resorts in the country. It features 10 slopes — ranging from a vast beginner's area to the Highlands, a three-slope complex designed for advanced skiers only.

Skiers may be restricted from certain slopes, depending upon ability. To ski the 4,125-foot Wild Turkey run, for instance, skiers must first demonstrate their ability to make controlled, parallel turns down very steep slopes. The way Wintergreen carefully segregates slopes according to ability level keeps the more advanced slopes relatively uncongested. Safety on the slopes is a primary concern at Wintergreen. Its ski patrol was ranked tops in the nation in 1992 by the National Ski Patrol Association.

Free beginner lessons are offered to those who rent skis from Wintergreen. Children 5 and under ski for free when accompanied by an adult. Wednesday is "Family Day," when children 17 and younger ski for free when accompanied by an adult.

You can ski in the morning and golf at the Stoney Creek course in the afternoon for the price of a ski ticket.

A summit ski area, the resort's accommodations and facilities sit at the top of the slopes. Restaurants and condominium complexes offer extraordinary views up the spine of the Blue Ridge and off to each side. To the west is the Shenandoah Valley, and to the east, the piedmont.

The resort's headquarters is the Mountain Inn, where guests can check in, enjoy a drink or sandwich at the Gristmill Restaurant, and browse at an array of shops selling everything from exquisite hand-knit sweaters to Blue Ridge Mountain crafts and quilts.

"Hibernia"
Holiday Home
Blue Ridge Mountain Retreat

"Hibernia" is a secluded, family owned mountain home nestled in the Blue Ridge Mountains — perfect for a relaxing vacation or weekend getaway. Here, you'll will find yourself surrounded by the **George Washington National Forest**, which offers thousands of acres of hiking, hunting and fishing. You are only ten minutes away from **Wintergreen Ski Resort** and two minutes away from **Sherando Lake** recreation area. **The Blue Ridge Parkway** and **Appalachian Trail** are right in your backyard.
Hibernia is your home in the Blue Ridge.

Call Ed or Joan Quillen at
(703) 943-0070
for more information or reservations

 Hibernia • PO Box 136 • Lyndhurst, VA 22952

You can park your car for the duration of your stay. Shuttle buses serve all the lodging complexes day and night—a good thing since parking space is in short supply.

The Wintergarten sports complex features an indoor pool, a small exercise room, a sauna and whirlpool — all in a building with skylights and huge windows through which you can see the Blue Ridge. There are also several hot tubs on the deck outside, where you can soothe aching muscles while stargazing.

Dining at Wintergreen is exceptional. The Garden Terrace offers fine dining in the evenings, and children can eat for free from 5:30 to 6:30 PM. Wintergreen has seven other cafeterias and restaurants. The Confectionery delivers a surprisingly good pizza from 5 to 9 PM, and the Blackrock Market grocery store stocks sandwiches, muffins, and other quick food.

Programs for children at Wintergreen are outstanding — rated tops in the country by *Family Circle* and *Better Homes and Gardens* magazines. The Treehouse, which actually houses a real-live treehouse, is right next to where ski equipment and lift tickets are bought. This is the headquarters for child care for children from ages 2 1/2 to 7 years old. It's also where day-long ski programs for children begin. "Ski and Splash" offers ski lessons, lunch, swimming and snacks to 8 to 12-year-olds on the weekends and holidays.

Wintergreen takes MasterCard, Visa and American Express credit cards.

Directions: From areas north or east of Wintergreen, follow I-64 west to Exit 107 (Crozet, Rt. 250). Take 250 west to Rt. 151 south and turn left. Follow Rt. 151 south to Rt. 664, 14.2 miles. Turn right, and Wintergreen is 4.5 miles ahead on Rt. 664.

You can also get to Wintergreen from the Blue Ridge Parkway. Head south on the Parkway after leaving I-64 at the top of Afton Mountain at the Waynesboro exit. After roughly 12 miles look for signs to Wintergreen at Reed's Gap.

Alleghany Highlands Region

THE HOMESTEAD

Hot Springs, VA 24445
    (800) 336-5771 (hotel reservations)
    (703) 839-7721 (ski information)
Hours: 9 AM - 5 PM weekdays, 8 AM - 5 weekends; 6 PM - 10 PM Tuesday through Saturday.

This elegant hotel became the South's first true ski resort when it opened its slopes in 1959. Daniel Ingalls, the Homestead's board chairman, had dreamed for years of bringing the exciting sport to his already famed resort.

But Mother Nature needed some help before skiing could take off in Virginia's Blue Ridge, with its erratic snowfalls and occasional balmy winter days.

In the 1950s Northern ski resorts were experimenting with snow making to augment the real thing. Ingalls seized upon the chance to turn his resort into a four-season operation, and hired some Yankee engineers to bring their snow-making technology to the

Homestead.

He invested nearly $1 million to develop a 3,000-foot slope on Warm Springs Mountain, along with side trails, a ski-mobile and a glass-walled lodge with a circular fire pit, ski equipment shops and a rental service. Since then, the slopes have grown 200 feet steeper and the runs more challenging and diverse. The four-wheeled ski mobile has been replaced with modern ski lifts. An Olympic-sized ice-skating rink sits at the base of the slopes, with instructors close at hand.

Sepp Kober, a native of Igls, Austria, was hired in 1959 to help design the slopes and develop what would quickly become a premier ski school. Known as the Father of Southern Skiing, Kober imports about a dozen young Austrian ski instructors each season to teach at his ski school. Kober offers group, private and children's lessons. Nine runs are open for both day and night skiing, and half day rates are also available.

All skiers who spend the night at The Homestead may of course take advantage of its many sporting facilities and services, from its his-toric spa—with aroma and massage therapy, to an 18-hole golf course and high tea in the afternoon. Some of the most exquisite dining in the Southeast is offered at the Homestead.

The nearby Cascades offers lodging packages and is an economical alternative to staying at The Homestead. There are other small inns, motels, and bed and breakfasts nearby.

A range of ski packages is available, with extra savings for weekday stays. Discounts for skiing are available for groups of 15 or more. And on Sundays, church groups can even have religious services on the slopes when arranged in advance.

All major credit cards are accepted.

Directions: The Homestead is about 200 miles from Washington, D.C. Take the Bridgewater Exit (Rt. 257) off I-81; go south on Rt. 42 then west on Rt. 39 to Rt. 220 into Hot Springs. Or take I-64 west off I-81 near Lexington, and take 39 northwest to Rt. 220 into Hot Springs for a lengthier, but highly scenic route to the Homestead.

Photo: Prince Michel Vineyards

The French oak barrels at Prince Michel Vineyards.

Inside
Wineries

America's first true connoisseur of fine wine was Thomas Jefferson, a Virginian born in the foothills of the Blue Ridge. And so it is fitting that the region is now home to so many fine wineries. In fact, with few exceptions the state's most highly acclaimed wineries are in the foothills of the Blue Ridge. This is no coincidence. Higher elevations help ensure healthy growing conditions for grapes, minimizing summer heat and lengthening the growing season.

Jefferson himself experimented for 30 years with grape growing and wine making at Monticello, believing that Virginia provided a suitable environment for wine making. But it wasn't until the 1980s that the wine making industry really took off in the state. In 1973, Virginia had only 59 acres of grapes; by 1981, the total had grown to 581 acres. Today, there are 1,400 acres of vines and 43 wineries scattered across the state.

Just as the acreage has expanded, so have sales. In 1992, sales of Virginia wine soared 20 percent; the year before, an increase of 29 percent meant a record 115,000 cases were sold. Generally speaking, Virginia wine sells best in Richmond, the Tidewater and the Charlottesville area.

The Blue Ridge is home to roughly 27 wineries, with most concentrated in that gorgeous stretch of rolling farmland from the Charlottesville area to Culpeper.

Most are small, family-owned and operated establishments. They are located in mountain coves, on mountain tops and along rolling hills in the Shenandoah Valley. If you're lucky you'll be in the area when one of the wineries hosts a festival or open house. Rebec Vineyards in Amherst County throws a big party in the fall with the Virginia Garlic Festival, for instance, and several wineries get together for the annual Montpelier Wine Festival on the grounds of James Madison's estate in May. Chateau Morrisette in Southwest Virginia hosts summer and fall jazz concert series on its grounds, offering tastings, tours and gourmet lunches.

We recommend an excellent guide to Virginia's wineries that includes maps, complete directions and a calendar of events. It's available for free and updated annually. Just write to the Virginia Wine Marketing Program, VDACS, Division of Marketing, P.O. Box 1163, Richmond, VA 23209 or phone (804) 786-0481.

The following is a complete list of wineries of the Blue Ridge region, beginning with those in the Shenandoah Valley. Wineries are organized geographically, from north to south and east to west.

Wineries of the Shenandoah Valley

DEER MEADOW VINEYARD
199 Vintage Lane, Winchester, VA 22602
(703) 877-1919
or (800) 653-6632

Owner Charles Sarle built his own winery and made his first commercial wines in 1987, after retiring from a career as a mechanical engineer. He had been a home winegrower for 10 years. He and his wife, Jennifer, operate the winery on their 120-acre farm southwest of Winchester. They make Chardonnay, Seyval Blanc, Chambourcin and "Golden Blush" — a wine from an American hybrid. They invite you to tour their winery and bring along a picnic lunch and a fishing pole. Deer Meadow Vineyard is open from March through December. Tours are offered from 11 AM to 5 PM Wednesdays through Sundays and most Mondays.

NORTH MOUNTAIN VINEYARD & WINERY
Rt. 1 Box 543, Mauertown, VA 22664
(703) 436-9463

This winery and vineyard is situated on 20 acres of western Shenandoah County that has been farmed since the late 1700s. The vineyard was established in 1982, when proprietor Dick McCormack planted some 8,000 vines of Chardonnay, Vidal and Chambourcin.

At the winery building, which was built in 1990 and modeled after a European-style farmhouse, you can taste some of his wines for free. The winery produces several table wines, including a spiced apple wine. North Mountain is open for tours and tastings on weekends and holidays from 11 to 5.

SHENANDOAH VINEYARDS
Rt. 2 Box 323, Edinburg, VA 22824
(703) 984-8699

This is the Shenandoah Valley's first winery, growing Chardonnay, Riesling, and some French-American hybrids such as Chambourcin and Vidal Blanc. The winery itself is on the lower level of a renovated Civil War-era barn, which also houses a small gift shop and tasting room. Owner Emma Randel grew up on the Shenandoah County farm, which also contains an old log cabin where her mother was born. Free tastings are available and leisurely unguided tours are encouraged. The winery is open from 10 to 6 every day except Thanksgiving, Christmas and New Year's Day.

GUILFORD RIDGE VINEYARD
Rt. 5, Box 148, Luray, VA 22835
(703) 778-3853

Owners John Gerba and Harland Baker use hybrid grapes and Bordelaise methods to produce their Page Valley Red, Delilah (light red), Pinnacles (crisp white) and other wines. Call ahead to arrange a visit and purchases. On August 8 Guilford Ridge plans to throw a

"Fete Champetre" western-style festival featuring grape-stomping, games, live music and wine tastings. Two plays will also be performed on site: "Pecos Bill" and Chekhov's "The Bear."

ROCKBRIDGE VINEYARD
P.O. Box 14, Raphine, VA 24472
(703) 377-6204

Shepherd and Jane Rouse are the new owners of this five-acre winery, Virginia's newest. Shep is the wine maker at Montdomaine, but here he is trying his hand on his own patch of land, located between Staunton and Lexington. The Rouses produce Chardonnay, Riesling, and two blends called "St. Mary's Blanc" and "Tuscorora." Call in advance for tours. The winery's first annual Autumn Fest will be held Oct. 23.

Wineries of East of the Blue Ridge

NAKED MOUNTAIN VINEYARD
P.O. Box 131, Markham, VA 22643
(703) 364-1609

This chalet-like winery is nestled on the east slope of the Blue Ridge, east of Front Royal in Fauquier County. A picnic area on the five-acre vineyard offers sensational views. Owners Bob and Phoebe Harper produce Chardonnay (one of the best in Virginia, according to some), Riesling, Sauvignon Blanc and Cabernet Sauvignon. They use traditional methods of wine making — including fermentation in French oak barrels. The winery has a spacious tasting room on the second floor surrounded by a deck. Tours are offered in January and February on weekends and holidays from 11 to 5. From March through December tours are available Wednesday through Sunday and holidays from 11 to 5. For groups of 10 or more,

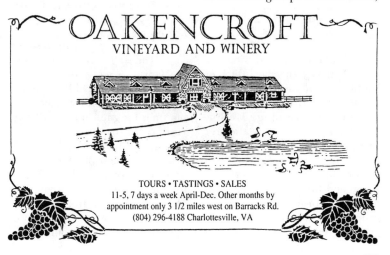

OAKENCROFT
VINEYARD AND WINERY

TOURS • TASTINGS • SALES
11-5, 7 days a week April-Dec. Other months by
appointment only 3 1/2 miles west on Barracks Rd.
(804) 296-4188 Charlottesville, VA

call ahead for an appointment.

LINDEN VINEYARDS
Rt. 1 Box 96, Linden, VA 22642
(703) 364-1997

Linden has 12 acres of vineyards and leases six acres at Flint Hill, producing about 4,000 cases a year of Chardonnay, Seyval, Cabernet, Sauvignon Blanc and Riesling-Vidal. The latter is a blend that does not require aging and produces a young, fresh wine, with 48 percent Vidal and 52 percent Riesling. The small, well-designed winery, which was started in the spring of 1987, includes a comfortable tasting room, which enjoys a view over the vineyards into the mountains. There are also picnic areas outdoors. Tours are offered on weekends in January and February. From March through December the winery is open for tours from 11 to 5 on Wednesdays through Sundays. The winery is also open most Mondays, but it is closed to the public on major holidays.

OASIS VINEYARD
Hwy. 635, Box 116, Hume, VA 22639
(703) 635-7627

This vineyard and winery is located on a spectacular stretch of land facing the Blue Ridge mountains. The winery produces Chardonnay, Riesling, Merlot, Gewurztraminer, Cabernet Sauvignon and two types of Champagne, using traditional "methode champenoise". Owners Dirgham Salahi and his charming, Belgian-born wife, Corinne, purchased the property in the mid 1970s and planted French hybrid grapes as a hobby. They soon learned that the soil was well suited for wine grape growing, and the rest is history. Although much of Oasis' wine is sold at the winery, it is also carried by some independent wineries and served by many restaurants in Washington, D.C. Tours are offered daily from 10 to 4, but sales are available until 5.

FARFELU VINEYARD
Rt. 1, Box 23, Flint Hill, VA 22627
(703) 364-2930

This is a small winery not far from Oasis Vineyard that is being revitalized. It was one of the first Virginia wineries to receive a commercial license as a farm winery and produced its first wines in 1975. Owner Charles Raney, a former United Airlines pilot, produces Cabernet Sauvignon, Chardonnay and a couple of "picnic" wines. Tours and tastings are available from 11 to 5 daily, but Raney asks that visitors telephone in advance.

ROSE RIVER VINEYARDS AND TROUT FARM
Rt. 2, Box 186, Syria, VA 22743
(703) 923-4050

This is a 177-acre farm winery in Madison County that borders Shenandoah National Park on the east. There are picnic sites and hiking trails for guests to enjoy. The vineyards produce Cabernet Sauvignon, Chardonnay, Mountain Peach, Mountain Blush and other wines. Fresh or smoked trout is also for sale. Tours are offered from March to November from 11 to 5 on Saturday and Sunday. The winery is open daily in October from 10 to 5, and at other times or days, by appointment.

PRINCE MICHEL VINEYARDS
HCR 4, Box 77 (Rt. 29), Leon, VA 22725
(800) 869-8242
or (703) 547-3707

Just south of Culpeper, along Rt. 29, sits Prince Michel Vineyards, the largest wine producer in the state. So popular are its wines that Prince Michel runs out every year.

Prince Michel is also the only Virginia winery with an extensive museum about wine and an exclu-

sive restaurant with a French chef. The winery's owner, Jean Leducq, lives in Paris and made his fortune in the industrial laundry industry. His dream was to have his own winery, and he started one here in the Blue Ridge foothills in 1983.

The French influence can be felt in many corners at Prince Michel, which is located north of Charlottesville and about 70 miles southwest of Washington, D.C. All the employees receive French language instruction. The museum's

Photo: Virginia Wine Marketing Program

There are over 40 farm wineries located in the valleys and slopes of Virginia.

diverse collection includes a series of photos showing the process of grape-crushing; some eye-opening photos taken in Burgundy show two naked men in a barrel with the grapes, stirring and ventilating them. (Rest assured, this is not a technique applied here at Prince Michel!) There is also a fascinating collection of every Mouton Rothschild label from 1945 to 1984 – many of whom were designed by famous artists such as Picasso, Salvador Dali and Georges Roualt.

The winery also has a special room for viewing a video documentary about the history of wine, the process of making it, and about Prince Michel Vineyards.

The winery's self-guided tour takes visitors throughout the winery and features displays that describe the wine-making process.

The tour ends at the gift shop, which sells everything from elegant wine canisters to scarves, wine-related jewelry, and of course, the wine itself. Visitors can sample wine or drink it by the glass at an attractive bar inside the gift shop.

Prince Michel produces about 40,000 to 45,000 cases a year, while it has the capacity to produce nearly double that amount.

The winery won four gold medals last year in the Virginia Wineries Association Festival: the 1991 Chardonnay, 1990 Reserve Cabernet Merlot, along with Rapidan River's (its sister winery) 1990 Semi-Dry Riesling and the 1991 Dry Riesling (Rapidan River Vineyards produces Rieslings and Gewurztraminer nearby in Orange County). Prince Michel also won a

gold medal for its 1990 Barrel Select Chardonnay in the Virginia Governor's Cup Competition. This is just a sample of the awards won by this ambitious winery.

The Prince Michel Group owns 105 acres on site, 45 acres at the nearby Rapidan River property, and 13 acres in the Napa Valley.

Prince Michel is open to visitors daily from 10 to 5 daily, except major holidays. The annual Fete des Vendanges harvest festival takes place in October – call for details.

And for more details about the fine Prince Michel Restaurant at the vineyards, please refer to our restaurants chapter or call (800) 800-WINE for reservations.

MISTY MOUNTAIN VINEYARDS, INC.
SR 2 Box 458, Madison, VA 22727
(703) 923-4738

According to *The Wine Spectator*, Misty Mountain's owner Michael Cerceo makes some of the state's best red wines. Cerceo, a physicist, refurbished a 19th-century barn to make roughly 3,500 cases of wine a year from his 12 acres of vines. The winery produces barrel fermented Chardonnay, Merlot, Cabernet Sauvignon and Riesling. Tours are offered Monday through Saturday from 11 to 4, and on Sundays by appointment. Tours are offered by appointment only from November through January.

AUTUMN HILL VINEYARDS/BLUE RIDGE WINERY
Rt. 1, Box 199 C, Stanardsville, VA 22973
(804) 985-6100

This is a small, award-winning winery located on the plateau of a hill northwest of Charlottesville. Owners Avra and Ed Schwab left Long Island for Virginia in the mid 1970s — Ed had been head of an interior design firm and had grown weary of the rat race. They decided to grow grapes and make wine, and planted the first stage of their vineyards in 1979. Their European-style wines include Chardonnay, Riesling, Blush and Cabernet Sauvignon. They are open to visitors three weekends during the year from 11 to 5: April 24-25, Aug. 7-8, Nov. 6-7.

BARBOURSVILLE VINEYARDS

P.O. Box 136 , Barboursville, VA 22923
(703) 832-3824

The giant Italian wine firm Zonin owns this winery outside Charlottesville, which includes a cattle farm and the imposing ruins of a mansion designed by Thomas Jefferson for Virginia governor James Barbour. The site is a registered Virginia Historic Landmark and has endless perfect spots for picnicking. The winery produces 10,000 cases of wine a year from 75 acres of grapes. According to *The Wine Spectator,* the whites are clean and crisp, while the reds are light and fruity in style. Wines include Chardonnay, Riesling, Sauvignon Blanc, Cabernet Sauvignon, Cabernet Blanc and Pinot Noir. The Malvaxia dessert wine is also popular. Barboursville won the Virginia Governor's Cup last year for its Cabernet Sauvignon Reserve 1988. Tours are available on Saturdays from 10 to 4. Tastings and sales are offered seven days a week from 10 to 5.

BURNLEY VINEYARDS

Rt. 1, Box 122, Barboursville, VA 22923
(703) 832-2828

This is one of oldest vineyards in Albemarle County, producing Chardonnay, Cabernet Sauvignon, Riesling, Rivanna White, Rivanna Red, Rivanna Sunset (blush) and Daniel Cellars Somerset (dessert) wines. Lee Reeder and his father planted the

Simeon Vineyards

VINTAGE WINES

From Charlottesville, 1¼ mile past the entrance to Monticello on Route 795 off Route 53.

Open 11 a.m. — 5 p.m. for tours and tastings daily March 1st through November 30th, except major holidays. Others by appointment. Christmas Open House held on the weekend following Thanksgiving from 10 a.m. — 5 p.m.

(804) 977-0800 • 1-800-272-3042 Charlottesville, Virginia 22902

first vines in 1976, the year after nearby Barboursville Vineyards opened. In 1984, father and son started their own winery. Today, they produce about 5,000 cases a year from grapes grown on both their own 20 acres and from Ingleside and North Mountain Vineyard. They expect to be totally self-sufficient in a couple of years, with plans to plant another five acres. Tours are available and tastings offered in a room with a cathedral ceiling and huge windows overlooking the countryside. The winery is open from March through December, Wednesday through Sunday, from 11 to 5. In January and February the vineyards are open on weekends only. Group tours or evening visits can be arranged in advance.

OAKENCROFT VINEYARD AND WINERY
Rt. 5, Charlottesville, VA 22901
(804) 296-4188
Owner Felicia Warburg Rogan heads the Jeffersonian Wine Grape Growers Society—a group that won Charlottesville the title of Wine Capital of Virginia and initiated the annual Monticello Wine and Food Festival about 12 years ago. The winery is situated on a bucolic farm west of the city, with a lake in front and rolling hills behind. A big red barn houses the winery, tasting room and gift shop. The winery produces Chardonnay, Blush, Cabernet Sauvignon, Countryside White-Seyval Blanc, Sweet Virginia and Jefferson Claret. Tours are available from April through December from 11 to 5 daily. From January through March you must schedule

an appointment.

SIMEON VINEYARDS, LTD.
RFD 9, Box 293, Charlottesville, VA 22902
(804) 977-3042
Near Monticello, this vineyard is situated on the same stretch of rolling land once owned by Filippo Mazzei, the 18th century wine enthusiast who helped convince Thomas Jefferson to plant vines. Today the vineyard belongs to Stanley Woodward, Jr., son of the former owner who recently passed away. His father, the Honorable Stanley Woodward, was a retired U.S. Foreign Service Officer, Ambassador to Canada and Chief of Protocol under President Harry Truman.

Woodward Sr. hired an Italian viticulturalist, Gabriele Rausse, from the University of Milan to grow grapes and make wine for him in the early 1980s. Rausse was also Barboursville's first winegrower, and has worked with growers statewide for 15 years. Today he produces Pinot Grigio, Pinot Noir, Cabernet Sauvignon, Chardonnay and Riesling at Simeon. Tours are available from March through November from 11 to 5 daily, except major holidays. From December through February you must make an appointment. The schedule could change in 1994. The winery also has a small gift shop, tasting room and picnic area under a grape arbor.

Don't miss the market owned by the vineyard a few miles away on Rt. 53 (halfway between Monticello and Ash Lawn-Highland). It sells all the wines made at the vineyard along with homemade breads, imported cheeses, crackers and cookies and fresh produce when in season.

MONTDOMAINE CELLARS
Rt. 6, Box 188 A, Charlottesville, VA 22902
(804) 971-8947

Wine maker Shep Rouse's Bordeaux-type reds are among the best in Virginia, according to *The Wine Spectator* magazine. One of Virginia's largest wineries, Montdomaine produces Chardonnay, Cabernet Sauvignon and Merlot. It has become known for its Merlot, a difficult vine to grow in Virginia. Both it and the Cabernet are aged in French oak.

Montdomaine also has a new label, Horton Vineyards, whose first release is the Vidal Blanc – a light, fruity white wine with a slight oaky accent.

Montdomaine's winery building is partially built into a hillside for natural cooling. Visitors are welcome year round for tours and tastings, and the place is only about 10 miles from the Thomas Jefferson Visitors Center off Interstate 64. Tours are from 10 to 5 daily from March through December. In January and February tours are available Thursday through Sunday from 10 to 5.

TOTIER CREEK VINEYARD
Rt. 6, Box 188-B, Charlottesville, VA 22902
(804) 979-7105

This family-owned vineyard, located off Rt. 20 about 10 miles south of Charlottesville, produced its first wine last year from grapes planted in 1982 and '83. The owners consider themselves growers and vintners of fine, premium wines. Jamie Lewis, owner and vintner, uses Virginia white oak barrels to age his wines, which include three types of Chardonnay, Merlot, Cabernet, Riesling, and blush – a blend of Riesling and Merlot. Of the estate's 45 acres, 19 are planted with grapes so far. Totier Creek's wine can only be purchased at the vineyard or at wine festivals.

The vineyard is situated in

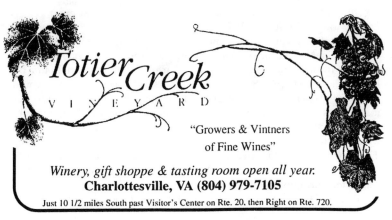

Totier Creek
VINEYARD
"Growers & Vintners
of Fine Wines"
Winery, gift shoppe & tasting room open all year.
Charlottesville, VA (804) 979-7105
Just 10 1/2 miles South past Visitor's Center on Rte. 20, then Right on Rte. 720.

the Green Mountain range – a series of foothills east of the Blue Ridge. Tours and tastings are available from Tuesday through Saturday from 11 to 5 and on Sundays from 12 to 5.

AFTON MOUNTAIN VINEYARDS
Rt. 3, Box 574, Afton, VA 22920
(703) 456-8667

This winery is located just minutes from the end of Skyline Drive and the beginning of the Blue Ridge Parkway near Afton, a village known for bargains in antiques and mountain crafts. The vineyards and winery offer magnificent views of the Rockfish River Valley and the mountains immortalized in Edgar Allen Poe's, *Tale of the Ragged Mountains*. Wines include Chardonnay, Cabernet Sauvignon, White Zinfandel, Gewurztraminer and Riesling. It's open daily except Tuesday from 10 to 6 (5 during winter), and closed on major holidays.

CHERMONT WINERY, INC.
Rt. 1, Box 59, Esmont, VA 22937
(804) 286-2211

This small winery in the rolling hills of Southern Albemarle County was established in 1978 by Josh Sherman, a career pilot and retired Navy captain. Sherman planted 10 acres of Chardonnay, Riesling and Cabernet Sauvignon grapes over a period of three years, making his first wine in his basement in 1981. He has since built a winery with a large tasting room. The winery produces Chardonnay, Riesling (dry and semi-sweet) and Cabernet Sauvignon. Tours are offered Tuesday through Saturday

from 12 to 5 most of the year. Tours from January through March and on Sundays are by appointment only. The winery is closed on major holidays.

MOUNTAIN COVE VINEYARDS
Rt. 1, Box 139, Lovingston, VA 22949
(804) 263-5392

Owner Al C. Weed, II was the first in Central Virginia to plant grape vines, starting his operation in 1974. A native of Brooklyn, N.Y., Weed left his career in investment banking and moved with his family to the Nelson County farm in 1973. He planted French hybrid grapes, believing that they were more hardy and proliferous than vine. Today he produces several blends called "Skyline White," "Skyline Red" and "Skyline Rose." His peach wine is also popular. Weed built most of the little log cabin tasting room and the winery himself. Tours are available from April through December from 1 to 5 daily, and from January through March, Wednesday to Sunday, from 1 to 5.

REBEC VINEYARDS
Rt. 3, Box 185, Amherst, VA 24521
(804) 946-5168

This tiny, family-owned winery is about halfway between Charlottesville and Lynchburg on Rt. 29. Ella Hanson once could laughingly boast that her and her husband's winery is the smallest in Virginia, but with the advent of Rockbridge Vineyard near Lexington, she can no longer make this claim. Both are tiny, with only five acres planted with vines. The Hansons produce white, blush,

Chardonnay, Cabernet Sauvignon and Riesling. Rebec Vineyards hosted Virginia's first Garlic Festival in September, 1991, and it was a rollicking success. The festival takes place this year Oct. 9 and 10, and will feature a garlic queen contest, a garlic-eating contest, live music, good food, and lots of Virginia wine.

The Hanson home was built in 1742, and has been home to the descendants of three governors of Virginia: Thomas Nelson, William Crawford and William Cabel. Tours are available from March 15 through December 15 daily from 10 to 5. From December 15 to March 15 tours are by appointment only.

STONEWALL VINEYARDS
Rt. 2, Box 107 A, Concord, VA 24538
(804) 993-2185

This is a family operated winery within easy driving distance from Appomattox and Lynchburg. Owners Larry and Sterry Davis produce Claret, Cayuga White, Chambourcin, Vidal Blanc and Pyment, a medieval wine made of wine, honey and spices. Tours are offered March through December from Wednesday to Sunday from 11 to 4 or by appointment. The winery also throws an annual celebration in early May featuring wineries, foods, crafts and live music. In mid-October, it holds a "Jazz on the Lawn" festival, with gourmet food, live music and of course, plenty of wine. Call for the exact dates, because they vary from year to year.

CHATEAU MORRISETTE WINERY, INC.
P.O. Box 766, Meadows of Dan, VA 24120
(703) 593-2865

This winery is set on a hilltop on a 40-acre farm in Floyd and Patrick counties that borders the Blue Ridge Parkway. A French restaurant on the premises is reportedly fabulous. The Morrisettes' first wines were produced in 1983. They are made in a traditional European style, using stainless steel tanks for fermentation and French and American oak for aging. The winery, built of native stone and wood, resembles a miniature German castle. The wine cellar is underground, and there is a tasting room, deli and a large deck for picnicking.

Chateau Morrisette also hosts the monthly "Black Dog" jazz concert series every summer, beginning in June and ending in October. Live jazz, tastings, tours and gourmet lunches make this an exciting event.

Tours, tastings and sales are available daily from 12 to 5, except on major holidays.

The famous Natural Bridge of Virginia is located 15 miles south of Lexington, on U.S. Route 11. Towering 215 feet high, 90 feet in length, this great arch was carved by a mountain stream over thousands of years.

Inside
Other Attractions

With so many and varied attractions to see in the Blue Ridge area as a whole, there are a few that deserve a chapter of their own: Covered Bridges, Zoos, Caverns and Spectator Sports.

Covered Bridges

Virginia's first covered bridges were built around 1820 and during the following century, hundreds were erected across both wide and narrow rivers and streams. Since, they have nearly disappeared from the Virginia scene. Happily, a few picturesque covered bridges, favorite courting spots for couples of yesteryear, have been carefully preserved on Virginia's side roads to recall the past. Of the seven covered wooden bridges made accessible to the public, the Blue Ridge claims the bridge deemed the oldest and most unusual, Humpback Bridge in Covington, Alleghany County. Don't forget your camera! Here's a rundown of these beauties, from north to south:

Meems Bottom Bridge
North of Harrisonburg, less than half a mile from busy I-81, visitors can step back in time at Meems Bottom Bridge, a 204-foot,

single span Burr arch truss over the North Fork of the Shenandoah River, two miles south of Mount Jackson, Route 11. It takes its name from the Meems family that owned the Strathmore estate west of the Shenandoah River. Rebuilt in 1979, almost three years after arsonists burned the original 1893 structure, the one-lane bridge still caters to automobiles on quiet Sunday drives. It previously was burned in 1862 when Stonewall Jackson went up the valley ahead of Union General John C. Fremont, prior to the battles of Harrisonburg, Cross Keys and Port Republic. Rebuilt, the bridge was again destroyed in a flood in 1870. Six miles south is New Market, a major tourist destination for Civil War buffs.

HUMPBACK BRIDGE
Known as the "Granddaddy of them all," as Virginia's oldest standing covered bridge, Humpback is the nation's only surviving curved-span covered bridge. Built in 1835 as part of the Kanawha Turnpike, it is a graceful, 100-foot arched span with an eight-foot rise over Dunlap Creek in Alleghany County, within viewing distance of I-64, off the Callaghan Exit between Covington, VA, and White Sulphur

Springs, W. Va. Its hump-like design is unique in the western hemisphere. Only one other bridge, located in France, is similarly constructed. During autumn, the Humpback Wayside, between Virginia's breathtaking Allegheny and Blue Ridge Mountains, is a popular picnic area. Visitors can stroll through the bridge and wade in the shallow creek below to admire the bridge's hand-hewn oak timbers. Milton Hall, an historic bed and breakfast with gorgeous gardens, is close by.

SINKING CREEK BRIDGES

Near the breathtaking Appalachian Trail in the New River Valley's Giles County stand two modified Howe trusses built across Sinking Creek, north of Newport. Built in 1912 and 1916, the 55-foot Link's Farm Bridge and 70-foot Sinking Creek Covered Bridge spans were left in place when a modern bridge was built in 1963. The Newport countryside is worth exploring for its quaint, country setting, and is considered choice farm real estate by professors at nearby Virginia Tech. Northwest is Mountain Lake Resort, made famous by the movie, "Dirty Dancing."

Zoos

There are enough natural sites in this area to keep anyone happy, and when you add in the wonderful zoos, even the most avid naturalist has something to howl about.

NATURAL BRIDGE ZOO
Natural Bridge, VA. 24578
(703) 291-2420

Located next to Natural Bridge Village and Resort, this 25-acre zoo is also an endangered species breeding center, with the largest petting area in Virginia and elephant rides for the kids. For 19 years, the zoo has been raising generations of endangered species including four generations of the Scarlet Macaw, Siberian tigers and ring-tailed lemurs. For $2, on weekends, children can ride an eight-year-old African elephant. They'll get a real thrill mingling with llamas, ostriches and peacocks. The family also will enjoy large covered picnic pavilions and a well-stocked gift shop. Open from 9 AM to 6 PM, seven days a week, admission is $5 for adults and $3 for children.

MILL MOUNTAIN ZOO
P.O. Box 1384, Roanoke, VA 24034
(703) 343-3241

Located on top of Roanoke's Mill Mountain, off the Blue Ridge Parkway and right below the famous star, is a small but energetic zoo operated by the Blue Ridge Zoological Society of Virginia. Its main star is Ruby the Tiger, who received national attention while zookeepers struggled to build the non-pedigreed tiger a habitat bigger than a cage, where she languished after she was confiscated from her owners. Everyone rallied to the cause, and the 10-acre zoo recently celebrated its grand opening of a new tiger habitat, thanks to pennies from school children and several large donations. Thanks to more dona-

ROANOKE VALLEY

Attractions

Virginia Museum of Transportation Downtown Roanoke (703) 342-5670

Mill Mountain Zoo Three miles off the Blue Ridge Parkway (703) 343-3241

Dixie Caverns & Pottery Salem, VA (703) 380-2085

Historic Farmers Market Downtown Roanoke (703) 342-6025

Festivals
Recreation

Culture
Excitement

"The Capital of the Blue Ridge"

114 Market Street, Roanoke, VA 24011-1402   800-635-5535

tions, Ruby also will have her own watering hole for use in the summertime. In addition to Ruby, there are 43 species of exotic and native animals. The main attraction is the prairie dogs, who pop up and down out of their burrows, much to the delight of schoolchildren. Other residents are Japanese monkeys, tree kangaroos and a Red Panda. The zoo is open to the public April through September, seven days a week from 10 AM to 6 PM. Admission is $3.50 for adults and $2 for children over age two. A Zoo Choo-Choo train operates on busy weekends, and a concession stand also is open weekends. Picnic facilities and a breathtaking overlook view of Roanoke are located nearby. Access also can be taken from I-581. Follow the signs off the Elm Ave. exit and go up the mountain by going under the Walnut Street bridge.

FANTASYLAND

Hobby Horse Farm, Inc.
Rt. 6, Box 358, Bedford, VA 24523

This isn't really a zoo, but it's an attraction so unusual that we've included it in this section for animal lovers. Located three miles from the city of Bedford, off Rt. 746, Fantasyland is open April through October. Picture real, live horses so small that even a tot can reach down and pet them. No kidding! That's the scenario at Fantasyland over at Hobby Horse Farm, just open this spring. Featuring the world's smallest horses, Hobby Horse Farm is the culmination of more than 20 years of selective downsize breeding by Bob and Jean Pauley. After having tons of visitors stop by in disbelief

after hearing about the animals or spotting them from the road, the Pauleys finally decided to start charging admission for the curious. Various breeds include miniature Clydesdale, Appaloosa, Arabian, Pinto, Draft and Buckskin. There are also miniature donkeys, goats, sheep, mules, pigs and Dexter bulls. Lots of other animals are on hand, including llamas, Tennessee fainting goats, prairie dogs, rabbits, peafowl, exotic chickens and a goldfish pond. Bus tours and school groups are welcome. There's a train ride, gift shop, picnic area, clean restrooms and refreshments for guests. Admission is $4.50 for adults and $3.50 for children. Seeing is believing. This place delights both old and young alike.

Caverns

America's history does not end at ground level. Just ask any cave-lover. There is another world beyond, with a history 30 million years older than America. Exploring caves, or spelunking, can be an unearthly quiet, surreal experience surrounded by ever-growing stalactite icicles and stalagmite gardens in year round temperatures that average 54 degrees. A sweater is a good idea. Unlike our above-ground gardens, these require no sun, but mineral water is a must, enabling painstaking growth of only one cubic inch every 125 years. Under Virginia's soil are so many miles of caves that spelunkers themselves say the end has never been found to some of them. The Blue Ridge of

Shenandoah Caverns, near New Market, offers a world of subterranean beauty.

the Appalachians boasts the highest number of caves in North America. Six are easily accessible from major interchanges of Skyline Drive, I-81 or I-66.

As with most of the Blue Ridge, Thomas Jefferson also left his mark and was an early spelunker. He wrote about Madison's Cave (closed to the public) near Grottoes in his "Notes on the State of Virginia."

How the caves were discovered is often one of their most interesting aspects. They often involve stories of Indians, soldiers and adventurous children with disappearing pets who become unsuspecting eyewitnesses to another nether world directly under ours. Unfortunately, some caves show signs of vandalism from eager souvenir hunters. The Virginia Cave Act ensures that the Blue Ridge Caverns endure for many more generations of the adventuresome. On a hot day, you can't beat the caverns for comfort and an awe of the world under our feet.

SKYLINE CAVERNS
P.O. Box 193, Front Royal, VA 22630
(703) 635-4545

Sixty million year old Skyline Caverns, at the foothills of the Blue Ridge that border Skyline Drive, has a unique solarium entrance, where green shrubs border the cave, creating a most attractive welcome. Three running streams are in the core of the cave, unbelievably stocked with trout as an experiment in adaptation. Fat and thriving, they require chopped pork each week to make up for Vitamin D. Another unusual aspect is anthodites, called "orchids of the mineral kingdom," the only such rock formations known to exist in the world and growing at a rate of one inch every 7,000 years. Skyline is noted for its simulated scenes of reality, such as The Capitol Dome, Rainbow Trail and The Painted Desert. Kids enjoy the outdoor Skyline Arrow, a miniature train that carries them on a half-mile journey through a real tunnel. Skyline is also near the north entrance of Shenandoah National Park, where more fun awaits adventuresome families. Take Exit 6 off I-66. Open year round. Hours depend on season. Adults $9. Children 6-12 $4.

SHENANDOAH CAVERNS
Shenandoah Caverns, VA 22847
(703) 477-3115

Shenandoah Caverns, taking the name from the Indian "Daughter of the Stars," were discovered in 1884 during the building of the Southern Railway. The caverns are an estimated 11 million years old and are the closest major caverns located off I-81 and the only ones in Virginia with an elevator, a real boost to the handicapped, elderly and just-plain-tired! One formation, "Bacon Hall," hanging slabs of striped iron oxide and calcite, was featured in National Geographic. Other incredible sights are Grotto of the Gods, Vista of Paradise and Rainbow Lake. Nearby attractions are plentiful, including Skyline Drive, New Market battlefield and its two Civil War museums, Tuttle & Spice 1880 General Store and the Meems Bottom covered bridge. Take Exit

269 off I-81. Open year round. Hours depend on the season. Adults $8. Children 8-14 $4. Wheelchair accessible.

LURAY CAVERNS

P.O. Box 748-STG, Luray, VA 22835
(703) 743-6551

Luray Caverns, the largest known cave on the East Coast, is a colorful cathedral of natural beauty with the world's only Stalacpipe Organ. Stalactites are tuned to concert pitch and accuracy and are struck by electronically controlled rubber-tipped plungers to produce music of symphonic quality. You must see this amazing instrument to appreciate it. A one hour conducted tour transports you through nature's underground wonderland in vast chambers of 140 feet in height. Memorable formations include the "Fried Eggs," the enormous Double Column and Pluto's Ghost. Placid, crystal-clear pools, such as Dream Lake, remarkably reflect the thousands of stalactites from above. One of the largest chambers, the Cathedral, has been the site for nearly 250 weddings. A wishing well has produced nearly half a million dollars from tourists, with proceeds donated to charity. There is a gift shop and restaurant as well. Outside, don't miss the Luray Singing Tower, a carillon of 47 bells, the largest weighing 7,640 pounds, the smallest 12. Recitals are given seasonally by Carillonneur David Breneman. A self-guided tour of the Historic Car & Carriage Caravan is included in your caverns admission. 10 minutes from here is the Central Entrance to Skyline Drive in the Shenandoah National Park. Luray Caverns is on U.S. 211, 15 minutes from I-81, exit 264. Open year round. hours seasonal. Admission: $10.75 adults, $5.00 ages 7-13. 12 & under free.

ENDLESS CAVERNS

P.O. Box 859, New Market, VA 22844
(703) 740-3993

On the first of October, 1879,

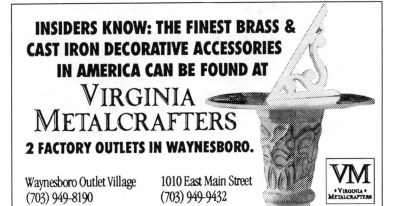

INSIDERS KNOW: THE FINEST BRASS & CAST IRON DECORATIVE ACCESSORIES IN AMERICA CAN BE FOUND AT

VIRGINIA METALCRAFTERS

2 FACTORY OUTLETS IN WAYNESBORO.

Waynesboro Outlet Village
(703) 949-8190

1010 East Main Street
(703) 949-9432

VM
• VIRGINIA •
METALCRAFTERS

two boys with their dog chased a rabbit up the slope of Reuben Zirkle's farm. The rabbit disappeared under a boulder. The boys moved the boulder, and before their astonished eyes appeared a great shaft of Endless Caverns. No end has ever been found to the labyrinth of winding channels and vast rooms, which now are lighted artfully and dramatically for visitors. Snowdrift and Fairyland are two of the most popular formations. Of all the caverns, Endless most seems as if you are venturing into uncharted, rugged territory, and its outdoor scenery is the most beautiful. Just as interesting are the historic native limestone buildings constructed during the 1920s. Relaxation is first class on the wide porches of the Main Lodge which invite you to rest, rock and relax awhile enjoying Endless Caverns' breathtaking view of the Shenandoah Valley. The big, stone lodge is cooled in the summer and warmed in winter by pure, fresh air direct from Endless Caverns. Nearby Endless Caverns Campgrounds is a beautiful facility at the foot of Virginia's Massanutten Mountains, adjoining George Washington National Forest. Over 100 campsites are available. Driving on I-81, you can't miss the sign for Endless Caverns, the largest outdoor sign in the Eastern U.S., 500 feet long and 35 feet high. Take Exit 257. It's open year round except Christmas. Hours from March 15 - June 14, open 9 AM to 5 PM, June 15 - Labor Day, 9 AM to 7 PM, after Labor Day to Nov. 14, 9 AM to 5 PM, Nov. 15 - March 14, 9 AM to 4 PM. Admission is $8 for adults and $4.50 for children ages 3-12.

GRAND CAVERNS

Grottoes, VA 24441   *(703) 249-5705*

Grand Caverns, within Grand Caverns Regional Park, is one of the oldest and most spectacular caverns. The public has been coming here since 1806, including Thomas Jefferson, who rode horseback from Monticello to visit. During the Civil War, Gen. Stonewall Jackson quartered his troops within its massive stone walls after the Battle of Port Republic. Union soldiers also visited the cave. Their signatures still can be seen in pencil on the walls. In better times, The Grand Ballroom, which encompasses 5,000 square feet, was the scene of many early 19th century dances for the socially prominent. Cathedral Hall, 280 feet long and 70 feet high, offers visitors a look at one of the largest rooms of any cavern in the East. Massive columns and the rare "shield" formations, whose origins are a mystery to geologists, are highlights.

Grand is a hauntingly beautiful cave. Its origins are also haunting. Its unique, vertical bedding is believed to be the result of Africa's collision with Virginia, millennia ago. Rocks from Virginia have been found in West Africa. Take Exit 235 from I-81. Open year round, from 9 AM to 5 PM, admission is $9 for adults, $6 for children 3-12. Discounts to AAA Auto Club, Senior Citizens and Active Military.

NATURAL BRIDGE CAVERNS

U.S. 11 Highway   *(703) 291-2121*

Here's a cavern with its own

ghost! For more than 100 years, people have been hearing the plaintive voice of a woman, deep within the underground limestone formations. The first time it happened, in 1889, men working in the caverns abandoned their ladders, fled and refused to go back. Their tools and lanterns were found in 1978. The last time the ghost was heard was as recently as 1988, when six people on the last tour of the day heard a distinct moaning sound, which continued throughout the guide's narrative. In all cases, it is documented that those present had an eerie feeling and fled the premises without hesitation. Located at the immensely entertaining Natural Bridge Village complex, take the guided, 45-minute tour 347 feet underground after you've seen awesome Natural Bridge and the Wax Museum above. Tours of the Caverns require some strenuous physical activity. The pathways are winding and steep in areas, so walking shoes are suggested. The Caverns Gift shop features some of the most unusual gifts in the Blue Ridge, including rock and mineral candy, sure to delight the young ones. Colonial-style Natural Bridge Hotel features sumptuous buffets. The Cavern is open March through November, 10 AM to 5 PM daily. Admission is $7 for adults; $3.50 for children (6-15); special combination tickets to see all three attractions at $13 Adult; &7.50 Child (6-15). Take Exit 175 or 180 off I-81.

DIXIE CAVERNS
5753 West Main St., Salem, VA 24153
(703) 380-2085

Just south of Roanoke, Dixie Caverns tour guides initially take you up, instead of down, into the mountain, where you will see a shaft of light from the outside. Your guide will point out where a pet dog fell down through the hole in the mountain, much to the astonishment of its owners, who discovered the cavern when they rescued their pet. They also found evidence that the Indians of Southwestern Virginia used the cave heavily for shelter and food storage. Some of the most popular formations are the Turkey Wing, Magic Mirror and Wedding Bell, where dozens of couples have been united, dodging dripping water. On the outside, there's lots to do and see as well. The Dixie Caverns Pottery offers a huge display with thousands of gifts. There's a special Basket Shop and another shop named Christmas in Dixieland. Students love the Rock and Mineral Shop, with its famous polished stone wheel. Campers enjoy a complete facility with a new bath house. It is open all year for RV's and campers. For fishermen, there's the adjacent Roanoke River. Open year round, from 9 AM to 5:30 PM daily, adult admission is $5.50 while children 5-12 cost $3.50. Take Salem Exit 132 off I-81.

Spectator Sports

Believe it or not, some people do tire of watching spectacular sunsets on Virginia's mountains and yearn for something more to do. For them, the Blue Ridge offers fine college sports, ice hockey, baseball, Virginia's $12 million Horse Center and more. Here is a sampling:

College Sports

JAMES MADISON UNIVERSITY
BASKETBALL
Harrisonburg   *(703) 568-DUKE*

Men's basketball is James Madison University's most prominent sport. The Dukes had their fifth season under Charles G. "Lefty" Driesell in the 1992-'93 season with 21 wins and 9 losses.

Driesell, formerly head coach at the University of Maryland and Davidson College, won his 600th game in the 1991-'92 season. The Dukes have won their regular season championship four years in a row. Games are played at the Convocation Center on the east side of Interstate 81.

UNIVERSITY OF VIRGINIA FOOTBALL,
BASKETBALL AND OTHER SPORTS
Charlottesville   *(800) 542-UVA1*
                        or (804) 924-UVA1

Football games at Scott Stadium have gotten so popular that it's hard to get tickets at the last minute. The Cavaliers boasted six consecutive winning seasons as of 1993, and competed in four Bowl games during that time. For those reasons, orange-dressed UVA alumni are flocking to the games in record numbers, hollering "Wahoo-Wah!" at all the right moments.

Increasingly, season tickets are sold out even well in advance, so

if you're interested, call them after you read this. For ticket information call: (800) 542-UVA1 (in-state) or (804) 924-UVA1. The same number should be called for information and tickets to basketball, soccer and other games at UVA.

In the 1992-93 season, the men's basketball Cavaliers advanced to the "Sweet 16" of the NCAA tournament. The women's team excelled even further, winning the Atlantic Coast Conference Championship. Under head coach Debbie Ryan the women advanced to the final four in NCAA tournaments in the 1990, '91 and '92 seasons, and advanced to the final eight this past season. Basketball games are played inside the 8,864-seat University Hall.

If you're a soccer fan, you can watch the top team in the nation if you catch a home game at UVA. The men's soccer team won the national championships in 1991 and 1992 and the women's team advanced to the final four in 1991. The new Klockner Stadium for soccer opened in the fall of 1992. Klockner, a leading U.S. plastics firm, donated funds for the stadium.

Lacrosse is another winning sport at UVA; women's lacrosse is the top team in the nation, having won the NCAA tournament in 1991 and 1993.

And for the slower sport of golf, UVA hosts the Cavalier Classic Golf Tournament every spring. Some of the top teams and players in the country come to Charlottesville to play in the tournament at the Birdwood Golf Course.

VIRGINIA TECH HOKIE BASKETBALL
Virginia Tech, Blacksburg, VA
(703) 231-6726

A Division I NCAA team and member of the Metro Conference, Tech had an illustrious basketball legacy in its 32nd season of play in Cassell Coliseum, having won 318 of 390 games played there. Needless to say, the Hokies have never had a losing season at home in 31 years, and Cassell is often packed to capacity. Tech's top two all-time scorers are All-American guard Dell Curry, who helped Tech to four post-season tournaments and finished his career with 2,389 points. Following his senior season in 1986, he was a first-round draft pick by NBA's Utah Jazz. The second Tech player to have his jersey retired was Olympian Bimbo Coles. He finished his collegiate career in 1990 as the leading all-time scorer in school and Metro Conference history and also having set an all-time scoring mark for Division I players in Virginia. To get to Cassell Stadium, take the U.S. 460 bypass off I-81 and follow the signs.

VIRGINIA TECH HOKIE FOOTBALL
Virginia Tech, Blacksburg, VA 24060
(703) 231-6726

Virginia Tech Football is Big in western Virginia, so big that if you want to catch a game, go as early as you can to miss the less-than-adequate roads leading off I-81 onto U.S. 460 to Lane Stadium (capacity 51,000). You won't be alone. There will be thousands of tailgating fans to join you in the parking lot. It's simply the event for this part of the Blue Ridge, with wild, roaring crowds and lots of pageantry and fun! For those interested in the game itself, be aware that Tech is in the Big East Conference. Its mascot is a turkey sporting maroon and orange. A 1990 game with the University of Virginia, the Gobblers' arch rival, set a stadium record of 54,157, the largest crowd ever to see a football game in the state. Famous Tech football player graduates include Bruce "The Sack Man" Smith, who won the Outland Trophy in 1984, George Preas with the Baltimore Colts, Ricky Scales with the Houston Oilers, Don Strock of the Miami Dolphins and Bill Ellenbogen of the New York Giants. To get to Lane Stadium, get off I-81 to the Blacksburg Exit and take U.S. 460. Just follow the crowd!

Polo

VIRGINIA POLO CENTER
Old Lynchburg Road, Charlottesville
(804) 979-0293
or (804) 977-POLO

It's not surprising that polo's a popular sport among the genteel society of Charlottesville. But students, as well, flock to the Virginia Polo Center — especially when their own Virginia Polo Team holds games on Friday nights during the school year.

From late May through Sept. 7, the Charlottesville Polo Club also holds matches at 6:30 and 8 PM. Tickets are $3 per person.

Charlottesville resident and fiction writer Rita Mae Brown — author of *Rubyfruit Jungle* and other colorful works — played a key role in launching the Piedmont Women's

Polo Team several years ago. The women's team holds games in July and August every Saturday at 6:30 PM.

ROANOKE SYMPHONY POLO CUP

Green Hill Park   *(703) 343-9127*

Roanokers "Ponder the Ponies and Promote the Notes" at this festive way to raise money for the Roanoke Symphony. Held on October 2 at Green Hill Park in Roanoke County, the polo tournament not only provides a unique cultural experience, but also allows patrons of the arts to enjoy good food and fun together. General admission is low (about $10) so that the revelry is accessible to everyone. However, you may rent tables for "tailgate" parties and tents for private groups. The cost ranges from approximately $170 to $1450, depending on the size of tent or table you choose. Concessions are available during the activities. Tent and tailgate patrons have their names listed in the program as a gesture of appreciation.

Steeple Chase Races

FOXFIELD RACE COURSE

Garth Road, Charlottesville   *(804) 293-9501*

The Foxfield Race Course hosts exciting horse races twice a year, attracting a crowd of around 20,000 people from as far away as New Jersey. The races are held the last Saturday in April and the last Sunday in September. Usually about 75 horses race in the event, which involves leaping over brush hurdles and timber fences. Races start at 1 PM, with horses taking off every half-hour.

Although hot-dogs and soft drinks are sold at the course, sophisticated tail-gate parties have become the norm. Increasingly, the scene looks like something straight out of Town and Country magazine, with women adorned in hats and smart outfits. It's not unusual here to see folks sipping on champagne and feasting on pate by the light of a candelabra on the back of a BMW.

General admission costs $12 in advance and $15 at the gate, and an extra $5 for parking. Depending upon parking location, you can also reserve a spot for anywhere from $55 to $200. This prices includes four admission tickets.

The Foxfield Race Course is five miles west of the Barracks Road Shopping Center.

Foot Hunting

THE BOAR'S HEAD INN & SPORTS CLUB

Charlottesville   *(800) 476-1988 or (804) 296-2181*

The Boar's Head Inn & Sports Club west of Charlottesville hosts this old English sport the Saturday after Thanksgiving every year. The Farmington Beagles and the Hunt Staff and Field Master at the Boar's Head Inn lead the foot hunt over 53 acres (many stray dogs and cats are scared out of hiding). After the hunt, the Inn serves a traditional Hunt Tea. On Thanksgiving morning, many of the hunters head to the age-old "Blessing of the Hounds" services at Grace Episcopal Church in Cismont. Afterwards, guests are welcome to watch the traditional fox hunt that takes place at a neighboring farm.

Horse Shows

VIRGINIA HORSE CENTER

P.O. Box 1051, Lexington, VA 24450

(703) 463-2194

A showcase for the Virginia horse industry and one of the top equine facilities in the U.S., the $12 million World Class Virginia Horse Center hosted the 1988 Olympic Dressage Trials and is home to several premier national horse shows as well as the annual Virginia Horse Festival. There are exciting horse events every month. The Indoor Arena Complex has 4,000 spectator seats with a 150-ft. x 300-ft. show arena. There are 610 permanent stalls, 110 portable interior stalls, two winterized barns, an enclosed schooling area, on-grounds restaurant and 48 camper hook-ups. The Outdoor Wiley Arena is lighted with four all-weather dressage arenas, speed events ring and pavilion. Outside courses are pre-novice through preliminary cross-country, with a Hunter Trial Course, five miles of trails through the woods. The schedule of events here includes living history Civil War encampments, Jack Russell Terrier Races, Therapeutic Riding demonstrations and Fox Hound Demonstrations, along with the usual horsing events. Off I-81, take Lexington Exit 191, proceed on I-64 West to

Photo: Richmond Newspapers

As one of the premier college football programs in the state, the Virginia Tech Hokies compete against the nation's top collegiate powers.

Exit 55, then follow signs for only two miles to the Horse Center. Tours are offered but be sure to call beforehand.

Hockey

THE ROANOKE EXPRESS HOCKEY ROANOKE, INC.
4502 Starkey Rd., SW
Suite 110, Professional Park
Roanoke, VA 24018   *(703) 989-GOAL*

Roanoke has a new professional hockey franchise for the 1993-94 season, thanks to a group of seven civic-minded business owners. The team replaces last year's Roanoke Rampage. The new season starts October 20th through March 23 at the Roanoke Civic Center on Tuesdays, Fridays and Saturdays, with a few exceptions. The team will perform in the East Coast Hockey League, 19 teams from nine different states.

Season tickets are available. Individual tickets are $4 to $8 a person. There won't be a lack of action, both on the ice and in the stands. Bring the entire family!

Baseball

SALEM BUCCANEERS
620 Florida St., Box 842, Salem, VA 24153
(703) 389-3333

A Class A team for the Pittsburgh Pirates, the Buccaneers live happily in the sports-crazed Roanoke Valley City of Salem. They were Carolina League champs in 1987. Beginning in April, 140 games are on the agenda until Sept. 4, half at home at Salem Municipal Field.

The Buccaneers are excellent Valley citizens and plan numerous promotions benefiting area charities. You can hear the Buccaneer games on WROV-AM 1240 Radio. General admission is $3 with seniors and children getting $1 off. Take Salem Exit 141.

LYNCHBURG RED SOX
City Stadium, Lynchburg, VA 24500
(804) 528-1144

Lynchburg has had a baseball team in its midst for over 100 years. Since 1966, this group has been in the class A level of the Carolina League, along with other Virginia cities like Salem and Woodbridge. The Lynchburg team has been affiliated with many different clubs along the way including the Chicago White Sox and the New York Mets. But, since 1988, these "boys of summer" have been a part of the Boston Red Sox. The team, also know as the "L-Sox," plays in City Stadium, which has a capacity of 4,200. They play 140 games per season, half of which are played at home. All games are broadcast on radio station WLLL-AM. General Admission is $3.75.

Race Car Driving

NEW RIVER VALLEY SPEEDWAY
Route 2, Box 278, Radford, VA 24141
(703) 639-1700

Once known as Pulaski County Speedway, this track now is known as the New River Valley Speedway. A NASCAR sanctioned event, drivers race on a four-tenths of a mile, paved oval track. Every Saturday night from April to September, the Speedway packs in visitors from all over the New River Valley. The featured race division is late model stock, but other divisions include limited sportsman, modified mini, mini stock and pure stock. A family atmosphere is prevalent here, with over 2,000 children showing up each Saturday. And, no matter your preconceptions about racing, this is a sport for everyone to enjoy. Doctors, lawyers, farmers and schoolteachers all make the Speedway a part of their weekends! Admission is $8 for adults and $1 for children 12 and under.

Photo: Virginia Dept. of Tourism

The Bonnie Blue National, "A" rated for all divisions, is one of the most prestigious events held at the Virginia Horse Center just north of Lexington.

Inside
Annual Events

January

VIRGINIA SPECIAL OLYMPICS
Wintergreen   *(804) 325-2200*

**BIRTHDAY CONVOCATION FOR
ROBERT E. LEE**
Lexington   *(703) 463-3777*

**BIRTHDAY CELEBRATION FOR
STONEWALL JACKSON**
Lexington   *(703) 463-3777*

February

**GEORGE WASHINGTON'S BIRTHDAY
CELEBRATION**
                        (703) 662-6550
This is an open house at George Washington's Office Museum in Winchester. Held every February on the weekend closest to Washington's birthday.

VALENTINE CRAFT SHOW
Lynchburg   *(804) 847-1499*

VALENTINE'S DAY WEEKEND
Wintergreen   *(804) 325-2200*

March

HIGHLAND MAPLE FESTIVAL
Monterey   *(703) 468-2550*
This festival is celebrated across Highland County—that rugged, gorgeous region bordering West Virginia west of Staunton. During the festival you can visit local sugar camps and watch the actual process of syrup-making. There's also an arts and crafts show, a maple queen contest and ball, dances including the maple sugar hoedown, and plenty of opportunities to scarf down pancakes with maple syrup, maple donuts and fresh fried trout.

ST. PATRICK'S DAY PARADE
Staunton   *(703) 885-8504*

ST. PATRICK'S DAY PARADE
Roanoke   *(703) 981-2889*

**CIVIL WAR REENACTORS'
BOOT CAMP**
Newbern   *(703) 674-5888*

**WHITETOP MOUNTAIN
MAPLE FESTIVAL**
Mt. Rogers National Park   *(703) 388-3294*
Usually held on two weekends in late March, here you'll find live country and western music, tours of maple tree tapping areas, arts and crafts, and pancake dinners.

April

HISTORIC GARDEN WEEK
Locations throughout Virginia (804) 644-7776

This late April event throws open the doors of more than 200 private homes and gardens throughout the Commonwealth for tours. Many Blue Ridge area cities participate in this state-wide event, which is always held during the last full week of April. Charlottesville, Staunton, Harri-sonburg, Roanoke and the Front Royal area always participate.

OLD TOWN EASTER EGG HUNT
Winchester   (703) 665-0079

Held on the Saturday closest to Easter, this egg hunt delights youngsters from age 2 to 7 on the lawn next to the Godfrey Miller Center in downtown Winchester.

CHAMPAGNE AND CANDLELIGHT TOUR
Charlottesville   (804) 293-9539

This enchanting evening tour of the Ash Lawn-Highland home of President James Monroe is always held during Historic Garden Week. Period music is performed during tours of the Federal-style home and beautiful gardens, which are illuminated with 2,000 candles.

THOMAS JEFFERSON BIRTHDAY COMMEMORATION
Charlottesville   (804) 295-8181

Admission to Monticello's grounds and gardens is always free on April 13, the birthday of Virginia's best known renaissance man — U.S. President, Secretary of State, scholar, architect, collector,

and horticulturist. A major celebration is being planned for April, 1993, the 250th anniversary of Jefferson's birth. Opening April 13 is a major exhibition of paintings, drawings, maps and more that once belonged to Jefferson but are now in private hands. The exhibition continues through December.

FOXFIELD RACES
Charlottesville   (804) 293-9501.

THE DOGWOOD FESTIVAL
Charlottesville   (804) 295-3141

This popular community event features a queen's coronation, fashion show, fireworks, carnival, barbecue and, finally, a grand parade on Saturday. The attraction shows off Charlottesville at its springtime best. It's usually held in mid-April and lasts nearly two weeks.

EASTER AT WINTERGREEN
Wintergreen   (804) 325-2200

Every Easter weekend Wintergreen Resort holds a variety of activities for families: *Egg-Stravaganza* games for kids, a Ukrainian egg decorating workshop, culinary workshop, and an Easter morning worship service.

VIRGINIA HORSE FESTIVAL
Lexington   (703) 463-4300

This event showcases the state's horse industry with breed exhibits, a large equine trade show, terrier races, an equine art contest, a draft horse pull and more. It's held at the posh Virginia Horse Center, just outside Lexington on VA 39.

Spring Garden Show

Lynchburg   (804) 847-1499

This is a gardener's field day in early April at the Community Market, where landscapers, florists and nursery operators display their products and where gardening techniques are demonstrated. There's also entertainment and food.

Spring Balloon Festival

Bedford   (703) 586-9401

Franklin County Spring Arts and Crafts Festival

Rocky Mount   (703) 483-9542

Franklin County Court Days

Rocky Mount   (703) 483-9211

Brush Mountain Arts and Crafts Fair

Blacksburg   (703) 552-4909

River Run and Bicycle Ride

Narrows   (703) 921-1544

Honaker Redbud Festival

Honaker, Russell County   (703) 889-8041

This tiny community of 1,000 celebrates spring every year with a month-long festival, featuring gospel singing, arts and craft shows, a canoe race down the Clinch River, a car show, homecoming dinner, beauty pageant and parade. The redbud tree, indigenous to the Southwest Virginia county, blossoms this month.

Lonesome Pine Arts and Crafts

Big Stone Gap   (703) 523-0846

This community close to Kentucky is home to a wonderful annual celebration of mountain heritage. Here you will find craft making demonstrations and the display and sale of homemade arts, crafts and food.

May

Shenandoah Apple Blossom Festival

Winchester   (703) 662-3863

This four-day celebration is a salute to the area's apple-growing industry. You'll find high quality arts and crafts shows, numerous parades, live music, a 10-kilometer race and a circus. Back in the old days Winchester's festival leaders crowned as queen such Presidents' daughters as Luci Baines Johnson and Susan Elizabeth Ford. These days the Apple Blossom Queen is usually a young woman with blood-ties to a famous person — the '92 queen was the daughter of "Designing Women" star Dixie Carter. This festival is usually held the first week of May.

Spring Fly-In

Winchester   (703) 662-5786

This festival is always held the Sunday of Apple Blossom Festival. Aircraft owners compete for various pprizes and share their aviation interests with the public. The festival is held at the Winchester Regional Airport.

Antique Car Show

Winchester   (703) 869-7475

Held always in May, this show, flea market and car corral draws hundreds to the Jim Barnett Park in Winchester. It is sponsored by the Shenandoah Region Antique Auto club of America.

North-South Skirmish
Gainesboro (703) 888-7917

This is the spring nationals event of the North-South Skirmish Association, held at Ft. Shenandoah in Gainesboro. This year marks its 43rd year. It's always held in May.

Virginia Mushroom Festival
Front Royal   (800) 338-2576

Held usually the second weekend in May, this Main Street festival features arts and crafts, great food, wine tastings hosted by four or five area wineries, live music, clogging, and open air theatrical performances.

Wildflower Weekend
Shenandoah National Park   (703) 999-3482

This event celebrates the arrival of spring. Guided walks, exhibits, slide programs and workshops are held at the 195,000-acre park during the third weekend in May.

New Market Heritage Days
New Market   (703) 740-3432

Virginia Poultry Festival
Harrisonburg   (703) 433-2451

Memorial Day Horse Fair and Auction
Harrisonburg   (703) 434-4482

Folk Arts and Crafts Festival
Weyers Cave   (703) 886-2351

Annual Kite Day
Charlottesville   (804) 293-9539

At Ash Lawn-Highland, home of President James Monroe, the fields are open to children and the young at heart for kite flying. Both designs and flights are judged for prizes. Usually held in early May.

Crozet Arts and Crafts Festival
Crozet   (804) 977-1783

Spring Wildflower Symposium
Wintergreen   (804) 325-2200

Every May Wintergreen Resort invites prominent specialists to lead workshops, lectures and other educational programs about wildflowers. There are guided hikes, wildflower sales, photography displays and entertainment.

Memorial Day Celebration
Wintergreen   (804) 325-2200

Every year the resort kicks off its summer season with the Stoney Creek Valley Parade, a kite festival, a Firemen's Ball and an opening day celebration at Lake Monocan.

Montpelier Wine Festival
Montepelier Station   (703) 832-2828

Regional wines are showcased on the grounds of Montpelier every May. The festival provides an opportunity to enjoy one of the state's premier products, its wine, as well as equestrian events, crafts, music and food.

Dolley Madison's Birthday
Montpelier Station   (703) 672-2728

This is an annual celebration at Montpelier, four miles from Orange on Rt. 20 South.

Spring Arts and Crafts Fair
Waynesboro   (703) 942-2320.

INTERNATIONAL SPRINGTIME CELEBRATION

Staunton (703) 332-7850

Four "mini-festivals" at the Museum of American Frontier Culture coincide with Europe's traditional May Day celebrations. Come dance a jig and munch on a meat pasty while watching baby lambs frolic in a nearby pasture. Activities at the museum's working German, Scotch-Irish, English, and American farms include traditional dancing, music and foods. This happens on either the first or second Saturday in May.

OUTDOOR ART SHOW

Staunton (703) 886-2351

THEATER AT LIME KILN

Lexington (703) 463-3074

Memorial Day begins the summer season at Lime Kiln, an outdoor theater that's nationally recognized for presenting original plays and musicals that relate to Virginia's culture and history. Plays and concerts are held under the stars in an enchanting setting—the ruins of an actual lime kiln built in the 1800s. Plays are performed Monday through Saturday until Labor Day. On Sunday nights, some of the best and brightest in the eclectic music business perform at Lime Kiln — from jazz and blues to folk and bluegrass.

NEW MARKET DAY CEREMONY

Lexington (703) 464-7207

BASS BONANZA

Covington (703) 962-2178

Held every year at Lake Moomaw in the Allegheny Mountains.

PIONEER DAY

Covington (703) 962-8943

AN EVENING OF ELEGANCE

Lynchburg (804) 847-8688

This annual fund-raiser for the Virginia School of the Arts is always held in early May. Internationally acclaimed dancers perform with local students at the E.C. Glass auditorium.

CHILDREN'S DAY AT THE MARKET

Lynchburg (804) 847-1499

Also in early May, bring your kids to the Community Market to watch clowns and touch the animals at the petting zoo. There's lots of entertainment, games, and food, and an annual poster contest.

MEMORIAL DAY OBSERVANCE

Lynchburg (804) 847-1811.

MAY FEST

Stonewall Vineyards, Concord (804) 993-2185

THE VIRGINIA CHILI COOK-OFF

Roanoke (703) 981-2889

Thousands of connoisseurs pour into Roanoke's historic farmer's market the first Saturday in May to participate in the taste-testing for this cook-off. Don't forget to head down the block for some homemade strawberry shortcake at Community School's Strawberry Festival.

FESTIVAL IN THE PARK

Roanoke (703) 342-2640

This is a two week-long celebration beginning Memorial Day

weekend. It hosts one of the East Coast's largest sidewalk art shows, a river race, concerts, fireworks, children's games, ethnic foods, bike and road races, and a children's parade. During the second week, there's also a carnival at the Civic Center.

VINTON DOGWOOD FESTIVAL
(703) 345-9616

This community next to Roanoke celebrates spring in early May every year with a parade, a band competition, an antique car show, music, food, crafts, bike races, a long-distance run, an evening country music concert and more.

FRANKLIN COUNTY FESTIVAL
Rocky Mount   *(703) 483-9542*

ARTS AND CRAFTS FESTIVAL
Wytheville   *(703) 228-5541*

Usually held around the first few days of May.

WINE AND CHEESE FESTIVAL
Wytheville   *(703) 228-3111*

Includes an auction.

WYTHE COUNTY GUN SHOW AND FLEA MARKET
Fort Chiswell   *(703) 228-5586*

PLUMB ALLEY DAY
Abingdon   *(703) 628-8141*

This arts and crafts jamboree is always held the Saturday of Memorial Day weekend.

MOUNT ROGERS RAMP FESTIVAL
Whitetop Mountain   *(703) 388-3294*

This is a tribute to the pungent wild mountain onion. Bring a bottle of listerine to the festival if you plan to try some of the many ramp-laden foods. There'll be ramps in stews and salads, ramps fried with trout and ramps roasted with bear meat. Mountain crafts and quilts are on display and bluegrass music keeps things hopping on this mountaintop. This event is always held the third weekend in May.

MOUNT ROGERS NATURALIST RALLY
(703) 783-2125

This is a weekend retreat for discovering the natural history and wildlife of Southwest Virginia. It features a naturalist speaker and hikes led by college professors. It is usually scheduled in mid-May to coincide with the Ramp Festival.

APPALACHIAN TRAIL DAYS
Damascus

This three-day, rollicking event in tiny Damascus draws A.T. hikers from far and wide, making it a standard reunion for many. The hikers stage an amusing parade and talent show. Arts and crafts shows, street dances, clogging demonstrations and live music keep little Damascus hopping for days. Usually held in mid-May.

RALPH STANLEY BLUE GRASS FESTIVAL
Coeburn   *(703) 395-6318*

Held on Memorial Day weekend in a community along the edge of the Jefferson National Forest in far southwest Virginia.

BIG STONE GAP COUNTRY FAIR
(703) 523-4950

Always held on Mother's Day

Photo: Donald Roakes

The James River Bateau Festival is held every June in Lynchburg.

weekend at Bullit Park.

June

MOUNTAIN HERITAGE ARTS AND CRAFTS FESTIVAL
Near Harper's Ferry, W.Va. (304) 725-2055 or (800) 624-0577 outside West Virginia.

Nearly 200 artists and craftspeople demonstrate and sell their products at this event, held usually in mid-June. There is also singing, apple-butter making and live bluegrass.

SHENANDOAH VALLEY FARM CRAFT DAYS
Middletown   (703) 869-2028

CONFEDERATE MEMORIAL SERVICE
Winchester   (703) 662-1937

This year marks the 127th annual program to honor the memory of the more than 3,000 Confederate soldiers buried in the Stonewall Jackson Cemetery. This is sponsored by the United Daughters of the Confederacy, Chapter 54. It's always held on a Sunday in June.

BLUEMONT CONCERT SERIES
Winchester   (703) 665-0079

This Friday night free outdoor concenrt series begins in late June on the lawn of the old Frederick County Courthouse in Old Town Winchester. You can hear folk, cajun, bluegrass and other types of acoustic music performed under the stars—a relaxing way to end the work week. Concerts are held every Friday night in June, July and some of August.

COURT DAYS FESTIVAL
Woodstock   (703) 459-2542

This event, also held in mid-June, recreates the days when the old-time "County Judge" came to town to settle cases. The festival features a dog show, pig roast, street dances, exhibits, live music, a bike-a-thon, 5-K run and more.

NATURAL CHIMNEYS JOUST
Mt. Solon   (703) 350-2510

Here's an anachronism if you've ever seen one. This is the National Hall of Fame Jousting Tournament. "Knights" hailing from several states congregate here to joust for a shining ring. Bluegrass or country music fills the air, and the seven castle-like towers of Natural Chimneys form a spectacular backdrop. This happens the third Saturday in June every year.

NELSON COUNTY SUMMER FESTIVAL
(804) 263-5392

Held in late June, this is a family-oriented, upscale festival held on the lovely grounds of Oak Ridge Estate, Rt. 653, south of Lovingston.

SUMMER FESTIVAL OF THE ARTS AT ASH LAWN-HIGHLAND
Charlottesville   (804) 293-4500

This festival is a potpourri of music with its opera and musical theater productions, a Music at Twilight concernt series with traditional and contemporary musical performances, and a Summer Saturdays family entertainment series.

ANNUAL SUN AND SAND BEACH WEEKEND
Stuarts Draft *(703) 337-1911*
At Shenandoah Acres Resort, you'll need plenty of energy for this one. There's volleyball, mini-golf, sand castle building contests, various water contests and a D.J. dance on Saturday night. This is always held the third weekend in June.

RAIL ROAD DAYS
Clifton Forge *(703) 862-2210*
Celebrate the railroad heritage of the C&O with the Gandy Dancers, a train excursion, exhibits and all kinds of activities.

BLUE RIDGE MUSIC FESTIVAL
Lynchburg *(804) 948-1639*
Folk, classical or jazz concerts are held every evening during this week-long event in mid-June at Randolph Macon Women's College.

CENTRAL VIRGINIA INVITATIONAL TENNIS TOURNAMENT
Lynchburg *(804) 384-8179*

DINNER AT DUSK
Lynchburg *(804) 847-1459*
Dine with the crew members of the *James River Bateau*— the resurrected flat-bottomed boat and crew that once hauled tobacco to Richmond and beyond before canals were built. Participants dress up in full costume and tell tales of the river, perform folk music and celebrate the start of the Festival by the James.

FESTIVAL BY THE JAMES
Lynchburg *(804) 847-1811*
This is a downtown festival that celebrates the James River and what it means to the Lynchburg area. Always held in mid-June, it includes a foot race, exhibitions and demonstrations by costumed artisans, Civil War reenactments, horse-pulls, canoe races and more.

EAGLE ROCK FESTIVAL
Fincastle *703) 992-8280*

CONSERVATION FESTIVAL
Roanoke *(703) 343-3241*
Held every year in mid-June at Mill Mountain Zoo.

ROANOKE VALLEY HORSE SHOW
Salem *(703) 389-7847*
Held in mid-June, this is one of the top all-breed horse shows on the East Coast. Usually attracts about 1,000 entries from across the United States.

MONTGOMERY COUNTY HISTORICAL FESTIVAL
Blacksburg *(703) 552-4061*
Held the second Saturday in June at the Smithfield Plantation.

CAMBRIA WHISTLESTOP ARTS FESTIVAL
Christiansburg *(703) 382-4251*

FESTIVAL AROUND TOWN
Pearisburg *(703) 921-1324*

GILES AND MOUNTAIN LAKE BICYCLE RIDE
Giles County *(703) 921-4381*

CIVIL WAR WEEKEND
Newbern *(703) 674-4835*

Held usually the third weekend in June, this event features an afternoon tea, living history demonstrations, marches, a church service and lectures. A battle reenactment happens Sunday afternoon at Tabor Farm. Other events are held at the Wilderness Road Regional Museum.

RENDEZVOUS

Radford (703) 639-3619

Appalachian folkways and mountain storytelling are the focus of this all-day festival on the fourth Saturday in June. Events are held at the Long Way Home Outdoor Theater.

CHAUTAUQUA FESTIVAL IN THE PARK

Wytheville (703) 228-3111

This is the biggest annual event in Wythe County, with nine days and nights of entertainment. Other than arts and craft shows, there are antique sales, ballets and big band, bluegrass and classical music performances.

GRAYSON COUNTY OLD TIME FIDDLER'S CONVENTION

(703) 655-4144

BEST FRIEND FESTIVAL

Norton (703) 679-0961

This event features music, games, arts and crafts and is always held on Father's Day weekend.

CRAFTERS FAIR

Waltons Mountain Country Store
(804) 325-2200

This fair is held in mid-June.

July

SAFE AND SANE 4TH OF JULY CELEBRATION

Winchester (703) 465-5757

This is a mid-day party at the downtown pedestrian mall, with patriotic speeches, cake, balloons, carriage rides, a bike decorating contest and a parade.

FREDERICK COUNTY FAIR

Clearbrook (703) 662-9002

This will be the 59th year of this regional event, held at the county fairgrounds on Rt. 11 north.

4TH OF JULY CELEBRATION

New Market (703) 740-3432

This Shenandoah Valley town hosts a big celebration for the whole family, with lots of food, games, children's rides, a parade and fireworks.

SHENANDOAH VALLEY MUSIC FESTIVAL

Orkney Springs (703) 459-3396

During the last two weekends in July the Fairfax Symphony Orchestra performs pops and classical music under the stars in an outdoor pavilion next to the Orkney Springs Hotel, a massive pre-Civil War building. Get there early for the ice-cream socials that are held before every concert. Arts and crafts shows are also held those weekends.

SHENANDOAH VALLEY BICYCLE FESTIVAL

Harrisonburg (703) 434-3862

This festival is usually held the last two weekends in July.

FREEDOM FEST AT MONTPELIER
(703) 672-5216
Celebrate an old-fashioned, family-style Fourth of July on Saturday, July 3. There will be a horse show and children's games, as well as music, concessions and crafts. A musically choreographed fireworks extravaganza caps off the event.

INDEPENDENCE DAY CELEBRATION
Charlottesville   (804) 295-5191
Held every year at McIntire Park, there are softball and baseball games, band concerts, children's rides and games, a picnic and, of course, fireworks.

INDEPENDENCE DAY CELEBRATION
Charlottesville (Monticello)   (804) 295-8181
About 50 new citizens from the Charlottesville area are naturalized each 4th of July on the grounds of Thomas Jefferson's Monticello. A fife and drum corps provides music at this moving event attended usually by nearly 1,000 people.

FOURTH OF JULY JUBILEE
Wintergreen   (804) 325-2200
At Wintergreen Resort you'll find greased watermelon races, clogging demonstrations, and arts and crafts show and a grand fireworks display.

PLANTATION DAYS FESTIVAL
Charlottesville   (804) 293-9539
At Ash Lawn-Highland, James Monroe's 535-acre estate, merchants, craftspeople, servants and soldiers are depicted in a celebration of early American life. More than 20 crafters and artisans in period costumes demonstrate and sell

their work. Visitors can also enjoy 18th-century music and games, and a dressage performance, "Dancing with Horses."

ANNUAL RAFT RACE
Stuarts Draft   (703) 337-1911
At Shenandoah Acres Resort, folks of all ages race around a measured course in inflatable rafts. Cash prizes are offered to winners. This always happens in late July.

HAPPY BIRTHDAY U.S.A.
Staunton
As corny as it sounds, this is an old-fashioned, flag-waving, apple-pie 4th of July celebration spawned by Staunton's hometown heroes, The Statler Brothers. You can be sure to hear plenty of good country music at this event, held at Gypsy Hill Park.

ROCKBRIDGE REGIONAL FAIR
Lexington   (703) 463-3777

JULY 4TH CELEBRATION
Clifton Forge   (703) 862-4246

INDEPENDENCE CELEBRATION
Lynchburg   (804) 525-1806
This is not your typical 4th of July party. At Poplar Forest interpreters will portray the lives of local citizenry during Thomas Jefferson's time. There will be early 19th-century craft demonstrations and lots of food.

JULY 4TH CELEBRATION
Bedford   (703) 586-7161

BUCHANAN CARNIVAL
Buchanan   (703) 992-8280

MUSIC FOR AMERICANS

Roanoke   (703) 343-9127

At Roanoke's Victory Stadium, this July 4th celebration features a performance by the Roanoke Symphony Orchestra, the community chorus and fireworks.

MISS VIRGINIA PAGEANT

Roanoke   (703) 981-1201

VINTON JULY 4TH CELEBRATION

(703) 342-6025

Held every year at the Vinton War Memorial.

SALEM FAIR AND EXPOSITION

Salem   (703) 375-3004

This is an old-time country fair held at the Salem Civic Center, both indoors and outside. For nearly two weeks there are carnival rides, games, food, concerts and livestock judging. There's also a bake-off that attracts some of the best cooks in the Roanoke Valley.

ROCKY MOUNT INDEPENDENCE CELEBRATION

(703) 483-9542

FOURTH OF JULY CELEBRATION

Shawsville   (703) 268-5547

FOURTH OF JULY CELEBRATION

Radford   (703) 731-3677

At Radford's beautiful Bisset Park there will be gospel music, craft shows, food vendors and fireworks. All events take place along the New River.

RIVERFEST

Radford   (703) 639-2202

This event features a raft race down the New River. There's a barbe-cue cooking contest, a craft show and live music. It's always held the second Saturday following July 4.

4TH OF JULY CELEBRATION AND WATER CARNIVAL

Narrows   (703) 726-2423

NEW RIVER VALLEY HORSE SHOW

Dublin   (703) 980-1991

FOURTH OF JULY CELEBRATION

Pulaski   (703) 980-8200

BLUE RIDGE HERITAGE FESTIVAL

Fort Chiswell   (703) 228-3111

This event represents Southwest Virginia's 19 counties, with mountain music, arts and crafts, and representatives from the many attractions of the Blue Ridge and Highlands.

JULY 4TH CELEBRATION

Rural Retreat   (703) 228-3211

HOTTEST FUN IN THE SUN BEACH DAY

Wytheville   (703) 228-3111

Always held the third Saturday in July.

FOURTH OF JULY CELEBRATION AND CARNIVAL

Galax   (703) 236-3573

CHILI COOK-OFF & INDEPENDENCE DAY CELEBRATION

Marion   (703) 783-3881

HUNGRY MOTHER STATE PARK ARTS & CRAFTS FESTIVAL

Marion   (703) 783-3161

Always held the third weekend in July.

August

OLD TOWN HOE DOWN

Winchester   (703) 665-0779

Always held in August, this annual farmers' day celebration features displays of farm implements, live music, craft deminstrations, fresh produce, and a petting zoo in Old Town Winchester.

GREAT AMERICAN DUCK RACE

Winchester   (703) 662-4118

Held every August at Jim Barnett Park, this is an annual fundraiser by the Winchester-Patrick County Chamber of Commerce, featuring games, music, refreshments and duck races.

SHENANDOAH VALLEY MUSIC FESTIVAL

Orkney Springs   (703) 459-3396

Several jazz groups perform under the stars in this mid-August, Saturday night festival. Come early for the ice-cream social, complete with homemade cakes and pies.

ROCKINGHAM COUNTY FAIR

Harrisonburg   (703) 434-0005

NATURAL CHIMNEYS JOUST

Mt. Solon   (703) 350-2510

The third Saturday in August welcomes the oldest continuously held sporting event in America—so they say. Local "knights" joust for a shining ring, as they have for the past 170 or so years. A medieval skit sets the stage for the event. The local fire department supplies the food, and country or bluegrass bands make music.

ANNUAL SAND CASTLE & SAND FORM CONTEST

Stuarts Draft   (703) 337-1911

ROCKBRIDGE COMMUNITY FESTIVAL

Lexington   (703) 463-3777

THOMAS JEFFERSON'S TOMATOE FAIRE

Lynchburg   (804) 847-1499

This early August agrarian festival starts at 6 AM, with tomato and canned good competitions, live entertainment and handmade crafts. It's held at the downtown Community Market.

ANNUAL ROANOKE BEACH PARTY

                              (703) 981-2889

STEPPING OUT

Blacksburg   (703) 552-4061

This major downtown festival is always held the first weekend in August.

NEW RIVER VALLEY FAIR

Dublin   (703) 674-5421

NEWPORT AGRICULTURAL FAIR

                              (703) 544-7469

One of the oldest agricultural fairs in Virginia, this Giles County community features judged food and agriculture exhibits and livestock competitions, bluegrass, and horseshoe and jousting tournaments.

VIRGINIA HIGHLANDS FESTIVAL

Abingdon   (703) 628-8141

This festival in beautiful, historic downtown Abingdon features one of the largest antique shows in the country. There are historic tours, workshops, and fine arts and crafts. This is always held the first week in August.

OLD FIDDLER'S CONVENTION

Galax   *(703) 236-8541*

This is the real McCoy — the oldest and largest old-time music festival in the country. It's always held during the second week in August. You'll find bluegrass and folk bands, clogging and flat-foot dancing day and night.

VIRGINIA KENTUCKY DISTRICT FAIR

Wise   *(703) 328-9772*

APPALACHIA COAL AND RAILROAD DAYS

Appalachia   *(703) 565-0361*

This is a must-do for railroad and coal buffs. It's always held the second weekend in August.

September

APPLE HARVEST ARTS & CRAFTS FESTIVAL

Winchester   *(703) 662-4135*

This fall festival offers apple butter-making and pie contests, live music and, of course, arts and crafts galore. It's held at Jim Barnett Park.

ANNUAL INTERNATIONAL STREET FESTIVAL

Winchester   *(703) 665-0079*

Usually held in late September, this festival features costumes, native gourmet dishes and crafts and entertainments from around the world.

BOTTLE AND POTTERY SHOW AND SALE

(703) 877-1093

This year marks the 20th annual show and sale of antique bottles, pottery, postcards and small collectibles by the Apple Valley Bottle Collectors Club.

ANNUAL HARVEST FESTIVAL

Edinburg   *(703) 984-8699*

Shenandoah Vineyards hosts an all-day festival every September, giving you a chance to stomp on grapes, munch on barbecue, take a hayride, dance and, of course, sample some wine. There's also an arts and crafts exhibit.

EDINBURG OLE' TIME FESTIVAL

Edinburg   *(703) 984-8521*

ANNUAL FOOD & MUSIC FESTIVAL

Luray   *(703) 743-3915*

NEW MARKET ARTS & CRAFTS SHOW

New Market   *(703) 740-3329*

This is a show of high quality arts and crafts from the Blue Ridge and Shenandoah Valley region. It happens every year in late September.

SHENANDOAH VALLEY MUSIC FESTIVAL

Orkney Springs   *(703) 459-3396*

Held on Labor Day weekend, folk music is performed outdoors on Saturday night, and a Big Band concert happens Sunday night. Musicians vary every year.

ANNUAL SPORTSMAN'S FAIR AND BIG GAME TROPHY SHOW
Harrisonburg   *(703) 828-3393*

ALBEMARLE COUNTY FAIR
North Garden   *(804) 296-5803*
Usually held the first few days of September.

CONSTITUTION DAY CELEBRATIONS
(703) 672-2728
Enjoy free admission to tour Montpelier, the home of President James Madison, the father of the Constitution. This is an opportunity to better understand the man who contributed so much to the founding of our government. In 1993 the event takes place Sept. 17.

FOXFIELD RACES
Charlottesville   *(804) 293-9501*

LABOR DAY SPECTACULAR
Wintergreen   *(804) 325-2200*
Wintergreen Resort also throws a huge weekend party around Labor Day, with a boat race, a cookout with bluegrass, a goofy talent show and family scavenger hunts.

TRADITIONAL FRONTIER FESTIVAL
Staunton   *(703) 332-7850*
This is a good time to visit the Museum of American Frontier Culture, which hosts this festival the weekend following Labor Day every year. Come and enjoy traditional crafts, food, and entertainment from

The annual Old Fiddler's Convention is the oldest and largest old-time music festival in the country.

Germany, England, Ireland, and America at the museum's "living history" farms.

BUENA VISTA LABOR DAY FESTIVAL
(703) 463-5375

This is a huge event that usually attracts some of the state's leading politicians. There are band concerts, arts and crafts, tennis and horseshoe tournaments, amusement rides and more.

KALEIDOSCOPE
Lynchburg   (804) 847-1811

This is Lynchburg's big annual fall festival that lasts nearly three weeks. It includes a children's festival on the third Saturday, a major antique show with 100 dealers, a river-front music jamboree with barbecue, a craft show and bike race and Teddy Bear parade. Thousands of runners participate in the 10-mile race.

FALL FOOD FESTIVAL
Lynchburg   (804) 847-1499

Held on a mid-September weekend.

CENTERFEST
Bedford   (703) 586-2148

FINCASTLE FESTIVAL
(703) 473-8280

HENRY STREET HERITAGE FESTIVAL
Roanoke   (703) 345-4818

This is an annual celebration of African-American culture in a neighborhood close to downtown Roanoke. There is ethnic food, music, entertainment and children's activities.

OLDE SALEM DAYS
Salem   (703) 387-0267

This is a downtown celebration held the second Saturday in September, whose focus is antiques, crafts and health care.

WINE FESTIVAL
Smith Mountain Lake   (703) 721-1203

On the last Sunday in September nearly a dozen of Virginia's best wineries converge at Bernard's Landing and Resort for a festival on the beautiful lake. Chamber music, wine tastings and good food make this one of the area's more sophisticated festivals.

WILDERNESS TRAIL FESTIVAL
Christiansburg   (703) 382-4251

SEPTEMBERFEST
Radford   (703) 731-3656

This is a two-day downtown festival with jazz, wine tastings, sidewalk sales and competitions with a variety of bands. Septemberfest always happens the second Friday and Saturday in September.

CLAYTOR LAKE ARTS AND CRAFTS FAIR
Pulaski County   (703) 980-7363

A Labor Day Weekend event.

HERITAGE DAY
Pembroke   (703) 626-3689

DOCK BOGGS MEMORIAL FESTIVAL
Wythe County   (703) 328-0100

This is always held the second weekend in September.

SALTVILLE LABOR DAY CELEBRATION
(703) 496-7038

Here you will find an 1800s fashion show and Civil War reenactment. There will also be salt-making demonstrations, a street dance, parade, and live entertainment.

GRAYSON HIGHLANDS FALL FESTIVAL
Mouth of Wilson   *(703) 579-7092*

Held at the Grayson Highlands State Park, this is an old-time festival with apple butter and molasses-making demonstrations and presentations by a blacksmith. There is bluegrass and gospel music, barbecue chicken, and other foods.

CHILHOWIE APPLE FESTIVAL
Chilhowie   *(703) 646-8213*

This Smyth County celebration is always held the last weekend in September.

WASHINGTON COUNTY FAIR AND BURLEY FESTIVAL
(703) 676-2282

October

NORTH-SOUTH SKIRMISH ASSOCIATION FALL NATIONALS
Gainesboro   *(703) 666-7917*

Civil War reenactors fire old weapons at breakable targets in an original manner, wearing authentic uniforms. There is also a ladies' dress competition. This will be the 43rd year of this event at Ft. Shenandoah.

ANTIQUE SHOW AND SALE
Winchester   *(703) 662-4996*

This show is held in early October at the War Memorial Building.

BATTLE OF CEDAR CREEK LIVING HISTORY & REENACTMENT
Middletown   *(703) 869-2028*

This is a panorama of Civil War-era living history including the only reenactment held on an original battlefield of the Civil War. This takes place at Belle Grove Plantation on the weekend closest to Oct. 19, 1864, the anniversary of the Battle of Cedar Creek.

HERITAGE FESTIVAL
Luray   *(703) 778-3230*

This festival brings to mind the old-time county fair. There's country music, clogging shows, wagon rides, apple cider, home-cooked food, a steam and gas engine show, and a Saturday Chili Cook-Off. More than 100 crafts workers also display their wares.

ELKTON AUTUMN DAYS ARTS & CRAFTS FESTIVAL
Elkton   *(703) 298-9370*

This is an outdoor festival that's usually held during the best weekend for enjoying the brilliant colors of autumn.

BACCHANALIAN FEAST
Charlottesville   *(804) 296-4188*

This evening feast at the Boar's Head Inn includes a seven-course meal with Virginia wines and entertainment. It's usually held on one of the first Fridays in October to kick off the Monticello Wine and Food Festival.

MONTICELLO WINE AND FOOD FESTIVAL

Charlottesville   *(804) 296-4188*

Held also at the Boar's Head Inn, this is a chance to taste many of the wines made in Virginia and view exhibits of the state's many wineries and vineyards.

CROZET ARTS AND CRAFTS FESTIVAL

Crozet   *(804) 977-1783*

VIRGINIA FESTIVAL OF AMERICAN FILM

Charlottesville
     (804) 924-FEST or (800) UVA-FEST

Film makers, scholars, movie stars and the public explore trends in American film making at this event, which usually happens around the end of October. In the past, such stars as Gregory Peck and Sissy Spacek have graced the festival. (See our Arts & Culture chapter for more information.)

VIRGINIA HERITAGE WEEKEND

Wintergreen   *(804) 325-2200*

Wintergreen Resort hosts this event the first weekend of October. There will be a country cook-out and an outdoor bluegrass concert, Appalachian heritage crafts workshops, clogging demonstrations, folklore and storytelling.

APPLE BUTTER MAKING FESTIVAL

Nelson County   *(804) 277-5865*

This festival is held both at the beginning of October and in the middle of the month.

HALLOWEEN WEEKEND

Wintergreen   *(804) 325-2200*

Take the eerie Ghost Express chairlift; then share hair-raising stories around the campfire at Wintergreen this weekend. There's also a children's haunted house, a costume contest, and opportunities for families to carve pumpkins.

VIRGINIA FALL FOLIAGE FESTIVAL

Waynesboro   *(703) 949-6505*

This happens usually the first two consecutive weekends in October. This is a major event featuring a 10-K run, an arts and crafts show with more than 200 exhibitors, a chili cook-off, and lots of good foods made with apples. It also includes a gem and mineral show.

OKTOBERFEST

Staunton   *(703) 886-2351*

German beer, Virginia wine, food and an Oompah Band playing traditional German music make this a special festival. There's also a *Bach Bash* presented by the Mid-Atlantic Chamber Orchestra and arts and crafts displays.

FALL FOLIAGE FESTIVAL

Clifton Forge   *(703) 862-4969*

SORGHUM MOLASSES FESTIVAL

Clifford   *(804) 946-5063*

This little town east of the Blue Ridge salutes the dark, gooey sweet substance in October with a festival that includes a jousting tournament, country music, arts and crafts and a flea market. You can also watch molasses and apple butter being made.

VIRGINIA GARLIC FESTIVAL

Amherst   *(804) 946-5168*

The five-acre Rebec Vineyards hosts this mid-October celebration. Several Virginia wineries participate, and there is wonderful food for epicures. A Garlic Queen dressed in a giant bulb with sprouts shooting from her head has been known to make an appearance.

JAZZ ON THE LAWN

Concord   *804) 993-2185*

Just east of Lynchburg is another winery, Stonewall Vineyards, which hosts this relaxing weekend event in mid-October. Enjoy live jazz, gourmet food and local wines.

LYNCHBURG HISTORICAL FOUNDATION ANTIQUE SHOW AND SALE

Lynchburg   *(804) 528-5353*

OKTOBERFEST

Lynchburg   *(804) 845-6604*

HARVEST FESTIVAL

Lynchburg   *(804) 847-1499*

This end-of-October festival features Virginia-made products and crafts, square dancing and country music. Children go crazy with the costume contests and community pumpkin-carving.

HARVEST FESTIVAL ON THE MARKET

Roanoke   *(703) 342-2028*

Every October folks pour into the streets of Roanoke's historic City Market for horse-drawn carriage rides, lessons in scarecrow-building, hot cider and live bluegrass.

ROANOKE RAILWAY FESTIVAL

Roanoke   *(703) 342-2028*

The city celebrates its railroad heritage every year with a Columbus Day festival all weekend. You can take a ride on an old steam train then have a bite of pork at the pig roast. There's also nostalgic entertainment, a car show and a huge rail-related crafts show at the nearby Civic Center.

ANNUAL ZOO BOO

Roanoke   *(703) 343-3241*

Halloween party at the Mill Mountain Zoo.

EXPLORE FESTIVAL

Vinton   *(703) 342-1295*

HAUNTED CAVERNS

Dixie Caverns   *(703) 380-2085*

This Halloween tour of Dixie Caverns will make your hair stand on end. Grinding chain-saws, shrieks and lots of fake blood make this event a blast for those who thrive on horror.

SMITH MOUNTAIN LAKE FALL FESTIVAL

(703) 721-1203

Also on Columbus Day weekend, Smith Mountain Lake's six or so communities all host festivals — forming a virtual ring of festivals around the lake. There are arts and crafts shows, an antique car show, a flea market, traditional folkway demonstrations and more.

FALL FESTIVAL - FRANKLIN COUNTY

(703) 721-1203

WILDERNESS TRAIL FESTIVAL

Christiansburg   *(703) 382-4251*

COUNT PULASKI DAY
Pulaski County   (703) 980-1991

BLUE RIDGE FOLKLIFE FESTIVAL
Ferrum   (703) 365-2121
Ferrum College hosts this annual event the last Saturday in October. Widely attended, the festival showcases regional traditions with crafts workers showing time-honored skills, old-time musicians and traditional Appalachian competitions.

WHITETOP MOUNTAIN SORGHUM AND MOLASSES FESTIVAL
                                  (703) 388-3294
This festival at Mt. Rogers National Recreation Area features molasses and apple butter made the old-fashioned way. There are games, bake sales, arts and crafts and old-time gospel and bluegrass music.

WISE FALL FLING
                                  (703) 328-4470

MECC HOME CRAFTS DAYS
Big Stone Gap   (703) 523-2400
Two days of arts and crafts at Mountain Empire Community College feature bluegrass and country music, clogging, whittling, broommaking and other mountain heritage displays.

November

OLD TOWN CHRISTMAS PARADE
Winchester   (703) 667-2409
This parade is held in late November.

MONTPELIER HUNT RACES
                                  (703) 672-2728
This will be the 59th year of these famous races that take place on the beautiful grounds of Montpelier, home of James Madison. The traditional races feature two flat track and five overjumps, as well as a Jack Russell terrier race and the Dolley Madison tailgate competition.

THANKSGIVING AT WINTERGREEN
                                  (804) 325-2200
If cooking for a crowd is not what you want, spend the weekend at Wintergreen. They'll deliver turkey and all the trimmings to the door of your rented condo. Or you can partake of traditional buffets and dinners at all the resort's restaurants. There's also a turkey trot square dance, a hayride sing-along and a musical revue cabaret.

CHRISTMAS CRAFT FAIR
Waynesboro   (703) 949-8203

CHRISTMAS AT THE MARKET
Lynchburg   (804) 847-1499
Always held at the end of November at the downtown Community Market.

FRANKLIN COUNTY FALL ARTS AND CRAFTS FESTIVAL
Rocky Mount   (703) 483-9542
This festival is usually held the weekend before Thanksgiving.

ARTS AND CRAFTS BAZAAR
Wytheville   (703) 228-3111
This bazaar is usually held the weekend before Thanksgiving.

ANNUAL CHRISTMAS BAZAAR
Galax   (703) 236-2184

December

ABRAM'S DELIGHT
CANDLELIGHT TOUR
Winchester   (703) 662-6550
Take the tour at Abram's Delight, Winchester's oldest home.

CHRISTMAS OPEN HOUSE AT
STONEWALL JACKSON'S
HEADQUARTERS
Winchester   (703) 662-6550
Members of the United Daughters of the Confederacy are your costumed hostesses at this Confederate Christmas.

FIRST NIGHT WINCHESTER
(703) 662-3884
This is an annual New Year's Eve celebration of the arts in town. More than 40 different artists perform at sites throughout Winchester in this family-oriented, alcohol-free celebration.

CHRISTMAS CANDLELIGHT TOUR
Middletown   (703) 869-2028
At Belle Grove Plantation.

ANNUAL CHRISTMAS ARTS
& CRAFTS SHOW
Harrisonburg   (703) 879-9417

ANNUAL YULETIDE TRADITIONS
Charlottesville   (804) 977-1783
These special events at Ash Lawn-Highland, historic Michie Tavern and Monticello are held throughout December. There are *Christmas By Candlelight* evening tours and historic reenactments at Ash Lawn-Highland. Also at Ash Lawn is *Gingerbread and Lace*, a celebration with caroling, ornament making, tree trimming and refreshments. At Michie Tavern, an array of Christmas delicacies are served in "The Ordinary" for a Yuletide Feast. Monticello holds a candlelight open house several evenings before Christmas, with refreshments and music. There's also a holiday wreath workshop at the Monticello Visitors Center. The first few days after Christmas there are afternoon holiday concerts at Ash Lawn-Highland.

FIRST NIGHT VIRGINIA
Charlottesville   (804) 296-8269
This is a family-oriented New Year's celebration of the arts in the downtown area from 6 PM to midnight.

APPALACHIAN MOUNTAIN
CHRISTMAS
Wintergreen   (804) 325-2200
During Christmas week, the resort celebrates with horse-drawn carriage rides, ornament and Appalachian craft workshops, wandering minstrels, jugglers and clowns, and an old-fashioned carol sing. There is a candlelight Christmas buffet and a grand lighting ceremony.

FIRST NIGHT WAYNESBORO

TRADITIONS OF CHRISTMAS
Museum of American Frontier Culture
Staunton   (703) 332-7850
Throughout the month there are opportunities to tour the museum's living farms by lantern at

night, and to learn about how America's early settlers and their kin in the old country prepared for Christmas. There are also gift-making workshops for children.

CHRISTMAS AT THE MANSE
Staunton (703) 886-2351
At the Woodrow Wilson Birthplace.

HOLIDAY IN LEXINGTON WEEKEND CELEBRATION
Lexington (703) 463-3777

CHRISTMAS AT POINT OF HONOR
Lynchburg (804) 847-1459
This is a celebration of the joyous season as it would have been in the 1820s. Held at Point of Honor, a mansion built by Patrick Henry's doctor, George Cabell, you can revel in the color and aroma of festive greens and sing along with a local group performing 19th-century carols.

SCROOGE DAY
Lynchburg (804) 847-1499
Always the last Saturday before Christmas, this is the day to take care of last-minute shopping at the downtown Community Market. You'll find handmade gifts, stocking stuffers, home-baked treats, wreaths, greenery and trees.

ROANOKE CHRISTMAS PARADE
(703) 981-2889
Always the first Saturday in December

DICKENS OF A CHRISTMAS
Roanoke (703) 342-2028
Always the second Saturday in December, Roanoke's City Market is the place for carriage rides, chestnut-roasting, ice-carvings, hot cider and holiday music.

FIRST NIGHT ROANOKE
This is a non-alcoholic New Year's celebration in the downtown City Market area. There's ice-skating for kids, holiday music, hot cocoa and a "Resolution Wall" where you can write your New Year's resolutions for the world to see.

DECK THE HALLS OPEN HOUSE
Newbern (703) 674-5888
At the Wilderness Road Regional Museum.

CHRISTMAS CANDLELIGHT TOUR OF HOMES
Abingdon (703) 676-2282
In mid-December Abingdon's loveliest homes are open for tours. There are also holiday music parties, carolers and horse-drawn carriage rides.

CHRISTMAS AND FLOWER SHOW
Big Stone Gap (703) 523-1235
The show is held on the first weekend in December.

Inside
Arts and Culture

*W*hew! For a relatively sparsely populated region, the Blue Ridge of Virginia's opportunities for arts and cultural events are legion! Listing the best and brightest is a difficult task, since they're all backed by energetic people who believe strongly in the cause they promote.

The diversity of arts and culture is a pendulum of interesting events. Elvis Presley lives on in Roanoke, where he is honored by a private citizen at Miniature Graceland, while maple sugar is celebrated at its own museum in Highland County. Also in Highland, you can attend Bear Mountain Outdoor School and learn Blue Ridge country survival skills such as building a log cabin. In Alleghany County, there's one of the largest railroad archives in the U.S., through the C&O Railroad Historical Society.

If music is your leisure salvation, you can choose Friday night flat-footing at Cockram's General Store in Floyd County with fiddles, autoharps and a 1940 juke box that still works. Or, you can attend chamber music fests at Garth Newel in Bath County, where you may find yourself in an audience with Jackie Kennedy or other New York City residents who jet into the Homestead Resort for the mountain ambiance in the beautiful hills of Bath.

Historically speaking, the Charlottesville area is one of the country's best-known tourist cities with such attractions as Montpelier, Monticello and Ash Lawn-Highland, the former homes of three of our greatest presidents. Half a million visitors a year make the trek to the neo-classical mansion designed by the third president of the United States, Thomas Jefferson. Farther south, you can travel to Jefferson's summer getaway at Poplar Forest in Bedford County. In the hills of Pulaski County, you can stroll through an 1810 village in Old Newbern and see what life was like nearly two centuries ago.

History buffs shouldn't overlook an important source of information at our nation's libraries. In Lynchburg, Jones Memorial is one of the nation's foremost genealogical libraries and offers research and lending services by mail. Virginia Tech's Carol Newman Library has the fifth largest microforms collection in the U.S. and Canada.

Theatre opportunities range from movies to live performances. World chic Charlottesville, home to numerous movie stars and directors, annually hosts the biggest names in the movie business with its Virginia Festival of American Film. "The Reel South and Other Worlds" was last year's theme, and more than 20,000 people showed up for the event. Here's a chance to view film classics and hob-nob with celebrities who usually attend the closing bash.

If historical drama is more to your liking, you can attend Virginia's only outdoor drama, "The Long Way Home." This stirring true saga of Mary Draper Ingles' capture by the Indians and escape home through nearly 1,000 miles of wilderness to Radford, has been riveting audiences to their seats for 22 years now.

It seems that, no matter how small, nearly every community in the Blue Ridge has its own performing theatre group, some comprised of as few as a dozen people in, for example, sparsely populated Giles County. In small town Lexington, Lime Kiln Theatre enjoys a national reputation for its open-air plays and musical performances in a magical setting. Robin and Linda Williams, from public radio's "A Prairie Home Companion" with Garrison Keillor and Lake Wobegon, are regulars.

If you're a museum buff, the range and quality of museums here are beyond belief for an area the size of the Blue Ridge. The Mennonite-influenced work of world-famous artist P. Buckley Moss, "the people's artist,"whose annual revenues have been estimated at $11 million, can be seen in her private retreat and museum at Waynesboro.

There's probably not a small town in the U.S with as many military museums as Lexington, with its VMI Museum, George C. Marshall Museum, Stonewall Jackson House and Lee Chapel.

In the Roanoke Valley, an international tribute to the millions of lives touched by the volunteer rescue squad movement, "To the Rescue," honoring the father of the movement, Julian Stanley Wise, can be seen in the Roanoke Valley History Museum.

Some museums honor a way of life we tend to forget about, such as the Cyrus McCormick Museum in Rockbridge County. It is dedicated to the inventor of the first successful reaper, which revolutionized agriculture. Each county seat seems to have its own museum for recording local history. One, in Botetourt County, records the history of a county seat that once was an English land grant stretching the whole way to the Mississippi River!

Not to be underestimated for the role they play in the region's arts and culture are the wonderful, diverse programs underwritten by colleges and universities. Enough cannot be said about the influence of academic giants such as Virginia Tech in Blacksburg and the University of Virginia in Charlottesville. Yet, the largest colony of artists in residence in the country, the Virginia Center for the Creative Arts, affiliated with Sweet Briar College, is located in the remote foothills of the Blue Ridge in Amherst County. And then there's tiny Ferrum College in Franklin County, that has taken upon itself to become the nation's most important repository of Blue Ridge Culture through its Blue Ridge Farm Museum, Institute and Folk Life Festival.

Photo: Richmond Newspapers

A basketweaver demonstrates his skill at the Virginia Highlands Festival.

Education in the arts doesn't begin on the college level. Nearby, in culturally-rich Lynchburg, is the Virginia School of the Arts, one of the few select secondary schools in the nation tailored for the study of the arts.

The cultures of many ethnic groups are celebrated here. African-American poet Anne Spencer was a celebrity in her time in Lynchburg, constantly entertaining a steady flow of world dignitaries at her renovated home and grounds, open to the public by appointment. In her meticulous garden, she chatted with Martin Luther King, Paul Robeson and Marion Anderson, Thurgood Marshall, Dr. George Washington Carver and Jackie Robinson. Congressman Adam Clayton Powell even honeymooned there. In Roanoke, the Harrison Heritage Museum for African-American Culture exists to celebrate and remind western Virginia of the rich contributions of the Afro-American culture.

Enjoy selecting attractions from our list below of the best and the brightest. Since many attractions are rural and some under-staffed and underfunded, you may want to call ahead to be sure of hours. Admission prices, of course, also may change. Good luck if you're trying to see it all!

Shenandoah Valley Region

Winchester-Frederick County

Theater

SHENANDOAH SUMMER MUSIC THEATRE
Shenandoah University, 1460 University Drive
Winchester, VA 22601   (703) 665-4569

Student actors, singers and dancers perform four lively musicals every summer on Wednesday through Sunday nights at the university. The 1993 slate includes "A Chorus Line and "Lil' Abner." There are also afternoon matinees.

WAYSIDE THEATRE
P.O. Box 260,
Middletown, VA 22645   (703) 869-1776

The second oldest professional theater in the state brings the best of Broadway to the valley from May to December. The company's professional actors from New York and around the country perform comedies, dramas and mysteries in an intimate downtown theater. In 1993, "Lettuce and Lovage" is on stage from July 1 through 17; "I Hate Hamlet" from July 22 through Aug. 7, "The Diviners" from Aug. 12 through 28, "Arms and the Man" from Sept. 2 through 18 and Shakespeare's "Twelfth Night" from Set. 23 through Oct. 10. There will also be a Christmas performance in December. The theater is in the middle of the little town on Main Street, which you'll find by taking exit 302 from I-81.

Dance

MASSANUTTEN MOUNTAIN CLOGGERS
P.O. Box 423,
Harrisonburg, VA 22801   (703) 434-1251

This small clogging group performs at such posh places as the Homestead, the Greenbrier and the Commonwealth Club in Richmond, as well as at local craft shows. They're looking for new members and will give lessons on the traditional dance form.

PLAINS PROMENADERS SQUARE DANCE GROUP
Rt. 3, Box 316,
Luray, VA 22835   (703) 743-6792

This group of about 60 dancers meets every Tuesday night at the Plains Elementary School in Timberville for classes and workshops from September through

May. Some of the more advanced dancers also perform at special events around the area. The group's been around for 19 years. Nora and Leroy Plaugher are presidents this year.

Museums

ABRAM'S DELIGHT MUSEUM
1340 Pleasant Valley Road,
Winchester, VA 22601   (703) 662-6519

This is the oldest house in Winchester, built in 1754 of native limestone with walls 2 1/2 feet thick. There's also a restored log cabin on the lawn from the same period. Abram's Delight is beautifully restored and furnished with period pieces. It's open daily from 9 to 5 from April 1 through October. Admission is $3.50 for adults, $3 for seniors and $1.75 for children from ages 6 to 12. You can save by buying a block ticket for entrance to this museum and two other historic sites in town, Stonewall Jackson's Headquarters and George Washington's

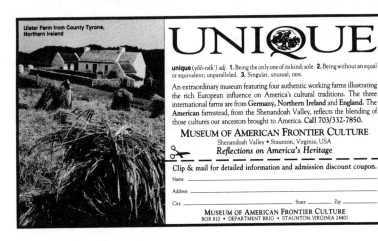

Ulster Farm from County Tyrone, Northern Ireland

UNIQUE

unique (yōō-nēk') adj. **1.** Being the only one of its kind; sole. **2.** Being without an equal or equivalent; unparalleled. **3.** Singular, unusual; rare.

An extraordinary museum featuring four authentic working farms illustrating the rich European influence on America's cultural traditions. The three international farms are from **Germany, Northern Ireland** and **England.** The **American** farmstead, from the Shenandoah Valley, reflects the blending of those cultures our ancestors brought to America. Call 703/332-7850.

MUSEUM OF AMERICAN FRONTIER CULTURE
Shenandoah Valley • Staunton, Virginia, USA
Reflections on America's Heritage

Clip & mail for detailed information and admission discount coupon.

Name _____

Address _____

City _____ State _____ Zip _____

MUSEUM OF AMERICAN FRONTIER CULTURE
BOX 810 • DEPARTMENT BRIG • STAUNTON, VIRGINIA 24401

Office Museum. Block tickets cost $7.50 for adults, $6.50 for seniors and $4 for children.

KURTZ CULTURAL CENTER
2 N. Cameron St.
Winchester   (703) 722-6367
Admission is free to this newest addition to Winchester's cultural life. The center is a short walk from the downtown pedestrian mall.

Downstairs in the building is a permanent interpretive exhibit called "Shenandoah–Crossroads of the Civil War." Numerous displays detail the Shenandoah Valley's major battles. Upstairs is an art gallery whose exhibits change regularly. The cultural center is open Monday through Saturday from 10 to 5 and on Sundays from 12 to 5.

WASHINGTON'S OFFICE MUSEUM
Braddock and Cork Streets,
Winchester   (703) 662-4412
Part of this old log and stone building was used by Washington when he was Colonel of the Virginia Regiment protecting the 300-miles frontier to the west. It's open daily from 9 to 5 from April 1 through October. Admission is $2 for adults, $1.50 for seniors and $1 for children from ages 6 to 12.

Other Cultural Attractions

BELLE GROVE PLANTATION
P.O. Box 137,
Middletown, VA 22645   (703) 869-2028
Belle Grove (circa 1794) is an 18th-century plantation, working farm and center for the study of traditional rural crafts. It was the home of Major Isaac Hite, Jr. and his family for more than 70 years. Hite was a grandson of one of the first permanent settlers in the Shenandoah Valley. Thomas Jefferson was actively involved in Belle Grove's design, thanks to some family connections. Hite married the sister of James Madison, who was a close friend of Jefferson. In fact, James and Dolley Madison spent part of their honeymoon visiting the Hites at Belle Grove.

Belle Grove hosts a variety of special activities throughout the year, from the Shenandoah Valley Farm Craft Days in early June to the Battle of Cedar Creek Living History Weekend in mid-October. There's also a very nice gift shop and quilt shop at the site.

The plantation is open to the public from mid-March through mid-November from 10 to 4 daily and on Sundays from 1 to 5. Admission is $3.50 for adults, $3 for seniors and $2 for children ages six through 12. Belle Grove is one mile south of Middletown on U.S. 11. Take exit 302 from I-81, then head west on Rt. 627 to U.S. 11.

STONEWALL JACKSON'S HEADQUARTERS
415 North Braddock St.,
Winchester, VA 22601   (703) 667-3242
Jackson used the private home of Lt. Col. Lewis T. Moore as his headquarters during the Civil War from 1861 to 1862. Jackson's office is much as it was during his stay, and the house contains artifacts of Jackson, Turner Ashby, Jed Hotchkiss and other Confederates. The house is open daily from 9 to 5 from April 1 through October. Ad-

mission is $3.50 for adults, $3 for seniors and $1.75 for children.

Shenandoah and Page Counties

Museums

BEDROOMS OF AMERICA MUSEUM
P.O. Box 977, 9386 Congress St.,
New Market, VA 22844   (703) 740-3512
This sounds like a sleeper of a museum, but actually it's a fascinating place if you like old furniture and want to learn more about American antiques. There are 11 different rooms of authentic furniture showing every period of America's bedrooms, from William & Mary (circa 1650) through Art Deco (circa 1930). The rooms are also furnished with period accessories, bed coverings, curtains and wall coverings. The museum is housed in a restored 18th-century building that was used for a time by Confederate General Jubal Early as his headquarters during the Civil War. It's open daily from 9 to 8 from Memorial Day to Labor Day and the rest of the year from 9 to 5. The museum is closed on Christmas Day. Admission is $2 for adults and $1.25 for children from ages 8 to 14.

STRASBURG MUSEUM
King Street   (703) 465-3175
This museum was originally a steam pottery (circa 1891) and is a registered historic landmark. Strasburg was once famous for its pottery, and its old nickname Pottown can still be seen around

town on various business signs. The museum displays blacksmith, copper and pottery shop collections and artifacts from Colonial farms, homes, barns and businesses. There are also Civil War and railroad relics. The museum is open daily from 10 to 4 from May through October. Admission is $2 for adults and 50 cents for children.

TUTTLE & SPICE GENERAL STORE MUSEUM
Four miles north of New Market at
Shenandoah Caverns exit   (703) 477-9428
The museum features nine shops set up to resemble a 19th-century country village. These include a tobacco store, doctor's house, haberdashery, millinery, apothecary shop and ice cream parlor. The items in the shops are museum pieces and not for sale, but there is a large gift shop. Admission is free, and the museum is open daily from 9 to 6.

WOODSTOCK MUSEUM
137 West Court St.   (703) 459-5518
This downtown museum features artifacts of country life in Shenandoah County, including tools, pottery, hardware, linens and handmade furniture. Admission is free.

Music

SHENANDOAH VALLEY MUSIC FESTIVAL
P.O. Box 12,
Woodstock, VA 22664   (703) 459-3396
This 31-year-old outdoor summer music festival features symphony pops, classical masterworks,

folk, jazz and big band music – all performed on the grounds of the grand, historic Orkney Springs Hotel. This was a popular spa and mineral springs resort at the turn of the century. Evening concerts are held on weekends from mid-July through Labor Day in a rustic open-air pavilion. Arts and crafts shows take place on the hotel's front lawn on the symphony concert weekends and feature handcrafts by artisans from the Shenandoah Valley and greater region. Another festival tradition is the old-fashioned ice cream social held next to the pavilion prior to each concert. Admission prices and concert times vary. For information and a free season brochure contact the Festival's Woodstock headquarters. By the way, the Orkney Springs Hotel serves country-style buffet dinners on all concert nights. Reservations are required and can be made by calling (703) 856-2141. Lots of guests also like to picnic on the grounds before the concerts.

Other Cultural Attractions

JOHN SEVIER GALLERY
Congress St. and Old Cross Rd,
New Market   (703) 740-3911
Set in a little log cabin in the heart of the downtown, this gallery specializes in watercolors and oil paintings by three local artists. It also sells locally made crafts such as woodwork, ornaments and stained glass windows, and fine photographs. One wall is set aside for an "Artist of the Month" display. The gallery is open seven days a week.

LURAY CAVERNS CAR AND CARRIAGE CARAVAN
U.S. 211 Bypass,
Luray, VA 22835   (703) 743-6551
Right next to Luray Caverns is a car buff's haven – rooms full of all kinds of automobiles from the vehicle's first 50 years of existence. The museum grew out of the car collecting hobby of Caverns president H.T.N. Graves. You'll see Rudolph Valentino's 1925 Rolls Royce, a Conestoga wagon, an ornate sleigh, an 1892 Benz, one of the oldest cars in the country, and much much more. All 140 items–cars, coaches, carriages and costumes–are fully restored. Admission is included in your ticket to Luray Caverns. The Caravan is open every day, beginning at 9 and closing 1 1/2 hours after the last cavern's tour.

Harrisonburg-Rockingham County

Visual Arts

DONOVAN'S FRAMERY
130 University Boulevard,
Harrisonburg   (703) 434-4440
This shop behind Valley Mall is the site of permanent exhibitions of the Rockingham County Fine Arts Association.

SAWHILL GALLERY
James Madison University   (703) 568-6407
This gallery exhibits five or six shows of fine art a year. It's open during the academic year on weekdays from 10:30 to 4:30 and weekends from 1:30 to 4:30. In the summer, it's open only on weekdays from noon to 4. There is no admis-

sion charge.

Museums

JAMES MADISON UNIVERSITY LIFE SCIENCE MUSEUM
Burruss Hall   *(703) 568-6378*

This museum displays Native American relics, sea shells, birds and butterflies from around the world. It's open during the academic year and the hours vary, depending upon the schedules of student volunteers.

REUEL B. PRITCHETT MUSEUM
Bridgewater Community College
         (804) 828-2501

A collection of rare artifacts here includes a three-volume Bible printed in Venice in 1482 and a medieval book of Gregorian Chants made and hand-copied by a monk. Admission is free, and the museum is open Tuesday through Thursday from 2 to 4 PM.

SHENANDOAH VALLEY HERITAGE MUSEUM
115 Bowman Rd.
Dayton, VA 22821   *(703) 879-2616*

This museum features a 12-foot electric relief map that depicts Stonewall Jackson's Valley Campaign of 1862. the map fills an entire wall and lets you see and hear by campaign battle by battle. The museum also displays many artifacts revealing different aspects of the Shenandoah Valley's history. It is open Monday through Saturday from May 1 through October from 9 to 4 and Sundays from 1 to 4. The rest of the year it is open only on weekends. Admission is $4 for adults

and $2 for children ages 6 through 12.

Theater

JAMES MADISON UNIVERSITY DINNER THEATER
Gibbons Hall   *(703) 568-6740*

Every summer the drama department puts on three plays seven nights a week. There's also a nice spread of food to enjoy while you're watching the light dramas.

LATIMER-SHAEFFER THEATRE
James Madison University   *(703) 568-6260*

This theater presents dance, live music, and plays throughout the academic year and in the summer.

Other Cultural Attractions

THE DANIEL HARRISON HOUSE (FORT HARRISON)
P.O. Box 366,
Dayton, VA 22821   *(703) 879-2280*

This historic stone house (circa 1749) just north of Dayton was a natural fort to which Daniel Harrison added a stockade and an underground passage to a nearby spring. Loopholes for firing rifles at Native Americans may have been set in the house's stone walls, giving rise to the name Fort Harrison. Guided tours of the house are available, and there is no admission charge.

The site also hosts community events, such as a Family Craft Weekend the second weekend in June and the Dayton Autumn Festival the first Saturday in October.

The Daniel Harrison House opens in late May and closes the last Sunday in October. It is open for special events from November to April. Hours are Saturdays and Sundays from 1 to 5 PM.

LINCOLN HOMESTEAD
Rt. 42, Harrisonburg

Abraham Lincoln's father, Thomas Lincoln, was born in Rockingham County and his ancestors were buried here in a little cemetery 7.5 miles north of Harrisonburg on Rt. 42. The house now standing at the old Lincoln homestead is privately owned, so please respect that when you visit the cemetery.

Staunton-Waynesboro-Augusta County

Visual Arts

THE FRAME GALLERY
21 N. Market St.   *(703) 885-2697*

This small gallery inside a downtown Staunton frame shop displays paintings, prints, sculpture, tapestries and artifacts. It's open weekdays from 9:30 to 5 and on Saturdays from 9:30 to 2.

SHENANDOAH VALLEY ART CENTER
600 W. Main St.
Waynesboro, VA 22980   *(703) 949-7662*

This nonprofit cultural center provides a forum for artists of all diversities to exhibit their works. Located in a beautiful, old downtown house, the center holds art exhibits, music and drama performances, workshops and classes for children and adults. It is an affiliate of the Virginia Museum of Fine Arts. You'll also find readings of prose

P Buckley Moss MUSEUM ® Waynesboro, Virginia

Exhibiting works by one of America's most popular artists...

Free Admission * Guided Tours * Museum Shop

Open daily, 10-6; Sunday 12:30-5-30
I-64, Exit 94/17. (703) 949-6473

and poetry and even music appreciation lectures here. The galleries are open Tuesday through Saturday from 10 to 4 PM and Sunday from 2 to 4 PM. Admission is free.

STAUNTON-AUGUSTA ART CENTER
I Gypsy Hill Park   (703) 885-2028

An old pump house at the entrance to the beautiful Gypsy Hill Park in Staunton is headquarters for this art center, an affiliate of the Virginia Museum. It puts on 10 exhibitions every year, some of which are shows on tour from the Virginia Museum. It also displays art work by area elementary and high school students every May and exhibits works of local artists. In addition, the art center offers classes and workshops for children and adults throughout the year. In May there's an Outdoor Art Show on the third Saturday. During the holidays, there's an Art for Gifts Exhibit and sale. It's open weekdays from 9 to 5 and on Saturdays from 10 to 2. Admission is free.

WHARF GALLERY
125 S. New St.   (703) 886-0271

This fabulous gallery in an old mill (atop Mill Street Grill) in Staunton displays paintings, prints, ceramics, jewelry and other crafts by local and regional artists. It's open Tuesdays through Saturdays from 11 to 7 and Sundays from 1 to 5. Admission is free.

Dance

SHENANDOAH CLOGGERS
Staunton Parks and Recreation Department
(703) 245-5727

This group of 26-odd dancers practices every Thursday night at Staunton's Gypsy Hill Park. They teach lessons to children and adults from 6 to 6:45, then practice until 9. The cloggers perform all over the place, from nursing homes and civic meeting halls to arts festivals and parades.

Museums

MUSEUM OF AMERICAN FRONTIER CULTURE
Exit 222 off I-81, then Rt. 250 West (follow signs), Staunton, VA   (703) 332-7850

Somehow museum doesn't seem an appropriate word for the living, breathing outdoor Museum of American Frontier Culture. Authentic farmsteads have been painstakingly brought from the Old World and reconstructed here. Original gardens, hedges, pastures and even road layouts have been duplicated, along with the old ways of survival. There are Scotch-Irish, 17th-century German, and early American farmsteads and an English farmstead is now under construction. The staff of knowledgeable, articulate interpreters is what makes a visit truly exciting. All kinds of critters make their home at the museum – from lambs and chickens to cows and kittens – and this helps make for a thrilling day for children. Dozens of special events take place throughout the year, such

Photo: Virginia Dept. of Tourism

Monticello, Thomas Jefferson's plantation home near Charlottesville, Virginia.

as Lantern Tours at Christmas and the Traditional Frontier Festival in mid September, with crafts, food and entertainment. This year, the museum was awarded the coveted "phoenix" from the National Writers Association. That tells you just how special this place is. The museum is open daily from 9 to 5 except Thanksgiving, Christmas and New Year's. Admission is $5 for adults, $2.50 for children, and $4.50 for seniors. Special rates for group of 15 or more are available.

P. BUCKLEY MOSS MUSEUM
2150 Rosser Avenue,
Waynesboro, VA 22980   (703) 949-6473

The museum dedicated to this former resident of Augusta County resembles many of the large, tall houses built by early 19th-century settlers. Since the early 1960s, Moss has found her inspiration and much of her subject matter in Shenandoah Valley scenery and in the Amish and Mennonite peoples of the area. Although the artist was born in New York, she moved here in the mid-60s when her husband got a job at DuPont. Hers is a moving story. Born with what later was diagnosed as dyslexia into a family of high achievers, Moss was ridiculed and taunted as a child for her lack of academic prowess. she hid her childhood sorrow in her artwork and eventually her family recognized her artistic genius. As a result, she now uses her foundation profits, guided by the world-wide Moss Society, to help needy children. Whenever she travels, she makes it a point to visit pediatric hospital centers to encourage chil-

dren. She and her first husband lived here for about 20 years. She married her English manager after her divorce. The museum's displays examine the symbolism in her work and her sources. Her mother works at the museum and Moss often visits when she's not traveling. The museum and shop are located just south of I-64 at the Waynesboro West exit. The hours are Monday through Saturday from 10 AM to 6 PM and Sunday from 12:30 PM to 5:30 PM. Admission is free.

WOODROW WILSON MUSEUM AND BIRTHPLACE
18-24 N. Coalter St.,
Staunton, 24401   (703) 885-0897

This museum is a tribute to our nation's 28th president, who was born right next door to a Presbyterian minister and his wife in 1856. The museum chronicles in detail Wilson's life as a scholar, Princeton University president, governor and statesman. Seven exhibit galleries include rare artifacts, photographs, personal possessions and a replica of Wilson's study at Princeton. The displays do not shy away from the controversies Wilson generated in his lifetime – from the way in which he alienated wealthy trustees and alumni as Princeton's president to his lack of support for women's suffrage as U.S. President. Of course, the displays also highlight the reforms Wilson brought about as the nation's leader.

The museum houses Wilson's beloved Pierce-Arrow automobile, which is brought out yearly in the Happy Birthday USA parade down Main Street and also travels to the

Pierce-Arrow Convention in California. His birthplace has been carefully restored to appear as it would have when he lived there as a child. Throughout the Greek Revival-style house are furniture, silver, and other personal items belonging to the Wilsons and period pieces typical of Presbyterian manses in the antebellum era. The museum and birthplace are open daily from 9 to 5 except Thanksgiving, New Year's and Christmas. Admission is $5 for adults, $4.50 for seniors and $1 for ages 6 to 12.

Music

JAZZ IN THE PARK

Free jazz concerts are held at the beautiful Gypsy Hill Park on Thursdays at 8 PM during the summer months.

MID-ATLANTIC CHAMBER ORCHESTRA

This Washington, D.C.-based orchestra of professional musicians performs three or four times a year in Staunton at the Robert E. Lee High School auditorium. For more information, call Bob Link at (703) 885-1232.

SHAKIN'

All kinds of bands – from rock 'n' roll to country – perform downtown at Mary Baldwin College every other Friday during the summer months from 5:30 to 7:30. This is another freebie!

STONEWALL BRIGADE BAND

This is reportedly the oldest continuously performing band, hav-

ing thrown its first concert before the Civil War. The local musicians perform every Monday at 8 PM at Gypsy Hill Park during the summer months. There's no admission charge.

Theater

FLETCHER COLLINS THEATRE
Deming Hall, Mary Baldwin College,
Staunton, VA 24401   (703) 887-7189

Every academic year, the theater department at this women's college produces five plays, from musicals such as Gilbert and Sullivan to Shakespeare and new, modern plays.

OAK GROVE PLAYERS
232 W. Frederick St.,
Staunton, VA 24401   (703) 885-6077

This amateur theater company produces five plays every summer in the middle of a grove of oak trees two miles west of Verona. Founded in 1954 by Fletcher Collins, the retired head of Mary Baldwin College's Theater Department, this is one of the oldest outdoor theaters in the country. Lots of patrons picnic on the grounds before the plays, which are mainly comedies. Admission is by season subscription only, although patrons are allowed to buy tickets for their guests from out of town. The Oak Grove Players were the first to perform "The Nerd," a play by the late Larry Shue, a native of Staunton.

SHENANARTS, INC.
Rt. 5, Box 167-F,
Staunton, VA 24401   (703) 248-1868

This is a not-for-profit performing arts company that produces all kinds of plays and musicals and hosts a retreat for playwrights every summer at the historic Pennyroyal Farm (circa 1808) north of Staunton. Performances take place at the Pennyroyal Farm in warm weather, and in the winter, at McCormick's Cabaret at Frederick and Augusta streets in downtown Staunton. The arts corporation also offers theater programs for youth – one of which led to a full-blown production of a rock opera, The Wall, in 1992. A touring company performs throughout Virginia and West Virginia. One of the traveling shows is a play about AIDS that's geared for teens, performed entirely by teenaged actors. The annual Shenandoah Valley Playwrights Retreat has been going on for 17 years and hosts writers from all over the world.

THEATER WAGON, INC.
437 E. Beverley St.,
Staunton, VA 24401   *No phone*
Through this grant-funded program, Fletcher and Margaret Collins encourage the development of new plays and translations of old ones. Fletcher Collins headed Mary Baldwin College's theater department for 32 years and founded the local Oak Grove Players. He and his wife critique new play scripts and occasionally produce them, using local talent, at their downtown historic home.

WAYNESBORO PLAYERS
P.O. Box 937, Waynesboro, VA 22980
Contact: Bill Robson at   (703) 885-4668
This is a nonprofit amateur theater group made up of actors from Waynesboro, Staunton and Augusta County. They perform three plays a year, in addition to some dinner theater offerings at Waynesboro-area restaurants. Most of the plays are performed at the Waynesboro High School auditorium.

Other Cultural Attractions

STATLER BROTHERS COMPLEX
501 Thornrose Ave.,
Staunton, VA 24401   (703) 885-7237
The Statler Brothers, the world-famous down-home country singers, make their home in Staunton and have their own museum and office complex in town. Their annual July 4th concert brings 100,000 people into town and rooms are reserved a year in advance. The last concert is set for 1994, so if you want to catch this famous event, next year's will be the last. Tours are free and are given only at 2 PM on weekdays. You can see all kinds of Statler Brothers' memorabilia collected over the past 25 years that they've been playing. A gift shop sells their albums, cassettes, compact discs, t-shirts, sweaters and other souvenirs. A tip from those in the know....if you really want to see the Statler Brothers in the flesh, hang out until after the museum closes. That unusual tour time does serve a purpose.

SWANNOANOA
University of Science & Philosophy,
Waynesboro, VA 22980   (703) 942-5161
A mountain-top marble palace and sculpture gardens is head-

quarters of a new-age school of transcendental thinking, founded by Walter and Lao Russell. The palace and gardens are open to the public year round from 9 to 5 daily. Admission is $3 for adults and $1 for children. The University also offers a range of workshops and seminars on such topics as the science of centering and ways to develop your own unique "Light Center."

Lexington

Visual Arts

ART FARM GALLERIES
Rt. 39 (near the Virginia Horse Center)
(804) 463-7961
Chinese artist and teacher Sing Ju started the Art Farm in 1975 as a "farm to raise young artists." A retired professor of art at the local Washington and Lee University, Dr. Ju conducts summer workshops in the traditional Chinese method of painting. Students come from all over the country to live for a week at the farm and learn from Dr. Ju. The gallery is on the first floor of a rambling house and displays the artist's paintings. Many are reasonably priced; all are astonishingly beautiful.

ARTISTS IN CAHOOTS
1 Washington St. *(703) 464-1147*
A cooperative gallery for local artists and craftspeople, Artists in Cahoots offers local arts and crafts and has ongoing demonstrations. Browsing is encouraged and artists are happy to take you for a tour. You'll find metalwork, jewelry, hand-

blown glass, photography, sculpture, pottery and paintings here.

HARB'S BISTRO
19 W. Washington St. *(703) 464-1900*
Harb's Bistro is a sophisticated cafe whose walls are adorned with paintings by artists from up and down the East Coast. The exhibits change every month or so. Gallery operator and painter Agnes Carbrey moved to Lexington a few years ago from New York City, and many of the shows are of New York-based artists. Carbrey also showcases the work of noteworthy artists from the local area, of which there are quite a few. Gallery openings are a great way to meet Lexingtonians, enjoy fine hors d'oeuvres, and pay tribute to the artist(s). Of course, it's also a great place to have lunch or dinner.

Museums

GEORGE C. MARSHALL MUSEUM AND LIBRARY
VMI Parade Grounds *(703) 463-7103*
The Marshall Foundation was founded in 1953 at the suggestion of President Harry Truman to honor the memory of Gen. George C. Marshall, the only military hero to win a Nobel Peace Prize, for his plan to reconstruct Europe following World War II. None other than Winston Churchill himself said that, "Succeeding generations must not be allowed to forget his achievements and his example." Marshall also was former Army chief of staff and secretary of state and defense. Presidents Johnson and

Eisenhower dedicated the museum in 1964. Visitors can see a stirring movie of Marshall and a striking photographic display. The stark, black and white photos of the faces of children of war-torn Europe will haunt you and remind you of why Marshall should be remembered forever for his humanitarian efforts that gave the US. the reputation of an upstanding, moral nation with a gigantic heart. Open daily from 9 AM to 5 PM.

LEE CHAPEL AND MUSEUM
Washington & Lee University, Main St.
(703) 463-8400

Civil War buffs won't want to miss the beautiful Lee Chapel and Museum, the focal point of the campus where the great Confederate served as president for five years after the war. It contains the remains of Lee and the famous pose of the recumbent Lee, sculpted by Edward Valentine. Open Daily 9 AM to 5 PM, Sunday 2 to 5 PM.

STONEWALL JACKSON HOUSE
8 East Washington Ave.   (703) 463-2552

Stonewall Jackson House is the only home that the famous Confederate general ever owned. Restored in 1979 by the Historic Lexington Foundation, the house is furnished with period pieces, including many of Jackson's personal possessions. The house, which is listed on the National Register of Historic Sites, is open to the public daily for guided tours of the period rooms. In addition to tours and exhibits, the Stonewall Jackson House sponsors a variety of educational programs through the Gar-

land Gray Research Center and Library located on the office level of the museum. Educational activities include in-school programs, internships, lectures, workshops and scholarly symposia.

Open daily Monday through Saturday from 9 AM to 5 PM, Sunday from 1 to 5 PM, until 6 PM in June, July & August. Closed on major holidays. Adults \$4, ages 6-12, \$2.

VMI MUSEUM
VMI Parade Ground, N. Main St.
(703) 464-7232

The VMI Museum, on the lower level of Jackson Hall on the VMI Campus, brings to life our nation's history. Stonewall Jackson's horse, Little Sorrel, a wonder of state-of-the art taxidermy, probably is its most curious and popular display. Other displays and exhibits tell American history through the lives and service of VMI faculty. Both Gen. Stonewall Jackson and Gen. Robert E. Lee taught at VMI.

Open daily Monday through Saturday from 9 AM to 5 PM, Sunday 2 to 5 PM. Closed holidays.

Music

LENFEST CENTER FOR THE PERFORMING ARTS
Washington & Lee University (703) 463-8000

W&L's Lenfest Center is the cultural heart of Lexington, offering lively arts from national concert performers as well as W&L's own University-Rockbridge Symphony Orchestra and other music department concerts. The center offers a Concert Guild Series, Theatre Series, and Lenfest Series featuring performances to appeal to all artistic tastes.

ROCKBRIDGE CONCERT-THEATRE SERIES
(703) 463-9232

For 46 years, the Rockbridge Concert-Theatre Series has continued to bring outstanding performers to the Rockbridge area community for both the public and local schools. Selections may include ballet, classical dance and popular ensembles.

Theater

LIME KILN THEATRE
Lime Kiln Rd. Box Office at 14 S. Randolph St. P.O. Box 663, Lexington, VA 24450
(703) 463-3074

Performances at the outdoor Lime Kiln Theatre celebrate the history and culture of the Southern mountains. What makes the place unique and even enchanting is its setting in what was once a limestone quarry. Lime Kiln is best known for its annual musical, "Stonewall Country," a rollicking tribute to local Civil War hero Stonewall Jackson. Robin and Linda Williams, favorites of Garrison Keillor's "A Prairie Home Companion," sometimes star in the performances. And if you've never heard the two sing together, you have not lived. Also to be performed this summer is "Apple Dreams," a play by a local drama professor, Tom Ziegler, that is on its way to Broadway. A new play workshop about an Appalachian version of the Oedipus myth will also be offered.

Lime Kiln's popular Sunday night concert series always offers an eclectic slate of musicians. This summer's schedule includes Alison Krauss, a Grammy Award-winning bluegrass musician, the Johnson Mountain Boys, a Zydeco band and a group of musicians from Haiti.

Lime Kiln has some beautiful picnic areas with tables and grills and sells some food and drinks.

It will begain sponsoring an annual play writing contest this year to encourage the creation of plays that are relevant to this region and that can be performed at Lime Kiln. Performances begin at 8 PM nightly on scheduled dates and are held rain or shine. There's a big tent with plenty of seating in bad weather. Call ahead for information.

Other Cultural Attractions

HISTORIC GARDEN WEEK
April date changes yearly
(703) 463-3777

History and garden aficionados flock to Lexington in the spring for its incomparable Historic Garden Week. Each year, civic-minded residents open their historic homes and gardens to an appreciative public. Many are furnished with family heirlooms, gorgeous antiques and ornate gardens. We highly recommend it!

HOLIDAY IN LEXINGTON
December date changes yearly
(703) 463-3777

For one weekend in December, this 19th-century college town welcomes you to its historic downtown district with mini-lights and white candles. Events include tours of historic properties and homes, music, galas, theatre and overall festivity. If you like Christmas in Williamsburg in eastern Virginia, try it western Virginia style.

HULL'S DRIVE-IN THEATRE
RFD 5   *(703) 463-2621*

One of the last auto drive-in theatres left in Virginia, Hull's is worth a visit for nostalgia. From the well-groomed grounds to the syrupy snowballs, Hull's Drive-In is one of the premier mom-and-pop operations anywhere. Nothing's changed since 1950. Open weekends at dusk mid-March through November.

McCORMICK FARM
Steeles Tavern   *(703) 377-2255*

This is the home of world celebrity Cyrus McCormick, who invented the first successful mechanical reaper. A few miles north of Lexington, McCormick Farm is part of the Virginia Tech College of Agricultural and Life Sciences and a Virginia Agricultural Experiment Station. Visitors may tour the blacksmith shop, gristmill, museum and McCormick family home.

McCormick was 22 when he invented the reaper in 1831. The invention launched a new era in agriculture, an age of mechanization that not only changed life on the farm, but also made it possible for millions of people to leave the land and enter an industrial society.

The entire family will enjoy visiting MCormick Farm and learning about an invention that revolu-

tionized the world. Open daily 8:30 AM to 5 PM.

MOCK CONVENTION
Washington & Lee University (703) 463-8460

This is an event worth waiting for every four years! It's a tremendous party and long, incredible parade straight from the '50s. Students try to outdo each other with outlandish floats. 1992's included one of Elvis, with live donkeys in tow! It should be a mandatory event for all civics students. Held only during presidential elections, W&L's nationally known mock convention in spring attracts national politicians and celebrities. It is written up internationally as "the nation's foremost and most accurate predictor in presidential politics." The convention has earned this respect by correctly predicting the presidential nominee 14 times in 19 attempts since its inception in 1908. It has been wrong only once since 1948, when it predicted Edward Kennedy would receive the Democratic nomination in 1972. And once again, the students were right in 1992 with the selection of Bill Clinton. New York Gov. Mario Cuomo and former Speaker of the House Tip O'Neill were among the illustrious, inspiring speakers of the 1992 convention.

Botetourt County

Museums

BOTETOURT MUSEUM
Court House Complex,
Fincastle, VA 24090   *(703) 992-8223*

Botetourt County (pronounced Bot-uh-tot), named in 1770 for Lord Botetourt of England, stretched the whole way to the Mississippi River, encompassing what is now parts of West Virginia, Kentucky, Ohio, Indiana and Illinois. Fincastle was the historic county seat. Thousands of people come to this historic town and its museum to look up and find fascinating historical information. The museum is sponsored by the Botetourt County Historical Society, an active group proud of the county's heritage. Programs, especially those dealing with genealogy, are open to the public. The museum plays an important role in Historical Fincastle's Old Fincastle Festival each fall, one of the largest festivals in the Roanoke Valley. Open 2 to 4 PM on Sundays and upon request.

Craig County

Museums

CRAIG COUNTY MUSEUM
Main & Court Streets,
New Castle, VA 24127   (703) 864-5296
Dedicated Craig County residents are lovingly restoring this old circa 1910, three-story brick hotel as a repository for Craig County's past. They've already restored a bedroom just as the old hotel used to be and have a genealogy library for those tracing their roots in this rural, scenic town. Operated by the Craig County Historical Society, which also sponsors the Craig County Fall Festival in October, (the county's largest), the museum's potential as a first-class attraction is

just beginning to be fulfilled. Open Monday through Wednesday, 1 to 4 PM.

Roanoke

Visual Arts

THE ARTS COUNCIL OF THE ROANOKE VALLEY
Center in the Square, Center on Church, Level 1
20 East Church Ave.   (703) 342-5790
The heart and soul of Roanoke's art community, this dedicated council brings exciting cultural and educational events to the region. It showcases local artists in an annual juried art exhibition and lets artists know about opportunities. Its major task the past two years has been "Blueprint 2000," outlining the direction of art in the future. This group of dedicated volunteers keeps the Roanoke arts scene lively and informed. Every year, it also presents the Perry Kendig Award for outstanding support of the arts. Open 9 AM to 5 PM, Monday through Friday.

ART MUSEUM OF WESTERN VIRGINIA
Center in the Square, Levels 1 & 2
One Market Square   (703) 342-5760
The Art Museum of Western Virginia is a gathering place for the large colony of Valley artists who migrate here both for the beauty and for the artistic opportunities. Permanent galleries emphasize American Art of the 19th and 20th centuries. There are impressive collections of sculpture in the Sculpture Court. The Folk Art Gallery features works by artisans of the

southern mountains. Museum education programs feature dialogues, family days, tours, films, performances, classes and workshops. Its rotating exhibitions are of regional, national and international significance. There's also a store which is stocked with regional American crafts and folk art. Open 10 AM until 5 PM, Tuesday through Saturday, 1 to 5 PM on Sunday.

VICTOR HUGGINS GALLERY
125 East Campbell Ave.   (703) 345-1462

If you want to enjoy art that exemplifies the mountain beauty of the Blue Ridge, go to this famous artist's new gallery. You won't be able to leave empty-handed. His blue and green banded mountains grace the Shenandoah Valley Travel Association's Travel Guide classic cover. Huggins' work is in every important public and private collection in the Blue Ridge. The works of Joni Pienkowski, Maryann Harman, Jim Yeatts and many of the area's noted artists also have been exhibited. This gallery serves as an educational and cultural asset to the Roanoke Valley through participation in "Art by Night," special gallery talks and hosting tour groups and field trips. Exhibits rotate about every six weeks.

Museums

HARRISON MUSEUM OF AFRICAN-AMERICAN CULTURE
523 Harrison Ave. NW   (703) 345-4818

A Roanoke Valley showcase for the region's African-American culture, the Harrison Museum of African-American Culture is on the National Historic Record Register as the first public high school for blacks in western Virginia. The museum's mission is "To research, preserve and interpret the achievements of African-Americans, specifically in western Virginia, and to provide an opportunity for all citizens to come together in appreciation, enjoyment and greater knowledge of African-American culture." The museum accomplishes its mission with aplomb!

Its most popular undertaking is the proud Henry Street Heritage Festival in Autumn, a celebration of the Henry Street area that used to rock weekends in the days of integration with the leading black jazz singers of the time. The museum takes an active role in the restoration of the historic Henry Street area. It also plans Black History Month Events and sponsors a Kwanzaa Celebration.

Since its opening in 1985, the museum's visitors have included young and old, black and white and other ethnic groups, as well as rural and urban. Colorful and sobering exhibits can be viewed in The Jayne Thomas Auditorium and The Hazel B. Thompson Exhibit Room. The museum's volunteers are its backbone and, along with its enthusiastic staff, the Harrison Museum has established itself as a center of information, entertainment, joy and understanding. Open 10 AM to 5 PM Monday through Friday and on weekends during special events, or by appointment.

ROANOKE VALLEY HISTORICAL SOCIETY AND MUSEUM CENTER IN THE SQUARE, LEVEL 1 AND 3

One Market Square   *(703) 342-5770*

The rich heritage of Roanoke unfolds before you in the galleries of the Roanoke Valley Historical Society and Museum, run by a dedicated group of preservationists. Prehistoric artifacts acquaint you with life in the Valley before Colonial settlement, through the Frontier Days into the boom days of the NW Railroad, and on into the present. There's a charming recreation of an 1890 country store, intriguing fashions from the 1700s to the 1990s, archives and a library. Its changing exhibits are both resourceful and sensitive and relevant to the Roanoke Valley.

A blockbuster exhibit is planned for Elvis Presley's birthday in January, 1994. For the first time ever, the private Elvis collection of Roanoker Kim Epperly, inventor and nurturer of "Miniature Graceland," will be displayed here, a curator's dream. Buy your Gala tickets early!

The museum membership conducts tours of historic sites offered to the public. Its shop, "Past Presents," on the first floor, offers handmade quilts, historical maps, genealogical charts and archival supplies. You can also buy the dogwood pattern china used at Hotel Roanoke. In addition, it's home to the permanent national "To the Rescue" exhibition described below.

Open 10 AM until 4 PM Tuesday through Friday, 10 AM to 5 PM Saturday, and 1 to 5 PM Sunday. Adults are $1, ages 6-12 & mature adults are $1.

SCIENCE MUSEUM OF WESTERN VIRGINIA AND HOPKINS PLANETARIUM

Center in the Square, Levels 1, 4 and 5
One Market Square   *(703) 342-5710*

The Science Museum teaches the wonders of science through hands-on experiences. Its enthusiastic volunteers play a special role in making the museum a really fun experience for both parents and children. You can broadcast a weather report and see yourself on TV, enjoy the touch tanks and Tot and Parent Learning Center and see the stars in the Hopkins Planetarium. You'll explore the reaches of the universe and then come back down to earth to enjoy lectures, concerts and movies. Children also like the first floor Science Museum Shop with real educational toy bargains that are so much fun, kids don't have a clue that they're learning while they play. Where else can you get a bag of seven model plastic dinosaurs for $3.50!

Exhibits change frequently, ranging from roaring mechanical dinosaurs and real sharks to animated life-size animals of the future. Special attention is taken to provide exhibits teaching care of the environment, such as the Wetlands. The first-class planetarium has been filled with everything from dancing laser shows to imaginative narratives on the creation of earth and the stars. It's a great way to spend an entire afternoon in Roanoke.

Open 10 AM to 5 PM Monday through Saturday, Sunday 1 to 5 PM. Planetarium shows are Friday and Saturday from 6:30 to 9:30 PM. Admission is $4 for adults and $2.50 for ages 5-12.

ST. ANDREWS CATHOLIC CHURCH MUSEUM

624 N. Jefferson St.   (703) 362-2245

A major Roanoke landmark, the stunning St. Andrews Catholic Church will be 100 years old in 1993 and is celebrating by opening its Parish Center as a three-room museum. The museum is operated by the Catholic Historical Society of the Roanoke Valley. The stunning Gothic style cathedral looms above and beyond the commercial landscape downtown as a daily reminder of serene spirituality.

Open 9 AM to 5 PM Tuesdays, or by appointment.

FIFTH AVENUE PRESBYTERIAN CHURCH WINDOW

301 Patton Ave. NW

(703) 342-0264

After the Civil War, in 1903, the pastor of an African-American church, Fifth Avenue Presbyterian, commissioned a stained galss window in his church to honor Confederate Gen. Stonewall Jackson. The Rev. Lylburn Downing had been a member of the Sunday School class Jackson had established for slaves at his own church in Lexington. Although the church burned down during the 1920's, it was rebuilt and the unusual window was spared and today is a symbol of racial harmony.

Open 10 AM to 11 AM Tuesday and Thursdays.

TO THE RESCUE NATIONAL EXHIBITION

Roanoke Valley Historical Society and Museum Center in the Square, Level 3
One Market Square   (703) 344-5154

"To the Rescue," the only permanent national exhibition dedicated to volunteer lifesaving, brings an international spotlight to Roanoke as the birthplace of the rescue squad movement. As a nine-year-old Roanoker, Julian Stanley Wise never forgot standing helplessly by as two men drowned when their canoe capsized on the Roanoke River. He vowed then that he would organize a group of volunteers who could be trained in lifesaving. He did. In 1927, he and his crew of NW Railway workers became the first volunteer rescue squad in America to use both medical techniques and transport on victims. Later, they were the first to use iron lungs during the polio epidemics that struck the country. They pioneered the Holger method of lifesaving and modern day CPR.

The creation of the exhibit, which includes breath-taking hands-on interactive videos and displays, was overseen by the famous museum expert Conover Hunt, a Virginia native whose last project was The Sixth Floor, the JFK Museum in Dallas. The quality and brilliance shows. The exhibit includes artifacts from 31 states and three countries. "To the Rescue" also houses the National Rescue Hall of Fame, which will recognize Emergency Medical Services heroes during National EMS Week the second May of each year. This exhibit has the potential to make Roanoke the inter-

Center in the Square in Roanoke.

national center of EMS activities, and efforts to do so are underway.

See History Museum, above, for same hours and admission.

VIRGINIA'S EXPLORE PARK
Headquarters, 101 S. Jefferson Street
(703) 345-1295

Virginia's Explore Park, a unique recreational and educational experience, is being built in eastern Roanoke County, near Vinton. It is expected to be open to the public in 1996, after the National Park Service completes a road to the area. Nevertheless, many events are being held there now including astronomy field trips, bird watching, Sierra Club hikes and Scout projects. The restored Hofauger Farmhouse, the focus of the park, is complete and available for use with advance reservations.

Explore's three main parts include a frontier settlement, a North American wilderness zoological park and an environmental education center. The park will be completed in various phases, with a major emphasis on environmental preservation. Call headquarters for a list of upcoming seasonal events. The beauty of the meadows and riverway the project is preserving is worth a visit in itself.

VIRGINIA MUSEUM OF TRANSPORTATION
303 Norfolk Ave.   *(703) 342-5670*

Roanoke proudly displays its railroad heritage with the Virginia Museum of Transportation, located in a restored freight station next to the NS mainline. It chronicles the formation of transportation over the lives of generations. Here, you can come face to face with steam engines, vintage electronic locomotives and classic diesels. You can climb on board a caboose and stroll through a railway post office car.

Inside, you can walk down Main Street to see early autos, freight trucks, fire engines and carriages. You'll see the way passenger cars looked at their peak in the 40s, before the automobile took over as king of the highways. Everywhere, from posters and photographic displays, there's nostalgia and a yearning for a time when life rolled along more smoothly on tracks to an unquestioned destination. There's also a fabulous carved wooden miniature circus with thousands of figurines to appreciate and the largest collection of museum rolling stock on the entire East Coast. The Gift Shop offers unique prints, books and toys for railway buffs.

Open daily 10 AM to 5 PM Monday through Saturday, Noon to 5 PM Sunday. Adults are $4, students are $2 and children 3-12 are $1.75.

Music

OPERA ROANOKE
111 W. Campbell Ave.   *(703) 982-ARIA*

Opera Roanoke produces operas of consistently high quality. The company engages up-and-coming professional singers in innovative new productions. Artistic Director Victoria Bond, who also serves as the Music Director of the Roanoke Symphony, enjoys a national reputation. The Opera offers season subscriptions with performances both in Roanoke and Salem. Perennial favorites such as Bizet's "Carmen," Verdi's "Aida," and Lehar's "The Merry Widow" are showcased with top talent, who convincingly portray passion, emotion, laughter and the beauty and tragedy of life. Sondheim's "Sweeney Todd" will make an area premier in September. Mozart's "Marriage of Figaro" will be presented in May, 1994. Standing ovations are the norm.

Opera Roanoke takes the extra step, with English translation subtitles projected over the stage, to ensure opera-goers can follow every twist and turn of the plot. Operatifs, on the order of intermissions features at the Met, are enlightening lectures for each opera hosted by Bond at the historic Radisson Patrick Henry Hotel. Opera Roanoke is the icing on the cake of Roanoke Valley culture!

The Roanoke Symphony Orchestra

111 W. Campbell Ave.   (703) 343-9127

The Roanoke Symphony Orchestra continues to receive national fame for two reasons; first, for its successful outreach into the community in clever ways, and second, for the success of its director, the diminutive but mighty media darling Victoria Bond. You'll find Bond and her symphony everywhere that they can bring the joys of fine music to the people. She and her symphony may be recording with THE Ray Charles (Uh Huh!) who flew his entire entourage to Roanoke in 1992, or cavorting with country star

Chet Atkins' magical flattop on stage at the summer series, "Picnic With the Pops."

The Symphony was responsible for bringing competitive polo to the Valley through sponsorship of the Roanoke Symphony Polo Cup, where you can "Ponder the Ponies and Promote the Notes" each fall. There's a never-ending round of school performances, get-togethers and fun events in the name of the symphony. It goes without saying that the Roanoke Symphony Orchestra is the most popular and involved grassroots cultural organization in the entire Roanoke Valley. Having one of the wealthiest women in America as a major benefactor enabled them to achieve this lofty status. Even with her unfortunate death last year, the Symphony's popularity should ensure that its quality doesn't miss a beat in the years ahead.

Theater

Grandin Movie Theatre

1310 Grandin Rd.   (703) 345-6177
Daily Performances in multi-theatres

Yes, you CAN see a movie in a gorgeous movie theatre like the ones that the wrecking balls have destroyed throughout America, thanks to Julie Hunsaker and the Lindsey family. Comedian Bill Murray of Saturday Night Live and Ghostbusters fame did a benefit for it recently, remarking that places like the Grandin should never be forgotten or destroyed. Classics and modern movies can be seen for the best prices in town, often with 99 cent specials. This cavernous, popcorn-scented architectural masterpiece will thrill everyone, especially children who have never seen anything quite like the tiled floors, mahogany candy cases and ornate decor of the Grandin. This is one of Roanoke's greatest cultural treasures.

MILL MOUNTAIN THEATRE & THEATRE B

Center in the Square, Level I
Box Office   *(703) 342-5740*

Admission charges vary with each play, time and date of performance.

A Roanoke institution, having been both burned down, (when located on Mill Mountain), and flooded out, (during the Flood of '85), Mill Mountain Theatre has been a Roanoke institution for 30 years, attracting cutting-edge visiting artists and scholars for the cultural enrichment of western Virginia.

Offered is the Main Stage, with productions featuring world premieres such as "All I Really Need To Know I Learned in Kindergarten," adapted by Robert Fulghum; Norfolk Southern's Festival of New Works in the exciting Alternative Theatre B; Centerpieces lunch readings; and children's musicals. The theatre offers a new play competition, drama enrichment programs, youth ensemble, guest speakers and jurors. Mill Mountain Theatre's dynamic presence in the Roanoke Valley makes it a cut above any theatre group in the Blue Ridge and makes a visit to the Star City well worthwhile and guaranteed enjoyable.

Other Cultural Attractions

CENTER IN THE SQUARE

One Market Square   *(703) 342-5700*

Resident organizations' hours vary. See above.

In all the U.S., only Roanoke has Center in the Square, visited by

OPERA ROANOKE

Victoria Bond, Artistic Director

1993 • 1994 Season

Sweeney Todd   *The Marriage of Figaro*

Write or call for information:
P.O. Box 1014 • Roanoke, VA 24005
703-982-ARIA

nearly 400,000 annually, making it the best-attended cultural center in western Virginia – more, even, than Richmond's Valentine Museum. Five resident organizations coexist in a restored 1914 warehouse that is the anchor of Roanoke's historic city market. A dramatic sculptural spiral staircase symbolizes how these five organizations have come together to create a richer cultural life in western Virginia. A confetti-like sculpture, a gift by the famed Dorothy Gillespie, hangs on the wall. In the heart of shops, galleries and restaurants, Center in the Square is the binding cultural tie in the life of a growing, vibrant downtown and a "must see" while in Roanoke. The shopping in its three member stores is also terrific, with some real bargains in science, art and history.

MILL MOUNTAIN ZOO

PO Box 1384   (703) 343-3241
Open April - Sept. 10 AM - 6 PM Daily
Adults $3.50 Ages 3 & Up, $2

Mill Mountain Zoo, located off the Blue Ridge Parkway on Mill Mountain, is a 10-acre zoo operated by the Blue Ridge Zoological Society, whose dedication is legend. Its main attraction is Ruby the Tiger, who received national attention after she was confiscated from her owner and adopted by the zoo, which had only a small cage to house her in. Now, thanks to the pennies of school children and a few major donations, Ruby grandly roams her new tiger habitat, looking for all the world like she can't believe how much her world has expanded. Having her there has certainly expanded Roanoke's.

Although this zoo serves a noble purpose of nurturing endangered species, small children best love the ordinary, such as the pygmy goats and the frisky prairie dogs who pop in and out of their holes like a large calliope. A Zoo Choo-Choo train operates on weekends, and is a real thrill for the tiny tots. Picnic facilities, Roanoke's famous gigantic metal star, and a breathtaking overlook view of Roanoke are also on Mill Mountain. It makes for a very pleasant afternoon.

MINIATURE GRACELAND

605 Riverland Drive   (703) 342-6025
Visitors welcome anytime

The King lives! You'll find him in miniature in this Southeast Roanoke neighborhood, complete with an adoring audience of Barbie dolls seated in a miniature auditorium as he revolves on stage, under the light of the Mill Mountain star. This private collection of Kim Epperly and her husband, Don, has been visited by people from 14 countries and featured in foreign tabloids.

Epperly, editor of the international "The Wonder of You" newsletter, dedicated to the late Elvis Presley, is the heart and soul behind keeping the memory of the entertainer alive. Epperly's husband has handcrafted replicas of the entire estate and placed it in their side yard. It is lit nightly and fans are invited to stroll through the grounds and hear an Elvis song wafting over the loudspeaker. She selects a different musical tribute each night.

Inside the basement of her home, Epperly maintains her own

personal museum of Elvis artifacts, including "Love Me Tender" shampoo and conditioner, full-size mannequins sculpted with auto body compound to look like Elvis' features, and newspaper clips of when The King first visited Roanoke. Each year, the Epperlys add something new to the yard. Don Epperly does most of the building from scrap wood, based on pictures or descriptions from his wife. Right now, they're finishing up his airport and a privacy fence. Some very big news for the city is that the Epperlys have consented to show their private collection at an opening on Jan. 10, The King's birthday, at the Roanoke Valley History Museum. It's guaranteed to be a blockbuster! There are two things you can't doubt – the popularity of Elvis and the sincerity of the tribute the Epperlys provide.

THE ROANOKE VALLEY HORSE SHOW

Junior League of Roanoke Valley
(703) 774-3242

Rated "A" by The American Horse Show Association, for 21 years this show has been a national standout in horse-lovers' country. Sponsored by the Junior League of Roanoke Valley and Roanoke Valley Horsemen's Association, it is held in June and attracts more than 1,000 entries nationwide for a purse of over $250,000 and grand prix of $100,000. It's the only indoor, air-conditioned show in Virginia and continues to be one of the top multi-breed shows in the U.S. This is a truly special community effort which, over the years, has plowed $1 million back into community projects.

East of the Blue Ridge Region

Washington and Sperryville

Visual Arts

MIDDLE ST. GALLERY

Corner of Gay and Middle streets,
Washington, VA 22747   (703) 675-3440

This is a nonprofit artists' cooperative featuring museum quality painting, photography and sculpture. Exhibitions change monthly, and classes are offered for adults and children. It's open from Friday through Sunday from 11 to 6 and by appointment.

SOUTHERN DRAWL ARTWORKS

Main St., P.O. Box 271,
Sperryville, VA 22740   (703) 987-9333

This fine arts gallery features original works and limited edition prints on wildlife, nature, Civil War and aviation. Both regional and local artists are represented. "No bad white wine, stale cheese, or pretentious conversation," reads its brochure. "Just fine art and good manners." The gallery is open Saturdays from 10 to 5:30 and Sundays from noon to 5:30 and by appointment.

Music and Theater

THE THEATRE AT WASHINGTON
Gay and Jett Streets, P.O. Box 322,
Washington, VA 22747   (703) 675-1253

This is the site of cultural activities ranging from high quality films to plays and performances by gospel choirs, chamber music ensembles, folk rockers and other musical groups.

THE OLD TOWN HALL
Gay St., P.O. Box 203,
Washington, VA 22747   (703) 675-1616

This is actually a performing arts center that serves as home to the Ki Theatre, a multi-media performance troupe made up of leaders in the fields of theatre, dance, music, storytelling and the visual arts. The artists create and perform original theatrical productions based on stories, and perform locally and tour across the country.

Formerly an old Methodist church, the building is also where virtually the entire community gathers the first weekend in December to see Christmas nativity plays. The "Shepherd's Play" and "Three Kings" are 14th-century Christian dramas that are performed by more than 30 members of the Washington community.

This will be the second year Ki Theatre (pronounced "Kee") has co-sponsored "Crossroads: Soul and Soil–the Arts and the Land," a Columbus Day weekend festival. Held the second weekend in October, the festival celebrates farming and the arts with farm tours, performances at farms, and workshops on growing and marketing produce.

Rain won't stop this festival from happening. It's also sponsored by the Rappahanock County Farmers Association.

Also at Old Town Hall is the popular "Exchange" program, in which artists from across the country (and sometimes from other parts of the world) perform January through April on the third Sunday of the month. At the end of the shows the audience always has an opportunity to converse with the performers.

Charlottesville and Surrounding Area

Visual Arts

BETH GALLERY AND PRESS
Barboursville   *(703) 832-3565*

Artist Frederick Nichols Jr. has his studio and gallery here just off Rt. 33 in a renovated general store across from the railroad tracks. He calls his work "photo-impressionism." He does enormous colorful landscapes of Blue Ridge scenes using either oil paint or a silk-screen process. A friendly fellow, Nichols will give tours through the gallery and studio on the weekends and during the week when he's open. Nichols' career has taken off since he won top honors at a recent international print exhibition in Japan.

FAYERWEATHER GALLERY
Rugby Road   *(804) 924-6122*

This university gallery next to the Bayley Art Museum has regular exhibits by faculty and student artists, so it's naturally where the

UVA Art Department likes to hang out. Admission is free, and it's open Monday through Friday from 9 to 5.

FRANCES CHRISTIAN BRAND GALLERIES
111 Washington Ave.   *(804) 295-5867*

Call before you drop by this eclectic gallery, which is actually a private home containing the art collection of Frances Christian Brand, now deceased. Cynthia Brand, her granddaughter, lives here and likes to have people over for coffee while they admire the rooms full of pre-Columbian pottery, Mexican art, African masks and sculptures, and paintings done by Frances Brand.

McGUFFEY ART CENTER
201 Second Street, N.W.   *(804) 295-7973*

This is an arts cooperative that began in 1975 with city support. It's located in a renovated elementary school within walking distance from historic Court Square and the downtown pedestrian mall. Its light airy rooms have been transformed into more than 40 studios where you can sometimes watch artists work. There are also galleries and a gift shop. Exhibits, tours and gallery talks are available to the public year round. The center also offers classes for the public in children's art, printing, painting, drawing and more.

NEWCOMB HALL ARTS SPACE
University of Virginia   *(804) 924-3601*

This student-run gallery in the UVA Student Union building is open daily from 12 noon to 9 and admission is free.Last year's many exhibitions included a display of the heart-breaking AIDS quilt.

PIEDMONT VIRGINIA COMMUNITY COLLEGE
Rt. 20 and I-64   *(804) 977-3900 x203*

An art gallery here displays regular exhibits by student and professional artists. Admission is free, and the gallery is open from 8 AM to 10 PM weekdays.

SECOND STREET GALLERY
Inside the McGuffey Art Center
        (804) 977-7284

This sophisticated gallery presents the work of regional and national artists–from paintings and prints to more avant-garde art forms such as site-specific installations. The gallery hosts lively receptions, art talks, slide presentations, workshops and tours. It's free and open Tuesday through Saturday from 10 to 5 and Sundays from 1 to 5.

Dance

CHIHAMBA
P.O. Box 3286   *(804) 296-4986*

The Chihamba Dance Company of Dancescape celebrates and educates people aboout African cultures through music and dance. Programs include concerts, lecture demonstrations, workshops and African craft sessions. One six-week program offered last winter, called Discover Africa through the Arts, taught African beading, weaving, tie-dying, leather work, mask making and sand painting.

CONTRA CORNERS
        (804) 295-1847

Contra Corners puts on a

dance the second and fourth Sunday of every month at the Greenwood Community Center. A dance workshop happens from 5:30-6:30, and a dance from 6:30 to 9:30.

DANCESCAPE

P.O. Box 3801   *(804) 296-4986*

Dancescape not only offers instruction in various African art forms (see Chihamba above) but it also gives classes in flat foot clogging, modern dance and jazz to adults, teens and children. One of the instructors hails from Guinea, West Africa. Mohamed Dacosta danced for several dance companies before moving to Charlottesville. Another instructor, Sheila Stone, apprentices with a 78-year-old flatfooter who lives near Elkins, West Virginia.

THE MIKI LISZT DANCE COMPANY

(804) 973-3744

Based at the McGuffey Art Center, this nonprofit company performs annual dance concerts, conducts workshops with guest artists and offers lectures and demonstrations in nursing homes, schools, hospitals, libraries and museums. The company also sponsors the annual Community Children's Dance Festival.

Museums

BAYLY ART MUSEUM

Rugby Road   *(804) 924-3592*

This is the University of Virginia's own modern museum that has both a permanent collection of ancient pottery, sculpture and some paintings, along with spe-

cial, short-term exhibitions. String quartets and other classical music groups perform certain times during the year. Admission is free, and it's open Tuesday through Sunday from 1 to 5.

JAMES MADISON MUSEUM

129 Caroline Street,
Orange, VA 22960   *(703) 672-1776*

The downtown museum offers four permanent exhibits dealing with the life and times of Madison and his important contributions to the American political system. Artifacts include furnishings from his nearby home, Montpelier, some of his correspondence when he served as president and a few of Dolley Madison's belongings. The museum is open weekdays from 10 to 5 and weekends from 1 to 4 from March through November. The rest of the year it's open only on weekdays from 10 to 4. There's a nominal admission fee.

THE VIRGINIA DISCOVERY MUSEUM

East End of Downtown Mall   *(804) 293-5528*

This is a dynamic place for children and their families filled with hands-on exhibits, science programs, costumes in which the children can play "dress-up," and a real-live log cabin from Rockingham County. Special exhibits change every few months. An art room, complete with all kinds of materials, invites children to create at their own pace, and a gallery space displays their creations for about three weeks.

The Discovery Dash children's race is held in May. There are many other special events, such as photo contests and a Halloween party.

The museum aims to "nurture the self-worth, success, and feelings of confidence of all who enter through its doors."

It's open Tuesday through Saturday from 10 to 5 and Sundays from 1 to 5. Admission is $3 for adults and $2 for children up to age 13 and seniors. Parking is free at the Market Street Parking Garage or Water Street outdoor lots.

THE WALTONS MOUNTAIN MUSEUM
At the Schuyler Community Center, Rt. 617
Schuyler, VA   (804) 831-2000
Earl Hamner, whose early years are chronicled in the heartwarming television series, grew up in tiny Schuyler. A new museum dedicated to Hamner and the Waltons opened to great fanfare last October in the same school where the Hamner youngsters learned their ABCs. The museum is actually a series of former classrooms that recreate sets from the TV program. You'll find copies of actual scripts, photo displays that juxtapose Hamner's real family with the television actors, and all manner of memorabilia.

Visitors can also sit back and watch a video documentary which shows interviews with Hamner, former cast members and episodes from one of the most enduring television series ever.

A $30,000 state grant and support from Hamner and community leaders have made it all possible.

The school is on Rt. 617 in Schuyler, a stone's throw from the old Hamner homestead. Schuyler

is half-way between Charlottesville and Lynchburg, a few miles off Rt. 29.

Visiting hours are from 10 to 4 and admission costs $3 for adults and $2 for children. The museum is open daily from the first Saturday in March through the last Sunday in November, except major holidays.

Music

ASH LAWN - HIGHLAND
(804) 293-9539
The restored home and gardens of President James Monroe host a chamber music series every summer, as well as three light operas. Other special events throughout the year bring pianists, singers and dancers who perform to 18th-century music. For more information about Ash Lawn, refer to the "Other Cultural Attractions" section for Charlottesville.

CHARLOTTESVILLE AND UNIVERSITY SYMPHONY ORCHESTRA
112 Old Cabell Hall   (804) 924-6505
Seventy musicians form this volunteer orchestra, which has received rave reviews. Professional principal musicians perform alongside outstanding student and community players. Concerts are held in the Cabell Hall auditorium located on the historic lawn at UVA.

CHARLOTTESVILLE GAMELAN ENSEMBLE
(804) 979-4818
This group performs traditional Javanese music as well as more contemporary "American Gamelan." The Ensemble includes

around a dozen musicians performing on various bronze gongs and xylophone-type instruments.

MONTICELLO TRIO
(804) 924-3052

This is a professional chamber music trio that performs regularly in Charlottesville and also tours across the state and nation.

OLD CABELL HALL
UVA   *(804) 924-3984*

Located at the south end of the lawn, this auditorium is the scene of all kinds of concerts throughout the year, from avant-garde jazz to internationally acclaimed chamber music. The Tuesday Evening Concert Series – a Charlottesville tradition for more than four decades – is held here every year and has presented such artists as Yo Yo Ma, the Tokyo String Quartet and the Juilliard String Quartet.

ORATORIO SOCIETY OF CHARLOTTESVILLE-ALBEMARLE
(804) 286-2150

This is Central Virginia's largest community chorus, performing major classical choral works in at least one concert annually.

PIEDMONT CHAMBER PLAYERS
(804) 973-2194

This is a local group of professional musicians that presents a concert series every year at Cabell Hall and also appears in schools and colleges throughout Central Virginia.

THE PRISM COFFEEHOUSE
214 Rugby Road   *(804) 97-PRISM*

This nonprofit volunteer organization presents folk, traditional and acoustic concerts in a casual smoke-free, alcohol-free setting. Formed in 1966, the Prism is one of America's oldest surviving coffeehouses. Concerts are held on the weekends. The group holds its bimonthly meetings and jam sessions every second Monday at the Prism. Local song writers also meet regularly at the Prism, and a monthly percussion jam session invites players at all levels of experience to make noise together. You can also occasionally hear jazz and even African drumming performances here.

THE SWEET ADELINES
(804) 973-7203 (night)
or 924-0276 (day)

This a four-part harmony barbershop chorus for women only. They perform around town and compete in barbershop competitions nationally. All women interested in barbershop harmony are invited to attend.

THE WESTMINSTER ORGAN CONCERT SERIES
(804) 293-3133

Held every year at Westminster Presbyterian Church, this series of concerts offers a variety of organ music combined with other instruments and singers. Concerts are free.

YOUTH ORCHESTRA OF CHARLOTTESVILLE-ALBEMARLE
(804) 924-6505

This orchestra has been

around for more than a decade, providing the best in musical direction and coaching for elementary and high school musicians. It includes a youth orchestra, jazz ensemble, string ensemble and the Evans Orchestra for younger musicians.

Theater

COMMUNITY CHILDREN'S THEATRE
(804) 971-5671
For 40 years this company has brought affordable family theatre to the Charlottesville community. Performances often sell out well in advance, but individual tickets, when available, are sold at the door an hour before curtain call and at other locations. The 1992-'93 season included such hits as "Fred 'Zeplin' Garbo–The Inflatable Man" and a full-scale musical production of "The Wiz." Local youngsters dazzled the audience in "The Wiz," a gospel/rock/soul version of Dorothy's adventures in the land of Oz. Theatre workshops for children are also offered in the winter. Performances are held at the Charlottesville Performing Arts Center.

FOUR COUNTY PLAYERS
(703) 832-5355
This theater company out of Barboursville produces Shakespeare, full-scale musicals and children's productions. In August, Shakespeare productions are staged in a most magical setting: the ruins of what was once the estate of James Barbour, governor of Virginia (1812-

1814), Secretary of War, and Ambassador to the Court of St. James. Thomas Jefferson, a friend of Barbour's, designed the house, but it was destroyed by fire on Christmas Day, 1884. Towering, overgrown boxwoods surround the ruins, adding to the air of enchantment about the place. The award-winning Barboursville Vineyards are located within walking distance.

In cooler months, Four County Players operates a dinner theater in conjunction with Toliver House in Gordonsville.

HERITAGE REPERTORY THEATRE
1 Culbreth Rd., UVA
Charlottesville, VA 22903   (804) 924-3376
The highly acclaimed Heritage Rep produces a series of plays every summer at the University of Virginia. The 1993 schedule includes such works as "Angel Street," "My Friend Mr. Jefferson," "Les Maisons dans Gereuses," and "Love Letters," the latter slated to feature a different well-known guest star each week.

LIVE ARTS
609 East Market St.,
Charlottesville, VA 22902   (804) 977-4177
Located one block off the downtown mall, Live Arts is home to a resident theater company, the Live Arts Theater Ensemble (LATE). LATE produces everything from original avant-garde plays to well-known Broadway musicals like the Fantastics. LATE started two years ago in Charlottesville and aims to become a professional theater. It also hosts poetry readings, music events and provides a space in which

The Miller-Claytor House, built in 1792, is one of Lynchburg's oldest houses and was the city's first public library.

other groups may perform.

THE OLD MICHIE THEATRE
609 East Market Street   (804) 977-3690
This is a new home for theater and puppetry arts for children and teens in Central Virginia. A summer theatre school offers weeks of instruction in drama, music, storytelling, puppetry and clowning. The theater also produces summer musicals.

UNIVERSITY OF VIRGINIA DEPARTMENT OF DRAMA
(804) 924-3376
This is UVA's main student theater group, producing six main stage shows every academic year. The UVA Spanish Theater Group also performs plays entirely in Spanish every spring. Last year's productions included "All My Sons" by Arthur Miller, "My Three Sisters" by Anton chekhov, and "Top Girls," a contemporary satire by Cary Churchhill.

Other Cultural Attractions

ASH LAWN-HIGHLAND
Rt. 6, Box 37,
Charlottesville, VA 22901   (804) 293-9539
This 535-acre estate was the home of James Monroe, our nation's fifth president who fought in the Revolution under George Washington and went on to hold more offices than any other U.S. President.

As ambassador to France, Monroe negotiated with Napoleon for the "Louisiana Purchase"–an acquisition of western territories which doubled the size of the country. During his presidency, Monroe articulated the nation's first comprehensive foreign policy, later termed the Monroe Doctrine, to prevent further European colonization of the Americas.

Ash Lawn-Highland is just about two and a half miles from Thomas Jefferson's Monticello, right off I-64. Visitors can tour the home that is full of Monroe possessions and stroll through the boxwood gardens, where magnificent peacocks strut around. Livestock, vegetable and herb gardens, and colonial craft demonstrations recall what life was like on the Monroe's plantation. Special events at the estate include summer opera performances sung in English, an early American festival–"Plantation Days"–held on July 4th weekend, and Christmas candlelight tours.

Monroe purchased the 1,000-acre plantation in 1793 because he wanted to be closer to his friend and mentor, Thomas Jefferson. Monticello's property then bordered Highland. Jefferson had personally selected the site and sent his gardeners to start orchards for Monroe. In late 1799 Monroe and his wife, Elizabeth Kortright of New York, moved to their tobacco plantation, where frequent guests included James and Dolley Madison who lived nearby at Montpelier.

Today, the Monroe estate is owned and maintained as a working farm by Monroe's alma mater, the College of William and Mary. This is a good year to visit the estate. It is the 200th anniversary of the Monroe purchase of Ash Lawn-Highland, the 300th anniversary of the College of William and Mary, and the 250th anniversary of Thomas Jefferson's birth. A special exhibit commemorating the three, called "Monroe and Jefferson: A Society to Our Taste," will be shown through December in the main entrance.

Ash Lawn-Highland is open daily from 9 to 6 from March through October and from 10 to 5 daily from November through February. Admission is $6 for adults, $5.50 for seniors and $2 for children ages 6 to 12. A special "President's Pass" costs $16 (children and adults) and gets you into Ash Lawn-Highland, Monticello and Michie Tavern. Groups of 25 or more receive a special rate.

MICHIE TAVERN

Rt. 6, Box 7-A,
Charlottesville, VA 22901   (804) 977-1234

Historic Michie Tavern (pronounced "Micky") is one of the oldest homesteads remaining in Virginia and was originally located along a well-worn stage coach route near Earlysville about 17 miles away. To accommodate the many travelers seeking food and shelter at their home, the Michie family opened it up as a tavern in 1784. The tavern was dismantled piece by piece, moved to the present site and reconstructed in 1927.

Today, visitors to Monticello and Ash Lawn-Highland can stop by this tavern for a hearty Southern-style meal. It's located on Rt. 53 on the way to both attractions. Visitors can also see a fine collection of 18th-century Southern furniture and artifacts and learn about the tavern's lively history from both tour

guides and audio recordings. Next door, a 200-year-old converted slave house called "The Ordinary" serves fried chicken, black-eye peas, stewed tomatoes, cole slaw, potato salad, green bean salad, beets, homemade biscuits, cornbread and apple cobbler every day of the year from 11:30 to 3.

Michie Tavern also features 18th-century craft demonstrations every weekend from April through October and houses the small Virginia Wine Museum in its basement.

Next door, the Meadow Run Grist Mill houses a General Store where visitors can buy Virginia wines, specialty foods, crafts and all kinds of gifts.

The Michie Tavern Museum is open year round from 9 to 5 except Christmas and New Years. Admission to the museum costs $5 a person, unless you have lunch, in which case you get a $2 discount to the museum. Lunch costs $8.95, not including beverage, dessert and tax.

MONTICELLO

P.O. Box 316,
Charlottesville, VA 22902   (804) 295-8181

Monticello celebrates the 250th anniversary of Thomas Jefferson's birth this year, so it is an extraordinary time to tour the estate. A unique loan exhibition will return to the elegant homestead more than 150 of Jefferson's possessions that are dispersed in public and private collections throughout the nation and Europe. For the most part, all the objects have been absent from the mountaintop since Jefferson's death. Opening on

Jefferson's birthday, April 13, and continuing until Dec. 31, "The Worlds of Thomas Jefferson at Monticello" will recreate Monticello as it has not been seen for over a century and a half and as it may never be seen again in our lifetimes.

In and around Monticello, a number of other significant events will honor the birthday. A new $1 million roof restoration executed to Jefferson's specifications will be completed, and Shadwell, Jefferson's birth site nearby, will be opened for special programs following two years of archaeological research and planning. Other programs planned for this year include musical events, living history demonstrations that describe slave and plantation life, and an after-hours series of evening conversations exploring Jefferson's varied interests in cuisine, wine, law, politics, education, archeology and other topics.

Another important annual event is July 4th at Monticello, which hosts festivities on the mountaintop, including a naturalization ceremony for new U.S. citizens.

Jefferson's wide-ranging interests made him an avid collector of sculpture, maps, paintings, prints, Native American artifacts, scientific instruments and fine furniture – and these objects kept his house quite cluttered. With all the nieces and nephews and other relatives and visitors also filling his home, it's no wonder the man liked to escape to his wooded retreat, Poplar Forest, in nearby Lynchburg.

Jefferson, our nation's third president, the author of the Declaration of Independence, and international statesman, reportedly detested politics. He wrote to his daughter Martha in 1800, "Politics is such a torment that I would advise every one I love not to mix with it." But he refused to shirk his duty to his country and its fragile democratic system.

He began construction of Monticello in 1769 when he was just 26, and often longed to retire there during the most active part of his political career. Work on Monticello continued for 40 years thereafter, during which Jefferson made many alterations. Evidence of his interest in architecture, science, agriculture, the arts and much else can be found throughout the estate, which includes an eight-acre orchard, 1000-foot vegetable garden and vineyard.

The Thomas Jefferson Center for Historic Plants operates a garden shop at Monticello from April through October that sells historical plants and seeds. There is also a fine museum shop at Monticello offering a varied selection of brass, porcelain, crystal, pewter and silver gift ware, plus reproductions made exclusively for Monticello.

During the 1980s more than five million visitors toured Monticello. It's such a popular destination for tourists that long lines are inevitable during the peak season of summer and early fall. Monticello's popularity has soared even more due to the publicity surrounding President Clinton and Vice President Gore's visit to the mountaintop as their starting point to Washington in January. This year it is expected that 10 percent more visitors will come to Monticello than did last year. So it's advisable to start early in the day to avoid a long wait. A lunch stand selling good picnic food is open from 10:30 to 3:30 daily from April through October.

Monticello is located on Rt. 53, three miles southeast of Charlottesville. Take exit 121 off I-64 and follow the signs. It's open daily from 8 to 5 from March 1 through October and from 9 to 4:30 the rest of the year. It's closed on Christmas Day. Written tours are available in foreign languages.

Admission is $8 for adults, $7 for seniors, and $4 for children (ages 6-11). As mentioned earlier, it's possible to save on the cost of adult admission to Monticello, Ash Lawn and Michie Tavern by buying at $17 President's Pass at the Charlottesville/Albemarle Convention and Visitors Bureau. This bureau is located at Rt. 20 South and I-64, near Monticello.

THOMAS JEFFERSON VISITORS CENTER
Rt. 20 south (exit 121 - I-64)(804) 293-6789

A permanent exhibition on Jefferson's domestic life here is an ideal introduction to nearby Monticello. Nearly 400 objects and artifacts, from his pocketknife to a porcupine quill toothpick, are on display, many for the first time. Also, an award-winning film entitled "Thomas Jefferson: The Pursuit of Liberty," is shown daily at 11 and 2 in the exhibition theater. The hours are 9 to 5:30 daily from March

through October, and 9 to 5 the rest of the year. Admission is free.

MONTPELIER
P.O. Box 67,
Montpelier Station, VA 22957
(703) 672-2728

The gracious home of President James Madison and his beloved wife, Dolley, opened for public tours in 1987. The estate is in the early stages of restoration, and extensive archeological work and architectural research are ongoing. This is what makes Montpelier such an interesting, even exciting, place to visit. Someone touring the estate might hear about a new discovery on the 2,700-acre property the same day it happened! (the staff are an enthusiastic, friendly bunch).

For these reasons, a tour of Montpelier is the perfect complement to a visit to Monticello. Unlike Jefferson, Madison did not document the fine details of his everyday existence, from his gardening techniques to his diet. So the process of uncovering (and literally, in some cases, unearthing) what Montpelier was like in Madison's time is slow and painstaking. Unlike Monticello, where lines form for hours and tours are rather regimented, you can dally at Montpelier and even brainstorm with a tour guide.

Montpelier was owned by the DuPont family for decades before it was bequeathed to the National Trust for Historic Preservation in the 1980s. The DuPonts built major additions to the home and planted elaborate formal gardens. The biggest challenge for Montpelier's new owners, the National Trust, was what to do about all the new rooms and interior changes. They considered doing away with the DuPont imprint and restoring the property to its original Madisonian form. But a compromise was struck, with the exterior and the landscape keeping their 20th-century appearances, along with three DuPont rooms in the house. The rest of the mansion's museum is being reconfigured as Madison-period rooms, based on the results of research in progress.

The estate offers breathtaking views of the nearby Blue Ridge mountains. Visitors are given guided tours of the main floor of the 55-room mansion and may also stroll throughout the grounds and see the barns, stables, a bowling alley, and the garden temple Madison built over his ice house. The cemetery where a number of Madison family members are buried, including Dolley and James, may also be visited.

Montpelier's energetic and imaginative staff have big plans for the museum: a full-scale educational center for children to be in a renovated barn, a winery, extensive walking trails, and displays in the mansion using the newest technology. For instance, you may one day see a hologram in a hallway, suggesting how the space used to look when it was Madison's bedroom.

Special events throughout the year include the famous Montpelier Hunt Races, which take place on the first Saturday in November. This will be the 59th year of the steeple chase races.

For some historical information: Montpelier was first settled by

Madison's grandparents in 1723. After the completion of Madison's second presidential term, Dolley and James retired to Montpelier where their legendary hospitality kept them in touch with world affairs. Madison was the primary author of the Constitution and one of the authors of the Federalist Papers. He was a proponent of freedom of religion and education in Virginia, and served as second rector of the University of Virginia. Madison's public life spanned 53 years and included services as a delegate to the Continental Congress, a member of the Virginia House of Delegates, a U.S. Congressman, Thomas Jefferson's Secretary of State, and U.S. president for two terms.

Montpelier is about 25 miles north of Charlottesville near Orange. It is open daily from 10 to 4, except Thanksgiving, Christmas, and New Year's and the first Saturday in November. Admission is $6 for adults, and $1 for children 6 to 12 years of age.

OAK RIDGE

Rt. 1 Box 152,
Arrington, VA 22922   (804) 263-4168

This estate, more than two centuries in the making, is now open to the public for the first time. Located in the rolling hills of Nelson County, the estate was once the private kingdom of Thomas Fortune Ryan, one of the nation's 10 wealthiest men at the turn of the century. The estate once employed hundreds of people and boasted its own railroad station, dairy, race track, post office, 18-hole golf course, power plant and water system. Many of the out-buildings are still standing – such as the rotunda greenhouse, carriage house, railroad station, dairy complex and spring house. Visitors can tour the first floor of a 14,275-square-foot mansion and sections of the grounds. Many guests enjoy having a picnic lunch on the front lawn beforehand or afterwards. The estate's new owners, John and Rhonda Holland, want to put Oak Ridge and Nelson County on the map as a major tourist spot. They plan to renovate the horse race track on the property, having passed a local referendum to allow parimutuel betting. They hope the track will host fairs and other cultural events, as well. They also plan to restore the 18-hole golf course. In June, 1992, they hosted a wine festival and in April, the Jaycees threw an Easter egg hunt on the grounds. Plans also call for the large carriage house and barn to become a restaurant with space for large parties and wedding receptions. Total restoration of the fabulous property is the Hollands' goal, and the process will take decades. But it seems the sky's the limit for Oak Ridge's potential as a cultural attraction and vital center for community events.

Oak Ridge threw a big Railroad Festival in May, and a steam excursion from Washington with hundreds of passengers stopped at the estate for the first time in 50 years. June saw the Nelson County Summer Festival at Oak Ridge, and a major Fall Festival is planned for Oct. 2 and 3. Christmas is an especially enchanting time at Oak Ridge-

-a formal children's tea party and hayrides are among the events planned for this year.

Oak Ridge is open for tours during the summer months from Tuesday through Thursday from 10 to 4. Tours cost $10 per person, with discounts for senior citizens and school groups and visitors to the nearby Walton's Mountain Museum.

THE ROTUNDA/THE UNIVERSITY OF VIRGINIA
(804) 924-7969

Free tours of Mr. Jefferson's "Academic Village" are offered daily from the Rotunda, which Jefferson designed after the classical Pantheon. Begun in 1819 and opened in 1825, the university is renowned for its magnificent and unique architectural design. In fact, in 1976 the American Institute of Architects voted Jefferson's design for the University as the most outstanding achievement in American architecture.

Along with his authorship of the Declaration of Independence and the Statute of Virginia for Religious Freedom, the university was the third achievement Jefferson wished to be remembered for. He called it the hobby of his old age, but this is quite an understatement. Not only was he the principal architect, Jefferson also helped select the library collection, hire faculty and design the curriculum. He was also one of the largest financial contributors and succeeded in securing public funding for the school.

It was his ardent lobbying for public education in Virginia that led to the establishment of the university in the first place. Jefferson had studied at the College of William and Mary in Williamsburg but he felt the state, which then encompassed West Virginia, needed a major university. All of this he accomplished during his retirement at Monticello, from which he often watched the university's construction with his telescope. The magnificent Rotunda was completed in 1826, the year Jefferson died.

Tours are conducted daily from the Rotunda at 10 and 11 AM and 2, 3 and 4 PM except for about two weeks around Christmas. The tour also includes a look at Edgar Allan Poe's old dorm room, which appears much the same as it did when Poe was a student in 1825. By the way, Poe had to leave the university prematurely after running up a huge gambling debt that he couldn't pay.

THE VIRGINIA FESTIVAL OF AMERICAN FILM
University of Virginia, P.O. Box 3697
Charlottesville, VA 22903 (800) UVA-FEST

This five-year-old festival held at UVA is dedicated to celebrating and exploring the unique character of American film. It lasts for four days, bringing leading actors, filmmakers, scholars and the public together to discuss American film in a serious way.

The 1993 festival's theme will be "Film Noir," and invited guests include Faye Dunaway and Kirk Douglas. "Thumbs up" Film critic Roger Ebert will also participate. The festival happens from Oct. 28 through the 31–a colorful time to be in the

Blue Ridge.

The event has attracted national attention by featuring special events that honor the history of American film. These have included a 50th anniversary "encore premiere" of "Mr. Smith Goes to Washington," with its star, James Stewart, in attendance.

Other renowned actors and filmmakers who have participated in the festival have included Gregory Peck, Sissy Spacek, Charlton Heston, Sidney Poitier, Robert Duvall, John Sayles and Robert Altman. Writers William Styron and Rita Mae Brown participated in panel discussions last year, as well as scholar and civil rights leader Julian Bond.

As usual this year a strong roster of independent feature and documentary premieres will also be shown. Such screenings and discussions in the past have included "Roger and Me" with Michael Moore (about General Motors' lay-offs and its infamous president, Roger Smith) and the Academy Award-winning "American Dream" with Peter Miller. This year, "Chinatown," "Double Indemnity," "Out of the Past" and "Body Heat" are among the classic examples of the film noir genre that will be shown.

This is such a stimulating, ecxciting event–well worth planning your fall vacation around. Special discount hotel-and-event package rates are available. Call 800-UVA-FEST for more information.

SCOTTSVILLE ON THE JAMES
The Albemarle County seat until 1762, Scottsville is an old river

town right on the James, about 20 miles from Charlottesville on Rt. 20. In and around the town are 32 authentic Federal buildings – one of the four or five largest concentrations of Early Republic architecture in the state. The town also has a museum that was originally a Disciples Church built in 1846.

Lynchburg

Visual Arts

ARTS COUNCIL OF
CENTRAL VIRGINIA
Greater Lynchburg Chamber of Commerce
(804) 847-1597
Coordinating the huge wealth of cultural events of Lynchburg and Central Virginia, the Arts Council serves as a clearinghouse for information about area artists, musicians, actors and dancers and offers calendars of their performances. It is active in preservation and advancement of the arts with a mission to make Lynchburg a model cultural center, a goal well within reach by the year 2000.

LYNCHBURG FINE ARTS CENTER
1815 Thomson Drive   (804) 846-8451
An affiliate of the Virginia Museum of Fine Arts in Richmond, the Fine Arts Center has provided Lynchburg with an environment where the arts have flourished. Programs have included arts and music with opportunities for instruction or performance in dance and drama. Membership in FACination, the Center's Pop chorus, is open to residents. The Regional Ballet The-

atre is the Center's resident dance company. The Alliance for Visual Arts, the resident art organization at the Center, presents year round exhibits and classes. Professional instruction is available in all media. The Center's auditorium seats 500 and the costume shop is open to the public for costume rentals.

VIRGINIA CENTER FOR
THE CREATIVE ARTS
Amherst, VA 24595   (804) 946-7236
A surprising artistic treasure is located just outside of Lynchburg in Amherst County. It is the Virginia Center for the Creative Arts, the largest working retreat for professional writers, artists and composers in the country, who come seeking the solitude conducive to creative work. Artists who visit from abroad are often the leading artists in their own countries and some of the most important exchanges between artists worldwide take place here. The Virginia Center for the Creative Arts is affiliated with an elite private women's college, Sweet Briar, known for its international programs, and is supported by the National Endowment for the Arts.

The VCCA is not frequently open to the public but does have exhibits at Camp Gallery, located in the renovated barn that also houses the artists' studios. There are three different shows each summer with meet-the-artists receptions on Sunday afternoons. Special events are also open to the public, such as a summer exhibit by a Mozambican sculptor in residence. Many public events, such as poetry readings with Russian writers in residence, are co-sponsored with Sweet Briar.

Camp Gallery hours are 2:30 to 4 PM Sundays.

MAIER MUSEUM OF ART
Randolph-Macon Woman's College
1 Quinlan St. (804) 947-8136

Known for its collection of 19th- and 20th-century American paintings, the Maier Museum at prestigious Randolph-Macon is also the site of The Blue Ridge Music Festival, which brings a continuing rich and varied schedule of internationally recognized musicians to the area. This is a tremendous community asset well worth the visit for arts lovers.

Open Tuesday through Thursday, 1 to 5 PM.

Museums

LYNCHBURG MUSEUM AT OLD COURT HOUSE
5th St. (804) 847-1459

One of Virginia's outstanding Greek Revival civil buildings, the Lynchburg Museum headquarters Lynchburg's fine museum system. The courtroom has been restored circa 1855. It traces Lynchburg's history through each successive period and is an outstanding collection for both scholars and history buffs, especially for the Civil War period.

Open daily from 1 to 4 PM. Closed holidays. Adults are $1, students are 50 cents.

PEST HOUSE MEDICAL MUSEUM AND CONFEDERATE CEMETERY
Old City Cemetery,
4th and Taylor Streets (804) 847-1811

In the 1800s, Lynchburg residents who contracted contagious diseases such as smallpox or measles were quarantined in the Pest House. Medical care and cleanliness were virtually non-existent then and most patients died and were buried a few yards away. By 1861, the Pest House was used for Confederate soldiers. Dr. John Jay Terrell, 33, volunteered to assume responsibility for the soldiers and changed their wretched conditions. His office shows the state of medicine during that era. You can see an 1860s hypodermic needle and one of the first chloroform masks ever used. This is a fascinating medical journey through history and a sobering reminder of humankind's mortality and just how far we've come in a little over 130 years.

Open sunrise to sunset. Guided tours are available by appointment.

Music

BLUE RIDGE MUSIC FESTIVAL
Randolph-Macon Woman's College
(804) 947-8000

The Blue Ridge Music Festival has been created as a celebration of musical diversity. Now in its fourth season, the blue Ridge Music Festival continues to inspire and challenge music-lovers of all ages and tastes with concerts of the world's great chamber music, with jazz improvisation, and with folk music from Tex Mex ballads to Appalachian melodies. An unparalleled week of concerts awaits you on the campus of Randolph-Macon Woman's College.

COMMUNITY CONCERTS
E. C. Glass High School   (804) 384-3184

The 50th Anniversary of Lynchburg's Community Concerts will be held at the Lynchburg Civic Auditorium through an association with Columbia Artists Management. Many special events, ranging from singers, pianists, ballet and ethnic performances, are part of this special subscription series that is an asset to Central Virginia. No single tickets are sold.

POINT OF HONOR
112 Cabell St.   (804) 847-1459

You can usually find Lynchburg's history elite, some of whom are from historical families themselves, at this restored 19th-century mansion in the afternoon. Lovingly restored by the Lynchburg Historical Foundation, the Garden Club of Virginia and the Katharine Garland Diggs Trust, Point of Honor shows today's families what life was like in the days of Dr. George Cabell, Sr., Patrick Henry's personal physician. It also was home to Mary Virginia Ellet Cabell, one of the founders of the Daughters of the American Revolution. Its name comes from the gun duels fought on its lawn.

Open daily 1 to 4 PM. Closed holidays. Admission is $1 for adults and 50 cents for students.

Theater

CHERRY TREE PLAYHOUSE
Seventh at Church St.   (804) 528-0715

A new theatre, the Players is a group of artists, musicians, business people, directors, technicians and others who formed to advance the arts and theatre in the Lynchburg area. There is an active children's and youth theatre as well. Their theatre, in the Community Room in the YWCA, is similar to off-Broadway in New York City. The Playhouse seats 100.

Admission: $7.50 for adults; $6.50 for students. No children under age 6 are allowed.

Other Cultural Attractions

ANNE SPENCER HOUSE AND GARDEN
1313 Pierce St.   (804) 846-0517

Anne Spencer was an internationally recognized African-American poet of the Harlem Renaissance period in the 1920s. Her poems are included in the *Norton Anthology of Modern Poetry*. Behind her home is the garden and the garden cottage, "EdanKraal," built for her by her husband as a place where she could write. The garden has been beautifully restored by Hillside Garden Club. Revered the world over for her brilliance and intellect, she entertained many great leaders and artists of her day including Dr. Martin Luther King, Supreme Court Justice Thurgood Marshall, scientist Dr. George Washington Carver, sports legend Jackie Robinson, Congressman Adam Clayton Powell, (who honeymooned there), and the legendary singers Paul Robeson and Marion Anderson. Her son, Chauncey, still lives in the family home, so hours are by appointment only. Call him at (804) 846-0517.

JONES MEMORIAL LIBRARY
2311 Memorial Ave.   *(804) 846-0501*

The second oldest library in Virginia, Jones Memorial is also one of Virginia's foremost genealogical libraries. With 30,000 volumes specializing in genealogical, historical and Lynchburg holdings, the Jones is known for its vast records. These include Revolutionary War records, family histories, enlistments and Virginia county and state court records. Records from England, Ireland and Scotland include heraldry information. It offers research and lending services by mail. This gem is probably one of the most underutilized treasures of the Blue Ridge.

Open 10 AM to 5 PM Tuesday through Saturday with additional evening hours on Tuesday.

RED HILL
Patrick Henry National Memorial
Brookneal   *(804) 376-2044*

Who can ever forget Revolutionary War hero Patrick Henry's speech "Give me liberty or give me death!" Red Hill was home to the famous lawyer and his 17 children and is also his burial ground. The original plantation of nearly 3,000 acres showcases the largest collection of Patrick Henry memorabilia in the world, including the famous P.H. Rothermel painting, "Patrick Henry before the Virginia House of Burgesses." You can see Henry's

home, original law office, kitchen and overgrown boxwood garden as they were before Henry's death in 1799.

Open daily from 9 AM until 5 PM except November through March, when it closes at 4 PM. Closed holidays.

VIRGINIA SCHOOL OF THE ARTS
Columbia & Rivermont Ave.   *(804) 847-8688*

Virginia School of the Arts, a private residential secondary school, is dedicated to preparing young people for careers in dance, theatre and the visual arts. It is one of only six such schools for the arts in America and students come from throughout the U.S. Its arts faculty includes prominent professional performers and artists who contribute greatly to Lynchburg's culture.

Smith Mountain Lake

Other Cultural Attractions

SMITH MOUNTAIN VISITORS CENTER & DAM
Route 908   *(703) 985 2416*

At Appalachian Power's Visitors Center overlooking Smith Mountain Dam, you'll enjoy both the view and learning how electricity is generated – the whole purpose of why the largest lake in Virginia was created by APCO. The entire experience provides insight into the relatively recent lake culture of western Virginia. An audiovisual presentation shows how the dam was constructed. You can spin zoetropes and watch how APCO uses the water cycle to generate electricity. The

Photo: Richmond Newspapers

Square dancing and clogging are popular forms of dance in the Blue Ridge region.

ramp in the overlook offers a spectacular view of the dam and gorge. Picnic facilities are nearby.

Open daily 10 AM to 6 PM. Closed holidays.

SMITH MOUNTAIN LAKE STATE PARK & VISITORS CENTER
Route 1, Huddleston   (703) 297-5998
In addition to camping and the only public swimming area on the lake, Smith Mountain State Park offers a continuing variety of educational programs aimed at lake and nature lovers. The Visitors Center offers a schedule of programs and lectures.

Open daily 8 AM to 10 PM.

Bedford County

Museums

BEDFORD CITY/COUNTY MUSEUM
201 E. Main St.,
Bedford, VA 24523   (703) 586-4520
Visitors will enjoy a collection showing the story of Bedford, a charming Virginia city at the foot of the Peaks of Otter, a Blue Ridge Parkway attraction. It begins with early Indian natives and progresses through the mid 20th century. Here, you'll see Indian relics, Revolutionary War and Civil War artifacts, clothing, flags and quilts, among other interesting, well-displayed artifacts. Research assistance is available for genealogists outside Bedford.

Open 10 AM to 5 PM Tuesday through Saturday. Adults are $1 and children 50 cents.

Other Cultural Attractions

ELKS NATIONAL HOME
Bedford, VA 24523   (703) 586-8232
A spacious retirement home used recently as a set in the Disney movie, "What About Bob?," the Elks National Home for retired members of this fraternal organization is best known for its annual Christmas light display. Men from every state work all year to give western Virginia's children a Christmas show worth driving to see. The rest of the year, the beautiful grounds are open for visitors.

HOLY LAND USA NATURE SANCTUARY
Route 6,
Bedford, VA 24523   (703) 586-2823
A 400-acre nature sanctuary, where the religious can imagine the journey and deeds of Jesus Christ, is located in the beautiful Blue Ridge close to the Peaks of Otter. You have to use your imagination to envision the Biblical scenes outlined for Bible research and study, but many find inspiration from the visit.

POPLAR FOREST
Route 661,
Forest, VA 24551-0419   (804) 525-1806
Thomas Jefferson's summer home, Poplar Forest, has been under renovation for several years now and visitors are invited to watch the painstaking excavations and historical restoration. During Jefferson's time, Poplar Forest was a working plantation of nearly 5,000 acres tended by slaves who grew corn and tobacco. Although Monticello was Jefferson's pride and joy, Poplar

Forest was where he came to get away from it all, riding three days from Charlottesville by horseback to reach it. As Mikhail Gorbachev said when he visited in the spring of '93, "This is the first Camp David!" Restoration of the Main House has begun and is expected to take four years.

Jefferson himself designed the unusual building. History and Jefferson buffs will be fascinated with seeing his office, library and even two domed "necessaries" that were part of day-to-day life. July 4th is the best time to visit, since historical actors staff the home in period attire and speak the language of the day, transporting you right back to 1815. The event is free and takes place from noon to 5 PM. Picnicking is encouraged. Poplar Forest's huge, ancient boxwoods are incredible to see on the beautiful grounds. The staff's enthusiasm for this cultural treasure is highly contagious.

Open 10 AM to 4 PM, April through November, Wednesday through Sunday and major holidays except thanksgiving. Group tours may be arranged year round. Adults are $5, $1 for students.

SEDALIA CENTER
Rt. 638,
Big Island, VA 24526   (804) 299-5080

The Sedalia Center for the art of living and the living arts is a regional, non-profit organization offering programming in the arts, culture, environmental awareness, health and inner development. It offers classes, workshops, seminars and special events to ignite and nourish the creative process in each per-

son, according to its mission, and it does it well. The center's modern building is set on seven acres of land at the foot of Flintstone Mountain near big Island. Special events include dance, storytelling, music festivals and a country fair. The Sedalia Coffeehouse is every fourth Saturday and contradancing is every second Friday. At least once a quaarter, you'll find the coffeehouse being an open jam in keeping with Sedalia's mission to ignite and nourish the creative process in each person.

Here, you can take classes in everything from Cajun cooking and Tai Chi to Introduction to Mountain Dulcimar and Fundamentals of Instrument Construction. Lectures may include "How Native American Indians Lived with Nature and How Some of Their Approaches Might Work for Us." A small but very dedicated group of creative people makes the Sedalia Center the heart of a special culture for people of the Blue Ridge foothills.

Franklin County

Museums

BLUE RIDGE FARM MUSEUM
Ferrum College,
Ferrum, VA 24088   (703) 365-4416

The Blue Ridge Farm Museum presents the history and culture of early Virginia settlements in the southwestern mountains of the state. There's an 1800 German-American farmstead with log house, oven, outbuildings, pasture and garden that reveals the daily life of colonists who came from the German settlements of Pennsylvania and the Shenandoah Valley. All buildings are authentic and were moved from their original Blue Ridge locations. Heirloom vegetables flourish in the gardens, vintage breeds of livestock shelter by the barn, and costumed interpreters work at farm and household chores true to early life in the region.

Open weekends from mid-May through mid- Aug., Saturdays from 10 AM to 5 PM, and Sundays from 1 to 5 PM. Admission for adults is $3, and students are $2.

Theater

Blue Ridge Dinner Theatre
Ferrum College, Sale Theatre, Schoolfield Hall
Ferrum, VA 24088   *(703) 365-4335*
Celebrating its 13th season at Ferrum College, the Blue Ridge Dinner Theatre operates on three guiding principles: theatre as discovery, theatre as wholesome family entertainment and theatre as celebration. It also serves up a great luncheon or dinner in combination with everything from murder mysteries to great historical masterpieces. Adjacent to the nationally-known Blue Ridge Institute, tours of this facility are also offered to theatre-goers.

Performances are varied, with hours at 12:15 PM and 6:45 PM.

Other Cultural Attractions

Booker T. Washington National Monument
Route 122 N., Hardy   *(703) 721-2094*
Booker T. Washington was born into a legacy of hard work during his first nine years on a small tobacco farm, living in slavery. It was from this unlikely beginning that Washington achieved international recognition as an educator, founder of Tuskegee Institute, presidential advisor and leader. Begin your tour of this famous African-American educator's birthplace by watching the slide show and seeing the exhibits at the Visitor's Center. This is the most famous attraction in Franklin County, and with good reason. From the beautiful, restored farm and its animals to the hike up Plantation Trail, Booker T. offers a scenic, historic sojourn about a time in America when slavery was a way of life.

Open daily 8:30 AM to 5 PM except holidays. Adults are $1.

Blue Ridge Folklife Festival
Ferrum College,
Ferrum, VA 24088   *(703) 365-4416*
On the fourth Saturday of October, Ferrum College showcases the rich culture of regional folklife here. In 1993, this blockbuster festival will mark its 20th aniversary. Visitors can experience the tastes,

When you've got your heart set on seeing an attraction in a rural area, call ahead to avoid disappointment. Some are underfunded and understaffed or open by appointment only. Admission prices also change.

Insiders' Tip

sights and sounds of western Virginia folk culture as demonstrated by local residents. More than 40 Blue Ridge craftspeople demonstrate and sell rugs braided by hand, baskets, shingles and other folk arts. The South's thriving auto culture is featured along with vintage steam and gas-powered farm machinery. Among the most popular events for spectators are the horse pulling contests and coon dog water races. Many of these demonstrations are getting to be extinct as the old-timers die, so if you want to see the Blue Ridge as it was, make it a point to go to the festival. It's crowded, but lots of fun.

Open 10 AM to 5 PM. Adults $3, students $2 (includes tour of the Farm Museum).

BLUE RIDGE INSTITUTE

Ferrum College,
Ferrum, VA 24088   *(703) 365-4416*

It is often astounding to visitors that a small Methodist-related college in Franklin County, VA, has taken on the role of preserving a cultural heritage to the extent and level of visibility that Ferrum College has done. The result, the Blue Ridge Institute, along with the Blue Ridge Farm Museum and its Folklife Festival, places Ferrum among the nation's most important colleges culturally. Its archives contain thousands of photos, videotapes, phonograph records, vintage books and manuscripts. The archive is recognized for its special holdings and documentations of Appalachian photos, Shenandoah Valley beliefs, Southwest Virginia folktales and

The north front of the mansion at Oak Ridge, a fabulous Nelson County estate under renovation that hosts special cultural events. The estate is also open for tours. This photo was taken in 1940.

African-American and Caucasian folk music from throughout Virginia.

Ferrum's theatre group, the Jack Tale Players, continues the legacy through acting out legends of the South. BRI Records, which presents the diverse musical heritage of Virginia's folk culture, has been nominated for several Grammys.

People of English, Scotch, Irish, African and German descent will especially be interested in the distinct identities reflected in Blue Ridge music, crafts, foods, beliefs, and customs formed after emigrating from their homelands.

Open Monday through Friday, 8 AM to 4:30 PM. Archives are open by appointment.

New River Valley Region

Blacksburg

Visual Arts

Virginia Tech features several art galleries with good reputations that are worth visiting.

ARMORY ART GALLERY
201 Draper Road   (703) 231-4859
Virginia Tech's Department of Art and Art History operates the Armory Art Gallery as an educational and outreach program. The gallery is located in the Old Blacksburg Armory and has 1,000 square feet of exhibition space. A year round rotation calendar features work by national or regional artists, work by student artists and other shows of community interest.

PERSPECTIVE ART GALLERY
Squires Student Center   (703) 231-5200
Perspective Gallery offers a wide variety of styles and media by artists ranging from internationally-known professionals to students. The gallery is a program facility of the University Unions and Student Activities. The showcase gallery provides a spotlight for special interest exhibits and works from selected artists. Gallery talks and receptions where the public can meet featured artists are also offered.

XYZ COOPERATIVE GALLERY
223 N. Main St., Above College Inn
(703) 953-3435
A lively exhibitory gallery, XYZ sponsors continuing exhibitions of intriguing works of art. You'll enjoy the vitality of the changing exhibitions.

Theater

THEATRE ARTS DEPARTMENT
Virginia Tech   (703) 231-5615
The New River Valley's cultural richness comes in great part from Virginia Tech's presence, and theatre is no exception. The only Theatre Arts Department in Virginia to have both its graduate and undergraduate programs accredited by the National Association of Schools of Theatre, it has received more awards from the American College Theatre Festival than any

other college or university in the Southeast. The Theatre Arts Department at Tech stages about 20 productions each year, including comedies, dramas, musicals and reviews. Virginia Tech hosts four subscription shows within the academic year. There are three theatres, Haymarket Theatre at Squires Student Center, Black Box Theatre in the Performing Arts Building, and Squires Studio Theatre. All productions are open to the public. Don't miss Tech's Summer Arts Festival held throughout each summer.

Christiansburg

Visual Arts

New River Valley Arts Council
(703) 381-1430
An active group which publishes an Arts Directory, which is a lively magazine, and Calendar of Local Artists. The New River Valley Arts Council is a complete source of information on the wide range of arts within the New river Valley. If you're planning a visit there and want to see what the area offers, give them a call first.

Palette Art Gallery
Roanoke Road, just off U.S. Route 11/460
(703) 382-8861
For 30 years, Palette Art Gallery has provided a showcase for Southwest Virginia artists at its rambling building specializing in local art. Begun by Vance Miller, an 80-year-old impressionist artist, the Palette has no pretense, and is chocked full of art, quaint and con-

servative. There's no indoor plumbing and a coalstove provides the heat. You'll find many of Miller's paintings in Virginia Tech offices. In addition to being a great source of art, the Gallery has returned nearly $100,000 back to the community for charitable causes since opening in 1961.

Museums

The Montgomery Museum and Lewis Miller Regional Art Center
300 S. Pepper St.   *(703) 382-5644*
A Valley-wide project to promote Montgomery County's rich history and arts, this center is located in a mid-19th-century home of American and Flemish bond brick made from local materials, with hand hewn oak beams and rafters. A curious aspect of the manse portion of the house is a "step-up" feature in the back rooms, thought to be a carry-over design from Colonial days when it was believed that evil spirits bearing illness traveled the night air along floors. The house contains both historic and contemporary work including exhibits and shows of southwestern Virginia artists and craftspeople. It also houses a genealogical research area, historic small press library and an archive.

Open weekends, May through October, 2 to 5 PM, or by appointment.

Other Cultural Attractions

CAROL M. NEWMAN LIBRARY
Virginia Tech Campus   (703) 231-6170
Virginia Tech's Carol M.
Newman Library has a microforms
collection of nearly 5 million, making it the fifth largest in the U.S.
and Canada. Contained within this
store of information are rare books
and magazines, government documents, newspapers, Virginia Confederate Service Records and issues
of the campus newspaper back to
1903.

SMITHFIELD PLANTATION
*Virginia Tech campus, Off US 460 Bypass onto
Va. 314   (703) 951-2060*
Built by Col. William Preston
in 1772, Smithfield Plantation has
been extensively restored and is a
Virginia Historic Landmark. It was
the birthplace of two Virginia governors, James Patton Preston and
John Buchanan Floyd, and was
briefly the home of a third, John
Floyd, Jr.
Open April 1 through November 1, 1 to 5 PM, Wednesday,
Saturday and Sunday. Adults are $4,
under age 12, $1.50.

VIRGINIA TECH DUCK POND
Virginia Tech campus
If you took a poll of where
many people went on their first
date or fell in love in the New River
Valley, it would be the Virginia Tech
Duck Pond, hands down! It's a Tech
landmark beside the golf course,
where mothers take their babies,
couples hold hands and picnic and
the fattest ducks in the world hold
court over bread crumbs and crack-

ers. This place gives a whole new
meaning to the cliche "Lucky
Duck," and is the most popular
stroll on campus.

Floyd

Visual Arts

OLD CHURCH GALLERY
Rt. 221   (703) 745-4849
In this 1850 Greek Revival
building, various art work exhibits
are adjacent to the history room. A
century-old copper still (used to
make moonshine whiskey) is on
display. There's an active quilter's
guild, monthly literary group, arts
and crafts workshop and children's
programs in the summer.

NEW MOUNTAIN MERCANTILE HERE AND NOW GALLERY
114 N. Locust St.   (703) 745-4278
For art and crafts definitely
out of the ordinary, don't miss New
Mountain Mercantile and its Here
and Now Gallery. Located in the
100-year-old Boyd Store building,
six miles off Milepost 165.2 at the
Blue Ridge Parkway, this collage of
colorful creations has a gallery in
one corner that highlights the art of
one individual each month. What
looks like an ordinary building on
the outside is extraordinary inside.
It's just down the block from
Cockram's General Store.
Open Wednesday through
Saturday 10 AM to 6 PM, Sundays
noon to 5 PM.

Theater

FLOYD THEATRE GROUP
Route 4, Box 497,
Floyd, VA 24901   (703) 745-3158

This theatre group started with a Skit Night for locals and ended up an enthusiastic collection of folks who present outstanding plays and still make Skit Night an annual event. Productions are scheduled with tremendous community support and participation. It's yet another facet of the far-reaching culture of Floyd County.

Other Cultural Attractions

COCKRAM'S GENERAL STORE
South Locust St.   (703) 745-4563

The culture of mountainous Floyd County doesn't get any better than this! At 7 PM Friday nights, folks start showing up with fiddles, harmonicas, banjos and guitars and what follows is a Floyd County tradition. The flatfooting begins, the old-timers reminisce and the music that is the lifeblood of the Floyd County mountain spirit soothes the brow and heals the wounds of the work week. This is an endangered cultural species that is personally financed by Freeman Cockram, who believes Floyd Countians need such a place to gather. Don't miss this New River Valley landmark.

MABRY MILL
Mile 176, Blue Ridge Parkway
                          (703) 745-4329

Undoubtedly the most scenic and most-photographed place on the Blue Ridge Parkway, Mabry Mill has been called one of the most picturesque water mills in the entire U.S. It still grinds flour for buckwheat cakes and cornpone and produces some of the most delicious cornmeal you can buy for Southern-style cornbread. Mabry Mill also is a workshop of live crafts, music and exhibits that shows a way of life a century ago. There's also arts, crafts and a restaurant. If you're traveling through Floyd County, don't miss it!

Giles County

Visual Arts

THE MOUNTAIN LAKE SYMPOSIUM & GALLERY
Mountain Lake, VA 24136   (703) 626-7121

In the rarefied air on the second highest mountain in Virginia, Mountain Lake provides the picturesque setting each year for The Mountain Lake Symposium, begun by the Virginia Tech Department of Art and Art History, which has gained national recognition as an art criticism conference. Supported by the Virginia Museum of Fine Arts, it is yet another jewel in the culture of the Blue Ridge. While at Mountain Lake, also check out its Gallery, the home of the popular Bob Evans Knobbits make-believe creatures.

NEW RIVER VALLEY ARTS AND CRAFTS GUILD
U.S. 460, Pembroke   (703) 626-3309

Handmade treasures in the mountain tradition are both made and sold in the New River Valley Arts and Crafts Guild in the heart of

Pembroke. There's usually a quilt in the making, as well as rug weaving and other activities going on among the 60 artists who display and sell here.

Open 10 AM to 5 PM Tuesday through Saturday, 1 to 4 PM Sunday.

Museums

ANDREW JOHNSTON MUSEUM & RESEARCH CENTER

Main St.,
Pearisburg, VA 34134   (703) 921-5000

Located next to the Post Office on Main St., this restored brick house is home to a genealogy library and historic Giles County displays.

Open by appointment.

Theater

GILES LITTLE THEATRE

PO Box 193,
Pearisburg, VA 24134   (703) 921-4818

In sparsely populated Giles County, there's a driven group of little more than a dozen people who work feverishly to establish terrific theatre in this rural county. Over the years, they've lost several places to perform and hope to relocate into the renovated community center at old Narrows High. Call for the latest schedule!

Radford

Visual Arts

FLOSSIE MARTIN GALLERY

Radford University   (703) 831-5754

This state-of-the-art facility occupies 2,000 square feet of space on the beautiful Radford University campus. The combination gallery/ museum features rotating exhibits of both regional and nationally known artists. In its short three-year history, the gallery has had on its roster such important guests and international figures as the avant-garde John Cage and Dr. Jehan Sadat, wife of the former leader of Egypt, who displayed her own personal Egyptian art collection. The gallery sponsors CLAY, USA, an annual survey of contemporary ceramics.

Open 10 AM to 4 PM Tuesday through Friday, noon to 4 PM on Sunday.

Theater

THE LONG WAY HOME OUTDOOR DRAMA

Ingles Homestead Amphitheater
*   (703) 639-0679*

For 21 years now, the only outdoor theatre drama in Virginia has been wowing audiences with the Earl Hobson Smith historic epic, "The Long Way Home." This exciting drama focuses on local history, with a true heroic adventure depicting Mary Draper Ingles.

Ingles was captured after fleeing from a 1755 Indian attack on the north fork of the Roanoke River, where she saw her mother and infant nephew murdered by the Shawnee Indians. Forced to travel west 800 miles to make salt for the Shawnee, the story tells of her courageous escape and long trek back to Radford to warn of an upcoming attack. This breath-taking saga of honest, hardworking pioneers who labored to tame the American frontier is reenacted in the Ingles Homestead Amphitheater at her home site and grave. There's overnight camper parking available. This is a "must see" production for theatre and history buffs.

Open June through Labor Day. Adults are $6.50, ages 1-12 are $3.

Other Cultural Attractions

RADFORD UNIVERSITY COLLEGE OF VISUAL AND PERFORMING ARTS
(703) 831-5141
The university offers the public solo music performances, theatre, art exhibits, classical ballet, big band music, jazz and modern dance. Call the university for a schedule of culturally enriching events featuring students and nationally known guest artists.

Pulaski County

Visual Arts

THE FINE ARTS CENTER FOR THE NEW RIVER VALLEY
21 W. Main St.   *(703) 980-7363*
The New River Valley Fine Arts Center is the cultural hub of the New River Valley, featuring con-

temporary works, music shows, private collections and amateur and professional artists. It is housed in a storefront building considered a prime example of Victorian commercial architecture. Built in 1898, the center has been designated a Virginia Historic Landmark. This Center is also a prime example what can be accomplished when a community bands together to found and fund a grassroots fine arts center. Pulaski can be proud indeed of this facility.

Other Cultural Attractions

HISTORIC OLD NEWBERN & WILDERNESS ROAD REGIONAL MUSEUM
New River Historical Society (703) 674-4835
Nineteen original 1810 buildings comprise part of the 57 properties of the Old Newbern National Historic District, a neighborhood originally planned by early settlers. Newbern served as Pulaski County's seat from 1839-1893, when the courthouse was destroyed by fire. This interesting tour takes you through the historic buildings, some already renovated and some in the process, including a slave cabin, old jail, rose garden, pre-Civil War church, buggy shed and small weatherboarded barn. The museum contains artifacts of this era and sponsors a full annual agenda of everything from a Civil War Reenactors' Boot Camp and Civil War Weekend (Pulaski County was the site of the famous Battle of Cloyd's Mountain) to flea markets, dinners and holiday events.

Nearby are some great shops and restaurants including Valley Pike Inn, Granny Swain's Country Store, and PJ's Carousel Village, the world's largest manufacturer of carousel horses and animals, found at major amusement parks and fine gift shops around the world. With the tour, shops and restaurants, this makes for a wonderful day!

Open 10:30 AM to 4:30 PM, Tuesday through Saturday, 1:30 - 4:30 PM Sunday.

Alleghany Highlands Region

Visual Arts

ALLEGHANY HIGHLANDS ARTS & CRAFTS CENTER
439 East Ridgeway St., Clifton Forge   *(703) 862-4447*

The Galleries' changing exhibits feature works produced by Alleghany Highlands' and other artists. It is a not-for-profit volunteer organization that encourages creative experiences and appreciation of the visual arts.

Open Monday through Saturday, 10:30 AM to 4:30 PM summers, all other months Tuesday through Saturday same hours.

THE HIGHLAND COUNTY ARTS COUNCIL
PO Box 175, Monterey, VA 24465   *No phone*

The Highland County Arts Council provides artistic enrichment and enjoyable programming for all ages. HCAC has provided children's programs and also sponsored artists in residence who go into the schools. Other projects are a Maple Festival Crafts Booth, Highland Dance Classes and story-telling. Various events are scheduled throughout the year.

Museums

BATH COUNTY HISTORICAL SOCIETY MUSEUM
Courthouse Square   *(703) 839-2543*

Artifacts of Bath County and the Indian and Civil wars are prominent here. You'll see books, apparel and photographs. There's also a genealogy library. The group just published a history of Bath County for its 1991 Bicentennial.

Open May through November, Monday, Wednesday and Friday 9 AM to 4:30 PM, Tuesday noon to 8 PM.

MAPLE MUSEUM
U.S. 220, Monterey   *(703) 468-2550*

In the land of Maples, there's a museum celebrating old-time sugaring. See a replica of a Sugar House, where there are sugar and syrup-making demonstrations. Also on display are tools and equipment used by sugar makers throughout the years. Old-timers who can't otherwise get to the real sugar camps will especially find this interesting.

Open daily.

Music

GARTH NEWEL MUSIC CENTER
Hot Springs   *(703) 839-5409*

From among the giant hemlocks, the hills of Bath County come alive with the sound of music, envied by music-lovers the world over. The importance of the Garth Newel Center to the culture of the Alleghany Highlands and western Virginia cannot be underestimated. Musicians, students and awe-inspired audiences come together in this unspoiled mountain area to hear beautiful music, such as Mozart, Haydn and Dvorak in an enchanting mountain setting.

Featured are the Garth Newel Chamber Players and Garth Newel Piano Trio. Garth Newel provides an intensive residential Chamber Music Study Program for serious young musicians who receive a full scholarship. The architecture and acoustics of Herter Hall provide a wonderful ambiance for chamber music and create a unique sense of being outdoors while actually indoors! Before the performance, many visitors have made it a tradition to join friends for a picnic on the grounds. Its concerts have long been reputed to be not just music, but an entire experience. Garth Newel also sponsors holiday weekends that are a feast for lovers of chamber music, with gourmet meals, fine wine and convivial company. This is a Blue Ridge gem visited regularly by dignitaries the world over.

Other Cultural Attractions

BEAR MOUNTAIN OUTDOOR SCHOOL
Hightown   *(703) 468-2700*

Real mountain culture and crafts can be learned at Bear Mountain, located 4,200 feet up in Highland County. You can attain practical building skills, rural living pursuits such as log cabin building, blacksmithing and stone masonry, and take natural history hikes. Or, perhaps organic gardening, beekeeping, mushroom cultivation or spinning and natural dyeing are your cup of herbal tea. Workshops are one-on-one and hands-on, stressing real projects. Students actually build a log cabin or timber frame. This is a place to experience country living, rather than being lectured to about it. The school centers around a modern lodge 560 acres up in the clouds. Here's everything about the Blue Ridge that is unique!

C&O RAILROAD HISTORICAL SOCIETY
PO Box 79,
Clifton Forge, VA 24422   *No phone*

This organization in an historical railroad town is dedicated to preserving and interpreting the history of the Chesapeake & Ohio Railroad. It has one of the best archive collections of material pertinent to the history of a single railroad. It comprises over 100,000 ink-on-linen engineering and mechanical drawings, 50,000 photos and thousands of books and publications surrounding the industrial roots of the railroad that made this town boom long ago. The group publishes a monthly magazine and has a collection of historic passenger and freight cars covering the period of 1920s-1950s. It has 2,500 members in 49 states and is one of the largest organizations devoted to the study of a single railroad that traces its roots from 1836. The railroad's logo, the Chessie cat, from its "Sleep Like a Kitten" ad campaign in 1933, is one of the most famous logos in America.

Photo: Opera Roanoke

(Left to right) Jeffrey Ambrosini as Don Giovanni and Rod Nelman as Leporello in Opera Roanoke's sell-out Don Giovanni, May, 1992.

A few minutes south of Blacksburg is PJ's Mercantile in the historic community of "Old Newbern." Visitors will find PJ's famous carousel collection, 1900's style hand-carved miniatures, quilts, rugs, antiques and much more.

Inside
Shopping

Whether you're looking for antiques, handcrafts or outlet malls for bargains in clothing and housewares, the Blue Ridge region has it all. Of course there are the usual shopping malls, Walmarts, and K-Marts. But practically every town in the Shenandoah Valley, the foothills or other regions of the Blue Ridge has at least one quaint little antique shop and a place that sells locally made handcrafts.

Some fine furniture makers in the region, such as E.A. Clore in Madison or Suter's in Harrisonburg, sell directly to the consumer. You must visit their showrooms to see what they make, because you won't find their beautiful furniture elsewhere.

Likewise for the shops selling fine handcrafts. Places like the Blue Ridge Pottery on Rt. 33 near Skyline Drive and Limeton Pottery in Front Royal specialize in ceramics that are crafted literally right next door. Other shops, such as Forever Country in New Market and the Handcraft House in Madison, represent dozens of artisans whose creations also cannot be found in department stores.

Charlottesville is known for its fine downtown shops that sell crafts and other objets d'art from around the globe. There, you can just as easily find an African mask as a bar of American soap.

If you're visiting from out of state and want a Made-in-Virginia souvenir, there are plenty of shops specializing in such products. Virginia Born and Bred in Lexington is one fine example, selling beautiful brass and silver items as well as folk art, woven goods, peanuts, jams and jellies.

The following is a description of some of the best shops in the cities, towns, and rural areas we've covered in this guidebook. This is in no way a comprehensive listing, and we may have inadvertently missed your favorite shop. If so, drop us a line and give us your "Insider's" perspective. More will be added in subsequent editions of this book.

Shenandoah Valley Region

Winchester

One of the finest places in the region to find handcrafted jewelry, clothing, ceramics and home

The **U**niversity **Corner**

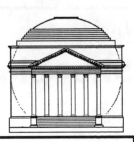

107 14th Street • (804) 295-1212

22 Elliewood Avenue • (804) 295-1242
(804) 295-4246

1327 West Main Street
(804) 293-4507

Heartwood

Rare & Used Books
Since 1975

5 Elliewood Avenue
(804)295-7083

1505 University Avenue
(804) 971-3558

Mincer's

UNIVERSITY SPORTSWEAR

Since 1948
University of Virginia Imprinted Sportswear
1527 University Ave • (804) 296-5687

The Universityversity Corner

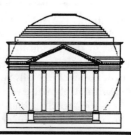

Freeman-Victorius

Professional picture frames and print sellers since 1938
1413 University Ave., (804) 296-3456

The Garment District

1509 University Ave • (804) 296-1003

1329 West Main Street • (804) 977-4885

THE PHOENIX

111 14th Street • (804) 296-1115

littlejohn's
New York **Delicatessen**
Open 24 Hours • (804) 977-0588
1427 University Avenue

Bike Rentals

Since 1974
19 Elliewood Avenue • (804) 977-1870

furnishings is Winchester's Hand-works Gallery (703-662-3927), located in the Loudoun Street Mall (for pedestrians only). Around the corner on W. Piccadilly Street is the beautiful Colonial Art and Craft Shop (662-6513), which sells fine china, crystal and silver, elegant lamps and picture frames. Kimberly's Antiques and Linens (662-2195) is not too far away on North Braddock Street. Located in historical Sheridan's Headquarters, Kimberly's sells early American and Victorian furniture, antique quilts and crochet spreads, fine bed linens and Civil War relics and literature. Virginia food products, such as honey, preserves and apple butter, are also sold here. The Happy Goose (662-0344) is one of several shops in Creekside Village, a new Williamsburg-style shopping development on U.S. 11. Here you will find Rowe Pottery, braided rugs, afghans, wreaths and other "country" items.

Strasburg

Strasburg considers itself the antique capital of Virginia. We don't necessarily endorse this claim, but we do agree that very fine antiques can be found here at fair prices. Whether you're a serious collector or someone who just likes to drool at beautiful things, you must visit the Strasburg Emporium, a 65,000-square-foot downtown building that houses about 100 antique and art dealers. The building, right on North Massanutten Street, used to be a silk mill. Along with high qual-

ity formal and country furniture, you'll find a lot of unusual items at the Emporium, such as old carnival horses, hobby horses, carriages, stoneware and iron beds. The Strasburg Emporium is open daily from 10 to 5, and has plenty of free parking (703-465-3711).

Bits, Bytes & Books on West King Street (465-4200) has a vast collection of old and new mysteries, westerns, science fiction and children's books, locally crafted gifts and glass collectibles. The Cedar Creek Relic Shop (869-5207), a couple of miles away in downtown Middletown, claims to have the largest collection of authentic Civil War relics for sale in the Shenandoah Valley. If you're hankering for a sword, bayonet, musket or artillery shell or two from that bloody war this is the place to shop.

Front Royal

The Limeton Pottery studio and gallery (703-636-8666) features locally made stoneware and earthenware pottery, along with note cards, baskets and other handcrafted items. One of downtown Front Royal's most interesting shops is the Bizarre Bazaar (636-6845), located in a 100-year-old home on Chester Street and open only on the weekends and some evenings. Here you'll find handmade crafts, folk art, pillows, quilts, wall hangings and more. Across from the Visitors Center on Main Street is Valley Crafters (635-4699), a shop selling baby doll clothes, quilts, and all kinds of country handcrafts.

Mount Jackson

Farther south, the little town of Mount Jackson off I-81 offers a number of quaint antique shops within walking distance of one another. Wolftrap Antiques (703-477-3250), situated in a pre-Civil War building on Main Street, specializes in walnut Victorian furniture. The Widow Kip's Bed and Breakfast and Antique Shop (477-2400) decorates its six rooms with antiques that are all for sale. It's located on Rt. 698, within walking distance from the downtown.

Luray

In downtown Luray, Mama's Treasures (703-743-1352) has an extensive collection of colorful glassware and old costume jewelry, along with some antique furniture and quilts. Zib's Country Connection on East Main (743-7394) features a unique collection of Victorian greeting cards, handcrafted gifts, collectibles and some antiques. Five miles east of Luray on Rt. 211, at the entrance to the Shenandoah National Park, sits the Pine Knoll Gift Shop (743-5805). This is an old-time store that's crammed with all kinds of Elvis and Hank Williams souvenirs, knives, quilts, baskets, coonskin caps, Indian moccasins and jewelry, jams and jellies, fireworks, great fudge and peanut brittle.

New Market

About two miles north of New Market on scenic U.S. 11 are two showrooms of Antiques by Burt Long (703-740-3777). Long specializes in country, oak and art deco furniture and also peddles pie safes, iron beds, cupboards, pottery, baskets and other accessories.

New Market's downtown Paper Treasures (740-3135) is a fascinating place to browse through old books, magazines and prints. The last time we checked, the store was selling old copies of *Colliers Weekly*, the *Saturday Evening Post*, *Ebony*, *Life*, and old Civil War maps and books. The store also sells some of the best in contemporary children's literature.

Shenandoah Valley Crafts and Gifts on Congress Street (or Rt. 11, 740-3899) sells everything from country furniture and fireworks to hand-loomed rugs, quilts and Virginia hams. Also on Congress Street is The Christmas Gallery (740-3000), which sells handmade crafts, wreaths, exquisite porcelain dolls and hundreds of ornaments, and Quarter Creek (740-4431) which specializes in 18th-century furniture.

Woodstock - Edinburg

Seven Bends Gallery (703-459-5525) in downtown historic Woodstock displays and sells original watercolors and photographs of the valley, along with stoneware pottery, hand-woven coverlets, stained glass lamps, wooden toys and other handcrafted items. Woodstock is also home to an Aileen Stores, Inc. outlet (459-3077), that sells women's sportswear for up to 70 percent off retail.

Every Saturday and Sunday a popular huge flea market takes place between Woodstock and Edinburg, offering antiques and collectibles both inside and out-doors. To get to The Flea Market (459-4723), take exit 283 from I-81. It's held on Rt. 11 on Landfill Road.

Richard's Antiques (984-4502) one mile south of Edinburg on Rt. 11 specializes in fine country and formal antiques and paintings.

Harrisonburg-Rockingham County

ANTIQUES

Nearly two dozen antique shops can be found throughout this area, which includes not just the thriving university city of Harrisonburg, but also the little towns of Mt. Crawford, McGaheysville, Dayton and Elkton.

Chalot's Antiques (703-433-0872) is a mecca for lovers of fine old furniture. Right on Main Street in tiny Mt. Crawford, in a building nearly 200 years old, the shop deals in high quality 18th- and 19th-century furniture. There are hundreds of pieces of "Flow-Blue" China in this shop, along with Victorian bric-a-brac, primitive accessories and old glassware.

The Antique Mart in McGaheysville (289-MART) is a re-stored old bank building that houses 25 shops with furniture and other collectibles. Farther east in Elkton is one of the area's finer antique shops, the Curiosity Shop (298-1404), where you'll find antique furniture, folk art, primitives, quilts

and old tools for the most discrimi-nating buyer.

Jeff's Antiques in Dayton (879-9961) specializes in oak and walnut furniture, and also carries pottery, primitives, toys and oil lamps.

In the Dayton Farmer's Mar-ket you will find Log Cabin An-tiques (434-8510), along with other shops selling freshly baked breads, candies, lace and handcrafted items. The antique store in the market specializes in primitives and painted country furniture.

In downtown Harrisonburg you'll find several shops selling an-tiques and collectibles, most nota-bly James McHone Antique Jewelry (433-1833). Here you will find ex-quisite estate and antique jewelry, sterling flatware and oil paintings. Villager Antiques (433-7226) sells painted country glassware and pot-tery, along with oak and walnut for-mal furniture.

HANDCRAFTS

The Mennonite-operated Gift and Thrift Shop (433-8844) in down-town Harrisonburg takes you around the globe with its selection of gor-geous weavings, ceramics, clothing and other crafts made in about 35 developing nations. Many of the craft makers are refugees, disadvan-taged minorities, or people with physical disabilities. The proceeds go toward the Mennonite Central Committee, the relief and develop-ment wing of the church. The prices are great, and spending money here helps people who are truly in need.

Suter's at 2610 S. Main Street (434-2131) has been around since the early 1800s, when Daniel Suter, a skilled Mennonite cabinetmaker and carpenter, settled in the Harrisonburg area and began making furniture. Today, William Suter and his daughter, Carol, are carrying on the family tradition of quality craftsmanship. The company makes gorgeous Colonial reproductions in cherry, mahogany and walnut, using the finest techniques. There are showrooms here and in Richmond, or you can send for a beautiful color catalog.

Tucked away in the Skyline Village Shopping Center on East Market Street is an unexpected place to find unique handcrafted porcelain jewelry, pottery, wooden ware, rugs and other crafts. The Bay Pottery (432-1580) also has a store in nearby Broadway on South Main Street.

It's definitely worth driving to the little town of Dayton just south of Harrisonburg for the Dayton Farmer's Market (879-9885), a place where the merchants are extraordinarily friendly. Inside the indoor market on Rt. 42, peddlers sell fresh poultry, seafood, beef, home-baked goods, fresh fruits and vegetables, cheeses, nuts and other dried goods. Specialty shops carry early American tin lighting, pottery, quality antiques and handcrafts, clothes, and even grandfather clocks. You can have a hearty, delicious lunch at Huyard's Country Kitchen inside the market. Nearby also in Dayton is the Clothes Line (879-2505), a fabric shop that also sells brilliantly colored handwoven rugs and quilts. There's a hitching post out front where buggy-riding Mennonites keep their horses while they shop.

East of Harrisonburg in McGaheysville is the Country Goose

Photo: Roanoke Convention and visitors Bureau

The historic Farmers Market in Roanoke.

Gift and Craft Shop (289-9626), that sells fine crafts made in the Shenandoah Valley. The place is a short drive from Massanutten Resort on Rt. 996. Here you will find salt-glazed pottery, handmade country furniture, folk art, baskets, benches, pillows, quilt racks, weavings and much more.

OTHER UNUSUAL SHOPPING SPOTS

The central business district has some specialty shops worth a visit, such as Touch the Earth (434-2895) with its Indian clothing, African jewelry and other exotic gifts and Reminisce (433-1889), which offers Victorian-era clothing and accessories.

North of Harrisonburg around Timberville are great places to partake of the region's sweet crop of the fall — apples. Showalter's Orchard and Greenhouse on Rt. 881 (896-7582) has its own cider mill, and sells freshly pressed cider from late September through December 1. There are also many varieties of apples to choose from, available from mid-August through the winter. Ryan's Fruit Market on Rt. 613 (896-1233) northwest of Timberville sells apples, sweet cider and pumpkins from the first of September to mid-November.

Locals flock to the Green Valley Book Fair (434-4260), which is held several weekends in the spring, summer, fall and winter at a warehouse near Mt. Crawford. Every spring and fall there is also a record fair, lasting only a single weekend. New books and records are sold at cut-rate prices.

Staunton-Augusta County

ANTIQUES

Historic downtown Staunton is full of interesting boutiques, including many antique shops – so many that Staunton has just issued a new brochure on antique shopping alone! Staunton has a treasure trove of architectural delights packed into five National Historic Districts, offering numerous places to hunt for antiques. Twenty-two shops are listed in the new brochure. Many are within walking distance of one another. One centrally located place is the Rose Street Interiors (886-0578) at 2 East Beverley, which sells some exquisite furniture but mostly curios, lamps, pillows and other accessories.

A few blocks away at the renovated Wharf Area sits the Freight Depot Antiques (885-8326), a lovely shop with folk art, glass, collectibles, linens, quilts and country furniture. Across the street, you can get lost in the Jolly Roger Haggle Shop (886-9527), a collector's paradise with coins, jewelry, china, old money, weapons, Civil War and Indian artifacts and much more. And around the corner at 112 New Street a quaint little shop called Of Things Past sells prints, jewelry, lamps and some furniture. The names of all of these shops are as much fun as looking in their doors. Just a few...Corner Cupboard, Honeysuckle Hill, Dusty's, Mint Spring, and Once Upon a Time Clock Shop, open "by chance or appoinment." Another great place to buy antiques, where you can stay

Shop Barracks Road

KRISSIA

Ladies Dresses
Sportswear
Swimwear
Great After Five
Lingerie

Christian Dior & DKNY
Hosiery & Tights

(804) 295-9249

**Toys, Miniatures,
Dolls & Books**

SHENANIGANS

North Wing Barracks Road
Charlottesville

804 295-4797

VIRGINIA'S BEST
VIRGINIA SHOP

THE VIRGINIA SHOP.
A must-visit store featuring
Virginia hospitality, gifts,
foods, wines, books, music,
and much, mouch more.

THE VIRGINIA SHOP
On "The Island"
(Behind Ruby Tuesdays Restaurant)
Open 7 days   977-0080

The Book
Gallery

VOTED CHARLOTTESVILLE'S
"BEST" BOOK STORE

(804) 977-2892

overnight, eat in a gourmet restaurant and enjoy a sophisticated nightclub is the Belle Grae Inn, 515 W. Frederick St.

Just north of Staunton, Dusty's Antique Market (248-2018) houses more than a dozen dealers of oak and walnut furniture, tools, quilts, primitives and other old things, and the nearby Rocky's Antique Mart (234-9900) also is headquarters for dozens of dealers selling everything from brass beds and china presses to gorgeous estate jewelry and sterling silver.

Also just north of Staunton is the Verona Flea Market (248-3532), which is open Thursday through Sunday. Thirty dealers sell a large variety of oak, pine, cherry, walnut and other antique furniture, along with quilts and linens, old books, china and more.

HANDCRAFTS

The Virginia Made Shop (886-7180) off exit 222 from I-81 has an extensive collection of foods, wines, handcrafts and other souvenirs from the Commonwealth. It's located right next to The Bacova Guild, (800) 544-6118 famous for silkscreened handcrafts and Rowe's Family Restaurant, an excellent place to sample down-home regional cooking and a favorite hangout for The Statler Brothers. The cookies here are big, homemade and delicious and the pies melt in your mouth.

Silver Linings on W. Beverley (885-7808) in the downtown is a popular shop with Mary Baldwin students, selling exotic jewelry and folk art from around the world,

along with clothes, pocket books and funky bric-a-brac. Across the street is the fascinating Once Upon a Time Clock Shop (885-6064), which sells antique wall clocks of every variety.

Elder's Antique and Classic Autos on New Street (885-0500) has a big window out front through which you can see the sleek old Rolls Royces and other beauties. Farther up New Street and across from the train station sits Naked Creek Pottery, where you can watch Jim Hanger work at his wheel if you're lucky. Several other potters work in this space, which has a small shop selling the pottery.

OTHER UNUSUAL SHOPPING SPOTS

Also new this year is "The Gift Connection," a brochure of 15 unique shopping experiences in the historic downtown district. People into the outdoors will enjoy Wilderness Collection at 20 Byers St. (886-0320), with name brands like Wigwam, Coloeman and Jansport. It carries everything you need for the great outdoors.

The first block of East Beverley in downtown Staunton is a fun place to browse through shops and have lunch. The Pampered Palate (886-9463) sells gourmet sandwiches and also has an unusually good selection of Virginia, French and Italian wines. Next door, Grandma's Bait Clothing Store (886-2222) carries fine clothing for infants and children, and the Golden Tub Bath Shop (885-8470) sells everything from elegant bath fixtures to soaps and towels. The Emporium (885-1673), 101 E.

Beverley, features a large selection of toys and antique gifts. Turtle Lane (886-9313) at 10 E. Beverley is a distinctive gift shop with unusual paper dolls, christening gowns, antique lace and reproductions. Arthurs at 3 E. Beverley (885-8609) has a dazzling collection of lamps and brass, pewter and silver items. West Beverly sports Silver Linings (885-7808), jewelry and folk art of the world, at 16 West. Down by the train station, don't miss Rails, 123 August St. (885-6575), which bills itself as more convenient than a trip to Paris, Rome or Rio, with the same shopping experience. There are many unusual items and chances are, you won't leave empty-handed.

Waynesboro-Stuarts Draft

The Waynesboro Village Factory Outlets (703-942-2320) right off I-64 houses dozens of specialty shops carrying discounted name-brand clothing, shoes, luggage, home furnishings, lingerie and more. Liz Claiborne, Royal Doulton, Dansk, Corning/Revere, Bass Shoes and London Fog are but a few of the stores at this attractively designed outdoor mall. The center is also popular for its quality arts and crafts exhibitors who sell their work Thursday through Sunday from April through December.

The Antique Barn (943-3756) opened in the spring of 1992 at the Waynesboro Village Factory Outlets; it's open Thursday through Sunday.

A number of Mennonite-operated businesses make shopping a

real pleasure in the Stuarts Draft area. Kinsinger's Kountry Kitchen (337-2668) on Rt. 651 sells breads, cookies, cakes and pies made from scratch. The hummingbird cake and cheese herb bread are out of this world. About a half mile away on Rt. Rt. 608 is the Cheese Shop (337-4224), an Amish-Mennonite family business since 1960. The tidy little store in the back of a simple brick house sells more than 30 varieties of cheese at great prices, along with nuts, dried fruits and other dry foods in bulk. The Cheese Shop is closed on Wednesdays and Sundays.

The Candy Shop on Rt. 608 near U.S. 340 (337-1438) sells a complete line of Hershey products, including reproductions of early tins and glass. There are no tours at the nearby Hershey plant in Stuarts Draft, but some of the items made there include Reese's Pieces, Whatchmacallits and Bar None. The Candy Shop also carries quilts, which they will custom make, along with handmade furniture. This year, the shop is featuring lawn furniture such as gazebos, porch swings like "Grandma used to have," and love seats.

Another shopping attraction based in Waynesboro is the Virginia Metalcrafters Factory Showroom (949-9432) at 1010 E. Main St. You can watch the age-old technique of pouring molten brass into molds through an observation window, and buy imperfects and discontinued items at reduced prices. There are items such as handcrafted solid brass and iron candlesticks, lighting fixtures, fireplace equipment and wooden accessories.

Lexington

ANTIQUES

The Lexington Historical Shop at 9 East Washington St. (463-2615) is the only shop of its kind in Virginia, specializing in Confederate-related original materials. Autographs, documents, books, prints, soldiers' letters, flags, belt buckles, uniforms and more will awe any Civil War buff. Owner Bob Lurate also offers Virginia-related histories, maps and other documents along with antique quilts and other collectibles. If you can't make it to Lexington, call to receive a catalogue so that you can order by mail.

For one of the finest antique stores in the Rockbridge County region, visit Old South Antiques, Ltd. (348-5360) in the charming village of Brownsburg, 15 minutes north of Lexington via US 11 and 710 or State Rt. 39 and 252. Old South specializes in New England, Pennsylvania and Southern antiques in original paint and refinished cherry, walnut and pine. The shop is recommended by American Country South for its country style wares and is known for its large selection of American Country furniture and accessories. Within walking distance is Brownsburg Tavern Antiques and Augusta Antiques (348-1192), a shop in the tavern room of a c. 1820 home. Here you will find distinctive 19th century American furniture, quilts, and country accessories. Both Brownsburg shops are open most

weekends and by appointment.

Braford Antiques on Hwy. 130 (703-291-2217) is another exquisite shop down the road from Natural Bridge. The Brafords have a fine collection of 19th-century American furniture and pieces from Asia.

GENERAL STORES

Enjoy a step back in time with the Lexington area's two real general stores, The General Store on 2522 Beech Ave. in Buena Vista (703-261-3860) and Maury River Mercantile, located on Va. Byway 39 (348-1300) in historic Rockbridge Baths. Both have been in business 100 years and, in many ways, actually are working museums. Don't miss the made-in-Virginia items and country crafts. Maury River even offers you the once-in-a-lifetime opportunity to visit an old fashioned working outhouse! And just next door is a swinging bridge across the river — a rare find in this day and age. In Buena Vista, visitors love The General Store with its early farm and transportation exhibit and century-old display cases. Aromas waft through the old building, where you can find everything from blue jeans and bulk seed to fabric and kitchenware.

HANDCRAFTS

Artists in Cahoots, is a cooperative gallery of local artists and craftspeople downtown at 1 Washington St. (703-464-1147). You'll find oil and watercolors, pottery, metalwork, hand-blown glass, photography, sculpture, hand-painted silk scarves and porcelain jewelry.

Photo: Harrisonburg Chamber of Commerce

The Farmers' Market in Harrisonburg.

OTHER UNUSUAL SHOPPING SPOTS

Downtown shopping is a panorama of boutique-type shops that will keep you looking all day. For gifts, try Fantasies at 21 Nelson St. (703-463-7222) for the new, subtle and dazzling. Virginia Born & Bred at 16 W. Washington St. (800-437-2452) is a sophisticated shop that is chock full of Old Dominion handcrafts, wine, fine brass work, linens and more. For sleek or funky dresses and exotic jewelry and accessories, don't miss Pappagallo at 23 N. Main, (463-5988). If new and used books are your idea of a perfect afternoon of browsing, go to the Second Story, 7 E. Washington St. (463-6264) or the Bestseller on Nelson St. (463-4647).

T.G.I.F., 30 S. Main (463-9730) is a popular destination for Washington & Lee students with its "seconds" from J. Crew, Tweeds and other fashionable clothing manufacturers.

If you're hankering for chocolate, head down to Cocoa Mill Chocolates (464-8400) on West Nelson St. Hand-dipped, scrumptious confections are sold individually or by the box, and the owners also have a mail-order service.

In Rockbridge County, on Route 606 at Racine, Don Haynie and Tom Hamlin welcome you to the wonderful world of herbs in a big way. They are the darlings of the local garden club set for the way they have renovated Buffalo Springs Herb Farm (348-1083), an extraordinary 18th-century stone house and garden open for herbal teas, luncheons and tours. These two perfectionists have a huge following for their herb workshops that always feature flawless food (such as hand-pressed herbal cookies) and decor. There is a gorgeous gift shop in a big red barn that features herbal products, dried flowers and garden books. Their display gardens look like something out of Williamsburg. You'll see a culinary garden, springhouse tea garden and four-square heirloom vegetable and herb garden. To make a wonderful trip even better, Buffalo Springs is located next to historic Wades Mill, a working water-powered flour mill that is listed on the National Register of Historic Places. The mill (348-1400) is open from April to mid-December and produces and sells all kinds of bread flours, cornmeal, cereal and bran. Gift boxes are also sold.

Botetourt County-Troutville-Fincastle

ANTIQUES

Many a Roanoker loves to take a trip out to the cool, crisp countryside in Autumn, buy apples from the county orchards and go antiquing. The opportunities are numerous on U.S. 11 heading into Troutville and on U.S. 220 on the way to historic Fincastle. Both towns have more than their fair share of terrific little antique shops. In Troutville, the Troutville Antique Mart (703-992-4249), beside the Troutville Fire Station and Goodwill Tinker Mountain Industries, offers the best opportunity for browsing under one roof. Here, a dozen dealers display fine antiques and collectibles and the prices are some of the lowest you'll find. How about a first-class antique 1890s leather and wooden trunk for $100? You can find it here.

HANDCRAFTS

A real gem in a rural area, Amerind Gallery (703-992-1066), Route 220 North, Daleville, features artwork of Native American and western artists. It is a member of the Indian Arts and Crafts Association and guarantees the authenticity of every Indian handmade item in the gallery. Amerind offers a unique cultural opportunity to learn about American art forms and cultures. Original works decorate the walls and the collectibility of the art is superb. Across town, in Troutville, there's a breath of fresh air in every gift at Al and Rachael Nichol's Apple Barn (992-3551) off Route 11. Located on a working apple farm, you can browse through country collectibles sipping a complimentary cup of hot, spiced cider, and buy or pick your own bag of apples before you leave the picturesque orchard setting. Shopping at Nichol's is an experience for your spirit and soul in the fresh Botetourt County country air.

ORCHARDS

Botetourt County is apple orchard country. There's nothing more beautiful than the acres of delicate apple blossoms that signal the coming of spring in the Blue Ridge. The county has quite a few orchards, large and small. Probably the biggest and best known are Ikenberry (703-992-2448), and Layman's (992-2687), both on U.S. 220 in Daleville. In addition to apples of every kind, you can buy seasonal specials such as pumpkins, sweet corn and peaches.

Craig County

Whatever your need, you'll find it at New Castle Mercantile (703-864-5560), located at 325 Main

Catalogue clothing for men & women 50%-75% OFF the catalogue prices, everyday.

BARR·EE STATION CATALOGUE OUTLET

NINE well-stocked stores in Virginia & North Carolina! CHAPEL HILL, CHARLOTTESVILLE (2), DUCK, HARRISONBURG, KILL DEVIL HILLS, RICHMOND, NORFOLK, VIRGINIA BEACH

St. In this tiny mountain community, New Castle Mercantile fills the bill for seeds, animal feed, hardware, housewares and toys. It's open every day but Sunday, from 7:30 AM to 6 PM.

Roanoke

ANTIQUES

The Roanoke Valley is a treasure trove for top-notch, low-cost antiques. When movie star Debbie Reynolds' daughter, star and author Carrie Fisher, came to visit at her mom's Roanoke home, that's the first place she wanted to go and she spent all day! What you'll find is a tremendous variety downtown. Trudy's Antiques (703-343-2004), 12 Wells Ave., NE, specializes in old prints and advertising, dolls, jewelry and glassware. Sandra's Cellar (342-8123), 120 Campbell Ave. SE, is a nostalgia trip specializing in vintage clothing, furniture and toys. Bob Beard Antiques, "Open By Chance or Appointment," (981-1757), 105 Market St., is a find for the unexpected. Russell's Yesteryear (342-1750), 117 E. Campbell Ave., has the slogan, "When you visit the Market, stop in and see us. If you don't, we both lose money." Civil War antique lovers will want to visit historian Howard McManus' shop, Magic City Station (344-2302), at 11 S. Jefferson St., to see his collection of Civil War memorabilia. McManus is an expert on the Battle of Cloyd's Mountain in Pulaski County and the war in Southwestern Virginia. For a complete list of antique shops in the Valley, call (342-6025).

HANDCRAFTS

If fine handcrafts are what you're looking for, look no farther than the historic City Market. You will find the perfect gift and probably end up buying something for yourself as well. Gallery 3 (703-343-9698), 213 Market St., offers the epitome of art for the kitchen, wood, glass, gifts and clothing. Gallery 3 is a favorite shopping spot for corporate art collectors as well, offering both local artists as well as nationally-known artists such as Wolf Kahn. The first Fridays of each month, Gallery 3 offers "Art By Night," featuring local artists and their work. Custom framing also is available Also located on the market, at 206 Market Square, is Studios on the Square, (345-4076), a second floor studio where 18 working artists demonstrate and sell wares including pottery, paper, fiber, wood, textiles, jewelry, baskets, stained glass, photography and fine paintings. The climb upstairs to this treasure trove of arts and crafts stores is well worth it. You'll think you're in a loft in New York and chances are, you won't leave empty handed.

OUTLETS

Roanoke offers some interesting outlets for unusual items ranging from camouflage to jewelry. On US 220 South, hunters and those who like the camouflage look won't want to miss Trebark Outfitters (703-774-9007), 3434 Buck Mountain Rd. Jim Crumley, the inventor of Trebark camouflage, lives in Roanoke and offers good deals at his store. Hunting and fishing lovers and fans of the sporting life will also enjoy the Orvis Factory Outlet (344-4520) downtown at 21-B Campbell Ave. Summers are an especially good time to shop, when you can get discounts of up to 80 percent on winter items offered in their national catalog and in the Orvis Retail Store just a block away. Other tremendous buys can be found at an Emerson Creek Pottery outlet (see Bedford shopping chapter), (342-7656), gorgeous handmade pottery on the market at 108 Market Street. Also downtown, but a little more difficult to find, is Design Accessories (344-8958), a custom-made Austrian crystal jewelry outlet store at 406 Luck Ave. Again, you can find discounts of 70 percent or more on fascinating watches, jewelry and accessories featured in national bridal magazines. For household items, go to Crossroads Mall on Williamson Rd. to Waccamaw Pottery (563-4948).

SPECIALTY STORES

There are great specialty stores and boutiques throughout the Roanoke City Market. You will find clothing at Patina (703-344-3836), 24 E. Campbell Ave., surplus Army gear at Sam's On the Market (342-7300), 304 Market St., a shop just for people who like birds, For the Birds (345-9393), 303 Market St. and specialty stores in the Market Building, which anchors the shopping area. Other favorites of all generations are branches of Blacksburg stores in the New River Valley. Mish Mish (345-1020), at 14 E. Campbell specializes in art supplies. Books, Strings & Things (342-5511), 202 Market Square, is a great place to browse among tapes and CDs, books, cards and calendars. The Children's Corner, with its own little rocking chair, endears parents who bring their prodigy to read and rock while they pick out their favorite oldies. The major malls in the area, Crossroads, Tanglewood and Valley View, also have some specialty stores of a more commercial nature.

East of the Blue Ridge Region

Washington

This tiny community of fewer than 200 residents boasts a number of sophisticated galleries, antique shops and places to buy fine handcrafted gifts.

Peter Kramer (703-675-3625) at Gay and Jeff streets has been making beautiful furniture for 23 years in town. Each of his creations is one-of-a-kind, a hand crafted creation made from native American wood. Some of the furniture is rather whimsical, while other pieces are more classical and austere. Kramer also has showrooms on Cape Cod.

The Rush River Company, a crafts gallery on Gay Street (675-1136), displays and sells works of more than 20 artists. You'll find furniture, fabrics, photographs, paintings, pottery, jewelry, baskets and clothing here.

Country Heritage specializes in American folk art, quality

Peter Kramer, a Washington, Virginia, cabinet maker for 22 years, works on a table-top in the back yard of his studio.

handcrafts, country and primitive furniture and fine antiques. More than 100 craft makers are presented at this shop on Main Street (675-3738).

Sperryville

Just south of Washington in Sperryville, you'll find scores of antique and craft shops, including the Trading Post (703-675-3990), which sells Native American quilts, beadwork, jewelry, pipes and crafts, and the Sperryville Emporium (987-8235), a series of connecting buildings where you can find everything from antiques and apples to country hams and honey.

Faith Mountain Herbs and Antiques (987-8547) sells flowers, herbs, crafts and fashions for women, with many items priced well below retail. The Church Mouse (987-9106) is a charming, turn-of-the-century Gothic church that has been converted into a gallery and craft shop. Springhouse Antiques (987-3177) on Main Street specializes in country pine and oak antique furniture, flow blue china, quilts, linens and kitchen collectibles. Elmer's Antiques (987-8355) sells walnut, cherry and oak antiques and also sells apples and presses its own cider in season. Country Manor is the last shop on Rt. 211 west before you get to Skyline Drive. Here you can browse for hours among carvings and baskets, including white oak baskets woven locally and grape vine baskets woven by the Manor's owner, Phylis Swindler.

North of Charlottesville — Greene and Madison Counties

Two major rural highways intersect through this area — Rt. 29 and Rt. 33 — and along both roads are dozens of shops chock full of antiques and handcrafts.

Starting in Madison, the Bleak-Thrift House (703-948-3645) is a restored old home (circa 1838) where you will find some antique furniture, glassware, primitives, lace and linens. English boxwoods surround the home, which is in downtown Madison on Main Street (29 Business).

Madison is headquarters for E.A. Clore Sons, Inc., makers of simple, but handsome furniture since 1830. "We don't make any fancy furniture," says company president Edward Clore, "but we try to make it last ... and by golly it does." Nestled in a hollow, three-tenths of a miles from Rt. 637, E.A. Clore (948-5821) specializes in handmade Early American furniture from walnut, cherry, oak and mahogany. Clore sells directly from its factory to the consumer, and its showrooms are right next door.

Just to the north in the tiny mountain town of Criglersville sits the Mountain Store (923-4349), open only on weekends. It's a truly wonderful place with books, handmade crafts and an interesting selection of children's toys and jigsaw puzzles.

Two miles south of Madison on Rt. 29 are several shops worth visiting. Spring Hill Farm Antiques

(948-4647) has dozens of quilts, ironware, blue and white stoneware, twig, tramp and folk art and old American "country" furniture. The store also has a fabric and upholstery service and a huge selection of lamp shades. Next door, the Madison Antiques Center (948-3428) represents about 55 dealers from around the country.

Handcraft House (948-6323), situated in an unassuming building right on Rt. 29, sells very fine crafts made by more than 300 artisans from across the nation. You'll find handwoven afghans and rugs, stoneware, hand painted china, wooden games and toys, lamps, tinware and much more. Handcraft House also has a mail-order service.

About seven miles south of Madison on Rt. 29 is Country Garden Antiques (948-3240), another fine store in a restored old home. This place sells exquisite antique furniture — both American and European, imported colorful tiles, old prints, old wrought iron gadgets, English lawn ornaments, antique jewelry and framed art work. The place also sells hard-to-find pillow covers from France that are copies of old tapestries.

When Rt. 29 arrives in Ruckersville, it intersects with Rt. 33 and forms a crossroads that bustles with activity for antique lovers. The three-story Greene House Shops (804-985-2438) houses at least 50 dealers of antiques, crafts, quilts and all kinds of gifts. It's open every day and even accepts credit cards. Across the road is the Country Store Antique Mall (804-985-3649), and the new kid on the block,

Antique Collectors (985-8966).

Lord Browne Antiques (804-985-7797), located on Rt. 29 about 1/3 mile south of this intersection, specializes in period Virginia mantles and accessories for the hearth.

Early Time Antiques and Fine Art, also in Ruckersville (985-3602) has a good reputation for its 18th- and 19th-century furniture, oil paintings and accessories.

Farther west on Rt. 33 toward Skyline Drive is a popular wayside called the Blue Ridge Pottery (985-6080), located in what was once the Golden Horseshoe Inn (c. 1827). The Inn, located along what was once called the Spotswood Trail, used to serve travelers making the difficult climb over the mountains. General "Stonewall" Jackson reportedly stayed here during the war, using the inn as his temporary headquarters only a few weeks before he was killed.

Alan Ward throws his stoneware pottery in a little studio right next door to Blue Ridge Pottery and welcomes visitors. His pottery, which is modelled after traditional Valley styles but painted with modern, vibrant glazes, is sold in the shop, along with locally made crafts, Virginia wines, apple butter and jams and Christmas decorations.

Closer to Stanardsville is the Edgewood Farm Nursery (804-985-3782), which stocks one of the largest selection of herbs and perennials in the state. You can walk to the nursery from Edgewood Farm, an elegant, hospitable B & B run by Eleanor Schwartz. Norman Schwartz, her husband, operates the nursery.

Charlottesville and Surrounding Area

Antiques

There are at least two dozen antique stores in the Charlottesville area, and this does not count the dozens of "mini" shops that share a single roof.

You'll find several stores in the heart of the downtown: Alley Antiques (804-979-1554) and the Downtown Charlottesville Art and Antique Center (295-5503) on the Historic Downtown Mall and South Street Antiques (295-2449), only a block away. You could spend hours strolling through the 16,000-square-feet Downtown Antique Center, which represents dozens of dealers in decorative accessories, period furniture, vintage clothing, and more.

On the higher end of the scale, Ann Woods, Ltd. on Rt. 250 West (295-6108) specializes in 18th- and 19th-century English and American furniture and silver. Woods also offers an interior design service in her shop. Next door is another exclusive shop, 1740 House Antiques (977-1740), which sells 18th- and 19th-century furniture and accessories.

DeLoach Antiques at 1211 W. Main St. (979-7209) is a charming place to find stylish and unusual decorative objects and antiques at very good prices. An eclectic selection of neoclassical, French, English and American pieces are displayed throughout a beautifully decorated townhouse that was built by one of Thomas Jefferson's master craftsmen in 1817.

If you're interested in either antique or new rugs from the villages of the Middle East, stop by the Sun Bow Trading Company on 4th Street (293-8821). Saul, the owner, has many a tale to tell about these tribal textiles and nomadic oriental rugs and his journeys to find them, and will serve you a cup of Middle Eastern tea.

The very nice Greenwood Antique Center (703-456-8465) is located about 15 miles west of Charlottesville on U.S. 250, selling fine old furniture, primitives, glassware, Chinese porcelain, works of art and jewelry. Beltrone & Company at the Woodbrook Shopping Center (974-1861) sells original weapons and artifacts from the American Revolution to World War I.

If you're looking for out-of-print books, the Daedalus Bookshop on 4th Street (293-7595) has three floors of them. The Heartwood Bookshop on Elliewood (295-7083) has an impressive rare book collection, with an emphasis on Americana and literature (as well as all kinds of new books).

Handcrafts

Charlottesville is known for having an abundance of shops that sell exquisite crafts from around the world. Many of the shops seem more like galleries and some function as both.

The historic Downtown Mall is a good place to start exploring such stores. On the west end, close to the Omni, The Nicholas & Alexandra Gallery (295-4003) stocks dolls, rugs, toys, artwork and all kinds of other crafts made in Russia and other republics of the former Soviet Union. Right next door is Renaissance Gifts (296-9208), an unusual shop selling rugs, pottery, masks and other items from Africa, South America and Asia. If you're needing spinning and weaving supplies, look no further than Stony Mountain Fibers (295-2008) a stone's throw away.

Artworks (979-2888), centrally located on the mall, is another gallery of contemporary crafts that sells jewelry, art pieces and hand-woven clothing. Paula Lewis on Fourth Street and E. Jefferson (295-6244) also has a splendid collection of old and new quilts, along with country folk art, Pueblo Indian pottery, quilting supplies and books.

The McGuffey Art Center (295-7973) is a renovated elementary school within walking distance from the downtown mall with a contemporary gallery and workshops and studios where more than 40 artists and crafts makers create their art. There are some very gifted artists at work here who are represented by galleries in New York City and other major cities. A small gift shop sells some of their creations. You'll find pottery, photography, prints, stained glass, sculptures, jewelry and much more.

At the Barracks Road Shopping Center is the Peddler's Shop (971-4847), which also sells fine hand-crafted gifts made all over the United States.

The Crafter's Gallery (295-7006), located nine miles west of Charlottesville on Rt. 250, specializes in contemporary crafts, selling glassware, pottery, ironware, silver, weavings and leather goods. While you're heading west, it's worth a trip to Afton to visit Blue Ridge Terrace Gifts, Inc. on 250 W. (703-949-0988), which sells traditional and mountain crafts made locally.

Lewis Glaser, Inc. (973-7783) at 1700 Sourwood Place specializes in hand-cut Colonial style goose quill pens. Internationally known quill maker Nancy Floyd is the exclusive producer of quill pens used by the U.S. Supreme Court.

OTHER SPECIALTY SHOPS

(organized by neighborhood)

"On The Corner" is the local term for that tight little neighborhood of shops, cafes and restaurants only a half-block away from the Rotunda and original UVA campus. A number of specialty shops make the corner an interesting place to wander around for both guys and gals and even youngsters.

Arnette's at University and Elliewood avenues (977-8451) has three floors full of unique gifts, cards, clothing and accessories. There's something for everyone in this charming family-run store — even a science and nature shop for kids.

Barr-ee Station on University Avenue (979-7981), is a great outlet store that sells brand name, high quality clothing for men and women at cut-rate prices.

The Phoenix on 14th Street (296-1115) is a unique women's

boutique that sells exquisite and funky dresses, unusual t-shirts, exotic earrings, belts and other accessories. The Garment District on University Avenue (296-1003) caters to university women with its cute, fashionable clothing at reasonable prices.

For traditionalists, Eljo's at 3 Elliewood Avenue (295-5230) has been selling "preppie" clothes for over 40 years, offering the best of Ralph Lauren, Southwick, Corbin and Gitman.

On the athletic front, the "Go Pal" Bicycle Shop on 14th Street (295-1212) specializes in mountain and road bikes, with a wide selection of Trek and Bianchi models. They are also licensed to repair all kinds of bikes. Blue Wheel Bicycles at 19 Elliewood Avenue (977-1870) features fine bicycles at competitive prices, along with a good selection of accessories. This bike shop has been around for nearly 20 years. Ragged Mountain Running Shop on Elliewood Avenue (293-3367) has a huge selection of running and aerobic shoes at very competitive prices.

And for all your framing needs, head to Freeman-Victorious Framing (296-3456) at 1413 University Avenue. The shop also sells antique prints and posters, mirrors, and other fine gifts.

Heartwood Used Books at 5 Elliewood Avenue (295-7083) has a great collection of second-hand scholarly and popular books in both hardback and paperback. You'll find cookbooks, histories, literature, mysteries, nature, science fiction, an antiquarian collection and more.

Mincer's, at University Avenue and Elliewood (296-5687), is open seven days a week and has been selling university sportswear for over 40 years.

Also on University Corner is Willie's Hair Design for your hair styling needs.

HISTORIC DOWNTOWN MALL

We've already described some of the shops in the downtown pedestrian mall that specialize in exquisite handcrafts. There are also many other delightful specialty shops, most of which are owner-operated.

One of the most interesting places to browse is the Old Hardware Store (977-1518), a block-long building that houses a restaurant and soda fountain, several specialty food bars and shops selling everything from gold and silver jewelry to games and wrought iron. The Old Hardware Store is aptly named. It operated from 1895 to 1976, and was once the hardware store in central Virginia. Not only did it sell rope and tools and other hardware, but you could also find fine china and silver there, along with everyday crockery and eggs and other staples. Just like the old days, the Old Hardware Store still has something for everyone. You can even get your hair trimmed and your shoes shined at the place.

Other outstanding specialty shops on the Downtown Mall include Palais Royal (979-4111), which has the finest in French designer linens, robes, towels and blankets and The Jeweler's Eye (979-5919), an eclectic collection of jewelry dating from the 1700s through the 1900s.

K.M.H. Hightower (979-

0136) on the east end of the Mall sells Caswell-Massey, producers of bath products and colognes for the world's fashionable elite since 1752.

Pewter Corner (971-3788) claims to stock the largest selection of pewter in the United States. There are also two fine oriental rug shops right on the Mall: Purcell Oriental Rug Co., Ltd. (971-8822), and T.S. Eways (979-3038) right next door.

The Williams Corner Bookstore (977-4858), just a couple of doors down from the Old Hardware Store, is considered by some to be the best book store in town.

BARRACKS ROAD SHOPPING CENTER

Located at Barracks Road and Emmet Street, this is a crowded but worthwhile shopping destination because there are dozens of wonderful specialty shops and a few department stores within walking distance (just watch the traffic).

Mum's the Word (971-8201) is one of the finest maternity and babies clothing stores in the state. The shop sells exquisite handmade christening gowns, hand-knitted booties and hats, bedding for infants and children, as well as nursery furniture and accessories. The maternity wear is fashionable, and so is the clothing for infants and children. One of the owners will also custom design christening gowns.

Speaking of youngsters, Shenanigans (295-4797) is a great place to find children's books, toys, stuffed animals, dolls from around the world, and children's music — including sing-along videos. True to its name, Whimsies (977-8767) has fanciful and spunky children's wear, including clothes for infants and toddlers. It's next door to Shenanigans.

The Book Gallery (977-2892) also has a great selection of children's books, along with other books on topics ranging from Thomas Jefferson and Virginia history to home decorating and sports.

Nature by Design (977-6100) is a fascinating shop for folks of all ages, selling everything from polished rocks for less than a dollar to driftwood water fountains at $1,300. You will find jewelry, bird feeders, garden accessories, chimes, agate bookends, puzzles, games and more — and all with a touch of nature.

Keller & George (293-5011) is where you'll find the popular Jefferson cup, along with fine jewelry and distinctive and unusual gifts.

Plow & Hearth (977-3707) sells beautiful outdoor ornaments and furniture made of wrought iron, cedar and other sturdy materials.

Art Needlework, Inc. (296-4625) has a large selection of needlepoint and knitting patterns and supplies, selling Persian, Appleton, Medici, silk and metallic yarns in every color. The unique shop also sells hand-dyed yarns in wool, cotton, silk, mohair and angora.

For women's clothing, Krissia (295-9249) sells exquisite lingerie, chic swim wear and fine hosiery and slippers. Levy's (295-4270) sells gorgeous, sophisticated sportswear and bathing suits downstairs, and on the upper level, formal wear and snappy business suits.

Nearby Seminole Square is a

very fine furniture store that has been furnishing homes in Central Virginia since 1926. Gilmore, Hamm and Snyder, Inc. (973-8114) sells quality furniture by such manufacturers as Henkel Harris, Henry Link and Hickory Chair, along with hand-woven oriental rugs, lamps, pictures, mirrors and window treatments.

La Difference (973-3122) is another place to shop for the home at Seminole Square. Here you'll find lighting, closet systems and furniture and gadgets for your kitchen, bedroom and bath.

Lynchburg

ANTIQUES

A phenomenal array of antique stores, nearly 20 in all, can be found in this historic and cultural city. For a list of them all, contact the Visitor's Center at (804-847-1811).

For a quick downtown whirl, try Consignment Shop on 1122 Main St. (804-845-1122), Redcoat Antiques, 1421 Main St. (804-528-3182) and Sweeney's Curious Goods, 1220 Main St. (804-846-7839). There's also a concentration near River Ridge Mall off Candlers Mountain Road.

HANDCRAFTS

Virginia Handcrafts, Inc., part of The Farm Basket shopping complex at 2008 Langhorne Rd. (804-846-5839), will keep you wandering around all day. It's a casual shop where browsers and their children are welcome. The spacious store features a collection of American crafts including kaleidoscopes, game boards, pottery and jewelry. These are displayed among paintings, planters, fountains, lamps, rugs and much more than can possibly be described here. One room is devoted to crafts made by Virginians. The atmosphere is just plain fun! If you're looking for a relaxed, casual and friendly atmosphere, you'll find it at Virginia Handcrafts. At adjoining Farm Basket Shop (528-1107), you can browse through rooms of carefully chosen gift items from around the world. Children can entertain themselves with an imported wooden train in a Toy Department which also overflows with stuffed animals, dolls and baby gifts. Custom invitations and announcements can be created with a calligraphy computer. A mail order catalog is available. While you're at this shopping complex, visit S.P. Petites, Lynchburg's first boutique for women 5' 4" and under (846-5839). Then have a cucumber sandwich at the best homemade food restaurant in the area, located within the complex. Farm Basket's fruit stand supplies are locally grown from their own mountain orchards. This is a Lynchburg landmark not to be missed!

OUTLETS

There are 14 terrific outlets and discount stores in Lynchburg. A complete list is available from the Visitor's Center (804-847-1732).

The granddaddy of them all, the first shoe company south of the Mason Dixon line (founded 1888), and the most famous is Craddock-

Terry Shoe Factory Outlet at 601 12th St. (847-3535). You can get up to 70 percent off 300,000 pairs of shoes in stock from the national Masseys catalogs. You'll see the billboards with the gigantic plastic pairs of red high heel pumps as you come into town on major roads. The store specializes in hard to find sizes and widths, from 3-13, AAAA to EEEE. Shoe lovers will recognize national brand names like Rockport and American Gentleman. It's worth an overnight stay for an average family just to buy seasonal shoes and see the sights of Lynchburg at the same time. Another fine shoe outlet is Consolidated Shoe Store, 10200 Timberlake Rd. (237-5569).

For clothes and accessories, there's Carolina Hosiery, 525 Alleghany Ave. (846-5099) and Tultex Mill Outlet at Forest Plaza West Shopping Center (385-6477). For the largest Tultex collection, known world-wide, go to Martinsville, home of Tultex. It borders the Blue Ridge and also offers furniture outlets.

SPECIALTY SHOPS

For both specialty shopping and terrific eating, go to the Community Market (847-1499), Main at 12th Street, established 1783. You'll find homemade crafts, Virginia made goods and baked goods. Something is always going on, and the market is the hubbub of Lynchburg activity, as it was in the days of Thomas Jefferson, when he scared Lynchburg citizens here by biting into a tomato, long thought to be a poisonous fruit. This market and the one in Roanoke are center-

pieces of Blue Ridge life and a joy to behold.

Smith Mountain Lake, Bedford & Franklin Counties

SMITH MOUNTAIN LAKE

There are two major areas for shoppers at Smith Mountain Lake. Those is Bridgewater Plaza on Rt. 122 at Hales Ford Bridge, where the official Smith Mountain Lake Partnership Visitors Center is located, and Village Square, at Rt. 122 and 655, Moneta.

Hales Ford is really the center of lake life, and there are enough interesting little shops to take some time to see while the kids play miniature golf at Harbortown Golf or ride the carousel. In the summer, entertainment is offered weekends. The steady seasonal stream of boats and visitors from around the world are often entertainment enough.

Bridgewater Plaza's anchor, in addition to the miniature golf course (703-721-1203), is Bridgewater Marina and Boat Rentals and Bridgewater Para-Sail (721-1639). The Virginia Dare, a dinner cruise ship, also leaves port from here.

Art lovers will enjoy fine arts at The Little Gallery (721-1596). Here, you can find one of a kind treasures and enjoy the art of well known as well as emerging local artists. The Bear Hug (721-5303) will delight children and has the lake's most unique collection of gifts and greeting cards. The Plaza also has the great restaurant, Schooner's (see the Restaurant chapter), with terrific pizza and hamburgers fresh ground daily and the refreshing Ice Cream Cottage (721-1305), where your family can get everything from flavored shaved ice to your favorite ice cream in a waffle cone.

At Village Square, there's Village Accents (297-7751), a collector's showcase featuring figurines such as Emmett Kelly Jr. clowns and Indian sculptures. Needlecrafter Custom-made Sweaters (297-6334) offers everything for the hand-crafter and Smith Mountain Flowers (297-6524) has gifts, candy, fruit and flowers for any gift need you might have.

Beyond these two centers, other shops are either general or specialized and far-flung. Classic Collections (297-2804), on Route 122, north of Hales Ford bridge, has quilts, pottery, baskets, customer designed flags, teddy bears, bird carvings and oak rockers. The Old Country Store and Deli, nearly four miles north of Hales Ford bridge, has souvenirs, balloons, food, fishing and hunting equipment and just about anything else you need while enjoying the lake.

Bedford County

ANTIQUES

There are nearly 20 antique stores within a close radius in Bedford County. In downtown Bedford, there's Bridge Street Antiques (703-586-6611), at 201 N. Bridge St., specializing in furniture, tools, silver and primitives. Books, toys and Virginia antiques can be found downtown at Hamiltons (586-

5592), at 155 W. Main. Peaks Antiques (586-5089), on 1510 Longood Ave., is a hodge podge of just about everything old and collectible. Farther out of town, you'll find the same at Old Country Store (586-1665), a mile west of Bedford on Route 460. Twelve dealers are at The Peddlar Antiques (804-525-6030), on Route 854 between Route 811 and route 221. Many shops are between Lynchburg and Bedford. For a complete list, call the Bedford Area Chamber of Commerce at (703-586-9401).

OUTLETS

If you love pottery and seeing how it's made, it's worth a trip to Bedford to visit Emerson Creek's factory in Bedford County. The line is in all 50 states and is becoming widely collected as a fine art. The retail shop (703-297-7884) will give you a tour schedule and directions from where you are to their stores. If you're going just to shop, the seconds shop is located in an 1825 log cabin next to their factory on Rt. 727 East, 10 miles from Bedford. A new renovated showroom houses a permanent display of the pottery's 14-year-old private collection. Emerson Creek Pottery is known for its designs featuring fields of wildflowers dancing in a spectrum of pastel and vibrant hues. Each pot is hand-decorated. The line consists of earthenware pottery including vases, coffee mugs, pitchers, lamps, creamers and sugars, flower pots and lotion bottles in more than a dozen colors and patterns.

Franklin County

GENERAL STORES

If you're in Franklin County, the one stop you must make is Boone's Country Store (703-721-2478), a few miles from the intersection of 122 at Burnt Chimney and Rt. 116, Boones Mill, the winding mountain road to Roanoke. Run by German Baptists, the store has the most heavenly sticky buns, pies, cakes, rolls and homemade entrees this side of Amish country. There are also country items and piece goods. If you want to take home an authentic reminder of German Baptist country, don't miss Boone's.

HANDCRAFTS

For a tremendous buy on hand-smocked children's items and clothing, as well as good quality children's consignment clothing and juvenile accessories, travel the main road between Roanoke and Rocky Mount, U.S. 220, and stop at Kids Kastoffs (703-483-2496). You'll find the same quality as in specialty stores at about a third of the cost. Downtown Rocky Mount has From the Heart (703-489-3887), 176 Franklin St., a store with a unique assortment of gift items, local art, toys, pottery, linen and antiques.

OUTLETS

Southern Lamp & Shade Showroom (703-483-4738), on U.S. 220, near Wirtz, has a great selection of lamps and shades at below retail prices. It's well worth visiting if you're shopping for lighting. In Rocky Mount, Virginia Apparel Outlet (703-483-8266), 721 N. Main St., has a fine selection of clothing for the entire family at outlet prices.

New River Valley Region

Blacksburg

ANTIQUES

Antique stores are spread out all over the New River Valley, especially the Blacksburg area. Downtown, there's Grady's Antiques (703-951-0623), at 208 N. Main St., Other Times LTD (552-1615) at 891 Kabrich St., and Heirloom Originals (552-9241), 609 N. Main. You'll find a good selection of collectibles and decorative antiques at all of these shops.

OUTLETS

There are two good clothing outlets in the downtown area that cater to the Virginia Tech crowd. TGIF Outlets (703-951-3541) on North Main sells returns and overstock for clothing catalogs with sporty clothes. You'll find J. Crew, Clifford & Wills, Smythe & Co. and Lands End. On South Main, in the Blacksburg Square Shopping Center, there is Virginia Apparel Outlet (961-2889), which manufactures and retails for major catalog companies including L. L. Bean, Vanity Fair, Bugle Boy and Botany 500.

SPECIALTY SHOPS

Downtown, a very special store

that started out as a hole in the wall several decades ago has since grown to be one of the most popular art supply and overall "neat stuff" stores in western Virginia. Everyone "in the know" in the New River Valley (and Roanoke, where there's a second store,) knows this is Mish Mish (703-552-1020) —which probably should be renamed Hodge Podge, located at 204 Draper Rd. Shoppers of any age could spend the entire day there looking at everything from the finest art supplies and watercolors to a rainbow of Silly Putty. Getting more general, 60 specialty shops and Peebles Department Store are among the stores at New River Valley Mall (381-0004) on 782 New River Road off US 460 in Blacksburg. The specialty stores here and Peebles really are a cut above those you find in other western Virginia shopping malls. The mall also wins your heart with free wheelchairs, high chairs in the Food court, strollers and special programs.

Christiansburg

ANTIQUES

Cambria Emporium (703-381-0949) at 596 Depot St. in Christiansburg, is the best place in Montgomery County to find tiny antique treasures and surprises. The big red, three-story building is a landmark in itself, constructed in 1908 and recently renovated as an antiques mall housing 20 dealers in the historic Cambria area of the county seat. Here, among 20,000 square feet, you can find every an-

tique imaginable in a pleasant, old-time setting that will remind you of the good old days. It's open, airy and uncluttered. You'll find broad categories of glassware, furniture, dishes, quilts, vintage clothing and fine china. Along with those, you'll run across small reminders of the past that will make you ooh and ahh! Cambria Emporium is definitely worth an overnight in this charming town for the antique-lover. The Oaks B&B nearby is the perfect place to stay. Don't miss going upstairs to see Casey's Country Store, a room laid out like a circa 1900s general store. A counter sign reads, "If it ain't priced, it ain't for sale, folks!" That's the spirit of Cambria Emporium.

OUTLETS

Both irregular and first quality fashions from chic brand name Donkenny's women's wear can be purchased for dollars at the Donkenny Fashion Outlet (703-382-8538) on North Franklin St. You can buy irregular clothing for up to $6.25 (yes, that's what I said!) and regular clothing for up to $45. Don't miss it if you want top fashion for few dollars. For cast-offs of every kind, don't miss Big Lots (382-3443) at the Hill's Shopping Center on U.S. 11. It's one of a chain filled with discontinued merchandise and overstocks from insurance claims, buy-outs and bankruptcies. You can get unreal prices if you hit the store at the right time, but constant vigilance is the key that pays off!

Floyd County

GENERAL STORES

Without a doubt, counterculture Floyd County has the most diverse, interesting shopping of any area in the New River and, some might say, the entire Blue Ridge. Cockram's General Store (703-745-4563) is the epitome of that fact. For 75 years, Cockram's has been the center of Floyd County entertainment, night life and culture. It has become famous not only for its merchandise, but for its famous Friday Night Flatfooting Jamboree at South Locust St. At 7 PM, folks start showing up with fiddles, mandolins, banjos and guitars for some pickin' and grinnin' over good conversation and the music that is the life-blood of the Floyd County mountain spirit.

Cockram's is dedicated to keeping traditions alive, but nearly died itself this year when owner Freeman Cockram found himself in debt after people who owed him money came upon rough times. The community rallied in support of the cultural institution, in a way reminiscent of old-fashioned note burnings and barn raisings, and Cockram's is still in business. By the way, as a general store, Cockram's offers everything from potted possum to bib overalls, sold from an old-fashioned candy counter. If you live in Floyd and need it, you'll find it here!

Down the road a piece, there's another interesting general store, Poor Farmers Market, a combination grocery store, deli and gift shop on US 58 in Meadows of Dan, just off the Blue Ridge Parkway. It's a hub for locals and tourists alike. The store began when owner Felecia Shelor, 30, told a local farmer she'd buy his produce and then peddle it wholesale. The idea boomed, so since 1983, the store has grown 10 times its original size. It serves great lunches at the deli—everything from fried apple pies to the Hungry Hillbilly sandwich. The owner's life story is as interesting as the store, having risen from a life of poverty as a bride of 15 to a store owner with 15 employees. You'll love this place and the prices are great!

HANDCRAFTS

When you're traveling the Blue Ridge Parkway looking for a unique Blue Ridge gift, don't miss New Mountain Mercantile (703-745-4ART), a shop at 114 Locust St., six miles from milepost 165.2 in Floyd. Its filled with many, many handmade items. Browse through stunning clothing (tie-dyed and batik). Then go on to dolls, pottery, jewelry, Native American handcrafts, perfume made of essential oils, candles (both herbal and decorative), stained glass, quilts, field guides and books on subjects such as herb gardening and gift-making. You'll also find music, instruments and hand-tuned windchimes. The store is run by three sensitive, saavy women, Theresa Cook, Kalinda Wycoff and Christine Byrd, who know great buys when they see them. Their store also serves as a Floyd County Information Center of sorts. Their "Here and Now" Art Gallery features new exhibits monthly. New

Mountain Mercantile rates as one of the outstanding handicraft stores in the entire Blue Ridge. They've also got a branch store at Tanglewood Mall in Roanoke, and you never know which Bluegrass artist will be performing out front to lure you.

SPECIALTY STORES

A direct contrast to a simple country mountain way of life, Chateau Morrisette (703-593-2865), the sixth-largest winery in Virginia, is a delightful stop, not only to buy wine and baked goods at wholesale prices, but as a terrific gourmet place for lunch (see the Restaurant and Winery chapters).

Another really specialized, interesting place is Brookfield Christmas Tree Plantation (703-382-9099), on Route 8, which sells trees by mail across the U.S. Fresh wreaths, pine roping and other gifts are also available or you can make your own in workshops. Trips to the 800-acre farm are encouraged. Free hayrides and pre-selection of your tree are offered every weekend in October and November. It's a wonderful storybook outing for the whole family, and a memory children will never forget! Also in the spirit of the holidays is Country Christmas House (703-745-3565) on Route 615. Formerly the Possum Hollow School House, you'll find everything there to decorate your tree and home.

Bluegrass and old-time music-lovers won't want to miss seeing the largest distributor of such music in the world, Country Records (703-745-2001), on Main Street.

Request come in from the four corners for their old-time fiddle music and gospel albums.

OUTLETS

Better than an outlet store, with more fabric than you could ever find in any retail store, School House Fabrics (703-745-4561) on Locust St. is a cloth addict's dream. A huge, three-story-high old schoolhouse has been renovated and filled with everything from specialty fabrics to buttons and beads. What is amazing is how organized and well-grouped this mass mania of cloth goods is for shoppers. Each room is arranged according to fabric. For example, downstairs there is a large room devoted to bridal fabrics, lace, veils, beading and wedding goods. Out back, an extra building contains large reels of upholstery fabric, tapestry and some remnants. Don't expect to leave without buying enough fabric and bric-a-brac to last well into the year 2000.

Giles County

ANTIQUES

You can't miss White Horse Antiques (703-726-7021), at U.S. 460 between Pearisburg and Narrows. There's a huge, plaster white horse in the window. You'll find a wide range of quality and prices, sets of Florentine dishes priced up to $100 as well as $1 china plates. Another interesting antique store is Woodland (921-1600) in tiny downtown Pearisburg. You can find some real gems among the rural offerings.

HANDCRAFTS

The New River Valley Arts and Crafts Guild operates a dynamic Fine Arts Center (703-626-3309) shop in the Old Pembroke School on the main drag of U.S. 460. More than 50 categories of handcrafts are available from 60 working artists, ranging from snake canes to Knobbits. In addition to a huge variety of first-class items for sale, the Guild has a floor loom in operation, on which beautiful rugs can be woven from old rags and discarded clothing. The service is open to the public for a small fee. There's also a year round Christmas Corner.

Radford

ANTIQUES

Some dandy antique shops can be found in Radford including Grandma's Memories (703-639-0054), 237 First St. and Collector's Corner (639-9185), 327 First St. Uncle Bill's Treasures (731-1733) at 1103 Norwood St. rounds out a great selection of antique stock.

SPECIALTY SHOPS

The combined Norwood Art Gallery and Encore Gift Shop (703-639-2015) on 1115 Norwood St. is the best place in the city to find unique gifts and original fine art. Their offerings range from the very unusual to the very trendy. There's eclectic folk art, Toys that Touch the Senses, and truly unique cards, gift items and packaging. After you're done shopping, have some artfully prepared cuisine in a casual gallery setting at Gallery Cafe.

Pulaski County

Pulaski County and Main Street Pulaski offer the most tremendous shopping surprises of any-place in the rural Blue Ridge. It's a Blue Ridge town where time seems to have stood still just for the benefit of tourists. While the Pulaski County's unusual shops have been established for some time, newcomers to Downtown Pulaski within the last year will think they're dreaming when they see what has happened to a formerly run-down downtown area.

Seventy-year-old Roscoe Cox, a former Pulaski native and retired executive, took up the town's languishing Main Street program and within eight months, had 20 new stores and restaurants within two blocks of the town's newly rebuilt courthouse, which burned down a few years ago. You'd have to see it to believe it! A former military man who gets paid $5 an hour to work 20 hours an week (and works 60-70), Cox literally has become a one-man downtown revivalist.

Some stores already there even before the revival are worth a trip in themselves. Theda and Rudolph Farmer have been in the portraiture business for 55 years and a visit to their shop is like taking a trip through time, from the original tin-roofed ceilings to the arresting pictures of brides from the 50's and 60's. With an outside barber pole that still turns, Sani-Mode Barber Shop is like looking through the window into a Norman Rockwell painting. The prices of hair-cuts are a throw-back to that time, as are the lines of barber chairs from the 40s and 50s. This is a priceless, we repeat, priceless experience that, if you don't hurry, may not be on the Americana landscape for much longer.

New stores include specialty stores such as Aloma's Snap Shop Photography (980-1079), work of a former journalist; Main Street Galleries and C&S Galleries (980-6603), an authorized B. Buckley Moss dealer; The Colony of Virginia, Ltd. (980-8932), specializing in items hand-crafted in Virginia; and New River Fine Arts Gallery, run by the Fine Arts Center for the New River Valley (980-7363), which has been serving the arts and culture of the New River Valley for 15 years. In this spacious setting, you'll find furniture, glassware, rugs,

quilts, baskets and jewelry. Nationally-known artists Annie Moon and Pam Tyrell are represented here. Also, don't miss Upstairs, Downstairs, hand-painted furniture upstairs and a a series of small boutiques upstairs. You'd find furniture like this for four times the cost in the metropolitan areas.

Main Street Pulaski's main thrust, however, is attracting first-class antique stores. It has succeeded wildly in this area. The list is long and still growing. While visiting, don't miss Memories (589-6559), full of country kitchen and primitives and "antiques and uniques;" Briarpatch Antiques (980-0270), with the Quesenberrys of Fancy Gap, Va.; Court Square Antiques and Collectibles (980-3784); and Mountain Man (325-2378), specializing in antiques, fur-

Shoppers can find handmade Virginia crafts at one of the many craft shops in Virginia's Blue Ridge.

niture, cabinetry, restoration and repair. After you've browsed, refresh yourself at Daynell's Delite, between the historic courthouse and theatre building. By the time you ready this, who knows how many first-class, unusual stores Roscoe Cox will have attracted to Main Street Pulaski!

General Stores

Pulaski County offers some unusual specialty shopping in unique settings. Draper Mercantile (703-980-0786), on Route 658, two minutes of I-81 at Exit 92, is a revitalized 1880s general store, doctor's office and fire station in what was old Downtown Draper. Now it's a discount place to buy, among other things, the largest display of Ridgeway brand grandfather, wall and mantle clocks in Virginia. You also can buy, at a 40 to 60 percent discount, High Point, N. C. showroom furniture, gifts, crafts, floral arrangements, reproduction toys and Christmas ornaments. If you can't take it with you, the gracious owners, Lee and Katie LaFleur, will arrange to have it shipped back home.

Services Unlimited (980-7350) keeps busy finding lots of beautiful places for a memorable wedding or reception in the New River Valley. The many students at nearby Virginia Tech and Radford University have taken advantage of Mildred Laine and her staff's knowledge in "handling it all" in a timely manner with aplomb!

Specialty Stores and Outlets

Christmas store buffs, don't you dare miss the opportunity of a lifetime at the trio of PJ's Carousel Collection Christmas stores at Newbern in Pulaski County (703-674-1249), Fort Chiswell (703-637-NOEL) and Wytheville (703-228-ELFS), both in Wythe County. All are just off I-81 in different towns. PJ's Carousel Village in historic Newbern is the original home of the famous full-size and miniature Carousel horses, right next to the factory where they are manufactured. Factory seconds are available. The Carousel Village is 3,500 square feet of fun! Be sure to have some ice cream in the old-fashioned parlor. The stores down the road offer the world's only Christmas carousel (Wytheville) and a 150-year-old Christmas House (Fort Chiswell).

Alleghany Highlands Region

Antiques

You'll find many charming little shops in charming downtowns, as well as in unexpected, out-of-the-way country roads in the counties of Alleghany, Highland and Bath. It's a junket you're bound to enjoy, whether you're hunting for top-quality antiques or just out enjoying the scenery.

Special items can be found at Always Roxie's, 622 Main St., Clifton

Forge, Alleghany Co. (703-862-2999), which specializes in dollhouses and miniatures. Their slogan is, "We can help make your mini house a mini home." You can find railroad items, crocks, jewelry and glassware.

Quilt lovers and lovers of first-class, unusual quilted gifts and handcrafts won't want to miss Quilts Unlimited, a Homestead Resort shop located on Cottage Row (703-839-5955) in Bath County. There are both new and antique quilts, as well as a fine selection of regional handcrafts.

In Highland Co., try Chicken Coop Antiques at Bobbie's Bed and Breakfast in Monterey (703-468-2308) and High Valley Antiques and Collectibles, located in a pre-Civil War era log home (703-474-5611). The Woodlane Craft Shop, Route 84 (703-499-2230), offers antiques, crafts and "junque."

GENERAL STORES

There are two super general stores not to be missed for nostalgia shoppers, both in Highland County. Hevener's, circa 1800, in Hightown, (703-468-2360), prides itself on carrying "a little bit of everything and not much of anything." It is located at the headwaters of the James and Potomac rivers at the intersection of Routes 250 and 640.

Over in McDowell, just off Route 250, (703-396-3469), there's Sugar Tree Country Store and Sugar House, a 19th-century country store featuring maple products, apple butter, pottery, baskets and some antiques. Located in the scenic Bullpasture Valley, the store is of special interest during the annual Highland Maple Festival, when they have demonstrations of old-timey methods of making maple syrup in iron kettles.

HANDCRAFTS

In Alleghany County, visit the Highlands Arts & Crafts Center in downtown Clifton Forge, located off I-64 (703-862-4447). Here, you can see displays of fine arts, handcrafts, antiques and collectibles. The Center is a not-for-profit volunteer organization that encourages creative experiences and appreciation of the visual arts. Included for sale are pottery, wooden wares, jewelry, stained glass, needlework, quilts, fiber arts and watercolors and oils.

In Bath County, the Homestead shops offer country crafts at The Virginia Building (703-839-3264). You can buy country dolls, rugs, candles, baskets, tin and pottery.

Highland County's Gallery of Mountain Secrets on Main St. (703-468-2020), in Monterey, is a treasure trove for traditional arts and fine crafts. It's a very special store, down from the historic Highland Inn, that offers jewelry, pottery, wooden and quilted items and decorative accessories. In the Highland Inn, the Glass Slipper (703-468-2305), features finely crafted stained glass gift items along with other quality handcrafts. Also on Main St., Highland County Crafts (703-468-2127) gives a touch of country to all its gifts. It offers a Christmas corner and maple syrup and homemade preserves and pickles.

OUTLETS

It's worth a trip to the Alleghany Highlands just to shop at the Bacova Guild Factory Outlet on Main St. (703-839-2105) in Hot Springs in Bath County. You've seen the Bacova Guild's wide variety of silk-screened gifts, including mailboxes and doormats, in leading outdoor catalogs such as Orvis and L.L. Bean. Every family in Bath County received a silk-screened mailbox free of charge from the Bacova Guild's owners, a county trademark undoubtedly unmatched in the U.S and perhaps the world! The wildlife motif items are made in Bacova, a charming village built in the early 1920s as a lumber mill company town. In 1965, the village was completely restored by philanthropist Malcolm Hirsh, whose brother, Philip, owns Meadow Lane Country Lodge in Warm Springs. A complete line of decorative, yet useful, gift items are at least 20-40 percent off regular prices. Summer shopping can yield an incredible Christmas gift bonanza!

SPECIALTY STORES

Across the Alleghany County border, in Greenbrier County, W. Va., the Greenbrier Resort shops will remind you of New York City. There are charming shops including a toy store, and fabulous boutiques.

Bath County's Homestead Resort offers a great array of shops including Ashleys, located just off the main lobby (703-839-3286), with products from Crabtree & Evelyn. Other Homestead shops are The Captain's Cabin (839-5447), a Bootery, Men's Shop, Tower Shop with logoed items, and linen and children's shops.

Highland County has the unique Ginseng Mountain Farm storefront off U.S. 220 (703-474-5137), with erratic hours. Call ahead for an appointment for choice spring lamb cut to your specification, sheepskin products, stoneware, maple syrup and stove and fireplace bellows. Another great place is The Personal Touch, Main St., Monterey (703-468-2145), that carries country fabric art, lampshades and stained glass.

Inside
Resots

*R*are is the region, anywhere in this country, where such a variety of famous and soon-to-be famous resorts can be found. They range from two ultra-posh Mobil Four and Five Star resorts within a half hours' drive from each other — the world-famous Homestead and Greenbrier — to mile-high Mountain Lake, which the movie, "Dirty Dancing," made famous...along with Patrick Swayze's biceps. Another resort, Bernard's Landing on Smith Mountain Lake, was the site of Bill Murray's recent zany hit, "What About Bob?"

To visit most of these resorts is to experience a lush lifestyle, your every wish the command of staffs that may provide a two-to-one guest ratio. European royals such as the Duke and Duchess of Windsor, and Prince Rainier and Princess Grace were 'regulars' at the Greenbrier. Most of America's Presidents have been 'regulars' at the swankier resorts including The Homestead. Prepare to drop big bucks at some of them; others are surprisingly affordable.

The listing below, from north to south and east to west, tells you a little about the resort's history, its amenities, and what sets it apart in

the realm of accommodations.

Shenandoah Valley Region

BRYCE RESORT
P.O. Box 3,
Basye, VA 22810   (703) 856-2121

Directions: Bryce Resort is located 11 miles west of I-81, exit 273 on St. Rt. 263. From Washington, D.C. area, take Beltway to I-66 West, to I-81 South, to Mt. Jackson exit. Take Rt. 263 West to Basye and Bryce Resort. Also, Sky Bryce Airport is a five-minute walk away.

AMEX, MC and VISA honored. No out of state checks.

Bryce Resort, built along the beautiful mountains of the Shenandoah Valley, offers a wide range of family recreation with modern, privately-owned studio condominiums, townhouses and chalets to please individual tastes. All units offer interesting decor and history in this colorful and friendly valley. Many are furnished with kitchenettes.

Bryce is especially attractive to the golf and outdoor lover. Well known as a winter skiing recreation getaway (see the Skiing chapter), it is also unique for its grass skiing (yes, I said 'grass'), for athletes 12 years and older.

Bryce's golf course is a par 71, 18-hole championship course, 6,175 yards in length. Facilities include a driving range, putting green, club and cart rentals, professional instruction, individual club storage and a fully stocked golf shop. Greens fee is $27 Monday through Thursday and $37 weekends & holidays. A great golf package is offered for three days including 18 holes of golf with cart per day and two dinners.

While Mom and Dad are on the course, the children can enjoy Lake Laura, a 45-acre manmade private lake with its own sandy beach offering swimming, boating, windsurfing and fishing. Beach admission is $3. Windsurfing is taught at a certified school, on a dryland simulator, before you head for the water. The beginning package costs $30.

Horseback riding is another family outing at T. J. Stables, open Memorial Day Weekend to Labor Day, weather permitting afterwards. Pony rides are available for children age 3 to 6.

Mountain biking and rollerblading are new sports at Bryce Resort. "Diamond Back" mountain bikes can be rented at the ski shop for $13 for up to 3 1/2 hours and rollerblades for $10 for the same amount of time. Tennis is another favorite activity, with lighted outdoor courts and a well-stocked pro shop. Court time per hour is $10 with light tokens $3.

Lodging prices vary according to accommodations. Condos on the ski slopes with a great fireplace, bedroom and bath rent for $95 nightly (there's a three night minimum during ski season); two-bedroom townhouses on the golf course rent for $115 nightly; and scattered chalets range from $250 to $700 for a two-night stay.

MASSANUTTEN
Harrisonburg, VA 22801   (703) 289-9441

Directions: From I-81, take Exit 64, go right on Rt. 33 E, 10 miles to Rt. 644 & entrance on left.

VISA, MC & AMEX accepted.

Massanutten bills itself as "More than a Mountain, Your Place in the Fun..." with 5,300 acres of unspoiled beauty and unequaled recreation. The Massanutten experience can't be said any better than that! Massanutten is probably known best for its superb skiing and winter recreation (see the Skiing chapter) and also for its exchange program with Vail and Beaver Creek Resort in Colorado.

Golfing is probably what Massanutten is second-best known for, with its semi-private 18-hole PGA Championship golf course and its scenic splendor. Greens fee is $20 with $22 per cart.

Guests also enjoy Massanutten's multi-million dollar sports complex, Le Club, which provides a full gym, fitness center, racquetball and everything you need to stay in top physical condition. Year round swimming is available. Tennis buffs will enjoy lighted outdoor courts at no fee.

Kids enjoy putt-putt at $2.50 and love pond fishing for free. There also is a host of programs geared to children including tubing, canoeing, nature hikes and arts and crafts. Mountain bikes are available for $5 per hour.

Dining opportunities are sparse, with a cafeteria-style restaurant in the sports complex available. Nearby Harrisonburg, however, home of James Madison University, offers a bonanza of great restaurants.

It is best if you call (703) 289-9441 for current rates, since they were being restructured at our press time.

WINTERGREEN

P.O. Box 706,
Wintergreen, VA 22958   (800) 325-2200

Directions: The resort is 43 miles southwest of Charlottesville, bordering the Blue Ridge Parkway. Off I-81, west or east, on Rt. 250, take Route 250 east to Route 151 south, turn right. Follow Route 151 south to Route 664, 14.2 miles. Turn right and Wintergreen is 4.5 miles ahead on Route 664.

AMEX, MC, VISA and personal checks accepted.

Wintergreen, an 11,000-acre resort along the solitary spine of the Blue Ridge, enjoys the reputation of one of the most environmentally conscious resorts in the Blue Ridge. The resort embodies the idea that conservation is good for development, and the philosophy has paid off. Wintergreen was the recipient of the National Environmental Quality Achievement Award in 1987.

Wintergreen's name also appears on the list of "Top 50 Favorite Family Resorts" by *Better Homes and Gardens* and "Top 10 Family Mountain Resorts" in the country by *Family Circle* magazine. Furthermore, *Golf Digest* rated the resort's new Stoney Creek course as one of the best new resort courses in the country in 1990 while the same year, *Tennis* magazine selected Wintergreen as one of its "Top 50 Tennis

One of America's Truly Great Inns.

•AAA 4 Diamond•
53 acre estate near
Monticello, UVA•
Golf, tennis and aerobics,
massage & more
•175 spacious rooms, 3
restaurants
•Inviting rates.

The Boar's Head Inn
& Sports Club

Route 250 West
Charlottlesville, VA 22901
800-476-1988   804-296-2181

Resorts."

Needless to say, recreational amenities are legendary. Wintergreen is known as a great place to ski and golf on the same day (see the Skiing chapter to read about its 10 slopes). In addition to Stoney Creek, there's Devils Knob, Wintergreen's 18-hole championship golf course, the highest in Virginia. The course rate is $60 and the cart fee is $20 per single player.

Tennis buffs have their pick of 20 composition clay and five all-weather hard surface courts. The court rate ranges from $12 to $28 and tennis clinics, workouts and ball machine rentals are available.

Swimmers can take advantage of a superb indoor pool at Wintergarden Spa and five outdoor pools. Water enthusiasts also have 20-acre Lake Monocan for swimming and canoeing. Mountain Bikes can be rented by the hour for $8, $50 daily, and there is a 25-mile network of marked hiking trails. Horseback riding and pony rides are offered seasonally, with new lessons on vaulting, the European sport of horseback gymnastics. And, after all that activity, you might want to take advantage of their therapeutic and sports massages at $35 a half hour.

Special events, such as the Spring Wildflower Symposium, are featured throughout the year and include holiday celebrations such as the spectacular Appalachian Mountain Christmas with horse-drawn carriage rides and candlelight dinners.

Babysitting services are avail-able. In summer, a special children's program is offered that introduces youngsters to the beauty and wildlife of the Blue Ridge.

Dining out is no problem with six full-service restaurants. There are Cooper's Vantage, The Garden Terrace and the Gristmill for casual dining and The Copper Mine for continental cuisine. Rodes Farm Inn offers country and family style meals while the Verandah specializes in regional cuisine. There also are seasonal restaurants, following the golf and skiing schedules, and three lounges, one with live entertainment.

Wintergreen offers 350 rental homes and condominiums ranging from studio size to seven-bedroom. Most have fireplaces and fully-equipped kitchens and many have spectacular views. Rates range from $100 to $455 nightly out of season, to $130 to $550 in season. Various packages are available including golf, tennis, family, sports and romance getaways.

NATURAL BRIDGE OF VIRGINIA
P.O. Box 57,
Natural Bridge, VA 24578   (703) 291-2121
or (800) 533-1410

Directions: Natural Bridge is 13 miles from the Blue Ridge Parkway, minutes off I-81, 12 miles from Interstate 64 and 39 miles north of Roanoke. Traveling up or down I-81, you can't miss it.

All major credit cards accepted; personal checks are accepted for advance deposits only.

One of the seven wonders of the natural world, Natural Bridge Resort isn't posh in the same sense as some of the other great five-star resorts of the Blue Ridge, but it's definitely worth seeing and staying overnight because of its unique character. Many make the trip just for the unique Sunrise services, as well as for the nightly Dramas of Creation, a spectacular light and sound show, both held under the 23 stories-high, 90-foot long structure.

The story of Natural Bridge, a 36,000-ton limestone structure carved millions of years ago, is a historian's delight. Early on, the bridge was worshipped by the Monocan Indians. Thomas Jefferson was the first American to own the bridge, which he purchased from King George III in 1774. George Washington surveyed the bridge as a lad. In fact, you can still see the spot where he carved his initials. Colonists made bullets by dropping molten lead off the bridge into the cold creek water below. During the War of 1812, soldiers mined the nearby saltpeter cave to make explosives.

Additional attractions are the 34-stories high caverns (it is said they are haunted with ghostly voices still heard as late as 1988), and the Natural Bridge Wax Museum, which houses life-like figures including a gallery of American presidents. A huge gift shop, featuring everything from Homemade Fudge to candy made to look like rocks along with fine gifts. For lunch or a snack, a Deli is available featuring several fast food stations in this Gift Shop. For recreation, the Tennis Courts, Indoor Heated Swimming Pool and new 18-Hole Mini-Link Indoor Golf Course are available. Each attraction costs $7 per adult and $3.50

per child (6-15); special combination rates are $13 Adult and $7.50 per child to visit all three attractions.

Accommodations feature 180-rooms in the newly refurbished hotel, Annex and cozy Hillside Cottages. Room rate ranges from $46-$88, to $195 for a 3-room suite.

East of the Blue Ridge Region

THE BOAR'S HEAD INN & SPORTS CLUB
Route 250 West,
Charlottesville, VA 22905   (800) 476-1988

Directions: From I-64, take Exit U.S. 250 West. Go West 1 1/2 miles and turn left into the Inn. Amtrak and major airlines provide service to Charlottesville.

All major credit cards accepted.

Built to perfection in Old English tradition, this inn is any Anglophile's delight. In case you didn't already know, the Boar's Head symbolized festive hospitality in the days of Shakespeare's England. A beautiful old grist mill symbolizes the Boar's Head Inn's link with Virginia's proud past. If visiting Jeffersonian Country or the University of Virginia, this Four-Star Mobil, AAA Four-Diamond complex is the place to stay! The Boar's Head is also for tennis lovers, being rated one of the top 50 tennis resorts by *Tennis* magazine. Unique to Blue Ridge resorts is its hot air balloon flight over the Blue Ridge countryside, which is almost de rigueur.

A quarter-century ago, Boar's Head President John B. Rogan brought the old mill to its present spot from near Thomas Jefferson's historic Monticello home. Today, the 1830s mill is the resort's main dining and social room called, in quaint understatement, the "Ordinary." Public rooms are furnished with antiques brought from England and guest rooms contain custom designed period furniture. Gardens feature traditional southern flowers and greenery.

Within this 43-acre country estate atmosphere, there are 175 guest rooms and suites, 12 meeting rooms, a grand ballroom, five dining rooms, specialty shops and a Sports Club. Resort facilities include three indoor Grasstex tennis courts, 10 Lee Fast-Dry clay courts and six all-weather courts, along with two platform tennis and four squash courts. Golf (18-hole), swimming, fishing and horseback riding are available nearby.

Three public dining rooms are located in the Inn — The Old Mill Room, Garden Room, and the Tavern, the latter of which is open nightly for live entertainment. The real highlights of the year are the traditional Thanksgiving and Christmas celebrations, the most unique of any Blue Ridge Resort. The former, a Thanksgiving feast, is preceded by the "Blessing of the Hounds," of the Keswick Hunt at Grace Episcopal. After the hunt, there is a Hunt Tea. The Merrie Olde England Christmas Festival is a pageant of how the English celebrated Christmas in days of yore. Unique is the "Feast Before Forks," the bringing in of the boar's head, wassailing and torchlight parades. The Boar's Head Resort is a true historical spectacle of America's past, and a great place to bring visitors from foreign lands for an experience they'll never forget!

Boar's Head offers a variety of packages, ranging from bed and breakfast at $99 during value season, to Bed, Breakfast & Ballooning at $375 during high season. There are accommodating specials including the traditional golf and tennis packages, but the special ones unique to Jeffersonian Country are the Historic Tour and Bacchanalian Feast packages.

BERNARD'S LANDING
Route 3, Box 462,
Moneta, VA 24121   *(800) 572-2048*

Directions: Nestled on Smith Mountain Lake, Bernard's Landing is 45 minutes from either Roanoke or Lynchburg. From Roanoke, take 220 south to a left on Rt. 697 at Wirtz. Follow 697 to its intersection with Route 122. Take a left on Route 122 and continue for approximately seven miles and then take a right on Route 616 at Central Fidelity Bank. Drive seven miles and take a left on Rt. 940, which will dead end at Bernard's. From Lynchburg, take Rt. 460 west to Rt. 122 and drive about 25 miles to Rt. 616. Turn left and follow above directions to Bernard's.

All major credit cards accepted.

Bernard's Landing is a relatively new resort on a relatively new lake. The largest in Virginia, with 500 miles of shoreline, it has become a water playground getaway for people from all over the East Coast. Known as a piece of paradise, its majestic view and magnificent sunsets sinking into the crystal clear lake have drawn artists from around the world.

Bernard's Landing was built in 1981 on what was once a prosperous farm worked by slaves of the Parker family. A descendent, Phyllis Parker, manages sales and marketing for the resort today. The family home, an old brick plantation house, still stands at the center of Bernard's activity. Appalachian Power filled the lake in 1966, covering over 22,000 acres and making many Franklin, Bedford and Pittsylvania county farmers instantly wealthy. Bernard's was built on the widest part of the lake and is one of few places where you can see the magnificent view of the seven-mile-long Smith Mountain.

Walt Disney Productions searched the entire U.S. looking for a lake resort with just the right combination to portray Lake Winnipesaukee, N.H., an out-of-the-

The Boar's Head Inn and Sports Club, Charlottesville.

way vacation spot that still had luxurious amenities. In 1990, a staff of 100, including Bill Murray and Richard Dreyfuss, stayed nearly half a year for the filming of "What About Bob?" Many were so impressed with the pristine beauty of the lake that they stayed even longer. That's because Bernard's has become known as the place where people come to get away from it all. Although friendly, Franklin County residents grant you privacy, whether you're sailing, swimming or just drinking in the silence.

The well-planned waterfront community sits on its own peninsula and is designed to take advantage of its natural surroundings of mountains reflected by the sparkling lake. As you drive up, the resort impresses you with its huge expanse of lawn that separates the buildings. This could be a premier location for an international kite-flying competition. There are sandy beaches for swimming and sun bathing and an Olympic-size swimming pool. The original brick plantation home serves as a clubhouse. A health club with exercise equipment, indoor handball courts and six tennis courts complete the complement of recreational activities. Clearly, the draw is the water. But if you want more than a splendid view, there's plenty to keep you entertained.

Smith Mountain is a fisherman's paradise. Nationally known for its striped bass fishing, the lake boasts the state's record striper — weighing 44 pounds, 14 ounces. If you're into fishing (see Fishing under our Recreation chapter), Bernard's operates a marina and rents fishing, pontoon and ski boats right at the dock. The Virginia Commission of Games and Inland Fisheries manages and maintains an adjoining 5,000 acres for hunting enthusiasts.

The resort's restaurant, The Landing, serves gourmet meals, packs many a picnic lunch for boaters and consistently earns *Roanoker* magazine's "Best Restaurant on the Lake" award. Probably every resident at the lake has enjoyed Bernard's sumptuous Sunday brunch, truly worth a tasting trip. The savory omelettes are the most requested item. Prices are reasonable for great sandwiches at the dockside restaurant or evening entrees. Bernard's rental facilities run from one- to three-level townhouses, to single-level homes, or one- to three-bedroom condos. They feature fireplaces, decks, skylights and cathedral ceilings. Nightly rentals in peak season range from $105 for a one-bedroom condo to $195 for a three-bedroom townhouse.

New River Valley Region

MOUNTAIN LAKE RESORT
Mountain Lake, VA 24136   (800) 346-3334
Directions: Take U.S. 460 Bypass around Blacksburg, home of Virginia Tech, to Rt. 700. Follow Rt. 700 for seven winding, scenic country miles to Mountain Lake.

All major credit cards and personal checks accepted.

If you saw the great, nostalgic

sandstone lodge in the hit movie, "Dirty Dancing," you saw Mountain Lake Resort. The majestic beauty of this grand old hotel was forever captured in 1986 after filmmakers, searching for a gentle, romantic circa-60s resort, saw an ad for Mountain Lake in a magazine. The rest is history. Dirty Dancing Weekends sell out quickly and everyone wants to know where Patrick Swayze slept when he stayed there.

But there's far more history than that to Mountain Lake, one of only two natural fresh water lakes in Virginia and one of the highest natural lakes in the East. It was formed when a rock slide dammed the north end of the valley. The lake, 100 feet deep, is fed by underground streams which rarely allow the water temperature to rise above 72 degrees.

The first report of a pleasure resort here was in 1857, and the first hotel was wooden. In the early 30s, William Lewis Moody of Galveston, Texas, purchased the property and built the present huge hotel from native stone. His elderly daughter, Mary, who died in 1986, loved to sit under the great stone fireplace in the lobby, which still says "House of Moody." Since her death, Mary's foundation has contributed $200 million to charitable organizations and Mary ensured her beloved Mountain Lake, where she stayed each summer, would keep its 2600 acres of natural paradise into perpetuity.

Mountain Lake's motto is "We'll Put You On Top of the World." And they do. When you stay at Mountain Lake and sit on the great stone front porches in a rock-

ing chair overlooking the lake, you can't help but feel refreshed and renewed. Summer offers the opportunity to relax in cool mountain air and in the autumn, few fall foliage vistas can compare to Mountain Lake's.

A year round resort, its winter cross-country skiing and horse-drawn sleigh rides are incomparable. The other seasons offer a variety of boating, fishing (guests must furnish own equipment), hiking, tennis, swimming and lawn games. A health club is equipped with a whirlpool, exercise equipment and sauna. There is a Recreation Barn with games and snacks and several shops featuring Appalachian arts and gifts. Mountain Lake is also known for its special weekends, with themes such as Dirty Dancing, Mardi Gras, Appalachian Culture and Murder Mysteries.

The food is always superb in the newly decorated, stone dining room where guests lucky enough to get window tables will see a panorama of bluebirds, canaries and redbirds scolding spoiled squirrels waiting for guests to feed them.

MOUNTAIN LAKE

Located on a Natural lake at 4000 ft. El. - 2600 acres, hiking, swimming, boating, fishing & family fun.

Hit movie "Dirty Dancing" filmed here!

MOUNTAIN LAKE

Mountain Lake, Virginia 24136
703/626-7121 or 1-800-346-3334

Deer are common visitors to the grounds and other wildlife is prevalent. Jacket and tie is suggested for evening meals, which are a gourmet's delight and unbelievably priced for such fare in a beautiful setting. Lunch entrees range from $6.95 for Orange Roughy with Lemon Pepper Glaze to $11.95 for broiled New York strip. This includes rolls and a choice of soup, salad or vegetable du jour. Many nearby (17 miles away) Virginia Tech parents make the trip just for the meal, which can be booked with a reservation.

Accommodations include the 50-room hotel, whose room amenities may include fireplace and whirlpool, the 16-room Chestnut Lodge, and 15 wooden cottages with fireplace. Prices for couples range from $125 nightly to $175 in the lodge, with a small additional charge for each child. Most guests stay on the Modified American Plan, which includes lodging, breakfast, dinner and use of all facilities and equipment. The air is rare, and so is the experience!

Southwest Virginia

DOE RUN LODGE RESORT AND CONFERENCE CENTER

Mile 189 Blue Ridge Parkway,
Hillsville VA 24343   (703) 398-2212
                    or (800) 325-M189

Just across the border of Floyd County, in Patrick County, Doe Run

Lodge Resort and Conference Center and its High Country Restaurant are nestled in the most beautiful part of the Blue Ridge Parkway. With Groundhog Mountain as the midpoint on this road of pastoral beauty, your senses will be overwhelmed by what this year round resort has to offer. Azaleas, rhododendron, dogwood and mountain laurel are in the air in spring and early summer. The foothills below reveal a burst of color from apple, peach and nectarine orchards and grape vineyards. You may hear animals of the forest–deer, fox, hawks, eagles, groundhogs and raccoons–scampering through the woodlands.

Doe Run Lodge Resort and Conference Center was built to fit the beauty of this environment. The chalets were built utilizing stone and wood beams. Floor-to-ceiling windows allow magnificent views. These large suites have a fireplace, two bedrooms, two full baths and living/dining area, a real buy for the money! The chalets, townhouses and single family residences are furnished and have complete kitchens. Millpond Hideaway, designed for executive use or honeymooners, has a whirlpool tub, luxury shower and steam cabinet, full suite stereo and TV, fireplace and enclosed garage. To realize the true value of their accommodations, share a chalet with another couple or with your family as it can accommodate up to six people with two bedrooms and two full baths.

High Country Restaurant offers a unique menu of seafood, steak and other regional recipes including venison, duck, fresh rainbow trout from their stocked pond, pheasant and country ham. Picnic lunches are packed to go. For the best the Blue Ridge Parkway has to offer, park yourself at Doe Run Lodge Resort and Conference Center and let the magic of the Blue Ridge happen! All major credit cards are accepted.

Alleghany Highlands Region

THE HOMESTEAD RESORT

Hot Springs, VA 24445   (703) 839-5500
Directions: From I-81, take Mt. Crawford exit, Rt 257 west to Rt. 42. Take 42 south to Millboro Springs, then Rt. 39 west to Warm Springs and U.S. 220 south to Hot Springs. By air, there is ground service from Roanoke Regional Airport. Also, Ingalls Field, Hot Springs, is located nearby and serves private and corporate aircraft.

All major credit cards accepted.

The Homestead, one of the South's major resorts on 15,000 acres in the Allegheny Mountains, received the Mobil Five-Star Award for more than 30 years and, for the first time, a Four this year. It's as "homey" as its name, famous for its afternoon teas in its long, wide lobby. Washington and Jefferson strolled these grounds and Lord and Lady Astor honeymooned here. The most

unusual guests of all began their visit December 29, 1941, three weeks after the attack on Pearl Harbor, when 363 Japanese diplomats, along with many Japanese citizens in the U.S., were placed at The Homestead for a three-month internment.

The Homestead has been pampering guests since the late 1700s, when the aristocracy of Virginia went to the mountains instead of enduring the lowland heat with the common folk. In those days, it was fashionable to move from one mountain spring to another, virtually en masse, in a group composed of high society. Originally valued for medicinal purposes by the Indians, the springs became centers of social activity.

Hot Springs, where The Homestead has been for more than a century, was one of the most prominent springs in Virginia. The lineage of The Homestead as a resort and its tradition of 'taking the waters' can be traced back to 1766. The spa of today was built in 1892, the dream of M. E. Ingalls, great-great grandfather of the present owner. Designed with the grandeur and technological expertise of today, the spa treatments are still one of the most popular services. The two covered pools and the sheltered "drinking spring," have been preserved in their natural condition. Eleanor Roosevelt's special chair is still at one of them. There are still legions of visitors who swear by the springs' curative properties. The magnificent, ornate indoor pool is fed continuously by waters of the Octagon Pool, which can be viewed in front of the spa. The most popular spot is where the natural mineral waters come rushing out under the see-through canopy. There are two outdoor pools as well.

Today, it is often the golfers who swear by the Homestead's magical abilities to renew youth and vigor. And no wonder! Golf is king at this resort! There is championship playing on three 18-hole courses, one of which has been the site of the U.S. Amateur and boasts the oldest first tee in continuous use in the *U.S. Golf Digest* and *Golf* magazine rank the Cascades Course among the top in the nation. John D. Rockefeller used to spread his wealth here by tossing shiny dimes into the pool of water in back of the first tee for the caddies to fight over. President William Taft nearly created a scandal by playing the "frivolous" game of golf on the Fourth of July holiday here at the turn of the century. Golf carts are included in the rates, which range from $65 to $75.

Tennis is also superb at The Homestead, with 19 courts including four all-weather courts. Singles are $7.50 per person, per hour.

Fishing is another favorite sport, with permits costing $20, as is skeet and trap at The Shooting Club, where a round of 25 birds costs $19. Hiking and horseback riding are other popular activities, with carriage rides in fringe-topped surreys on scenic trails a pleasant option. Bowling and movies are indoor activities guests enjoy.

Winter brings a whole new round of sports with skiing (see the Skiing chapter), considered some of the best in the South, and ice-skating. Half-day skating sessions

cost $5.50 weekends and holidays. There are fabulous winter weekends priced for the budget-minded pocketbook. Bring the kids!

The Homestead is a classic. Six hundred spacious guest rooms are offered at the sweeping Colonial-style building topped by a modern high-rise clock tower. Inside are white Corinthian columns, high-ceiling rooms and turn-of-the-century crystal chandeliers. Daily room rates in high season are $195 to $320 for double occupancy; in value seasons, $120 to $245. Children under 12 may share their parents' room with no charge. The Homestead has a meal option for $45 per person, per day that includes breakfast in the Main Dining Room or in the casual atmosphere of Sam Snead's Tavern in the Village.

THE GREENBRIER

White Sulphur Springs,
W.Va. 24986   *(800) 624-6070*

Directions: Take White Sulphur Springs exit off I-64. Turn left at the exit; turn right and travel two miles to entrance on the left. The Greenbrier's entrance is across the street from Amtrak Station, a stop for the luxurious American-European Express Railway Train Deluxe, a match for the Orient Express. Accessible by air from Roanoke Regional Airport, the resort is two hours away by limousine.

All major credit cards accepted.

"Monumental" is the first word that comes to mind about this Mobile Five-Star, AAA Five Star National Historic Landmark set in 6,500 acres of breathtaking scen-

The famous Homestead Resort in Hot Springs.

Photo: The Homestead

ery. Both its history and its present, as well as its star-studded guest list, have enchanted people for two centuries. The Greenbrier has hosted world summits and celebrities in the midst of the sleepy little town of White Sulphur Springs. One never knows when TV star Bill Cosby or former British Prime Minister Margaret Thatcher will be seen on the grounds. In 1981, when the U.S. government wanted the ultimate in rest and recreation for its former Iranian hostages, it chose the Greenbrier.

Its history has been nothing short of incredible, beginning in the 18th century, when aristocratic Southerners came to drink the mineral waters, stroll and chat while avoiding the summer sun. Twice during wartime, the U.S. government took over and used the resort as a hospital, first in 1861, when the Confederacy also claimed it as its military headquarters. It came perilously close to total destruction during the 1864 occupation by Union troops, when it was ordered burned. Only a plea from a U.S. senator saved it. Later, Gen. Robert E. Lee used it as his summer home. During World War II, former guest Gen. George Marshall (for whom the museum in nearby Lexington, VA, is named) turned it into a 2,200-bed hospital named Ashford General. According to locals, many a wounded soldier, upon awakening, thought he had died and gone to Heaven. After the war, again a resort, The Greenbrier was refurbished and redecorated. Its interior designer used over 30 miles of carpeting, 45,000 yards of fabric, 40,000 gallons of paint, 15,000 rolls of wallpaper and 34,567 individual decorative and furniture items on the job. The outstanding results still stand today.

Last spring, the Pentagon confirmed that a secret underground bunker large enough to house the President, his Cabinet and Congress was constructed here during the nuclear attack threat of the Cold War. Locals have known of its existence for years, but it's a fact the Greenbrier won't discuss.

Staff outnumber the guests with 1,600 employees and a 1,200 guest capacity. There are 650 guest rooms (no two of them furnished alike), 69 cottages (some come with use of a Cadillac), 51 suites, 30 meeting rooms, three championship golf courses, 20 tennis courts and a $7 million spa. To ensure you are adequately fed, there are 120 chefs (no kidding...120!) to serve you six-course dinners in The Greenbrier's acclaimed combination of classical, Continental and American cuisine, in six different settings. The list of culinary awards is endless. The Greenbrier is acclaimed for its own cooking school, La Varenne.

Adjacent is the world-famous Greenbrier Clinic, a diagnostic center where CEOs can have a checkup in the morning and play golf in the afternoon on a course designed by Jack Nicklaus.

Golf also gets a lot of attention at this resort. Sam Snead was the club's pro and played his best game ever here, setting a PGA record of 59 in the third round. Bob Hope, Bing Crosby, Arnold Palmer and the Prince of Wales were regular golfers. In 1979, the course served as the site of the International Ryder Cup matches. Golf is complimentary during winter months, with the fee ranging from $34 to $65 in peak season, and the golf cart extra at $32.

For the tennis set, 15 outdoor Har-Tru courts and five indoor Dynaturf courts await play. Doubles are $38 per hour indoors. Recreational offerings are rounded out with croquet, indoor and outdoor swimming, bowling, billiards, trout fishing, hiking, horseback riding, carriage rides, biking, cross-country skiing, trap and skeet shooting and shopping in a large gallery of

wonderful stores. For a touch of heaven, treat yourself to the 18 different treatments of the new Spa and have your own nutritionist and exercise trainer design an individual program for you. A five-day spa package costs $2,100.

You won't miss a meal at The Greenbrier. Nobody does. Rates are based on a Modified American Plan, which includes breakfast and dinner in the Main Dining Room. Nowhere else is The Greenbrier's southern heritage more apparent than at the breakfast table, with fresh brook trout, hominy grits, Virginia ham and bacon, cornbread and biscuits. Dinner of six courses is truly an event. A string ensemble provides

Photo: The Greenbrier Resort

The Greenbrier Resort in White Sulphur Springs, W. Virginia.

music and dinner is served with candlelight and chandeliers. The vichyssoise is a favorite of Greenbrier regulars, along with its famous peaches and cream for dessert. In 1989, The Greenbrier delivered 10,000 of its famous hand-made chocolate truffles for George Bush's Presidential Inaugural dinner.

The Greenbrier's multitude of accommodations are available in a variety of packages, including golf, tennis and family. Its tariff schedule ranges from a low of $120 nightly per person during value season on the Modified American plan.

You don't have to stay overnight to enjoy the Greenbrier. Dessert and beverage for two can be had for about $16. Have a snack and then tour the President's Cottage Museum or visit the Miniature Gift Shop, a little dollhouse that sells only miniatures. Then, save your pennies to experience the total experience!

Inside
Bed and Breakfasts

*I*sn't it time you got away from it all? This is the perfect time to slip into the tranquility of country life. From an old stagecoach inn on the Valley Turnpike in Woodstock, the Inn at Narrow Passage, to Elmo's Rest, a working Bedford County farm where you can help pick apples each fall, you can find the perfect place to relax, no matter what your interests.

Each of these grand old bed and breakfast inns has its own distinct charm. The histories are as varied as the decor. How many of us dream of spending the night in a real mansion? You may experience just that at Lynchburg's Mansion Inn B&B. You may stay on the former site of an ancient Indian village at Silver Thatch Inn in Charlottesville. Or you may be swept away by the beauty of bubbling springs at Meadow Lane in Warm Springs, on land that has remained in the Hirsh family for over three generations.

We don't think you'll find hosts so genuinely concerned with your well being anywhere else in the world. And, only these antiquated country manors can afford you such tranquility. The soothing countryside and warm hospitality

of the Blue Ridge's bed and breakfasts are the perfect remedy for the headaches of modern living.

Reservation Services

These services are available to assist you in selecting a bed and breakfast and making reservations. Most B&Bs run in the same price range of between $50 and $100 dollars per night.

BED & BREAKFAST ASSOCIATION OF VIRGINIA
P.O. Box 791,
Orange, VA 22960   (703) 721-3951
BLUE RIDGE BED & BREAKFAST
Route 2, Box 3895,
Berryville, VA 22611   (703) 955-1246
GUEST HOUSE BED & BREAKFAST
Charlottesville, VA   (804) 979-7264
          Princely Bed & Breakfast, Inc.
Alexandria, VA   (703) 683-2159
SHENANDOAH VALLEY BED & BREAKFAST RESERVATIONS
P.O. Box 634,
Woodstock, VA 22664   (703) 459-8241
SHENANDOAH VALLEY LODGING SERVICES
Route 3, Box 119F,
Luray, VA 22835   (703) 743-2936

Shenandoah Valley Region

Woodstock

COUNTRY FARE
402 Main Street
Woodstock, VA 22664   (703) 459-4828

You'll travel the historic Lee Highway (Rt. 11) to find this small-town bed and breakfast. A half acre of glorious magnolia, boxwoods and Japanese cherry trees encircle the home. Proprietor Bette Hallgren will greet you at the door. Her old-fashioned hospitality will surely soothe a road-weary traveler. The home is full of old country charm and history. Country Fare was built in the late 18th century. An addition was built in 1840. From 1861 to 1864, the building served as a hospital. An old log cabin, the original dwelling, was an auction house for years. The house has been restored and is now as beautiful as ever.

The three guest rooms are furnished with antiques and country collectibles. Each has been hand-stenciled in original designs. The master bedroom has a private shower, another room has twin beds and a Boston rocker. The double room has its own fireplace. A Continental breakfast is served each day. You can sit by the inviting fire in the common room and eat homemade breads, or you can have your coffee on the brick patio.

After breakfast, take a walk into the village of Woodstock to explore the town's history. George Washington presented the town's charter to the Virginia House of Burgesses on March 31, 1761. The 8th Regiment emanated from Woodstock during the Revolutionary War. The courthouse was designed by Thomas Jefferson in 1792. This is the oldest building of its kind still in use west of the Blue Ridge Mountains. There are also attractions of natural beauty such as Shenandoah National Park, Skyline Drive, Luray Caverns and various vineyards. Visit New Market Battlefield, Belle Grove Plantation and Wayside Theater. Seasonal activities include the Shenandoah Music Festival in July and the Shenandoah County Fair in August. A deposit is required with reservations.

THE INN AT NARROW PASSAGE
I-81 & U.S. 11 South
Woodstock, VA 22664   (703) 459-8000

This log inn overlooking the Shenandoah River has been welcoming and protecting travelers since the 1740s, when it was a haven for settlers against Indians. Later this historic building would become a stagecoach inn on the Valley Turnpike and headquarters to Stonewall Jackson during the Valley Campaign. Travelers today will still find The Inn at Narrow Passage to be an inviting and warm place to stay in order to relax and revive. Ed and Ellen Markel have taken great care in restoring the inn to its 18th-century look. As a bed and breakfast, this landmark is enticing guests with its charming Early American character.

The interior is decorated with

The Inn at Monticello

"A Cozy Charmer" — Country Inns Magazine, June '92

Route 19, Box 112 Charlottesville, Va. 22902 804-979-3593

SLEEPY HOLLOW FARM

You Are Invited
to Experience
Virginia
Hospitality

c. 1740

16280 Blue Ridge Tnpk., Gordonsville, VA 22942 (703) 832-5555

NORFIELDS FARM

500 Acres at The Blue
Ridge Foothills

Rt. 1 Box 477
Gordonsville, VA 22942
(703) 832-2952

c. 1850

gorgeous antiques and Colonial reproductions. Each bedroom gives all of the comforts of home plus more. Some rooms have wood-burning fireplaces for a cozy evening. For your comfort, the inn is centrally heated and air conditioned. Join other guests in the Colonial dining room for breakfast in front of a cheery fire. For a calm, soothing day, you can rest by the massive limestone fireplace in the living room or sit on the porch and view the beautiful sloping lawns and river. However, there is no lack of activity. Hiking and fishing are options right at the inn itself. There are also historic battlefields, wineries, caverns and skiing at the famous Bryce Resort. The Markels will be happy to suggest a day's activities for you or you can just sit on the porch and chat as the sun sets across the Valley.

Stanley

JORDON HOLLOW FARM INN
Route 2, Box 375,
Stanley, VA 22851   *(703)778-2209*
or (703)778-2285

Jordan Hollow Farm Inn is a beautifully restored Colonial horse farm, converted into a country inn. The farm has 45 acres nestled in a secluded "hollow" surrounded by the Shenandoah National Park and the George Washington National Forest. Marley and Jetze Beers have personally created the inn and say that, "Jordan Hollow is the kind of place in which we most want to live . . . ." The buildings, except for Rowe's Lodge, are the original farm buildings, renovated to provide cozy

but modern facilities. There is an overall family farm environment that is nurtured by the Beers. The property is a blend of rolling hills, lush meadows and fragrant woods.

In the spring and early summer, foals and kittens can be seen soaking up the sunshine and frolicking in the fields. The sun deck surrounding Rowe's Lodge is perfect for overseeing all of the farm's activities. This lodge was named for Rowe Baldwin, a relative who came to help for a few weeks and has been there ever since! There are 16 beautiful guest rooms, decorated with country antiques and artifacts. All have private baths and some have fireplaces and Jacuzzi tubs. You'll enjoy dining in the Colonial farmhouse, where two of the dining rooms are two-hundred-year-old log cabin rooms, and the other two are the one-hundred-year-old Fox and African rooms.

The food is described to be "country cosmopolitan" and it is outstanding. The flavor is part good old home cooking with a little bit French and a unique touch of African and Mideastern seasonings. There is a large selection of dishes including quail, chicken, veal, steak, fish and pasta. There is also home baked bread, a garden salad and fresh vegetables. Top off your meals with tasty desserts and a fine selection of wines and beers.

For indoor entertainment, there is a library, a cable TV lounge and a pub. Known as The Watering Trough, the pub was originally a stable. There is live entertainment on Friday and Saturday nights, and you may find yourself challenged to

Virginia's Inns

Irish Gap Inns

Small, romantic, European - Style Country Inn. 5 deluxe rooms, Mountain Top, & Adjoining Blue Ridge Pky.

Rt. 1, Box 40, Vesuvius, VA. 24483

Virginia's

Fassifern
Bed & Breakfast

"Our staff makes the difference"

RR5, Box 87 Lexington, VA. 24450 **(703) 463-1013**

Virginia's Inns

Llewellyn Lodge at Lexington

- Full Gourmet Breakfast
- Walking distance to downtown
- Trout fishing packages

- Nearby Hiking, horseback riding, & cycling
- 11 miles from Blue Ridge Parkway
- A retreat for private parties and reunions

603 S. Main Street Lexington, VA 24450 1-800-882-1145

a game of pool or chess by Jetze. There is a stable located on the property. Horses are available for the beginner or the expert rider, as well as pony rides for children under eight years of age. There is also a wide variety of activities near the farm such as swimming, hiking, canoeing, fishing, skiing, museums, antiques and craft shops. The farm is within a short drive of Lake Arrowhead, Luray Caverns, Shenandoah National Park and George Washington National Forest. Room reservations must be guaranteed by the equivalent of one night's stay. Limited boarding facilities are available for pets. You need to let them know if you are bringing children prior to making your reservations.

Harrisonburg

JOSHUA WILTON HOUSE
412 S. Main Street,
Harrisonburg, VA 22801   (703) 434-4464
Roberta and Craig Moore will welcome you to the Joshua Wilton House in historic Harrisonburg. Their inn is found in an elegantly restored Victorian home right in the heart of the Shenandoah Valley. Restoration efforts have preserved much of the original architecture.

The Moores will spoil you with complimentary wine and cheese, and their gourmet breakfast including homemade pastries, fresh fruits and a delicious pot of coffee is enough to summon anyone out of bed in the morning. The bedrooms are furnished with period antiques

to give them the charm of the 1880s. You can choose from three dining rooms, a sun room or an outdoor terrace, and dine on food that is famous across the Shenandoah Valley. All five of the bedrooms have private baths and a reading area.

The Wilton House is within walking distance of James Madison University and fascinating downtown Harrisonburg. There is also a variety of athletic activities such as golfing, biking, hiking, swimming and skiing accessible from the inn. This old mansion is "an oasis of quiet charm and gracious living" surrounded by the Blue Ridge Mountains.

Staunton

BELLE GRAE INN
515 West Frederick Street
Staunton. VA 24401   (703) 886-5151
This authentically restored, 17-room inn built in 1870 will please you with its luxurious rooms and appetizing menu. It is named after two of the surrounding mountains, Betsy Belle and Mary Grae. The Scotch-Irish settlers in the area, reminded of their homeland, named the mountains for Scottish landmarks. Belle Grae sits atop a hill in the historic town of Staunton. Wicker rockers invite relaxation on the veranda; white gingerbread decorates the porch of the main, original building. You will be mesmerized by the four dazzling stained glass panels found in the double entrance door. Engraved inside a crystal oval is the inn's name. Period reproductions and antiques,

Virginia's Inns

Fountain Hall

609 S. East St., Culpeper, VA 22701 (800) 476-2944

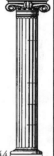

THE INN AT MEANDER PLANTATION

Mansion sits majestically on 40 acres of rolling pasture and woodland. Full gourmet country breakfast. Dinner available. Near Montpelier, wineries, antiques.

ca. 1766

James Madison Highway, U.S. 15
Route 5, Box 460
Locust Dale, VA 22948
(703) 672-4912 Voice or Fax

GRAVES' MOUNTAIN

Experience The Bounty

Our Blue Ridge Mountain country inn specializes in home-cooked food and gracious hospitality. Enjoy hiking, fishing, swimming and good old-fashioned fun.

Rt. 670 Syria, VA 22743 (703) 923-4231

which are for sale, are found throughout the dining rooms, bistro, lounge and other lovely rooms. The bedrooms are each furnished a little differently, but all fit the period. You can sit in front of your cozy fireplace and sip complimentary sherry from long-stemmed glasses. Many of the rooms have private baths with such amenities as English herb soap, shampoo, moisturizer, toothbrush and herb bath foam. The annex features rooms furnished for corporate clientele. They feature desks, dressing rooms, phones, queen size beds and color televisions.

The popular chef at this fine establishment will get you going with his delicious, full American breakfast — prepared for a day of sightseeing or business. Or, if you prefer to relax, a Continental breakfast with newspaper will be delivered to your room. Private parties and weekend dining get a special flair from live entertainment and candlelight meals. An extensive dinner menu will keep even the most refined palate happy. You could find cream of asparagus soup, charcoaled swordfish, tenderloin of beef covered with backfin crab or bourbon carrots. Homemade breads and desserts complete the menu with such specialties as Amaretto mousse, chocolate peanut butter pie or smudge pie. Activities in the area include walking tours through gorgeous historic Staunton, shopping at a gigantic antique warehouse or chess and backgammon in the quiet of the inn's sitting room.

FREDERICK HOUSE

Frederick and New Streets, P.O. Box 1387
Staunton, VA 24401   (703) 885-4220

Three stately old townhouses were rescued from demolition to be transformed into Frederick House. These Greek revival buildings have been restored and the rooms inside have been decorated with antiques and paintings by Virginia artists. The oversized beds add an extra special touch of comfort. Each of the 14 rooms and suites has its own private bath, cable TV, telephone, radio and air conditioning and many have a private entrance. A full, delicious complimentary country breakfast is available each morning and may be served in guests' rooms.

One activity we recommend is to take a relaxing stroll through the town and photograph Staunton's gorgeous architecture. Woodrow Wilson's birthplace is only two blocks away and Mary Baldwin College is right up the street. There is also terrific cycling, hiking and touring accessible in the surrounding Blue Ridge and Allegheny Mountains. Hosts Joe and Evy Harman will point out places of interest and provide a bit of history as well. Ask the Harmans to help you plan a day on the town to suit your curiosity and show the great beauty of this fair city.

THORNROSE HOUSE

531 Thornrose Avenue,
Staunton, VA 24401   (703) 885-7026

Carolyn and Ray Hoaster are the innkeepers at this family-owned and operated bed and breakfast in the heart of Staunton's historic Gypsy Hill area. The couple, along

Virginia's Inns

The Inn At Union Run

Stay and dine in
Victorian country
splendor.
A 6 room Inn
with a full service
restaurant.

Union Run Rd. Rt. 674 • Lexington, VA • (703) 463-9715

The Keep

Like the Keeps
of old enjoy refuge
& comfort in the
mode of Home stay.

(708) 463-3560 116 Lee Avenue Lexington. VA 24450

Seven Hills Inn

Gracious
Hospitality -
Sophisticated
Accommodations

(703) 463-4715
408 South Main St. Lexington, VA 24450

with their two daughters, designed this home after a favorite B&B they once visited in Devon, England. But it was Staunton's history and gorgeous surroundings that lead the Hoasters to settle here. The moment you step into the grand entranceway, you will begin to discover the charm of this Georgian Revival brick home. Family heirlooms, German-American furniture and salvaged antiques from old Staunton homes decorate the dining and sitting rooms and all of the three guest rooms. The guest rooms are air conditioned and all have private baths. "Canterbury" has a king size bed; "Windermere" features a queen size bed, antique standing closet and a telephone case now used as a washstand; "Yorkshire," named in tribute to the "vet" James Herriot, offers English lace at the windows and a four-poster bed. Yorkshire's bathroom has a footed tub.

After a good night's sleep, you will love waking up to the smell of a hearty breakfast. The morning meal begins with the house specialty, Birchermuesli. This Swiss cereal is made of oats, fruit, nuts and whipped cream! Then a large breakfast platter follows with bacon, sausage, eggs and toast. With an advanced request, special diets can be catered to. And, in complete English tradition, afternoon tea is served on Royal Albert china.

After you've satisfied your tastebuds, it's time to venture out and see the sites that make Staunton so beautiful. Across the street is the 300-acre Gypsy Hill Park where you can play golf, tennis (rackets and balls provided) or swim. Watch for the mama duck and her ducklings as they waddle from their nest under a shade tree in the front yard of Thornrose to the park where they might meet up with a peacock, swan or even some deer. Thornrose House also has a beautiful yard with bittersweet entwined pergolas in the landscaping. The wrap-around veranda with rocking chairs is perfect for a lazy chat in the company of fellow rockers. And, the sitting room is inviting with its fireplace and grand piano. Thornrose House is a magnificent place to stay while visiting this town. And as Carolyn and Ray say: "Our aim is to make your stay at Thornrose House the most memorable of your journey."

Rockbridge/Lexington

IRISH GAP INNS
Rt. 1, Box 40
Vesuvius, VA 24483   (804) 922-7701

Irish Gap Inns is a quiet, romantic secretive place priding itself on "No Night Life." Innkeeper Dillard Saunders opens her 285-acre retreat with nearly four miles of hiking trails for fishing, swimming and just enjoying the surrounding quiet of the woods. Animals abound, both wild and domestic.

Five fantastic rooms are available, each with its own private balcony. There are lakeview rooms and gardenview rooms. The Heartroom is the most romantic, often chosen by honeymooners. The four poster pine rice bed is queensize and quilt-covered. In the

Virginia's Inns

JORDAN HOLLOW FARM INN

In Virginia's lovely Shenandoah Valley only 2 hours west of Washington. D.C. and 8 miles south of the Luray Caverns and Skyline Drive.

703-778-2209 or 703-778-2285
Route 2, Box 375, Stanley, Virginia 22851

FORT LEWIS LODGE

Come settle back in the total privacy of a vast 3200 acre mountain farm. Miles of river trout and bass fishing, extensive hiking trails, swimming, magnificent views, abundant wildlife and food better than Mom ever thought of fixing!
• *Private fly fishing lessons*
• *Business conference facilities*
• *Open April thru mid October*

Call for color brochure Millboro, VA   **(703) 925-2314**

Looking for something different to do on the weekend?

summer, the private balcony is shared by nesting barn swallows and cascading window box flowers. The Fox Hunter guest room is very English, done in dark red with two pencil post double beds. The game table is a British antique example of marquetry. Chintz fabrics used here enhance the artwork of horses, dogs and foxes. The Rabbit Garden room is on the main floor with direct access to the frolicking Lop rabbits living in the garden beyond the porch. The Orkney Island Shepherds chairs appear to be for children until you sit in them and they cradle your tired back. Plus, there's a gatehouse with three rooms. Each also has private bath and refrigerator. The Woodland room is Germanic in feeling with stucco walls and pillows of tapestry animals welcoming you into the alcove bed. Look outside when there's a full moon and you may catch a glimpse of deer grazing on the hill.

Breakfast is included with room cost in the timber-framed Great Hall. Dinner is available at $20 per person with 48-hour advance reservation. Half of room cost deposit is required at time of reservation. A full game room is available. Guests may avail themselves of nearby hiking, trout fishing, canoeing and horseback riding, all within the area.

THE KEEP BED AND BREAKFAST
116 Lee Ave.
Lexington   (703) 463-3560
This B&B sits on a quiet corner in the heart of Lexington's historic residential district. Owners Bea and John Stuart opened the gorgeous Victorian home to guests last October, offering two suites and a double-bedded room, all with private baths. Don's expect a lot of frou-frous here; the decor is elegant and understated. The Stuarts put on a lavish breakfast, complete with linens on the table, and also serve dinner upon request. At tea time, the owners are always happy to share tea, coffee or sherry with their guests. "We like to spoil nice people," says Bea Stuart.

Summertime travelers to Lexington will be grateful for the central air-conditioning at the Keep, which is a short walk from museums and shops in downtown Lexington. The B&B does not allow children under 12 but does welcome small, well-behaved pets on a request basis. Rates are $75 a night for the double room and $100 for the suite.

THE INN AT UNION RUN
Rt. 3, Box 68
Lexington   (703) 463-9715
A friendly, down-to-earth couple, Roger and Jeanette Serens opened their inn two years ago and have won rave reviews for the service and enticing cuisine they offer. The inn is situated roughly on 12 acres about four miles from town and borders on a bird sanctuary. Union Run Creek winds through the property, named for the Union Army who camped on the grounds in June of 1963.

The Federal-style home was built in 1885. There is also a newly built carriage house with four rooms, all with private baths. The main house has a small dining area

Virginia's Inns

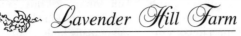

Lavender Hill Farm

Offers English country charm, hospitality, and outstanding food. Located near historic Lexington on a working farm. Enjoy horseback riding packages, fishing, hiking, and birding. Dinner available to inn guests.

RR 1 Box 515
Lexington, VA 24450

(703) 464-5877
(800) 446-4240

Joshua Wilton House

Harrisonburg's most elegant lodging dining facility in a beautifully restored Victorian home. Within walking distance of James Madison University and historic Downtown Harrisonburg. Eat our fine cuisine in the Restaurant or dine casually in The Cafe.

**412 S. Main Street
Harrisonburg, VA 22801
(703) 434-4464**

Escape for a weekend getaway at any one of Virginia's Inns.

downstairs, along with a living room and den for guests and three rooms upstairs with private porches. Two of those rooms are equipped with jacuzzis. American and Victorian antiques fill the rooms in both the carriage house and the main building. Other interesting collectibles include an array of Toby mugs dating from 1755, a walnut desk piece that belonged to Winston Churchhill, Meissen porcelain figurines and Henry Wadsworth Longfellow's clock. The Serens serve tea in the afternoon if requested, and wine or beer upon arrival. A full gourmet breakfast features such specialities as French toast made with English muffins and topped with fresh strawberries, whipped cream and powdered sugar, and an Eggs Benedict-type of dish with spinach and artichokes instead of Canadian bacon. They also offer gourmet meals to guests and to the public in a romantic dining room. For more details refer to the chapter on Restaurants. Rates are $85 a night for a room with a jacuzzi and $75 a night for all the other rooms. The Serens offer special packages for guests who want to combine their stay with fox hunting, horseback riding or a trip to see a play or concert at the outdoor Lime Kiln Theater nearby.

SEVEN HILLS INN

408 S. Main St.,
Lexington, VA 24450   (703) 463-4715
This inn's seven guest rooms are named after the seven historic estates in Rockbridge County that are connected to the Grigsby family who settled here in the 1700s. The estates themselves are as magnificent as any plantation home to be found in Virginia, and the Seven Hills Inn reflects this grandeur. It's a southern Colonial-style home that was actually built by a Washington and Lee fraternity in 1928. It passed through several hands before being purchased by its current owners, Ben and Carol Grigsby, several years ago. Ben's mother, Jane Daniel, is the executive innkeeper.

All of the guest rooms are furnished with either the family's antiques or with 18th or early 19th-century hand-crafted reproductions. A gorgeous handmade needlepoint rug from Portugal graces the living room, and decorative items purchased during the family's trips to the Orient are displayed throughout the house.

All of the rooms have private baths except for "Liberty Hill" and "Cherry Hill," which share an enormous connecting bathroom. Those rooms are often used as a suite by families. Speaking of families, the inn welcomes well-behaved children. Rates are from $75 to $95, depending upon the size of the room. Rates are based on double occupancy; a third person costs an extra $15. The rate includes a deluxe continental breakfast and afternoon tea, upon request. Guests can watch television, read or play games in the "Chapter Room" in the basement where the fraternity used to hold its meetings.

LLEWELLYN LODGE AT LEXINGTON

603 South Main Street,
Lexington, VA 24450   *(703) 463-3235*
    or (800) 882-1145

This charming 53-year-old brick Colonial home is located in the heart of Lexington, within walking distance of all the city's historic sights. Ellen and John Roberts are your hosts at this lovely home. Ellen is a gourmet cook who has been a part of the airline, travel, hotel and restaurant industries. John is a Lexingtonian who will be happy to share his knowledge of the surrounding area.

The friendly atmosphere is noticed right from the start as you are met at the front door with refreshments. The comfortable living room has a large fireplace — a perfect setting for a good conversation. There is a separate television and telephone room. And, for your comfort, there is air conditioning in the summer months. The six bedrooms are distinctly different from one another, designed to meet the needs of a wide variety of guests. All have extra firm beds, ceiling fans and private bathrooms. Room 1 has a pencil post queen bed with a tub/shower. Room 2 has wicker furniture, a queen bed and a stall shower. Room 3 has an oak spindle queen bed, an easy chair and stall shower. Room 4 has a king bed, a sitting area, a television and a tub/shower. Room 5 has two brass double beds and a stall shower (great for a family). And Room 6 has two four-poster twin beds with a tub/shower. This last room is located in the first floor and can accommodate handicapped persons, not requiring a wheelchair.

A gourmet breakfast awaits you each morning. You can feast on fantastic omelettes, Belgian waffles, French toast, Virginia maple syrup, homemade muffins and breads, bacon, sausage, ham, juice, coffee and teas. After breakfast, take on the great outdoors! There is hiking on the Chessie Trail, bicycle riding, canoeing on the Maury River, tubing at Goshen Pass and golf and tennis at Lexington Golf and Country Club. (You might even find that John is willing to share his "secret" fishing spots with you!) In the summer you can visit the drive-in movie theater or the Lime Kiln Arts Center, featuring regional historical dramas and concerts.

A one night's deposit is required to hold a reservation. Smoking in the guest rooms or dining room is not permitted, nor are pets of any kind. The Lodge is designed with adults in mind. Call about children (6 years of age or older).

FASSIFERN

Rt. 5, Box 87
Lexington, VA 24450   *(703) 463-1013*

Visitors to the Virginia Horse Center pass right by Fassifern on Va. 39. It's a place of striking beauty: tall weeping willows surround a small pond, and bright flowers abound when the weather is warm.

Fassifern is situated on three and a half acres, just across the road from the Art Farm, a gallery with summer workshops where traditional methods of Chinese painting are taught. On the other side of the Art Farm is the Horse Center.

The B&B's main building is a

beautiful old home, built in 1867. There's also the "dependency" which used to be an ice house and servants' living quarters, and which now houses two guest rooms.

Owners Ann Carol and Arthur Perry assumed ownership of Fassifern in July, 1989, and they live on the property in their own separate quarters. Guests need not feel they must tip-toe around someone's private home, because this house is set up for guests and their needs. The guest living room is elegant but cozy, furnished with an old pump organ and piano, a stuffed leather chair and sofa and lots of magazines and books.

A hearty continental breakfast is served in the beautifully decorated dining room, and includes fresh squeezed orange juice, homemade granola, fresh fruit, croissants and other breads, country ham spread, and hot chocolate, coffee and tea.

All five guest rooms are air-conditioned and have private baths. The Austrian Room is furnished with gorgeous European antiques, while the Country Room is more casual, with golden oak furniture and bright reddish print wallpaper. The three other rooms are also beautifully furnished and appear to be very comfortable. There are two other private sitting areas in the house besides the living room.

Rates range from $79 to $87, which includes breakfast. Children aged 8 and older are welcome. The owners recommend calling as far in advance as possible to make reservations.

THE HUMMINGBIRD INN

P.O. Box 147
Goshen, VA 24439   (703) 997-9065

This unique Victorian villa has operated on and off as an inn since it was built in 1853. Its new owners, Jeremy and Diana Robinson, opened it again this spring to overnight guests and have done a beautiful job redesigning the interior. Its four guest rooms, furnished with antiques, are colorful and spacious and all have private baths. Full breakfasts include country bacon or sausage, homemade bread, and foods unique to the area. There are wrap-around verandas on the first and second floors, original pine floors of varying width, and a rustic den, solarium and music room.

During Goshen's boom days in the late 1800's and early 1900's, the inn was directly across from the town's railroad station, and the steps from the tracks to the inn's private road are still in place. Trains still come through several times a week, but never at night to disturb guests' sleep.

In the 1930's the inn played host to Eleanor Roosevelt (one of the rooms is named after her) and Ephraim Zimbalist, Sr., among other notables.

A wide trout stream defines one of the property lines, and only five minutes away is the gorgeous Goshen Pass, a popular spot for kayaking, picnicking and sunbathing in warm weather. This place is not to be missed when the rhododendron are in bloom!

Guests can also enjoy a relaxing float along Mill Creek, which flows behind the inn, in inner tubes. Historic Lexington is only 20 minutes away, offering fine restaurants and shops, the Virginia Horse Center, the George Marshall Museum, Stonewall Jackson House and Cemetery and other historic sites.

Rates are between $50 and $65, including the sumptuous breakfast.

LAVENDER HILL FARM

Rt. 1, Box 515 (Rt. 631)
Lexington, VA 24450   *(703) 464-5877*
or (800) 446-4240

Cindy and Colin Smith have restored a 200-year-old farmhouse on about 20 acres of beautiful land a few miles outside Lexington. The house is situated on the banks of Kerrs Creek, and has three light, airy guest rooms with private baths. One of the queen rooms can be rented as a suite; it connects to a second room with a double bed.

What makes this bed and breakfast unique is the chance to combine an overnight stay with horseback trips led by Virginia Mountain Outfitters. Packages are offered for riders of all levels of experience, and are focused around such activities as trail rides, riding workshops and fox-hunting weekends.

The B&B was designed with animal lovers in mind. Sheep, cows and friendly nubian goats roam over the land that surrounds the farmhouse, and a dalmatian and cat stay close by.

Colin Smith is a gourmet chef who loves to cook with fresh herbs that are grown on the farm. In fact, his first book on cooking with herbs

is scheduled for release this year. Four course dinners cost $20 per person and are optional. A sample menu: poached rainbow trout for an appetizer, a Greek salad, an entree of boneless pork loin stuffed with apricots, and a chocolate raspberry tart for dessert.

Rates for two at the farm range from $60 to $70 per night, and this includes a full country breakfast.

The Horse Lovers Holiday package costs $225 per person based on double occupancy, which includes a two-night stay, breakfast, dinner, and picnic lunches both days, along with the use of horses, tours, and all instruction.

Special theater packages are offered during the summer months, when the local Lime Kiln Theater puts on its outdoor plays and Sunday night concerts. The Smiths will purchase tickets and pack a gourmet picnic dinner to take along to Lime Kiln, whose bucolic grounds are conducive to sipping wine and feasting.

The Smiths don't allow pets or smoking inside the house. But, quips Cindy, they do welcome children with "well behaved adults."

Roanoke/Salem

THE MARY BLADON HOUSE

381 Washington Avenue, SW,
Roanoke, VA 24016   *(703) 344-5361*

This 1890s Victorian home is nestled in the heart of the Old Southwest neighborhood in Roanoke. Bill and Sheri Bestpitch want The Mary Bladon House to be your home away from home as you explore the beautiful Roanoke Valley. The Rococo Revival, Renaissance Revival and Eastlake style furnishings, the antique English china, the original brass light fixtures and even the Victorian playing cards on the writing table in the parlor combine to recapture the charm of "a time when elegant comfort was a way of life." Guests will feel the spirit of the Victorian age while relaxing in the rocker in their room or on the swing found on the wrap-around front porch.

The guest rooms are decorated with crafts and period antiques. Families travelling with children are welcome in the roomy suite. For your comfort, modern conveniences are to be found, such as air conditioning and a 24-hour telephone answering service.

A delicious breakfast will help you start your day. The meal features the cook's choice of eggs, pancakes, waffles or French toast served with bacon, ham or sausage. Home fries, hot and cold cereals, juice, coffee and tea are also available. The cook will be happy to accommodate special dietary requests with advance notice.

Afterwards, spend the day in downtown Roanoke. Visit the restored Farmers' Market and Center in the Square, an arts and entertainment mecca. The home is also only five minutes from the Blue Ridge Parkway. There is also easy access to Natural Bridge, Dixie Caverns, Mabry Mill, Smith Mountain Lake, Peaks of Otter and more! After a busy morning, return to the inn for afternoon tea, served from 4 to 6 PM. And, with advance reserva-

tions, you can savor a terrific dinner in the dining room.

Pets cannot be accommodated. Smoking is permitted on the verandas only. A deposit is required with reservations.

THE INN AT BURWELL PLACE
601 W. Main Street,
Salem, VA 24153   *(703) 387-0250*

Michel Spence Robertson is the innkeeper of this turn-of-the-century mansion at the southern end of the Shenandoah Valley. The magnificent front porch allows for a panoramic view of the Blue Ridge Mountains and the Roanoke Valley. Each of the five bedrooms is decorated with queen size beds, period furniture and antiques and each has a private bath. A large suite with fireplace and whirlpool is perfect for families with children, or couples desiring privacy and romance.

After a large country breakfast of eggs, French toast or pancakes, fresh fruit, home fries, muffins and more, visit the sights of Salem. The historic downtown area is full of antique shops. Roanoke College and Salem's Farmers' Market are within walking distance. A short drive away are Dixie Caverns, the Blue Ridge Parkway, Mabry Mill, Peaks of Otter, Natural Bridge and historic downtown Roanoke. Return after a day's exploring to afternoon tea on the porch.

Pets are not permitted and smoking is not allowed inside the inn. One night's deposit is required with reservations.

East of the Blue Ridge Region

Sperryville/Washington

BLEU ROCK INN
US 211, Route 1, Box 555
Washington, VA 22747   (703) 987-3190

This cozy country inn is situated on 80 rolling acres in Rappahannock County. The gorgeous scenery will have you calling this place home in no time. Lush green meadows, a clear pond and tall shade trees are all surrounded by majestic mountains. There are seven acres of carefully cared for vineyards, where the inn grows grapes for its wine. The farmhouse has been renovated into an inn with five guest bedrooms, each with private baths. You can enjoy dining fireside in one of the three dining rooms, or relax in the lounge. The open air terrace overlooks the vineyards of Cabernet Sauvignon, Chardonnay and Seyval grapes. At the large pond, you can try your hand at catching bass, catfish and blue gill. Or stroll through the open grazing lands and watch the horses run free. There is plenty of adventure to be found in Rappahannock County. Try skiing, bicycling, canoeing, golfing, hiking and caving. There are also historic sites and wineries for you to tour and explore.

Bernard and Jean Campagne are the owners and operators of Bleu Rock Farm and Inn. Master Chef, Jean Campagne, has been honored with the Medals of Merite Agricole de France, Academie Culinaire de France, Cordon Bleu and Maitre Cuisinier de France. But you won't need his credentials to tell you that the food here is delicious. Breakfast, which is only served to overnight guests, is spectacular. It begins with fresh orange juice and coffee served with hot biscuits, croissants and muffins. Next is a fruit plate, no doubt full of fruit picked from their own orchards. Then the main course is served. It could be an omelette of ham, shiitake mushrooms and cheddar cheese, or Santa Fe French toast served with maple syrup and creme fraiche. Both are accompanied by a spicy pork sausage, made in-house, and sauteed apples. This breakfast will really knock your socks off. Their dinners are superb as well.

Children over ten years of age are welcome, but supervision by an adult is requested when they are outdoors near the pond or horses. Pets are not allowed. One night's deposit is required with reservations.

THE INN AT LITTLE WASHINGTON
Middle and Main Streets, P.O. Box 300
Washington, VA 22747   (703) 675-3800

If you are looking to be pampered beyond your wildest dreams and eat food more delicious than you thought possible, then The Inn at Little Washington should certainly be number one on your list. This inn, located in a cozy, quiet town in Rappahannock County, is the only Mobil Travel Guide Five Star Inn in the United States. Its praise has come from far and wide,

and it has been written about in *USA Today*, *People* magazine, the *New York Times*, the *San Francisco Chronicle* and *Hemispheres* (United Airline's magazine). All of that, and there isn't even a sign over the door.

Reinhardt Lynch and Patrick O'Connell are the owners of this Heaven on Earth. Lynch takes care of the day-to-day operations at the Inn...you know, little stuff like making sure that the 3,000 requests for Saturday night dinner are narrowed down to 65. O'Connell is the cause for all of the commotion. His culinary masterpieces are the main reason Inn at Little Washington is in business. The dinners are prix fixe, which means that there's a fixed price no matter what you order. The evening meal consists of cocktails, wine, five to six courses, and after-dinner drinks. Normally when a restaurant has a fixed price, the cost remains high, but your selection is minimal. Not true at Little Washington. There are 11 entree choices and 15 desserts. Not bad. The only problem is choosing among such devilish delights as peppered tuna and swordfish grilled rare, local rockfish, salmon and sea scallops with a sauté of silver queen corn, and veal medallions with purées of black olives, sundried tomatoes and pesto. Desserts range from warm custard bread pudding with Wild Turkey sauce to the white chocolate mousse in passion fruit purée. It will make your mouth water just reading about it.

The rest of the Inn should not be shadowed by the success of the restaurant. The consistently excellent service and the luxury of the rooms are certainly entitled to praise. There are only ten guest rooms and each is spectacular enough to stand on its own. The rooms are filled with antiques, overstuffed reading chairs, canopied beds and elegantly decorated with faux bois woodwork and draped fabrics. The scent of freshly-cut flowers mingles with that of potpourri and drifts across the room. Old-fashioned silhouettes hang on the wall. Colorful pillows form a mountain of comfort on the bed. But do not succumb to them yet. First soak in packets of pine-scented bubbles in the marble and brass bathroom. Pamper yourself with the heated, fluffy towels. Then wrap yourself in the plush white robe and watch the fountain from your balcony. You will pinch yourself to see if you're still awake. It will truly feel as if you've died and gone to heaven. The Inn is very popular so advance registration is a must.

Culpeper

FOUNTAIN HALL BED & BREAKFAST
609 S. East Street,
Culpeper, VA 22701-3222 (703) 825-8200

George Washington, the first County Surveyor of Culpeper, was quoted referring to Culpeper as "a high and pleasant situation." And this bed & breakfast in Culpeper County is no exception to that rule. Fountain Hall is built on land with a long and interesting history. It was originally part of a large tract owned by Virginia's Royal Governor, Sir Alexander Spotswood. In 1923, the house was sold to Jackson

Lee Fray, founder of the local telephone company. Fray hired an architect to build the Colonial Revival house from the older, Country Victorian structure.

Steve and Kathi Walker are the hosts of the home today. They take special pride in the fact that Fountain Hall became the first bed and breakfast in Culpeper. The guest rooms are all elegantly decorated and named in order to make each truly unique. Rooms range from a single with shared bath to a two-room suite with private bath and porch. All rooms have individual telephones.

Fountain Hall can accommodate board-style meetings and small receptions as well. Pets are not allowed and smoking is permitted in designated areas only. Guests are required to send a one night deposit.

THE INN AT MEANDER PLANTATION

James Madison Highway
U.S. Route 15
Route 5, Box 460
Locust Dale, VA 22948   (703) 672-4912

Cradled in the heart of Jefferson's Virginia, The Inn at Meander Plantation offers a rare opportunity to experience the charm and elegance of Colonial living at its best. This historic country estate, built in 1766 by noted Virginian Joshua Fry, allows guests to return to an earlier, more romantic time when hospitality was a matter of pride and fine living was an art practiced in restful surroundings.

The stately Colonial mansion, sitting majestically on 40 acres of rolling pastures and woods, was converted to a country B&B in 1993. The sun-drenched bedrooms, each with private bath, welcomes you with elegance, warmth, romance and comfort. Four-poster queen-size beds piled high with plump pillows beckon you to snuggle beneath down comforters.

Throughout the house are plenty of private nooks for reading, writing or quiet contemplation. Guests often gather in the parlor where Thomas Jefferson and Gen. Lafayette were frequent visitors. A baby grand stands ready for impromptu concerts.

A full country gourmet breakfast is served daily in the formal dining room or under the arched breezeway on sun-warmed mornings. Fresh-baked muffins topped with homemade apple butter or fruit preserves compliment tantalizing and creative entres which vary with the seasons and the mood of the morning. Full dinner service and take-along picnic baskets are available with advance notice. The graceful rooms and gardens are available for special events.

Outdoors, white rockers line both levels of the expansive back porches, providing peaceful respites for sipping afternoon tea. Boxwood gardens are dotted with secluded benches and a hammock for spectacular views. Croquet, volleyball, badminton and horsehoes can be played on the lawns. Wildlife and birds abound in surrounding woods and fields. Trail rides and English riding lessons are offered at the stables.

Innkeepers are Suzanne Thomas and Suzie Blanchard;

Suzie's husband, Bill, and their daughter, Kelly. Suzanne, a former newspaperwomen, continues a duel career in historic preservation and food-writing. She writes a weekly food column for 40 newspapers and welcomes a chance to share recipes from her 400 cookbooks. Bob loves sharing his passion for classical music and rehabilitating old houses while Kelly most often can be found in the stables. Golden retriver, Honey, and Bojo the sociable Siamese offer their own special greetings to guests.

The inn is a smoke-free environment, located in the bend of the scenic Robinson River. It is located in Madison County on Route 15, nine miles south of Culpeper and six miles north of Orange. The best of the countryside is close at hand, including wineries, antique shops and history sites.

Stanardsville

EDGEWOOD FARM BED & BREAKFAST
Route 2, Box 303,
Stanardsville, VA 22973   (804) 985-3782
A quiet and secluded 130-acre farm at the foothills of the Blue Ridge is the site of this bed and breakfast in Greene County. The murmur of nearby streams provides solace for the weary traveler, and the surrounding woods are the perfect place for exploring the natural beauty of the area.

The home itself is a step back in time. Originally built in 1790, the house was doubled in size in the 1860s. Restoration of the glorious

old building began almost ten years ago in 1984. The period-decorated bedrooms come complete with fireplaces and private baths. The bathrooms are furnished with pleasantly-scented goat's milk soap, lotion and shampoo made in nearby Charlottesville. Upon arrival, Norman and Eleanor Schwartz, your hosts at Edgewood Farm, will greet you with refreshments and smiles. Each morning you will be treated to a full country breakfast, including an unbelievably generous array of homebaked muffins, coffeecakes and other breads, and an exotic fruit compote.

But before you even head downstairs for breakfast, open your door and you'll find an urn of fresh, hot coffee on a beautiful silver service with fresh flowers and linen.

Gardeners and nature lovers alike will love the plant nursery that specializes in herbs and perennials.

An abundance of historical and natural attractions are within a 30-mile radius of the farm. Skyline Drive, Monticello, Montpelier, Ash Lawn-Highlands and University of Virginia are only a few. There are also vineyards and antique and craft shops close by. Special arrangements can be made for meals other than breakfast, so call ahead. A deposit is required with reservations.

Orange

NORFIELDS FARM BED & BREAKFAST
Rt. I Box 477,
Gordonsville, VA 22942   (703) 832-2952
or (703) 832-5939
This is a moderately priced,

but perfectly charming and comfortable B&B that's nestled on 500 acres in the foothills of the blue Ridge. Norfields is in its fourth generation of dairy farming, and the bed and breakfast dates back to 1850. Green pastures with 250 holstein cows and wildlife make this an especially ideal retreat for city folk. There is a two-bedroom suite downstairs with a private bath that holds an old clawfoot tub. The suite is perfect for a couple with children. A large, bright and sunny living room is available for reading, relaxing or watching television, which has cable. It's separated from the dining room with French doors. The kitchen is also quite enticing with antiques and stenciling. Upstairs are two more country bedrooms. All the rooms are air-conditioned. A full country breakfast is served every morning at the guest's convenience. Proprietress Teresa Norton invites her guests to relax on the front porch swing, take a long walk, or fish in the well-stocked pond. Whether for business or pleasure, enjoy the quiet seclusion and warm hospitality at Norfields Farm, located 30 minutes from Charlottesville and one hour from Richmond. Rates are $65 to $75 a night based on double occupancy. The cost of a single room is $50. Children are welcome, and so are pets by prior arrangement. Norfields is a non-smoking home.

HOLLADAY HOUSE
155 West Main Street
Orange, VA 22960   (703) 672-4893
                     or (800) 358-4422
Pete and Phebe Holladay run this friendly B&B in their restored 1830 federal-style home in downtown Orange. Guest rooms are spacious, comfortable, and furnished with antiques. Phebe is an artist, and many of her works decorate the walls, along with an interesting collection of prints by other artists. The living room is an especially inviting place to sit and read.

Fine china and silver are used for breakfast, which is served in the privacy of guests' own rooms. The bountiful breakfasts include juice and coffee or tea, homemade muffins, fresh fruit and a main course like eggs and bacon.

There are five rooms and one suite available, and rates range from $75 to $185, including the full breakfast.

The Holladays welcome families with children at their B&B and are happy to talk to guests about the Orange County area and all there is to see and do.

Holladay House is only a 10-minute drive from James Madison's Montpelier and within walking distance to the James Madison Museum. Two wineries, Barboursville and Burnley, are also nearby.

WILLOW GROVE INN
14079 Plantation Way
Orange, VA 22960   (703) 672-5982
                     or (800) WG9-1778
If you want to live and breathe history while you're staying overnight in Orange County, consider this antebellum mansion with formal gardens and sloping lawns.

Willow Grove Inn is listed on the National Register of Historic Places. It was built by the same craftsmen chosen by Thomas Jefferson for work on the University of Virginia.

The mansion, whose exterior is a prime example of Jefferson's Classical Revival Style, fell under siege during the Civil War. You can still see trenches near the manor house, and a cannonball was recently removed from its eaves.

Nestled on 37 acres, the original atmosphere of the mansion has been carefully preserved. Fine American and English antiques decorate the manor house, and English boxwood, magnolias, and willows grace the lawns.

But don't let this intimidate you. Owners Richard Brown and Angela Mulloy have figured out just how to help their guests wind down and truly enjoy their visit. For example, there is no check-out time - -you can sleep until noon and have a full breakfast at 2 or 3 if you like. A newspaper and pot of fresh coffee will be at your door in the morning, along with fresh baked muffins if you want something before the hearty breakfast.

Several dining rooms offer distinct atmospheres: Clark's Tavern is dark, cozy and casual, while the Dolley Madison Room is formal and elegant, with delicate china and crystal.

Antique furnishings, wide pine flooring, and original fireplace mantels preserve the traditional character of each of the inn's seven bedrooms. You'll also find fresh flowers in the rooms, and down pillows and comforters for extra comfort. Coconut milk baths await guests in private bathrooms.

By the way, Chef Warren Volk prepares the most exquisite food you will find in any restaurant for many miles around. This is THE place to dine in Orange County. A pianist and vocalist provide romantic background music many nights.

As with virtually all bed and breakfasts in the area, rates aren't cheap. They range from $95 to $155, which includes breakfast. But a special deal on Sundays and Thursdays allows guests to enjoy a five-course meal, stay the night, and eat breakfast for only $55 per person, plus tax.

SLEEPY HOLLOW FARM
16280 Blue Ridge Turnpike
Gordonsville, VA 22942   (703) 832-5555

This is a cozy 18th-century house filled with nooks and crannies and bedrooms that feel like private hideaways. Flower and herb gardens surround the house, and the broader surroundings are woods and rolling fields with cattle grazing. Beverley Allison and her daughter, Dorsey Allison-Comer, run the bed and breakfast, which has been the Allison family home for decades.

The atmosphere here is casual and comfortable. Three dogs and two cats serve as the palace guards, quips Beverley Allison. Guests find a welcome basket in their rooms stocked with Virginia peanuts, fruit, and a homemade chocolate chip cookie. If this isn't enough to snack on, a freshly baked cake awaits the hungry at all times in the sitting area. The formal dining room is one of the prettiest you'll find anywhere, and it overlooks the herb garden and distant rolling hills.

All of the rooms have private baths, and one has a working fireplace and whirlpool. A beautiful pond on the grounds can be used for swimming or for fishing for catfish, bass or brim. Ducks and their babies can be seen gliding around the pond much of the year. Speaking of babies, Sleepy Hollow is one of the few B&Bs in the area that caters to children. A baby crib and playpen are available, and there are two suites that are popular with families.

Rates range from $60 to $95 and include a full country breakfast and afternoon tea, if requested. Private dinners are also offered by prior arrangement. The owners like to do wine tastings if there are several guests who stay more than more night.

Another plus at Sleepy Hollow is the late check-out time – 1 p.m. Skyline Drive is only a 20 minute drive away, and the Massanutten Ski Resort only 45 minutes away, across the mountain by way of Rt. 33.

THE SHADOWS BED AND BREAKFAST INN

14291 Constitution Highway
Route 1, Box 535,
Orange, VA 22960   (703) 672-5057

Barbara and Pat Loffredo are the innkeepers of this restored 1913 stone house. The inn is surrounded by old cedars on forty-four acres in Orange County. If you want to relax and forget about the hassles of modern life, stay at the Shadows. You can curl up in front of the large stone fireplace with a cup of hot cider or enjoy a good book from the library. Relish the romance of holding hands on the porch swing and chat with other guests while enjoying the ritual of afternoon tea in the gathering room.

The four artfully-decorated guest bedrooms are individually named and decorated, and each has its own special charm. In addition, the Loffredos had the good fortune to discover two cottages a few steps away from the house. These, too, have been lovingly restored. The two-room Rocking Horse Cabin is decked in country crafts while The two-room Cottage, a former cook's quarters, sports it own deck providing a quiet view of the country retreat. The Blue Room has a queen size pre-Civil War walnut bed and a day bed. The natural cedar bathroom has a lady's vanity, clawfoot tub and pedestal sink. The Rose Room is full of frills and lace. There is a full size antique highback oak bed and a private upper deck. The Peach room is art deco and has two twin burled walnut beds and a private hall shower. The Victorian Room has a full size iron and brass bed with ruffled bed and window dressings. There is a private hall bathroom with a tub/shower and pedestal sink. A full country breakfast is served each morning.

The Shadows is conveniently located near Montpelier, Civil War battlefields and local wineries. Pets are not allowed. Reservations are accepted with one night's deposit.

Charlottesville

CLIFTON--THE COUNTRY INN
Rt. 13, Box 26,
Charlottesville, VA 22901   (804) 971-1800

Clifton is winning rave reviews around the country for its elegance, comfort, wonderful amenities and gourmet dining. So outstanding is this inn that *Country Inns* magazine called it one of the top 12 in the nation. And Judith Martin, Miss Manners herself, listed Clifton as one of her four favorite hotels in the world in her latest book, *Miss Manners Guide to the Turn of the Millennium.* Clifton is an imposing 18th-century manor house with pillared veranda and a clear view to Monticello when the trees are not in bloom.

Clifton was built by Thomas Mann Randolph, husband of Thomas Jefferson's daughter, Martha, on land that once adjoined the Shadwell Plantation, Jefferson's birthplace. It is believed to have been built as an office for Randolph,

but it became his home in his later years. Clifton offers overnight guests a gracious escape from the here and now, a chance to slip away to a less hurried Jeffersonian life. At Clifton, decisions become no more demanding than whether to play a few wickets of croquet, or to read a long-intended book by the fire; whether to float around the lake on an innertube, or to practice a Chopin prelude on the grand piano.

Innkeepers Craig and Donna Hartman set the mood at Clifton with their obvious and genuine affection for people. They will greet you with a willingness to help with luggage, an explanation of all the options for filling your time, and even a tour of the house, if there is time. Tea is served at 4 every afternoon, complete with gourmet teas, fresh fruits and freshly-baked treats. Every room has its own fireplace and they aren't just for show. Firewood is freshly laid in each guest's room in the cool season, ready for

SILVER THATCH INN

Turn an ordinary evening into an extraordinary night.

Dine with us and spend the night in one of our romantic rooms.

Rita & Vince Scoffone
Your Innkeepers

3001 Hollymead Dr., Charlottesville, VA 22901 • (804) 978-4686

· Clifton Country Inn ·

"One of the 12 best inns in America."
—*Country Inns*, February 1993

"Clifton ranks in the top three or four historic inns in the world."
—*International Living*, July 1992

"Outside [Charlottesville] are many country inns. Best choice: Clifton, near Jefferson's birthplace at Shadwell."
—*Forbes*

"In Charlottesville, Clifton reigns supreme."
—*Andrew Harper's Hideaway Report*

14 gracious accommodations in a historic 18th century manor house.

Serving *prix-fixe* dinner to the public
Wednesday through Sunday by reservation

(804) 971-1800

250 East, Right on SR 729, 1/3 Mile on Left

the strike of a match. Guests are also warmed by down comforters on each of the antique beds. All the rooms and suites have private baths, as individual and unusual as the rooms themselves. One of the most popular rooms, the Martha Jefferson, features walls, bed hangings and a rug the color of rich vanilla ice cream. The carriage house is a spectacular guest suite featuring a stair railing and other architectural artifacts from the recently dismantled Meriwether Lewis home. This seems especially fitting because Martha and Thomas Randolph's affection for Lewis was such that they named their fourth son after him.

Outside, flower beds surround a manicured croquet court. Down the lawn from the enclosed veranda is a spacious gazebo, and a little farther is a tennis court and a lap pool for serious swimming. All of this is surrounded by 45 acres of dense forest, through which a short walk brings you to a dock on the private, pristine lake. This is the perfect point from which to begin a swim or a lazy float in an oversized innertube. The cost of a stay at Clifton ranges from $143 to $193 per night for two. Some of the suites have sofa beds, and children may share their parents' accommodations for no extra charge. Pets are not allowed, and neither is smoking. Full breakfasts are included in the price of a room and feature fresh fruit, sausage or bacon, a lavish entree, juice and coffee or tea. Clifton also operates a restaurant which serves gourmet dinner to the public Wednesday through Sunday. Exquisite meals consist of four or five courses and are prepared by Craig Hartman and assistant Ron Miller, both award-winning chefs and graduates of the Culinary Institute of America. Light refreshments are also always available for guests, from fresh-baked cookies to a self-serve refrigerator stocked with wine, sodas, beer and water. Clifton is also happy to prepare luncheons and private dinners to order.

200
South Street
A VIRGINIA INN

Charlottesville, Virginia 22901
804-979-0200
800-964-7008

Clifton is just off Rt. 250 East, on State Rt. 729 in Shadwell. It is only four miles from Charlottesville and three miles from Monticello.

THE 1817 ANTIQUE INN

1211 W. Main St.
Charlottesville, VA 22903   (804) 979-7353

If you suspect this inn in a historic townhouse might be too stiff and formal for your fancy, consider this:

The friendly black lab who sits quietly in the hallway, so happy for a scratch behind the ears. The fact that owner Candace DeLoach Wilson, in her early 30s, loves nothing more than for her guests to sit back and relax in the living room and munch on the M and M's she keeps in a big bowl.

Eclectic decor makes this place unique in tradition-bound Charlottesville. For instance, the living room is decorated with items as disparate as Biedermeier chairs, American Empire chests, Venetian tables, and a big zebra skin rug. The total effect is exciting, but comfortable.

This is precisely the aim of Wilson, who grew up in Savannah, attended college in South Carolina, then moved to New York where she worked as an interior designer for 10 years.

She met her husband, Jon, a fellow Southerner, in New York and the two married and moved to Charlottesville for his job in industrial engineering last year.

Candace Wilson opened DeLoach Antiques next to the inn in an adjoining townhouse in the spring of 1993. Most all the antiques and furnishings in the inn are for sale – and at reasonable prices for the Charlottesville area.

Both buildings were built by one of Thomas Jefferson's master craftsmen, James Dinsmore of Northern Ireland, in 1817. Dinsmore was the principal carpenter at Monticello and several original dormitories at the University of Virginia.

Prospect Hill ...1732

The Virginia
Plantation
Inn
ca. 1732

The Sheehan Family Innkeepers • Telephone (800) 277-0844

Along with another master builder, Dinsmore was Jefferson's principal carpenter for the Rotunda, which is only a few blocks from The 1817 Inn.

Prices are reasonable at the inn, given the luxurious surroundings and the bountiful breakfast and the wine and cheese that are offered in the early evening. Rates range from $89 for a double room to $129 for a king.

On weekends, breakfast includes either Eggs Benedict or Eggs Florentine with a rich grits dish, or Plantation Eggs with sausage gravy and biscuits. Also offered are pumpkin bread with cinnamon cream cheese, hearty muffins, granola, yogurt, piles of fresh fruit, juice, and coffee. Weekday breakfasts include everything listed above except for the egg dishes.

The inn's convenient location will likely make it a popular destination for parents of UVA students. Within easy walking distance is "The Corner," a block or two of restaurants, clothing stores, and other shops across from campus. Some of Charlottesville's most appealing restaurants are along Elliewood Avenue in this neighborhood.

Back to the inn: all the bedrooms offer a mood of romance, whether it be the spacious Mattie Carrington room with French antiques and a glass chandelier, or the exotic Lewis and Clark room with an African cowhide rug, fur pillows and English hunt pictures.

My personal favorite is Mrs. Olive's Room in the back, whose many white shuttered windows are hung with silk balloon valances, and whose love seat, chair and tufted ottoman make for a comfortable place to read and write letters.

Perhaps most appealing are the warm, unpretentious personalities of Candace and Jon Wilson and their manager, Vickie Gresge. You will be left alone as much as you like at The 1817 Inn, but you will also be treated like a welcome friend.

INN AT MONTICELLO
Highway 20 South,
Route 19, Box 112
Charlottesville, VA 22902   (804) 979-3593

Carol and Larry Engel invite you to "Spend the day at Thomas Jefferson's beloved Monticello. Spend the night with us." This country manor house was built in the mid-1800s and is cradled in the valley of Thomas Jefferson's own Monticello Mountain. The gorgeous grounds are full of dogwoods, boxwoods, azaleas, a lush, manicured lawn and beautiful Willow Lake. The croquet set is set up neatly on the lawn and a lazy hammock summons you for a mid-afternoon nap.

Inside there are five elegant bedrooms, each furnished with period antiques and reproductions. The beds are made with crisp cotton linens and down comforters. Some have special features such as a working fireplace, a four-poster canopy bed or a private porch. Every room has a private bath. For your comfort, a smoke-free environment and central air conditioning are provided.

Let the aroma of freshly brewed hazelnut coffee lure you

from your warm bed. Breakfast each morning includes fruits and juices, hot tea and coffee, sugar and cream. Their changing menu of such delicious entrées as Crab Quiche and Orange Yogurt Pancakes provides for the best of seasonally available specialties.

You will never run short of things to do or see here. Within moments you can visit Monticello (the home of Thomas Jefferson), Michie Tavern, Ash Lawn-Highland (the home of James Monroe) or Montpelier (the home of James and Dolley Madison). There are also vineyards and wineries, recreational activities and a long list of seasonal events. Your visit to historic Charlottesville will definitely be more memorable with a stay at the Inn at Monticello. A two-night minimum stay is required on certain "peak season" weekends.

PROSPECT HILL INN

Route 3, Box 430,
Trevilians, VA 23093   (703) 967-0844
or (800) 277-0844

A graceful English tree garden shades the manor house. A boxwood hedge lines the entrance way to this 1732 mansion. A few steps away are the slave quarters, the overseer's house, slave kitchen, smoke house and carriage house. A large open lawn rolls on for a quarter mile. This is Prospect Hill, a plantation that is more than two and a half centuries old. You will begin to feel the country spirit the moment you breath the sweet, clean air. Mirelle and Bill Sheehan, along with their children Mike and Nancy, are the innkeepers today, but the tradition of hospitality began long before their time.

After the end of the Civil War, the son of the plantation owner returned to find Prospect Hill overgrown and run down. In order to make ends meet, he was forced to take in guests from the city. In 1880

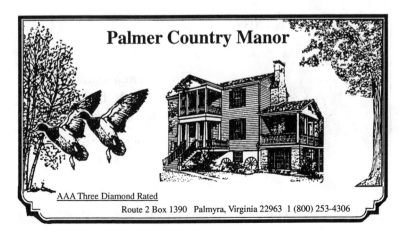

Palmer Country Manor

AAA Three Diamond Rated
Route 2 Box 1390 Palmyra, Virginia 22963 1 (800) 253-4306

he built onto Prospect Hill and re-modeled the old slave quarters for guest bedrooms. This renovation made the interior of the buildings as beautiful as the extraordinary magnolias, tulip poplars and giant beeches in the yard. The slave quarters have beamed ceilings and warm, crackling fireplaces. The rooms in the manor house are adorned with antique furnishings and lovely quilts and most have a fireplace. A private veranda looks over the hillside. There are 11 guest rooms in all. All have modern bathrooms and some are even equipped with Jacuzzis in which you can soak all of your cares away.

A full country breakfast is served in bed or at a table in your room. Dinner is served as well, and a bell will ring to announce it. The Sheehans keep with the old tradition of serving the guests the same meal they have made for their family. There are three candlelit dining rooms and your four to five course feast is served there. The

blessing is given and then leisurely dining begins. There are basic country dishes with a French Provincial twist to them. Tea time is a ritual at Prospect Hill. You can also enjoy a glass of sherry before dinner while you are curled up next to the fireplace. There is plenty to do and see from here.

The inn is located in the Green Springs Historic District of Louisa County, so there is plenty of natural beauty around. Try hunting, biking, hiking swimming or driving along Skyline Drive and the Blue Ridge Parkway. Or you can visit Monticello, Ash Lawn, University of Virginia, Montpelier, the Barboursville Vineyards or Oakencroft Vineyard and Winery. A deposit of one night's lodging is required.

SILVER THATCH INN
3001 Hollymead Drive,
Charlottesville, VA 22901   (804) 978-4686

Built in 1780 by Hessian soldiers, the Silver Thatch Inn's cen-

BLEU ROCK INN

Fine French-American Cuisine & Lodging complete with a **Blue Ridge Vista**

U.S. Rt. 211, Rt. 1, Box 555, Washington, Virginia 22747, (703) 987-3190

tral house brings to mind the architecture of colonial Williamsburg. It is an immaculately restored white clapboard building with beautiful landscaping, including dogwood, magnolia and pine trees all around.

The Hessian soldiers, who were captured during the Revolutionary War in New York, had been marched south to Charlottesville. They built a two-story log cabin on the site of a former Indian settlement. This section of the inn is now known as the Hessian Room. In the 19th century the inn served as a boys' school, then a tobacco plantation, and after the Civil War, as a melon farm. A wing was added in 1937, and a cottage built in 1984 to complement the main building.

Owners Vince and Rita Scoffone stand firm on their promise os providing a smoke-free environment. Smokers are welcome to go outside to smoke but no exceptions are made indoors.

Telephones and a television are available in common areas of the Inn. The idea here is to withdraw from the rat race, to rest and recuperate.

The interiors are decorated with early American folk art, quilts, reproduction furniture and antiques. Each of the seven guest rooms are named for Virginia-born presidents, with the "star" room being The Thomas Jefferson, of course – complete with a pencil-post queen canopy bed and fireplace. The remaining six rooms are elegantly decorated but not overly formal. All have private baths and several have fireplaces. Guests will find scrumptious homemade cook-

ies waiting for them in their rooms.

The Silver Thatch Inn has a restaurant with three dining rooms, a sun room and a bar, where guests can enjoy a complimentary glass of wine or beer before dinner.

Chef Gordon Carlson changes the gourmet menu frequently, but always includes a vegetarian special and some entrees to satisfy conventional tastes such as grilled filet mignon. Two of the more exotic items on one winter menu this year included roasted quail Sonoran (served with a Southwestern sauce of tomatoes, onions, olives, bacon and garlic) and lamb chops Fez (grilled with Merguez sausage, Moroccan tomato sauce and couscous). Homemade desserts will surely tempt the most stoic of dinner guests: a hazelnut/brown sugar tart with Frangelica cream and a flourless chocolate cake with pecans sat on a platter with a other equally tempting desserts.

Silver Thatch is only a short driving distance from UVA, Monticello, James Madison's Montpelier and Ash Lawn-Highland. Both Skyline Drive and the Blue Ridge Parkway are about a half-hour's drive away. Athletes of all ages can use an outdoor swimming pool and tennis courts near the inn when weather permits. A two-night minimum stay is required on weekends.

Advance deposits are required for reservations. Rates range from $105 to $125 and include a generous continental breakfast

200 SOUTH STREET

South Street,
Charlottesville, VA 22901   (804) 979-0200

200 South Street is comprised of two restored houses in historic downtown Charlottesville. The restoration was completed in 1986 and every detail of the Inn was meticulously recreated or renewed, including the classical veranda and a two-story walnut serpentine hand rail. The larger of the two buildings was completed in 1856 for Thomas Jefferson Wertenbaker, son of Thomas Jefferson's first librarian and close friend, and remained a residence until the 20th century. In the following years the building was believed to house a girls finishing school, a brothel and then a boarding house before it was transformed into the Inn.

The rooms are decorated with lovely English and Belgian antiques. If you wish, you could have a room with a whirlpool bathtub, a fireplace, a canopy bed or a private living room suite. Every room has a private bath. The Inn's main gallery houses an ongoing exhibition of Virginia artists and a part of the private collection of Holsinger photos (of historic Charlottesville). A complimentary Continental-style breakfast, afternoon tea and wine are available to tempt your taste buds each day. And, if you are looking for action, you'll find it in Charlottesville! 200 South Street is only blocks from the finest restaurants, shops and entertainment in the area. It is also less than five miles away from both the University of Virginia and Monticello. Of course, if you prefer to relax, you can curl up with a book in the Inn's library or sitting room, daydream in the upstairs study or lounge on the veranda or garden terrace. Innkeepers Brendan and Karen Clancy will make your stay memorable and delightful. Come here to get away from it all without leaving any luxury all behind.

Palmyra

PALMER COUNTRY MANOR

Route 2, Box 1390,
Palmyra, VA 22963   (800) 253-4306

One hundred and eighty acres of wooded wilderness await you in this country paradise, once a part of a 2500-acre ranch known as "Solitude." Palmer Country Manor has had a widely varied list of owners through the years. Perhaps the most interesting of these was Richard McCary, a mason who built the Palmyra Stone Jail, Carysbrook Plantation and the house which is now know as Palmer Country Manor. McCary prospered quickly and within 20 years he and his wife owned 583 acres. However in 1858, Richard was arrested for murder and put in the jail he built. On September 16, 1858 he was forced to sell the entire plantation.

Eventually the land was bought by Kathy and Greg Palmer from the estate of a previous owner. They opened the Palmer Country Manor in July of 1989 and since then, its tradition of excellence has been growing. The furnishings and the ambience reflect a 1834 plantation house. There is a library, a parlor and a screened porch. You can stay in the historic plantation house, which is decorated to fit the period, or in one of the private cottages. Each air-conditioned cottage comes complete with a fireplace, a king or queen size bed, a color television, a full bath and a large private deck. Each room can sleep up to four people. A complimentary breakfast is served every morning and a lavish dinner is available every night. Adventurous types can find all they need to whet their appetites minutes away, such as white water rafting in the James River. You can also hike, picnic, fish or relax in the nearby woods. Or if you are feeling a little romantic, take a champagne balloon ride at sunset. Everything you could want in a vacation or weekend retreat is awaiting you here.

Nellysford

ACORN INN
P.O. Box 431,
Nellysford, VA 22958   (804) 361-9357
Kathy and Martin Versluys have done their fair share of traveling and they know how great it can be to find those off-the-beaten-path wonders along the way. They have also experienced the pleasure of finding truly accommodating hosts in these places, as they did while touring South America, snapping photos for a Dutch publishing company. These are among the reasons why the couple decided to open their own bed and breakfast in Nelson County, in the gorgeous Blue Ridge. The Acorn Inn is a unique stop for vacationers or just a

relaxing weekend get-away. There is a choice of three different lodging styles, including the Inn itself (which is a remodeled horse stable), the Acorn Cottage and the Farmhouse. The rooms in the inn are decorated to be comfortable and contemporary. Each of the 10 bright, has a double bed, a wardrobe, a desk, a large window and the original stall door.

A large Continental-plus breakfast is available each morning with fresh fruit, coffee, teas and a variety of home-baked breads. After enjoying this ample meal and the friendly conversation, most guests take off to explore the area — and there's plenty to choose from to keep the active or the not-so-active happy. There are crafts festivals, local vineyards and beautiful golf courses. If you bring your bicycle, you can follow a bike route mapped out by Mr. Versluys. Or, in the winter, you can swoosh down the famous ski slopes at Wintergreen. After a long day, we suggest that you come back and relax around the Finnish soapstone stove found in the Mexican decor of the A-frame room. You may even get to sample the delicious cookies that Mr. Versluys makes. Then it's time to retire to your inviting room and let the countryside sing you to sleep.

Economy and convenience are only two of the many reasons to stay here. No matter the adventure you choose, the Acorn Inn is the place to stay. One night's deposit or 50% of the anticipated bill is required at time of reservation.

THE MEANDER INN AT PENNY LANE FARM

Routes 612 & 613/Box 443,
Nellysford, VA 22958   (804) 361-1380

The Rockfish Valley in Nelson County is home to this country farmhouse on 50 acres of horse-grazed pasture and woods. Rick and Kathy Cornelius are the innkeepers of the Meander Inn, an 80-year old Victorian farmhouse in the heart of the foothills of the Blue Ridge Mountains. Hiking trails and the Rockfish River distinguish the land. The five rooms offered are tastefully decorated with Victorian or country antiques and four-poster beds. You'll wake each day to the gorgeous sight of the morning sun on the breathtaking mountains. If you rise early enough you can help fetch the morning eggs from the henhouse and give the horses their breakfast grain. Or you can just wake in time to savor a scrumptious country breakfast prepared for all of the guests.

Leisurely afternoons can be spent taking tea on the porch or watching the guinea hens play in the brush. As the name suggests, you can "meander" along Skyline Drive and behold the spectacular scenery. If you are an adventure lover, choose from the many activities offered on the farm or minutes away. There is skiing, canoeing, horseback riding, tennis, golf, fishing, hiking, swimming, biking and more! Then, after a fun-filled afternoon, enjoy a glass of Virginia wine and sit around the wood stove listening to the antique player piano. A trip to Meander Lane and Penny Lane Farm is a great escape from the hustle and bustle of every day life.

Amherst/Monroe/Lynchburg

DULWICH MANOR

Route 5, Box 173A,
Amherst, VA 24521   (804) 946-7207

Flemish bond brickwork and fluted columns adorn the outside of this late 1880s English-style manor house. Nestled in the countryside and surrounded by the Blue Ridge Mountains, Dulwich Manor is abounding with beauty and country appeal. You will know your journey is over when you turn onto the winding country lane and see the inviting porch of this estate, set on five secluded acres in Amherst County. Hosts Bob and Judy Reilly will be there to welcome you into a world away from the hassle of every day life. Period antiques decorate the rooms and there are large fireplaces to relax by in the living room and study. The bedrooms are reminiscent of an English country home. The beds are canopied brass or antiques. You can choose a room with a fireplace or window seat for relaxing afternoons or evenings. The Scarborough room also offers a whirlpool tub and a canopied queen-sized bed.

Each day begins with a full country breakfast including fresh fruits and juices, inn-baked muffins and breads, country sausage, herb teas and hot coffee. Take a stroll after breakfast and see the natural beauty of the Washington and Jefferson National Forests. The nearby Blue Ridge Parkway is perfect place for hiking, picnicking or photographing the view. Natural Bridge and Caverns, Peaks of Otter and Crabtree Falls are all wonderfully scenic spots for a lunch. This area of the country is also full of history . . . Washington, Jefferson and Patrick Henry were all born near here. The Appomattox Courthouse, Monticello, Ash Lawn and Poplar Forest are all within a short distance of Dulwich. Bob and Judy ask you to: "Leave it all behind for a brief sojourn into a turn of the century world of pampering and comfort."

FAIRVIEW BED & BREAKFAST
Route 4, Box 117,
Amherst, VA 24521   (804) 277-8500
Casual living and friendly conversation are staples of living at Fairview. Surrounded by green pastures and rolling fields, this Italian influenced home is the perfect place to forget all of your cares. There are cats, dogs, burros, llamas and cows roaming the pastures and Sara, the black Lab, oversees all. Judy and Jim Noon enjoy their porch whenever possible because of the beautiful view and crisp, clean air. The home is the only one in Amherst County with a tower. The Italian influence can be seen in the architecture of the house: in the woodwork, in the ell and dentil moldings and in the oculus windows. The inviting rooms have high ceilings and large windows to preserve the feeling of the Victorian age. The hand-made bricks were fired right on the property and the dining room window pane is inscribed "This house was built in 1867. Fairview

July 22 in '87."

The three guest bedrooms, all with a private bath, are filled with antiques, but the Noons maintain that these are to be used and enjoyed by all. All of the bedrooms have fireplaces. The entire house is air conditioned for your comfort.

A hearty breakfast of juice, coffee or tea, homebaked muffins or bread and fresh fruit compote is served wherever you wish — in your room, on the porch or in the dining room. Picnic lunches and light evening foods are available as well. There is plenty of activity around, as Fairview is only 15 miles from the Blue Ridge Parkway, 22 miles from Wintergreen, and Sweet Briar College is just minutes away. A 50% security deposit is required along with reservations. Smokers and children are welcome.

"ST. MOOR" HOUSE
BED & BREAKFAST
Route 1, Box 136
Monroe, VA 24574   (804) 929-8228
Warm Virginia/British hospitality will greet you at this lovely house. It sits among large trees facing majestic High Peak Mountain in Amherst County. The nature lover will enjoy strolling along the acres of fields and woods and seeing the pastures, horses, cows and the clear, cool pond. The sight is even more breathtaking when the peach and apple orchards on the adjacent land are in full bloom. One may also sit on an outside deck and enjoy the birds and landscapes. The home's interior is every bit as lovely as the vistas outside. The old chestnut post-and-beam architec-

ture makes "St. Moor" House unique. A cathedral ceiling, a handmade brick fireplace and plenty of gorgeous antiques and orientals make the atmosphere inside warm and inviting. For the comfort of the guests, the building is centrally air conditioned, and private or semiprivate baths are available.

The aroma of a scrumptious breakfast will wake you each morning. The serenity of this getaway will be perfect for afternoons spent reading a favorite book, wandering across the meadows or chatting on the porch. Nearby are the natural wonders of the Blue Ridge Parkway, Natural Bridge and the James River. Advance registration is required.

LANGHORNE MANOR

313 Washington Street,
Lynchburg, VA 24504   (804) 846-4667

Share in the comforts and heritage of this 27-room classical mansion, built circa 1850. The Langhorne family had this home constructed for them and it stands today in the heart of Lynchburg's historic Diamond Hill neighborhood. Antebellum architecture, mahogany and walnut furnishings, and crystal and brass chandeliers decorate the interior of Langhorne Manor. The bedrooms are full of massive antique furniture and Langhorne family heirlooms. Each room has a private bath, most with clawfoot tubs, and all are air conditioned for your comfort. A delicious homemade breakfast is served in the gorgeous oak-panelled dining room. Ask about romantic dinners, late night snacks and picnic lunches. The gallery displays chang-

ing exhibitions of sculpture and other works by Virginia artists.

Proprietors Jaime and Jaynee Acevedo will be happy to point out the history in this home, on the National Register since 1979, and the others in the quiet neighborhood. There are beautiful mountains, orchards and antique shops all around. Whether strolling through the neighborhood or traveling to such places as Poplar Forest, Fort Early, Natural Bridge and Crabtree Falls, you are sure to find entertainment to suit your interests. You will never run out of things to do here in the heart of Lynchburg!

Reservations are accepted with the receipt of one night's fee. Smoking is not allowed on the upper floors and pets are not allowed. Call to discuss children before bringing them along.

LYNCHBURG MANSION INN BED AND BREAKFAST

405 Madison Street,
Lynchburg, VA 24504   (804) 528-5400
or (800) 352-1199

"Welcome to the Lynchburg Mansion Inn Bed and Breakfast where you can return to a finer yesterday." Built in 1914 for James R. Gilliam, Sr., this 9,000-square-foot Spanish Georgian Mansion is located on a half acre in the Garland Hill Historic District. A six-foot-high iron fence surrounds the main house and the carriage house. Three separate entrance gates are anchored in massive piers and guests drive under the columned porte-cochere upon arrival. Large concrete front steps lead to the six-columned entry portico. The front door opens onto the 50-foot grand hall with its restored cherry columns and wainscoting. There are 219 spindles in the cherry and oak staircase.

Bedrooms here are the ultimate in luxury. Some rooms have fireplaces and all beds are king or queen sized. Every room has a full in-room bathroom, plenty of storage space, air conditioning, padded satin clothing hangers, color television, telephone and even a night light. Decor varies from the Victorian style Gilliam Room with mahogany four-poster bed with steps, a rose strewn comforter, plump pillows and billowing lace to the light and airy Country French Room done in crisp Laura Ashley prints with a bleached four-poster bed and armoire.

Each morning the newspaper is delivered to your door along with a freshly-brewed pot of coffee and a pitcher of juice for those who would like to "wake up" privately before venturing forth. A full breakfast is served in the dining room with fine china, crystal and silver. There is an information center in the back hall where brochures and newspapers on local events are provided. Go for a fun-filled day of sightseeing and shopping and then retire to the elegant living room and sink into an overstuffed fireside chair. The Lynchburg Mansion Inn really "aims to satisfy your every need ." One night's deposit is required for reservations. Smoking is permitted only on the veranda. The request is for "well-behaved children" and no pets.

THE MADISON HOUSE BED & BREAKFAST
413 Madison Street,
Lynchburg, VA 24504   (800) 828-MHBB
The Madison House, c. 1874, is the ultimate in comfort and style. The mansion was built by Robert C.

Winridge Bed & Breakfast in Madison Heights.

Burkeholder for wealthy tobacconist George Flemming. It is a brilliant example of Italianate and Eastlake Victorian architecture. The home is located in the historic Garland Hill District of Lynchburg. The elaborate New Orleans-style cast iron porch welcomes you to a world apart from modern hassles and hustles.

Irene and Dale Smith will greet you and invite you into this ornate home. For over a century, the interior floor plan has remained untouched. Crystal chandeliers hang delicately from the ceiling. An intricate peacock stained glass window and numerous fireplaces and original woodwork are only a few of the details that make Madison House distinctive. There are antique-filled parlors and a library of books from as early as the late 1700s.

Each bedroom is individually decorated and features a mixture of antiques with modern conveniences, such as telephones. A lush, soft robe is provided in your room so that you may relax in total comfort. The Gold Room has a bay window, a king size brass bed, sitting area and antique vanity. The Madison Suite has a private sitting room with TV and writing desk and a bed chamber with a queen size canopy bed. The Rose Room has an 1840s handcarved mahogany antique bed with matching dresser and armoire and a fireplace. The Veranda Room features a screened-in sitting porch with Victorian-style white wicker. Each has a private bath, two of which feature with original bathroom fixtures from the turn

of the century. Bed linens and bath towels are all 100% cotton, and the rooms are centrally air conditioned.

A leisurely breakfast in the dining room can consist of such tasty treats as freshly perked cinnamon coffee, a fresh fruit cup, homemade muffins and bread, spinach quiche, French toast or Eggs Benedict. After breakfast, you can visit some of the fascinating historical sights in and around Lynchburg such as Poplar Forest, Old Western Hotel, The Old Court House Museum and Appomatox Court House. The Blue Ridge Parkway, Skyline Drive and underground caverns are also close by. Check with the Smiths about walking tour brochures and other points of interest. Smoking and pets are prohibited. Children are discouraged, although some exceptions may be made. Reservations are strongly recommended and a deposit is required.

WINRIDGE BED & BREAKFAST
Route 1, Box 362,
Madison Heights, VA 24572(804) 384-7220

Winridge Bed and Breakfast, 14 miles off the Blue Ridge Parkway, offers a panoramic view of the Blue Ridge Mountains and the simple elegance of country living. The Colonial Southern home is a fourteen-acre country estate built in 1910 by Wallace A. Taylor, president of the American National Life Insurance Company of Richmond. LoisAnn and Ed Pfister are the hosts now, and the landmark has been restored to its original grandeur. The outside of the home is gorgeous, with four massive columns adorning the entry portico. Grand windows are in abundance so that the beauty of the surrounding countryside is visible from anywhere in the home. The three guest rooms are furnished with your comfort and privacy in mind. The Habecker Room has a queen size four-poster bed and private in-room bath with ceramic tiled shower. The Walker Room has a queen-size cannonball bed and the Brubaker Room has two twin beds. The Walker and Brubaker Rooms share a hallway bath with footed tub and brass and porcelain shower.

A delicious, hot breakfast is served every morning in the lovely old dining room. There is plenty of entertainment to be found on the estate. Explore the meadows, swing under the big shade trees or relax on the porches. The library and living room are full of books, magazines and games for your amusement. Or, if you prefer to venture off of the grounds, the Blue Ridge Parkway, the National Historical Park at Appomattox Courthouse, Poplar Forest (Thomas Jefferson's summer home), and several colleges are all within a short drive. There are also sites of engrossing natural beauty like Crabtree Falls, the Peaks of Otter and Natural Bridge and Caverns.

A deposit equal to one night's stay is required to hold a reservation. Outside smoking only is requested. Children are welcome and are invited to play with the Pfister children.

Bedford

ELMO'S REST
Bedford, VA 24523   (703) 586-3707

Ignore the name. Rest is the last thing you'll want to do at this 250-acre farm in Bedford County. Proprietors Nancy and Danny Johnson operate this self-sufficient southern farm, reminiscent of the 1940s. Elmo's Rest features beef cattle, sheep, chickens, goats, rabbits, horses and ponies, an adopted burro and her baby, an elkhound (who stands on his hind legs and acts like a bear), a miniature jackass, ring-necked pheasants (that the Johnsons release into the wild) and a 600-pound pet hog (that Nancy calls "a Vietnamese potbellied pig with a thyroid problem). Whew! That's a large group of animals! But, the primary crop at Elmo's has nothing to do with all of those animals. Instead, it's apples, and guest assistance is welcome come picking time.

The guest house was built in the late 1800s. It's a two-story, white-frame farmhouse with a tin roof. But there's no worry for space. The guests have the run of the house. The Johnson home rests unobtrusively in a corner of the property. However, Nancy and Danny do not make themselves scarce. One guest was quoted as saying, "If you have problems, they'll take care of it right away. They'll do anything for you." Guests are responsible for their own meals, but Nancy comes by each morning with the paper and goodies like homemade applesauce, honey, fresh bread, molasses or a jug of cider. This is really being away from it all, especially for city folks. There is no TV and no telephone. And after you spend the day feeding animals, picking apples or haying, you won't want to do much else but drink a nice cup of tea and hit the sack. Of course all work done on the farm is on a volunteer basis only. You can spend the day just wandering through the lush green meadows or lounging in the house. But if you want to work up a good, clean sweat, come during September and October for apple-picking or between June and the first frost for haying. Week or long-weekend reservations only are accepted.

Rocky Mount/Wirtz

THE CLAIBORNE HOUSE BED AND BREAKFAST

119 Claiborne Avenue,
Rocky Mount, VA 24151   (703) 483-4616

English gardens surround the 1895 Victorian Claiborne House, an elegant turn-of-the-century home in Franklin County enhanced by 130 feet of wrap-a-round porch with white wicker furniture in the southern tradition. This tranquil getaway is nestled between the Blue Ridge Parkway and glorious Smith Mountain Lake. In the spring you will be mesmerized by the azaleas and dogwoods in the yard. And in the cooler months, the beauty of the autumn colors will leave you breathless. The best place for enjoying the scenery is the porch.

Inside, the lovely Victorian-era furnishings are celebrations of days past. The bedrooms are no exception to that beauty. Each room comes with a king, queen or twin size bed and a private bath. A full gourmet breakfast is served each morning and may include fresh berries or other home grown fruits in season, or home made bread. Specialties are eggs benedict, blueberry crepes, spinach souffles or sourdough pecan waffles. A special service provided guests is fresh hot coffee each morning outside their doors as they prepare for a romantic candlelight breakfast. The table colors change dailly to accent a different set of china.

Many guests spend their day reading a book from the lending library. Or you can watch the house cat, Rascal, spend his day observing the goldfish in the pond. Margaret and Jim Young are your hosts, and they will be pleased to help you plan a day's excitement. If you are looking for adventure, visit Smith Mountain Lake. There are a variety of activities for all ages on its 500 miles of shoreline. Year round activities include fishing, golf, tennis and biking. Booker T. Washington National Monument is just moments away. Ferrum College and its Blue Ridge Farm Museum, Mabry Mill, Peaks of Otter, Mill Mountain Zoo and Roanoke's historic Farmer's Market are all within a short drive. Well-behaved children are welcome. Sorry, no pets are allowed. Smoking is restricted to the outside only, and advance reservations are requested with a one-night deposit required.

THE MANOR AT TAYLOR'S STORE
Route 1, Box 533,
Wirtz, VA 24184   (703) 721-3951

In 1799, Skelton Taylor first established Taylor's Store as a general merchandise trading post at this site in Franklin County. It served the community and travelers alike for many years. Later the building functioned as an Ordinary and a US Post Office. The original manor house was built in the early 1800s as the focus of a prosperous tobacco plantation. The present-day home, featured this summer in "Southern Living," has emerged as a lovely blend of the periods in which it has been restored. Lee and Mary Tucker are your hosts at this 120-acre utopia. The manor itself features several common areas, a formal parlor with a grand piano, a sunroom full of plants and a great room with a large fireplace. You may also enjoy the billiard room, guest kitchen or the fully-equipped exercise room. The home is furnished with period antiques, which lend a romantic atmosphere.

There are several types of bedrooms to choose from, each with its own unique decor and ambience. You can stay in the Castle, Plantation, Victorian, Colonial or English Garden Suite. The Toy Room is decorated with antique toys, quilts and an extra-high queen size canopied bed with bed steps. The Christmas Cottage is ideal for families with children. Three bedrooms, two baths, a fully equipped kitchen, den with stone fireplace and a large deck with gorgeous views of the six ponds and wilderness area are enough to take anyone's breath away. All guest rooms have private baths and some have a private balcony or kitchen.

After a fresh gourmet breakfast, plan your day. The estate offers hiking, picnicking, canoeing and fishing in one of its spring-fed ponds. There are also swimming docks, a gazebo and even a resident flock of geese! If you prefer to relax, soaking in the hot tub or lounging on the sun decks seem to be the best methods. Nearby are Smith Mountain Lake, Booker T. Washington National Monument, the Blue Ridge Parkway and all of Roanoke's sights. Smoking is not allowed in the Manor house, and pets are not allowed in the house or the cottage. Children are welcome in the cottage. Advanced reservations are important, and a one-night deposit is required.

Scottsville

HIGH MEADOWS
Rt. 4, Box 6
Scottsville, VA 24590   (804) 286-2218

High Meadows, just outside Charlottesville, is a terrific restoration of a 1832 Federalist-Victorian home that is a Virginia Historic Landmark and National Historic Home, as well as a full-service country inn. High Meadows offers the discriminating guest a rare opportunity to look at both 170 years of architectural history and 10 new and exciting years of viticultural happening. The inn's management offers today's guests the same hospitality, service and warmth which travelers experienced at its opening – for a decade, the hallmark of comfort and good food owned and operated by the Suska/Abbitt team. There are 12 guest rooms, three with whirlpools and seven with fireplaces, all furnished with period antiques. Guests will enjoy the copious flower gardens and pinot noir grapevine vinyard with charming footpaths leading to ponds and creeks. Guests are welcomed with champagne and stay in individually appointed rooms, furnished with period antiques and art, each with private bath. Expect a four-course breakfast and dinners by candlelight or gourmet picnic baskets on request. Dining is a sensuous experience. Breakfast might be gourmet egg dishces, scones or freshly squeezed orange juice. All foods are prepared for the health conscious...yet offer Alaskan smoked salmon, crusty breads, tenderloins of pork and venison, homemade ice cream pies and sinful chocolate desserts. The multi-course dinners offer distinctive cuisine featuring northern European and Mediterranean dishes. Take exit 121 South off I-64. Follow Rt. 20 for 17.6 miles; turn left at inn's sign. To confirm reservations a deposit of one night's lodging is required.

New River Valley Region

Christiansburg

THE OAKS

311 E. Main Street,
Christiansburg, VA 24073   (703) 381-1500

Massive oak trees, believed to be 300 years old, surround this majestic estate in Christiansburg which holds a three-star from Mobil, a three-diamond from AAA and a 4-crown from the American Bed and Breakfast Association, the top rating in its category.   A rich green lawn stretches for what seems like miles. The home itself stands like a fairy-tale castle. Major W.L. Pierce built the magnificent buttercup yellow Queen Anne Victorian for his family. Construction was complete in 1893. The home remained in the Pierce family for almost 90 years. The Hardies purchased the home in 1982 and performed a year-long renovation.   This added several modern bathrooms and other amenities, but the original floor plan and interior were carefully preserved.

Margaret and Tom Ray have recently converted The Oaks into a bed and breakfast country inn. The luxurious manor is well-suited for both leisure and business travelers. Guest rooms feature queen or king canopy beds with posturepedic mattresses, fireplaces and window nooks. The private baths in each room are stocked with plush towels, fluffy terry robes and toiletries. The garden gazebo houses a new hydrojet hot tub. A small separate cottage has a sauna, efficiency kitchen and bathroom with shower. Each morning guests awake to freshly ground coffee and a newspaper. Breakfast is a real pleasure at The Oaks, with a menu that is varied and features such delicious specialties as curried eggs, shirred eggs in spinach nests, rum raisin French toast or whole wheat buttermilk pancakes in praline syrup. Oven-fresh breads, sausage, bacon, ginger-braised chicken breasts are all favorites. A bounty of fresh fruits and juices are available in season.

Take some time after breakfast to lounge on the wrap-around porch with Kennedy rockers and wicker chairs. Investigate the books and games in the parlor or study. Or have a nice chat in the sunroom. Cable television and a VCR are also provided, but considering the attractions in the surrounding area, you probably will feel guilty turning the TV on. There is hiking on the Appalachian Trail and boating or fishing on Claytor Lake. The historic Newbern Museum, Long Way Home Outdoor Drama, Mill Mountain Theatre, Center in the Square, Smithfield Plantation and Chateau Morrisette Winery are all only a short drive away. Don't miss the Oaks' Victorian Christmas each December!

Alleghany Highlands Region

Clifton Forge/Covington

FIRMSTONE MANOR BED & BREAKFAST

Route 1, Box 257,
Clifton Forge, VA 24422   (703) 862-0892

Stone gates welcome you to Firmstone Manor's grounds. The winding drive is lined with flowering plum trees while closer to the house there are multitudes of flowers and exotic shrubbery. Marko and Danica Diana Popin will give you a warm greeting in the magnificent entrance hall. The Popins are avid antique and art collectors, and Firmstone is full of their treasures. The rooms are decorated with furnishings and fabrics selected by Diana. Laurel-leaf embellishment enhances the eleven-foot ceilings. Embossed iron door hinges and brass carbide chandeliers with etched-glass globes can be found throughout the house. There are hand-painted marble fireplace mantles on each of the eight fireplaces. Floor-to-ceiling windows provide for a view that will leave you breathless. The nine bedrooms are decorated in Victorian, European or Southwestern decor. Newlyweds or second-honeymooners will love the romance of a private suite furnished in white wicker and muted peach and grey tones.

A delicious English or Continental breakfast is served each morning in the dining room or in individual rooms. Picnic lunches are available. In the best English tradition, guests may take afternoon tea in the garden. There is plenty to do at Firmstone. Children can romp in the play yard while their parents play croquet beneath century-old shade trees. The nature lover will enjoy strolling on the manor's twelve acres. The grounds are rich with wildflowers, deer and songbirds. If you decide to venture away for the day, Longdale National Recreation Area offers hiking tails and a sandy beach along a mountain lake for swimming. The North Mountain Trail is perfect for photographers who won't want to miss this view of the Shenandoah Valley's southern tip and the Blue Ridge. Daytrippers can soak in the mineral waters at Hot and Warm Springs and Sweet Chalybeate Springs. Then after a day's adventures you can return to Firmstone for a tasty four-course dinner. You'll be able to savor fresh herbs and vegetables from the gardens outside and crisp watercress from a nearby stream. Weddings and social gatherings can be accommodated.

MILTON HALL BED & BREAKFAST INN

Rural Route 3,
Covington, VA   *(703) 965-0196*

The Honorable Laura Marie Theresa Fitzwilliam, Viscountess Milton, built this manor in 1874. Lord Milton was ill and Lady Milton hoped that the peace and tranquility of the countryside and beautiful mountain scenery would help return him to health. Today, Milton Hall still stands on forty-four acres, just west of Covington, in the community of Callaghan. Nestled in the Allegheny Mountains, the house presents an exotic contrast to its rustic surroundings. There are many gables, buttressed porch towers and Gothic trimmings, which suggest the design came from across the Atlantic. However, the inside of the house is not as ornate. It is spacious, but more of a large country home than a mansion. It is believed that the plain interior was purposely executed by Lady Milton, due to her sensitivity and graciousness, in perhaps not wanting to overwhelm the local residents with the elegance and affluence to which she was accustomed.

A roomy living area and equally large dining room each have two sets of French doors that open to the gardens in the south lawn. The guest bedrooms, with one exception, have private baths. The one exception is the center bedroom with the oriel window that has become the Milton Hall logo. Addition of a bathroom would require a drastic change in the original floor plan, and no one advocates that. There are rooms with a queen size bed, fireplace and private bath. The second floor master bedroom suite has a private bath, queen size bed and sitting area. One of the original bedrooms in the servants' quarters has been converted into a bath suite complete with whirlpool and fireplace. Some rooms have telephones and a central hall phone is available to all guests.

Every morning guests have the choice of a full English breakfast or a Continental breakfast, which can be served in your room. Complimentary afternoon tea is provided as well. Picnics or elegant basket lunches are available to sightseers. Dinner may be provided by special arrangement. There are plenty of attractions in the area: Lake Moomaw, national forests and state wildlife management areas are just a few. There is also the famous Humpback Bridge, Virginia's oldest standing covered bridge, which is within walking distance. The bridge is the nation's only surviving curved span covered bridge. Children are welcome with proper supervision. Pets that are "accustomed to an environment such as Milton Hall" are also welcome. Smoking is not regulated, but left up to the guests to give their opinion. A one day deposit is required with reservations.

Millboro/Warm Springs

FORT LEWIS LODGE
Star Route A,
Millboro, VA 24460   (703) 925-2314
In 1754, Col. Charles Lewis built a stockade to protect the southern pass of Shenandoah Mountain from Indian raids. This frontier outpost became a vast 3200-acre farm, situated deep within the Allegheny Mountains. For over two hundred years this area has remained virtually unchanged. The spectacular scenery and rushing mountain streams are enough to take your breath away. About 15 years ago, John and Caryl

Cowden moved from Ohio to manage and operate the farm. Today, they are your gracious hosts at this mountain paradise. They have restored the old red-brick manor house and the Lewis gristmill, dating back to 1850. They have also taken the time to build a new guest lodge. A large "gathering room" framed with massive beams of oak and walnut will invite you to relax with a cup of coffee and enjoy a chat with the Cowdens. A gorgeous view "in the round" of the grounds can be obtained from an observation tower, made of an enclosed stairway leading to the top of an adjoining silo. The twelve bedrooms are decorated with wildlife art and handcrafted walnut, cherry, red oak and butternut furniture. Much of the furniture was made by local craftsmen from wood cut right on the property. All of the guest rooms have a private or semi-private bath.

Venture out to the nineteenth-century gristmill for a scrumptious feast. Three meals are included in the room rate and all dishes are handmade and delicious! A full country breakfast includes freshly baked breads, eggs, sausage, bacon, fruits and French toast with locally-made maple syrup poured over top. Lunch is served in the lodge or you may opt to take a box lunch along with you. The buffet dinners offer fresh vegetables from the farm's garden. The outdoor activities are abundant here. There are over two miles of the meandering Cowpasture River flowing through this fertile valley, which provides for swimming, tubing and sport fishing (catch and release) for small mouth bass and trout. Several state-stocked trout streams are nearby. There are miles of marked trails and old logging roads for you to stroll along or explore. Camping is another special option at Fort Lewis. With advance notice, the lodge will outfit overnight camp-outs anywhere along the property. Deposit of one night's stay is required.

MEADOW LANE LODGE

Star Route A, Box 110,
Warm Springs, VA 24484 (703) 839-5959

"A little jewel of a country inn, set in meadows and mountains . . . " Meadow Lane Lodge is the keystone jewel in the crown of heritage tourism country inns. There is no question as to why this is true. You will know it from the moment you lay eyes on Meadow Lane. The estate cannot be seen from the road. You must wind your way up a narrow road, between meadows and woods. Finally you will emerge upon a large clearing, and there it is. A three-part white frame house with green and yellow trim beckons you near. The stone dairy house and the old ice house are right out of the days before refrigeration. The deck, out behind the 1920s barn, is an overlook which provides for a most impressive view. From here, guests can observe a nature preserve, where you can find almost any plant or animal native to Virginia. Two miles of the pure Jackson River flow through the property. One and a half miles up the river is a limestone spring, the origin of Meadow Lane's water supply. Across the lawn you'll see some unusual animals — like peacocks, a pet duck and Japanese Silkies (a type of

chicken with black skin and white feathers) roaming the grounds. There is even a half-breed cat, part domestic and part bob.

The history of Meadow Lane is just as impressive as the scenery. The land was part of the original grant given to Charles Lewis, an early Virginia settler, by King George III. An old log cabin, built in 1750, is visible from the west side of the Jackson River. A stockade built around the cabin during the French and Indian War eventually became known as Fort Dinwiddie. Today, Philip and Catherine Hirsh are the owners and innkeepers, with Meadow Lane having been in the Hirsh family for three generations.

The guest rooms are decorated in a combination of modern comfort and antique grandeur. There are double rooms, suites with fireplaces and private cottages. Some rooms have surprising little extras such as a 19th-century walnut dropleaf table, engravings or a private porch. The Common Room has a fireplace at each end. The Breakfast Room serves you from a 1710 oak sideboard. A full southern breakfast is served each morning.

The Bacova Guild showroom is nearby, as are The Garth Newel Music Center, the Homestead and Lake Moomaw. But, many guests just like to stay put and play croquet on the lawn - it is the house specialty! The 1600-acre expanse provides for hiking, fishing, canoeing and "creative loafing." Children over age six are welcome. No pets are allowed without prior approval. A deposit is required with reservations.

Inside
Other
Accommodations

After you've had a great day and are looking for an equally great place to stay, the Blue Ridge of Virginia has a wide selection of comfortable, pleasing general accommodations to top off your sightseeing. In this chapter, we are providing a good cross section of accommodations in the region — motels and hotels, bed and breakfasts, and resorts. Since the Blue Ridge region is so large, we are not including every option available to travelers...also, don't forget that this is a guide, not a directory, so we want to point you toward some of our favorites, not just what's there. But, the properties we are presenting here will more than get you started in your search for the perfect place to lay your head. And, there are some truly perfect spots to be found.

Room rates are varied throughout the Blue Ridge since some accommodations are in small towns and some in the larger cities, some are simple motels and others are knock-you-dead-extravagant resorts. Most rates range from $30 on up for a double. We've categorized the rates for each property we've included so you'll have a good idea of what to expect. Here's what

our dollar signs mean, for two people to a room per night:

$30 - $40	$
$41 - $60	$$
$61-$85	$$$
$85 and up	$$$$

Now that your pocketbook is taken care of, let's explore the vast array of accommodations that will take care of the rest of you.

Shenandoah Valley Region

Strasburg

HOTEL STRASBURG
201 Holliday Street,
Strasburg, VA 22657   (703) 465-9191
$$$ and up   All major credit cards

This white clapboard structure was built after the Civil War as a hospital. Its Victorian history and charm is evident—from the antique furniture in the rooms to the unique second-story balconied porch. The public rooms have been decorated with period furniture and the walls are covered with folk and fine art. Hotel Strasburg is perfect for a short romantic getaway or a longer vacation.

The 25 cozy guest rooms feature private baths and are decorated with period furniture, Victorian wall and floor coverings and classic window treatments. Other special touches are toiletries, fresh flowers, basketed greenery, telephones and big, fluffy towels. Suites and staterooms also include a sitting area.

This grand old hotel is located near Strasburg Emporium (see Shopping), Hupp's Hill Battlefield Park, Wayside Theatre and Half Moon Beach. A variety of golf packages is also offered.

Front Royal

Quality Inn Skyline Drive
10 Commerce Avenue,
Front Royal, VA 22630   *(703) 635-3161*
                          or *(800) 228-5151*
$$ *All major credit cards*

Located at the beautiful northern entrance to Skyline Drive,

Quality Inn will give you excellent service and attractive accommodations. Each of the 107 rooms comes equipped with cable television, including HBO. Guests can enjoy meals in the dining room and there are banquet and conference rooms available with advance notice. The clean, cool swimming pool is a great place for a road-weary traveler to relax. Ask about discount rates.

Basye

The most recommended accommodation in Basye is the Bryce Resort, (703) 856-2121, described in detail in the Resorts chapter.

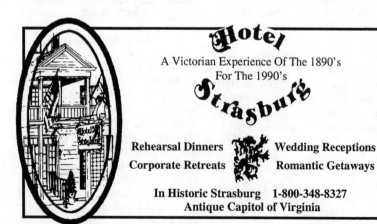

A Victorian Experience Of The 1890's For The 1990's

Hotel Strasburg

Rehearsal Dinners   Wedding Receptions
Corporate Retreats   Romantic Getaways

In Historic Strasburg   1-800-348-8327
Antique Capitol of Virginia

Photo: Wintergreen Resort

Learning to ski at Wintergreen.

New Market

NEW MARKET BATTLEFIELD DAYS INN

9360 George Collins Parkway,
New Market, VA 22844   (703) 740-4100
or (800) 325-2525
$$ All major credit cards

On May 15, 1864 Union Troops occupied Manor's Hill. Confederate Troops were south on Shirley's Ridge. The Rebel troops enlisted the help of young cadets from Virginia Military Institute and pushed the Yankees north. Ninety percent of the battle and casualties occurred here. Today, the New Market Battlefield Days Inn stands in that very spot on Manor's Hill. The New Market Battlefield Park Hall of Valor & Military Museum, dedicated to the cadets of VMI, is adjacent to the hotel. Other attractions in the area include Shenandoah and Endless Caverns, New Market historic district and championship golfing. A short drive away are Shenandoah National Park, Skyline Drive, Luray Caverns and Bryce and Massanutten Ski Resorts.

The 92 guest rooms feature king or double beds and remote control color cable TV. Complimentary coffee and danish are served to guests each morning. An outdoor pool is on site and handicap facilities are available. Groups and buses are welcome.

QUALITY INN SHENANDOAH VALLEY

P.O. Box 100,
New Market, VA 22844   (703) 740-3141
or (800) 228-5151
$$ All major credit cards

The Johnny Appleseed Restaurant and Apple Core Village Gift Shop are special attractions of this motel. You will be treated like a VIP with red carpet service and complimentary sunrise coffee and sunset cider. The 100 spacious rooms have free in-room movies and the outdoor pool and sauna are perfect for relaxing afternoons. Or, you can enjoy the game room and miniature golf course. The property is located near Historic New Market, Luray Caverns, New Market Battlefield and more. AAA and AARP discounts are offered.

THE SHENVALEE GOLF RESORT

9660 Fairway Drive,
New Market, VA 22844   (703) 740-3181
$$ All major credit cards

This lovely lodge is a golf-lover's delight! Motels are located right along the golf course. Or, for those not here to enjoy the ranges, there are poolside motels. The 18-hole PGA golf course features a practice driving range and a fully-equipped pro shop. Three regulation tennis courts, a large swimming pool, a fishing pond and a hair salon are located at the resort for your pleasure and convenience. Take your meals in the dining room, or visit the Sand Trap Tavern for a casual evening. All rooms are air conditioned and carpeted and come equipped with telephone and TV.

Luray

Skyland Lodge
Shenandoah National Park
P.O. Box 727,
Luray, VA 22835   (703) 743-5108
$$$ MC, VISA

Skyland Lodge is located in the midst of natural beauty in gorgeous Shenandoah National Park. Known as "Virginia's Mountain Playground," the Park will awe a first-time camper or a seasoned mountaineer. From every window and doorway of this lodge there are incredible views of the surrounding Shenandoah Valley. And, Skyland knows how important it is to educate the public on the need to care for this land. Park Naturalist programs are conducted so that guests can learn how to keep this stunning vista clean and attractive.

The multi-unit lodge provides 186 rooms. There are no telephones and few televisions found in rooms or lodge units. However, a TV lounge and public phones are located on the premises. There is a full-service restaurant, a taproom featuring nightly entertainment and a mountain craft shop on site at the Lodge. A 50 percent advance deposit is required eight week prior to your stay.

Harrisonburg

Holiday Inn Harrisonburg
1 Pleasant Valley Road,
Harrisonburg, VA 22801   (703) 434-9981
                          or (800) HOLIDAY
$$ All major credit cards

This beautiful, two-story roadside hotel is found in the heart of historic Harrisonburg. From here, Massanutten Ski Resort, Skyline Drive, New Market Battlefield and Museum and Shenandoah and Endless Caverns are only a moment's trip away. There are 130 rooms, all with air conditioning and color TV with Showtime.

Special group services are available with advance notice. These include complimentary bus parking, group meals and pre-registration for groups with keys in envelopes. A full service restaurant, the River Mill Cafe, is located on site. Holiday Inn is handicapped accessible and pets are allowed.

Massanutten Resort
                          (703) 289-9441

This is a very popular resort in this area and is detailed in the Resorts chapter of this book.

Staunton

Sheraton Inn Staunton
Rt. 275 & I-81 Exit, 225, P.O. Box 3209
Staunton, VA 24401   (703) 248-6020
$$$ All major credit cards

Historic downtown Staunton is less than five minutes away from this luxurious hotel. Sheraton Inn is only three miles from attractions like Woodrow Wilson Birthplace and the Museum of American Frontier Culture. Staunton is also home to the Statler Brothers' "Happy Birthday U.S.A." celebration each year. Other attractions in the area include Waynesboro Outlet Mall, the Blue Ridge Parkway and Skyline Drive. Of course, you don't have to leave this hotel to find things to do.

There are tennis courts and an indoor/outdoor heated pool to keep you busy. And, the Sheraton overlooks an 18-hole PGA Championship golf course.

There are 112 spacious rooms available, some for nonsmokers and handicapped persons. A full-service restaurant located in the hotel serves international cuisine. The lounge features weekend entertainment. A 30-day advance deposit is required.

Lexington

BEST WESTERN
KEYDET-GENERAL MOTEL
US 60 West,
Lexington, VA 24450   (703) 463-4715
$$ All major credit cards

Best Western is located 1 1/2 miles from the Lexington Visitor's Center and not much farther from Virginia Military Institute, home of the Keydets. This hotel gives a few conveniences not found at all other hotels. For example, they will accept pets and many rooms have refrigerators and wet bars. There is also air conditioning and a television in each room. A restaurant is located on the property and senior citizen discounts are available.

COMFORT INN
I-64, Exit 13 (US 11 South),
Lexington, VA 24450   (703) 463-7311
                   or (800) 228-5150
$$ All major credit cards

Conveniently located near the Virginia Horse Center, Comfort Inn offers a complimentary continental breakfast. There is an indoor pool, enclosed corridors, glass elevator and free local calls.

This place is great for families with children because kids under 18 stay for free! Several restaurants are nearby.

HOLIDAY INN LEXINGTON
I-64 and US 11 North,
Lexington, VA 24450   (703) 463-7351
                   or (800) 465-4329
$$ All major credit cards

Located 1 1/2 miles from the Lexington Visitor's Center, the 72 rooms at this Holiday Inn come complete with air conditioning and televisions. There are non-smoking and handicapped-accessible rooms available. A full restaurant and pool are located in the hotel for the convenience of the guests. Pets are allowed. Ask about the senior citizen's discount.

HOWARD JOHNSON LODGE AND
RESTAURANT
I-64 and I-81, Exit 53 (US 11),
Lexington, VA 24450   (703) 463-9181
                   or (800) 654-2000
$$ All major credit cards

This mountaintop hotel is located near Washington and Lee University, Virginia Military Institute and Natural Bridge. Good for smaller business and social functions, its meeting room can hold up to 135 people. There are 88 regular rooms, ten non-smoking and two handicapped-accessible rooms. All have complimentary HBO.

There is an on-site restaurant and guest laundry. The gift shop features local handcrafted items. AAA and AARP discounts and group rates are available.

RAMADA INN

I-81 at US 11, P.O. Box 703
Lexington, VA 24450   (703) 463-6666
                or (800) 228-2828
$$ All major credit cards

The business traveler as well as families and tour groups will appreciate the convenience and comfort of this hotel, located near Washington & Lee University, Virginia Military Institute and historical sites. There are 80 guest rooms and three suites. The suites or double bedrooms are ideal for families with children. Two of the guest rooms are handicapped accessible and there are 12 non-smoking rooms.

Rockbridge Restaurant (see Restaurants), a full service restaurant and lounge, is located within the Ramada. Other amenities include an indoor swimming pool and cable TV. The banquet facilities are able to accommodate up to 200. AAA and AARP discounts are available.

Natural Bridge

NATURAL BRIDGE OF VIRGINIA

U.S. 11 Highway
$$ (703) 291-2121

Natural Bridge of Virginia, containing the Natural Bridge Hotel, the Annex and Hillside Cottages, is detailed in the Resorts chapter of this book.

Roanoke Valley/Roanoke/ Troutville/Salem

COMFORT INN - ROANOKE/TROUTVILLE

US 11 South, P.O. Box 7332
Roanoke, VA 24019   (703) 992-5600
                or (800) 228-5150
$$ All major credit cards

Wake to a complimentary continental breakfast, served each morning to guests of Comfort Inn. The 72 guest rooms have all of the conveniences of home. All are equipped with satellite television. Non-smoking rooms are available and there is an outdoor pool, en-

EXPLORE THE HEART OF THE BLUE RIDGE FROM ROANOKE'S HISTORIC LANDMARK HOTEL. Located downtown, just 5 minutes from the Parkway and within walking distance of Roanoke's best shopping, dining and entertainment, including the Historic Market Area and Center In The Square.

· 800-333-3333 ·

Radisson

PATRICK HENRY HOTEL

The Star City's Star Hotel

closed corridors and gift shop provided. Senior citizen discounts are honored.

HAMPTON INN

3816 Franklin Rd., SW   (703) 989-4000
                or (800) 426-7866
$-$$ All major credit cards

Hampton Inn is so sure you'll be completely satisfied that it offers a 100 percent Satisfaction Guarantee. Just three miles from downtown, close to Roanoke Memorial Hospital, and across the road from Tanglewood Mall, the Hampton Inn offers an expanded Continental breakfast, HBO and ESPN, VCR's, direct dial phones, copier and FAX service, meeting room, hair dryers, refrigerator/freezer and micro-

wave, and no-smoking rooms in its 59-room motel. Excellent restaurants are nearby and health club passes are available. Hospital and commercial rates are offered.

TRAVELODGE - ROANOKE NORTH

2444 Lee Highway SouthTroutville, VA 24175
                (703) 992-6700
            or (800) 255-3050
$$ All major credit cards

Travelodge wants you to feel at home, so they provide a free continental breakfast, free coffee, tea and popcorn and free local calls. Your private room contains lovely furniture, cable TV (with CNN and Showtime), executive work areas and direct dial telephones. Children under 18 stay free when shar-

1-800-426-7866
Toll-Free Reservation Number

Featuring all the amenities you have grown to love and expect:

Now Open
ROANOKE/ TANGLEWOOD

**3816 Franklin Road, S.W.
Roanoke , VA 24014**
Offering Easy Access From Blue Ridge Parkway Motel is on intersection of US 220 & Franklin Rd. on Frontage Road (703) 989-4000

Children 18 years and under stay free when sharing your room

Complimentary continental breakfast each day of your stay

Free local phone calls

**To Open December , 1993
ROANOKE/AIRPORT
6621 Thirlane Road , N.W.
Roanoke , VA 24019
(703) 265-2600**

ing a room with their parents. Efficiency rooms are available for relocating personnel or longer term visitors. Pets are welcome and rooms for the physically impaired and non-smokers are available.

COLONY HOUSE MOTOR LODGE
3560 Franklin Road,
Roanoke, VA 24014   (703) 345-0411
or (800) 552-7026
$$ All major credit cards
Colony House is situated just two miles north of the Roanoke entrance to the spectacular Blue Ridge Parkway. This small, quiet inn specializes in personal service. The 67 rooms are air conditioned and carpeted and have direct dial phones, cable TV (with HBO and ESPN) and king, queen or double size beds. There are a few suites available. You're close to great restaurants and terrific shopping, close to the interstate and downtown as well.

Colony House is a wonderful base for business travelers and tourists. After a complimentary continental breakfast, visit Tanglewood or Valley View Mall, Center in the Square, Mill Mountain Zoo or Roanoke Memorial Hospital. Call for special discounts and rates.

Peaks of Otter Lodge

Relax with us and enjoy the serenity of a high country vacation where the rates are great and so is the food.

Our location at milepost 86 on the Blue Ridge Parkway is ideal. You can walk a trail, photograph the spectacular scenery, fish the lake or climb a mountain. You can also sit on the porch, listen to the birds, watch for deer or visit the NPS Visitor's Center.

We're open year-round. Call us at (703)-586-1081. In Va. call toll-free, 1-(800)-542-5927 or write PO Box 489, Bedford, VA 24523.

Put yourself in our place.

An authorized concessioner of the National Park Service.

FRIENDSHIP INN

526 Orange Avenue,
Roanoke, VA 24016   (703) 981-9341
                         or (800) 327-5887
$ All major credit cards

Access to the Roanoke Civic Center is about as simple as it gets from this hotel, since it's located just across the street! The Friendship Inn is also less than one mile away from Center in the Square, the historic Farmers Market and the Virginia Transportation Museum. Free coffee will be served to you each morning. The cozy guestrooms have cable television with HBO. FAX service and shuttle pick up are available as are group,

discount and seasonal rates.

HOLIDAY INN HOTEL TANGLEWOOD

4468 Starkey Road,
Roanoke, VA 24014   (703) 774-4400
$$ All major credit cards

Holiday Inn Tanglewood is conveniently located just minutes away from Tanglewood Mall, downtown Roanoke and the Roanoke Regional Airport. Complimentary limousine service to the airport is available as well as rental cars, private limos and taxi service.

The 196 guest rooms are traditionally furnished. Each comes with climate control, color TV (with Showtime, CNN and ESPN), AM/FM radio and two vanity dressing areas. Starkey's Bistro, located in

The Colony House
Travelers Bed & Breakfast

❖ Large, Quiet Rooms
❖ King Rooms and Suites Available
❖ Meeting/Conference Room
❖ Swimming Pool
❖ Free HBO & ESPN
❖ Excellent Restaurants Within Walking Distance

(703) 345-0411
In VA Only — 1-800-552-7026

Convenient from the Blue Ridge Parkway
Take Exit Marked US 220 North
Motel Location: 3560 Franklin Road, S.W.
Roanoke, VA 24014
(Take I-581 Franklin Road Exit)

the hotel, serves continental breakfast or regional cuisine. For some excitement, try the Elephant Walk lounge (see Night Life), which takes its atmosphere from a safari decor. The hotel offers outdoor swimming and tennis. Golf, horseback riding and hiking are accessible in the area.

INNKEEPER MOTEL
815 Gainesboro Road,
Roanoke, VA 24016   (703) 982-0100
or (800) 822-9899
$$ All major credit cards

The Innkeeper Motel knows that it's the little touches that make a stay more pleasant. That is why guests at this hotel are treated to a complimentary continental breakfast, coffee, newspaper and ice! Their 98 rooms feature firm, extra-length beds for a sound night's sleep. The furnishings are high quality. Each room has a remote control color television with cable, sofas, desks, AM/FM clock radios and electronic fire alarms. There are non-smoking rooms and handicap facilities available. Some rooms come with Jacuzzis. An outdoor pool is located on the grounds for guest use.

THE JEFFERSON LODGE
616 South Jefferson Street,
Roanoke, VA 24011   (703) 342-2951
or (800) 950-2580
$$ All major credit cards

The Jefferson Lodge is located in the heart of downtown Roanoke. A walk of only a few blocks will have you at the main public library, city and federal government buildings, hospitals and shopping. It is only

three blocks to the City Market and Center in the Square.

One hundred newly decorated rooms await guests. Free parking, coin-operated laundry and color TV are all provided for your comfort. An outdoor swimming pool and family dining room are on the property. Special group rates are available.

THE PATRICK HENRY HOTEL
617 South Jefferson Street,
Roanoke, VA 24011   (703) 345-8811
or (800) 833-4567
$$ and up   All major credit cards

On November 12, 1925, The Patrick Henry Hotel opened its doors for the first time. Its 11-story exterior was already a wonder. But, visitors and guests were astounded by the beauty of the interior. Wrought iron railings and accents of brass surrounded the lobby. Chandeliers hung from the towering 30-foot ceilings. And ornate carvings flowed along ceilings and walls. Today, the hotel has been restored to its previous splendor, and it is the only operating landmark hotel in Roanoke.

The guest rooms are more than spacious; they are actually over twice the size of typical hotel rooms. Each has been modernized, but in a way that reflects the historic heritage. Room have their own separate kitchenettes. Airport transportation, free parking, smoking and non-smoking floors and a restaurant are all a part of this hotel's special charm. And, rooms feature amenities most requested of hotel rooms, like full-length mirrors, hair dryers, irons and special bath items.

ROANOKE AIRPORT MARRIOTT

2801 Hershberger Road, NW,
Roanoke, VA 24017   *(703) 563-9300*
$$$ *All major credit cards*

The Roanoke Airport Marriott has been chosen as a AAA Four Diamond award winner, and the reasons are easy to see. The elegant lobby welcomes you. Sounds of casual conversation float over from Whispers, the lobby bar. You catch the scent of some delicious dish being served to a guest in Lily's or Remington's (see Restaurants). Soon, you open the door to your lovely room, one of the 320 guest rooms and suites available here. You will find all of the comforts of home and more. Every guest room has individual climate control, AM/FM radio, remote-control color cable TV, two direct dial telephones with message lights, video messages and complimentary personal care products. Twenty-four hour room service, valet service, airport transportation and free parking are just a few more of the luxurious benefits you will find.

After you unpack, you can relax in the special atmosphere of the Marriott. There are indoor and outdoor pools, a fitness center, sauna, whirlpool and two lighted tennis courts. Or if you feel like finding some action, try Charades, the entertainment lounge (see the Night Life chapter). If you are looking for activities outside of the hotel, golf, horseback riding, hik-

More Families "Resort" to The Roanoke Marriott!

Pack up the kids...head for the hills..and take in a great Blue Ridge mountain vacation!

And when day is done, come home to the Roanoke Marriott; relax in our sauna and whirlpool; exercise in our fitness center; play tennis; or take a swim. Then savor a casual family meal at Lily's or gourmet dining at Remington's.

So, when your family needs time to unwind, *"resort"* to Virginia's Roanoke Marriott, at far less than resort prices. Call for details on package plans!

FOUR DIAMOND AWARD

1-703-563-9300
or call toll-free
1-800-USA-WKND

ROANOKE AIRPORT Marriott.
I-581 & Hershberger Road, Roanoke, VA

ing and water sports are easily accessible. Also nearby is Center in the Square, the Blue Ridge Parkway and Mill Mountain Zoo.

The Marriott's Grand Ballroom, Shenandoah Ballroom and six meeting rooms can accommodate groups from 20 to 900. There is a total of 17 conference rooms available with over 12,800 square feet of flexible space. Special rates include Two For Breakfast Weekends, Honeymoon Packages, Super Saver and long-term rates.

SHERATON INN ROANOKE AIRPORT
2727 Ferndale Drive, NW,
Roanoke, VA 24017   (703) 362-4500
                          or (800) 325-3535
$$$ and up   All major credit cards

Indoor/outdoor pools, tennis courts, volleyball and golf are available at this outstanding hotel. For more adventure, there is a piano bar and a club, Miami's, the hottest place to dance the night away! Oscar's Restaurant will provide an extraordinary dining experience in the heart of this elegant hotel. Each of the 150 guest rooms and 4 suites is designed for your comfort. They are equipped with satellite TV, two phones, individual climate control, radio and two double beds or a king-sized bed. Pets are allowed in the room with a $25 deposit.

Sheraton has more than 7200 square feet in meeting and conference facilities. From a small dinner of 20 to a banquet of 350 people, the Main Ballroom will easily house your guests. A conference center and luxurious hospitality suites are perfect for business, meeting and social functions. AAA and AARP discounts are available.

QUALITY INN - ROANOKE/SALEM
I-81 Exit 41 & Route 419, P.O. Box 460
Salem, VA 24153   (703) 562-1912
                          or (800) 228-5151
$$ All major credit cards

Quality Inn is great for families with children. Here at their "Quality Park," kids can swing, play games and enjoy other activities, or swim in the children's pool. The 120 rooms have cable TV with HBO, and pets are allowed to stay with you. The dining room, Back To Berkeleys, serves tempting meals from breakfast through dinner. BTB's lounge features live entertainment. Nearby attractions are the Blue Ridge Parkway, Dixie Caverns, Natural Bridge, Center in the Square, Roanoke and Salem Civic Centers and shopping malls.

East of the Blue Ridge Region

Madison County/Syria

GRAVES MOUNTAIN LODGE
Syria, VA 22743   (703) 923-4231
$$$ and up (meals included)
                          All major credit cards

Graves Mountain Lodge is a family-owned resort tucked away in the beauty of the Blue Ridge Mountains. This is a complete resort with recreational facilities to please the whole family. There is swimming, tennis, softball, volleyball and ping pong to enjoy. Or you can try horseback riding, fishing, hunting and hiking. Visit the gift shop to see mountain crafts, Indian and folk carvings and jewelry. The recreation lounge has books, magazines, games, a piano and a television set. There is also an oldtime country store, Syria Mercantile Company, where you can buy groceries, dry goods and other everyday needs. If you decide to venture off the farm, the surrounding area has plenty to offer. You can enjoy sightseeing at Luray Caverns, touring gorgeous Skyline Drive, or observing authentic full-time farm operations at R. S. Graves Bros. Farm.

There are ten different accommodation styles for you and your family to choose from.

Ridgecrest Motel has 22 rooms and two conference rooms. Hilltop Motel has 16 rooms, some with TV sets. The Old Farm House has seven rooms with half-baths and a portico to the shower house. There are also seven cottages located in the vicinity of the Lodge. Perfect for families and groups, all come equipped with refrigerator or kitchen. Dormitory facilities are also operated in conjunction with the Lodge.

Charlottesville

HOWARD JOHNSON
1309 W. Main Street
Charlottesville, VA 22903   (800) 654-2000
$$ All major credit cards
Adjacent to the University of

DOE RUN LODGE

For a vacation, a weekend getaway or business conference, Doe Run Lodge offers the finest accommodations on the Blue Ridge Parkway. Top of the line amenities which include everything from hiking and tennis to championship golf packages.

A famous country restaurant adds to the unforgettable stay at Doe Run Lodge.

DOE RUN LODGE

Milepost 189
Blue Ridge Parkway
Hillsville, VA 24343

Come enjoy the scenic beauty and cool alpine setting offered at Doe Run Lodge.
For reservations or information please call
(800) 325-M189.

Virginia and University Hospital, Howard Johnson is designed to offer guests every convenience. It also offers easy accessibility to the sports complex and stadium. The Charlottesville historic district, shopping and restaurants are within walking distance. For the family, spacious rooms are decorated with comfort in mind. Studio rooms offer a large living area tastefully decorated for private parties. There are king-size beds available. For the business person, roomy accommodations provide a large work area in a relaxed atmosphere. Studio rooms have adjacent rooms which provide a conference table for either working or relaxation. A courteous staff is always on had to assist with all of your needs. An outdoor swimming pool is open during warm months. Tourists and business people alike will find everything they need at this fine facility.

BEST WESTERN CAVALIER
105 Emmet Street, P.O. Box 5647
Charlottesville, VA 22905-0647
(804) 296-8111
or (800) 528-1234
$$ *All major credit cards*

The 118-room Cavalier is located centrally in Charlottesville, right near the University of Virginia. The accommodations options include two suites, three handicapped-accessible rooms and 18 for non-smokers. A swimming pool is located on site. Continental breakfast is served each morning. Up to 150 people can be accommodated in one of the three meeting rooms. Two-day and special meeting packages are offered.

THE BOARS HEAD INN
Route 250 West,
Charlottesville, VA 22905   (804) 296-2181
$$$

This is a charming resort that is detailed in the Resorts chapter of this book.

HOWARD JOHNSON

Hotel   "IN THE MIDST OF EVERYTHING"

- Closest Hotel To UVA & Hospital
- For Room Reservations call 1 (800) 654-2000
- Ask About our Guaranteed Reservation Plan.
- Hotel number: (804) 296-8121
- 1309 West Main St., Charlottesville, VA 22903

On the Corner of 13th & W. Main

Holiday Inn®

University Area of Charlottesville

- historic getaway
- personal service with contemporary guest rooms
- Red Lobster Restaurant
- exercise room with treadmill, universal gym and sauna
- one mile to University of Virginia
- large outdoor pool and landscaped courtyard
- 18-hole public golf course nearby
- courtesy shuttle van
- laundry valet
- Nearby attractions include:

Monicello	Skyline Drive
Michie Tavern	Ash Lawn
The University of Virginia	Fashion Square Mall

1600 Emmet Street
(804) 293-9111   1-800-HOLIDAY

COURTYARD BY MARRIOTT
1445 Seminole Trail,
Charlottesville, VA 22901   (804) 973-7100
or (800) 321-2211
$$ All major credit cards

Shopping, historical sites and the University of Virginia are all close to Courtyard by Marriott. The 142 rooms feature color televisions with HBO and ESPN and free in-room coffee. The hotel has 75 non-smoking and two handicapped-accessible rooms, along with 12 suites. The indoor pool, whirlpool and exercise room are perfect for keeping up with your normal daily routine, or just for relaxing. A restaurant and lounge are found on the property.

HOLIDAY INN NORTH-UNIVERSITY AREA
1600 Emmet Street,
Charlottesville, VA 22901   (804) 293-9111
or (800) HOLIDAY
$$ All major credit cards

This historic getaway will please you with its personal service and contemporary rooms which, along with the rest of the hotel, have been handsomely decorated. They provide you with all of the comforts of home and feature air conditioning and color TV with Showtime. An exercise room with treadmill, universal gym and sauna is also available. A large outdoor pool and landscaped courtyard are both relaxing and pleasing to the eye. Red Lobster Restaurant is nearby for scrumptious dining. The Holiday Inn is located just one mile from the University of Virginia.

SHERATON INN CHARLOTTESVILLE
2350 Seminole Trail
Charlottesville, VA 22901   (804) 973-2121
$$$ All major credit cards

This 240-room palatial accommodation on 20 acres offers everything you need for rest and relaxation after seeing the sights in Charlottesville. That includes a casual restaurant, "Treetop," a formal restaurant, "Randolph," and a great nightclub, "Dooley's." There's also two indoor and outdoor pools. A great place to relax!

HOLIDAY INN CHARLOTTESVILLE/MONTICELLO
I-64 & 5th Street,
Charlottesville, VA 22901   (804) 977-5100
or (800) HOLIDAY
$$ All major credit cards

Located two miles from downtown Charlottesville and four miles from various historical attractions, this hotel is in a wonderful central location for tourists and businesspeople alike. The high rise building has 130 rooms and one suite. A restaurant, located on the property, serves hot, tasty meals daily. Meeting and banquet facilities are available for up to 150 people.

OMNI CHARLOTTESVILLE HOTEL
235 W. Main Street,
Charlottesville, VA 22901   (804) 971-5500
or (800) THE-OMNI
$$$$ All major credit cards

This spectacular hotel has been AAA Four Diamond rated. There are facilities for a cocktail party for 30 or a conference of 600 people. A restaurant and pub are located within the hotel for delicious dining at guests' ultimate leisure. An indoor/outdoor pool, whirlpool, sauna and health club are available for your enjoyment. The 208 grand rooms are decorated in elegant furnishings. There are 36 non-smoking rooms available, six suites and three handicapped-accessible rooms.

Wintergreen

Wintergreen Resort, (804) 325-2200 or (800) 325-2200, near Charlottesville, is also a fine resort in the Shenandoah Valley region offering a myriad of accommodation alternatives. See our Resorts chapter for full details.

Lynchburg

Comfort Inn

Route 29 Expressway at Odd Fellows Road,
P.O. Box 10729
Lynchburg, VA 24506   (804) 847-9041
$$ All major credit cards

A comfortable and clean room or suite awaits every Comfort Inn guest. Take advantage of the free shuttle from the airport, just a few miles down the road. A free continental breakfast is offered each morning and a VIP floor, meeting rooms and FAX machines are available as well. Located within 5 miles of Liberty University, Lynchburg College and Randolph Macon Woman's College, this hotel is a convenient choice for visiting parents or those doing business with the colleges.

Days Inn

3320 Candlers Mountain Road,
Lynchburg, VA 24502   (804) 847-8655
                                        or (800) 325-2525
$$ All major credit cards

The Days Inn Lynchburg is perfect for the executives conducting out-of-town business or for travelers looking for more that just a good night's sleep. There are 131 spacious guest rooms available which feature remote control television with HBO and in-room safes. The 20 King executive rooms come with recliners for ultimate relaxation. The hotel also provides complimentary transportation to the airport and local businesses, valet/laundry service, 24-hour guest wake-up calls and FAX service.

The DayBreak Restaurant, situated within the hotel, provides a discount to hotel guests wishing to take their meals here. A gift shop, pool and playground are also provided. Ask about the audio/visual equipment in the meeting rooms. The hotel is convenient to Liberty University, Lynchburg Municipal Airport, Lynchburg College, the Farmers Market and River Ridge Mall.

Hilton - Lynchburg

2900 Candlers Mountain Road,
Lynchburg, VA 24502   (804) 237-6333
                                        or (800) HILTONS
$$$$ All major credit cards

Families with children should consider the Lynchburg Hilton. Not only do they offer adequate amenities and prompt service, but children of any age stay for free when they occupy the same room as their parents. The 168 attractive guest rooms and suites are furnished with large, comfortable beds, color satellite TV and direct dial telephones. Suites also feature wet bars, refrigerators and double, full-length, mirrored closets. Wake-up service, a gift shop, a newsstand and a courtesy van are other comforts offered. An exercise room, heated indoor pool, spa and sauna are located on the premises.

Johnny Bull's Restaurant serves some of the finest cuisine in Lynchburg. There is a wide assortment of American, Continental and regional foods on the menu. Share a cocktail and conversation with friends in The Imbibery. The Hilton boasts being the closest hotel in the area to the airport. It is also convenient to River Ridge Mall, Poplar Forest and the Appomattox Courthouse.

HOLIDAY INN
Route 29 and Odd Fellows Rd., P.O. Box 10729
Lynchburg, VA 24506   (804) 847-4424
or (800) 465-4329
$$ All major credit cards

The Appomattox Courthouse, Natural Bridge, Poplar Forest and Rev. Jerry Falwell's Thomas Road Baptist Church are all within a short radius of this Holiday Inn. Your comfort is thought of first, and guest room amenities reflect that attitude. Writing desks, sleep sofas, direct dial telephones with computer jacks and remote control color television are all provided. If you are enrolled in Holiday Inn's Priority Club, you will also receive a steaming cup of morning coffee and newspaper delivery service. The on-site restaurant, The Seasons, offers an interesting menu for breakfast, lunch and dinner and the luncheon buffet appears to be a hit! Meeting and function space is available. AAA and AARP discounts are offered.

HOWARD JOHNSON LODGE
Route 29 North, P.O. Box 10729
Lynchburg, VA 24506   (804) 845-8041
or (800) 654-2000
$ All major credit cards

Howard Johnson Lodge is located near Sweet Briar College and just across the James River from Randolph-Macon Woman's College, Lynchburg College and Liberty University. There are 72 rooms available, all with oversized beds, plush lounge chairs, a writing desk and an extra vanity. Guests enjoy free in-room movies and cable television. Private patios and balconies will allow you to relax while viewing the breathtaking Blue Ridge Mountains. Next door is a Howard Johnson restaurant, open 24-hours for your ultimate convenience.

INNKEEPER LYNCHBURG
2901 Candler's Mountain Road,
Lynchburg, VA 24502   (804) 237-7771
or (800) 822-9899
$$ All major credit cards

The Innkeeper offers a free continental breakfast and comfortable, clean accommodations. The guest rooms feature extra-length beds, remote control color TV (with cable and HBO), custom-made desks, sofas and direct dial touch-tone phones. Also for your comfort, non-smoking rooms and handicapped facilities are available. Whirlpool baths or shower massages and swimming pools are here to tempt guests to relax. Children under 16 stay free, and roll away beds are complimentary. Corporate, senior citizen and tour/group rates are available.

Smith Mountain Lake

BERNARD'S LANDING
(703) 721-8870
or (800) 368-3142

Bernard's Landing, a leading resort in Moneta, is an excellent choice for accommodating travelers. See the detailed write up in the Resorts chapter of this book.

Bedford County/Bedford

PEAKS OF OTTER LODGE
P.O. Box 489,
Bedford, VA 24523   (703) 586-1081
$$$ All major credit cards

This lodge is like no hotel you've ever seen! Located at milepost 86 on the Blue Ridge Parkway, Peaks of Otter is surrounded by the natural beauty of the Blue Ridge Mountains, a gorgeous lake and unbelievably green countryside. The interior of the lodge is decorated to reflect that setting, with natural woods and subtly blended textures, tones and colors.

The 59 rooms offer double beds and private baths. Three large suites are also available. Each room opens onto its own private balcony. From here you will be able to see the stunning sight of the magnificent mountain range. There are no telephones in the Lodge so that you may truly unwind and relax away from the "modern world." Guests are welcome in the cocktail lounge and dining room for friendly conversation and delicious dining.

Franklin County/Rocky Mount

COMFORT INN
950 North Main Street,
Rocky Mount, VA 24151   (703) 489-4000
$$ All major credit cards

Beautiful Smith Mountain Lake is just 14 miles away from this lovely hotel. The red brick exterior and carefully trimmed lawn are welcome sights to road weary travelers. The 60 rooms feature cable TV with HBO and AM/FM radios. A complimentary continental breakfast is served each morning and sunrise coffee and sunset cider are available to all guest for no extra charge. There is an outdoor pool on the property, which is located near Ferrum College, the Blue Ridge Parkway, Franklin County and Martinsville Speedway and Blue Ridge Farm Museum.

New River Valley Region

Blacksburg

BLACKSBURG MARRIOTT
900 Prices Fork Road,
Blacksburg, VA 24060   (703) 552-7001
$$$ All major credit cards

The Blacksburg Marriott offers 148 outstanding rooms in the heart of the city, right across from

Virginia Tech. Included are one suite, two handicap rooms and 20 non-smoking rooms. The rooms are comfortable and stylish, with in-room movies and HBO. There is an indoor/outdoor pool, tennis courts and a putting green. A health club is located within the hotel for your convenience. Enjoy elegant meals in the restaurant downstairs or drinks and conversation in the lounge. Banquet facilities are available.

HOLIDAY INN OF BLACKSBURG

3503 S. Main Street,
Blacksburg, VA 24060   (703) 951-1330
or (800) HOLIDAY
$$ All major credit cards

Nostalgics will love this hotel for its railroad theme restaurant, and the 98 lovely rooms have all of the conveniences you'll need. There is one suite, one handicapped-accessible room and ten non-smoking rooms. Banquet and meeting rooms can accommodate up to 500. A lounge, coin-operated laundry, game room, pool and satellite cinema are available for guests.

SHERATON RED LION INN

900 Plantation Road,
Blacksburg, VA 24060   (703) 552-7770
or (800) 325-3535
$$ All major credit cards

This hotel is situated on 13 acres of beautiful wooded land. The perfect site for a meeting or banquet, there are facilities able to accommodate up to 400. There are 104 rooms available, including two suites and one handicapped-accessible room. Enjoy hearty meals in the dining room or relax with

friends in the lounge where there is nightly entertainment. Three tennis courts are located on the property for working out all that nervous tension!

Radford

BEST WESTERN RADFORD INN

1501 Tyler Avenue, P.O. Box 1008
Radford, VA 24141   (703) 639-3000
$$ All major credit cards

Hunters Restaurant and Dux & Company Lounge (see Restaurants) make Best Western the place to come in Radford. The restaurant serves delicious food for breakfast, lunch and dinner. Dux & Co. draws a crowd from all over the New River Valley with its generous hors d'oeuvres and live entertainment. The deluxe guest rooms here are decorated in Colonial Williamsburg colors. Each has a color television with satellite, two touch-tone phones, a wall-mounted hair dryer and full bath amenities. King or double and non-smoking rooms are available.

A gazebo-style indoor pool area with whirlpool, sauna and exercise facilities is provided for guest enjoyment. Free parking, ice and vending machines, babysitters, baby cribs and safety deposit boxes add to a list of amenities that make this an especially great choice to traveling families. Nearby is the Blue Ridge Parkway, Claytor Lake State Park and Dixie Caverns. Weekend and Honeymoon packages are available along with AAA and AARP discounts.

EXECUTIVE MOTEL
Route 11 West, P.O. Box 708
Radford, VA 24141   (703) 639-1664
$ All major credit cards
This small motel is clean and comfortable, and very affordable. Its location near St. Alban's Hospital and shopping provides added convenience. The 26 rooms feature two double beds, refrigerators, air conditioning, direct dial telephones and satellite color televisions.

SUPER 8 MOTEL
1600 Tyler Avenue,
Radford, VA 24141   (703) 382-5813
or (800) 848-8888
$ All major credit cards
Super 8 is called "North America's Finest Economy Lodging," and they live up to the title here by providing excellent amenities. The rooms feature cable television with the Movie Channel. Waterbeds are available upon request. There is 24-hour desk and wake-up call service. You will be treated to free coffee each morning. Non-smoking rooms and business singles are available upon request.

COMFORT INN RADFORD
1501 Tyler Avenue,
Radford, VA 24141   (703) 639-4800
$$ All major credit cards
Families, business travelers and tourists alike will appreciate the comfort and convenience of Comfort Inn. Its theme is "We Love Guests" and they really show it! Thirty-two large, spacious rooms with color cable television and tasteful furniture await you. An indoor pool, meeting rooms and an on-site restaurant are available for guest use. The hotel is near Radford University, historic Radford Mainstreet, an antiques mall and Virginia's only historic outdoor drama, "The Long Way Home." AAA and AARP discounts are available.

Pulaski County/Dublin

COMFORT INN
Route 1, Box 123F,
Dublin, VA 24084   (703) 674-1100
or (800) 221-2222
$$ All major credit cards
A special feature of this hotel is the Emily Virginia's restaurant located on the property! Motor Coach groups will enjoy the special Red Carpet greeting, apple cider reception and fresh apple farewell. Each of the 100 rooms has individual temperature control, satellite color TV, AM/FM clock radio and direct dial touch-tone phones. Some rooms feature Jacuzzi tubs. The conference room has a wet bar and a private banquet room is also available. New River Community College, Radford University and Virginia Tech are all within a short distance of the hotel. AAA and AARP discounts are offered.

Patrick County

DOE RUN LODGE RESORT AND CONFERENCE CENTER
Mile Post 189/Blue Ridge Parkway,
Hillsville, VA 24343   (703) 398-2212
or (800) 325-M189
$$$$ All major credit cards
Just across the border of Floyd County, in Patrick County, Doe Run

Lodge Resort and Conference Center and its High Country Restaurant are nestled in the most beautiful part of the Blue Ridge Parkway. With Groundhog Mountain as the midpoint on this road of pastoral beauty, your senses will be overwhelmed by what this year round resort has to offer. Azaleas, rhododendron, dogwood and mountain laurel are in the air in spring and early summer. The foothills below reveal a burst of color from apple, peach and nectarine orchards and grape vineyards. You may hear animals of the forest—deer, fox, hawks, eagles, groundhogs and raccoons—scampering through the woodlands.

Doe Run Lodge Resort and Conference Center was built to fit the beauty of this environment. The chalets were built utilizing stone and wood beams. Floor-to-ceiling windows allow magnificent views. These large suites have a fireplace, two bedrooms, two full baths and living/dining area, a real buy for the money! The chalets, townhouses and single family residences are furnished and have complete kitchens. Millpond Hideaway, designed for executive use or honeymooners, has a whirlpool tub, luxury shower and steam cabinet, full suite stereo and TV, fireplace and enclosed garage. To realize the true value of their accommodations, share a chalet with another couple or with your family as it can accommodate up to six people with two bedrooms and two full baths.

High Country Restaurant offers a unique menu of seafood, steak and other regional recipes including venison, duck, fresh rainbow trout from their stocked pond, pheasant and country ham. Picnic lunches are packed to go. For the best the Blue Ridge Parkway has to offer, park yourself at Doe Run Lodge Resort and Conference Center and let the magic of the Blue Ridge happen! All major credit cards are accepted.

Alleghany Highlands Region

Alleghany County/Covington

THE ARBORGATE INN

I-64 to Route 220, Exit 5,
Covington, VA 24426   *(703) 962-7600*
or (800) 722-7220
$$ *All major credit cards*

This motel is conveniently located within a two block radius of shopping and fine restaurants. The 75 rooms (including several suites) come with amenities like air conditioning, color TV with HBO and direct dial phones. A conference room is available with advance notice.

COMFORT INN

Mallow Road,
Covington, VA 24426   *(703) 962-2141*
or (800) 228-5151
$$ *All major credit cards*

A free continental breakfast is served each morning for all guests of Comfort Inn. Also, for your pleasure, coffee is available 24-hours a day. All of the 67 rooms are equipped with air conditioning, satellite TV with the Movie Channel and Showtime (VCR available) and direct dial phones — local calls are even free. Laundry service is available. Relax in the outdoor pool, Jacuzzi, sauna or health spa. A full service restaurant is located in the hotel. Shopping is found within a two block radius of the hotel.

HOLIDAY INN COVINGTON
Routes 220 & 60,
Covington, VA 24426   (703) 962-4951
                           or (800) HOLIDAY
$$ All major credit cards
Come to Holiday Inn and enjoy its wonderful restaurant or visit the lounge for nightly entertainment. The rooms are equipped with air conditioning, color TV with HBO, and direct dial phones. Ten non-smoking rooms are available. The outdoor pool and nearby shopping facilities are convenient amenities.

Bath County/Hot Springs

THE CASCADES INN
Hot Springs, VA 24445   (703) 839-5355
$$$$ MC, VISA, AMEX
Stunning scenery will draw you to the Cascades Inn. The excellent service and convenient location (less than 1,500 yards from The Cascades Course) will bring you back again and again. Golfers will love The Cascades Course, ranked among the top 30 courses in the nation. The Lower Cascades and Homestead Courses are only

three miles from the inn. The beautiful mountain scenery and the three-mile Cascades Stream are incredible assets to this inn, which is a beauty itself. The interior is tastefully and warmly decorated. There are three cottages available as well, each with bedroom accommodations, color television and sitting area. Since the property is operated by the Homestead Resort, you are assured superior service with a more affordable price.

Highland County/Monterey

HIGHLAND INN
Main Street,
Monterey, VA 24465   (703) 468-2143
$$ MC, VISA
Michael Strand and Cynthia Peel-Strand are innkeepers of this cozy spot, found in Monterey (fondly referred to as "Virginia's Switzerland"). This Victorian home was built in 1904 to serve the lodging needs of tourists escaping from the summer heat of nearby cities. Eastlake porches with gingerbread trim and rocking chairs are so inviting you will want to stay indefinitely.

All 20 guest rooms have their own private baths and are decorated with antiques and collectibles. Choose a standard room (double bed), deluxe room (king size bed or two beds) or a suite (two rooms). A complimentary continental breakfast is provided each morning with lunch and dinner served in the Monterey Room. The Black Sheep Tavern offers beer and wine every day but Sunday.

Inside
Restaurants

*I*f you think dining in the Blue Ridge region means just country ham, biscuits, fried chicken and apple pie, think again. Everywhere you turn there are old-fashioned restaurants offering hearty, conventional Southern fare. But there are also dining rooms whose chefs have won national and even international reputations for their innovative cuisine.

The latter tend to be concentrated in the Charlottesville area and in the northern foothills region, east of the Blue Ridge. These highly acclaimed restaurants include the Inn at Little Washington, just an hour from the "Big" Washington beltway, the C & O Restaurant and Memory & Company in Charlottesville, and the Homestead in Hot Springs.

Some of the region's finest restaurants are tucked away inside beautifully renovated country inns, such as the Joshua Wilton House in Harrisonburg, Prospect Hill in Trevilians and the Valley Pike Inn in Newbern. Others sit smack in the middle of downtown districts, and others along the major highway of the Blue Ridge, Interstate 81.

In this vast region you will find mountaintop restaurants with magnificent views from your table — especially Peaks of Otter in Bedford, Chateau Morrisette in Floyd County and the historic restaurants inside Shenandoah National Park.

If you have a hankering for exotic, ethnic cuisine, try the Maharaja or the Saigon Cafe in Charlottesville or one of the fine Brazilian restaurants in Roanoke, such as Carlos' in the downtown market area. Or if organically grown, vegetarian food is your preference, head to the Wildflour at Roanoke's Towers Mall.

The healthy, home-cooked food at Lynchburg's The Farm Basket is wildly popular, with people lining up as early as 11 AM for lunch on one of the place's few tables. The lunch spot grew out of a fruit stand and vegetable garden; it is famous for its cucumber sandwiches on dill bread and its gouda cheese biscuits.

Many restaurants throughout the region take pride in relying primarily on local products for their cuisine. The Highland Inn in Monterey specializes in fresh local trout and desserts concocted from Highland County maple syrup. Staunton's 23 Beverley uses local fruits and vegetables, herbs and cheeses, meats, poultry and even flour ground locally for its nouvelle style cuisine.

Many of Charlottesville's restaurants seem to be competing with one another for first place in offering the very finest, freshest, and most innovative cuisine. This writer would hate to be the judge of such a contest, because there are so many mouth-watering places to dine in and around town.

Because of the vastness of the region we have attempted to cover in this guide, we were unable to list all the good restaurants in every city, town and village. We hope your favorite is included. But if it is not, drop us a line with your suggestions. We will be updating this book every year and will add to this list.

Readers may also be able to challenge our pricing guidelines for the restaurants listed below. Personal choices and menu changes will prove us wrong in some cases. But we wanted to provide you with a basic idea of what you could expect to pay, so here are the guidelines (which do not reflect sales tax, gratuities, or alcoholic beverages):

A basic meal for two under $20:	$
A check for two of $21 to $35:	$$
A check for two of $36 to $50:	$$$
More than $51 for two:	$$$$

Note also that this chapter does not include restaurants in the Shenandoah National Park; those are listed instead in our chapter on the National Park and Skyline Drive.

The restaurants profiled in this guide are listed alphabetically under regional sections, then big cities like Charlottesville, Lynchburg and Roanoke. Others are listed according to their geographical location. As in other chapters of the book, we begin with the northern tip of the Blue Ridge — Winchester, and work our way south, zig-zagging east and west over the mountains and Shenandoah Valley.

Bon appetit!

Shenandoah Valley Region

Winchester

EL DORADO

1919 Valley Avenue	(703) 662-6488
$	All major credit cards

This place is run by Mexicans who aren't shy with their use of hot chili peppers. You can expect generous portions of hearty, spicy food here. Four-cylinder salsa and tortillas arrive at your table before the meal. The atmosphere is casual — laminated tables and chairs and walls hung with pinatas, Mexican hats and travel posters of the home country. Local Mexicans frequent this place, assuring that the food is authentic and good.

THE OLD POST OFFICE RESTAURANT & LOUNGE

200 N. Braddock St.	(703) 722-9881
$-$$	All major credit cards

This is a relatively new restaurant situated inside an original Winchester Post Office building, which was built in 1910. Lunch selections include gourmet sandwiches, salads, and pasta, and dinner offerings include fresh veal, pasta and seafood.

CAFE SOFIA

2900 Valley Ave.   *(703) 667-2950*
$-$$ All major credit cards

This lovely restaurant serves the only Bulgarian food in the Shenandoah Valley. They are open for lunch and dinner.

Middletown

WAYSIDE INN

7783 Main Street   *(703) 869-1797*
$$-$$$ *All major credit cards*

This restaurant is part of an elegantly restored 18th-century inn. Regional American cuisine is served in seven antique-filled dining rooms, including the old slave kitchen. Peanut soup, spoon bread and country ham, along with a variety of game and seafood dishes and homemade desserts, make this place a special place to dine.

Strasburg

HOTEL STRASBURG

201 S. Holliday St.   *(703) 465-9191*
$$ *All major credit cards*

This is a wonderful restaurant inside a restored 1895 Victorian hotel. The tables, chairs and paintings are supplied through the nearby Strasburg Emporium, and every item is for sale, so the furnishings are always changing. The restaurant has a strong following in the northern Shenandoah Valley, and is known for its generous portions, courteous service and delicious meals. Dinner specialties include

Chicken Shenandoah — chicken breast sauteed with country ham, peanuts, apples and an apple brandy/cream sauce. The Strasburg salad combines greens and vegetables with pecans, blue cheese, artichoke hearts, egg and croutons. Reservations are recommended on the weekends.

Front Royal

OLIVER'S

108 S. Royal Ave.
(U.S. 340 S)   *(703) 635-3496*
$$$ *MC, VISA, Discover*

The menu changes weekly at this popular new restaurant in town, situated in a renovated Victorian house. Four dining rooms are decorated with old Fiesta china and fresh flowers, and background music hails from the 30s and 40s. A typical entrée is the pan-roasted beef tenderloin with a confetti of sweet potato, Smithfield ham and celery. Desserts include a dark chocolate mousse cake and creme brulée. Children are always welcome. Oliver's is closed on Mondays and Tuesdays.

Woodstock

THE SPRING HOUSE

325 S. Main St.   *(703) 459-4755*
$$ *All major credit cards*

Word has it there used to be an underground spring on this property, and town folk came to fetch spring water from the lady who lived here. Folks still come here for refreshment, though the spring is now closed up. Breakfast, lunch and dinner are served seven days a week. Specialty entrées include Eleanor's Delight (a creamy seafood mixture on an open kaiser roll, with tomato and cheese). Dinners come with a complimentary glass of apple cider, homemade walnut rolls with honey butter, and a trip to a huge salad bar.

Luray

PARKHURST RESTAURANT
U.S. 211 (2 miles west of
Luray Caverns)   (703) 743-6009
$$$-$$$$ All major credit cards

This place is extremely popular with golfers who flock to Luray's great courses in the spring, summer and fall. The atmosphere is casual, although tables are set with cloth napkins, crystal, china and candles. Some of the specialties are escargots, tomato shrimp bisque, fettucine with shellfish and veal Oscar. Every meal comes with a wonderful relish tray, served with a fresh, light garden dip, homemade breads and more. Dinner is served every night, and children are welcome. Reservations are suggested.

New Market

SOUTHERN KITCHEN
U.S. 11   (703) 740-3514
$ MC, VISA

If you're up for good old Southern food, nothing fancy, this is the place. There's peanut soup — which some say is the best made anywhere, Lloyd's fried chicken, barbecued ribs of beef and much more.

Lacey Springs

BLUE STONE INN
Rt. 11 (exit 251 from I-81)   (703) 434-0535
$$ No credit cards

This is a popular place with professors from James Madison University, and people are willing to stand in long lines for a table. It specializes in fresh fish, such as Lacey Spring Trout, and tender steaks.

Harrisonburg

HUYARD'S COUNTRY KITCHEN
Hwy. 42, Dayton   (703) 879-2613
$ No credit cards

You really shouldn't miss this place. Owner David Huyard and his cooks serve up ham, beef, chicken and vegetables buffet-style. The food is homemade and very, very tasty — more than likely nothing comes out of a can. The "kitchen" is inside the Dayton Farmer's Market, where you can shop for kitchen items, lace, fudge, antiques, fresh cheese, homemade breads and much more.

JOSHUA WILTON HOUSE
412 S. Main St.   (703) 434-4464
$$$$ All major credit cards

The restaurant inside this beautifully restored Victorian home serves the most exquisite food in town. It's no exaggeration to say this is one of the best restaurants in Virginia. Hard to believe the place was once a frat house for James Madison University students.

Craig and Roberta Moore gutted the whole building and renovated it, and now it is a beautiful, romantic place to have dinner and spend the night.

A selection of about 140 wines includes a wide variety of American and French wines at very reasonable prices. Appetizer choices range from a salmon and scallop mousse to a confit of duck. The smoked duck salad features carrots, walnuts, raspberries, an artichoke bottom and Boston bib lettuce. Entrées range from trout with a country ham cream sauce to grilled smoked beef tenderloin with smoked oysters. Lamb, quail, pork, veal, duck, salmon and tuna are also offered, prepared in creative ways. Among the many freshly prepared desserts is the creme brulée—absolutely the best this writer has tasted anywhere. Reservations are suggested. (For more information on an overnight stay here, see our accommodations chapter.)

L'Italia Restaurant and Lounge
815 E. Market Street   (703) 433-0961
$$ MC, VISA, Disc.

Owner Emilio Amato runs a marvelous restaurant right off I-81 at exit 247-B. The pasta and sauces are all homemade, and many of the entrées are prepared with a light touch for those who need to keep their cholesterol levels down. We highly recommend the gnocci — tiny dumplings made with ricotta cheese and topped with a tomato and meat sauce, and the ravioli stuffed with meat.

The Village Inn
U.S. 11 South   (703) 434-7355
$ All major credit cards

The dining room at this small, family-owned motel serves simple,

delicious meals prepared by Mennonite cooks. The inn, which has a gorgeous view of the mountains, has a three diamond rating by AAA and Mobil.

El Charro
1570 E. Market St.   (703) 564-0386
$$ MC, VISA

This is a good Mexican restaurant with locations also in Covington and Fredericksburg. The staff is fast and courteous.

Waynesboro

The Fox and Hounds Pub & Restaurant
533 West Main Street
Waynesboro, VA 22980   (703) 946-9200
$$ Major credit cards

The Augusta County Court records of March 7, 1798, mentioned the present site of The Fox and Hounds as being located on "The First Main Street in a new town called Waynesborough." In 1837 a house was built on that site by John and Catherine Long, a house that was later used as a Civil War hospital facility for both Confederate and Union troops during the battle of Waynesboro. Today, this historic building is the second oldest structure still standing in Waynesboro. In 1987 the home was elegantly renovated to open its doors as The Fox and Hounds, rated three stars by the Mobil Guide. It's the perfect place to escape for great food. English decor helps raise your spirits. The menu will tempt your tastebuds. It includes favorites such as Filet Mignon Bearnaise, Fresh Salmon, Chuckling Oysters and Nutty Trout.

Desserts such as Chocolate Mousse, Turtle Cheesecake and the famous "Fox & Hounds Hot Fudge Swan" end your relaxing meal. Only the freshest ingredients are used in dishes which are Continental and American in style. Lighter dining and a wide variety of imported and domestic beverages (over 30 beers and five single malt Scotches) are available in the warm and welcoming atmosphere of the Pub. The Fox and Hounds is open Monday-Friday for lunch, 11:30-2 PM, with dinner served Monday-Saturday 5-9:30 PM. Closed Sundays.

Staunton

THE BEVERLEY
12 E. Beverley   *(703) 886-4317*
$ *MC, VISA*

This place has been around for a long time and is known for its luscious homemade pies and generous afternoon teas. It's a small, family owned place where you can also get real whipped potatoes and country ham on homemade bread. Tradition English tea is served from 3 to 5 PM on Wednesdays and Fridays and includes sandwiches, cake, cheese, fruit, scones and other pastries.

THE MILL STREET GRILL
1 Mill Street   *(703) 886-0656*
$ *MC, VISA, AMEX*

What a great family-style restaurant this is after a day of browsing in the historic Wharf area. Seat yourself within this converted grist mill, White Star Mill, soak in the atmosphere of stained glass signifying the old mill days and feast your eyes on a menu that offers something for everyone at an incredibly low price. The angel hair pasta will win the hearts of everyone. Steaks are cooked to your specification and bread fresh out of the oven is a staple at every meal. Bet you can't eat it all! Look for musical groups on weekends and special occasions.

The Fox and Hounds
Pub and Restaurant

Continental, American Regional Cuisine

Serving Lunch
Monday-Friday 11:30am-2pm

Serving Dinner
Monday-Saturday
5pm-9:30pm

Mobile Guide
3 Star Rating

533 West Main St.   Waynesboro, VA 22980   (703) 946-9200

PAMPERED PALATE CAFE
26-28 E. Beverley (703) 886-9463
$ *MC, VISA*

This is another great watering hole smack in the middle of the most interesting shopping area in the downtown. Here you will find gourmet deli sandwiches, such as roast beef and brie on French bread, bagels, stuffed potatoes, iced strawberry tea and luscious desserts. The place also sells a lot of wines, including the best Virginia wines, gourmet gift baskets and imported candies. Wine tastings are available.

23 BEVERLEY
23 E. Beverley (703) 885-5053
$$$ *MC, VISA, AMEX*

This newcomer to Staunton is a sophisticated dinner alternative to most other area restaurants. Lunch and dinner are served in an austere, grey-toned room with indirect lighting, decorated with contemporary paintings and sculptures. It's rather expensive, but you can't beat it for an elegant night out. Owners Lisa Joy and Doug Porter take pride in relying on fresh, local produce, herbs, meats, cheeses and trout for their regional American cuisine. There are more than 100 wines to choose from, about a quarter of which are made in Virginia. The restaurant is closed on Tuesdays and reservations are suggested.

Lexington/Rockbridge County

HARBS' BISTRO
19 West Washington Street (703) 464-1900
$ *No credit cards*

The sophisticated atmosphere, food and service at this bistro and gallery make it a popular lunch spot and evening watering hole for students and other locals. Harbs' really lives up to the definition of a bistro: an intimate, unpretentious club atmosphere. The cafe's walls are covered with art and its restroom signs modeled after a bull and the Statue of Liberty.

During the day, you choose from the menu of hearty sandwiches, salads and desserts, and other specials. Their hero sandwiches are served on freshly baked loaves. The dinner menu changes frequently, but you can count on fresh, delicious bistro fare. Reservations aren't necessary, but you may wish to call ahead for prompt lunchtime service. Open from 8 AM to 9 PM.

ROCKBRIDGE RESTAURANT AT RAMADA INN
I-81 and U.S. 11 North (703) 463-9655
  or (703) 463-6666
$$ *Most major credit cards*

The savory foods served here have been praised as unusually good for a hotel restaurant. The chef serves up fresh, contemporary dishes for lunch and dinner every day. The restaurant has a comfortable atmosphere, and the quality of the food far exceeds the prices. Choose such dishes as grilled tuna Mediterranean, New Orleans onion bloom, Shrimp Creole and grilled salmon. The pecan coated chicken with orange sauce is peppery and delightfully rich. There is also a list of American wines including several Virginia varieties. Open seven days a week from 6:30 AM to

2 PM for breakfast and lunch, and 5 to 10 PM for dinner.

SOUTHERN INN
37 South Main Street   (703) 463-3612
$$ MC, VISA, AMEX

This charming historical restaurant has been a tradition in Lexington for over 59 years. Located in the heart of the downtown, the inn specializes in Virginia wines. Visit this family restaurant for traditional Southern-style cooking, sandwiches or Greek and Italian dishes. It's also open for breakfast.

WILLSON-WALKER HOUSE
30 N. Main Street   (703) 463-3020
$$$ Most major credit cards

This 171-year old Greek-revival townhouse is an example of architectural beauty and sets the perfect scene for an elegant dinner or brunch. But you are welcome whether you're wearing coat and tie or shorts and loafers. The interior of the house is decorated with elegant antique furniture and artwork. Opening off of the foyer are the two dining rooms. Each room has a fireplace with a faux-marble mantel and two portraits circa 1840.

The menu offers such tempting favorites as medallions of venison stuffed with cherries, apples and currants, broiled Norwegian salmon with pink and green peppercorn sauce and mushroom pate with homemade walnut bread. Afterward, enjoy such scrumptious desserts as amaretto-pumpkin cheesecake and frozen chocolate-and-peanut butter mousse. There's also a children's menu. Second-floor banquet rooms are also available for private parties. The restaurant serves lunch from 11:30 AM to 2:30 PM and dinner 5:30 to 9 PM Tuesday through Saturday. (Lunch is not served on Saturday from January to March). Reservations are recommended for lunch and dinner.

LEE HI TRUCK STOP RESTAURANT
U.S. 11 North   (703) 463-3478
$ Most major credit cards

You'll enjoy substantial, hearty fare that is appreciated both by locals and the trucking crowd at this friendly spot. Order the daily special and go away happy. They're open 24-hours a day.

MAPLE HALL
U.S. 11 North   (703) 463-4666
$$$$ MC, VISA, Choice

Come to Maple Hall for fine dining in an elegant atmosphere. This antebellum mansion is full of gorgeous antiques and restorations. Their seasonal menu allows for the freshest and most delicious cuisine imaginable. Open seven days a week (for dinner only) from 5:30 to 9 PM. Reservations are required.

NATURAL BRIDGE VILLAGE RESTAURANTS
U.S. 11 South   (703) 291-2121
The Colonial Dining Room
$$ MC, VISA, AMEX

A wonderfully adequate oasis of good family food, the Natural Bridge Village restaurants are as popular with the locals as they are with visitors at this gigantic tourist attraction. Known for their Friday night seafood buffet and Sunday brunch, you can count on quality food here. Open Sunday through Thursday from 6 to 8:30 PM and on Friday and Saturday from 6 to 9:30 PM. They are also open in the mornings for breakfast and from 12 noon to 3 on Sundays.

Roanoke/Salem/Catawba

ALEXANDER'S

105 S. Jefferson Street   (703) 982-6983
$$$ MC, VISA

The excellent food and the renowned service make this restaurant well worth the trip into downtown Roanoke. Along with such tempting dishes as Chicken Scampi, Grilled Breast of Duck with Raspberry Butter and Veal Alexander, you can find homemade bread and desserts. Lunch is served Wednesdays, 11 to 2. Dinner is served Friday and Saturday from 5:30 PM to 10 PM. The restaurant is also open for private parties seven days a week. Reservations for dinner are recommended.

ASIAN FRENCH CAFE

32 Market Square   (703) 345-5593
$$ AMEX, MC, VISA

If you are looking for the best Vietnamese cuisine in the Roanoke Valley, then look no further. This cafe, located in the food court in historic Market Square, has a versatile menu of tempting food, thanks to the chef's two separate kitchens. You can choose from Asian, French or American style foods such as Grilled Sesame Chicken, Quiche Lorraine or fresh fruit plates with honey dip. You can also choose to eat in either the elegant dining room or in the large, neon star-decorated food court. The dining room is open from 11:30 AM to 2:30 PM and from 5-10 PM Monday through Saturday. However, if you're just hopping in for a quick bite, the cafe operates two counters in the food court as well, open 10 AM to 6 PM Monday through Saturday. Reservations for the dining room are suggested on Friday and Saturday.

BILLY'S RITZ

102 Salem Avenue, SE   (703) 342-3937
$ Most major credit cards

Once known as "The Ritz," this building has been a part of Roanoke for over 100 years and is a favorite with the lunch-time business suit crowd. Now this century-old hotel in historic downtown Roanoke houses Tex-Mex dining at its finest. Come in for a casual dinner with friends or a quiet dinner for two. Choose from such favorites as blackened red snapper, chicken teriyaki or Billy Bubba's Texas Chili — good enough to die for. The restaurant is open for lunch 11:30 AM to 2:30 PM Monday through Friday. Dinner is served from 5 to 10 PM Monday through Wednesday, 5 to 11 PM on Thursday, and 5 to 12:30 PM Friday and Saturday. Reservations are recommended for large groups.

BUCK MOUNTAIN GRILLE

Route 220 S., Off Blue Ridge Parkway
Exit 121 S.   (703) 776-1830
$$ MC, VISA, Diner's Club

They've done it again! Another smashingly successful restaurant even bigger and better than The Wildflour at Towers Mall opened in June just off the Blue

Roanoke
Restaurants

IN THE MARKET

★ EXPERIENCE ★
The Roanoke Market Building

A FESTIVAL MARKET PLACE
IN DOWNTOWN ROANOKE

*Featuring an international food court,
specialty shops, restaurants & lounge*

MARKET
R O A N O K E

Across from Center in the Square
Managed and Leased by F& W Management Corp.
774-1641

Lunch
11:30-2:45 M-Sat.
Dinner
5-10 T-Thurs., 5-11 F&S
Closed Sunday

309 Market Street
downtown Roanoke
(703) 343-0179
Voted Best Market Restaurant

**BRAZILIAN
INTERNATIONAL
C-U-I-S-I-N-E**

*Brazilian • French
Spanish • American
food at it's best.*

Lunch 11:00-2:00 Mon.-Sat.
Dinner 5:00-10:00 Mon.-Thurs.
5:00-11:00 Fri.-Sat.
312 Market St.
(703) 345-7661

YANUCCI'S

Lunch
11:00-2:00 M-Sat.
Dinner
5:00-10:00 T-Thurs.
5:00-11:00 F&S
Open Sunday
4:00-9:00

315 Market St.
(703) 981-0000

WARD'S ROCK CAFE

109 S. Jefferson St.
Roanoke, Virginia 24011

(703) 343-CAFE

102 Salem Ave. S.E.
Roanoke, Virginia 24011

(703) 342-3937

ON THE MARKET DOWNTOWN

Ridge Parkway at the old Parkway Restaurant. Doug and Evie Robison have duplicated the delicious, home-cooked food that keeps waiting lines at Wildflour and added even more to the menu line. You'll find the old standards of Evie's Red Beans and Rice, but you'll also find dishes as diverse as Dragon's Tooth, fresh eggplant dipped in parmesan cheese and grilled with veggies and spicy salsa, Hummus and Polenta with Roma Tomato Sauce. Everything is strictly homemade. The staff is very friendly, considering how the place is usually packed weekends, with brisk traffic on weekdays as well. There's a local flavor to everything, including their own brand of coffee from Mill Mountain Coffee and Tea, and steaks fresh from Mason & Hannabass Meats on the Roanoke City Market. For dessert, there's strawberry shortcake, huge brownies or other sinful temptations. With all the Roanokers eating there, tourists will know they've hit the culinary jackpot when they stop at Buck Mountain Grille. The restaurant also serves alcoholic beverages. Open for breakfast, lunch & dinner six days. Closed Mondays. Hours 7 AM - 9 PM Tuesday through Thursday and Sunday. Open 7 AM - 10 PM Weekends.

CORNED BEEF & CO.

107 Jefferson St.   *(703) 342-3354*
$$ *MC, VISA, AMEX*

Probably the most successful deli-type operation in town, Corned Beef & Co's hearty fare, served up by three former frat brothers who graduated from Roanoke College, is known both for its great food and downtown atmosphere. The name says it all. Don't look for anything pretentious here. What you will find is good, basic deli sandwiches served quickly in a first-class atmosphere. These guys know what Roanokers want, and their success shows it. Open from 11:30 AM to 11 PM Monday, Tuesday and Wednesday, and 11:30 AM to 2 AM Thursday, Friday and Saturday.

EL RODEO MEXICAN RESTAURANT

4301 Brambleton Avenue,
Roanoke   *(703) 772-2927*
260 Wildwood Road, Salem (703) 387-4045
$ *MC, AM EX*

This favorite family restaurant will whisk you away to Mexico with its south-of-the-border decor, Mexican food servers learning English who rarely get your order totally correct (but who cares, it's all good!) and ethnic foods. The menu lists each dinner with an individual list of ingredients for those unfamiliar with Mexican food. These special dinners are created to give the diner a taste of Mexican cuisine — on the mild side! Choose from such delicious dinners as Fajitas, Taquitos Mexicanos, La Chicana or Enchiladas de Polo (chicken enchiladas). There are vegetarian and a children's menus as well. You will find the service to be excellent, the food kept hot, and the chef always willing to accommodate your substitutions. There is a special "lunch only" menu served from 11 AM to 2:30 PM Monday through Saturday. Dinner is served from 4 to 11 PM.

THE HOMEPLACE

Catawba   (703) 384-7252
$$ MC, VISA

A grand old farmhouse situated just outside of Roanoke is the site of the Homeplace. Their slogan is "Down home cooking that makes you want to eat all your veggies," and you would have to agree. This family oriented establishment is the perfect place for a Sunday dinner. The delicious home cooking is served family style, in bowls placed right at your table. Fried chicken, mashed potatoes and gravy, pinto beans, baked apples and hot biscuits are the staples of the menu here. A neighborly and courteous staff will make you feel right at home. Always plan on a wait of at least 20 minutes, since Roanokers pack the place on weekends. But you won't mind it on the big front porch where you can pet the farm felines while you wait. Dinner is served Thursday through Saturday 4:30 to 8 PM and Sunday 11:30 AM to 6 PM.

LA MAISON DU GOURMET

5732 Airport Rd.   (703) 366-2444
$$$-$$$$ All major credit cards

Here, close to the Roanoke Regional Airport, is elegant dining in a gracious 1929 Georgian mansion. La Maison has been voted Roanoke's "Favorite Restaurant for a Special Occasion," and "Best Restaurant Interior and Exterior" by readers of *Roanoker Magazine*. This is a popular spot where business deals are closed and special events in the Southern tradition are held. Proprietor Rance Marianetti prides himself on ensuring that everything

is prepared as if it were for his own family. Outdoor weddings are popular here among the lovely landscaped boxwood garden. Inside, the mansion atmosphere continues. You may sample superbly prepared cuisine along with private label wines from the Barboursville Vineyard. Homemade Virginia seafood sausage is a house specialty.

Lunches are popular among the business crowd, with fresh fruit salads and a flaming spinach salad prepared at your table. Lunch also features all your favorite sandwiches. Entrées include Maryland crab cakes, beef peppercorn and catch of the day.

Dinner is exquisite. Appetizers might be fettucine carbonara or escargot a la Bourguingnonne. Onion soup grantinee is a favorite and lobster citrus salad with brandy mayonnaise could be the start of your meal. Specialties du Maison include roast rack of lamb for two, Chateaubriand Bouquetiere for two, a trio of beef, lamb and veal, Steak Diane and gourmet seafood. For dessert, expect a tempting array of pastries, Baked Alaska, Cherries Jubilee or sorbet with fresh fruit. At a place such as this, you expect fine service and you get it. Open for lunch and dinner Monday through Friday from 11 AM until 11 PM and Saturday for dinner only, 4:30 until 11 PM.

THE LIBRARY

3117 Franklin Road, SW   (703) 985-0811
$$$$ All major credit cards

One of the most elegant and exclusive restaurants in the Roanoke valley, The Library is known for its memorable dining experience. The AAA Travel Guide rates The Library one of the seven top restaurants in Virginia. Dine on delicious French cuisine by candlelight. The menu includes such classics as Veal Princess, Beef Admiral and English Dover Sole. The decor of the restaurant is that of a well-stocked library. Dinner begins at 6:15 PM Monday through Saturday. Reservations are recommended.

LILY'S

At the Roanoke Airport Marriott,
I-581 at Exit 3-W   *(703) 563-9300*
$$ *All major credit cards*

This casual, family restaurant is located in the Roanoke Airport Marriott. Lily's features a full range of moderately-priced menu items, as well as popular buffets and children's menus. Prime Rib is featured Friday and Saturday nights, and Champagne Brunch on Sundays. Reservations suggested. Open daily.

LUIGI'S

3301 Brambleton Avenue   *(703) 989-6277*
$$ *MC, VISA, AMEX*

This Italian gourmet restaurant was established after the tradition of Mama Leone's restaurant in New York City. Naturally, the spaghetti is wonderful, and coupled with the other pasta selections, it's an Italian gourmet's delight. Some of their special treats include Veal Luigi's, Shrimp Scampi and the ever popular Cappuccino L'amore, made with a blend of gin, brandy, rum, Creme de Cacoa and Galliano Liquor topped with a cinnamon stick, clove and whipped cream.

Homesick Northerners can get real Italian desserts here too, like cannoli and spumoni ice cream. Luigi's is definitely a cut above any other Italian restaurant in town, both for food and service. Each dish is prepared by your special order, so count on a leisurely dinner with lots of attentive service. Open 4 to 11 PM Sunday through Thursday and 4 PM to midnight Friday and Saturday.

MACADO'S

120 Church Avenue   *(703) 342-7231*
$$ *All major credit cards*

The decor is as interesting as the food at Macado's, where both keep the restaurant packed with a younger crowd. A big hot air balloon drops from the ceiling and pictures and keepsakes from local or nationally-known bands decorate the walls. You'll see the Three Stooges riding in an airplane, a section of a real classic car on the wall, old toys, posters and nostalgic collectibles and antiques. The extensive menu could take your entire lunch hour to read. It specializes in a delicious array of hot and cold deli sandwiches. The salads and chili also are exceptional. The owner of the Macados restaurant chain lives in Roanoke but has restaurants throughout the area including Blacksburg, Charlottesville, Harrisonburg, Salem and Radford. Hours are 9 AM to 12:30 PM Sunday through Thursday and 9 AM to 1:30 PM on weekends.

REMINGTON'S

At the Roanoke Airport Marriott,
I-581 at Exit 3-W   (703) 563-9300
$$$$ All major credit cards

Remington's features a superb menu of distinctive American cuisine, complemented with superior service and fine selection of wines. Rated 4-Diamond by AAA. Serving dinner Monday through Saturday evenings; reservations recommended.

THE ROANOKER RESTAURANT

Colonial Avenue at 581
and Wonju Street   (703) 344-7746
$$ MC & VISA

For over 50 years, this restaurant has held high standards for itself and the results show. It's busy day and night, every day of the week, and is filled with loyal customers whose parents and grandparents ate here. Run by the Warren family all those years, customers have come to expect quick service and farm-fresh quality food served by people who truly care when they ask how you're doing. Roanoker was voted "Best Place to Eat With Your Mother." And it is! Breakfasts are the real highlight and the same people can be seen every day enjoying it. Don't miss the red-eye gravy and ham with biscuits and grits! Open daily from 7 AM to 10 PM.

ROANOKE WEINER STAND

25 Campbell Ave.   (703) 342-6932
$ No credit cards

In 1916, when prohibition caused the decline of Salem Avenue by forcing its saloons to close their doors, brick-paved Campbell Avenue took over as Roanoke's main thoroughfare. The road was exciting and new with streetcars and electric street light. The Municipal Building on Commerce Street and Campbell Avenue opened to the public. And, the "Roanoke Hot Weiner Stand" opened for business at the location where it would remain for over 75 years. Harry Chacknes opened the stand with a six burner stove, a kitchen that measured 13x7 feet (including counter space) and six stools. And, right in the heart of the "Magic City" you could get a steaming, plump hot dog for just a nickel. Friendly smiles and neighborly conversations awaited every lunchtime customer.

Almost eight decades later, times have changed. What once cost you five pennies now runs you 85 cents. The original six stools increased to 19 in 1988 when the Weiner Stand became a part of Center in the Square. They even traded up for a more modern stove after using the old one for 72 years. But some things haven't changed a bit. The stand is still in the Chacknes family. Harry's wife, Elsie, ran it in the 1960s. Now his nephew, Gus Pappas, is the owner. Elsie's nephew, Mike Brookman, works in the kitchen. And, while John Liakos is not actually a blood relative, he is certainly a part of the family after working here for over 30 years. You can still get that delicious, plump hot dog. And we don't think that the friendly conversation and warm, honest smiles will ever leave the kitchen of the Roanoke Weiner Stand.

SUNNYBROOK INN RESTAURANT

7342 Plantation Road   *(703) 366-4555*
$ - $$ *MC, VISA*

Howard and Janet Schlosser wanted to purchase a place that created an atmosphere to fit their "home cooking" style. And they found it. In 1983, the Schlossers bought Sunnybrook Inn. This large farmhouse was built in 1912 and served as home to owners of a 150-acre dairy farm. Each day homemade pies, cakes and rolls are baked in their kitchen. Their menu is a compilation of recipes from all over western Virginia, some 100 years old. Their special Peanut Butter Pie is a legend at the Inn. Other favorites are oysters fresh from the Chesapeake Bay, which are served year round. Every Friday and Saturday, there's a spectacular seafood buffet with crab legs and fried oysters. There are separate children's prices. The restaurant is open 8 AM to 8 PM Monday through Thursday, 8 AM to 9 PM Friday and Saturday, and 8 AM to 6:30 PM on Sundays. Reservations are required for large groups.

TEXAS TAVERN

114 W. Church Ave.   *(703) 342-4825*
$ *No credit cards*

As soon as you open the door to this 62-year-old white brick Roanoke landmark, the scent of hamburgers and hot dogs cooking on the grease coated grill hits you. You will notice that the countertop is dented and dull and that some of the stools are in need of long-overdue attention. Sometimes it seems as if the floor hasn't been swept for weeks. Men in industrial-white tee-shirts, workpants and aprons shout "hello" to newcomers over the popping grill, bubbling chili and chattering customers. The staff is neighborly and will "shoot the breeze" with you — that is if they have the time. But, don't try to rush another customer or break ahead in the line. Texas Tavern frowns on such impolite behavior, and they might just tell you so! They proudly display a sign that reads, "We serve 1,000 people ten at a time." No, you certainly won't be pampered here. But what you'll find is some of the best chili this side of Texas! The Tavern is the perfect place to stop for a quick, hot lunch or a midnight snack. They serve all of the favorite standards: hot dogs, hamburgers and of course chili. And if you order a nice cool drink, you won't get a styrofoam cup or even an aluminum can. Only glass soda bottles and straws found here! Texas Tavern is conveniently located near three (pay) parking lots, which is a bonus since they have little parking space of their own. It is also just a few blocks away from the Farmer's Market and Center in the Square. The restaurant is open 24-hours a day, seven days a week. Don't miss it!

THREE O NINE FIRST STREET

309 First Street   *(703) 343-0179*
$$ *Major credit cards*

Dining at 309 First Street is like having your favorite meal with an old friend. If there's one thing that stands out about this place, it's the repeat business it seems to do as a downtown Roanoke favorite on the historic City Market. It's undoubtedly one of the top choices for lunch by downtown professionals.

With a pleasant contemporary atmosphere and excellent service, lunch and dinner are served bathed in sunlight under a skylight filled with green plants. Each day offers a menu special ranging from a famous Seafood Salad to Chicken Fingers. It seems that one of the most popular dishes here is a selection of gourmet hamburgers. Try the Burgundy Burger, a daily special with a hint of fine wine, a Tex Mex Burger, well seasoned with Jalapenos, hot sauce and cheese, or First Street Favorite, a top-of-the-line gourmet burger with bacon and Swiss.

Dinner selections include the old favorite of Filet Mignon or Chicken Teriyaki and Sauteed Seafood Supreme, a delightful combination of fish, crab, scallops and shrimp sauteed in herbs and butter. Also available to the vegetarian taste is a popular Ratatouille and Vegetable and Rice Medley. All dinner selections include hot bread and butter, fresh steamed vegetables or seasoned rice, baked potatoes, onion rings or fries. 309 First Street will stay first in your mind after you've dined here.

VANUCCI'S ITALIAN CUISINE

315 Market Street SE   (703) 981-0000
$ Major credit cards

There's nothing better than inexpensive, fine Italian eating. That's what visitors to Roanoke's historic market will find at Vanucci's Italian Cuisine, a new restaurant with masterfully prepared and beautifully presented Italian dishes, which are complemented by excellent service and a warm, welcoming atmosphere. Host Walter Vanucci offers daily lunch and dinner specials at unbelievably low prices. Emphasis is on the northern Italian white sauce dishes. Pollame/Poultry might be Pollo Donatello, a breast of chicken topped with thin slices of eggplant and mozzarella cheese with house marina sauce, all for $5.25. Beef/Carne could be a succulent Veal Piccato sauteed in white wine, capers and lemon, for the same inexpensive luncheon price. Frutti Di Mare/Seafood features Seafood Pasta, a butterfly pasta with shrimp, fresh basil and mushroom cream sauce, also for $5.25. House salad and bread is served with each entree. Zuppa di Conchiglie (clam chowder) for $1.95 and Zuppa Di Granchi (crab soup) for $2.95 are popular favorites with the lunch and dinner crowds, along with a delicate Caesar Salad. From the ample entrees to the excellent coffees, Vanucci's offers a memorable dining experience every visit. Lunch is noon to 2 PM Tuesday through Saturday. Dinner is served 5-10 PM Tuesday through Thursday and 5-11 PM Friday and Saturday. Open Sundays from 4-9 PM.

WARD'S ROCK CAFE

109 S. Jefferson St.   (703) 343-CAFE
$ MC

Shake it up, baby! Roanoke's latest addition to the night scene is Ward's Rock Cafe, featuring groups such as "Cows in Trouble," "Big Idea," and even Magician Travis Winkler and his traveling magic show. Ward's is helping to make a Jefferson Street section of restaurants become THE hangout for young Roanokers. It features a rooftop section where the latest hot groups are featured. Ward's promise is to serve appetizing food consisting of the freshest ingredients available, with an entertaining atmosphere and service with a smile.

Food is served in an atmosphere of rock greats. You may choose from "Costello's Chicken Salad," a tangy concoction of all white chicken breast with walnuts, red onions and tarragon, or "The Orbison," roast turkey with Swiss cheese, thousand island dressing, cole slaw and spicy mustard on whole wheat. Other greats whose names are affixed to food are Ringo, Elvis and Mick Jagger. This must be a watering hole for Democrats since Al Gore and Bill Clinton have their own sandwiches named for them too! Dessert might be homemade brownies or buttermilk spice cake. A full range of beverages also is served, from healthful juices to hot chocolate and domestic and imported beer.

Ward's Rock Cafe has a goal of becoming the home of the best food, greatest music and most fun in the Roanoke Valley. Ward Holland and his family are well on their way to making this dream come true.

WILDFLOUR CAFE AND CATERING
Towers Mall (703) 344-1514
$$ MC

If you're going to eat at Wildflour, which everyone in Southwest Roanoke off the Colonial Avenue Exit at 581 appears to do, be sure and get there before 11:30 AM. A small operation with limited seating, what has been called the best food in Roanoke (by those who like healthy and homemade), is made from scratch early, so the smell of fresh baking bread lures in people who've been thinking about eating there since morning. It keeps getting more and more popular and the only liability is that it's too small for the throngs who haven't seen food prepared like this since their organic 60s days. Each day, the breads du jour are arranged in a flower pot at the cash register for all to smell and admire. The best red beans and rice in the world comes out of this place and you could eat it every day and not tire of it. To top it off, the young owners take the time to chat and get to know everybody, yet run an extremely efficient operation. Open 11 AM to 8 PM Monday through Saturday.

East of the Blue Ridge Region

FOUR & TWENTY BLACKBIRDS
Routes 522 and 647,
Flint Hill (703) 675-1111
$$$ MC, VISA

This wonderful restaurant is on the border of the Shenandoah Valley region and East of the Blue Ridge, a short drive from Front Royal down Rt. 522 south. Owners Heidi Morf and Vinnie DeLuise prepare creative American cuisine at reasonable prices. The menu completely changes every three weeks in order for cooks to take advantage of the best available seafood and local produce. The first-floor dining room is small but offers privacy for romantics — the tables are in nooks with screens of lace or floral prints.

The restaurant serves Sunday brunch and lunch and dinner Wednesday through Saturday. For dinner, guests have a choice of four appetizers, seven entrées and three desserts. Appetizers might include corn crepes filled with morels and shiitake mushrooms served with a smoked red pepper sauce. One acclaimed entrée is the beef filet kebabs, with a red wine sauce sparked with blue cheese and walnuts, and served with lemony sauteed potatoes and snow peas. Morf used to be the dessert chef at the highly acclaimed Inn at Little Washington, and her work is sensational. Chocolate pecan tart, mango mousse, pecan shortcakes with sautéed apples and maple cider cream are a few of her creations. Reservations are suggested for dinner.

THE INN AT LITTLE WASHINGTON
Middle and Main streets,
Washington (703) 675-3800
$$$$ *VISA, MC*

This highly acclaimed country inn is a favorite of Washington, D.C. media stars and politicians — being only a little more than an hour's drive from the city. Be prepared to spend big money here for exquisite regional American cuisine. The five-star restaurant has been praised by Craig Claiborne, the dean of food writers and restau-

rant critics, by the Relais & Chateau, a sort of Bible for the sophisticated European traveler, and countless other publications. The menu changes daily, and guests are served a seven-course meal for a fixed price. Here's an example of what one Richmond food critic rhapsodized over: the "fragrant, plump, explosively juicy little rabbit sausages" and the filet of salmon, wrapped in strudel pastry, flavored with mushroom duxelle, and accompanied by a delicate watercress butter.

On Saturday nights, dinner costs $88 per person, not including tax, tip, or alcoholic beverages. On weekday nights, the price drops to $78 per person. It's open for dinner daily except on Tuesdays. But in June and October, the busiest season, dinner is served daily. Reservations are required. See our chapter on Accommodations for information about the inn.

BLEU ROCK INN
U.S. 211, Washington (703) 987-3190
$$$$ *VISA, MC, AMEX*

Owned by brothers Jean and Bernard Campagne, who also operate La Bergerie in Alexandria, the Bleu Rock Inn is situated on 80 acres about an hour from the Washington, D.C. beltway. The inn's three dining rooms have fireplaces, and in warm weather, the terrace is a wonderful place to have dinner, drinks or dessert. From November through April Chef Scott Carr offers a five-course, fixed price menu on the weekends, and a three-course, less expensive dinner on Wednesday and Thursday nights. The rest of the year the restaurant serves dinner a la carte Tuesday through Sunday nights. The duck foie gras on a crisp potato cake has received rave reviews, as well as the grilled sea scallops, blackened grouper, loin of lamb with madeira and rosemary sauce, and desserts. Reservations are suggested. For more information about an overnight stay at the Bleu Rock Inn, see our Accommodations chapter.

Madison County

PRINCE MICHEL RESTAURANT

Rt. 29, between Culpeper and Madison

(800) 800-WINE
or (703) 547-9720

$$$$ *Major credit cards accepted*

Prince Michel, the state's leading winery, opened this exquisite French restaurant last September. Its fixed price menu emphasizes contemporary versions of traditional French cuisine and includes a choice of several imaginatively presented dishes for each course.

The restaurant offers the extraordinary cuisine of Alain Lecomte, a Frenchman who took first place in the prestigious Concours National de France des Chefs de Cuisine in 1990. Recreating his highly acclaimed French specialities using local products and pairing these dishes with Prince Michel and Rapidan River wines has been very exciting for the chef.

Lunch is $20, or $30 for the "gourmet" lunch, which offers an extra appetizer course and more choices for the entree. Dinner is $50 per person, exclusive of wine, spirits, taxes and gratuity. Reservations are recommended.

Guests enter through Prince Michel's wine shop where they may taste wine at the attractive wine bar. The stairway leading to the restaurant sets the stage for a unique experience. Styled by Parisian designer Ariane Pilliard in collaboration with local artist Marie Taylor, the decor focuses on trompe l'oeil effects including floor-to-ceiling murals which transport guests to the Bordeaux region of France. Opulent table settings with French linen add to the atmosphere of elegance.

The restaurant is open for lunch from noon to 2 p.m. and dinner from 6 to 9 p.m. Wednesday through Saturday. Lunch only is served on Sundays.

Travelers coming from the north will find the Prince Michel Restaurant ideally situated at the gateway to approximately 20 of Virginia's 40-plus farm wineries. The smart dinner guest will arrive early to tour the winery and enjoy the fascinating displays of its wine museum.

THE BAVARIAN CHEF

P.O. Box 375,
Madison, VA 22727   *(703) 948-6505*
$$-$$$ *MC, VISA, AMEX*

This restaurant a few miles north of Charlottesville serves huge portions of German cuisine, family style. The food is extraordinary, especially the Sauerbraten and the homemade desserts, which include a Bavarian nutball and Tiroler apfelstrudel with vanilla sauce. You can also enjoy conventional American seafood dishes. Reservations are suggested.

BERTINES NORTH
RT. 29, MADISON

(703) 948-DINE
$$-$$$ *No credit cards*

After 10 years on St. Martin's island Bernard and Christine Poticha started this Caribbean restaurant in, of all places, rural Madison County. This is a popular place with a menu that includes such dishes as blackened shrimp and swordfish, "Steak on a Hot Rock," and Veal Mustard. Don't miss Christine's famous chocolate mess pie with a hint of Amaretto. Bertines is open Wednesday through Sunday from 3 to 9 p.m.

Orange County

WILLOW GROVE INN

14079 Plantation Highway,
or Rt. 15 North - Orange   *(800) 949-1778*
                               or (703) 672-5982
$$$-$$$$ *No credit cards*

Limoges china, crystal chandeliers, Chippendale chairs ... get the picture? This plantation home, built in 1778, is now a bed and breakfast with quite a restaurant. The regional American cuisine of Chef Warren Volk, formerly of the Boar's Head Inn, is the most contemporary thing about this magnificent place. The menu changes frequently, depending upon the season, but last winter's included such items as baked chevre with toasted brioche and red pepper conserve and grilled aged tenderloin of beef with fines herbes butter. Truly scrumptious desserts include dark chocolate cake with mocha creme and warm chocolate sauce, French lemon tarte, and a white chocoate praline mousse. One of the most inviting things about this place is the friendly (and handsome) bartender who helps guests select an appropriate wine for their dinners. The menu also suggests a particular wine for each entree, and offers a full range of dessert wines, after dinner liqueurs and dessert coffees. This is the ideal place to dine after a full day touring Mont-

RoCoCo'S
PIZZA AND PASTA
(804) 971 7371

Mesquite Grilled Seafoods
Cappucino
Extensive Wine List

Corner of Hydraulic Rd. & Commonwealth Drive in the Village Green

Brunch, Lunch, Dinner • Serving All Day

pelier and other Orange County sites. Reservations are recommended. Dinner is served Thursday through Sunday, with brunch also offered on Sunday.

Charlottesville

Aberdeen Barn
2018 Holiday Drive across from
Holiday Inn north (804) 296-4630
$$-$$$ *Most major credit cards*
This is a well-established restaurant known for its roast prime rib and charcoal-grilled steak. But you can also have Australian lobster tail, crab cakes, shrimp scampi and other seafood delights here. The atmosphere is intimate, with candles on every table, and the Sportsman's Lounge features live entertainment nightly. Reservations are suggested.

Awful Arthur's
333 W. Main St. (804) 296-0969
$ *MC, VISA, AMEX*
A newcomer to Charlottesville, this casual seafood restaurant opened in January near the "Corner," that thriving district next to the oldest part of the UVA campus. It specializes in fresh seafood and a raw bar, and offers live music two nights a week. Awful Arthur's also serves brunch on both Saturdays and Sundays.

Baja Bean Co.
1327 W. Main St. (804) 293-4507
$ *MC, VISA*
This lively restaurant opened last February on the Corner near the Rotunda. California-style Mexican food is its specialty, meaning meals are lighter than the usual Mexican fare. Owner Ron Morse hails from San Diego, and he brought the healthier California sensibility with him to Charlottesville. The vegetarian specialities for lunch and dinner are especially popular. A full bar features 12 different kinds of Mexican beer and 15 different brands of tequila. Everything is made fresh, including both hot and mild salsa.

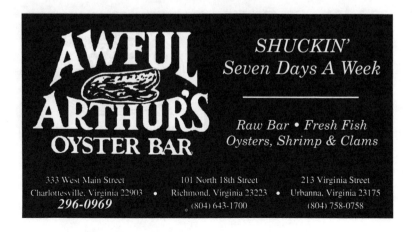

AWFUL ARTHUR'S OYSTER BAR

SHUCKIN'
Seven Days A Week

Raw Bar • Fresh Fish
Oysters, Shrimp & Clams

333 West Main Street
Charlottesville, Virginia 22903 • 296-0969

101 North 18th Street
Richmond, Virginia 23223 • (804) 643-1700

213 Virginia Street
Urbanna, Virginia 23175
(804) 758-0758

The festive restaurant is decorated with banners and t-shirts from Puerta Vallarta, Cancun, Cozumel, and other Mexican hot spots. Baja Bean Co. is open seven days a week from 11 AM to 2 AM, with live music every night except Sunday and Tuesday.

Biltmore Grill

Elliewood Avenue   (804) 293-6700
$ - $$ Most major credit cards

One of the most attractive things about this restaurant is the beautiful, thick, wisteria-covered arbor that covers an outdoor dining area during the warmer seasons. A popular restaurant for UVA students, the place serves creative pasta dishes and other entrees, white gourmet pizza, unusual and hearty salads and much more. There's a wide selection of imported and domestic beer and an outdoor bar. The dessert menu includes such yummy items as apple maple pecan tart and the great American chocolate brownie.

Blue Ridge Brewing Company

709 W. Main St.   (804) 977-0017
$$ VISA, MC, AMEX

If this place smells like a brewery, that's because it is. A friendly, casual restaurant, its home-brews are named for Blue Ridge mountain peaks, such as Humpback (stout), Hawksbill (golden lager), and Afton (red ale). The eclectic menu includes such dishes as bourbon steak, smoked trout wontons, pesto lasagna, Thai pork chops and blackberry cobbler. The bar's open every night until 2 AM and reservations are suggested.

Blue Bird Cafe

625 W. Main St.   (804) 295-1166
$-$$ MC, VISA

Neon lights decorate this relaxed restaurant on West Main. The place has wonderful desserts, especially the Chocolate Whisper — two layers of chocolate souffle with whipped cream between, topped with chocolate mousse. There's both a set menu and a special menu

estive FARE

CATERING & RENTALS
1745 Allied St.
296-5496

Oregano Joe's

TRADITIONAL ITALIAN CUISINE IN A CASUAL ATMOSPHERE

Lunch/ Dinner/ Take-Out

1252 Emmet St.
971-9308

Visa/MC/Amex/Diners/Disc.

that changes weekly. Entrées include grilled filet of beef with cognac bearnaise and grilled lamb chops with sundried tomatoes, chevre and rosemary purée. Reservations are required for groups of five or more.

THE BOAR'S HEAD INN AND SPORTS CLUB

Rt. 250 West   (804) 296-2181
$$$$ (Old Mill Room)
$$ (The Tavern)   All major credit cards

The Boar's Head Inn's Old Mill Room used to be an actual grist mill. Now it's a formal establishment — one of the few places in the area that requires men to wear jackets in the evenings. Some of the chef's specialties are roasted striped bass with wild greens, crab and a sorrel sauce, and grilled Madison County veal with country ham, leeks and fried tomatoes. A popular dessert is the chocolate pecan tart with bourbon ice cream. The less formal Tavern offers an old English pub-type atmosphere. Reservations are required in the Old Mill Room for dinner and are suggested for lunch. If you want to have lunch or dinner in The Tavern, reservations are suggested. Sunday brunches here are impressive, offering a spread of food that includes omelettes and Belgian waffles made-to-order, pastries, breads, cheeses, smoked fish, breakfast meats and egg dishes.

C AND O RESTAURANT

515 E. Water St.   (804) 971-7044
$$$$ (upstairs dining room)
$$ (Bistro)   MC, VISA

"I can confidently assure you that not since Jefferson was serving imported vegetables and the first ice cream at Monticello has there been more innovative cooking in these parts than at the C&O Restaurant," said William Rice, Editor-in-Chief of *Food and Wine Magazine*.

This celebrated restaurant is proudest of its upstairs dining room, whose menu features such French cuisine as Coquilles St. Jacques au mangue and smoked duck breast with apricots. Dessert offerings on a typical Saturday night include mint chocolate cheesecake and lemon strawberry torte. Reservations are required upstairs, but not in the downstairs Bistro. While more casual, the Bistro's menu also leans toward French cuisine, offering beef tornados with red wine mushroom glaze and sea scallops steamed with grapefruit dijon cream sauce. Hundreds of wines, including some very old ones, are available both upstairs and downstairs.

CLIFTON -- THE COUNTRY INN

Off 250 E., on Rt. 729   (804) 971-1800
$$$$ MC, VISA, AMEX

This elegant, historic inn also has a restaurant that serves a prix-fixe dinner on Wednesday through Sunday nights to some of the most demanding palates in the area. Craig Hartman and Ron Miller, award-winning chefs and graduates of the Culinary Institute of America, are considered masters in the kitchen. Craig's reputation, in fact, earned him an invitation to prepare dinner as guest chef at the James Beard House in New York City last March. He was a resounding critical success, and will appear in an upcoming issue of *Country Inns* magazine.

A typical winter dinner might start with smoked duck, move on to a soup of pureed winter vegetables, a salad of organic greens, continue with a passion-fruit ice and a choice of either rack of veal with wild mushrooms or grilled swordfish, and end with a chocolate terrine.

Reservations are required.

THE COFFEE EXCHANGE
120 East Main   *(804) 295-0975*
$ *MC, VISA*

This bakery/cafe on the downtown mall is an elegant place to hang out, sip coffee, and read the paper or spy on attractive grad students. Coffees from around the world are served all kinds of ways, from cappuccino to frozen mochaccino. This is also a popular lunch spot, serving what some say is the best potato soup money can buy. The cafe also serves salads, sandwiches, light meals, beer, wine and desserts. Unfortunately, it is often short on cookies and pastries in the evenings (the demand is clearly as high as this spot's reputation)...just when you want something to nibble on with that coffee...so go earlier in the day to buy your goodies then hoard them until you have time to sit and drink your java.

COURT SQUARE TAVERN
5th and Jefferson Streets   *(804) 296-6111*
$ *No credit cards*

This bar on historic Court Square is a watering hole for lawyers and other professionals in town. No wonder — there are more than 130 imported bottled beers and Bass, Guiness, Sam Adams and Spaten on tap. You can also enjoy roast beef chili, grilled bratwursts and homemade cheesecake here. The British pub atmosphere features antique mirrors and engravings, a stained glass window and copper-topped bar.

COUPE DE VILLE'S
#9 Elliewood Avenue   *(804) 977-3966*
$ *No credit cards*

This is a hip place that attracts scores of UVA students. The

The Famous Old
HARDWARE STORE
RESTAURANT
A Charlottesville Landmark
Since 1895...
SIMPLY A GREAT PLACE TO EAT.
The Largest, most Imaginative, Popularly Priced Menu in Charlottesville. You'll find Old Favorites as well as Exciting New Dishes, Enormous Deli Sandwiches, Burgers and Salads, Scrumptious Desserts, Generous Mixed Drinks, and our famous "Meters" of Beer. In all—*The Food Is Wonderful*—*The Atmosphere Unique and Relaxed...And You're Sure To Have a Great Time.*

804-977-1518 • 800-426-6001

316 E. Main St. Downtown
Historic District Mall
Visa - MC • Casual Dress

food is inexpensive, but sophisticated. The restaurant serves fresh pasta that's made locally, along with sandwiches, seafood and homemade soups. An acoustic rock band pumps up the volume at 10 PM, except on Wednesday nights, when a country music singer performs (and there's never a cover charge). You can dine indoors or outdoors on the garden terrace (even in the rain since there's an awning) Coupe de Ville's is open every night until 2 AM but closed on Sundays.

DURTY NELLY'S PUB

2200 Jefferson Park Ave.   *(804) 295-1278*
$ *No credit cards*

This is a great place for sandwiches. One of the tastiest is the Lady Godiva, a pita stuffed with turkey, bacon, Muenster, lettuce, tomato, onion and pepper-parmesan dressing. The pub also serves beer, wine and champagne.

THE HARDWARE STORE RESTAURANT

316 E. Main St.   *(804) 977-1518*
$-$$ *MC, VISA*

The Grand Old Hardware Store Building, a city landmark since 1895, houses this restaurant, which offers an astounding variety of foods to suit every palate. You enter the restaurant from either the downtown mall or Water Street. Inside the central dining area, you'll see the same ladders and shelves that belonged to the old hardware store, which operated continuously from 1895 to 1976. This was the original sales area. On the Water Street end of the restaurant, the hardware store's offices have been trans-

formed into dining rooms, and you can see the original typewriters and adding machines used by the store's clerical workers decades ago.

The restaurant is known for its generous portions, whether they be beverages, sandwiches or salads. The menu's backbone is its array of marvelously concocted sandwiches, such as the Pavarotti. This robust creation is a hoagie stuffed with several types of ham, Genoa salami, provolone, onions and peppers. The restaurant also serves barbecued ribs, pasta, mesquite grilled meats and a variety of crepes. If you simply want to satisfy your sweet tooth, there is a vast selection of pastries to choose from, or you can order a malt from the old-fashioned soda fountain. There are many other luscious desserts to choose from.

There is plenty of free parking at the Water Street door. For more information about the shops in the Hardware Store building, see our chapter on Shopping in Charlottesville.

KAFKAFE

20 Elliewood Ave.   *(804) 296-1175*
$-$$ *MC, VISA*

This airy new place is a sophisticated restaurant-cafe-bookstore in one. You could also almost consider it a gallery, with its changing exhibits of works by local artists. You can dine indoors or outside on the patio, and order as little as a cappucino or an appetizer. For the latter, we highly recommend the rich, creamy pate served with olives, capers, cornichons, red onions and French bread. Salads are both creative — combining meats and diverse vegetables, nuts, cheeses or fruits — and generous, a rare combination. One of the most popular entrées is the chicken satay and Szechuan shrimp served with a hot peanut sauce. Desserts are made daily, and include English trifle, Kahlua cheesecake, carrot cake and lots of wicked treats made with Callebaut chocolate from Belgium. The Chocolate Regal, a rich, dense cake served on a pool of raspberry purée, will make your toes curl it's so rich.

Daily newspapers from Madrid, London, Hamburg, Frankfurt and other great cities of the world are also available here. Kafkafe also holds fiction and poetry readings at night on a regular basis.

LITTLE JOHN'S

1427 University Ave.   (804) 977-0588
$ No credit cards

Be it lunchtime or the middle of night, Little John's is the place to go if you've got a hankering for a New York style deli sandwich. Open 24 hours a day, Little John's is conveniently located on "The Corner," a short walk from the Rotunda at U.V.A. Don't miss the Nuclear Sub with cold slaw, turkey, barbeque and mozzarella, or the Baby Zonker, a bagel with cream cheese, bacon, tomatos and onions.

MACADO'S

1505 University Ave.   (804) 971-3558
$ MC, VISA, AMEX

Like its sister restaurants in

PRINCE MICHEL RESTAURANT

Enjoy fine French Cuisine in the congenial ambience of Virginia's leading winery.

Serving lunch 12-2 p.m. Wednesday-Saturday
Dinner 6-9 p.m. Wednesday-Sunday
Located 10 Miles
South of Culpeper on Rt. 29 South

Reservations

1 (800)-800-WINE   (703) 547-9720

Roanoke, Farmville, Radford and elsewhere, this is a casual place to have a sandwich and beer or sundae made with Haagen-Dazs ice cream. It's "on the Corner," close to campus and UVA Hospital.

Maharaja

Seminole Square   (804) 973-1110
$$ VISA, MC, AMEX

If spicy, rich Indian cuisine is your desire, this is the place to dine. Located in the Seminole Square shopping center near Barracks Road, the place has a cozy, but spartan atmosphere. "Curry and spice and everything Indians think nice can be found on this restaurant's extensive menu," wrote one local critic. You'll find a variety of curries and chicken, shrimp and fish tandoori, which means marinated in herbs and spices and grilled in a clay oven, and more. Ginger, garlic, onions, cilantro, lemon, tamarind, cashews, almonds and yogurt are some of the ingredients that are blended together and served with meats, fish or vegetables, making this cuisine exciting to the palate. You can ask for your food to be chili hot, mild or medium temperature. Reservations are suggested for dinner.

Main Street Grill

1329 West Main St.   (804) 977-4885
$ No credit cards

This is a diner for the 90's, with pastel colors and modern art on the walls but good old classic American cooking. Word has it this grill serves the best grilled cheese sandwiches anywhere. Open from 7 AM to 2 AM, the grill welcomes

families, with plenty of high chairs and booster seats for children. Its desserts alone are worth a visit: homemade key lime pie, hot fudge sundaes, mousse cake, and cheesecake imported from the Bronx. The Main Street Grill has live music Thursday through Sunday nights, and serves brunch on Saturdays and Sundays. It's open seven days a week.

Martha's Cafe

11 Elliewood Ave.   (804) 971-7530
$ No credit cards, but personal checks accepted.

This is a highly popular place on "the Corner," and it's no wonder. The food is homemade, interesting and reasonably priced, and the atmosphere is casual but never boring. The place has been around since 1976, and served cappucino long before it was in vogue in this city. The menu emphasizes chicken and fish, and nothing is deep fried. It's known for its crab cakes, but other popular items are barbecued shrimp, jambalaya and spinach lasagna. All the desserts are made at the restaurant, and they include white chocolate mousse with Frangelica and chocolate decadence cake. Children's portions are available, and children and babies are welcome. The cafe is situated in an old house with an enormous elm tree out front. You can dine indoors, or in spring or summer, outdoors on a cobblestone patio under the elm tree.

Inside, weavings from around the world and musical instruments hang from the walls. There's a fireplace in the front room, and a bathtub full of goldfish. Owner Ken Waxman loves to play old jazz on the stereo system. Though the cafe is within walking distance to the UVA campus, it does not necessarily cater to students. The clientele is older — lots of grad students, doctors and professors. As with most of the restaurants on the crowded Elliewood Avenue, you need to park in the centrally located parking garage.

MEMORY & COMPANY
213 Second Street S.W.   (804) 296-3539
$$$ VISA, MC

Owner Ann Memory used to operate a cooking school out of this restaurant, situated in a renovated brick home within walking distance from the downtown mall. Trained at L'Academie De Cuisine in Washington, Memory has established one of the finest restaurants in the city. One room is decorated simply with a colorful quilt hanging from a wall; another small dining room adjoins the open cooking area where Memory does her chopping and sautéeing. In warmer weather, guests can dine outdoors on the patio next to an herb garden.

The menu, which changes weekly, features French country cuisine. Memory uses local produce, game and other ingredients as much as possible. As in the French style, there is a prix fixe for a four-course meal, with a selection of appetizers, entrées, and desserts to choose from. Asparagus tart and strudel of pork and wild mushroom are two typical spring appetizers, and local rabbit Corsican style and veal ragout with carrots two entrées listed on a spring menu. The restaurant also serves brunch on Sundays, and has an award-winning wine list. Reservations are recommended.

MICHIE TAVERN
Thomas Jefferson Parkway   (804) 977-1234
$

At Michie Tavern, a 200-year-old converted log house called "The Ordinary," serves fried chicken, black-eyed peas, stewed tomatoes, cole slaw, potato salad, green bean salad, beets, homemade biscuits, cornbread and apple cobbler every day of the year from 11:30 to 3 PM. Lunch costs $8.95, not including beverage, dessert or tax.

OREGANO JOE'S
1252 Emmet St.   (804) 971-9308
$-$$ VISA, MC

This is a popular, informal Italian restaurant one block north of Barracks Road shopping center. Owners Carl and Victoria Tremaglio and Roberta Corcoran use fresh local ingredients and imported Italian products, making all sauces, soups and dressings from scratch. Daily specials feature fresh seasonal ingredients and often include such seafood as salmon, swordfish, tuna and red snapper. Cappucino, espresso and international coffees are served here, along with Virginia and Italian wines and domestic and imported beer. Children are welcome, and so are take-out orders. Oregano Joe's also serves lunch on weekdays. Tremaglio runs a catering business called "Festive Fare" out of the restaurant which handles everything from formal wedding receptions to picnics and business meetings.

ROCOCO'S

Hydraulic and Commonwealth Roads,
in the Village Green   *(804) 971-7371*
$$ *MC, VISA, AMEX*

This elegant, but casual, Italian restaurant features homemade ravioli, fettucine, stromboli, calzone, gourmet pizza and more. Some of its specialties are the white cheese and pesto pizza and the mesquite grilled half chicken marinated in balsamic vinegar and rosemary. Another favorite is the chocolate toffee ice cream pie. The restaurant has an extensive wine list and a full-service bar. It's open for brunch on Saturdays and Sundays, and the full menu is available for take-out orders. The restaurant accepts reservations for parties of five or more except on weekends after 6 PM, after which no reservations are made.

SAIGON CAFE

1703 Allied Lane   *(804) 296-8661*
$ *MC, VISA*

This is a new restaurant in town, and the first offering Vietnamese cuisine. The atmosphere is easy, comfortable and relaxing. Some of the specialties of the house are the Vietnam egg rolls, grilled lemon chicken and shrimp Saigon style. The soups are especially noteworthy.

SILVER THATCH INN

3001 Hollymead Drive
(at 29 N)   *(804) 978-4686*
$$$$ *MC, VISA*

The menu changes every six weeks or so at this exquisite restaurant in a beautiful old inn (circa 1780). The Silver Thatch serves regional American cuisine, with an emphasis on fresh produce. Two typical entrées are the peppered and charred veal carpaccio with asparagus and mushroom compote and grilled lamb chops with minted apple and roasted corn relish. The wine list is All-American, with an emphasis on California and Virginia. Desserts are all homemade, beautifully presented, and mouth-

RESTAURANT

AND

For the Most Perfect Day... There is Only One Selection.

515 E. Water St.   Charlottesville, VA   (804) 971-7044

watering. The atmosphere is intimate and candlelit, and reservations are recommended.

THE SMOKEHOUSE
16 1/2 Elliewood Ave.   *(804) 977-3024*
$ *No credit cards*

This place offers quick, delicious sandwiches piled with freshly smoked meats. The casual atmosphere attracts lots of tourists and students, who eat outdoors on picnic tables in warm weather. The sandwiches and barbecue here are considered the best in town.

SOUTHERN CULTURE
633 W. Main St.   *(804) 979-1990*
$$ *MC, VISA*

This is a hip cafe and restaurant with delicious food that leans toward the Cajun variety of Southern cuisine. Fettucine Claire, with artichoke hearts, green chilies, red peppers, ricotta, and roasted pecans, is a real hit here, along with the crab and corn chowder and sweet potato fries. The atmosphere is dark and artsy – an exciting place for dining and chatting with good friends or a lover. The bar here appears to be a lively watering hole for intellectuals and artists of all sorts.

ST. MAARTEN'S CAFE
1400 Wertland   *(804) 293-2233*
$$ *MC, VISA, AMEX*

This is a favorite of UVA students—a place to forget your troubles and imagine you're far away on a tropical island. It has a late night menu till 1 AM. The cafe serves lots of fresh seafood and burgers. All the soups are made from scratch

and the cheesecakes are also made on the premises. It's open every night till 2 AM and every day for lunch. St. Maarten's is on "the Corner," near the college campus and hospital.

LE SNAIL
320 W. Main St.   *(804) 295-4456*
$$$$ *All major credit cards*

This is an intimate restaurant with a country French atmosphere. Classic French cuisine is served here, with specialties that include beef Wellington, chateaubriand, crepes suzettes and Caesar salad. Reservations are recommended and jackets are required.

TASTINGS
502 E. Market St. (next to downtown parking deck)   *(804) 293-3663*
$$-$$$ *MC, VISA*

This is a restaurant, wine bar and wine shop combined, run by William Curtis, who also owns the popular Court Square Tavern nearby. You can stop first at the bar and sample a wine to order with your dinner, or simply drink and munch on a few crackers.

The place has a wood grill, which adds a delicate flavor to meats and fish. Foods are straightforward, fresh and deeply satisfying. Crabmeat casserole, grilled salmon with bearnaise sauce and herb crusted rack of lamb are some of the best entrées, and strawberry rhubarb pie is a delicious dessert. There are more than 600 wines in the shop to choose from for dinner. Or you can order a half or full glass from a list of between 80 and 100 wines. Better yet, have Curtis prepare a "flight" of three wines to sample during dinner. Reservations are recommended.

THE VIRGINIAN

1521 W. Main St.   *(804) 293-2606*
$$ *Most major credit cards*

Locals say this restaurant is about the only thing in Charlottesville that hasn't changed over the past decade. But if you assume this is a grits and ham kind of joint, think again. There's no country ham on the menu. Instead, you'll find spinach fettuccine with clam sauce, Boursin and bacon omelettes, couscous salad, stir-fried vegetables and more. The Virginian serves lunch and dinner, brunch on Saturdays and Sundays, and a late night menu from 11 PM to 1 AM every night.

Other restaurants near Charlottesville

PROSPECT HILL

Rt. 3, Box 430,
Trevilians, VA 23093   *(800) 277-0844*
$$$$ *MC, VISA*

This historic plantation inn, located 15 miles east of Charlottesville, houses a beautifully decorated, candlelit restaurant. Classic French cuisine is served here, with Provençal and American accents. A spring dinner menu listed, among its many entrées, tenderloin of beef tornados, served with a port wine, sundried tomato and morel sauce. Or for a lighter dinner, you could have tried the Volaille Farcie au Provence — a chicken breast stuffed with spinach and boursin cheese and served with Provençal sauce. Desserts are also French, and include a chocolate cappuccino mousse and a classic mille feuille, which means 1,000 layers. The fixed price, five-course dinners cost $40 a person, not including wine, taxes or gratuities. The chef will cater to people whose diet is restricted with advance notice. Innkeepers Michael and Laura Sheehan invite dinner guests to arrive one-half hour earlier for a glass of wine or cider and to stroll the grounds or sit by the crackling fire. Reservations are required.

PIG 'N STEAK

17 Valley St.,
Scottsville, VA 24590   *(804) 286-4114*
and Washington St. in
Madison, VA   *(804) 948-3130*
$ *No credit cards*

The Southern Farmers Almanac lists Pig 'N Steak as one of the top 50 barbecue places in the south and one of the top five in Virginia. You can also get real hickory pit smoked ribs here, and steaks, hamburgers and tons of french fries. By the way, this is the home of the original "Dew Drop Inn" mentioned in The Waltons television show. Remember the place? It's where "Jason Walton" used to play the piano. The Pig 'N Steak is closed on Mondays, but open the rest of the week.

Lynchburg

BATEAU LANDING

Main at 12th Street   *(804) 847-1499*
$ *No credit cards*

Lynchburg's historic community market, Bateau Landing, offers a vast array of country fare — fresh eggs, country ham and homemade jams and jellies with breakfast and lunch. Produce changes seasonally. After having a piece of homemade cake, pie or a cookie, browse the market and whet your appetite for shopping. This is truly a fun place for the whole family with ever-changing vendors and seasonal goods. The market is open 8 AM to 2 PM Monday through Friday and Saturdays from 6 AM to 2 PM.

CAFE FRANCE
3225 Old Forest Road (804) 385-9865
$$$ MC, VISA, AMEX

Jazz music helps to create an upbeat atmosphere in this cafe. From the art deco design to the wine bar, this restaurant is fresh and original. Both the lunch and dinner menus are extensive. Lunch calls for sandwiches, soups and burgers. An additional menu is available with the day's specials, which could include a French dip, soft shell crab sandwich or seafood au gratin. There is also a soup, dessert and coffee du jour. The dinner menu is even more varied. Delicious entrées like Jamaican Prime Rib and Cornish Game Hen are available on the standard menu. A special dinner menu with the night's specials is listed as well. Some of their more popular dishes are Rack of Lamb with Pommery mustard and seasoned bread crumbs and Virginia Jumbo lump and backfin crabmeat served with buerre blanc sauce. A deli take-out menu is available as well. Lunch is served Monday through Friday from 11:30 AM to 3 PM. Cafe France is open for

dinner Tuesday through Saturday from 5:30 to 10 PM. Deli take-out is available on Monday from 11 AM to 3 PM and Tuesday through Saturday from 11 AM to 5:30 PM. Reservation are suggested for dinner.

CHARLEYS
3405 Candlers Mountain Road
(804) 237-5988
$ MC, VISA, AMEX

There is always something special going on at Charleys. A new calendar comes out each month with a long list of special happenings. There's live entertainment every Wednesday through Saturday with karaoke on Wednesday, solo artists on Thursday and live bands on Friday and Saturday. Every Tuesday is seniors day and all persons 55+ receive 15 percent off of their entree. There is also a special $.99 children's menu every Sunday through Thursday. The menu is just a varied as the entertainment. You can choose from such favorites as fajitas, seafood fettucini, chicken cordon bleu and beef stroganoff, all homemade. Dining is available in the greenhouse dining room or in the more elegant back room. Open Sunday through Thursday from 11:30 AM to midnight, and Friday and Saturday from 11:30 AM to 2 AM Reservations are suggested for parties of six or more.

CROWN STERLING
6120 Fort Avenue (703) 239-7744
$$ All major credit cards

Experience the tradition of excellence and personal attention established by this charming restaurant. Their steaks are their specialty and are charcoal-broiled. There is also a full salad bar and mixed drinks and wine are available. Open Sunday through Thursday from 6 to 8:30 PM and Friday and Saturday from 6 to 9:30 PM.

CLAYTON'S
3311 Old Forest Road   (804) 385-7900
$ MC, VISA

Clayton's is a casual table service style restaurant. A friendly staff serves up a delicious breakfast and lunch daily, and dinner twice a week. Choose from chicken Tina, grilled marinated shrimp, grilled vegetable sandwich or one of their other tasty sandwiches. There are two hot specials daily. The restaurant is open for breakfast and lunch from 6 AM to 3 PM daily. Dinner is served on Wednesday and Friday from 5 to 9 PM.

EMIL'S
Boonsboro Shopping Center   (804) 384-3311
$$ (cafe) $$$ (rotisserie)All major credit cards

Whether you dine in the informal surroundings of the cafe or in the more elegant rotisserie, Emil's is an excellent choice for fine dining. Each has its own special menu and atmosphere. The cafe is casual and bright with plenty of lovely green plants. Its menu is full of dishes like G'Schnatzlets, roestis, seafood au gratin and crabmeat imperial. The rotisserie is very elegant with candlelight and a white setting. Here you can enjoy Veal Zurich, roast rack of lamb, chateaubriand maison, Norwegian salmon and entrées flambéed tableside. There is also a special lunchtime menu. Indulge yourself

and try one of the many delicious desserts made in Emil's in-house bakery. Open Monday through Saturday from 10 AM to 10 PM.

THE FARM BASKET
2008 Langhorne Road   (703) 528-1107
$ No credit cards

Don't miss the Farm Basket while you're in Lynchburg! Regardless of your age or nature, it's the kind of place that will fascinate you for hours with its shopping opportunities. Then it will amaze you once again with its teeny tiny restaurant that stays packed with locals and others who keep coming back for the homemade food made by cooks who look like your Grandma. The place is famous for its cucumber sandwich on dill bread that melts in your mouth, Gouda cheese biscuits and Brunswick stew. Have a dessert of lemon bread with cream cheese and then go shopping! Lots of Lynchburg matrons stop by this beautiful neighborhood and get box lunches to go. Open daily except Sundays 10 AM to 3 PM.

THE LANDMARK STEAKHOUSE AND LOUNGE
6113 Fort Avenue   (804) 237-1884
$$ Most major credit cards

The Landmark will allow you to have an elegant dinner in a casual atmosphere. The rustic decor of this restaurant will make you feel at home while special touches, like linen tablecloths, will enhance your dining. Their steak and ribs have a terrific flavor because they are cooked over hickory charcoal. You can also choose from chicken and seafood dishes. The restaurant holds an ABC license and there is a full bar and extensive wine list. A no smoking section is also available. Open for lunch from 11:30 AM to 2 PM daily. Dinner is served from 5:30 to 10 PM Sunday through Thursday and 5:30 to 10:30 PM on Friday and Saturday. Reservations are suggested on weekends and during busy seasons (Christmas, prom, etc.).

RED LOBSTER RESTAURANT

3425 Candlers Mountain Road
(804) 847-0178
$$ *Most major credit cards*

A nautical American theme perfectly matches the name of this seafood restaurant, which also has a Roanoke Valley location. Although the restaurant is casual, it is still well suited for business, banquets or special occasions. A traditional array of fine seafood is offered. However, after dinner you may like to try some very creative desserts. Try their Sensational 7 Cake, made with seven different chocolates; the Fudge Overboard, a brownie pie topped with French vanilla ice cream, whipped cream and Hershey's chocolate syrup; or Key Lime Pie. Open Sunday through Thursday 11 AM to 10 PM and 11 AM to 11 PM on Friday and Saturday. Reservations are not accepted but call ahead seating is available.

TEXAS STEAK HOUSE

4001 Murray Pl.   *(804) 528-1134*
$ *Most major credit cards*

A real Texas dinner awaits you at this steak house. A casual setting and a Texas theme set the stage for a delicious dinner. There is a vast variety of delicious foods, but this place is primarily a steakhouse serving up 7 and 9 ounce filets. Try a Yellow Rose of Texas or a Hershey Brownie for dessert. Open 11 AM to 10 PM Monday through Thursday, 11 AM to 11 PM Friday and 4 to 11 PM Saturday. Reservations are not accepted, but call ahead seating is offered.

Smith Mountain Lake Area

BERNARD'S LANDING RESTAURANT

Route 940, Moneta   *(703) 721-3028*
$$ *All major credit cards*

For the finest dining and best view on the lake, Bernard's Landing Restaurant has it all! It's truly a special place well worth the 45-minute drive from Roanoke or Lynchburg. Everything on the menu is a delight. Whether you want a sandwich (try the chicken salad) or a seafood platter of shrimp, scallops, flounder and deviled crab, you can expect a gourmet twist to your order. The Friday night seafood buffet is special and there probably isn't a soul on the lake who hasn't been to Sunday brunch, with waffles and fluffy omelets served to your precise instructions. If you're going to the lake to experience it the way lake fanatics do each weekend, don't miss this dining opportunity. You'll feel like you're in another world with the lake breeze, service by waiters and waitresses dressed in nautical garb, boat decor or outside dining beside the breeze. Open 11 AM to 10 PM Tuesday through Saturday and 11 AM to 3 PM Sundays.

PADDLE WHEEL CRUISES

20 Bridgewater Plaza,
Moneta   *(703) 721-7100*
$$$ *All major credit cards*

Glide across gorgeous Smith Mountain Lake while enjoying some of the best food around. You can ride on the luxurious Virginia Dare, a 19th-century side wheeler, or on the Blue Moon, a 51-foot motor yacht perfect for smaller groups. Bask in the sun on an afternoon cruise or relax with a cocktail or favorite wine while watching the sun set across the lake. Seafood buffets and gourmet food make up the tempting menu. Many trips feature live entertainment to create a festive atmosphere. The cruises run year round, but times vary. Call the company for specific information. This is a wonderful experience for lake lovers. Reservations are required.

COOPERS CORNER

Route 608 & 626,
Huddleston   *(703) 297-7104*
$$ *MC, VISA*

A pleasant setting specializing in German fare, Coopers Corner offers substantial family dining with a complete salad bar and special seafood, country and breakfast buffets. Angel hair pasta selections and chicken dishes are the specialties. Open seven days a week from 7 AM to 9:30 PM.

DUDLEY MART & RESTAURANT

Route 670 & 668, Wirtz   *(703) 721-1635*
$ *No credit cards*

This revamped country school built in 1931 is now home to one of Smith Mountain Lake's most delicious surprises. The homemade BBQ and roasted chicken are worth the trip here and it's a great place for a quick meal while you're touring the lake. Stop by Sunday through Thursday from 7 AM to 8 PM and Friday and Saturday from 7 AM to 9 PM.

SAL'S PIZZA RESTAURANTS

Fairway Village Shopping
Center   *(703) 721-8904*
South Lake Plaza, Union Hall *(703) 576-2263*
$ *MC, VISA*

Homesick Northerners will feel right at home at one of the best restaurants on the lake. Sal's is a family restaurant that you just seem to keep coming back to, whether you order the Italian family's spaghetti and pasta specialities or come for the fantastic salad bar. Naturally, the pizza is just what you'd expect from authentic Italian cuisine. There's an adequate wine list to complement your meal. Kids enjoy their own separate menu too and can choose from their favorite pasta dishes at a reduced price. When you visit on weekends, don't miss the $5 breakfast buffet for a tasty value. Open seven days a week from 6 AM to 10:30 PM.

SCHOONERS RESTAURANT

Route 122 at Hales Ford Bridge,
Moneta   *(703) 721-1752*
$ *No credit cards*

Whether you're driving down route 122 or cruising across the beautiful lake, Schooners is a casual and friendly stop for lunch or dinner. You can eat inside or sit outside under sun umbrellas until their loudspeaker announces your order is ready. This little nook near Hales

Ford Bridge is often chocked full of locals and visitors. In addition to Greek foods and rib eye steak, this restaurant makes some of the best pizza and hamburgers known to the Blue Ridge. Their hamburger meat is ground fresh and pattied daily, so you never get frozen burgers! Their mouth-watering pizza is created from scratch at the time of your order. The fresh tomatoes on cheese pizza add a special touch you can't find anywhere else on the lake. Open seven days a week from 10:30 AM to 10:30 PM.

Franklin County

OLDE VIRGINIA BARBECUE
108 Meadowview Street,
Rocky Mount   (703) 489-1788
$ MC, VISA

Come discover the most succulent pork, beef ribs and chicken barbecue in the county. This restaurant, a county landmark, has created their own Olde Virginia Barbecue Sauce and is a favorite hang-out for the Franklin County crowd. You've just never tasted better barbecued chicken and ribs than this place serves and people who don't even like coleslaw can't believe what Olde Virginia's tastes like – real Southern coleslaw that's irrestistable! Children have their own menu as well, with $3.95 specials. Open seven days a week from 11 AM to 9 PM.

Bedford County

BEDFORD STATION RESTAURANT
515 Bedford Avenue,
Bedford   (703) 586-6600
$$ MC, VISA, AMEX

This unique restaurant, located in a beautifully restored train station, is a perfect start to an excursion on the town to see Bedford's historic attractions. The exterior of this authentic old station is exactly the same as it was years ago. The tracks are still outside and trains run by daily. The interior has been revamped, but there are still antiques from the station left inside. Enjoy a wonderfully varied menu including a prime rib buffet, pasta, steak and seafood. The restaurant is able to handle large parties. Open for lunch from 11:30 AM to 2 PM Monday through Saturday. Dinner is served from 5 to 9 PM Monday through Thursday and from 5 to 10 PM on Friday and Saturday. Brunch is served from 11 AM to 3 PM on Sundays. (The restaurant is closed on Sundays during the summer.) Reservations are recommended.

New River Valley Region

Blacksburg

ANCHY'S
1600 N. Main Street   (703) 951-2828
$ MC, VISA, AMEX

A relaxing family atmosphere surrounds you as you dine in this college-town favorite. The menu consists of Euro-Asian favorites and treats like fresh seafood and steaks. Open 11 AM to 10 PM Tuesday through Friday, 4 to 10 PM Saturday and 10 AM to 9 PM Sunday. Reservations are suggested.

BOGEN'S

622 N. Main Street   (703) 953-2233
$ All major credit cards

Probably the most popular restaurant with both the college crowd and business people, Bogen's slogan is "Casual with Class." You can enjoy inexpensive food served in a great atmosphere. That includes gourmet sandwiches, charbroiled steaks, spicy BBQ ribs and chicken and tempting seafood. To top it off, get cappuccino and one of their outrageous ice cream desserts, sky high and wonderful! Open 11 AM to 1 AM Thursday through Sunday and until 2 AM Friday and Saturday.

BUDDY'S RESTAURANT

130 Jackson Street   (703) 552-6423
$ MC, VISA

Share a laugh with friends at this restaurant and comedy club in the heart of Blacksburg. You'll enjoy comedians and live music nightly in down to earth surroundings. The menu is full of favorites like hickory smoked barbecue sandwiches, buffalo wings, Buddy burgers and even Buddy's beer. Buddy's is open seven days a week from 11:30 AM to 3 AM

CRICKETT'S

216 N. Main Street   (703) 951-4003
$ Most major credit cards

Blacksburg's downtown college community is a sure place to find friendly faces, delicious food

and plenty of fun. A rustic setting gives you a warm atmosphere for dining at Crickett's. Sample such delights as live Maine lobster, charcoal steaks, Calamari and chocolate truffle mousse pie. Also try their famous Greek pasta. The restaurant is open 4 PM to 1:30 AM Monday through Saturday. Reservations are accepted but not required.

HOLIDAY INN BLACKSBURG

3503 S. Main Street   (703) 951-1330
$$ All major credit cards

Dine in Vicker's Switch while visiting the beautiful Holiday Inn Blacksburg. Conveniently located on Main Street, this restaurant has a comfortable atmosphere and a friendly staff which will make dining a pleasure. Taste their St. Louis barbecue pork, prime rib or bacon wrapped scallops. They're open Monday through Saturday 11:30 AM to 2:00 PM and 4:30 to 10 PM and Sunday 6:30 AM to 2 PM and 4:30 to 10 PM and reservations are suggested on special dates.

JACOB'S LANTERN

At the Marriott,
900 Price Fork Road   (703) 552-7001
$$ All major credit cards

Offering both fine dining with tableside service, Jacob's Lantern emphasizes excellence. Whether having a light meal or a complete dinner, both the food and service are consistently good. Open for breakfast and lunch from 6:30 AM to 2 PM and dinner from 5 to 10 PM seven days a week.

PEKING PALACE RESTAURANT

235 N. Main Street   (703) 552-4400
$ MC, VISA

For authentic Chinese cuisine in an elegant setting, you can't beat this restaurant in the heart of Blacksburg. Sample some of their delicious dinners like Hunan Double Delight, Dragon & Phoenix, General Tso's Chicken and Orange Beef. Also available on the menu are special selections for health minded diners, prepared in compliance with the guidelines of the American Heart Association. The dishes marked are lower in fat, cholesterol and calories and contain no MSG. These include Hawaii Chicken, Sizzling Triple Delight and Honolulu Scallops. The restaurant is open 11 AM to 11 PM Reservations are necessary for large groups.

SUNRISE HOUSE CHINESE RESTAURANT

1602 S. Main Street   (703) 552-1191
$ MC, VISA, AMEX

Another top notch Chinese restaurant in Blacksburg, the atmosphere at Sunrise is relaxing and makes for an enjoyable experience. Feast on Crabmeat Lagoon, General Tso's Chicken, Triple Delight and Hawaii Five "O." Prices are very reasonable. Open seven days a week from 11:30 AM to 1:30 AM. Reservations are accepted but not necessary.

Christiansburg

THE FARMHOUSE

Cambria Street   (703) 382-4253
or (703) 382-3965
$$$ Most major credit cards

Exceptional service is a trademark of this authentic farmhouse-turned-restaurant. The farmhouse was part of an estate built in the 1800s. It was opened as a restaurant in 1963, and in the early 1970s, an old train caboose was added for an even more unique dining experience. Now the staff provides their famous southern hospitality to all types of customers: families, corporate executives and college students. The rustic setting lends the perfect atmosphere to a first date or a 50th anniversary. The farmhouse is decorated with both antiques and country furnishings. The menu is full of country-style favorites such as prime rib, jumbo-size ocean shrimp cocktail, steak and their famous Farmhouse onion rings. A separate children's menu is available. The Farmhouse is open from Monday to Friday 5 to 11 PM and Sunday from noon to 9 PM.

THE HUCKLEBERRY

2790 Roanoke Street   (703) 381-2382
$$$ Most major credit cards

Convenient and luxurious, this restaurant is located near I-81 and several hotels in the Christiansburg area. Two lounges, Whispers and Sundance, offer Top-40 and Country and Western entertainment. Their succulent barbecue items are slow-cooked in "the finest hickory-smoking oven money can buy." The restaurant also guarantees the high quality and freshness of its beef. Choose from baby back ribs, dijon chicken, filet mignon and broiled lobster tail. There is also a special children's menu. Senior citizens receive a 15% discount on all entrées. Open daily 6:30 AM to 10 PM.

STONE'S CAFETERIA

| 1290 Roanoke Street | (703) 382-8970 |
| $ | No credit cards |

A long-time favorite with locals and tourists alike, Stone's gives you real country food as fast as you can go through the cafeteria line to get it. Lovers of dishes such as fried chicken, greens, mashed potatoes and pinto beans will be in their glory, both when they taste and when they pay. Open 6 AM to 7:30 PM Monday through Saturday.

THE OUTPOST

| US 460 and Rt. 11 off I-81 | (703) 382-9830 |
| $$$ | All major credit cards |

Since 1960, lovers of Lebanese food have been flocking to The Outpost every Wednesday for Lebanese Night. Other nights, The Outpost is full of people looking for their chicken, seafood, spaghetti and real Italian pizza. Imported beer, wines and cocktails top off a fine meal with excellent service. Open 4:30 until 11 PM Tuesday through Saturday.

Radford

BEST WESTERN RADFORD INN

| 1501 Tyler Avenue | (703) 639-3000 |
| $$ | All major credit cards |

Hunter's Restaurant is a warm, pleasant experience, with fireside dining and delicious food. It is open daily for breakfast, lunch, dinner and cocktails. Dux & Company Lounge is the gathering spot for the New River Valley. Enjoy live entertainment over generous cocktails and tasty hors d'oeuvres. The lounge is open nightly from 4 PM until everyone goes home! The restaurant is open for breakfast and lunch from 6:30 AM to 2 PM Monday through Friday and from 7 AM until 2 PM on Saturday and Sunday. Dinner is served from 5 to 9 PM daily.

GALLERY CAFE

| 1115 Norwood Street | (703) 731-1555 |
| $$ | MC, VISA |

Radford's trendiest restaurant, Gallery Cafe stays full with professionals and students who enjoy artfully prepared international cuisine served in a casual and memorable gallery setting. With a recent renovation from an old department store, what once was the Gallery Cafe Restaurant is now divided into Gallery Cafe, Books and More and Hot Chilies Restaurant and Bar. There's a variety of fresh ground and brewed gourmet coffees as well as pastries, fancy foods and a great selection of magazines and books. Hot Chilies downstairs has a southwest accent with an eclectic flair. The menu features selections by a vegetarian chef as well as owner Charlie Whitescarver, a three-time winner of the Virginia State Championship Chili Cookoff contest. Three types of hot sauces are on each table to challenge the meek or satisfy the bold. The Norwood Room is an elegantly appointed room and the Garden Room is an open area with soft music, serving a buffet lunch Monday through Friday. Soups, salads and sandwiches are available. It's the perfect place for a relaxing lunch; a haven from the rat race. Open for lunch Monday through Saturday from 11:30 AM to 3 PM. Dinner is served from 5 to 9 PM on Wednesday and Thursday and from 5 until 10 PM on Friday and Saturday. Brunch is served on Sunday.

MACADO'S RESTAURANT AND DELICATESSEN

510 Norwood Street   *(703) 731-4879*
$$ *Most major credit cards*
One of a chain of family-owned restaurants at various locations in the Blue Ridge, including Roanoke and Blacksburg, Radford's restaurant offers a fun alternative to any other type of dining in the New River Valley. Macado's is popular both with students and professionals for its overstuffed sandwiches and unique, antique and collectibles-filled decor. Gourmet items from many nations are available including cheese, wine and fine candies. Open 9 AM to 1 AM Sunday through Thursday and 9 AM to 2 AM Friday and Saturday.

Giles County

MOUNTAIN LAKE

Route 700, Mountain Lake   (703) 626-7121
                 or 1-800-346-3334
$$$ *All major credit cards*
If dining in absolutely gorgeous surroundings is your idea of a great evening, as many from nearby Virginia Tech do, then you should drive seven miles up the winding mountain, the second highest in Virginia, to Mountain Lake. This 2600-acre paradise is the home of the movie "Dirty Dancing" and that glorious scenery wasn't designed in the prop room. For miles, all you will see are tall trees, rolling hills, beautiful wildflowers and a clear mountain lake. And as if that wasn't enough, the dining is out of this world.

The elegant atmosphere matches the outstanding cuisine, which changes daily, and may include chilled blackberry soup, sauteed shiitake mushrooms, London Broil Madeira or Red Snapper with pecan butter. Breakfast could be a Giles County Platter of country favorites or Appalachian buttermilk pancakes. Call ahead to find out what culinary pleasures await you. Reservations are important, since guests dine there too as part of their resort stay.

Floyd County

BLUE RIDGE RESTAURANT

113 East Main Street   (703) 745-2147
$ *No credit cards*
Lunch time regulars and those just passing through will find plenty of friendly faces here. Generous servings and "real honest to goodness food" are awaiting discovery at this hometown restaurant in the heart of Floyd. They boast real mashed potatoes — not instant, and pinto beans that are always soaked, dried beans — not canned. Choose from delicious country style meals such as hotcakes, country

ham, grilled tenderloin and fried squash. There is also a special children's dinner plate at a reduced price. Open Monday through Saturday 5:30 AM to 8 PM and Sunday 7:30 AM to 8 PM May to October.

CHATEAU MORRISETTE

Meadows of Dan   (703) 593-2865
$$ All major credit cards

World-class Virginia wines are produced from this small family owned winery in the Rocky Knob growing district. Founded in 1978, this winery is small enough to remain in the family, yet large enough to produce several different varieties of award winning wines. At the restaurant at Chateau Morrisette, called Le Chien Noir, you can dine on both American and International cuisine in an elegant Old World atmosphere. Their special Jazz on the Lawn events are reminiscent of a Monet painting of a French picnic and the price is right at $5 a plate. Visitors are welcome to tour the facilities, sample the wines and enjoy a light meal surrounded by the magnificent Blue Ridge Mountains. Open for lunch from 11 AM to 2 PM Wednesday through Saturday and from 11 AM to 3 PM on Sunday. Dinner is served on Friday and Saturday evenings from 6 to 9 PM Reservations are requested.

PINE TAVERN

Floyd   (703) 745-4482
$$ No credit cards

Live music and theater are reason enough to lure one to Pine Tavern. Dinner theater is performed on Tuesday evenings for a price of $4, which is added to the price of dinner. Dinner is served before the show, and dessert and coffee are available during the intermission or after the show. Special nonsmoking evenings are set aside for those who would not be able to attend otherwise. Live music is played in the dining room on Saturday evenings. Various bands from the area perform and the Dave Figg Quartet plays jazz here several times a month. The menu is full of delectable dishes such as lasagna, eggplant parmigiana, Szechuan tofu and baby ganouj. Organic and locally grown vegetables are used whenever available. For the vegetarian, there is a special menu which includes vegetable stir-fry, black bean chili and French onion soup, which are all made with meatless recipes. The chef even uses separate cutting boards for vegetables and a separate deep fry with vegetable oil which is used for veggies only. Open Wednesday and Thursday 5 to 10 PM, Friday and Saturday noon for lunch and 5 to 10 PM for dinner, and Sundays 2 to 9 PM. Reservations are suggested on Fridays, Saturdays and holidays.

Pulaski County

NEW RIVER CRUISE COMPANY

Howe House Visitor's Center Dock,
Claytor Lake   (703) 674-9344
$$$ MC, VISA

Take a ride on the Pioneer Maid across stunning Claytor Lake and enjoy authentic foods made with recipes from our Colonial past. This vessel can provide a fully enclosed deck and an open starlight deck due to its size, which is 60 feet long and 18 feet wide. Each day, the boat departs from the Visitor's Center dock and cruises down the New River at approximately 5 m.p.h. There is a narrative of historical points along the world's second oldest river. Lunch cruises feature deli sandwiches and fresh salads. The Moonlight Dinner/Dance cruise is called "Virginia is for Lovers." Local talent performs for dancing under the stars. The dinner menu features such items as George Washington Ham, Thomas Jefferson Fried Chicken, cooked greens with garlic and tomato and Virginia Spoon Bread. The cruises are two relaxing hours of drifting through the fantastic Blue Ridge Mountains. Office hours are 9 AM to 5:30 PM Tuesday through Sunday. Reservations are required.

DAYNELL'S DELIGHT

Pulaski Main Street   (703) 980-2437
$ No Credit Cards

While visiting the newly-refurbished Pulaski Main Street to shop and Gallery-hop, take a refreshing break at Daynell's, between the Historic Courthouse and Theatre buildings. An unpretentious place, you can order up some pinto beans and cornbread or a super sub. Breakfast features scrumptious biscuits of tenderloin, tomato, smothered with gravy. It's every parent's delight. Kids can get mini corn dogs and beverages in a training cup. For dessert, order an old-fashioned banana split or Otis Spunk Meyer cookies. Don't ask what these cookies are, because you've just got to try them for yourself! Open weekdays 7 AM - 8 PM

and Saturdays from 11 AM to 5 PM. Closed Sunday.

VALLEY PIKE INN

Old Wilderness Trail,
Newbern   (703) 674-1810
$ MC, VISA

The charm and history of this beautiful old inn is reason enough to come visit. Built before 1839, this stagecoach inn and tavern has always been a welcome stop for weary travelers on the Old Wilderness Trail. This center of hospitality was once known as the "Famous Haney Inn," named after its owners John "the Jolly Irishman" and his wife, Cornelius Haney. At the turn of the century, this hotel was a home. In 1974, the property was purchased, renovated and renamed. In 1989, Marilyn Rutland, a prominent Louisiana belle, fell in love with the area and purchased the home. The Inn is decorated with sconce lights and a chandelier and dried Virginia wildflowers. Church pews were used to make the tables and all of the doors and windows are from a structure built in 1834.

All meals are prepared and cooked from scratch and the menu includes fried chicken, roast beef, country ham, spiced apples and homemade biscuits. You can also sample delicious Virginia wines with your meal. Summer hours (May through October) are from 4:30 PM to 9:00 PM Thursday, Friday and Saturday, and from 11:30 AM to 6:00 PM on Sunday. Winter hours (November through April) are 4:30 to 8:00 PM Thursday and Friday, 4:30 to 9:00 PM Saturday, and 11:30 AM to 6:00 PM Sunday.

Alleghany Highlands Region

Alleghany County

THE CAT & OWL STEAK AND SEAFOOD HOUSE
Low Moor Exit off I-64   (703) 962-9961
$$ All major credit cards

Antiques create the scene as you dine in this beautifully remodeled home. This steak and seafood house has a Victorian atmosphere which will please the eye as well as the palate. There is a wide selection of tasty dishes including their popular charbroiled shrimp, filet mignon and fresh tuna steak. Finish off your meal with delicious banana fritters. The restaurant is open Monday through Saturday from 5-10 PM. Reservations are suggested, and you can make them by calling (703) 862-5808.

DOUTHAT PARK RESTAURANT
Route 1, Clifton Forge   (703) 862-5856
$ No credit cards

This historic landmark is a vision of rustic beauty. The casual dining area has high beamed ceilings and a large gorgeous fireplace. A big porch overlooks a beautiful clear lake. Try their sandwich menu for lunch or their special buffets for dinner. Wednesday night there is a delicious Italian buffet and a tasty seafood buffet is featured on Friday nights. Open seven days from 11 AM to 8 PM.

EAGLE'S NEST RESTAURANT
Route 311, Crows   (703) 559-9738
$$$ MC, VISA

At Eagle's Nest, established in 1930, you can enjoy gourmet dining on a deck overlooking a waterfall! You'll feel like you're dining in Frank Lloyd Wright's private home. The nature lover and the adventurous tourist will love this place, in the middle of practically nowhere (about two hours from Roanoke west, 20 minutes from White Sulphur Springs, W.Va. east), and one of the most intriguing in the entire Blue Ridge! In an ancient log cabin decorated with antiques, beside a breathtaking waterfall filled with trout and ducks, you'll see purple irises lining the top of the falls, and overstuffed felines (the restaurant's charity cases) roaming the mountain crags seventy feet straight up. The scenery alone makes this place one you won't forget. But, nothing about the food is forgettable either!

Served on country blue speckled metal plates, dinners may be international in flavor one day, with a cucumber and mint salad, or fresh brook trout the next. Salads may be mandarin orange with pecan and the soup may be cream of leek. A full complement of house wines is available. The service, by fresh-faced country waitresses, is impeccable. This isn't just dining, it's an experience anyone in love with the Blue Ridge shouldn't miss. Fidgety children might not do well here, since nobody is in a hurry. The restaurant is open daily 5 to 10 PM and Sunday from 3 to 9 PM.

HOLIDAY INN
Route 60 & 220,
Covington   (703) 962-4951
$$ All major credit cards

A relaxing atmosphere and top-notch service accompany a meal at this restaurant. Choose from steak, seafood and other American favorites. Open seven days from 6 AM to 10 PM.

IMPERIAL WOK
348 W. Main Street,
Covington   (703) 962-3330
$ MC, VISA

A Chinese restaurant of high caliber, Imperial Wok is a favorite of Covington residents and is known for its quality for miles around. The more popular dishes include the Seafood Delight, chicken and shrimp combo and the mixed vegetables with shrimp. Another favorite is the Happy Family meal, which is made with chicken, beef, pork, shrimp and fresh vegetables. Open from 11:30 AM to 9 PM Tuesday through Thursday.

JAMES BURKE HOUSE EATERY
232 Riverside Street,
Covington   (703) 965-0040
$ MC, VISA

Stop in here for breakfast or lunch. The James Burke House Eatery serves soups, sandwiches, salads and desserts. They are open from 9 AM to 3 PM daily (closed Sunday).

MARION'S CAFE
804 S. Highland Avenue,
Covington   (703) 962-5022
$ No credit cards

Marion's serves terrific home cooked meals in a comfortable atmosphere. Their specialties are homemade pies and German dishes. The cafe is open from 5 AM to 10 PM every day.

Bath County

CAFE ALBERT
Cottage Row, Hot Springs   (703) 839-5500
$$ MC, VISA, AMEX

Come discover this small, intimate cafe in Hot Springs. Continental breakfasts and light lunches are offered, as well as a wide assortment of freshly baked breads, pastries and cookies from the Homestead kitchens. You can start off your day with fresh berries, sliced banana with cream or melon. Then try the scrambled eggs "Western Style" with cheddar cheese and fresh fruit, served with toast. Or sample the Cafe's Crepe Albert, paper-thin crepes with fluffy scrambled eggs and tomato butter sauce served with smoked sugar-cured ham.

Cafe Albert's lunch menu is just as wonderful as the breakfast. While waiting for your lunch, the cafe offers you its own Strawberry Spritzer or Virginia Apple Cider Cooler. You have a choice of sandwiches, like hot corned beef or chicken salad, all served on rye, white, whole wheat, brioche or croissant according to your preference. You will also receive your choice of macaroni, potato, fruit or tortellini salad, cole slaw or cottage cheese. Their lunch entrées include Spinach Salad Supreme, with mushrooms, chopped bacon, egg, croutons and nuts, Virginia's Highland County smoked beef frank with chili, sauerkraut and relish, and the Cafe's Shenandoah Croissant, a thinly sliced breast of turkey with spinach leaves on a Homestead croissant with watercress spread, pepper jelly and potato salad. Top off a great lunch with something tasty from the dessert menu like a soda float or a banana split. The cafe is open year round 9 AM to 6 PM and outdoor service is available in warm weather.

CASCADES CLUB RESTAURANT
Cascades Golf Course,
Route 220   *(703) 839-5670*
$ *MC, VISA, AMEX*
You don't even have to be an Arnold Palmer wanna-be to appreciate the beautiful scenery at the Cascades. You'll be dining in the clubhouse of this 18-hole masterpiece, rated as one of the top 30 golf courses in the United States. Light lunches and sandwiches are prepared from April through October, 11:30 AM to 5 PM daily.

THE CASINO
Homestead Grounds,
Hot Springs   *(703) 839-5500*
$$$$ *MC, VISA, AMEX*
Dining out on the lawn in view of the beautiful tennis courts, or indoor dining are both options at this elegant restaurant. You can treat yourself to the buffet luncheon, sandwich service or a champagne brunch while relaxing in style. Open April through October, the buffet luncheon is served from noon until 2 PM, sandwich service is from 2:30 to 5 PM and beverages are served noon to 6 PM. Sunday champagne brunch is served 11 AM to 2:30 PM.

THE GRILLE
The Homestead,
Hot Spring   *(703) 839-5500*
$$$$ *MC, VISA, AMEX*
If you're looking to get "all dressed up and go" — coat and tie are required — you'll appreciate the fabulous setting and gourmet dining found at the Homestead. Delicious dishes for lunch, dinner or late supper are served. From April through October, lunch is served from noon until 2 PM, dinner from 7 PM and late supper from 10 PM until midnight. Reservations are required.

THE HOMESTEAD DINING ROOM
The Homestead,
Hot Springs   *(703) 839-5500*
$$$$ *MC, VISA, AMEX*
Exquisite dining and dancing with dinner are featured at the world renowned Homestead. Ladies and gents are expected to dress for dinner, which is served from 7 to 8:30 PM. Breakfast is served from 7:30 until 9:30 AM; reservations are required for dinner.

LOWER CASCADES CLUB RESTAURANT
Lower Cascades Golf Course, Route 687,
Hot Springs   *(703) 839-5667*
$$ *MC, VISA, AMEX*
Overlook the beautiful Lower Cascades Golf Course while lunching in this clubhouse, six miles south of Hot Springs. If you time it right, you can enjoy the sandwich service before or after playing this world famous course. The restaurant is open from 11:30 AM to 5 PM April

through October.

SAM SNEAD'S TAVERN
Main Street,
Hot Springs   *(703) 839-7666*
$$ *MC, VISA, AMEX*

For a taste of Colonial Virginia, visit this tribute to Hot Springs' living legend and native son. An historic old bank building houses the tavern where lunch and dinner are served to a golf theme. The menu lists the foods as chip shots (appetizers), from the halfway house (sandwiches, burgers and light offerings), water hazards (fish), the main course (meat entrées), handicaps (desserts) and from the 19th hole (beverages). Appetizers include lump crabmeat cocktail, spinach salad and chili con carne. Light fare includes a seafood taco salad, the "Sam" burger and a delicious golden fried breast of chicken sandwich. Fresh Virginia Allegheny Mountain rainbow trout from Highland County and fresh swordfish steak are examples of the fish menu. Try the medallion of veal, a tender loin of veal sautéed and dressed with lemon butter sauce or the Tavern's hickory smoked barbecued spareribs and chicken. The tempting dessert menu will have you asking for more parfait creme de menthe, fudge fantasy (a freshly baked brownie with vanilla ice cream and hot fudge sauce) or a chocolate nut sundae. Then, you'd better hit the course for real... walking... not in the cart! Seasonal entertainment is offered. Homemade meals are served daily from 11:30 AM to 11 PM.

THE WATERWHEEL RESTAURANT
The Inn at Gristmill Square,
Warm Springs   *(703) 839-2231*
$$$ *MC, VISA, Discover*

Continental cuisine is served in the setting of an old mill here. This area, composed of restored 19th-century buildings, is full of rustic beauty. The restaurant's delicious fresh trout is a favorite. Visit for dinner Sunday through Thursday 6 to 9 PM and Friday and Saturday from 6 to 10 PM, or for brunch on Sunday, 11 AM to 2 PM.

Highland County

HIGHLAND INN
Monterey   *(703) 468-2143*
$$ *MC, VISA*

This historic inn is a wonderful setting for a delicious dinner in casual elegance. Formerly known as the Hotel Monterey, this three-story landmark is one of the few mountain resorts of its size still in operation in Virginia. Lace curtains, candlelight and classical music set the mood for your evening of dining. Choose from their menu featuring a variety of tempting dinners including local fresh mountain trout and grilled Brace of Quail. But be sure to leave room for their Maple Pecan Pie made rich with Highland County maple syrup—simply delicious. The Inn is open for dinner 6 to 8 PM Wednesday through Saturday and for brunch from 11:30 AM to 2:00 PM on Sunday.

Inside
Night Life

*P*eople don't come to the Blue Ridge of Virginia for the night life. Usually, instead it's to get away from big crowds, hustle and bustle and smoke-filled rooms. A survey of community leaders pretty much bears this out. Nobody seems to miss "night prowling" too much because there's so much to do and see during the daytime. Everybody who does miss it has moved, or is thinking about moving, to Washington, D.C. or Charlotte, N.C.

There are those who would argue with this premise, however, and indeed there is one very chatty, trendy monthly publication, *V Magazine*, that covers the night life in the middle Blue Ridge area. You'd do well to get a copy by calling (703) 343-5138 before visiting Charlottesville, Lexington, Roanoke, Staunton, Lynchburg or the New River Valley. You'll also find "*V*" at most all the "in" places to be.

The exceptions to this in-bed-at-a-reasonable-hour syndrome are the clubs in the college towns of Charlottesville and the New River Valley, the metropolitan areas of Roanoke and Lynchburg, and big resorts such as The Homestead, Greenbrier and Boar's Head Inn,

which offer something for everyone. Another exception would be Cockram's General Store in Floyd County, where everybody comes Friday nights for miles around for a real hoedown.

Shenandoah Valley Region

HARRISONBURG

We'll start our meandering journey in search of the big thrill and bright lights in Harrisonburg. Clayborne's (703-432-1717) at 221 University Blvd. is decorated with palm trees, water falls and skylights. This restaurant and bar with a dance floor is a popular night spot for James Madison University students. Occasionally live bands perform. On Main Street you will also find several popular spots — Joker's (703-432-6333), a downtown nightclub with live music and dancing, and JM's Pub and Deli (703-433-8537), with a big dance floor and either a DJ or a live band.

In the Sheraton Hotel on E. Market Street, you'll find Scruple's (that is, if you're behaving...703-433-2521). This lounge offers disc jockey-guided music every night except Thursday night, when there's a popular comedy club. Tully's Restaurant & Pub, located behind the Valley Mall (703-433-5151) is a restaurant well known for its baby back ribs and for drawing in the 25 to 40 crowd on the weekends for music and dancing with a DJ. College students flock to the place on Wednesdays, which is both Ladies Night and Karioke Night. If you're not yet familiar with this new form of entertainment, it's when common folk like you and me get to stand on stage and make a fool of ourselves singing solo to popular hits. Tully's also has live music on Thursday nights.

STAUNTON

Heading on down to Staunton, night prowlers will find that the action takes on a more refined air — which is just fine with most of us...most of the time. For a relaxing drink in an equally relaxing atmosphere, the Belle Grae Inn on Frederick Street (703-886-5151), a restored Victorian mansion, is a popular choice. The lounge in this historic downtown inn and restaurant has classical and jazz music on occasion. The decor is sophisticated and so is the service. We can't say enough about the Belle Grae! You'll have to experience this gem for yourself. For more action, head to McCormick's Pub and Restaurant on Augusta and Frederick streets (703-885-3111). This restaurant has a small dance floor and occasional live music. It becomes a cabaret with dinner theater performances during the winter months by ShenanArts, a local theatrical group. The piano lounge at the Sheraton Hotel (703) 248-6020 offers light background music for relaxing entertainment. Then, in the downtown area, 23 Beverley (703-885-5053), the new chic restaurant, is becoming a cultural watering hole, offering occasional art openings with live music and appetizers. The bar brings in blues, jazz and other live music on Thursday nights. Also try the new Mill Street Grill (703) 886-0656 with open mike Fridays. Mill Street Grill is located in the heart of the renovated downtown. It's a cozy restaurant in an enchanting old converted grist mill, the historic White Star Mill Building. The second floor is the Wharf Gallery.

LEXINGTON

In Lexington and Rockbridge County, local night-owls head for The Palms (463-7911), a rowdy downtown bar and restaurant with a big screen TV and juke box. This is a popular college hang-out, but local yokels also feel at home here.

A quieter, more sophisticated alternative is Harb's Bistro on West Washington Street, which serves wine, beer, cappuccino and extraordinary desserts (as well as a full menu). The patio makes for a perfect place to sip a cool drink on a hot summer night.

These days a younger crowd flocks to Sharks on East Nelson for a night of pool. Adjacent to Sharks is another new nightspot, The Bone, which features live music, a bar, and a decent dinner menu.

Without question the most exciting nightlife in Lexington in the summer happens at the outdoor Lime Kiln Theater (see our

Arts and Culture chapter). The Sunday Night Concert Series draws huge crowds to hear reggae, bluegrass or folk music. Most every other night Lime Kiln Theatre stages a play whose theme relates in some way to the culture of the Southern Mountains. Lime Kiln has great picnic spots for dining before the performances.

Visitors should also check with the Lexington Visitors Bureau to find out about other plays and concerts at Washington and Lee's Lenfest Center and other sites around town.

ROANOKE VALLEY AREA

Things definitely start getting livelier if you drive an hour south to the Roanoke Valley. Forget the bedroom communities of Botetourt and Craig counties, though—everybody's home with their families or sleeping or else moved here to get away from noise. However, you can find others with insomnia, or rub shoulders with young people on dates or the newly single seeking to be double at a variety of nightspots in this area.

A real gem, unique to the Blue Ridge, is Groucho's (703-982-5693), a combination comedy club/restaurant that has hosted some of the biggest names in comedy since it started business a decade ago. Located in downtown Roanoke on the City Market, Groucho's is a really fun place to go to get rid of the week's stress. The food is great, too. There's dancing every Wednesday and Thursday after the comedians perform.

If you're going to go bar-hopping in Roanoke, there are some very nicely appointed ones such as Charades (703-563-9300) at the Marriott off I-581 on Hershberger Rd., an action lounge with dancing, promotions and a hungry hour buffet. The Elephant Walk (703-774-4400) at 4368 Starkey Road, close to Tanglewood Mall, is also very popular. Scooch's, (703)-362-4065), 5010 Williamson Road, is one of Roanoke's oldest rock n' roll bars, close to Hollins College. But fellas, you can forget about picking up a Hollins girl here, because most of them are at private fraternity parties at the all-male enclaves of VMI or Washington & Lee and Hampden Sydney. There's a pool tournament every Thursday. Jazz-lovers congregate at Lowell's Restaurant and Lounge (703)-344-4884 at 2328 Melrose Ave. NW. At Lowell's, you'll think you're in New York City with R&B, soul, jazz and a DJ to spin out the music on Friday and Saturday. For real atmosphere, don't miss the Iroquois Club (703)-982-8979 at 324 Salem Ave. Downtown. There's a real variety of music and foot stomping or slam dancing. Big counterculture names are frequently booked here. It's a truly interesting place, considered to be one of the most "hip" in town with the younger set.

You can enjoy a quiet, inspirational moment (no children allowed) at the Third St. Coffeehouse, located in Old Southwest at the lower level of Trinity Methodist Church, Third St. and Mountain Ave. It's a throwback to the coffeehouses of the 60s, and you'll find many people from that era soaking up the good Karma amidst guitar-plucking and poetry readings.

In Salem, you can go to Cheers (703-389-4600) at Rt. 419 and Braeburn Drive, for three years voted "Roanoke's Best Bar." If Country Western dancing is your thing, wear your two-step dancing boots to The Top Rail (703-389-0917) at 1106 Kessler Rd. You also can go country at Billy's Barn (703-389-2508) Thompson Memorial Drive, where lots of West Virginians drive over Rt. 311 to come to the big city and dance to country music and country rock. Also try Valley Country, 3348 Salem Turnpike (703)-344-6510, Thursday through Saturday for dancing the two-step!

East of the Blue Ridge Region

CHARLOTTESVILLE

Lots of restaurants in town bring in musicians on the weekends and some weekday nights and usually don't charge admission. These include the popular Biltmore Grill on Elliewood Avenue (804-293-6700), the Blue Ridge Brewing Company on West Main (977-0017), the Tavern at the Boar's Head Inn on 250 West (972-2231), Coupe DeVille's on Elliewood (definitely an undergrad hang-out—977-3966), Eastern Standard on the downtown mall (295-8668), Fellini's on W. Market (295-8003), Macado's on the Corner (971-3558), and Durty Nelly's, kind of a dive on Jefferson Park Avenue that serves great sandwiches (295-1278). Schedules often change with the seasons, so we won't commit to print exactly when these restaurants turn into hopping nightspots. But, you can call if you're headed their way.

Other places where you'll find action at night in Charlottesville include Dooley's in the Sheraton on Seminole Trail (973-2121). On Wednesday nights, Dooley's hosts the only live comedy show in town, bringing in stand-up comics from across the nation. The club opens its floor to a dance contest on Saturday nights.

Katie's Country Club on 29 North by Office America (974-6969) is a hard drinking place with live country music on the weekends and some weekdays. It's popular with the Greene County locals and the 29 North suburban crowd. It's even been known to host wrestling matches.

Miller's, in the Downtown Mall (971-8511) is an excellent jazz club and restaurant with live music many week nights and always on the weekends. You'll also hear blues and country here. There's a big outdoor patio that can be nice in the summer if the heat isn't too withering.

We talked about the Prism Coffeehouse on Gordon Avenue (804-97-PRISM) in our Arts and Culture section, but mention it again here because it is such a great place to hear live bluegrass, folk and other acoustic music. The coffeehouse sometimes brings in nationally known musicians, but also provides a forum for the area's top folk, acoustic and traditional musicians to perform.

Two large nightclubs are

back-to-back in the building at 120 11th Street SW, close to campus — the country-oriented Max and rock 'n' roll hot spot Trax. Max (295-MAXX) boasts the largest dance floor in Central Virginia. It has DJs on weekdays nights and live country music on the weekends. Students pour in Thursday nights for country line dances and Wednesday night for lessons in two-step. Trax (295-TRAX) is the hot spot in town to listen and dance to some nationally known and popular regional artists. 38 Special, Bill Monroe and The Seldom Scene were just a few of the performers in early 1993. The Dave Mathews Band also performs for a huge, wildly loyal crowd every Tuesday night. There's live music virtually every night here.

If a calmer, more intellectually stimulating evening is your preference, several places around town offer poetry and fiction readings from time to time. Contact the Williams Corner Bookstore (977-4858) on the Downtown Mall, Kafkafe, a chic new restaurant/cafe/bookstore on Elliewood Avenue (296-1175), or the UVA Department of English (924-7105) to find out about upcoming readings.

New River Valley Region

Traveling south yet another hour, you'll hit College Town, USA, the New River Valley. If you'll feel self-conscious being around the young and tanned with perfect bodies and no wrinkles, stay in Roanoke where the crowd is older. If you don't, head for Blacksburg pronto!

There are two major universities within cruising distance of each other, Virginia Tech and Radford. Where to start? How about Blacksburg, home of 23,000 students, half of which are likely to be the opposite sex.

If you want something to do with your hands other than hold a drink, how about a sports bar on the scene, Champions Italian Eatery and Cafe in Blacksburg (703-951-2222), 111 North Main St., which features sports dart lanes, pool tables, food and drink and some live music. If you're not into the sporting scene and just want to dance, go to Buddy's (703-552-6423), 130 Jackson St., where there are bands, comedy and karaoke. The Balcony (703-953-2837), 217 College Ave., also features live bands, as does South Main Cafe (703-951-8202), 117 Main St. Here, you'll hear such bands as SCUM, Not Shakespeare, Baby Igor, Yams from Outer Space and The Rhinoz (no, we did not make up those names). For more sedate music (and band names), try Jacob's Nightclub (703-552-7001) at the Marriott at 900 Prices Fork Road.

If watching a loud, live band isn't your mug of beer, there's always the landmark Carol Lee Doughnuts (703-552-6706) at 133 College Ave., a nice, quiet place for terrific, fattening donuts. But who cares, since you wouldn't be doing the night life in Blacksburg with the college crowd if you had to worry about calories, right?

Actually, there is a place in Radford, half an hour south, where you can get non-fattening, super broiled seafood at the East Coast

Raw Bar, a downtown bar for "old salts" that features everything from stuffed fish to surfers. If you want to dance in Radford, Sackett's (703-731-0647), Norwood St., calls itself the most popular bar in southwestern Virginia. It does have a good-sized dance floor.

If you want to just sit and chat, and like espresso and glorious desserts, try Radford's Gallery Underground, a cozy downtown pub located under the Gallery Cafe (703-731-1555) at 1115 Norwood St. a favorite of university professors.

If country music is your thing, you'll fine plenty of it, good and loud, at The Walton House (703-731-1922), on Rt. 663, with first-class country groups who sing with the best of them to leave you crying in your beer.

Heading down to Floyd County, you'll do your rollicking and rolling country-style at the legendary Cockram's General Store's (703-745-4563) Friday Night hoedowns on Locust St. or at The Pine Tavern (703-745-4482), where anybody who's anybody hangs out on Saturday night to be entertained. The Pine Tavern, on U.S. 221 N., also has dinner theaters Tuesdays in June and offers non-smoking performances part of the time. Ray's (703-745-2501), also on U.S. 221 N., is another popular hangout for country western and bluegrass.

Alleghany Highlands Region

Traveling to the western limits of the Blue Ridge, in the Alleghany Highlands, the night life is limited to the great resorts of the Homestead and Greenbrier. The Homestead Club (703-839-5500) offers cocktails and entertainment on the prestigious Homestead. The Tuxedo Junction Orchestra entertains with dance music nightly from 9:30 PM. As elegant a club life also awaits at the Greenbrier's Old White Club (304-536-1110), where live bands of the contemporary or Big Band variety entertain with music and dancing under sparkling chandeliers. At either resort, it will be a night to remember.

Inside
Real Estate

An outstanding quality of life is available in a great variety of neighborhoods, farms, second homes and retirement getaways in the Blue Ridge. They offer nearby schools and shopping, and prices for every budget. Frequent is the story of visitors who just happened to be passing through the Blue Ridge, spied the small town, home or property of their dreams and moved without even having jobs. Finders' fees offered for Blue Ridge farmland, often held for generations, are not unusual.

Home sites in the Blue Ridge can be found to fit every taste. They range from architecturally spectacular secluded modern homes nestled in mountain ridges, such as Bryce, Wintergreen and Massanutten, to tin-roofed Victorian homes in Salem or Edinburg, which seldom reach the market. If you're looking for a farm spread, consider the gorgeous Catawba Valley near Roanoke or isolated country estates in Alleghany, Highland or Bath counties. If lots of water is your thing, you don't have to travel to the ocean to enjoy it. A visit to Smith Mountain Lake's Bernard Landing's condos or the townhomes at Mallard Point at

Claytor Lake's white sand beaches will convince you you're already there. If New York City's old brownstones are your ideal, visit downtown Lexington or Lynchburg. If what you want is a primitive log cabin to fix up yourself, visit Franklin or Floyd counties.

Virginia's history as the first, largest and wealthiest of the British colonies in America, as well as the preservation efforts of groups and individuals, have resulted in the state having more historic homes than all other states put together. As a result, while other states' historic homes were being overrun by burgeoning industry and population, Virginia has prized its structures, many of which are located in the Blue Ridge. Nearly a hundred are open for visitation and they do change hands. There are Realty companies which specialize in such prized homes, such as Mead Associates in Historic Lexington, an affiliate of Sothebys's International, and McLean Falconer in Charlottesville, of late the chosen city of movie stars and millionaires who live in such houses. Also in Charlottesville, there's "The Charlottesville Area Real Estate Weekly," issued by the Charlottesville Area Association of

Realtors. The publication covers seven counties and offers the most comprehensive guide to real estate in the area, including editorial. It's available at 420 locations or will be mailed to you if you call (800) 845-4114 or (804) 977-8206.

Lucky visitors may stumble upon their dream homes, but your best bet is to let local Realtors know that you're looking, since some homes, like those in Charlottesville, South Roanoke and Lexington, are sold by word of mouth before they ever see the marketplace. Realtors also can offer guidance on where the best schools are located, where people shop and an opinion on whether or not you'll be satisfied with the neighborhood you're considering.

Local boards of Realtors are your best resource to answer questions about major developments and fair market prices. We've included information for these boards for each region in this chapter. Also listed are local Homebuilder's Associations, in case you decide to remodel or build and want reputable contractors. Finally, we offer the average price of a home in each region, according to the Multiple Listing Service of the Virginia Association of Realtors. If you are interested in making regional or statewide comparisons, or have other real estate related questions, listed below is the address for the state organization of Realtors, which can give you guidance on the area where you're looking. The state Home Builders Association information also is listed.

Virginia Association of Realtors, PO Box 15719, Richmond, VA 23227, (804) 264-5033

Home Builders Association of Virginia, 1108 E. Main St., Suite 700, Richmond, VA 23219-3534, (804) 643-2797

Shenandoah Valley Region

WINCHESTER

The east end of this northern Shenandoah Valley city and the southern part of Frederick County are growing rapidly. This is in part a result of the westward migration of Washington-based workers—people willing to commute an hour or so to their jobs to live in an area that is less crowded and costly. But the Winchester area also has a good number of industries that keep the real estate market healthy.

Much of the historic city's beauty comes from the graceful old homes along tree-lined streets and row houses built before and during the Civil War era. Many of these row houses, which are a short walk from the pedestrian-only Downtown Mall, are being restored and remodelled. You'll also see a lot of old homes here that were built in part with stone.

In Winchester, the average price of a home up for sale in June, 1993 was $114,700. In Frederick County, where there are many developments of modestly priced homes on small lots, the average price of a home was $132,400.

Just to the east in Clarke County, prices were even higher in June 1993. The average cost of a home up for sale in that beautiful,

Find your new address here

or find it at one of the 420 other locations around town.*

Interested in moving to Charlottesville, Virginia? Pick up a **free** copy of the *Charlottesville Area Real Estate Weekly*, your complete resource for local real estate. A publication by the Charlottesville Area Association of REALTORS®, this handy guide contains the most current information about everything from residential properties to grand country estates. So for the best information all in one place, pick up a copy around town* or call (804) 977-8206 or1-800-845-4114.

* Includes Charlottesville and the counties of Albemarle, Buckingham, Fluvanna, Greene, Louisa, Nelson, Orange, and Madison

rural county was $154,200. Also in Clarke, one estate in the country was selling for $1.1 million. There are quite a few 19th century manor homes surrounded by rolling pastures in Clarke County. Some of the county's newcomers are wealthy Washingtonians willing to make the long commute to work or wanting to have a second home for the weekends. Oliver North is one of these new residents.

FRONT ROYAL AND WARREN COUNTY

Many federal employees and retirees have moved into this area, attracted by the beauty of the land and relaxed pace of life. The most prized properties here are those with a sense of privacy, with clear views of the Shenandoah River or the mountains. While vacation homes on the river or in the mountains could be bought for as little as $68,900 in the summer of '93, prices were as high as $350,000. An historic estate in the spectacularly beautiful county can cost in the millions, but it is rare when one comes on the market. Spacious new homes on the county's two golf courses — Shenandoah Valley Golf Club and Bowling Green, cost up to $400,000. But the average price of a home up for sale in Warren County was $114,700 in June, 1993.

For more information on real estate in Winchester, Front Royal and Warren, Frederick and Clarke counties, contact:

Blue Ridge Board of Realtors, 181 Garber Lane, Winchester, VA 22602, (703) 667-2606

Top of Virginia Building Association, 18 E. Piccadilly St., Winchester, VA 22601, (703) 665-0365

SHENANDOAH AND PAGE COUNTY

Shenandoah County encompasses several quaint, historic towns, including Woodstock, Edinburg and New Market, along with the Bryce Resort community in Basye. Page County is more rural, with much of its land tucked between Massanutten Mountain and the Blue Ridge range further east. A growing number of retirees and young couples out of Washington, D.C. seeking weekend retreats are buying property in both counties. The average price of a home runs about $100,000, but prices are much lower in Page County, where the average cost is closer to $85,000. Riverfront property is usually more expensive and is hard to come by (the south fork of the Shenandoah River runs through Page County and the north fork winds through Shenandoah County).

For the most part, architectural styles are very simple — this is a rural, no-frills kind of region. There are interesting old homes, but brick ramblers, Cape Cods and modest, plainly built homes are more the norm.

Bryce Resort, in western Shenandoah County, is an entirely different real estate market. The year round resort community features chalets, condominiums and townhouses within close range of the resort's ski slopes, lake and other facilities. Prices range from $30,000 to $300,000, depending upon the size of the property and its proximity to the slopes.

There are four timeshare developments at Bryce Resort but only one, Chalet High, is still selling. Managed by Alexander Properties, Chalet High is a development of chalets and townhouses on the northern end of Bryce Resort's golf course.

For more information about real estate in Shenandoah and Page counties, contact:

Massanutten Board of Realtors, 129-C S. Main St., Woodstock, VA 22664, (703)/459-2937

Shenandoah County Homebuilders Association, c/o Harris Thompson, Rt. 1 Box 1, Edinburg, VA 22824, (703) 984-4136

HARRISONBURG

In the heart of the Shenandoah Valley, Harrisonburg is a thriving university city that is also the seat of Virginia's leading agricultural county of Rockingham. Housing prices in this area accelerated during the 1980s but began levelling off in 1990-'91. In 1992, the average price of a home was about $96,000. That year you could buy a starter home for as low as $65,000, or a more luxurious house for anywhere between $100,000 and $350,000.

It's increasingly difficult to find nice, historic properties in many areas of the Blue Ridge, but not so in Harrisonburg and Rockingham County. There is still a good supply of old homes, some needing renovation, some already restored. It is also fairly easy to find farm properties. Dairy and poultry farming are the leading agricultural industries.

Massanutten Village, a year round mountain resort community, is a 15-minute drive east of Harrisonburg. Here you will find chalets, condominiums and townhouses near the resort's ski slopes, golf course, tennis courts and swimming pools. A property owners association maintains the roads, runs a police department and

Waterfront Luxury Townhomes

- Magnificent views of Claytor Lake in beautiful southwest Virginia
- Spacious contemporary floorplans
- Two and three bedroom units
- Fireplaces/wetbars
- Whirlpool baths
- Kenmore appliances

- Automatic garage door openers
- Cable TV ready
- Minutes off I-81
- Private tennis court
- Lighted individual boat slips
- Full basements in some units
- Electric heat pumps

Call:
(703) 639-9041
Days
(703) 674-5199
(703) 674-0103
Weekends

MALLARD POINT

For a free brochure write:
MALLARD POINT
Rt. 1, Box 253 M
Dublin, VA 24084

Photo: Richmond Newspapers

Built in 1893, Oakdene at 605 E. Beverley St. is one of many large homes that help make Staunton a town that inspires rich architectural interest.

manages the entire 600-home development. There are hundreds of lots still for sale.

A total of 300 villas and condominiums at Massanutten are timeshares. The units cost anywhere from $8,000 to $16,000, and allow purchasers to spend one week per year at the resort. Or, instead, timeshare owners can swap that week for a condominium in Germany, Key West, the Bahamas — any timeshare development that participates in an exchange program of Resort Condominiums International.

For more information, contact:

Harrisonburg-Rockingham Association of Realtors, 633 E. Market St. Suite B, Harrisonburg, VA 22801, (703) 433-8855

Shenandoah Valley Builders Association, 245 Newman Ave., Harrisonburg, VA 22801, (703) 434-8005

STAUNTON, WAYNESBORO AND AUGUSTA COUNTY

Augusta County is growing by leaps and bounds — especially in the Stuarts Draft area close to Waynesboro. A number of industries have built plants in the Stuarts Draft area over the past several years, including Hershey and Little Debbie Bakery, and this has led to a boom in housing growth. Further west, more and more people from Washington, D.C., New York, and other Northern states are looking to retire in the Staunton area, drawn to its rich history, pastoral beauty and a vibrant downtown.

While the average price of a home in quiet, historic Staunton is about $65,000, it is closer to $85,000 in the Stuarts Draft area. In Waynesboro, a city that's home to such industries as Dupont and Genicom, homes sell for an average of $75,000.

There is great demand from newcomers to the area for big old homes and farmhouses in the county, but they are both in short supply. It's not that they don't exist, they just rarely come on the market.

Two major developments in Staunton are worth mentioning. Ironwood is a private community next to the Staunton Country Club that features spacious, red cedar homes with private gardens. Baldwin Place is a planned community in Staunton's north end where the homes, streets, and even flora are reminiscent of early American villages. There are also many small, well-maintained developments throughout the county with five to 20-acre parcels.

It is expected that a major new hospital being built between Staunton and Waynesboro will spur commercial and residential growth in that area. Augusta Medical Center is scheduled to open in Fishersville in early 1994 and will serve the two cities and surrounding county. Staunton's downtown area is definitely on the way up, as it is being developed into a major tourist area worthy of many repeat visits. Developers and families have happily embraced the charming, architecturally sound commercial buildings and homes. They're being snapped up quickly, but this is an area where you still can make a difference and be in on the cutting edge if you hurry!

For more information contact:

Staunton-Augusta Board of Realtors, 1023 N. Augusta St., Staunton, VA 24401, (703) 885-5538

Waynesboro Board of Realtors, 531 W. Main St. Suite 15, Waynesboro, VA 22980, (703) 949-4904

Augusta Homebuilders Association, PO Box 36, Waynesboro, VA 22980

LEXINGTON

In Lexington, known for its historic downtown and rolling pastures, the average price of a home is estimated at $87,000, according to local realtors. Naturally, there are wide disparities in the cost of farmland estates, which can run anywhere from $200,000 to a cool million, to the historical homes downtown that can go for $370,000 on Marshall Street. Forty percent of Rockbridge County is farmland.

Lexington's historic downtown long has been popular for filming period movies. In 1938 Lexington's Virginia Military Institute was the film site for parts of "Brother Rat," and in the summer of 1992, dirt was poured on the streets for the Civil War movie "Sommersby." Lexington includes numerous buildings and homes that represent most of the architectural styles that were prevalent in American communities during the 19th century. You will find Victorian cornices and stoops on Main Street, turreted Gothic buildings at VMI, Roman Revival and slender Tuscan columns and bracketed pediments. There is even an Italianate villa at 101 Tucker St., which dates to the late 1850s. A central bell tower surmounts its bracketed overhanging roof. Many of these gems are open during the Holiday in Lexington tour and Historic Garden Week in the spring.

Lexington's proximity to the state's Virginia Horse Center has brought in many would-be gentleman farmers whose presence has driven up the price of farms. A restorable 1820 brick residence and cottage on 82 acres sold for about half a million dollars, but small family farms are still available for $100,000 (no house). With a house, you'll probably pay at least $50,000 more. Many such homes are sold by Mead Associates, local realtors located in the historic Jacob Ruff House at 21 North Main St., who offer samplers of Shenandoah Valley properties.

Average family developments may be found at Lexington at above-average prices. Homes in the Suburbia-type family neighborhoods of Birdfield, Mt. Vista and Country Club Hills start at $100,000, with many $150,000 and up. If you're looking for something in the price range of $80,000 to $100,000, neighboring Buena Vista offers some nice neighborhoods.

For more information, contact:

Lexington-Buena Vista-Rockbridge Board of Realtors, PO Box 311, Buena Vista, VA 24416, (703) 261-2176

ROANOKE VALLEY

The average price of a home in the Roanoke Valley runs $80,000. In the nearby area of Smith Mountain Lake, populated by retirees and second home owners, the average price is determined by whether or not a home is waterfront, with lake homes easily averaging $200,000. The nearby growing bedroom community of Botetourt County averages $73,500, and finders' fees are often offered for farmland. Others choose to live farther out in rural Craig County and the Catawba Valley, where a wide variety of homes average $50,000, and large spreads are easier to find.

Roanoke's neighborhoods are well defined, often bound together by civic leagues and The Neighborhood Partnership, an energetic organization uniting neighborhoods for the past dozen years, encouraging pride and fellowship. Popular areas of town range from pricey Hunting Hills in Southwest Roanoke County, with an average sales price of $270,000, to up and coming Wasena, where an average family home in a nice neighborhood can be purchased for $55,000. South Roanoke remains a favorite, with minuscule turnover in homes ranging from $90,000 to $350,000. More affordable, but equally as nice, family favorites include Raleigh Court and Penn Forest, where neighborhood block parties and nightly strolls are the norm. Nearby Salem offers everything from downtown-area tin-roofed Victorian-style homes with stained glass that can cost as much as the highest bidder offers (and we mean on the high side, not low!) to Beverly Heights, where young families congregate in ranch homes valued from $70,000 to $100,000. The adjoining Town of Vinton offers pricey subdivisions such as Falling Creek, with homes over $150,000, to charming downtown wonders you can still buy for under $50,000.

For more information, contact:

Roanoke Valley Association of Realtors, 4504 Starkey Rd. SW, Roanoke, VA 24014, (703) 772-0526

Roanoke Regional Home Builders Association, 1626 Apperson Drive, Salem, VA 24153, (703) 389-7135

East of the Blue Ridge Region

Heading south from Front Royal along the eastern side of the Blue Ridge Mountains you will see some of the most gorgeous, rolling land anywhere on the East Coast. Between Front Royal and Charlottesville, there are four counties: Rappahannock, Madison and Greene then Albemarle, home of Charlottesville.

Generally speaking, prices are higher in Rappahannock County because of the growing number of relatively affluent residents who commute to Northern Virginia to work. Prices drop further south in Madison County, then rise again in Greene County, which is becoming a bedroom community for fast-growing Charlottesville and overall Albemarle County. Orange County — just to the east of Greene and north of Albemarle—is also a popular area for people who want to buy property in the Charlottesville area but want a better buy for their money.

In this entire region, some of the most beautiful historic properties have been transformed into bed and breakfasts. Some say the number of "B&Bs" in the area has more than doubled in 10 years.

In Rappahannock County, the minimum requirement for developing land is 25 acres. Madison County's rules are more relaxed: three acres are the minimum. The median price of a home in Madison County was $90,000 in 1992; in Rappahannock County it was closer to $125,000. Up-to-date figures were not available from the Piedmont Association of Realtors; its new policy forbids the release of statistics to the public.

It is difficult to find historic Victorian or Colonial homes on the market in Madison and Rappahannock counties. Instead, the norm is the brick rambler or a simpler home with vinyl siding.

The real estate market in Orange County, home of James Madison's Montpelier and the Barboursville Winery, is more upscale. Here you will find a diversity of residential properties and prices that are generally lower than in Albemarle County. But the gap is closing. The median price of a home in Orange County is roughly $100,000. Generally, the homes are scattered across the county, because the local government does not allow the growth of residential neighborhoods.

More than 95 percent of Orange County is zoned agricultural, and land cannot be subdivided into more than four parcels in any five-year period of time. Thus, it is practically impossible to rezone agricultural land to residential. This is precisely what makes it such a desirable place to live for people who can afford the prices of some of the stately old estates.

For more information about real estate in Rappahannock, Madison, Orange and (further east) Culpeper counties, contact:

Piedmont Association of Realtors, 810 S. Main St., PO Box 279, Culpeper, VA 22701, (703) 825-3789

CHARLOTTESVILLE

Charlottesville has the dubious distinction of being one of the most expensive areas in which to live in Virginia, second only to Northern Virginia. People of great wealth are drawn to the area — captivated by the beauty of the land, its sprawling historic estates, and the city's cosmopolitan atmosphere. Plus, the many hospitals in the area mean lots of doctors. And jokes abound about the number of lawyers per capita — graduates of UVA who refuse to leave the area. In short, there's a lot of money floating around, and the real estate market has risen to the occasion.

This is especially true in that stretch of land west of the city along Barracks Road and toward Free Union and east of the city at the new Keswick development.

In that western area near Free Union, new homes on three- to six-acre lots in a subdivision named

Rosemont cost $600,000 and up. Near the Farmington Country Club, also west of the city, stately homes run anywhere from $500,000 to more than $1 million. Inglecress is another exclusive development along Barracks and Garth roads, where homes on three to five acres cost anywhere from $750,000 to $1 million.

Architectural styles of most of these new homes are not terribly innovative; here, white columns and symmetrical porticos abound. Jefferson's Monticello and University of Virginia are architectural models — at least on the exterior. But inside many new homes you'll find contemporary features such as vaulted ceilings, skylights and open spaces.

Back to Keswick – this development east of the city gives new meaning to the term "exclusive" in Charlottesville. Sir Bernard Ashley of the Laura Ashley group purchased the 600-acre old Keswick estate and is spending $36 million on a project to develop some homes around it. The project's show home is the estate itself, furnished with the nobleman's antiques and selling for a cool $1.5 million. The old golf course has been redesigned by Arnold Palmer, and he's not the only celebrity to grace Keswick's graceful lawns. Sissy Spacek, a county resident, is reported to have joined the Keswick Club, a facility offering tennis, swimming and golf and more. She likely had no problem paying the $25,000 per person membership fee.

Prices at Keswick will run between $600,000 to $800,000 for a house on a two to three-acre lot.

Nearby, Glenmore, a new development off Va. 250 east of town, has become a destination for many Charlottesvilleans wanting to relocate. Apparently, the glut of houses on the market this year is largely due to the local residents wanting to move into Glenmore. The development surrounds a nice golf course and country club and prices range from $300,000 to $500,000 for a house and lot.

More than 100 homes in the Charlottesville area were built between the early 1700s and the Civil War era. Wealthy families began migrating west from Richmond in the early 1700s — often given crown grants. Such estates as Plain Dealing, Estouteville and Edgemont are registered historic landmarks. Because there are so many historic homes in the area, there are usually one or two on the market at any given time.

Estates whose names are posted on signs at the road are not limited to rich historic properties. It's become the fashion to name your abode — no matter how new. This is an English tradition, of course. It started when many early settlers in the area — who were either from England or whose parents were from England — gave their new homes a name that often linked it somehow to their ancestral home in the old country.

In the city, where there is no more room for development, there are some beautiful neighborhoods. Gracious old homes are concentrated in the Rugby Road area, but there are also more modest, rambler type homes and Cape Cods in that neighborhood close to the university. Within a two-block range of Rugby Road you can find homes that sell for anywhere from $300,000 to $1 million.

In the city, the median price of a home in early 1993 was $90,000 — including condominiums and townhouses. In the county, median prices ran anywhere from the upper $120,000s to the mid $130,000s – not including farms and estates.

Albemarle County is very restrictive in allowing for growth. The local government has targeted Crozet and the Ivy area, west of the city by a few miles, as growth areas and is allowing some higher-density development. But the Free Union area and many other parts of the county are to remain as rural as possible, with minimum requirements of one residence per 20 acres.

For more information, pick up a copy of the Charlottesville Area *Real Estate Weekly*, a publication put out by the local association of realtors. It covers seven counties and is the most comprehensive guide to real estate in the area. It also features editorials about the area and about home ownership. It's available in 420 locations around the area. If you're moving to the area and would like a copy sent to you, phone (800) 845-4114 or (804) 977-8206.

And for some other important numbers:

Charlottesville Area Association of Realtors, 2321 Commonwealth Drive, Charlottesville, VA 22901, (804) 973-2254

Blue Ridge Homebuilders

Association, 2330 Commonwealth Drive, Charlottesville, VA 22901, (804) 973-8652

WINTERGREEN RESORT

Nestled in the mountains and foothills of Nelson County are two private communities that belong to the four-season resort: Stoney Creek, a year round valley development, and Wintergreen Mountain Resort, primarily luxury condominiums but also many single family homes.

Wintergreen is well secluded from any encroaching development, bordered on the west and north by the Blue Ridge Parkway and a 2,400-acre federal preserve and on the south by the George Washington National Forest. More than half of Wintergreen's 11,000 acres have been set aside as permanent, undisturbed wilderness.

Homes and condominiums are situated on ridges for spectacular views of the valley and mountains, and along private drives in Stoney Creek near the golf course.

The community has its own pre- and primary school and private police force. Property owners receive benefits and privileges that include special lift lines at the ski slopes and preferred reservations for golf tee times and tennis courts.

Condominiums cost anywhere from $60,000 to $360,0000, homes from $125,000 to more than $1 million, and land from $20,000 per lot to $280,0000 per lot. The posh resort is about a half hour drive from Charlottesville.

For more information, call (800) 325-2200 or (804) 325-2500.

LYNCHBURG

"In the Blue Ridge Mountains of Virginia" is a well-known ballad in Central Virginia, particularly in the Lynchburg area. Certainly the mountain views are one reason people choose to live in the City of Seven Hills, where the average price of a home is $79,000.

Lynchburg and surrounding Bedford County is one of the most rapidly growing regions in the state. According to Realtor Alice Smith of Smith & Thurmond, Inc., spokesperson for the Lynchburg Realtors, the average days on the market for a home is only 115 prior to sale.

Among the areas of growth are Ivy Hill, a planned community around Ivy Lake and Ivy Hill Golf Course; Poplar Forest, a neighborhood of fine homes on wooded lots carved out of Jefferson's land surrounding his home; Meadowwood, just outside the city on lots averaging 2 to 3 acres, and Meadowridge, on 2- to 3-acre lots nestled close to the mountains. Prices in these areas range from $125,000 to $350,000.

Campbell County, which is west and southwest of Lynchburg, continues to move out into previously agricultural areas. The largest and best-known subdivision is Wildwood, with mostly wooded lots ranging from 1/2 to one acre, and prices in the $100,000 to $125,000 range.

In the city of Lynchburg, there are many impressive, tree-lined streets filled with two-story brick colonials with well-manicured lawns. Among the most prestigious and desirable are Peakland Place, Linkhorne Forest, Link Road, Rivermont Avenue and Boonsboro Forest. New growth occurs west of the city because developable land is there.

Lynchburg is proud of its designated Historic Areas where many turn-of-the-century homes are being renovated into glorious showcases. Neglected for years, many are being restored to their original condition including tall ceilings, winding staircases and beautiful fireplace mantels. The most advanced of these historic districts are Diamond Hill and Garland Hill. Close behind are Federal Hill, College Hill and Daniels Hill.

Lynchburg homes sell well, according to Smith, because of overall good economic conditions, available land for new construction, a variety of neighborhoods and wide price ranges, from $40,000 for a small two-bedroom home to a million dollars. She also emphasizes outstanding scenery, the lowest interest rates in 20 years with available mortgage financing and, of course, a warm and friendly atmosphere.

For more information, contact:

Lynchburg Association of Realtors, 3639 Old Forest Rd., Lynchburg, VA 24501, (804)385-8760

Builders & Associates of Central Virginia, PO Box 216, Forest, VA 24551, (804) 385-6018

New River Valley Region

The average price of a home in the New River Valley runs $85,000. In both Montgomery County, Blacksburg and Radford, well-paid university professionals have driven up the price of homes and land, especially premium farmland in Floyd and Giles counties. The New River area is considered one of the five major growth areas of Virginia, according to noted Realtor E.R. Templeton of Raines Real Estate of Blacksburg. Requests for "Finders'" are often found posted on bulletin boards in little towns like Newport.

Potential homeowners will most likely find Christiansburg and Pulaski as the least expensive places to buy a home, according to the local Board of Realtors. The average price of a home was $20,000 higher in nearby Blacksburg.

The downtowns of Blacksburg and Radford offer a true small-town atmosphere conducive to nightly leisurely strolls, breathtaking parks, especially Radford's Bisset Park along the New River, and the likelihood of constantly meeting others who enjoy an academically stimulating lifestyle. They also are packed with apartment complexes and townhouses for the thousands of students here. The great majority of apartments are well kept, and the students are most pleasant and add immensely to the area's quality of life and diverse culture.

Popular family developments near Blacksburg are Foxridge, Heathwood, Toms Creek Estates and Westover Hills, where the average price of a home ranges from $90,000 to $95,000. In Christiansburg, the same type of development will cost between $70,000 and $85,000. Some of Christiansburg's better known developments are Craig Mountain,

Diamond Point, Victory Heights and Windmill Hills. In Radford, families can enjoy Sunset Village with prices on the low end for homes ranging from $40,000 to $70,000, and the newer developments of College Park and High Meadows, whose prices range from $100,000 to $150,000 per home.

Many New River Valley residents opt to live on the environs of Giles, Floyd and Pulaski counties, where rural living is the norm. Farms still aren't inexpensive, since lots of professionals also like to live out in the country. Farmland differs in each county, and is scarce, due to the area's beauty and proximity to the Blue Ridge Parkway. It probably is least expensive in Pulaski County, where good farmland sells for about $1,000 an acre. Much of the land there is devoted to dairy farms and raising cattle and hogs.

Numerous second homes have been built in Pulaski County's Claytor Lake. A recent development, Mallard Point near Dublin, is a luxurious waterfront community of gracious townhomes unique to the popular water playground. The spacious two- and three-bedroom units offer amenities such as whirlpool, individual lighted boat slips and a private tennis court.

Downtown Pulaski is definitely on the rise, due to its dynamic Main Street program which started up again this year. Professionals from Washington, D.C. and other metropolitan areas are already starting to come in to renovate some of the Prospect Street mansions with witches' caps and winding front porches. An area short on B&Bs,

Downtown Pulaski probably has more old mansions which would lend themselves to this cause than any other place in the New River Valley. It's the next hot spot of New River Valley tourism just waiting to happen!

If you're looking for a nice family development, consider Mountain View Acres and Newbern Heights, with houses that range from $70,000 to $120,000. Oak View is more expensive at $80,000 to $160,000, but considerably less than what you would pay for a similar development in neighboring Montgomery County.

For more information, contact:

New River Valley Association of Realtors, 811 Triangle St., Blacksburg, VA 24060, (703) 953-0040

New River Valley Home Builders Association, PO Box 2010 , Christiansburg, VA 24068, (703) 381-0180

Smith Mountain Lake, Bedford and Franklin Counties

The average price of a home in this area varies greatly from waterfront golf communities, second homes and retiree getaways. Most waterfront property lists for $150,000 to $200,000 for a home. Some of the more popular communities are Chestnut Creek, Waters Edge and the Waterfront and Waverly. Condos can cost from the low $80s at Bernard's Landing to the $60s at Striper's Landing.

It's worth a boat trip around Smith Mountain's 500 miles of shoreline just to see the architectural, custom-built splendor of some of the homes. One of the most noted specialist builders of cedar lake homes is Smith Mountain Cedar Homes, which placed fourth in sales volume and performance among 350 dealers world-wide earlier in 1991 with its parent company, Lindal Cedar Homes.

Rural farmsteads and homes in Bedford and Franklin counties are more affordable and available than in any of the other Roanoke bedroom communities. The average price of a home is less than in Roanoke, at around $63,000. Naturally, the cost of lake property brings up the median, but some real rural bargains still can be found.

For more information, contact:

Builders & Associates of Central Virginia (see Lynchburg)

Roanoke Regional Home Builders (See Roanoke)

Alleghany Highlands Region

There is no organized local board of Realtors in this area. No Multiple Listing Service records are kept on the average price of a home, but local Realtors say most homes typically sell for a fourth less than their urban counterparts. Another rule of thumb, from Highland County's Building Permits Office, is that the cost of building a new home there is $32 per square foot compared to $65 in Northern Virginia.

The area also is unusual in that much of the rural, mountainous property is owned by people who don't live there. For example, half of Highland County, the least populated county in Virginia, is owned by people who live elsewhere but come to vacation in the highest county east of the Mississippi.

The real estate is prized for its proximity to The Homestead, the Potomac and James rivers, and hunting and fishing preserves. Here, one can buy farms with miles of split rail fences on emerald green pastures, maple sugar orchards, wooded tracts, trout farms and cattle farms. It's obvious to visitors that the sheep outnumber the human population five to one. So, for those looking for seclusion, the Alleghany Highlands region is a perfect choice.

Inside
Retirement

"You can't turn back the clock, but you can wind it up again." – Bonnie Prudden.

*R*etirement is the time to start living, and there's evidence many seniors are living it up in the Blue Ridge of Virginia, with its temperate climate, leisurely lifestyle and access to health care and mature services.

People are living longer, healthier and more active lives and traditionally the Blue Ridge of Virginia has been a haven for retirees, especially Northerners. You can find them in picturesque Charlottesville with its cutting-edge medical facilities; the academically stimulating New River Valley (with lots of free university programs); and placid Smith Mountain and Claytor lakes. Access to a wide variety of medical care is also a big plus for Roanoke and Lynchburg and retirees in the Alleghany Highlands, who visit the world-famous Greenbrier Resort Clinic.

In any urban area, you can find scores of happy retirees who take advantage of the many activities offered. Away from the cities, you can find open areas and tiny towns as quiet and peaceful as any in America. The town of Blacksburg, home to

Virginia Tech, has been rated by Rand McNally (number 20) as one of the prime retirement communities in the nation. "Retirement Places Rated" author David Savageau has predicted that Blacksburg will soon become one of the most popular retirement locations in the entire U.S.

Or, if you feel that now is the time to move to a retirement community, you can live like a king or queen in many first-class facilities such as The Park at Oak Grove and Roanoke United Methodist Home in Roanoke or Westminster Canterbury in Lynchburg, Winchester of Charlottesville.

There even is a new Gerontology Center at James Madison University in Harrisonburg devoted to the study of aging. The center not only offers courses in gerontology, but provides a place where people who work with, or are part of, the older population, can meet, talk and study with professors who teach courses and conduct aging research. Call Director Dr. Dorothy Pomraning at (703) 568-6169.

If you enjoy golfing, hunting, fishing, boating, shopping or arts and culture, the Blue Ridge is the perfect place for you to retire. Armchair sports fans will cheer the wide variety of spectator sports the area provides while mature athletes will be glad to know there's a Golden Olympics held at Virginia Tech in the New River Valley, a special competitive and social event that combines sports and games with entertainment, dancing and fellowship. To find out more, call Golden Olympics at (804) 672-5156.

Determining the perfect retirement location takes planning. Individual tastes and personal needs must be taken into account if you're one of the 25 percent of seniors who decide to move after retirement. Too many seniors move to a retirement spot sight unseen. The Blue Ridge, however, offers numerous agencies and contacts to help you determine where you would be happiest. One good way is through Elderhostel programs available at many Blue Ridge colleges. Mary Baldwin in Staunton, Southern Seminary in Buena Vista and Radford University are some locations. You can get more information on Elderhostels by writing to PO Box 1959, Wakefield, MA, 01880, or by calling (703) 261-8413. Many agencies listed below keep catalogs in their libraries.

You can count on a warmer climate, safe neighborhoods and a better quality of life. Planning and the proper research can ensure that you lead the good life in the Blue Ridge after retirement, with never a dull moment! Many seniors volunteer their services. Councils on Community Service can help find just the place for your talents. One of the most popular with retired businesspeople is the Service Corps of Retired Executives (SCORE), of the U.S. Small Business Administration, which offers advice to entrepreneurs on how to start a business. For more information, call (703) 949-6990.

An excellent magazine, *Silver Service 1993*, for the Shenandoah Valley, is a resource guide of quality businesses and community resources for the mature market. Contact Ben Jones at (703) 779-2877 or call 1-800-762-8460.

In this chapter, we list by region any agencies or programs that can be helpful for area retirees. They can offer you tips ranging from broad, comprehensive service and personal care programs, to local perks such as Cox Cable Roanoke's free cable TV installation for seniors, "Enjoy the Prime Time of Your Life." Also check with local hospitals and county health departments and social service departments, since many offer ongoing senior services, programs and seminars.

Shenandoah Valley Region

Agencies

SHENANDOAH AREA AGENCY ON AGING
15 North Royal Ave.,
Front Royal, VA 22630   (703) 635-7141

This agency serves senior citizens in Winchester and the counties of Warren, Clarke, Frederick, Shenandoah and Page. It operates six senior centers where hot meals

Quality
live-in child care...

with a special European *flair*.

- carefully screened European au pairs
- about $170/week for any size family
- AuPairCare counselors in your area

800-288-7786

A U.S. Government-designated program.

and various recreational and educational programs are offered. These centers are in Winchester, Front Royal, Edinburg, Luray, Stephens City and Berryville. The agency also sponsors an elder abuse program, a homebound meals program, transportation services, legal assistance, volunteer programs for retirees, job training, screenings for federal benefits, and help with coordinating long-term care.

ROCKINGHAM COUNTY PARKS AND RECREATION DEPARTMENT
602 County Office Building,
Harrisonburg, VA 22801 (703) 564-3160
Rockingham County sponsors seniors groups that meet at churches or civic centers across the county for lunch and fellowship. A summer picnic for seniors is also organized every year, as well as numerous bus trips to places as far away as Amish country in Pennsylvania and Norfolk for the annual HarborFest. Through this program area seniors have also enjoyed train rides to various places and river boat trips.

AUGUSTA COUNTY PARKS AND RECREATION DEPARTMENT
P.O. Box 590,
Verona, VA 24482-0590 (703) 942-5113
Since January of 1993, the Augusta County Parks and Recreation has offered a variety of programs, classes and trips in response to requests and expressed interests of seniors in the county. Trips are offered by tour bus or van. Classes, crafts and lectures are offered as one-time sessions or as long-term programs, running over a period of weeks or months. Fall and early winter plans include line dancing, water

color and acrylic painting, ceramics painting, senior aerobics, Christmas card shop, beauty seminar, quilting, Appalachian singing fun, hayride, car care clinic and more. Trips are offered to destinations such as Peaks of Otter, Washington, D.C., State Fair, James Madison Museum and Carter's Planation. The big summer event of 1993 is the Old Tyme Fair to be held on Sept. 11. There will be free admission for all ages to enjoy Home Spun Fun at The Old Tyme Fair as seniors bring the past to the present generations. There will be live music, entertainment, food, a cake walk, exhibits, demonstrations, games and contests in harmony with life before WW II. The public is welcome to exhibit in various categories to be judged, such as garden produce, woodcarving and tatting.

AMERICAN ASSOCIATION OF RETIRED PERSONS (AARP)
(703) 942-4282
This Verona chapter of the national organization presents speakers who talk on issues related to senior citizens, sponsors bus trips to places like Washington, and participates in nonprofit work.

WAYNESBORO DEPARTMENT OF PARKS AND RECREATION
413 Port Republic Rd.,
Waynesboro, VA 22980 (703) 949-6505
Programs for seniors include a wide variety of fitness classes, including swimming lessons, hiking trips and day trips to such places as Washington, D.C., West Virginia, and trips to regional theatrical performances. Various instructional classes are also offered.

THE VALLEY PROGRAM FOR AGING SERVICES, INC.
325 Pine Avenue, P.O. Box 817
Waynesboro, VA 22980 (800) 868-VPAS

This agency provides a wide variety of services to adults age 60 and older, including legal assistance, adult day care in Waynesboro, scheduled transportation and guidance on insurance and financial matters. The agency also helps people 55 and older needing additional income to find jobs. Hot meals are delivered to the elderly in many areas. Other services include practical help for families who are taking care of a frail elderly person at home.

The services are offered in communities throughout the central Shenandoah Valley, and in Bath and Highland counties. The agency also operates 13 senior centers where older adults share a hot meal at noon, take field trips together and simply enjoy each other's company. The senior centers are located in Staunton, Waynesboro, Stuarts Draft, Harrisonburg, Goshen, Fairfield, Lexington, Bacova, Broadway, Churchville, East and Southwest Rockingham County and Monterey. VPAS also publishes a bi-monthly newspaper, "Sunburst," with information for seniors.

SENIOR CORPS OF RETIRED EXECUTIVES (SCORE)
(703) 949-8203
or (703) 434-3862

This is a group of retired businesspeople who act as a consulting establishment for those having trouble in their businesses or who are considering going into business. This group serves the Augusta County area, including Waynesboro and Staunton, and the Rockingham County-Harrisonburg area. Membership is open to any retired businessperson.

VOLUNTEER MEALS ON WHEELS - HARRISONBURG
(703) 833-5395

For seniors who live in Harrisonburg, this program delivers hot, home-cooked meals to peoples' homes. Contributions are accepted, and there are no eligibility restrictions.

ALZHEIMER'S SUPPORT GROUP
(703) 885-8818

This group is comprised mainly of family care-givers for Alzheimer's or other dependent patients. The group also provides information on the illness and helps with financial matters and housing for patients.

HOSPICE OF THE SHENANDOAH, INC.
(703) 943-6886

This is a nonprofit organization whose volunteer workers provide home-based support for those with terminal illnesses and their families.

MEALS ON WHEELS - STAUNTON
(703) 886-1219

Volunteers deliver hot, home-cooked meals to senior citizens' homes in Staunton on Monday through Friday for only $2 a day. This is a nonprofit program sponsored by local churches. Recipients must be city residents. There are no other eligibility restrictions, and volunteers lower the price for those who cannot afford the $2.

AMERICAN ASSOCIATION OF RETIRED PERSONS
Glasgow/Rockbridge Chapter (703) 463-1661

AARP offers a multitude of benefits and services. AARP is the nation's largest and oldest organization of Americans over 50, retired or not. It is a nonprofit, non-partisan organization with over 32 million members and serves its them through legislative representation at both federal and state levels. Educational and community service programs are also offered, as well as direct membership benefits.

FAMILY SERVICE OF ROANOKE VALLEY
3208 Hershberger Rd. NW, PO Box 6600, Roanoke, VA 24017   (703) 563-5316

Family Service, a member of Family Service America, offers a multitude of services to help older people remain independent in the community as long as possible. Their Older Adult Services Program offers outreach through social workers to evaluate the older person's situation. Help is provided through financial management assistance, case plan coordination with physicians, nurses and family, and consultations with other geriatric professionals. Counseling is provided, along with homemaker/home health aids and a Family Ties service that helps family members who live away to keep in touch. Family Service also offers Family and Alzheimer's support groups.

LEAGUE OF OLDER AMERICANS
706 Campbell Ave. SW, PO Box 14205, Roanoke, VA 24016   (703) 345-0451

The League of Older Americans, the area's agency on aging, is the place to start for finding out more about senior life in the Roanoke Valley and Alleghany, Botetourt and Craig counties. LOA helps newcomers settle in the valley and provides information on housing, adult centers, volunteer and employment opportunities. It provides a list of doctors who pay for Medicare and banks that cash seniors' checks. In addition, LOA offers its "Redbook" to newcomers and visitors, offering discounts at stores and senior business services. Its *LOA News* is an excellent monthly newspaper. Other helpful services include Meals on Wheels, an Ombudsman program, Foster Grandparents program, Diner's Clubs, transportation, tax counseling, daily telephone calls and legal assistance. A great gathering is LOA's annual Lunch on the Lawn in June, which offers gourmet fare, music, a silent auction and plenty of politicians!

Retirement Communities

WESTMINSTER-CANTERBURY
956 Westminster-Canterbury Drive, Winchester, VA 22601   (703) 665-0156

This is a nonprofit "life care" community affiliated with the Episcopal and Presbyterian churches. By "life care" we mean residents are assured of nursing care, when needed, at no extra cost. The entrance fee purchases the right to private living accommodations, services and programs, and residential health care services. Residents maintain their independence to the fullest extent possible.

There are seven levels of health care, including 24-hour emergency assistance, a clinic, home health care and advance nursing care.

The community is situated on a 65-acre campus with miles of walking trails, a 14-acre natural park, and vegetable and wild flower gardens. There are 20 spacious, brick, 2-bedroom cottages, 106 apartments and a health center and commons area. The monthly fee pays for one meal per day, housekeeping, maintenance, 24-hour security, scheduled transportation and all utilities except telephone. Monthly fees range from $1,367 for a studio apartment to $2,141 for a cottage. The second household member pays an additional $785 per month.

There are two different care plans: "extensive life care" or "modified continuing care." The first is more comprehensive and costly. The amount of the entrance fee depends upon the type of care plan chosen and the size of the apartment. Entrance fees range from $39,000 for a studio apartment on the "modified" plan to $153,000 for a cottage on the "extensive" life care plan. The second person of the family pays an extra $3,750 for the modified plan or an extra $5,000 for the extensive care plan.

The community is open to people of all religious denominations who are 65 years or older. It is much in demand; there was a waiting list in the spring of 1993. It is one of six Westminster-Canterbury retirement communities in Virginia.

SUNNYSIDE RETIREMENT COMMUNITY
P.O. Box 928
Harrisonburg, VA 22801 (703) 568-8200

This community is situated on 57 green, rolling acres outside Harrisonburg. About 450 residents live in cottages and residential suites at the facility, which has a 27-hole golf course at its back door as well as Lake Shenandoah. The cottages offer enough land for gardening. There is also a licensed health care center at the facility, and opportunities for assisted living.

Sunnyside's location was influenced by its ties with the Presbyterian Church. Next door is a Presbyterian Conference Center, and the Presbytery of the Shenandoah's office is in Harrisonburg.

In addition to 24-hour security, the community has a physician and dentist on site, bank, chapel, convenience store, dining facilities, pharmacy services, beautician and a barber shop. Housekeeping and maintenance services free retirees from the chores of home ownership, and scheduled bus trips to places like the Kennedy Center, the Peaks of Otter or the Homestead keep folks busy.

The entry fee is $25,000 and monthly fees vary from $230 to $1,585 for independent living arrangements. For assisted living or retirees needing full-time health care, the monthly fees range from $990 to $1,945.

This is a popular retirement community; there are waiting lists for all levels of care.

BRIDGEWATER VILLAGE
315 North Second Street
Bridgewater, VA 22812   *(703) 828-2550*

This is a life-lease community built by the Church of the Brethren, a congregation with many followers in the Harrisonburg area. Here, residents 55 and older live in modest brick cottages and apartments within walking distance of banks, shops and churches in the little town of Bridgewater.

There are 172 units, and the homes and grounds are maintained by the staff. A new, two-story, 28-unit apartment building opened in February. If more specialized care is required, a sister facility, Bridgewater Home, is right next door. Bridgewater Home was established in 1965 and provides health care services, including speech and hearing therapy, social services, and a chaplaincy program.

"Life lease" arrangements cost anywhere from $28,000 to $100,000. Monthly rentals range from $470 to $1,700, depending on the unit. Service fees are included in monthly rental costs. Under the life lease arrangement, residents pay anywhere from $118 to $280 a month in maintenance fees.

A certain percentage of the life-lease fee is refundable if residents either die or decide to move away.

VIRGINIA MENNONITE RETIREMENT COMMUNITY
1409 Virginia Avenue
Harrisonburg, VA 22801   *(703) 564-3400*

This community accepts people of all denominations and encompasses several types of living arrangements: cottages, townhouses, condominiums, a federally subsidized apartment complex, a nursing home with a special Alzheimer's unit and research center, and a home for adults.

Programs and services vary according to the living arrangement; they include spiritual counseling, home and yard maintenance, beauty/barber shops, gift shop, meals in a central dining area, and a variety of activities. A brand new community center serves as the central place for worship, reunions, music, exercise, share groups, travelogues and fun.

Cottages cost $3,500 plus $375 a month. Park Village townhouses cost anywhere from $80,000 to $95,000, depending upon the size of the unit, plus a $190 monthly service fee. Condominiums at Park Place cost anywhere from $55,100 to $81,700, depending upon the size of the unit, plus a monthly service fee of between $455 to $495 for one person.

BALDWIN PARK
21 Woodlee Rd.,
Staunton, VA 24401   *(703) 885-1122*

This retirement community close to downtown Staunton has studios apartments and one- and two-bedroom apartments with window boxes, patios or balconies. There is no entrance fee. Monthly rent includes two meals and a continental breakfast every day, weekly housekeeping, a wellness program and nursing consultations, laundry of bed and bath linens, all utilities except for telephone, and use of a community gardening plot and an activities room for ceramics, arts and crafts. Each apartment has a full kitchen and emergency call system. There's also a dining room, library and several lounges. Extra fees are charged for personal laundry services, guest meals and overnight accommodations, catering for private entertainment, and hair-styling at the beauty/barber shop.

Monthly rent ranges from $1,113 for a studio apartment to $2,449 for a two-bedroom apartment.

BRANDON OAKS

3807 Brandon Ave. SW, Suite 131
Roanoke, VA 24018-9969   (703) 989-1201

Just completed this spring, Virginia Lutheran Homes' life care community offers a variety of spacious floor plans, dining, housekeeping, 24-hour security and on-site professional health care. The community is located on 18 acres with a spectacular Blue Ridge Mountain view from every window of its 172 living units. Offered are one- and two-bedroom units as well as two-bedroom cottages. Amenities range from a beauty/barber shop and bank to reduced tuition fees at nearby Roanoke College, also Lutheran-related. There is a choice of entrance fee plans ranging from $51,500 to $152,000. Monthly service fees, ranging from $875 to $2,190, include dining options, housekeeping, utilities, 24-hour security and scheduled transportation.

ELM PARK ESTATES

4230 Elm View Rd.,
Roanoke, VA 24014   (703) 989-2010

Elm Park Estates is conveniently located to hospitals, medical facilities and shopping, with Tanglewood Mall across the street. Monthly rent pays for daily meals, housekeeping and linen service, utilities, cable TV, laundry and scheduled transportation. A resident management team lives on the premises for 24-hour security. Other amenities include a craft room, library, beauty salon and daily activities. There are no buy-in fees or leases. Studios and two-bedroom apartments are available and pets are permitted. The monthly price range is from $895 to $1,895 per person.

ROANOKE UNITED METHODIST HOME

PO Box 6339, 1009 Old Country Club Rd. NW,
Roanoke, VA 24017   (703) 344-6248

Roanoke United Methodist Home, a life care facility of the Virginia United Methodist Homes, Inc., has enjoyed an excellent reputation for 28 years. It's a beautiful setting, surrounded by dogwoods, towering oak trees and boxwood. Several types of facilities and levels of care are available to people of all faiths. There are private pay arrangements only. For independent apartments and resident rooms, there are refund options with the life-care contract. Entrance fees range from $42,500 and rentals go from $975 monthly. In assisted living and health care, there is a refund for 30 months. Meals are provided in some options. Transportation is provided for shopping and medical care. There are social rooms, a chapel and a library on the premises. Guest rooms are available.

THE PARK-OAK GROVE
4920 Woodmar Dr. SW, Box 21013,
Roanoke, VA 9501   (703) 989-9501

Tucked away in a nice, safe neighborhood, The Park-Oak Grove has wide expanses for leisurely walks. Locally owned and managed, the facility has such beautiful landscaping that the Roanoke Council of Garden Clubs presented The Park-Oak Grove with a commercial Beauty Spot Award!

Busy, bright and affordable, and requiring no entrance fee, this rental retirement community prides itself on superior fireproof stairwells, fire walls, fire doors, and, of course, sprinklers and smoke alarms. Health maintenance is emphasized with a 24-hour Wellness Program staffed for emergency response and other services to educate and encourage healthy choices in daily living. Evening meals are noted for nice linens, table service and choice of entree. Meal tray service to apartments can be arranged.

The Park-Oak Grove is known locally for its advertisements featuring pets belonging to residents, such as a cat named Rhett Butler and a doggie called Precious. There is a community garden, a lovely whirlpool, and each apartment has its own kitchen with refrigerator and stove. You may choose from seven spacious designs varying in size from studios, to one and two-bedrooms units. Rent ranges from $1,164 to $1,584 per month. Van transportation is a standard service, also weekly housekeeping and linen laundry service. Surprises, such as appearances by visiting opera stars, are thrown in, free of charge. A first floor art gallery

has been the scene of numerous exhibits, part of The Park-Oak Grove's ongoing Visual and Performing Arts Series. Inquiries are welcomed. Guided tours and complimentary lunches are easily arranged by calling during regular business hours.

East of the Blue Ridge Region

Agencies

THE JEFFERSON AREA BOARD FOR AGING (JABA)
2300 Commonwealth Drive, Suite B-1,
Charlottesville, VA 22901   (804) 978-3644

This not-for-profit agency provides advocacy, care planning and services to those 60 and older in Charlottesville and the counties of Albemarle, Fluvanna, Greene, Louisa and Nelson. The Thomas Jefferson Adult Health Care Center is a supervised, daytime program for impaired older people in Charlottesville. Jefferson Elder Care, a joint project with the University of Virginia's Center on Aging and Health, provides professional services such as advice on legal and financial issues.

JABA's Coolaid program loans fans and air conditioners to frail elderly who cannot afford to buy the equipment on their own. The agency also delivers meals to the elderly in their homes, helps people with complaints or questions about long-term nursing care, provides emergency financial assistance, and offers guidance with health insurance matters.

A home care program brings certified nursing aides into elderly people's homes, where they help with cooking, cleaning and other tasks. In addition, JABA matches volunteers over 60 with activities that suit their interests, and runs seven senior centers that offer lunch, recreation and fellowship.

THE SENIOR CENTER, INC.
1180 Pepsi Place,
Charlottesville, VA 22901   (804) 974-7756

This is truly a lively place, housing a gallery and a craft shop and offering workshops on everything from music therapy and coin collecting to injury prevention and management. Jitterbug dance classes, art lessons, ice cream parties, lectures, sing-alongs, various club meetings, Bible study groups, bridge and scrabble games keep the place hopping. The center also keeps people abreast of all kinds of events and programs in the Charlottesville area. It publishes a newsletter packed with information, including a monthly calendar of events.

ALZHEIMER'S DISEASE AND RELATED DISORDERS SUPPORT GROUP
(804) 973-6122

This is the Charlottesville/Piedmont chapter of the national organization, providing information and the chance for care-givers to get together and talk.

WIDOW/WIDOWERS SUPPORT GROUP
(703) 974-7756

This organization provides support to those who have lost their spouses. This is the number for The Senior Center; ask for Dela Alexander to find out more about this group.

MEALS ON WHEELS
(804) 978-3644

This private, volunteer program delivers hot, home-cooked meals to homebound elderly residents of Charlottesville. The fee is $4.50 per meal, but financial help is available for those who need it. Anybody who lives alone and can't cook for him or herself is eligible.

CENTRAL VIRGINIA AREA AGENCY ON AGING (SERVES BEDFORD CO.)
2511 Memorial Ave., Suite 301,
Lynchburg, VA 24501   (804) 528-8500

The Central Virginia Agency on Aging exists to develop, sponsor and provide services to the elderly, especially those who are at risk of having to leave their homes. They offer both information and services, including ombudsman care, Meals on Wheels and congregate dining, homemakers, transportation, legal and tax assistance, health insurance filing, home weatherization, employment, senior discounts and volunteer opportunities.

CITY OF LYNCHBURG DEPARTMENT OF PARKS & RECREATION
301 Grove St.,
Lynchburg, VA 24501   (804) 847-1640

To meet the diversified interests of Lynchburg's mature adults, the Lynchburg Parks and Recreation Department offers a wide array of opportunities including entertainment, nutrition, fitness, athletics, arts and crafts, classes and workshops in its "Life Begins at 55" program. The group has everything from a Writer's Club to a Billiards Club. The Department's "Senior Newsletter" is well read by locals.

Southern Area Agency on Aging (Serves Franklin Co.)

433 Commonwealth Blvd.,
Martinsville, VA 24112   (703) 632-6442

The Southern Area Agency on Aging is the first resort for persons seeking services for older individuals, or seeking information on age-related concerns. SAAA exists to promote maximum independence for persons age 60 and older by providing services that will assist them to live independently in their own homes. The Agency's tasks include advocacy and planning and coordination of services for older persons. Services include care management, home-delivered and congregate meals, in-home services such as personal care, homemaker/companion and respite for family members who provide care for elders with Alzheimers. Employment services, job training and ID discount cards are other services. Their chatty newsletter, "Senior Times," provides monthly service updates.

Retirement Communities

The Colonnades

2600 Barracks Road,
Charlottesville, VA 22901   (804) 971-1892

This Marriott retirement community is a newcomer to Charlottesville, opening in September 1991. The University of Virginia's real-estate foundation owns the land, and the UVA Health Sciences Center oversees health care for commu-

nity residents.

Situated on 59 acres west of the city, the Colonnades' Jeffersonian-style buildings are flanked by a 22-acre wooded walking area. The community offers "continuing care," which means you pay for the level of care you are currently using, rather than for any future need.

There are 180 apartments and 40 cottages, and every unit has its own medical alert system. Monthly fees include all utilities except telephone, linen services, weekly housekeeping, 24-hour security, maintenance of the grounds, scheduled transportation, and use of a heated pool, whirlpool, card room, cocktail lounge, arts and crafts room, woodworking shop and restaurant-style dining room.

There are three payment options at The Colonnades. You can deposit a certain amount of money for the entry fee, 90 percent of which is refundable, and thereby lower your monthly rate. Or you can simply pay a higher monthly fee and forego the entry fee.

The least expensive entry fee is $47,775 for a one-bedroom apartment. The additional monthly fee for the same unit would then be $1,280. Or, if you decided not to pay an entry fee at all, monthly rent would be anywhere from $1,525 to $1680 for a one-bedroom.

The highest entry fee for a two-bedroom cottage is $222,500. The additional monthly fee would then be $1,565. Or, you could simply pay between $2,960 and $3,310 a month in rent, depending upon the size of the unit. All of these prices are for one person only and do not include health care costs. A second person boosts the cost of living at The Colonnades by anywhere from $4,200 to $6,300 in entry fees, plus an additional monthly fee of either $315 or $420.

The Colonnades' health care programs are tailored to meet individual needs. Nursing care services include physical, speech and occupational therapy, and 24-hour availability. There's also a health care center for either short or long terms with private and semi-private rooms.

OUR LADY OF PEACE
751 Hillsdale Drive,
Charlottesville, VA 22901   (804) 973-1155

This is a non-denominational community sponsored by the Catholic Diocese of Richmond. A choice of seven floor plans is available, including a private studio, one- and two- bedroom apartments. All units have fully equipped kitchens and built-in emergency call systems. There is no entrance fee, and leases as short as 30 days are available. The monthly rental fee includes utilities (except for telephone and cable TV), weekly housekeeping and laundry of bed and bath linens, and at least one meal per day. The community also keeps nurses on staff 24 hours a day, seven days a week. A nursing unit is under construction. The community will also have a library, meditation chapel and studio for crafts and hobbies.

Three levels of care are offered: independent living, assisted living, and around-the-clock nursing care. For independent retirees, monthly rent ranges from $1,500 for

a small one-bedroom apartment to $1850 for a 2-bedroom apartment for one person. A second person has to pay an extra $350 per month.

For the "assisted" living arrangement, which includes three meals and a snack daily and 24-hour nursing assistance, prices range from $1,650 for a single room with kitchenette and private bath to $1,925 for a large one-bedroom apartment for one person. The second person pays an extra $525 a month. Residents also pay a $350 reservation fee, which becomes a refundable security deposit when the lease is signed.

Prices are expected to increase in November, 1993, but as of our publication deadline the amount of increase was not yet known.

UNIVERSITY VILLAGE
2401 Old Ivy Road,
Charlottesville, VA 22901   (804) 977-1800
or (800) UVA-LUXURY

The toll-free phone number says it all. An air of luxury permeates this community west of the city. Individual condominiums feature 8-foot picture windows, crown molding throughout, and French doors opening onto private balconies. Residents have their own full-service concierge, who handles everything from overnight dry cleaning to watering your plants while you're away on a cruise. A chauffeur and complimentary limousine services provide rides to the airport or trips to town for late-night dining. A porter will carry your groceries to your kitchen or start your car for you on a chilly morning.

The grounds are largely wooded, containing walking trails and gardens. The University Club, where you automatically become a member when you move in, has a health spa and fitness center, a heated indoor pool, sauna, whirlpool and steam bath. The Club also houses both formal and casual dining rooms, patio dining, a dance floor and piano lounge. There are both indoor and outdoor tennis courts and a pro shop. Residents' ages range from the early 50s to the late 80s.

University Village was designed to function as a traditional village, with nearly every necessity or convenience available within walking distance. The community has a library, billiard room, beauty salon and barber shop, art studio, bank and convenience store. There is also a 24-hour security patrol system.

Prices of condos range from $179,500 for a one-bedroom to $599,500 for the largest, most elaborate condo that overlooks the Farmington Country Club and the Blue Ridge Mountains. In addition, residents must pay monthly assessments ranging from $366 to $1,004, depending upon the type of dwelling unit. This fee covers utilities and the services, programs and amenities of the University Village Owners Association.

WESTMINSTER CANTERBURY OF THE BLUE RIDGE

250 Pantops Mountain Rd.,
Charlottesville, VA 22901   (804) 980-9100

This mountaintop community east of Charlottesville offers independent living in cottages and apartments, along with a full range of services and amenities to adults 65 and older. Like its sister facilities in

Winchester and Lynchburg, it's a "life care" community, meaning that there is no additional cost for on-site health and nursing care for as long as it is needed. The not-for-profit community is affiliated with the Episcopal and Presbyterian churches of Virginia.

Located high on a hill overlooking Charlottesville, the community's cottages have garden patios with views of the mountains. Each apartment or cottage includes an equipped kitchen, safety features in the bathroom, and a 24-hour emergency call system. The monthly fee includes one meal daily, weekly housekeeping and linen services, comprehensive nursing care if needed, all utilities except telephone, and maintenance.

The facilities include a chapel, dining room, library, beauty and barber shop, banking facilities, game room, and gardening and picnic areas. The 24-acre site also has an indoor pool, physical therapy and fitness room and exercise paths.

A comprehensive health care program includes preventive care, round-the-clock emergency services, and both short and long-term nursing care on the premises for life.

One thing that makes this facility unique is its Fellowship Fund, which provides financial assistance to residents who do not have enough money to pay the monthly maintenance fee. Residents pay an entrance fee of anywhere from $132,496 for a one-bedroom apartment to $237,715 for a two-bedroom cottage. This is the price for one person; a second person increases the entrance fee by at least $30,000, depending upon the size of the unit. In addition, residents pay a monthly maintenance fee of $1,645 for a one-bedroom apartment or between $1,930 and $2,045 for a two-bedroom cottage. These are the fees for one person. A second person in the same unit pays an additional $428.

VALLEY VIEW
1213 Long Meadows Drive,
Lynchburg, VA 24502   (804) 237-3009
Valley View is a month-to-month rental retirement community with no entrance fee. Services include meals, housekeeping, transportation, wellness programs and a community center with hot tub and visiting nurse, which are included in the monthly rental fee. A host of personal services are available, from medication monitoring to physical, speech and occupational therapy, with costs on an individual basis. There's a country store, barber/beauty shop, games and crafts area and exercise room. Pets are permitted, but those who don't care for them can live in a different part of the building. Apartments range from an efficiency at $825 monthly to a two-bedroom, two-bath at $1,425.

WESTMINSTER CANTERBURY
501 VES Rd.,
Lynchburg, VA 24503   (804) 386-3500
Located in a fine neighborhood on 21 rolling acres, Westminster Canterbury and its Drinkard Health Center are located between the Presbyterian Home and Virginia Episcopal School. The facility is convenient to hospitals, medical offices and shopping areas and provides scheduled transportation. It is affiliated with the Episcopal Diocese of Southwestern Virginia and the Synod of Virginias of the Presbyterian Church, USA.

Membership requires payment of an entrance fee ranging from $62,600 for a studio with a basic refund plan and unlimited health care to $148,500 for a two-bedroom of the same option. The lowest option, extended refund plan with modified health care, starts at $45,775 for a studio and goes up to $118,050 for a two-bedroom apartment. Plans include four refund and health care and nursing care options with monthly fees ranging from $982 for a studio to $1,447 for a two-bedroom apartment. Financial assistance is available to qualified seniors. Apartments are in eight different styles. Service includes medical and nursing care and help with insurance filing, all utilities and local telephone, beauty/barber shop, individual climate control, no-scald water control, housekeeping and dining of your choice, either in your apartment or in the central area. There's a crafts room, garden plot and walking trails and programs of social, recreational and religious activity.

New River Valley Region

Agencies

NEW RIVER VALLEY AGENCY ON AGING
143 Third St. NW,
Pulaski, VA 24301   (703) 980-7720
The New River Valley Agency on Aging is one of 25 in Virginia. Its

goal is to provide a spectrum of services which allow older persons to maintain maximum independence and dignity while enhancing their quality of life. It offers a Nutrition Program, serving noon meals to people 60 and over in seven nutrition sites. Transportation is provided by New River Valley Senior Services, Inc. In-home services also are offered through aides or meal delivery. Homemakers offer personal care and light housekeeping. NRV Agency on Aging also offers case management services, legal and employment services, an ID discount program and an Elder Abuse Prevention Program. There's a great newsletter, "The New Hope," and a wonderful inch-thick comprehensive guide, *Services for Seniors*, available for $5, one of the best retirement guides we've ever seen anywhere.

Retirement Communities

WARM HEARTH VILLAGE RETIREMENT COMMUNITY
2607 Warm Hearth Drive,
Blacksburg, VA 24060   (703) 961-1712
Located on a 220-acre wooded site, Warm Hearth has 46 one-level townhomes for independent living under a life-lease fee arrangement, apartments for independent living in three low-rise buildings and apartments for assisted living in a licensed home for adults. There are no entrance fees, life care or continuing-care contracts. All fees are on a rental basis ranging from $500 to $2,200 a month. Services offered depend on where a resident lives. Assisted living residents receive daily meals and weekly housekeeping. A full range of activities is provided, including transportation.

Alleghany Highlands Region

Agencies

LEAGUE OF OLDER AMERICANS
(Serves Alleghany – See write up under Roanoke in the Shenandoah Valley Region of this chapter)

VALLEY PROGRAM FOR AGING SERVICES, INC.
(Serves Bath & Highland – See the write up under Waynesboro in the Shenandoah Valley Region of this chapter.)

Inside
Airports and Bus Lines

With its beautiful mountains and interesting historical sites, Virginia is second only to Florida as the most popular tourist destination in the South. Airports are an important means for out-of-state tourists to conveniently visit the area.

There are more than 300 airports in Virginia, ranging from grass landing strips to large international facilities. Commercial airports generate 35 percent of Virginia's economic impact by the industry while General Aviation Airports account for only seven percent. Yet, the importance of general aviation in the Blue Ridge is recognized by a constant upgrading of the existing air transportation system.

Of the existing system in the Blue Ridge, three large airports — Charlottesville, Roanoke and Lynchburg — receive varied Commercial passenger service. They also provide a wide range of General Aviation services for corporate and private aircraft. Others, such as Shenandoah Valley Regional and Ingalls Field, next to The Homestead Resort in Bath County, have limited scheduled flights. The majority of Blue Ridge airports are designed to accommodate the single-engine and light twin-engine aircraft representing more than 90 percent of Virginia's fleet.

Below, the Commercial airports are listed, north to south, with the remaining Scheduled Service and General Aviation airports following.

Commercial Airports

CHARLOTTESVILLE-ALBEMARLE AIRPORT

201 Bowen Loop,
Charlottesville, VA 22901   (804) 973-8341

The Charlottesville-Albemarle Airport is located eight miles north of the City of Charlottesville in Albermarle County. It is accessible via U.S. Route 29 and State Route 649 and is served by four major airlines: American Eagle, Comair, The Delta Connection, United Express and USAir Express. These carriers provide 31 departures per day to six major hub airports including Raleigh/Durham, Charlotte, Pittsburgh, Greater Northern Kentucky/Cincinnati, Baltimore/Washington, and Washington/Dulles international airports. From these points, connections are available to an additional 175 domestic and international destinations. USAir Express also provides daily non-stop service to and from New York's LaGuardia Airport.

The terminal consists of a 60,000-square-foot building with four airline ticket counters, six airline gate areas, baggage claim space, a 500-space daily parking area, 61-space hourly parking lot and an on-site travel agency.

Ground transportation is available from Avis, Budget, or Hertz, and on-call taxi service is also provided. A number of hotels provide courtesy shuttle van service to and from their properties.

A food vending court and cafe-deli are also available.

The Charlottesville-Albemarle Airport's market area includes the cities of Charlottesville, Staunton, Harrisonburg and Culpeper, as well as the counties of Albermarle, Greene, Madison, Culpeper, Orange, Louisa, Fluvanna, Nelson, Augusta and Rockingham.

General Aviation services are provided by Corporate Jets of Pittsburgh, PA with aircraft fueling, hangaring, maneuvering as well as flight instruction services available. Navcom Aviation, Inc. provides aircraft repair services. Auto rental service is provided at Corporate Jets through Avis and courtesy vehicles are also available.

Major Airlines:

American Eagle	1-800-433-7300
Comair	1-800-354-9822
United Express	1-800-241-6522
USAir	1-800-428-4322

Car Rentals:

Avis	804-973-6000
Budget	804-973-5751
Hertz	804-973-8349
Parking:	804-973-5145

Lynchburg Regional Airport
4308 Wards Road,
Lynchburg, VA 24502   (804) 582-1150

The Lynchburg Regional Airport is located six miles south of the city of Lynchburg in Campbell County. It is accessible via U.S. Route 29 and is served by two major airlines, USAir Express and United Express. These provide 21 departures per day to four major hub airports including Charlotte, Pittsburgh, Baltimore/Washington, and Washington Dulles international airports. From these points, connections are available to an additional 175 domestic and international destinations.

The facilities at the airport consist of a new (1992) 35,000-square-foot terminal building with one airline ticket counter, six airline gate areas, second level boarding capabilities, 400-space daily parking area and on-site travel agency.

Ground transportation is available from Avis, Budget and Hertz and on-call taxi service is also provided. A number of hotels provide courtesy shuttle van service to and from their properties. A restaurant, lounge and gift shop also are available.

The Lynchburg Airport's west central Virginia market area includes the cities of Bedford and Lynchburg and the counties of Amherst, Appomattox, Bedford and Campbell.

General Aviation services are provided by Virginia Aviation, with aircraft fueling, hangaring, maneuvering as well as flight instruction services available. Virginia Aviation also provides aircraft repair services, aircraft rentals and charter services, parking and tie-down.

MAJOR AIRLINES:

United Express	*1-800-241-6522*
USAir	*1-800-428-4322*

GENERAL AVIATION:

Virginia Aviation	*1-800-543-6845*

CAR RENTALS:

Avis	*1-800-239-3622*
Budget	*1-800-527-0700*
Hertz	*1-800-654-3131*

PARKING:

Republic Parking Systems	*804-239-7574*

TAXI/LIMOUSINE:

Airport Limo	*804-239-1777*

ROANOKE REGIONAL AIRPORT
5202 Aviation Drive, NW,
Roanoke, VA 24012   *703-362-1999*

Roanoke Regional Airport is located three miles northwest of the city of Roanoke. It is accessible via I-581 and is served by six major airlines: USAir, USAir Express, United Express/Air Wisconsin, Comair, The Delta Connection, The Delta Connection/Atlantic Southeast Airlines and Nashville Eagle. These airlines provide 52 departures per day to 12 major hub airports with non-stop or direct service to 27 cities. From these points, connections are available to an additional 150 domestic and international destinations.

A new $25 million terminal opened in 1989. The dramatic glass-fronted, 96,000-square-foot building features four Jetway loading bridges, a modern baggage handling system and a panoramic view of the Blue Ridge Mountains. There are 772 daily and 227 hourly parking spaces, an on-site travel agency and a First Union Bank ATM.

Ground transportation is available from Avis, Dollar, Hertz and National. Three on-call limousine services are provided. A number of hotels provide courtesy shuttle van service to and from their properties.

A snack bar, restaurant and gift shop, video game room, lounge and conference center and nursery with diaper-changing table are also provided. There is a telephone hotel reservation system.

The Roanoke Regional Airport's market includes the cities of Roanoke and Radford and the counties of Alleghany, Bedford, Botetourt, Craig, Franklin, Floyd, Giles, Montgomery, Roanoke and Pulaski.

General Aviation services are provided by Piedmont Aviation. Provided is aircraft fueling, hangaring and maneuvering as well as flight instruction services. Aircraft maintenance is also provided by Piedmont, as well as Executive Air, Inc., and Roanoke Aero Services. Air charters are provided by Piedmont, Executive Air, Hillman and Saker flying services.

MAJOR AIRLINES:

American Eagle	1-800-433-7300
Delta Connection (ASA)	1-800-282-3424
Delta Connection (Comair)	1-800-354-9822
United Express (Air Wisconsin)	1-800-241-6522
USAir	1-800-428-4322
USAir-Express	1-800-428-4322

CAR RENTALS:

Avis	703-366-2436
Dollar	703-563-8055
Hertz	703-366-3421
National	703-563-5050

PARKING:

APCOA	703-362-0630

GROUND TRANSPORTATION:

Blacksburg Limousine	703-951-3973
Cartier Limousine	703-982-5466
Roanoke Airport Limo	703-345-7710
Yellow Cab	703-345-7711

General Aviation & Scheduled Service Airports

WINCHESTER REGIONAL AIRPORT
Route 1, Box 441,
Winchester, VA 22601   (703) 662-5786

This airport is located two miles south of Winchester and 42 miles northwest of Washington-Dulles International. The airport and a US Customs Service are open 24-hours a day. All-weather access (AWOW III, Localizer approach, Pan Am Weathermation) is available to pilots and there is a lighted runway. Executive fax, secretarial services and conference room with audio-visual equipment make business travel easier. There's on-demand air charter/taxi, overnight hangars, aircraft rentals and flight instruction. Crew car and courtesy vans provide transportation to nearby hotels and golf course. There's a $5 daily parking fee.

FRONT ROYAL-WARREN COUNTY AIRPORT
Route 4, Box 947,
Front Royal, VA 22630   (703) 635-3570

Located four miles west of Front Royal, this facility has a new terminal and hangars. A Duat weather system is available for pilots. Local car rental and cab service and maintenance are available. Parachuting trips are also offered. Tie-down is $3 overnight.

SKY BRYCE AIRPORT
P.O. Box 3,
Basye, VA 22810   (703) 856-2121

This unmanned airport with a 2,300-foot runway is walking distance from Bryce Resort, a large, family resort offering a myriad of recreational activities. There is no fuel. Do-it-yourself, no-fee tie-down is available.

LURAY CAVERNS AIRPORT
Luray, VA   (703) 743-6070

The 3300-foot paved lightened runway at the Luray Caverns Airport sells fuel and charges no fees for incoming craft. Located between the world famous Luray Caverns and the Caverns Country Club Resort, this facility offers free transportation to all Luray Caverns facilities.

NEW MARKET AIRPORT
P.O. BOX 599,
New Market, VA 22844   (703) 740-3949

This airport is outside historic New Market and the

Shenandoah Valley Travel Association Visitors Center, the largest in the Valley, features radio-operated lights, fuel (cheapest in the state at $1.49 a gallon, says the owner), tie-down at $3.50 nightly and cab service. There is a flying school and a $10 charter fee.

BRIDGEWATER AIR PARK
P.O. Box 7,
Bridgewater, VA 22812   (703) 828-6070

Operated by K&K Aircraft and close to Bridgewater College, this airport sells fuel and has limited overnight tie-down sites at no fee. Hours of operation are 8 AM to 5 PM weekdays, 9 AM to 4 PM Saturday and Sundays noon to 4 PM. Taxi service is available from Harrisonburg.

SHENANDOAH VALLEY REGIONAL AIRPORT
P.O. Box 125,
Weyers Cave, VA 24486   (703) 234-8304

This new 10,000-square-foot terminal building offers a restaurant and two car rental companies. A general aviation terminal has fixed base services including fuel and maintenance. There is air charter, corporate management services and two flight training schools. Information on hot-air ballooning and sail planes is available. Parking is free. There are no pilot fees. Free use of Weathermation, Duat and other flight-planning facilities is offered.

EAGLES NEST
Route 5, Box 14,
Waynesboro, VA 22980   (703) 943-3300

Close to Wintergreen Resort,

Eagles Nest offers fuel, car rental and mechanical service with three mechanics on the field. Tie-down fee is $3 nightly. There is a flying school and rides and glider plane rental are available.

VIRGINIA TECH AIRPORT
1600 Ramble Road,
Blacksburg, VA 24060   (703) 231-4444

Adjacent to the Virginia Tech Corporate Research Center and one mile from the main 24,000-student campus, the airport is situated on the Eastern Continental Divide at 2,134 feet above sea level. The runway is lighted and complemented by full instrument approach capabilities. Tech Airport offers a full line of maintenance services and refueling. Flight instruction is offered and Ground School students can earn three academic credits from Tech. Hard-surface tie-downs cost $5. Hangar space has a three-year waiting list. Two rental car services and taxi are available.

NEW RIVER VALLEY AIRPORT
P.O. Box 1617,
Dublin, VA 24084   (703) 674-4780

Two miles north of Dublin, New River offers fuel, maintenance and tie-down at $4 nightly. Hangar space is available. One plane is available for rental. A flight school also operates from here.

FALWELL AVIATION, INC.
4332 Richmond Highway, P.O. Drawer 11409,
Lynchburg, VA 24506   (804) 845-8769

Located within the city limits of Lynchburg, Falwell offers fuel, maintenance, hangar, charter, flight instruction, rental and air ambulance. No landing or parking fees are charged but there is a $5 tie-down for overnight.

NEW LONDON AIRPORT

Route 1, Box 485,
Forest, VA 24551 (804) 525-2988
Located between Lynchburg and Smith Mountain Lake, fuel and minor maintenance is available. There is no tie-down fee.

BROOKNEAL-CAMPBELL COUNTY AIRPORT AUTHORITY

P.O. Box 420,
Brookneal, VA 24528 (804) 376-2345
This unattended rural airport has a pay phone on the field. Rental cars are available nearby and there is no tie-down fee.

SMITH MOUNTAIN LAKE AIRPORT

Route 1, Box 85,
Moneta, VA 24121 (703) 297-4500
Adjacent to Virginia's largest lake, with 500 miles of shoreline, Smith Mountain offers fuel, sightseeing charters, limousine and car rental. Tie-down is $5 nightly.

INGALLS FIELD

Route 2, Box 147,
Hot Springs, VA 24445 (703) 839-5326
Gateway to the Mobil Five-Star Homestead Resort, Ingalls Field might have no planes one day and look like O'Hare the next, depending on which conventions are meeting. Two round-trips daily to Washington/Dulles are offered by a commuter and other trips are on demand. Rental cars and limo are available to Hot Springs, Warm Springs and other Bath County points of interest. Overnight tie-down is $3 and there's no landing or parking fee.

Metropolitan Bus Lines

Public transportation plays a vital role to major cities in the Blue Ridge. It provides an alternative to tourists or those with their own transportation and also provides the elderly and disabled with a means of getting around town.

Due to increased concern over energy consumption, ozone pollution and other critical issues facing the world today, public transportation is no longer just an alternative, but an environmentally responsible way to travel. Major cities in the Blue Ridge offer bus transportation which is clean, accessible and inexpensive.

For a guide to public transportation in Virginia, call the Virginia Division of Tourism (804) 786-4484) for an easy-to-read map prepared by the Virginia Department of Transportation.

Roanoke

VALLEY METRO GREATER ROANOKE TRANSIT COMPANY

PO Box 13247
Roanoke, VA 24032 (703) 982-0305
Valley Metro is Roanoke's regional transportation system which tries hard to accommodate everyone, ranging from eager tourists to the disabled, given special consideration with STAR service. It also oversees the city's five downtown parking garages.

Valley Metro serves more than 5,000 passengers daily, with a fleet of 40 buses. The modern main terminal, Campbell Court, is in the heart of the shopping district, located across from First Union Bank on Campbell Ave.

Riders may send for a bus guide in advance. Exact fare or ticket should be ready, since bus drivers carry no change. No smoking, eating or drinking are permitted. The bus operator should be signaled a block before you want to get off.

Charlottesville

CHARLOTTESVILLE TRANSIT SERVICE
PO Box 911
Charlottesville, VA 22902   (804) 296-6174

UNIVERSITY TRANSIT SERVICE
1101 Millmont St.
Charlottesville, VA 22901   (804) 924-7711

The City of Charlottesville's Transit Service and University Transit work together to provide dependable, efficient, convenient and safe transportation. The main terminal for Charlottesville transit is located at 104 Keystone Place.

Riders may send for a bus guide in advance. When they ride, they should have exact fare or ticket. Designated transfer points and routes are clearly marked on the guide in various colors. Eating, drinking and smoking are not permitted.

Two front seats may be reserved for senior citizens or those with disabilities.

Lynchburg

GREATER LYNCHBURG TRANSIT COMPANY
P.O. Box 797
Lynchburg, VA 24505   (804) 847-7771

Greater Lynchburg Transit serves both the City of Lynchburg and parts of Amherst County, carrying 3,500 to 4,000 passengers daily. Its fleet of 26 buses radiate from a main terminal at Plaza Shopping Center, the only transfer point, located between Memorial Avenue and Lakeside Drive. New bus guides, marked with colored routes, are available by mail. Exact fare or a pass is required.

Inside
Hospitals

Most acute care hospitals in Virginia's Blue Ridge region provide the latest in medical technology and innovative, cost-effective procedures. Almost all offer 24-hour emergency departments and ambulatory surgery units. Cancer programs, home health programs, hospices, physical therapy, sports medicine, open heart surgery, organ transplants and magnetic resonance imaging are available in many of the hospitals, along with traditional health services.

Pegasus, an emergency airlift service out of Charlottesville, travels quickly to the smaller, community hospitals in the region to whisk patients in critical condition to Charlottesville for more advanced care. Roanoke's three hospitals offer a similar helicopter service called Lifeguard 10.

In this chapter, we will give you a guide to each area's major and community hospitals, their basic services and special facilities.

Shenandoah Valley Region

WINCHESTER MEDICAL CENTER
1840 Amherst Street,
Winchester, VA   (703) 722-8000
This is a not-for-profit, acute care hospital with a staff of more than 170 physicians. Situated on 140 acres, the hospital offers wide-ranging specializations, from pediatrics to open-heart surgery, cardiac rehabilitation and chemotherapy. This 408-bed hospital has private rooms only and 24-hour acute care rooms.

WARREN MEMORIAL HOSPITAL
1000 N. Shenandoah Ave.,
Front Royal, VA 22630   (703) 636-0300
A traditional community hospital, Warren Memorial has 111 acute care beds and a 40-bed geriatric unit. It offers 24-hour emergency services, home health care, family-centered maternity care and in-patient and out-patient surgery. Thirty-three physicians staff this hospital.

SHENANDOAH COUNTY MEMORIAL HOSPITAL
955 South Main Street,
Woodstock, VA   (703) 459-4021
Built in 1951, this full-service community hospital has a staff of 30 physicians, 96 acute care beds and 34 long-term care beds. Located in downtown Woodstock in the heart of the Shenandoah Valley, it offers a 24-hour emergency room and full diagnostic services (MRI and CT scans). It is also one of the few hospitals in the region with a certified nurse midwife on staff in the OB unit.

AUGUSTA MEDICAL CENTER
P.O. Box 1000, Fishersville, VA 22939
(703) 887-2000 (from Staunton),
942-2273 (from Waynesboro)

This 225-bed acute care hospital located off Interstate 64 between Staunton and Waynesboro is scheduled to open in early 1994. It will replace King's Daughters' Hospital in Staunton and Waynesboro Community Hospital, which were built in 1951 and 1955, respectively. Until it opens, the older hospitals will continue to meet the health care needs of the Augusta County area.

In addition to standard healthcare services, the center will also offer rehabilitative treatment, home health nursing, comprehensive outpatient services, vascular and thoracic surgery, sports and industrial medicine and cardiology care.

WAYNESBORO COMMUNITY HOSPITAL
501 Oak Ave.,
Waynesboro, VA 22980   (703) 942-2273

This hospital, now owned by the Augusta Hospital Corporation, will serve patients until the day Augusta Medical Center opens in Fishersville in early 1994. It has a 24-hour emergency room and shares a staff of 116 physicians with King's Daughter's Hospital in Staunton (see below). Along with standard services, the hospital also offers fitness testing, home health services, physical therapy, a CT scanner and cardiac rehabilitation. Pegasus, an air ambulance service out of Charlottesville, can get patients to Charlottesville hospitals in a hurry if they need more advanced care.

KING'S DAUGHTER'S HOSPITAL
1410 N. Augusta St.,
Staunton, VA 24401   (703) 887-2000

This 179-bed community hospital offers the same services as Waynesboro Community Hospital, including air-lift service by Pegasus. It is also owned by Augusta Hospital Corporation and will be replaced by the new medical center in Fishersville. But it will serve patients until the day the new facility opens. Its emergency room serves patients 24-hours a day, seven days a week.

STONEWALL JACKSON HOSPITAL
102 Spotswood Drive,
Lexington, VA 24450   (703) 463-9141

Founded by Gen. Stonewall Jackson's wife as a hospital for convalescing women, this 130-bed facility naturally has undergone numerous renovations since those early times. It is nonprofit and community-owned. Services include a new emergency room staffed with four physicians, obstetrics with birthing room, mammography, social services, physical therapy, coronary care unit, home health and outpatient services.

COMMUNITY HOSPITAL OF ROANOKE VALLEY
101 Elm St., P.O. Box 12946,
Roanoke, VA 24029   (703) 985-8000

A member of the not-for-profit Carilion Health System, 312-bed Community Hospital enjoys a reputation for pioneering special services to women, with its Center for Women's Health, offering a vast network of programs and educational services. Carilion's Center for Women and Children is also at Community, providing a diversity of maternity, gynecological, pediatric and newborn services in a setting designed exclusively for women and children through age 17. There is a Ronald McDonald House nearby at little or no cost for families of those hospitalized. Community also is well known for its Sleep Lab, occupational health services, ophthalmology center, Western Virginia Laser Center, cardiac catheterization, and Center For Adult Life, designed for senior citizens. Communicare centers are located in North Roanoke, on Peters Creek Road, (563-4510), offering a Breast Diagnostic Center, and in Vinton, on Elm Ave. (981-1945). The hospital is served by Life-Guard 10, the region's only hospital-based helicopter.

ROANOKE MEMORIAL HOSPITALS
Belleview Ave. & Jefferson St. SE,
Roanoke, VA 24016   *(703) 981-7000*
     HealthCare Hotline 1-800-422-8482

The flagship hospital of the not-for-profit Carilion Health System, which employs 570 physicians, 644-bed Roanoke Memorial Hospitals is noted for its adult services including The Cancer Center of Southwest Virginia, The RMH Regional Heart Center and the Imaging Center of Southwest Virginia. Other specialities include cardiology, comprehensive rehabilitation, diabetic care, geriatrics, psychiatry, neurosurgical unit, hospice, lithotripsy, and an alcohol and drug dependency program. RMH houses Southwestern Virginia's only Level 1 trauma center, providing a full range of 24-hour emergency care services. Several intensive care units

provide specialized critical care for patients. A new wing under construction will provide additional space for surgery, cardiac services and a trauma center. Family Centers are also in Botetourt County and on Brambleton Avenue. Carilion also operates the Roanoke Athletic Club and Gill Memorial Eye, Ear, Nose and Throat Hospital. Carilion also funds the Ronald McDonald House located nearby, which offers housing at little or no cost for families of those hospitalized.

LEWIS-GALE HOSPITAL
1900 Electric Road,
Salem, VA 24153   *(703) 989-4261*
     Medline 1-800-422-0345

A subsidiary of Hospital Corporation of America, Lewis-Gale Hospital is a 322-bed hospital offering pediatrics, orthopedic and neurological specialties, mammography, lithotripsy, rehabilitation, heart and cancer treatment programs, magnetic resonance imaging and alcohol and drug treatment. Adjacent Lewis-Gale clinic is a multi-specialty group practice of more than 100 physicians at seven locations, representing more than 25 specialties and offering ancillary services such as diagnostic imaging and out-patient surgery.

VETERANS AFFAIRS MEDICAL CENTER
1970 Boulevard,
Salem, VA 24153   *(703) 982-2463*

The VA Medical Center is a 603-bed full-service facility that is affiliated with the University of Virginia School of Medicine. A nursing home was added in 1992. The VA provides acute and sub-acute medicine, surgical and psychiatric services, a 100-bed nursing home care unit, a hospice program, and a substance abuse center. Specialized services include cardiac catheterization, CT scanning, hemodialysis, a cardiac electrophysiology lab, sleep disorder evaluation, a cancer center, nuclear medicine, PTSD treatment unit, intensive care units, geriatric evaluation, respite care, day treatment, day hospital and a mental hygiene clinic. Partnerships with local agencies expand services to include 11 outpatient hygiene clinics, adult day health care and radiation therapy.

East of the Blue Ridge Region

MARTHA JEFFERSON HOSPITAL
459 Locust Avenue,
Charlottesville, VA   (804) 982-7000
This 221-bed hospital provides a full range of emergency, diagnostic, surgical, medical and rehabilitation services. Staffed by more than 150 physicians, the hospital offers a 24-hour emergency department, a family-centered maternity unit, pediatric care and much more. The Cardwell Ambulatory Care Center provides such outpatient services as same-day surgery, physical therapy and cardiac rehabilitation. There is also a women's health center, which was designed so that families can celebrate the birth of a child together or that cancer patients can experience the beginning of healing in a supportive environment. Included is a pri-

vate birthing suite complete with jacuzzis and large reading chairs.

UNIVERSITY OF VIRGINIA MEDICAL CENTER
Jefferson Park Avenue/Lee Street,
Charlottesville, VA   (804) 924-0211
The University Hospital, which opened in the spring of 1989, has 552 beds, 61 bassinets, 19 operating rooms, eight intensive care units and a 24-hour emergency room for adults and pediatric patients. The center's Blue Ridge Hospital on Rt. 20 South offers epilepsy, geriatric, adult rehabilitation and behavioral medicine programs. The Kluge Children's Rehabilitation Center and Research Institute on U.S. 250 West provides treatment to children with developmental disabilities, chronic illnesses and injuries.

In addition, the medical center provides outpatient care in more than 45 clinics. The Traveller Clinic, for one, offers education, treatment and immunizations for international travelers. The hospital also hosts a major helicopter program associated with its level I designation. The state has selected this hospital as a care provider for people with multiple traumas.

LYNCHBURG GENERAL HOSPITAL
1901 Tate Spring Rd.,
Lynchburg, VA 24501-1167 (804) 947-3000
An affiliate of Centra Health, Inc., formed to merge assets of Lynchburg General and Virginia Baptist hospitals, this 270-bed hospital is the parent system's emergency, critical care, mammography, hospice, cobalt therapy, neurologi-

cal intensive care and orthopedic center.

VIRGINIA BAPTIST HOSPITAL
330 Rivermont Ave.,
Lynchburg, VA 24503   (804) 947-4000
          Physician Referral Line (804) 947-4444

An affiliate of Centra Health, Inc., this 388-bed hospital has cornerstone programs in cardiology, oncology, pediatrics, women's health and mental health. Founded in 1924, it is the only Southern Baptist hospital in Virginia. Family fitness programs also are offered at Centra Health's Courtside Athletic Club (804) 237-6341). There is walk-in medical care at MedChoice, 8409 Timberlake Road (804) 947-5260), nursing home care at Guggenheimer (804) 947-5100) and numerous screening and education programs.

BEDFORD COUNTY MEMORIAL HOSPITAL
Oakwood St., P.O. Box 688,
Bedford, VA 24523   (703) 586-2441

Affiliated with Carilion Health System, this 166-bed hospital has 55 acute beds and 111 long-term. Services include family practice   (703)   586-4723) mammography, satellite breast imaging at Moneta (703) 297-7181), Special Beginnings, a family-centered maternity program, home health services, respiratory, speech and physical therapy, radiology, social services, lithotripsy and laparoscopic cholecystectomy.

FRANKLIN MEMORIAL HOSPITAL
124 Floyd Ave.,
Rocky Mount, VA 24151   (703) 483-5277

An affiliate of Carilion Health System, Franklin Memorial Hospital is a 62-bed facility in the heart of one of the fastest growing areas of Virginia, near Smith Mountain Lake. Key services include cardiac diagnosis and rehabilitation, family-centered maternity care, home health, industrial health, mammography, physical therapy, radiology, respiratory, social services, oral and eye surgery and outpatient clinics offering ear, eye, nose and throat services, neurosurgery, orthopedics and urology. They have locations at Family Physicians (703) 483-5168, Glade Hill (703) 576-2701, Wolfe Medical Group in Rocky Mount (703) 483-5212, Barrett and Quioco Surgical Clinic (703) 483-9017 and Boones Mill Medical Clinic (703) 334-5511.

New River Valley Region

MONTGOMERY REGIONAL HOSPITAL
US 460 South,
Blacksburg, VA 24060   (703) 951-1111

An affiliate of HealthTrust, Inc., Montgomery Regional Hospital is a 146-bed general acute-care facility in a large university town (Virginia Tech) providing medical, surgical, obstetrical, pediatric, emergency and outpatient services. MRH has four operating rooms, including an orthopedic operating room, a cystoscopic room, two general surgery rooms and a five-stretcher recovery room. Three labor rooms, one delivery room and two birthing rooms are provided. In addition to the general Emergency Room area, the Emergency Department has a minor surgery room, cast room, ENT room, OB/GYN room and an observation room. An expansion is underway which will house a new entrance, chapel and emergency room.

RADFORD COMMUNITY HOSPITAL
700 Randolph St.,
Radford, VA 24141-2430   (703) 731-2000

An affiliate of Carilion Health System, 148-bed Radford Community Hospital serves this university town (Radford University) and beyond with 80 physicians. It is home to the Heart Center of the New River Valley, Laser Surgery Center, Wellness and Fitness Center, Sleep Disorders Center, family-centered maternity care, imaging services including MRI, CT Scanner, nuclear medicine and mammography, home health services, a Level 3 Trauma Emergency Care Center and gastroenterology services.

PULASKI COMMUNITY HOSPITAL
2400 Lee Highway, (US Route 11)
(703) 980-6822

An affiliate of Health Trust, Inc., 153-bed Pulaski Community Hospital is a general acute care facility specializing in emergency medicine, oral surgery, orthopedics, outpatient surgery, cardiac catheterization and rehabilitation, cancer oncology and magnetic resonance imaging. Pulaski also offers a Family Birthing Center, lithotripsy, urology, neurology, home health and nursing services and a Seniority Program.

GILES MEMORIAL HOSPITAL
235 South Buchanan St.,
Pearisburg, VA 24134   (703) 921-6000

An affiliate of Carilion Health System, 65-bed Giles Memorial Hospital offers emergency room services, an intensive care unit, cardiac services, ambulatory surgery services and home health care services.

Alleghany Highlands Region

ALLEGHANY REGIONAL HOSPITAL
P.O. Box 7,
Low Moor, VA 24457   (703) 862-6011

Alleghany Regional is a community-owned, not-for-profit hospital offering 204 beds located in the heart of the Alleghany Highlands. Services offered include home health, diabetic care, mental health, a birthing center, intensive care, physical therapy and social service. Numerous seminars in areas such as parenting and various birthing classes are offered.

BATH COUNTY COMMUNITY HOSPITAL
P.O. Drawer Z,
Hot Springs, VA 24445   (703) 839-5333

One of the smallest hospitals in the Blue Ridge, with 25 beds, Bath County Hospital is a not-for-profit acute care facility located near The Homestead Resort. It offers 24-hour emergency services and an intensive care unit with telemetry capabilities. Other services include: physical therapy, respiratory care, social services, cardiac rehabilitation, EKG monitoring, stress testing, radiology and home health care. Monthly clinics are held for orthopedics, podiatry and urology. BCCH is a member of HeartNet of the Virginias, a system of hospitals that work together to provide emergency care and comprehensive heart treatment. There are six physicians on staff.

Nestled in the heart of the New River Valley
is one of Virginia's outstanding universities.

From September through May
we offer numerous concerts, lectures, exhibits and plays.

RADFORD UNIVERSITY

A World of Difference

◆ **Top-notch cultural entertainment,
  including national and
  international groups:**
  College of Visual and Performing Arts,
  (703) 831-5141.

◆ **Popular entertainment, lectures:**
  Heth Student Center Information,
  (703) 831-5420.

◆ **Exhibits and outdoor sculpture court:**
  University Art Galleries,
  (703) 831-5754.

◆ **See the exciting action of
  NCAA Division I Highlander
  and Lady Highlanders:**
  Ticket and information office,
  (703) 831-5211.

◆ **Elderhostels, adult learning program:**
  Office of Continuing Education,
  (703) 831-5483.

◆ **Tours for students and parents:**
  Office of Admissions, (703) 831-5371.

*For further information about
Radford University, call or write:*

*Office of Public Information
P.O. Box 6916
Radford, VA 24142
(703) 831-5324*

COME VISIT AND ENJOY OUR CAMPUS.

Inside
Education

Some of Virginia's finest colleges and universities can be found in the Blue Ridge region — foremost being "Mr. Jefferson's University" in Charlottesville. Both the School of Law and the Colgate Darden Graduate Business School at the University of Virginia consistently rank in the top 15 nationally and UVA's undergraduate program also wins top ratings. Virginia is also known for its respected college preparatory schools. Several in the Charlottesville area include St. Anne's-Belfield (804-296-5106), Woodberry Forest in nearby Orange County (703-672-3900), and the Miller School of Albemarle — a military boarding school for boys (804-823-4805).

Farther south in the foothills region, Lynchburg is home to five colleges and two business schools, drawing over 15,000 students each year. College preparatory schools in Lynchburg include Virginia Episcopal School (804-384-6221), one of the top independent schools in the southeast, and Seven Hills School (804-847-1013), a private, co-educational day school that stresses leadership, self-discipline and responsibility.

West over the mountains, every major city in the Shenandoah Valley has at least one college or university. There are also several college preparatory, parochial and military boarding schools.

Harrisonburg, the seat of Virginia's leading agricultural county of Rockingham, bustles with academic activity. James Madison University, Eastern Mennonite College and Seminary, and Bridgewater College are all located within a few miles here.

Further south in historic downtown Staunton are Mary Baldwin College, a Presbyterian-affiliated school for women, and Stuart Hall (703-885-0356), the oldest Episcopal preparatory school for girls in Virginia.

Farther south, Washington and Lee University and the embattled Virginia Military Institute sit in quaint, historic Lexington. As of August, 1992, VMI remains one of the nation's two public all-male colleges, but a pending court challenge could force the cadets to study, drill and sweat side by side with women.

A strict regime is also a way of life at two military boarding schools in the valley: Fishburne Military School in Waynesboro (703-943-1171) and Massanutten Military Academy in Woodstock (703-459-2167).

We've already mentioned Mary Baldwin College, but several other esteemed private women's colleges are nestled in the mountains and foothills of the Blue Ridge, including Hollins College in Roanoke, Randolph Macon Women's College in Lynchburg and Sweetbriar College in Amherst. South of Roanoke, the New River Valley is home to Virginia Tech and Radford University, two of the most popular choices in higher education for young Virginians.

The following list concentrates on the four-year colleges and some of the better preparatory schools in the Blue Ridge region. There are many two-year community colleges throughout the area and information on them may be obtained by calling the State Council on Education at (804) 2225-2628. Call the numbers listed for each college or prep school to get information on the ones that interest you.

Shenandoah Valley Region

SHENANDOAH UNIVERSITY
Winchester, VA 22601   (703) 665-4581

This small university sits on 62 acres at the southeast edge of Winchester. It offers eight undergraduate degrees — the Bachelor of Music being one of the most popular. The school also has a lively music theater program. Graduate study is also available; degrees offered include the Master of Business Administration, the Master of Music and the Master of Physical Therapy. Tuition at the Methodist

church-affiliated institution will be $9,800 in 1993-94.

CHRISTENDOM COLLEGE
Front Royal, VA 22630   (800) 877-5456

This is a tiny college founded in 1977 to inspire and educate Catholic students for church lay leadership. It has about 150 students and hopes to stabilize its growth at around 450 students to retain a close community life. The college is located on a 150-acre campus of gently rolling land that overlooks the Shenandoah River and is surrounded by the Blue Ridge Mountains.

The Bachelor of Arts degree is awarded in English, history, philosophy, political science and theology. The college also offers a two-year Associate of Arts degree. Tuition and fees in 1993-'94 will be $8,350.

EASTERN MENNONITE COLLEGE AND SEMINARY
Harrisonburg, VA 22801   (800) 368-2665
or (703) 432-4000

Christian values and global concerns are integrated with the learning process at this private college, which was founded in 1917 to serve the educational needs of the Mennonite Church. There are usually close to 1,000 undergraduates and around 100 seminary students. The most popular majors are business, education, biology, nursing and social work. Tuition will be $9,160 in 1993-'94.

JAMES MADISON UNIVERSITY
Harrisonburg, VA 22807   (703) 568-6211

This is a comprehensive public university that offers a wide range of courses on both the bachelor's and master's levels. The strongest academic areas include the arts, education, communications and health and human services. The beautiful 472-acre campus in the heart of the Shenandoah Valley is within walking distance of downtown Harrisonburg. Average enrollment is about 11,000 students. Tuition and fees for the 1993-'94 year will be $3,798 for Virginia residents.

BRIDGEWATER COLLEGE
Bridgewater, VA 22812   (703) 828-2501

This private Church of the Brethren-affiliated college is located seven miles south of Harrisonburg. Its average enrollment is 1,000 students, and the most popular majors are business and the general sciences for pre-med students. In 1993-'94 tuition and fees will be $10,770. Founded in 1880, Bridgewater was the first co-educational college in Virginia.

MARY BALDWIN COLLEGE
Staunton, VA 24401   (703) 887-7023

This private women's college enrolled about 650 students in the 1991-'92 academic year, and more than half were Virginians. Tuition is $10,654. Especially strong are the psychology and art departments, but the most popular program of study is what is called the "independent major." This is a focused, individualized program combining studies from more than one academic discipline. As of 1992, chemistry and biology majors at Mary Baldwin had maintained a 100 percent acceptance rate at medical schools. The

beautiful, rolling campus is within walking distance of downtown Staunton.

WASHINGTON & LEE UNIVERSITY
Lexington, VA 24450   (703) 463-8400

Washington & Lee University in historic Lexington was founded in 1749 and enrolls about 1,600 undergraduates and 400 law students. U.S. News and World Report has rated W&L as one of the top bargains for a quality private school education. The university offers both bachelors and juris doctor (law) degrees.

In 1796, George Washington contributed 100 shares of canal stock in the James River Co. to Liberty Hall Academy, a Presbyterian seminary. The grateful trustees changed the school's name to Washington Academy in 1798 and to Washington College in 1813.

Decades later, General Robert E. Lee rode into town on his horse, Traveller, in 1865 and became the college's president until his death in 1870. While there, Lee established the nation's first journalism program and its School of Law. W&L's gracious campus is designated a National Historic Landmark, with neoclassical brick buildings dating back to the generosity of Washington. Students still worship at Lee Chapel on the tree-lined colonnade. Lee designed the beautiful chapel and is buried there.

Although the student body is more diverse than ever, it is largely made up of the sons and daughters of wealthy Southerners and Easterners. This past year, students hailed from 33 states and five foreign countries.

W&L is a charter member of the 14-college Old Dominion Athletic Conference and is a member of NCAA's Division III. Tuition will be $13,100 in 1993-94.

VIRGINIA MILITARY INSTITUTE

Lexington, VA 24450   (703) 464-7000

Virginia Military Institute joins W&L in Lexington as a national treasure of tradition. Lt. Gen. Thomas J. Jackson, the immortal "Stonewall," taught here 10 years before leaving to heed the call of the South in the Civil War. It boasts one of the wealthiest alumnae per-capita giving groups in the U.S. and has some of the most famous military leaders in the world as graduates, including General George C. Marshall, Class of 1901 and author of the Marshall Plan to reconstruct Europe after World War II. A museum in his honor is next to the 12-acre parade ground. This is the school that was portrayed in Ronald Reagan's film, "Brother Rat," about VMI's infamous "Rat Line." However, tradition is being tested in the federal courts since state-supported VMI doesn't want to admit women, but Virginia and the U.S. Justice Department do. Just this spring, the Supreme Court denied a request to hear VMI's petition to remain all-male. So the case has bounced back to Federal District Court. Regardless of who wins next, the drawn out court battle is likely to continue for a long time.

VMI's 1,300 cadets are offered a baccalaureate degree in 13 disciplines and must also take four years of ROTC. They are encouraged to sign a formal contract during their last two years which normally leads to a commission. Degrees offered are in biology, chemistry, civil engineering, computer science, economics & business, electrical engineering, English, history, international studies, mathematics, mechanical engineering, modern languages and physics. Tuition is $2,920 in Virginia, $8,760 out of state. There are 13 intercollegiate athletic teams in NCAA Division I.

HOLLINS COLLEGE

Roanoke, VA 24020   (703) 362-6000

Founded in 1842, Hollins College was the first chartered women's college in Virginia. Enrollment is 991, with 826 undergraduate women and 165 co-ed graduate students. Hollins awards a bachelors of arts degree with 25 majors and offers graduate programs in five disciplines, English-creative writing, children's literature, psychology, liberal studies and certificate of advanced studies. It is known internationally for its clinic for stutterers, the Hollins Communications Research Institute, and also has a clinic for head injury patients, the Hollins College Rehabilitation Research Institute. Long known as a bastion for women from wealthy families, Hollins has worked hard to change its image by valuable community outreach programs to women through its adult studies, Women's Center and summer Program. It enjoys a strong liberal arts focus with nationally recognized programs in creative writing. Three Pulitzer Prize winners graduated from Hollins including Annie

Dillard, Henry Taylor and Mary Wells Ashworth. Other notable alumna include Time Publisher Lisa Valk Long and ABC News correspondent Ann Compton. Hollins is also noted for its international concentration. Nearly half of its graduates study abroad. Hollins sports programs are also well known in the NCAA Division III and Old Dominion Athletic Conference. Its Riding Center is popular for women who like to take their horses to college with them. No wonder, since its riding team won first place at the Nationals last year. Tuition is $12,950 annually.

ROANOKE COLLEGE
Roanoke, VA 24153   (703) 375-2500

Also celebrating its 150th anniversary in 1992, this Lutheran-affiliated college, the second-oldest such American college supported by the Lutheran religion, enrolls 1,600 students and offers bachelors degrees in 28 majors with a strong commitment to liberal arts and church-related values. For the fourth year in a row, U.S. News and World Report has named Roanoke College as the number one "Up and Coming Liberal Arts College in the South." Famous Roanoke College graduates include Henry Fowler, former secretary of the Treasury under Lyndon Johnson. Roanoke has 12 sports in Division III of the NCAA. Tuition is $12,625 annually.

East of the Blue Ridge Region

THE UNIVERSITY OF VIRGINIA
Charlottesville, VA 22903   (804) 924-0311

"Mr. Jefferson's University" is central to the Charlottesville community. With its neo-classical buildings, white porticos and graceful landscapes, the university's grounds are considered among the most beautiful in America.

A fall, 1992 survey by *U.S. News and World Report* hailed UVA as the second best public institution in the nation (next to U.C.-Berkeley). In the magazine's "best buys" category, UVA ranged fourth in the nation among both public and private universities.

It should be added here that the university has pretty much succeeded in shaking its reputation of being a party school, famous among *Playboy* readers and others for its annual Easter parties and famous mud slide near Fraternity Row.

This is due in part to the increasingly stiff entrance criteria; the number of applications far exceeds the space available for undergraduates. About half of all in-state applicants get in, and roughly two-thirds of the student body are Virginians. But they are smarter, and more studious and hard-working than ever.

Total enrollment is about 18,000 graduate and undergraduate students. Tuition and required fees for Virginia residents in the 1993-'94 academic year will be roughly $4,350.

The University of Virginia is especially noted for its schools of

Law and Medicine, and for the Colgate Darden Graduate School of Business Administration.

It's also known across the state for its Center for Public Service, which helps localities by collecting demographic and economic data for use in developing public policy. The university's relatively new Center for Liberal Arts provides continuing education for classroom teachers from across the state.

SWEET BRIAR COLLEGE
Sweet Briar, VA 24595   (804) 381-6100
Located 12 miles north of Lynchburg in Amherst and situated on 3,300 acres in the foothills of the Virginia Blue Ridge, Sweet Briar College is an independent liberal arts and science college for women. One of the most expensive colleges to attend in the U.S., Sweet Briar's tuition is $13,125 annually. Six hundred fifty women study for the bachelors degree in 43 majors including interdepartmental and self-designed. There are coordinate pro-

grams in European Civilization, Business Management, Arts Management and Public Administration. Sweet Briar is known for its study abroad programs in France, Spain, Germany, England and Scotland. Locally, it offers the Turning Point Program for women over age 25 and gives them an opportunity to enroll in courses for personal enrichment or a degree. Sweet Briar is the only college in the country to have a full-time artists' colony, The Virginia Center for Creative Arts, as an affiliate.

LYNCHBURG COLLEGE
Lynchburg, VA 24501   (800) 426-8101
Lynchburg College, an independent, coeducational institution related to the Christian Church (Disciples of Christ), is one of America's top 50 liberal arts schools, according to the "National Review College Guide." The school serves more than 2,000 undergraduates and 500 graduate students. Tuition is $11,600 annually. Two teaching

Lynchburg *is* Lynchburg's College

Offering undergraduate degrees in 47 fields in the liberal arts and professional studies with graduate degrees in business, personnel management, education and counseling.

A selective, independent, coeducational, residential college founded in 1903 as one of Virginia's first coeducational institutions.

LYNCHBURG COLLEGE
IN VIRGINIA

innovations at Lynchburg College are the Lynchburg College Symposium Readings course and the Senior Symposium. LCSR incorporates classical reading selections across the curriculum, while in the Senior Symposium, students read selections from the classics and attend weekly lectures to discuss major themes addressed in the readings. Small classes and one-on-one interaction with professors are among the many benefits of an education at Lynchburg College. Master's degrees are offered in business, personnel management, education and counseling. The Adult Center for Continuing Education and Special Services (ACCESS) program, for adults who want to earn an undergraduate degree, is specifically designed to address the special needs of persons age 25 and older. Services include admission, enrollment, advising, transfer arrangements, faculty contacts and program planning. The nursing program offers advanced degrees and specialization.

LIBERTY UNIVERSITY
Lynchburg, VA 24514   (800) 522-6225
Liberty University is a Christian, comprehensive, coeducational university committed to academic excellence. Liberty serves more than 10,000 students from 50 states and 31 nations at the undergraduate, graduate and post-graduate levels. The school was founded by Dr. Jerry Falwell, TV evangelist and also founder of the Moral Majority. Liberty is accredited by the Southern Association of Colleges and Schools and offers 75 areas of study from

which to choose. Liberty Baptist Theological Seminary offers master degrees in Christian education, divinity, counseling and theology. Liberty's facilities include a 12,000-seat football stadium and the 9,000-seat Vines Convocation Center, which are used by the Flames athletic teams who compete on the NCAA Division I level. Prospective students or anyone interested is encouraged to visit. For a free video tape, call the number above. Tuition is $5,250 annually.

RANDOLPH-MACON WOMAN'S COLLEGE
Lynchburg, VA 24503-1526 (804) 846-7392
Randolph-Macon Woman's College, a four-year liberal arts college affiliated with the United Methodist Church, serves 750 women from 42 states and 20 countries. It is located on 100 acres near the Blue Ridge and offers a 100-acre riding center nearby. For nearly a century, the school has prided itself on giving women the edge for a multi-faceted life. Many graduates pursue advanced degrees in science and medicine, a particularly strong area academically. Thirty major programs as well as minors in computer science, economics and business are offered. The Across-the-Curriculum Writing Program ensures every student has strong writing skills. The Prime Time program is offered for women of non-traditional college age. One of the school's most famous graduates is renowned author Pearl Buck. Several study abroad programs are offered including junior year in England. Tuition is $12,450 annually.

FERRUM COLLEGE

Ferrum, VA 24088   (703) 365-4290

More than any college in the Blue Ridge, Ferrum celebrates its ties to the local culture and brings national attention to Virginia, Franklin County, and a nearly extinct way of life. Located on 800 acres in Franklin County, near Smith Mountain Lake, Ferrum is a private, coeducational, liberal arts United Methodist Church affiliate. Founded in 1913, Ferrum offers the bachelor's degree in 31 majors to 1,208 students. It is nationally renowned for its Blue Ridge Institute and Blue Ridge Folk Festival each autumn. There, Coon Dog Trials and Jumping Mules are part of the program that brings thousands each year to Ferrum.

While educating students for success in modern society, Ferrum has remained attuned to those cultural traditions which give the region its sense of place and identity. In the early 1970s, the Blue Ridge Institute was established to document and interpret that heritage through research, fieldwork and educational outreach. Ferrum even was nominated for a Grammy Award for a recording series exploring Virginia folk music. Concerts have brought together traditional musicians, tale tellers and craftspeople. A Blue Ridge Archive preserves photos, recordings and printed materials important to Virginia folk culture. Tuition is $8,800 annually. The college is in Division III of the NCAA. Baseball and football are favorite sports.

New River Valley Region

VIRGINIA TECH

Blacksburg, VA 24061   (703) 231-6000

Virginia's most diverse and largest university, Virginia Tech's presence in western Virginia is pervasive, with 10,000 part and full-time employees and an annual payroll of $250 million. Virginia Tech enrolls nearly 24,000 undergraduate and graduate students with 76

A COMMUNITY OF EXCITEMENT AND DIVERSITY

Surrounded by the mountain beauty of Southwest Virginia, Virginia Tech is an exciting haven of academic and cultural diversity. If you have an interest, we probably have the program or event you're looking for. We are Virginia's largest university, with nine colleges, about 200 degree programs, and 23,000 students.

- Tours (Office of Admissions): **(703) 231-6267**
- Fine and performing arts events: **(800) 843-0332**
- University museums and galleries:
  Armory Art Gallery **231-5547**, Virginia Museum of Natural History **231-3001**
  Perspective Gallery **231-5431**, Museum of Geological Sciences **231-6521**
- Division 1A athletics: **(800) VA TECH 4**
- Donaldson Brown Center for Continuing Education **231-8000**

Virginia Tech

VIRGINIA POLYTECHNIC INSTITUTE
AND STATE UNIVERSITY

For further information about Virginia Tech, write:
Office of University Relations
315 Burruss Hall, Blacksburg VA 24061
or call
(703) 231-5396.

undergraduate and 124 graduate degree programs. There are seven colleges: Agriculture and Life Sciences, Architecture and Urban Studies, Arts and Sciences, Business, Education, Engineering and Human Resources. All 50 states and nearly 100 foreign countries are represented in the student body.

Tech's 2,600-acre main campus is located in a town of 32,000 in the scenic Blue Ridge Mountains. As would be expected, many students can't bear to leave Blacksburg after graduation, and legions of them stay to make it a top-notch, stimulating university town. Additional facilities include a 120-room conference center, 800-acre research farm, Equine Center, graduate centers in Roanoke, Hampton Roads and the Washington, D.C. metro area and 12 statewide agricultural experiment stations. Plans are underway to convert Hotel Roanoke in the City of Roanoke, 36 miles away, into a conference/continuing education hotel.

U.S. News and World Report has ranked Virginia Tech in its top 50 national universities. It also ranks in the national top 20 with National Merit Scholars and ranks in the top 50 nationally in annually sponsored research. Its Corporate Research Center is one of the best known in the South. As a land-grant university with a statewide mission, Tech is responsible for Virginia's Cooperative Extension, which is carried to 107 Virginia communities. Tech also ranks first among universities in the U.S. as an educational user of personal computers, with more than 12,000 PCs and 3,000 terminals on campus. It also is famous for its traditional Cadet Corps.

Tech is a member of the Big East Conference and has a 51,000-seat stadium, offering some of the most popular spectator sports in the Blue Ridge. Be prepared for hour-long traffic jams when the Hokies play football at home. Tuition is $3,812 in state and $9,680 out of state annually, fees included.

RADFORD UNIVERSITY
Radford, VA 24142-6903   (703) 831-5371

The New River Valley's other major state-supported educational institution, Radford University enrolls nearly 9,000 students in this residential section of Radford, (population 14,000), 45 miles southwest of Roanoke in the Blue Ridge Mountains. In addition to the Graduate College, there are five colleges offering Bachelor Degrees: Arts and Sciences, Business and Economics, Education and Human Development, Nursing and Health Services, and Visual and Performing Arts. Special pre-professional programs are offered in law, pharmacy, physical therapy, veterinary medicine, sports medicine, medicine and ROTC. As with Virginia Tech, many students elect to stay to live and work in this beautiful college community beside the scenic New River. Tuition in state is $2,746, out of state, $6270 annually. Radford belongs to the Big South Conference and NCAA Division I and offers 17 varsity sports.

Southwestern Virginia Region

EMORY & HENRY COLLEGE
Emory, VA 24327-0947   *(703) 944-4121*

Located in Southwestern Virginia, this historic, (1836) private, liberal arts college enrolling 850 was recently cited by *Money Guide* magazine as "One of the 100 Best Educational Buys in the U.S." Tuition is $7,900 annually. Emory & Henry offers 20 majors and special programs including Appalachian Studies, pre-med and pre-law. It also ranks with the top one percent of U.S. colleges and universities in alumnae giving. In addition to a small, intensive setting for education, it is ideal if you are interested in spectacular mountains and easy access to recreational opportunities including mountain climbing, hiking and bicycling. It is close to the historic town of Abingdon. Six varsity sports are in NCAA Division III, with membership in the Old Dominion Athletic Conference.

Preparatory Schools

THE MILLER SCHOOL OF ALBEMARLE
Charlottesville 22901   *(804) 823-4805*

This is a college preparatory and academic military school located on 1,600 beautiful acres 14 miles from Charlottesville. There are only about 114 students a year, with the majority enrolled in the Upper School for grades nine through 12. The rest of the students are in fifth through eighth grade. The Upper School is organized as a Cadet Squadron of the Civil Air Patrol, the official auxiliary of the U.S. Air Force. All students wear uniforms and are expected to conform to "modified" miliary procedures. Both girls and boys attend school, but only boys board there.

The Victorian-style buildings at the school are National Historic Landmarks, and the campus covers farmland, orchards, forests, a pond and a 12-acre lake for swimming, fishing and canoeing.

Eighty percent of the school's 1992 graduates were accepted by colleges and universities, with most entering schools in Virginia.

Tuition and other costs in 1993-94 will range from $8,400 for a five-day boarding program for younger students to $12,000 for new students in grades 11 and 12. This includes room and board, student services, uniforms and laundry. Financial aid is available; the average award is $4,500.

ST. ANNE'S-BELFIELD SCHOOL
Charlottesville 22903   *(804) 296-5106*

Formed in 1970 by the merger of St. Anne's School, a girls' boarding school, with the Belfield School, a co-ed elementary school, St. Anne's-Belfield is in its third decade of providing an excellent education for boys and girls in grades pre-school through 12.

A five-day boarding program is offered for students in grades seven through 12. In a nutshell, the school's guiding philosophy is as follows: "Although we expect our graduates to be prepared for the nation's finest colleges and universities, our true purpose is to create a challenging yet charitable atmosphere where students gain skills necessary for both creative and disciplined thought.... The transmission of knowledge, encouragement of curiosity, and the development of responsible, honorable behavior are the great ends of education."

Last year the school had 794 students, with 41 in the boarding program. The school limits the number of boarders to maintain a close, family-like environment.

A full range of advanced placement and honors courses are offered for upper level students, while younger children study basic subjects as well as French, art, drama, computers and physical education. Graduates advance to enroll in some of the nation's finest universities every year.

Tuition and fees range from $4,400 for a half-day session for preschool to $7,500 for grades 11 and 12. The five-day boarding fee is an additional $7,200. Financial aid is available to families who demonstrate need. About 19 percent of the students receive financial assistance.

WOODBERRY FOREST
Woodberry Forest (Madison County) 22989
(703) 672-6008

This is a prep school for boys on 1,400 rolling acres in Madison County, about 30 miles north of Charlottesville and 70 miles south of Washington, D.C.

Independent and non-denominational, the school prepares

"I've always loved math,

especially geometry, because there's usually more than one way to do something. I make a conscious effort to emphasize this point to my students. I always ask my students to explain why they did a math problem a certain way — whether it's right or wrong. I want them to discover their mistakes, to learn to support their answers, and to understand it's alright to make mistakes. To me, the process of learning is asking questions.
David Bard —

Upper School mathematics teacher
B.A. Hamilton College (mathematics)
M.S. Syracuse University (mathematics education)
Scott Master (award for exemplary teaching)
Summer School Director & teacher
Head football coach
Boys' J.V. lacrosse coach
Class sponsor
Advisor

We recognize the value of small class size and individual attention, but we cherish the value of our outstanding faculty. Like David Bard, all our teachers are gifted and dedicated individuals who enjoy what they do. They appreciate the importance of academic achievement and, in fact, 64% of our Upper School faculty hold master's degrees and 12% hold Ph. D.'s. For information about enrolling your son or daughter, please contact:

St. Anne's-Belfield School
FIVE DAY BOARDING GRADES 7-12• DAY SCHOOL PRE-SCHOOL - GRADE 12
2132 IVY ROAD • CHARLOTTESVILLE, VIRGINIA 22903 • (804) 296-5106

students for successful performance at some of the best colleges and universities in the country. This past year's graduates were admitted to 91 colleges and universities, including seven Ivy League schools.

Woodberry Forest offers a comprehensive Advanced Placement program and a curriculum that includes rigorous requirements in English, math, foreign language, history and science, plus art, music and religion.

This past year, 378 boys attended the school from 28 states and 13 foreign countries, with the majority coming from Virginia and North Carolina.

The school was founded in 1889 by Robert S. Walker, a captain in the Confederate army, who wanted a school to educate his six sons. Thomas Jefferson drew the floor plan for the headmaster's residence for his friend William Madison, brother of James Madison.

The average class contains about 12 students. Professors also live on campus and more than two-thirds have master's degrees, including four with doctorates.

The campus is gorgeous. Fine recreational facilities include an Olympic-size pool and a golf course. There are many teams in every sport, so each student has a chance to compete against other boys of similar athletic ability.

Tuition and fees for the 1992-93 school year were $15,000. One student in four receives tuition assistance.

Inside
Southwestern Virginia

*T*he unique mountain culture of Southwestern Virginia, comprised of 14 uniquely different counties, is a challenge to highlight in just one chapter and deserves a book of its own. This area is so close to the Blue Ridge Mountains, and offers such a refreshing cultural point of view, that a visit is an enticing daytrip, and easily much more!

Time-wise, don't let the map of Southwestern Virginia deceive you, however. A mountain mile can take considerably longer to navigate than the speedy miles on the efficient interstates of the Blue Ridge of Virginia. Besides, there's lots of rugged mountain scenery to enjoy as you go, so leave ample time to get to your destination.

Mountains formed the culture of this land, which has more miles of trout streams than roads. In the pioneer days, this beautiful mountainous country was the western frontier, romanticized with the legends of Daniel Boone. In 1775, Boone opened up the route to the west by carving out the Wilderness Road through the Appalachian Mountains.

Today, visitors can stand at various mountainous vantage points at 20,000-acre Cumberland Gap

National Historical Park and see why Boone's route through the Gap soon caught on with so many adventurous spirits. Or, they may visit the Kentucky border's "Grand Canyon of the South," Breaks Interstate Park, where a five-mile long, 1,600-foot-deep gorge prevented even the trail-blazing Boone from selecting this particular passage as the gate to the promised land.

Hardy, adventurous souls still practice and cherish a culture born and nurtured by isolation from outside influences. These are evidenced by the area's famous bluegrass music and hallowed arts and crafts passed on by generations of self-sufficient natives who learned to eke out a living from the land, either by farming or coal-mining.

The area's people, known for their genuine friendliness, are glad to share their culture with "outsiders" at special events throughout the region. Probably the most famous is the annual Old Fiddler's Convention in the city of Galax, always held for 57 years on the second weekend in August by Galax Moose Lodge 733. At this internationally-known event, string music, folk songs and clogging entertain visitors from around the world while contestants compete for thousands of dollars in prizes.

The area's other major attraction is the world-famous Barter Theatre in the town of Abingdon (an attraction in itself), the oldest professional repertory theatre in America. Founded during the Great Depression, the Barter began when a hungry young actor offered local residents theatre tickets in exchange for food. Although the Barter now offers cash for performances to many of the country's best young actors, it still continues its barter tradition as well.

Another popular attraction, the outdoor drama, "Trail of the Lonesome Pine," is also related to the mountains. Based on the famous novel of a proud mountain people by Big Stone Gap native John Fox, Jr., the drama is performed here each summer to show how the coming of modern civilization changed life for the local mountain folks, especially a romantic young girl, June Tolliver.

As you may expect, the highest mountains in Virginia are here. The steepest peak is 5,730-foot-high Mount Rogers, which sets the scenic stage for the vast acreage of this remote area. Not far behind in stature is lofty 5,520-foot-high White Top, host to both maple and ramp festivals. Driving up either is an adventure you'll never forget, and don't be surprised to still see snow on the ground as late as April and May! When you're headed for the high country, expect at the least a 10-degree temperature drop.

Virginia's mountains are home to numerous state and national parks including Hungry Mother, near Marion, Breaks Interstate on the Kentucky border in Coal Country and Natural Tunnel, an 850-foot-wide limestone tunnel winding its way through the Southwest Blue Ridge Highlands. Hunting, fishing, swimming, hiking, canoeing and, of course, mountain-climbing, are popular past-times for adventurous visitors.

What some say is the most beautiful stretch of the Blue Ridge Parkway also winds along the western edge of Patrick County. The picturesque landmark, Mabry Mill, is located nearby, with beautiful accommodations such as scenic Doe Run Lodge for the Parkway's many visitors.

The area's culture is carefully preserved by many institutions ranging from the Southwest Virginia Museum and Historical State Park in Big Stone Gap, to the Carter Family Fold, named for the famous Carter singing clan (June is married to singer Johnny Cash) and located between Gate City and Bristol near the Tennessee border.

As one travels farther up the winding Appalachians, Coal Country is all around in the counties near the tip of Virginia. America's black gold grips not only the history, but also the future of everyone living in the area. From the coke ovens of Buchanan County to the Harry Meador Coal Museum in Big Stone Gap, photos and equipment give you an awe and understanding of a way of life that has long centered around a boom or bust economy. These days, tourism, happily, is quickly taking hold as the isolated land's alternative industry.

Far Southwest Region

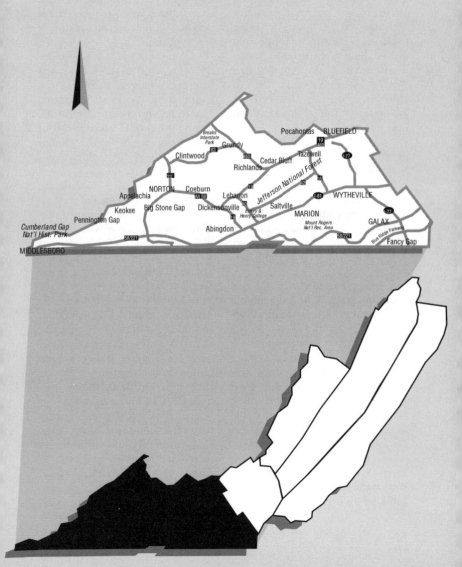

Breaks Interstate Park

Pocahontas   BLUEFIELD

Grundy

Clintwood

Cedar Bluff   Tazewell

Richlands

Jefferson National Forest

NORTON   Coeburn

Appalachia   Lebanon

Keokee   Big Stone Gap   Dickensonville   Saltville

Pennington Gap   Emory & Henry College   MARION   GALAX

Cumberland Gap Nat'l Hist. Park   Abingdon   Mount Rogers Nat'l Rec. Area   WYTHEVILLE

MIDDLESBORO   Blue Ridge Parkway   Fancy Gap

While sampling the best attractions the area has to offer, you won't be at a loss for places to eat, stay or shop. There are plenty. The four-star Martha Washington in Abingdon reigns supreme as the area's foremost accommodation while many quaint bed and breakfasts offer an alternative way to relax. Restaurants such as Mosby's, in Norton, are eager to please. Shopping can range from quaint shops offering hand-crafted items, such as the Appalachian Peddlar, also in Norton, to the vast shopping outlets offered at Wytheville, at the crossroads of two busy interstates, 77 and 81.

With far too much interesting information to give ample justice to Southwestern Virginia's unique culture, we offer you a synopsis of the best and brightest of attractions in the 14 counties that create this region, along with the names of tourism groups who are eager to send you enticing material so you'll visit and stay awhile.

These counties are, for the most part, parallel. In keeping with the rest of the book, the listing will go from north to south and east to west, starting with Patrick and ending with Lee. Some are grouped together, since they market themselves that way, as one entity for visitation. Others have so much going on that they stand well on their own. The 14 counties of Southwestern Virginia are: Patrick, Carroll, Grayson, the independent city of Galax, Bland, Wythe, Tazewell, Smyth, Buchanan, Russell, Washington, Dickenson, Wise, Scott and Lee.

PATRICK COUNTY

Unspoiled, pristine and sprawling, Patrick County, wedged between the Blue Ridge Mountains and the Piedmont, has always been a vibrant area where cultures collide. In the past, that included Iroquian Cherokees versus Siouan Indians; then Indians versus pioneers, trappers and settlers; and mountaineers versus planters.

The area still is as diverse today, offering attractions that range from archaeological artifacts to zoological exhibits and art to zithers. Named for the great orator Patrick Henry, the county has a wealth of American history from Colonial times to the present. Stuart, the county seat, was named in honor of a native son, dashing Confederate Cavalry Gen. J.E.B. Stuart.

Patrick County is home to one of the most beautiful sites on the Blue Ridge Parkway, Mabry Mill, at Milepost 176.1, made famous by artists and photographers the world over. The Parkway runs the length of Patrick County's western border. Its spectacular natural beauty, wildlife and foliage is highlighted by trails, waterfalls and sweeping overlooks of mountain ranges and valleys. At Fred Clifton Park, located off U.S. 58, you can picnic with a view of five counties from several scenic overlooks.

The eastern part of the county boasts Fairystone State Park, named for the small fairystone crosses found there. The crosses are much sought after as good-luck charms. Legend has it that the crystalline stones are teardrops that angels and fairies shed when Christ was crucified. Camping and cabins are available at the park, and there's a lake and beach. Rocky Knob at Milepost 174 also has cabins with electric kitchens. Other nice campgrounds are Deer Run, Dominion Valley, Lenglad, Round Meadow and Daddy Rabbit's.

With two-thirds of the county covered with woodlands, Patrick County is an outdoor-lover's delight. The "Top of the Mountain," a 3,000-foot plateau, is home not only to Lovers Leap and Fred Clifton Park, but to numerous shops in charming Meadows of Dan, with picnic spots and dining ranging from hot dogs to multi-course masterpieces at several fine restaurants including Chateau Morrisette Winery, Doe Run Lodge and Restaurant and Woodberry Inn near Mabry Mill. Five minutes from the Meadows of Dan juncture is yet another restored, operating mill, Cockram Mill, where you can picnic beside the placid mill pond or browse through the souvenir shop.

Other scenic points of interest include Mayberry Trading Post at Milepost 180, built in 1892. This white frame general store is stocked with wonderful food and aromas, including apple butter, each fall. Nearby is Mayberry Presbyterian Church, founded in 1924 and a magnet to artists who come to paint or photograph the picturesque rock landmark.

Visitors also enjoy the Reynolds Homestead, the ancestral home of R. J. Reynolds, founder of the tobacco company bearing his name. It sits in restored elegance on the Reynolds Plantation in Critz. The original house and contemporary Continuing Education Center, now an extension of Virginia Tech, welcome visitors for numerous annual events ranging from a Victorian Christmas celebration to art shows, live theatre and concerts.

Patrick County also is a sportsman's delight. It is known for Primland Hunting Preserve, a private, 10,000-acre hunting reserve stocked with thousands of game birds with hunt packages available for family outings and larger groups. Fishermen also will find the mountain streams sparkling with native and stocked trout at Philpott Reservoir, a manmade lake that stretches 15 miles and has a 100-mile shoreline with hundreds of campsites and a sandy beach.

The county has two of only a dozen covered bridges remaining in Virginia. Bob White, built in 1922, is located off Va. 8 near Woolwine. Jack's Creek Covered Bridge was built in 1914 two miles south of Woolwine on Va. 610. Both are beautiful examples of preserved Americana.

Next door to Patrick County is Henry County, home to Martinsville, an industrial center of textiles and furniture as well as the Virginia Museum of Natural History. Outlet shopping is excellent at Tultex Clothing and Stanley Furniture and the Martinsville Speedway packs them in for NASCAR races. The Natural History Museum is the state's center for research, collection and exhibits in the natural sciences with stimulating visuals and hands-on exhibits.

The county's most famous event is the Hillsville Flea Market, conducted each Labor Day Weekend. You'll spot cars lined up for miles before you get to the hundred acre-plus site where more than 2,000 vendors offer every type of collectible imaginable.

For more information on Patrick County, there are two groups to contact: Call the Blue Ridge/Piedmont Cultural Consortium in Martinsville at (703) 632-3221 or the Patrick County Chamber of Commerce at (703) 694-6012.

Carroll County/Grayson County/City of Galax

Carroll and Grayson counties and the City of Galax are bound together both by lay of the land as well as location.

CITY OF GALAX

An independent city, Galax is nestled in the Blue Ridge between Carroll and Grayson counties and serves as the commercial hub of the area.

Galax is a Main Street community with a charming downtown and is home to the oldest (since 1935) and largest "Fiddlers' Convention" in the world the second week of August, sponsored by the Galax Loyal Order of Moose Lodge #733.

Each year, about 30,000 people gather in Felts Park to see and hear the original music of pure American culture performed by a wide variety of nearly 2,000 talented artists competing for thousands of dollars in prize money. The program includes folk song, fiddle, guitar, bluegrass banjo, clawhammer banjo and mandolin.

Galax also is a major center of Virginia's furniture manufacturing industry. Textiles and clothing are also important industries. Consolidated Glass and Mirror Corp. operates one of the most modern, efficient mirror plants in the world.

CARROLL COUNTY

Carroll County is a rich agricultural area noted for fruit and vegetable production. Its gently rolling hills and well tended farms have become a well known destination for tourists and retirees, especially along the Blue Ridge Parkway.

Carroll sports numerous facilities for camping, swimming, fishing, horseback riding and hiking. There is an 18-hole golf course, Olde Mill, on the Blue Ridge Parkway.

GRAYSON COUNTY

Grayson County is rapidly becoming the recreational destination of Southwestern Virginia. It is home to Mount Rogers, the highest peak in Virginia, along with Grayson Highlands State Park and New River Trail State Park, Virginia's only linear state park featuring hiking, bicycling and horseback riding. All around are Fraser firs, the "king of Christmas trees," which sell for $100 each in big cities. Christmas trees are overtaking cattle as the area's biggest business.

The 60-mile-long Mount Rogers National Recreation Area stretches from the New River near Ivanhoe westward along the south side of Interstate I-81 to Damascus. Major access is off I-81 to Virginia 16 south from Marion and Virginia 600 south from Chilhowie. Headquarters for the area is on Virginia 16, south of Marion, and can be called at (703) 783-5196. Maps are available here for $3.

Grayson Highlands State Park contains 5,000 acres and provides facilities for camping, picnicking, swimming, horseback riding, hiking and nature study. To the delight to all visitors, several hundred ponies roam freely through the park. Each fall, they are herded up and auctioned off the last weekend of September at the park. Although the sale doesn't have the same visibility as the pony round-up at the eastern shore's Assateague-Chincoteague Islands, locals say their event is better, with a higher quality of pony.

The New River Trail State Park, the state's linear park, offers 57 miles of trails. Much of it parallels the scenic New River, the second-oldest river in the world.

Mount Rogers National Recreation Area is the real draw, however, with its 154,000 acres of beautiful, unspoiled land set in the Jefferson National Forest. People, many hiking the Appalachian Trail, come to the area, isolated by altitude and climate, to go back to another era and to see another ecosystem through alpine meadows and spruce-crowned summits. The town of Damascus is famous for its mid-May party during Appalachian Trail Days, when hikers are invited to join in a parade with the townspeople, indulge in barbecued chicken at the fire station and square dance in the post office parking lot.

A visitors center provides information on outdoor facilities, and many visitors say it's the closest thing they've ever seen to compare to terrain in Wyoming and Montana. Rhododendron Gap probably is one of the stiffest parts of the Appalachian Trail, but experienced hikers who make it to this point say the profusion of the wildflowers makes the hike well worthwhile.

Rangers warn visitors not to embark into the highlands wearing only light jackets and tennis shoes. When fog, cold rain or darkness fall, it's easy to get lost in the isolation. Most of the careless make it out of the wilds with just a cold, but there have been some tragic exceptions.

Family camping is available at sites including Beartree, Comers Rock, Grindstone, Hurricane, Raccoon Branch, and Raven Cliff. Horse camping can be found at Fox Creek Trailhead, Hussy Mountain and Raven Cliff.

Favorite picnic spots are Beartree, Comers Rock, Fox Creek, Raven Cliffs, Shepherd's Corner and Skull Gap. The most popular trails in addition to the Appalachian are Iron Mountain, Virginia Creeper and Virginia Highlands Horse Trail. Favorite hikes are to Mount Rogers Summit, Rhododendron Gap and Deep Gap.

For more detailed information, directions, points of interest, brochures and maps of the area, please contact: The Galax-Carroll-Grayson Chamber of Commerce (703) 236-2184); Mount Rogers National Recreation Area (703) 783-5196; Division of State Parks, Virginia (804) 786-2132; or Jefferson National Forest (703) 982-6270.

SOUTHWESTERN VIRGINIA

Town of Wytheville/Wythe County/Bland County

The Town of Wytheville and Wythe and Bland counties pride themselves on being the "Crossroads of America," with a convenient location at the intersection of I-81 and I-77 that brings in thousands of tourists for shopping and eating.

TOWN OF WYTHEVILLE

Wytheville cuts a sharp contrast between the scenic beauty of the rolling peaks and valleys of the Allegheny Mountain Highlands and the bright, modern, new construction of motels, restaurants, and industry. The area is a refreshing, welcome respite for a weary traveler.

Motorists enjoy the beauty of Bland and Wythe counties' forested lands for as far as the eye can see as they travel down the interstates. Pioneers heading west were so impressed that they settled here on a high, level plateau which became a natural crossroads for trappers and hunters as they made their way through Big Walker Mountain and Fancy Gap.

First called Wythe County Courthouse, the town later was named Wytheville for George Wythe, the first law professor at William and Mary College and designer of Virginia's state seal. The "Father of Wytheville," as he is called, was Colonel Thomas Jefferson Boyd. A museum stands in his honor today, a project of the Wythe County Historical Society. Edith Bolling Wilson, wife of President Woodrow Wilson, was born here in 1872, daughter of the judge of the Court of Wythe County.

Wytheville played a significant role during the Civil War because of its location and the fact that lead mines and the only salt mine in the South were nearby. It was the site of constant clashes between the North and South. Although many homes were burned, the stone house of the area's first resident physician, Dr. John Haller, was spared. Old Rock House, a National Landmark, is now a museum full of handcrafts and mementoes.

Wytheville Community College, an accredited two-year institution, is located in Wytheville. The town also has a modern library, and a well-established community center. Wythe County Community Hospital is located here. Along with Blacksburg, Wytheville was named one of the nation's best places to retire, with Asbury Center at Birdmont, a multi-level retirement community. There also are two charming parks located in the center of downtown.

Culturally, Wytheville is known for its recently-revived Chautauqua Festival, held the third week in June and gaining in recognition yearly for its celebration of music, education and the arts. During the 1920s, Wytheville was a regular stop on the "Chautauqua Circuit," a series of tours featuring lectures, plays and concerts originating from the Chautauqua Institution near Buffalo, New York. An important forum for adult education, the tent Chautauquas flourished until the development of radio, which made them a thing of the past.

Events take place in the Elizabeth Brown Park. Wytheville's charming downtown offers several walking tours in an old-fashioned and thriving business district. It is known for numerous shopping opportunities from local crafts to outlet shops. Another popular shopping site is Snooper's Antique and Craft Mall, where 50 local craftspeople display their work. Here, you will find a wide selection of antiques, quilts, hand-blown glass and pottery. Snooper's is located on the frontage road eight miles north of Wytheville. Ten miles north at Fort Chiswell is Factory Merchants Outlet Mall, featuring an array of discount shopping ranging from kitchenware to toys.

The most unique shop in the Wytheville area is P.J.'s Christmas Carousel, where children can ride a carousel of Christmas animals. P.J.'s offers hand-crafted holiday decorations and gifts. It's next to Snooper's.

While you're shopping, remember that there are 14 motels and 35 restaurants in Wytheville. Wytheville offers some very nice places to stay including The Holiday Inn Wytheville, Best Western, Ramada Inn and Days Inn. Wytheville also has the new Boxwood Inn Bed & Breakfast. This Inn is a lovely Georgian Colonial home located in the heart of scenic, historic Wytheville just off I-77 and I-81. There are eight spacious rooms tastefully furnished with a blend of traditional period and antique furniture each having a private bath.

Some of the most memorable restaurants are Scrooge's, just off I-81, the Log House Restaurant on Main Street downtown and Words and Music Irish Cafe. Scrooge's is fashioned after the Charles Dickens story. Also at Scrooge's Village is Tiny Tim's assortment of other novelties, and an ice cream parlor. The Log House was built in 1776 and features an antique menu with Appalachian flavor. Words and Music offers a taste of Ireland for both the palate and soul, with homemade apple dumplings and imported beverages served with eclectic live performances every other Saturday.

Wytheville also offers something for those hungry for outdoor beauty. Located midway between Claytor Lake State Park in Pulaski County and Hungry Mother State Park in Smyth County, there's fishing, boating and swimming in nearby Bland and Wythe counties. A great KOA campground is located there with kamping kabins, outdoor sports, farm animals for the kids and a large, heated swimming pool.

WYTHE COUNTY

Agriculture and manufacturing are Wythe County's leading industries, but tourism in the great outdoors is quickly gaining, since the county is a mecca for recreation. A large portion lies within the Jefferson National Forest. The Appalachian Trail crosses the county and part of Mount Rogers National Recreational Area lies in the southwestern corner.

Rural Retreat was the second town incorporated in Wythe County and offers a haven of natural beauty, especially at Rural Retreat Lake and Campground, located between Rural Retreat and Cedar Springs on Va. 749. The 90-acre fishing lake offers picnicking, boat rental and a Junior

Olympic swimming pool.

Anglers have it made in Wythe County. Trout fishing is popular at Cripple and Peak creeks. Hale Fishing Lake is 3,000 feet up Iron Mountain, south of Speedwell, just off U.S. 21. Part of the Jefferson National Forest, the lake is stocked regularly with trout. Cedar Springs Sportsmans Lodge, near Cedar Springs on Cripple Creek, is a popular place for fishermen to catch their limit. Wytheville State Fish Hatchery is located on Rt. 629, near Fort Chiswell. Visitors are encouraged to see the grounds and displays.

The county is home to one of the most unique landmarks in the world, the shot tower at Shot Tower Historical Park, located where U.S. 52 crosses New River at the Poplar Camp Exit, I-77. The 70-foot tower, the only one of its kind known in the world, was built in the early 1800s to make shot for the firearms of frontiersmen and settlers.

The tower is now the center of Virginia's newest state park, most of which is located in Wythe County. Its New River Trail offers the outdoor enthusiast opportunities for hiking, biking, horseback riding, canoeing and primitive camping.

Another great outdoor site is Big Walker Lookout, located between Wytheville and Bland on U.S. 52. There's a chairlift, swinging bridge, observation tower 3,600 feet up offering a view of five states, cabin and gift shop.

Wythe Raceway also is nearby, a few miles from Rural Retreat. The oval clay track seats 5,000 fans who like late model and mini-stock racing, bike races and tractor pulls.

BLAND COUNTY

Formed in 1861, Bland County, nearly 80 percent forest and with a population of 6,500, was named for Richard Bland, a prominent Virginia patriot of the Revolutionary War. Thomas Jefferson called Bland "the wisest man south of the James River." Situated on the West Virginia border, Bland County is close to the Bluefields of Virginia and West Virginia.

The "Blizzard of '93," which dumped 32 inches of snow in the nearby New River Valley, brought snow drifts of 10 feet with it, stranding nearly 2,000 travelers. Bland County High School, churches and homes opened up to the surprised travelers. Three hundred were forced to spend the night in Big Walker tunnel. Needless to say, Bland County deservedly got a national reputation for hospitality after the "Blizzard of the Century."

Bland County's population, though sparse, is heavily engaged in agriculture, with 350 farms encompassing nearly 100,000 acres. Beef and dairy cattle and sheep are what most farmers raise. In fact, 95.9 percent of the land is used for agriculture, conservation and recreation, with only one percent used for industrial purposes.

As you'd expect, hunting and fishing are popular and deer and turkey, brook and rainbow trout are the main attractions.

Hunters of beautiful scenery and those wanting a refreshing alternative to interstate driving will want to see Big Walker Mountain Scenic Byway, 16.2 miles of the natural beauty of Southwest Virginia, most of which passes through Bland County. The Byway takes travelers over some of the area's most scenic land, which is beautiful year round. There is camping, hiking, hunting and picnicking in the Jefferson National Forest along this route. To get on the Byway, take the intersection of Route 717 and I-77, about five miles north of Wytheville. Go west on 717. Landmarks along the way include Stony Fork Creek, Seven Sisters Trail and Big Walker Lookout, where you can see several states.

Big Walker Mountain and Bland County offer a recreational activity unmatched in the Blue Ridge — llama hiking! Bob and Carolyn Bane of Virginia Highland Llamas (703- 688-4464), with advance reservations, will lead you and your party up Big Walker's old Appalachian Trail section with a herd of llamas. On special saddles, the llamas will carry a picnic lunch you can enjoy after hiking through lush green meadows and up to a beautiful vista. The hike is about three hours up and two and a half hours down. An eerie aspect of the journey is listening to each llama hum in different monotones. Why do they hum? "Because they don't know the words," says Carolyn Bane. Actually, humming is how the llamas communicate.

Golfers preferring a more predictable and traditional past-time will enjoy Wolf Creek Golf Club in Bastian, an 18-hole, par 70 public golf course open year round. It is on Route 614, five miles west of I-77 Bastian Exit. Golfers will also have a wonderful golfing day at the Draper Valley Golf Club. A championship 18-hole course, Draper Valley Golf Club players enjoy panoramic views of the Blue Ridge Mountains while playing. A putting green and driving range is also open to the public. This golf course is located on the service road on I-81 between Exits 86 and 89.

For some good country fun, try the Bland County Fair and Horse Show in August or the Bland County Lord's Acre Sale in October. Visitors are made to feel welcome by members of this friendly agricultural community.

Shoppers can find some good antique stores on Main Street in Bland, Heritage House Antiques and Imagine That!, whose motto is "Bring your imagination and have a vision!"

If you're looking for a nice place to stay, blizzard weather or not, Bland County's Willow Bend Farm B&B is located just off I-77 and the Big Walker Mountain Scenic Byway. Rates range from $55 to $75 with breakfast. Call (703) 688-3719 for more information.

For more information on Wytheville and Bland and Wythe counties, contact: The:Wytheville Convention & Visitors Bureau at (703) 228-3211, Wythe Ranger District, Jefferson National Forest, (703) 228-5551. For regional tourism information, you also may call 1-800-446-9670 or write the Virginia Highlands Gateway Visitor's Center at Drawer B-12, Max Meadows, VA 24360.

SMYTH COUNTY

If you love the outdoors, breathtaking scenery and retracing the steps of soldiers in one of the most important counties in the Civil

War, by all means visit gorgeous Smyth County (population 33,000) and enjoy all the natural beauty and rich history it has to offer, along with a host of good country restaurants and inexpensive places to stay.

Smyth County was formed in 1832 and named for General Alexander Smyth. The county's important towns are the county seat, Marion, named for Revolutionary War hero "Swamp Fox" Francis Marion; Chilhowie, apple capital of the state's southwest, whose Indian name means "Valley of Many Deer" and Saltville, named for the salt ponds that have yielded mastodon bones with spear points embedded in them and nicknamed "Salt Capitol of the Confederacy." During the Civil War, there were 38 furnaces in operation and in 1864 alone, 4 million bushels of salt were produced. In addition to providing table salt and salt for animals, the salt ponds' most important function was providing salt to preserve meat in the days before refrigeration.

Saltville's copious salt production brought an attack from the North on Oct. 2, 1864. You still can see the trenches and fortifications from which the outnumbered Confederates nevertheless successfully defended the town's saltworks. One of the historic cannons stands at the entrance of Saltville's Elizabeth Cemetery, where some Confederate defenders are buried. The Saltville Historical Foundation, which restored some of the Confederate fortifications, also has various battle relics on display in the Saltville Museum and at Virginia Highland Community College. Visitors also can see a reconstruction of the historical, rough-hewn Madam Russell House, home of Patrick Henry's sister. All tours begin at Saltville Museum, located in the center of town behind the post office.

The week before Labor Day, Saltville residents observe Salt-Making Week. They heat up some of the town's old salt kettles and boil down the brine, just as their ancestors did several hundred years ago. Then, on Labor Day, they celebrate with four days of music and fun.

Other historical attractions have equally interesting origins. The area's leading recreational area, Hungry Mother State Park, was named for Hungry Mother Creek. The park is located five miles from Marion off I-81. As legend has it, pioneer Molly Marley and her small child were caught in an Indian raid that killed her husband. After eating only berries for many days, she collapsed at the foot of the mountain known as Molly's Knob. Her child, unable to rouse her, wandered down the creek and finally found a group of houses. The only words he could say were "hungry" and "mother." A search party found the child's dead mother and the creek took its name from this sad tale.

On a more upbeat historical note, Smyth County's town of Troutdale was journey's end to the famous author Sherwood Anderson, who helped shape the modern short story and wrote the famous Winesburg, Ohio, and other literary gems. The Sherwood Anderson Short Story Competition is sponsored annually and recognition is awarded to aspiring authors. Ripshin,

Anderson's home, is open by appointment by calling Tom Copenhaver at (703) 783-4192. Professor Charles Modlin at Virginia Tech (703) 231-8447 is also knowledgeable about Anderson and his impact on Southwestern Virginia's literary riches.

In addition to lots of history, Smyth County offers many ways to have fun. Marion and Saltville each have town pools. Boaters and swimmers also can choose from Hungry Mother and Beartree lakes. Hungry Mother offers 2,000 acres of lovely, unspoiled Virginia countryside. You can hike or rent and ride horses through its miles of trails, swim, rent rowboats or paddleboats or fish on its 108-acre lake. Or, you can relax in the sun on its beach and enjoy the sunset from the porch of one of its cabins. For cabin reservations, call early at (703) 783-3422. Hungry Mother Campground in Marion, a mile south of the state park on U.S. 16, also offers an especially nice camping area. Call (703) 783-2046. Other recommended campgrounds are Houndshell in Troutdale (703) 655-4639 and Interstate (703) 646-8384 off I-81 at Seven Mile Ford.

Each July, dozens of artists and craftspeople display their work at the Hungry Mother Arts and Crafts Festival. The festival lasts three days and offers leatherwork, handmade clothing and arts and crafts from throughout the Eastern United States.

Another famous celebration is Marion's July 4th Celebration and Independence Day Chili Championship. Cooks spend all morning preparing pots of their best chili, the start of a day of games and concerts topped off by fireworks.

Mount Rogers Recreation Area (See Grayson County Chapter) is accessible from the Chilhowie exit. Headquarters for Mt. Rogers Recreation Area is at Highway 16 South in Marion. Call (703) 783-5196.

Hunters and fishermen can pursue their dreams in gorgeous Tumbling Creek wildwater and the Clinch Valley Mountain Wildlife Area, which includes a 300-acre mountaintop lake set aside for fishing, hunting and primitive camping. For more information, call (703) 944-3434 or the Virginia Commission of Game and Inland Fisheries at (804) 257-1000.

For those who don't want to rough it, a very nice bed and breakfast, Clarkcrest, is located at Chilhowie on Highway 607. The four large rooms offer rates of $60 per double occupancy. Owners Doug and Mary Clark may be called at (703) 646-3707 or 3737. General accommodations can be found in Chilhowie at Econo Lodge (703) 646-8981, Budget Host Inn at Marion (703) 783-8511 or the Marion Holiday Inn (703) 783-3193.

Visitors staying at Chilhowie may be lucky enough to catch its Apple Festival each September, a three-day celebration that includes a huge parade and other festivities.

There are many nice restaurants including House of Hunan, Highway 16 S at Marion (703) 783-2186 or Corner Downtown Cafe in Marion (703) 783-7668.

For more information, call the Smyth County Chamber of Commerce in Marion at (703) 783-3161.

Washington County/Town of Abingdon

WASHINGTON COUNTY

Washington County, home of historic Abingdon, the oldest town west of the Blue Ridge, is alive with history, arts, music, education and Southern hospitality. It is indisputably the cultural center of Southwestern Virginia.

The area's pristine mountain streams and plentiful camping also attract outdoor lovers from all over. The Mount Rogers National Recreation Center is located here, its 115,000 acres offering breathtaking panoramic views, trails and cross-country skiing.

South Holston Lake, a large Tennessee Valley Authority Reservoir, forms part of Washington County's southern border, providing boating, swimming and fishing opportunities. The national Virginia Creeper Trail, which gently climbs from Abingdon to Whitetop Mountain, once was an Indian trail and then a railway. Many hikers, horseback riders and cross-country skiers tackle the former railroad bed's 34 miles for a fix of relaxation and nature watching. The Virginia Creeper Trail Club will send you information if you write them at P.O. Box 2382, Abingdon, VA 24210.

Another county landmark is White's Mill, a Virginia Historic Landmark and one of the few remaining water-powered working mills in the country, located three and a half miles north of Abingdon. With much of its original machinery still in place, the two-story mill is an excellent example of 19th-century milling. There's also a trout-stocked mill pond and early 20th-century general store. For more information, call (703) 676-0825.

Washington County is also home to Emory & Henry College, a private, four-year liberal arts school that is consistently rated among the top small colleges and most enjoyable colleges to attend in the Southeast. Virginia Highlands Community College is here, too.

ABINGDON

What truly makes Washington County a premier vacation destination, however, is Abingdon, beautifully and vitally alive with attractions of nationally-known theatre, arts, music, shopping, trendy restaurants, a Four-Star hotel and historic bed and breakfast inns.

Founded in 1778, Abingdon was once the most important town in western Virginia. The first Englishmen used Abingdon as a distribution point for mail and supplies on The Great Road to the wilderness. It is now a community of friendly people with historic homes, quaint shops and galleries, hoping you'll stay awhile and partake of their hospitality.

The two unequalled stars in Abingdon's multi-faceted crown are the Barter Theatre, celebrating its 60th anniversary, and the Martha Washington Inn, a lovingly-restored classic hotel known for hospitality, gourmet food and fine service. Traditionally, people from around the world come to see the Barter Theatre's acclaimed plays, stay at the Martha Washington or an area B&B

and then take their pick of the town's multitude of cultural offerings.

The Barter, the state theatre of Virginia, was founded during the Great Depression in 1933. It started when Robert Porterfield, an enterprising young actor, returned to his native Washington County with an extraordinary proposition: How about bartering produce for tickets to see a play? The idea of "exchanging ham for Hamlet" proved successful. The bounty of produce from the farms and gardens of Southwestern Virginia provided food and work to professional Depression-era actors. At the close of the first season, the company cleared $4.35 in cash, two barrels of jelly and a collective weight gain of over 300 pounds.

In keeping with the system of barter, the theatre exchanged Virginia's famous country hams for royalties to produce the works of such playwrights as Noel Coward, Thornton Wilder and Bernard Shaw. Shaw, a vegetarian, returned the ham and requested spinach. The Barter obliged him. As time passed, Barter earned a reputation for top plays performed by top professionals. For an upcoming schedule of playbills, call the Barter at 800-368-3240.

The Martha Washington, newly remodeled and refurbished, matches the historical charm and elegance of the year it was founded, 1832. The original home was built for Col. Francis Preston. After his death, it became the Martha Washington College for Women. After the college merged with Emory & Henry, the inn was used as a boarding house for actors at the Barter. In 1935, it opened as an inn. Its present owner, United Coal Company, recently spent more than $6 million on its renovation. The inn offers a restaurant, a nightclub, private club and gift shop.

For more information on the Inn, or reservations, call 800-533-1014.

You will also be very pleased with your accommodations at any of the area's super bed and breakfasts, Victoria and Albert Inn, (703) 676-2797, Silversmith Inn, (703) 676-3924, Cabin on the River (703) 628-8433, Maplewood Farm (703) 628-2640, River Garden (800) 952-4296 and Summerfield Inn (703) 628-5905. All are charming...but not guaranteed ghost-free!

There's also camping at Washington County Park, WolfLair Campground, Riverside Family Campground and Lake Shore.

You can call the Abingdon Visitors & Convention Bureau for a descriptive brochure of all the B&Bs and attractions at (703) 676-2282. You may want to take in the rest of Abingdon's sights on its scenic historic walking tour. A map is available by calling (703) 628-8141.

If shopping is your passion, try the Cave House Craft Shop, operated by the Holston Mountain Arts and Crafts Cooperative, located three blocks from the Martha Washington and a National Historic Site. It features the work of Southwest Virginia artisans. Another interesting shop is the Abingdon General Store and "The Plum Alley Eatery" at 301 E. Main Street. Abingdon Mercantile and Frame Gallery and Antiques offers three stories and 12,000 square feet of the wares of 19 antique dealers. Dixie Pottery, off I-81, five miles south of Abingdon, offers world-wide shopping under one large roof.

A very special shop which attracts a large following is the Antique Orchid Herbary a few miles outside the town. It offers everything from herbal barbecues to nature walks with an herbal picnic supper. Classes are held in fresh herb and flower bouquets, summer party planning and gardening. For a list of delightful and unusual offerings, call (703) 628-1463.

If you're hungry, in addition to the Martha Washington, also try the downtown restaurants of PJ Brown & Company, Hardware Company Restaurant, the modern Starving Artist Cafe and The Tavern, dating back to 1779.

The cultural heritage of the area has been celebrated since 1948 at the annual Virginia Highlands Festival held the first two weeks in August. The popular event offers everything from hot air balloons and live entertainment to arts and crafts. Other popular festivals are the Washington County Fair and Burley Tobacco Festival held during the fall and the Damascus Appalachian Trail Days Festival held every year since May to celebrate the famous trail.

The King William Regional Arts Center keeps art alive with offerings of exhibitions of national and regional interest, art camp, workshops and studios for adults and students and special events. Call for a schedule of events at (703) 628-5005. If this interests you, you'll also want to go to The Arts Depot featuring working artists in their studios, gallery exhibits, a performing arts series

and an Appalachian Center for Poets and Writers. Call (703) 628-9091.

Each Christmas, Abingdon also offers a charming candlelight tour of its historic homes. For information, call (703) 676-2282.

TAZEWELL COUNTY

Tazewell County, in the heart of mountainous Southwestern Virginia, is a center of education, commerce, medical care and travel. Its terrain encompasses the eastern edge of Virginia's Coal Country. Tazewell's combination of rustic beauty and bustling commerce has attracted 50,000 residents.

The county includes one of the twin Bluefields of Virginia and West Virginia. It's also noted for "The Garden Spot of the World," scenic Burke's Garden, where the spurned railroad tycoon, Cornelius Vanderbilt, originally wanted to build his famous Biltmore Estates. He later settled for Asheville, N.C., after local residents wouldn't sell. Asheville might have millions of dollars of tourist's money, but Tazewell still has this breathtaking spot!

Stories of the fiercely proud, independent people of Tazewell abound. Legend has it that Vanderbilt wasn't the only tycoon who didn't impress the locals. Auto magnate Henry Ford, in the company of inventors Thomas Edison and Harvey Firestone, couldn't get a check cashed by the locals while on a camping trip.

Tazewell County became famous in 1842 when Dr. Thomas English wrote the poem, "Sweet Alice, Ben Bolt," while visiting the county. The poem later became a world-famous hit song inspired by Tazewell's beauty.

Tazewell is known as a regional medical center with two hospitals providing state-of-the-art medical care for the area's residents. Opportunities for higher education also are here, with Bluefield College, a private, four-year college; Southwest Virginia Community College and National Business College.

Recreation abounds. The Jefferson National Forest and Clinch Valley Wildlife Preserve provide excellent year round hunting and fishing. There's also a variety of horse stables and gun clubs.

The Bluefield Orioles offer minor league baseball action at Bowen Field in Bluefield. Snow skiing is available within a one hour's drive and several recreational lakes are nearby.

Tazewell County has a rich mountain past. Native Americans lived an agrarian lifestyle in Tazewell. Later, the Cherokee and Shawnee tribes hunted here. The first pioneers to explore Tazewell County in the 1700s were hunters, surveyors and land speculators. The Burke's Garden area, about 50 square miles of beautiful, fine farmland encircled by a continuous mountain range, was the site of the county's first land survey in 1748. As the land west of the Blue Ridge Mountains was developed, pioneers of German, Scotch-Irish and English origins began building settlements and farming in the 1770s. The county was formed in 1799.

The town of Tazewell, the county seat, was founded in 1800. Beautiful homes were built in the early 1800s including the Bowen home in The Cove and the Gose house in Burke's Garden.

Burke's Garden, a National Historic District, is the largest rural historical district in Virginia. Those wishing to see the fabled area at its best, with produce, arts and crafts, should attend the September Fall Festival sponsored by the Burke's Garden Community Association. Call (703) 963-3385 for more information. To stay in the lovely valley, call the James Burke Inn B&B at (703) 472-2114.

Other important towns are Richlands, Bluefield, Cedar Bluff and Pocahontas. Another infamous town is Frog Level. It's so tiny, it's hardly on the map, but T-shirts sell briskly around the world and the Rescue Squad's entry is always the most popular in Virginia with its frogmen in lifeboats and their life jacket-clad Terrier mascot.

Richlands was named for its fertile land along the section of the Clinch Valley, where the town lies. The town was designed by Clinch Valley Coal & Iron, which envisioned Richlands as the "Pittsburgh of the South." Bluefield's name stems from a species of chicory that grows in abundance in the county. In the spring of 1993, the Tazewell County Board of Supervisors voted to make poke salad the county's official native vegetable. Poke salad was honored, according to one supervisor, "because the community couldn't be starved out" during tough times for coal miners. Along with coal mining, the railroad led to its growth, and there is a city with an identical name across the border in West Virginia. Cedar Bluff's name sprang from the profusion of cedar trees nearby. A resort and woolen mill aided in its growth. Pocahontas, with a glorious past as a coal-mining boom town, retains that image and has its own exhibition coal mine for visitors.

Tazewell also saw lots of action in the Civil War, as a route to Wytheville's lead mines and Saltville's saltworks. One young soldier, "Devil Anse" Hatfield, and his kin from the Tug Fork region of West Virginia, traveled to Tazewell, harassing Union troops. Later, Hatfield had his own war back home to contend with, thanks to the neighboring McCoy family. Who hasn't heard of the infamous West Virginia "Hatfields and McCoys?"

The history of Tazewell County and Southwestern Virginia is chronicled from prehistoric to present times at the Historic Crab Orchard Museum and Pioneer Park in Tazewell. The Park, with its eight log and two stone structures and horse-drawn equipment building is representative of the lifestyle of early pioneers. Call (703) 988-6755 for more information.

Another interesting historical area is Paint Lick Mountain, where Indians left their writing, pictures and artifacts.

The Bluefields, situated in two shallow valleys, offer scenery, shopping, commerce and the national reputation of "Nature's Air-Conditioned City." In 1939, Chamber of Commerce officials started serving free lemonade when the temperature hit 90 degrees, a promotion that still gets national air-time today, especially from Willard Scott of the Today Show.

Visitors to Bluefield can enjoy Graham Recreational Park and the Bluefield Area Arts and Crafts Center at 500 Bland St., the original City Hall and now on the National Register of Historic Places. Located here are artists' studios, a crafts shop, the Paine Art Gallery and Summit Theatre. Call (304) 325-8000 for more information.

Bluefield's Craft Memorial Library is the repository for the Eastern Regional Coal Archives, Southern West Virginia's research facility dedicated to collecting, preserving and making available the heritage of the coal fields. It's a fascinating collection of films, diaries, company records, scrip, rare books and railroad memorabilia. Call (304) 325-3943 for more facts. As the self-proclaimed documenter of the coal fields, The Bluefield Chamber hosts a Coal Show, held every two years, and called the "Best in the East." Call the Bluefield Chamber at (304) 327-7184 for dates.

Downtown Cedar Bluff, originally known as Indian, Virginia, was founded in 1800 and host to the historic district of the Old Kentucky Turnpike, as well as being the birthplace of Gov. George C. Peery. The town was also home to the C.E. Goodwin Sons' Woolen Mills, later known as the Clinch Valley Blanket Mills. The Goodwins began weaving coverlets in 1907, which was the beginning of one of the largest collections of blanket patterns in the world.

Water-ground meal was manufactured by Cedar Bluff Milling Company. This grist mill has been extensively renovated and is one of the region's major heritage tourist attractions. Another unusual attraction is the Wittle League Hall of Fame, built in 1980 by Bill H. Ascue to honor 40 years of local baseball. The building is in Ascue's front yard.

Fans of unusual phenomena may remember that Cedar Bluff was the home of the celebrated little girl, Nannie Ruth Lowe, an extraordinary child who walked and talked at the age of nine months and predicted her own death at age seven. People came from miles around to hear her read the Bible at age three. The tot led revivals and excelled in Biblical knowledge, spelling and arithmetic.

To experience the area's history first-hand, be sure to attend the Cedar Bluff Heritage Festival in September. Arts and crafts are center stage, along with a country store, antiques and vintage clothing. You can watch cider, apple butter and soap being made. Local historians and storytellers entertain. For more information on Cedar Bluff and the festival, call James K. McGlothlin at (703) 964-4889.

Visitors to the county will also want to see historic Pocahontas, the most interesting town in the county, designated a Virginia Historic Landmark. It has a colorful past as the early "capitol" of the famous and vast Pocahontas Coalfield and is the oldest mining town in the world. The first mine there was opened in 1882.

Proud citizens have since renovated many of its landmarks including the Pocahontas Exhibition Mine, showing a spectacular 13-foot-high coal seam. The mine's "smokeless" coal made it the chosen fuel of the U.S. Navy during the mine's 73 years of operation. In that time, it produced more than 44 million tons of coal, enough to fill a train 6,000 miles long. The mine is open May through October. For tour information, call (703) 945-5959. Also nearby is the Coal Miner's Memorial in Boissevain.

Hungarian and Southern black miners brought their rich culture into the mountainous wilds of the emerging coal field. Much of the beautiful, European-influenced architecture in Pocahontas dating from that period — the Opera House and the original Company Store — still stands today, a monument to a unique civilization. Built in 1895, the Opera House was the first theatre in the area, with many first-run Broadway shows. It was forced to close its doors during the Depression. Since, it has been restored by Historic Pocahontas, Inc. as a dinner theatre.

In the midst of Pocahontas is the Silver Dollar Saloon, a testimony to that boisterous and colorful era. On a more reverent note, another landmark to see is the ornate St. Elizabeth's Catholic Church, founded in 1898, featuring 10 life-sized hand-painted murals.

The town of Richlands boasts a 35-acre park adjacent to the town along the Clinch River. It includes a Junior Olympic pool, wading pool and multi-purpose sports courts. Richland is also known as the town of festivals, ranging from the Tazewell County Fair in August to the Richlands Festival, which is simply an excuse for five days of non-stop entertainment.

While visiting Tazewell, you'll find lots of good, old-fashioned family restaurants to visit. There's "RC's" on Main St. in Tazewell and Cuz' Uptown Barbeque in Pounding Mill, a restored barn that features a "Cow and Elvis" theme decor lounge. A nice place to stay is the Comfort Inn in Bluefield, Va. (800) 228-5150.

For more information on places to eat and stay, call the Tazewell Area Chamber of Commerce & Visitors Center at (703) 988-5091, the Richlands Area Chamber of Commerce at (703) 963-3385, or Greater Bluefield Chamber of Commerce at (304) 327-7184.

BUCHANAN COUNTY

Located in the Appalachian Plateau of Southwestern Virginia, this is real "Coal Country." The county of Buchanan, named for the former U.S. President James Buchanan, was explored about 1750 but sparsely settled until the 1930s, when coal mining made it big. So big, in fact, that Buchanan now produces nearly half of the entire state of Virginia's coal, which translates to nearly 50 million tons.

With towns with names such as "Dismal," one may expect a high unemployment rate (nearly 8 percent) among the county's 34,200 people. When they can work, many make their living from coal mining and companies that make roof bolts and mining equipment. Coal Country's industrial giants are located here, including Island Creek, Consolidated, United and Jewell Coal and Coke.

Buchanan County's people,

however, do know how to have a good time and are proud of the recreational opportunities they can offer visitors, ranging from the county's newest recreational facility, the William P. Harris, a park with a swimming pool, basketball and baseball fields, to Breaks Interstate Park, 4,200 acres nicknamed the "Grand Canyon of the South."

The park, which is shared by Kentucky and the Dickenson County border, sports the largest canyon east of the Mississippi, carved by the Russell Fork River to a depth of 1,600 feet guarded by sheer vertical walls. In a succession of waterfalls and rapids, the river lunges over and around massive boulders. Whitewater rafting is available, water conditions permitting.

Located 20 minutes from Grundy, the county seat, the park is open from April through October. In the spring, it is famous for its blooming rhododendron, foliage and wildflowers. Rhododendron Lodge, located here, has a restaurant, gift shop featuring lovely mountain crafts and a lodge with rustic rooms. Cottages and a camping area are also available. Call (703) 865-4413 for park information or (703) 865-4414 for the lodge.

Once at the park, the Visitor Center is the main feature of the interpretive complex. It houses exhibits and displays of the natural and historic features of the area. Its coal exhibit probably is the most popular. An amphitheater in a shaded setting offers visitors an opportunity to view dramas and nature slide and film programs. It also is the location of the annual, three-day Autumn

Gospel Sing Festival on Labor Day weekend.

Laurel Lake provides fishing opportunities and pedal boats for visitors who like the water. A pool is located near the lake and includes bath facilities and a children's pool. Breaks Interstate Park can be reached by U.S. Route 460 from Grundy to Harman Junction, then Route 609 to the Breaks. The state stocks trout in the stream at Dismal, which draws a large number of anglers when season opens in the spring.

A public golf course is also located here, Mountain Top, with nine holes located on 30 acres of previously strip-mined land in the Compton Mountain area on Route 639. It features artificial greens and is the first course of its kind in the U.S.

Another point of interest is Mountain Mission School, established in Grundy in 1921 for Christian education from ages one to 21, and famous for its choir, which is known throughout the world.

When visiting Buchanan County, there are five motels located along the Route 460 corridor, as well as family-style restaurants. General and speciality shopping can be found in the same area, as well as on Route 80 and 83.

For more information, call the Buchanan County Chamber of Commerce at (703) 935-4147.

RUSSELL COUNTY

Russell County, population 31,761 is famous for its coal mines, agriculture and incredible mountain scenery. Even the nomad, Daniel Boone, found Russell, "The Redbud Capital of the World," so beautiful that he put down roots here for a couple of years.

Wrote Teddy Roosevelt about the area's pioneers, "They were tough and supple as the hickory out of which they fashioned the handles of their axes." Long ago, however, the sturdy hickory made way for the coal industry.

In Russell County, you'll find the booming technology of the coal industry, headquarters of the nation's leading exporter of coal, Pittston, located in Lebanon. Appalachian Power, which uses the Blue Ridge lakes of Smith Mountain and Claytor for its northern energy sources, here turns southwest Virginia coal into power at its huge plant in Carbo. The manufacturing of furniture, clothing, shoes and interiors for the auto industry also provide employment to locals.

Russell County was founded in 1786 and named for Gen. William Russell, who assisted in the drafting of the Declaration of Independence. More than 20 historic homes still stand including the H.C. Stuart Mansion, built in 1913 at Elk Garden for Virginia's Governor Stuart; John Howard Mansion, on Route 71, five miles outside of Lebanon; Dickenson Bundy Log House, a public building standing beside the Old Court House in Dickensonville; and the present courthouse in Lebanon, in use since 1874. If you're a history buff, photographer, artist or just enjoy old architecture, don't miss seeing these Russell County landmarks.

Another landmark you won't want to miss is Russell County's unusual "House and Barn Mountain," a mountain named for these particular shapes.

Other places to see or go outdoors include the Clinch River, for some of the best fishing east of the Mississippi. The Clinch River is also well known for canoeing from Blackford to St. Paul. Camping facilities are offered next to the 300-acre Hidden Valley Lake. Big Cedar Creek, known as a "Big Bass Pond," is a fisherman's delight with camping, hiking and picnic facilities.

Lebanon's county park is home to a crystal clear waterfall. Camping is permitted and locals say there's nothing visiting campers remark about more than the pleasure of waking up to the soothing sound of a waterfall. Afterward, a pleasant morning walk can be taken at J.S. Easterly Park, which also offers hiking trails and tennis courts. Glade Hollow Park is another nice park. Near Cleveland, Lake Bonaventure Country Club has golfing on a nine-hole course, swimming and fishing.

Russell Countians celebrate on many occasions. The most popular is the Honaker Redbud Festival, named for the delicate Virginia budding tree that dots the mountains each spring. The month-long festival starts in March and goes into April with events as varied as an essay contest, canoe race, parade and homecoming dinner. The county's fair in Castlewood each September is another fun event, with a rodeo and drafthorse pulling contest taking top billing, along with the "Biggest Pumpkin" contest. The Southwest Virginia Music Festival in Belfast, held Labor Day Weekend, is another popular affair.

While staying in Russell County, consider the Carriage House Motel in Lebanon (703) 889-2884 and Town and Country Motor Lodge on Highway 19 (703) 889-2772. There are restaurants such as Bonanza and Western Sizzlin in Lebanon, all on Highway 19. For an interesting shopping event, visit the Russell County People's Market between Lebanon Elementary and Middle School each Saturday through September. It features farm produce and handicrafts made by the locals.

For more information about Russell County, call the Russell County Chamber of Commerce at (703) 889-8041.

DICKENSON COUNTY

Located in the heart of Virginia's coal fields, where many are employed by Pittston Coal Company, Dickenson County is rich in history and mountain heritage. Kentucky is its northwest boundary along the crest of the Cumberland Mountains, to the point where the mountain breaks up, allowing the Russell Fork River to flow through, carrying most of the water that flows out of Dickenson County through the "Breaks" Canyon to the north.

The Russell Fork provides world-class whitewater rafting, Class 3 to 5+, and some of the most breathtaking scenery east of the Grand Canyon! Business owners are confident that whitewater rafting will soon blossom into a multi-million-dollar industry.

Hundreds of people each weekend brave the river, putting in at historic Yellow Poplar Splashdam, where Route 611 crosses the Russell Fork river. Many rafting enthusiasts say it's the most challenging river they've ever tackled! Outfitters such as Russell Fork Whitewater Adventures take trips nearly each weekend down the ravine. Call or write the Dickenson County Chamber for a rafting schedule (703) 926-4328.

The internationally renowned Breaks Interstate Park encompasses an area of 4,500 acres surrounding the Breaks Canyon, referred to as the "Grand Canyon of the South." The park features a 122-acre campground, motel, restaurant and visitors center. Call (703) 865-4413 for more information.

Twelve miles south is John W. Flannagan Reservoir, a 1143-acre lake noted for monstrous walleye fish and surrounded by 7,500 acres of woodlands teeming with wildlife. The dam was finished in 1964. It is 250 feet high and 916 feet long and forms a lake of 1,145 acres, proclaimed one of the cleanest in the world.

Visitors enjoy outstanding fishing, boating and water-skiing. Campsites, picnic areas, tennis courts and a softball field are located near the lake. Horseback riding and hiking abound throughout the county. One of the most picturesque hikes is the 26-mile-long one along the crest of the Cumberland Mountains dividing Virginia and Kentucky from Pound Gap to Potter's Flats, near Breaks Park. For additional information, call the U.S. Army Corps of Engineers at (703) 835-9544.

Each fall, Pioneer Days and the county fair celebrate a rich Appalachian heritage. The Cumberland Museum and Art Gallery in the county seat of Clintwood is dedicated to the preservation of the area's vanishing art and artifacts, "Things of Toil and Love." You can see wood carvings, fossils, a miniature coal mine and hundreds of tools and survival items of early settlers in the mountains. It's been called "The Most Interesting Place in the Mountains." For more information, call (703) 926-6632.

Another interesting site is the historic Fremont Train Station, which has been restored near the original site at the intersection of Rt. 63 and 83. Yet another landmark is the homeplace of Ralph and Carter, "The Stanley Brothers," legends in bluegrass music. The old farm, located on Highway 643, is where Ralph holds his annual Bluegrass Festival.

If you're a railroad fan, also don't miss Dennis Reedy's own railroad museum in Clinchco. He'll show you around by appointment (703) 835-9593.

While in Clintwood, get some family-style food from the White Star Cafe, across from the courthouse. Here, you can sample the atmosphere, pace and pricing of a bygone era. For information on other restaurants, lodging and shopping, call the Dickenson County Chamber at (703) 926-4326).

WISE COUNTY

Wise County, like many nearby, is a wealth of scenery, culture and attractions. However, it has more of them than most of its neighbors, with numerous recreational areas, a major outdoor drama and four museums.

Located in the heart of the Appalachian Mountains, Wise County was named for Gov. Henry Wise. Its 50,000 people reside mostly in the towns of Wise, Norton, Appalachian, Big Stone Gap, Coeburn, Pound and St. Paul. Wise also is in the heart of coal country and a center of health care and higher education as well, with Clinch Valley College of the University of Virginia, a four-year, liberal arts college and Mountain Empire Community College.

Recreational opportunities abound in the Jefferson National Forest. Norton offers Flag Rock Recreational Area and High Knob, where you can see several states from one viewpoint. Another scenic overlook is Powell Valley. There's fishing and camping in North Fork Reservoir in Point and Oxbow Lake in St. Paul. The North Fork of Pound Lake is another recreational area where you can boat, fish, camp and picnic. The U.S. Army Corps of Engineers can give you more information by calling (304) 529-2311.

If you've got the bug to go backpacking but hate the thought of buying expensive equipment, call Joseph's Backpacking in Big Stone Gap at (703) 679-3532. They'll supply you with equipment "to go boldly on a new adventure" on High Knob Mountain, so there's no reason why you can't explore the highlands with nothing but sheer determination. Do call for reservations, however.

Locals also have taken to mountain biking in a big way. Ride and Stride Shop (703) 679-0118 can give you information. Holiday Inn of Norton (703) 679-7000 offers special mountain bike motel rates.

Car racing is another popular sport. Lonesome Pine International Raceway offers lots of fast cars in a continuing schedule of races featuring famous drivers such as Davey Allison, Mike Waltrip and Sterling Marlin. Call (703) 395-3338 for more information.

Wise County's towns are also worth exploring. You'll know Big Stone Gap is special when you see that its Visitor's Center is located in a restored Interstate Car, the #101, with a long, illustrious history. Built in 1870 for the South Carolina & Georgia Railroad, the car was retired in 1959 from the tracks and then transported to Wise for a hunting camp. In 1988, the car was donated to Wise by Humphrey's Enterprises. A successful community fund-raising effort resulted in the car being moved to Big Stone Gap, where it was restored to its present condition and used as the present Visitor's Center. It looks nearly exactly as it did in 1870! For information, call (703) 523-2060.

After you've seen the #101, it's time to see the rest of Big Stone Gap. The town is noted for its famous "Trail of the Lonesome Pine" outdoor drama, based on John Fox, Jr's book, and staged during July and August. It is performed on the historic site where the drama actually took place and has been telling the story of a proud mountain folk since 1964 at June Tolliver Playhouse. For more information, call (800) TRAIL-LP.

In addition to the drama, Lonesome Pine Arts & Crafts, Inc. was organized in 1963 for the histori-

Dickenson County, Virginia.
Rugged, Scenic, Different!

For Information, contact:
Dickenson County
 Chamber of
  Commerce
P. O. Box 1068
Clintwood, VA 24228
(703) 865-4443

SPONSORED BY: Dickenson County Chamber of Commerce, EREX, Gerald Gray Law Firm, Dickenson-Buchanan Bank, Pittston Coal

cal, cultural and economic benefit of all Southwestern Virginia. For nearly 30 years, it has impacted the lives of hundreds of young people through its touring theatre and artisans and craftspeople's marketing program. You can see their handiwork at the June Tolliver House and Craft Shop — weaving, painting, woodcrafts and other unique mountain handicrafts. Call (703) 523-1235.

Also stop by to see John Fox, Jr. Museum, a National and Virginia Historical Landmark which serves as both a museum and a memorial to the Fox family, where John, who eventually wrote 500 short stories, grew up. His "Trail of the Lonesome Pine" became the first American novel to sell a million copies and later became a popular movie. Call (703) 523-2747.

Big Stone Gap is also home to yet two other museums. They invite you to step across the threshold of the not-so-distant past to a time when "Gap Fever" brought a host of talented young men and women from all over the country, hoping to make their fortunes in the area's abundant natural resources. Among them was Virginia Attorney General Rufus Ayers, whose 1893 three-story, native cut stone home would eventually house the Southwest Virginia Museum. In it, you'll now see that Ayers spared no expense to build one of the finest homes in Virginia. The museum is operated by the Department of Conservation and Recreation's Division of State Parks. For hours of operation, call (703) 523-1322.

Another popular museum is the Harry Meador Coal Museum on East Shawnee St. and Shawnee Ave., which provides a fascinating history of this area's cornerstone industry. The museum contains artifacts painstakingly assembled from private homes and public buildings which illustrate the coal mining heritage of the area as well as its effect on the local lifestyle. Owned by Westmoreland Coal Company and operated by the Big Stone Gap Dept. of Parks and Recreation, admission is free. The department also oversees Miners Park, a moment to coal field workers in downtown. The museum is dedicated to Harry W. Meador, Jr., former vice president of Westmoreland Coal and a tireless advocate of the coal mining industry. Call (703) 523-4950 for more information.

Mountain Empire College in Big Stone Gap also celebrates a Home Crafts Day with traditional Appalachian crafts, demonstrations, storytelling, ethnic foods, dancing and music each October.

The town of Norton is another interesting area to visit for home crafts and historical preservation through the Appalachian Peddler and Country Cabin. The Peddler, at 903 Virginia Ave., promotes a positive message of Appalachia. Located in a three-story Victorian house with a wide front porch, owners Paul and Sheila Kuczko are dedicated to promoting the best of Appalachia. The Peddler specializes in art, antiques, books, crafts, music and artifacts indigenous to the Appalachian region. Call (703) 679-5927 for hours of operation. Each discipline claims its own area, with an Appalachian Music Room, Book Room and Antique

Room.

Country Cabin is co-sponsored by Clinch Valley College and Appalachian Traditions, a nonprofit organization dedicated to preservation, promotion and perpetuation of traditional Appalachian culture. It is used for everything from teaching clogging to a cultural exchange for tourists of other cultures. Here, you may hear the Sorghum Lickers Band or watch the Virginia Sugarcane Cloggers perform. The public is invited to visit the cabin each Saturday night for performances of traditional mountain music. Appalachian Traditions also sponsors the annual Dock Boggs Festival, a one-day celebration of traditional mountain music on the second Saturday in September at the Wise County Fairground. Call (703) 328-0100 for more information.

One of the nicest places to stay in Wise County is the Norton Holiday Inn, "The Friendliest Hotel in Southwest Virginia," a favorite gathering place for those who enjoy fine dining, luxurious accommodations and meeting facilities unparalleled in the area. This mountain oasis can be reached by calling (703) 679-7000. While you're staying in Wise County, you'll find great family places to eat. Mosby's at Norton Shopping Plaza has a varied menu ranging from traditional New York Strip to The General Lee Sandwich. Call for reservations at (703) 679-1046.

The town of Appalachia is another interesting place, with coal as the focus. Named for the mountain range, it sprang up at a railroad junction during the coal and land boom in neighboring Big Stone Gap.

Also be sure to see Bee Rock Tunnel, on U.S. 23-Business, featured in Ripley's "Believe It or Not" as the "Shortest Railroad Tunnel in the World." Other attractions are The Bullitt Mine Complex, Westmoreland Coal dump train and the Rotary Dump, a machine that turns railroad cars upside down and empties their contents into a bin below. You also can see coal camps on Route 68 at Imboden, Lower Exeter, Exeter and Keokee, built by coal mining barons of the early 20th century for their employees.

For more sites to see, call the Wise County Chamber of Commerce at (703) 679-0961.

Scott County

Scott County, where Daniel Boone passed through on the Wilderness Trail, still prides itself on being a land with scenery "the way Mother Nature made it," inspiring the famous country ballad of the "Wildwood Flower." It's also home to the "Eighth Wonder of the World," Natural Tunnel State Park.

Scott County, formed in 1814, was named after War of 1812 hero, Gen. Winfield Scott. The county's 24,700 citizens have their choice of enjoying mountain streams and backpacking trails through an unspoiled natural setting. There are laurel-lined mountains in Hanging Rock Canyon in the Jefferson National Forest near Dungannon. Outside Nickelsville, the Kilgore Fort House, a reconstructed fort from the frontier era, links the county to Boone's trek on the Wilderness Road. At Powell Mountain, on Highway 58, you can see a view of three states.

The centuries-old Holston and Clinch rivers flow through, lending themselves freely to the leisurely family activities of canoeing and fishing. Recreational areas are located at Scott County Park, which features a golf course and tennis courts, Hanging Rock Picnic Area, Bark Camp Lake and Devils Fork Recreational Area and its waterfalls are all overseen by the U.S. Forest Service.

The star attraction, however, is the Natural Tunnel Park in Duffield. Since 1880, when statesman William Jennings Bryan declared it the "Eighth Wonder of the World," Natural Tunnel has attracted sightseers from all parts of the country. Daniel Boone was one of the first to see it and the area was well known to Indians. However, the tunnel got its start long before people were on the scene, as it is believed to be about 1 million years old. The walls of the limestone basis are nearly vertical, rising to heights of more than 400 feet.

While you're at the visitor center, drop by and see the video, "Stay Awhile," which highlights historical and recreational attractions nearby. For more information, call the state park at (703) 940-2674.

Another major attraction is the Carter Family Fold, "Where Music Began," the homeplace of Sara and Maybelle Carter. Maybelle's daughter, June, is the wife of singer Johnny Cash. It features a country music museum and live music every Saturday night and is located on A.P. Carter Highway in Hiltons. Call (703) 386-9480.

While you're staying in Scott County, consider the Ramada Inn in Duffield, offering package rates. Call 1-800-VA-BYWAY. The Ramada also features Winfield's Restaurant. There are fast food places and markets in the Gate City, Nickelsville and Duffield area. For more information, call the Scott County Chamber of Commerce at (703) 386-6665

LEE COUNTY

Last but certainly not least, at the tip of Virginia, triangle-shaped Lee County, bordering Kentucky and Tennessee, offers beautiful rolling hills and valleys nestled in the Tennessee River Basin. It is home to 24,500 people and the Cumberland Gap, used by early settlers as the only means of passage during westward expansion. Cumberland Gap National Historical Park and the Jefferson National Park are also both located here.

People here frequently work either in the coal fields or on the farm. Tobacco is an important crop. Manufacturing is gaining more in importance, especially textiles. Tourism is also becoming a chief industry.

The northern part of Lee has nearly 12,000 acres of the Jefferson, which provide opportunities for hiking, hunting, camping, picnicking, backpacking and sightseeing. It contains Lake Keokee, a 92-acre waterway for fishing, boating and picnicking, and Cave Springs Recreation Area, a small lake for swimming and camping. Stone Mountain Trail, 11 miles long, is a difficult but popular trail here with one of the nicest natural settings in Southwestern Virginia. Call (703) 328-2931 for more information about the Jefferson.

The Cumberland Gap Park, commemorating early settlers and Daniel Boone, is located in the extreme western portion of the county. Also located on the edge of the park is Cudjo's Caverns, three levels of natural caves used by the Indians and Civil War soldiers. The camp features camping, hiking and the Hensley Settlement, a restored turn of the century mountain community that is a symbol of the determination and true grit of the early American pioneer. Shuttle bus service is provided or you can go by horseback. Call (606) 248-2817.

The 26-acre Cumberland Bowl Park in Jonesville has swimming facilities, picnic tables and pavilions, a walking trail and children's playground. Plays are performed regularly in the amphitheater. Leeman Field, in Pennington Gap, has swimming, tennis courts and a horse ring and is the site of the annual Lee County Fair in August and the Tobacco and Fall Festival in October.

Monte Vista Golf Course in Ewing, a nine-hole course, also has a swimming pool and clubhouse. It is located off U.S. Highway 58.

Another interesting site is the African American Historical Cultural Center in Pennington Gap, which contains a comprehensive collection of historical artifacts. A full-time curator presides. For more information, call (703) 546-5144.

A mile north of Pennington Gap on Old Harlan Road, Highway 421, look for Stone Face Rock, a fascinating attraction that can be seen day or night and looks like an Indian head. Widely believed to be a natural phenomenon, some theorists believe it is an ancient Cherokee Indian head which actually was carved by the Cherokees to mark the entrance of their holy grounds.

Lee is located a few hours away from the Great Smokey Mountains and the Tennessee Valley Authority lakes.

If you decide to trek along the Daniel Boone Heritage Trail, which starts in Duffield and ends in Lee County, there are several nice places to stay. The Jonesville Motor Court is on Highway 58, (703) 346-3210, as is Convenient Inn in Pennington Gap, (703) 546-5350 and Ritchie House Bed and Breakfast in Ewing, (703) 445-4505.

Family restaurants and fast food strips are located mostly in Pennington Gap and Jonesville.

For more information, call the Lee County Chamber of Commerce at (703) 346-7766.

ORDER FORM

Use this convenient form to place your order
for any of the Insiders' Guides® books.

Fast and Simple!

Mail to:
Insiders' Guides®, Inc.
P.O. Box 2057
Manteo, NC 27954 *or*
for VISA or Mastercard orders call
1-800-765-BOOK

Name _____

Address _____

City/State/Zip _____

Quantity	Title/Price	Shipping	
	Insiders' Guide® to the Triangle, $12.95	$2.50	
	Insiders' Guide® to Charlotte, $12.95	$2.50	
	Insiders' Guide® to Virginia Beach / Norfolk, $12.95	$2.50	
	Insiders' Guide® to the Outer Banks, $12.95	$2.50	
	Insiders' Guide® to Williamsburg, $12.95	$2.50	
	Insiders' Guide® to Richmond, $12.95	$2.50	
	Insiders' Guide® to Orlando, $12.95	$2.50	
	Insiders' Guide® to Virginia's Blue Ridge, $12.95	$2.50	
	Insiders' Guide® to The Crystal Coast of NC, $12.95	$2.50	
	Insiders' Guide® to Myrtle Beach, $12.95 (Summer '93)	$2.50	
	Insiders' Guide® to Charleston, $12.95	$2.50	
	Insiders' Guide® to Virginia's Blue Ridge, $12.95	$2.50	
	Insiders' Guide® to Civil War Sites In The Eastern Theater (Fall '93), $12.95	$2.50	
	Insiders' Guide® to Lexington, $12.95 (Spring '94)	$2.50	
	Insiders' Guide® to Wilmington, NC, $12.95 (Spring '94)	$2.50	

(N.C. residents add 6% sales tax.) GRAND TOTAL _____

*Payment in full (check, cash or money order) must accompany
order form. Please allow 2 weeks for delivery*

Index of Advertisers

200 South Street Inn	340
309 First Street Restaurant	394
Artists in Cahoots	89
AuPairCare	455
Awful Arthur's	405
Baja Bean Co.	262
Barr-ee Station	275
Billy's Ritz	394
Bleu Rock Inn	344
Blue Ridge Motor Lodge	17
Blue Wheel Bicycles	263
Boar's Head Inn	299
C & O Restaurant	413
Carlos Restaurant	394
Center In	
The Square	Inside front cover
Charlottesville Guide	47
Clifton Country Inn	339
Colony House Motor Lodge	370
Dickenson County Chamber	
of Commerce	519
Doe Run Lodge	374
Fantasies	89
Fassifern	317
Festive Fare	406
Fort Lewis Lodge	323
Fountain Hall	319
Fox and Hounds Restaurant	390
Freeman-Victorious Framing	263
GEICO	11
George C. Marshall Museum	89
Gilmore, Hamm	
& Synder	Inside back cover
Go Pal Bicycle Shop	262
Grave's Mountain Lodge	319
Hampton Inn	368
Hardware Store Restaurant	408
Heartwood Books	262
Hibernia	145
Holiday Inn-North	
University	376
Hotel Strasburg	362
Howard Johnson's-	
Charlottesville	375
Inn at Monticello	315
Irish Gap Inns	317
Jordan Hollow Farm	323
Joshua Wilton House	325
Krissia	269
Lavender Hill Farm	325
Lexington Historical Shop	89
Little John's	263
Llewellyn Lodge	317
Lynchburg Chamber	
of Commerce	53

Lynchburg College	488	Roanoke Market	394
Lynchburg Community Market	53	Roanoke Marriott	372
Lynchburg Museum	53	Roanoke Visitors Bureau	163
Macado's	262	Rococo's	404
Main Street Grill	263	Seven Hills	321
Mallard Point	441	Shenandoah Travel Association	17
Mincer's	262	Shennanigans	269
Ming Dynasty Restaurant	17	Signet Bank	32
Mountain Lake	305	Silver Thatch Inn	338
Museum of American		Simeon Vineyards	155
Frontier Culture	203	Sleepy Hollow Farm	315
New Market Battlefield		St. Anne's Belfield	493
Historical Park	92	Stonewall Jackson House	89
New Market Battlefield		The Book Gallery	269
Military Museum	17	The Garment District	263
New Market Cafe	17	The Inn at Meander Plantation	319
Norfield's Farm	315	The Inn at Union Run	321
Oakencroft	151	The John Sevier Gallery	17
Opera Roanoke	225	The Keep	321
Orange County Visitors Bureau	44	The Phoenix	263
Oregano Joe's	406	The Second Story Bookshop	89
P. Buckley Moss Museum	208	The Virginia Shop	269
Palmer Country Inn	343	Totier Creek	157
Pappagallo	89	Vanucci's Restaurant	394
Peaks of Otter	369	Virginia Born and Bred	89
Primland Hunting Reserve	113	Virginia Diner	13
Prince Michel Restaurant	410	Virginia Horse Center	89
Prospect Hill	341	Virginia Metalcrafters	167
Pulaski Main Street, Inc.	75	Virginia Tech University	490
Quarter Creek	17	Ward's Rock Cafe	394
Radford University	482	Willie's Hair Design	262
Radisson Patrick Henry Hotel	367	Willson-Walker House	89
Real Estate Weekly	439		

Index

200 South Street   346
23 Beverley   391, 432
4th of July Celebration and Water
   Carnival   188

A

Aberdeen Barn   405
Abingdon   508
Abingdon General Store   509
Abingdon Mercantile and Frame Gallery
   and Antiques   509
Abingdon Visitors & Convention
   Bureau   509
Abram's Delight Candlelight Tour   197
Accommodations   361

Acorn Inn   347
African American Historical Cultural
   Center   523
Afton Mountain Vineyards   158
Aileen Stores   265
airports   469
Albemarle County   46, 448
Albemarle County Courthouse   49
Albemarle County Fair   191
Alexander's   393
Alleghany County   77
Alleghany Highlands Arts & Crafts
   Center   257
Alleghany Highlands Region   451
Alleghany Regional Hospital   481
Alley Antiques   281
Alliance for Visual Arts   242
Aloma's Snap Shop Photography   293
Always Roxie's,   295
Alzheimer's Disease and Related
   Disorders Support   463
Alzheimer's Support Group   457
American Association of Retired
   Persons   456, 458
American Eagle   470
Amerind Gallery   275
Amherst County   56
Amherst County Historical
   Museum   57
An Evening of Elegance   181
Anchy's   421
Andrew Johnston Museum & Research
   Center   255
Ann Woods   281
Anne Spencer   52
Anne Spencer House and Garden   244
Annual Christmas Arts & Crafts
   Show   197
Annual Christmas Bazaar   197
Annual Food & Music Festival   190
Annual Kite Day   180
Annual Raft Race   187
Annual Roanoke Beach Party   189
Annual Sand Castle & Sand Form
   Contest   189
Annual Sportsman's Fair and Big Game
   Trophy Show   191

Annual Yuletide Traditions   197
Annual Zoo Boo   195
Antique Barn   271
Antique Car show   179
Antique Mart   266
Antique Orchid Herbary   510
Antique Show and Sale   193
antiques   264, 268
Antiques by Burt Long   265
Appalachia   521
Appalachia Coal and Railroad
   Days   190
Appalachian Center for Poets and
   Writers   510
Appalachian Mountain Christmas   197
Appalachian Peddler and Country
   Cabin.   521
Appalachian Power   515
Appalachian Traditions   521
Appalachian Trail   31, 112, 113
Appalachian Trail Days   182
Apple butter Making Festival   194
Apple Festival   507
Apple Harvest Arts & Crafts
   Festival   190
Appomattox Court House National
   Historical Park   97
Arborgate Inn   383
Armory Art Gallery   251
Arnette's   282
Art Farm Galleries   214
Art Museum of Western Virginia   218
Art Needlework, Inc   284
Arthurs   271
Artists in Cahoots   214, 272
Arts & Culture   199
Arts and Crafts Bazaar   196
Arts and Crafts Festival   182
Arts Council of Central Virginia   242
Arts Council of the Roanoke
   Valley   218
Arts Depot   511
Arts, Visual   206, 208, 227, 228,
   242, 251, 252, 254, 255, 256, 257
Artworks   282
Asbury Center at Birdmont   502
Ash Lawn-Highland   49, 231, 235
Asian French Cafe   393
Augusta County   20, 443
Augusta County Parks and Recreation
   Department   456
Augusta Homebuilders Associa-
   tion   444
Augusta Medical Center   443, 477
Autumn Gospel Sing Festival   514
Autumn Hill Vineyards/Blue Ridge
   Winery   154
Avis   470
Awful Arthur's   405

B

Bacchanalian Feast   193, 302
Bacova Guild,   270
Bacova Guild Factory Outlet   81, 296
Baja Bean Co.   405
Balcony   435
Baldwin Park   460
Baldwin Place   443
Barboursville Ruins   45
Barboursville Vineyards   41, 155
Barr-ee Station   282
Barracks Road Shopping Cen-
   ter   282, 284
Barter Theatre   496, 508
Baseball   174
Bass Bonanza   181
Bass Shoes   271
Bateau Landing   54, 416
Bath County Community
   Hospital   481
Bath County Historical Society
   Museum   257
Battle at Bull Run   85
Battle of Cedar Creek   87
Battle of Cedar Creek Living History &
   Reenactment   193
Battle of Cedar Creek Living History
   Weekend   204
Battle of Chancellorsville   95
Battle of Lantane   95
Battle of Little Big Horn   88
Battle of New Market   86
Bavarian Chef   403
Bay Pottery   267
Bayly Art Museum   230
Beale Treasure   61
Bear Hug   286
Bear Mountain Outdoor School   258
Beartree   501
Bed & Breakfast Association of
   Virginia   313
Bed and breakfast inns   313
Bedford Area Chamber of
   Commerce   287
Bedford City/County Mu-
   seum   98, 247
Bedford County Memorial
   Hospital   480
Bedford County.   60
Bedford Station Restaurant   421
Bedrooms of America Museum   18,
   205
Bee Rock Tunnel   521
Belle Boyd   15
Belle Boyd Cottage   92
Belle Grae Inn   270, 318, 432
Belle Grove Plantation   14, 90, 204
Beltrone & Company   281
Bernard's Landing Resort   57, 302
Bernard's Landing Restaurant   419
Bertines North   404
Best Friend Festival   186
Best Western Cavalier   374

Best Western Keydet-General Motel 366
Best Western Radford Inn 381, 423
Bestseller 274
Beth Gallery and Press 228
Beverley Restaurant 390
Big Lots 289
Big Meadows 106, 114
Big Meadows Lodge 103
Big Stone Gap 518
Big Stone Gap Country Fair 182
Big Walker Mountain Scenic Byway 504
Bikecentennial Trail 112
Billy's Barn 434
Billy's Ritz 393
Biltmore Grill 406, 434
Birthday Celebration for Stonewall Jackson 177
Birthday Convocation for Robert E. Lee 177
Bisset Park 74, 124
Bits, Bytes & Books 264
Bizarre Bazaar 264
Black Box Theatre 252
Blacksburg 67
Blacksburg Marriott 380
Bland County 504
Bland County Fair and Horse Show 505
Bland County Lord's Acre Sale 505
Bland, Heritage House Antiques 505
Bleak-Thrift House 279
Bleu Rock Inn 331, 402
Blue Bird Cafe 406
Blue Ridge Board of Realtors 440
Blue Ridge Brewing Company 406, 434
Blue Ridge Dinner Theatre 249
Blue Ridge Farm Museum 248, 250
Blue Ridge Folk Festival 490
Blue Ridge Folklife Festival 196, 249
Blue Ridge Heritage Festival 188
Blue Ridge Homebuilders Association 448
Blue Ridge Institute 63, 249, 250, 490
Blue Ridge Music Festival 185, 243
Blue Ridge Parkway 56, 101, 114
Blue Ridge Pottery 280
Blue Ridge Restaurant 84
Blue Ridge Terrace Gifts, Inc. 282
Blue Stone Inn 388
Blue Wheel Bicycles 283
Bluefield Area Arts and Crafts Center 512
Bluefield College 511
Bluefield Orioles 511
Bluefields 512
Bluemont Concert Series 184
Boar's Head Inn and Sports Club 301, 407
Boating 118
Bob Beard Antiques 276
Bob White 499
Bogen's 421
Bone 432
Bonsack 37
Book Gallery 284
Booker T. Washington National Monument 58, 63, 249
Books, Strings & Things 277
Boone's Country Store 288

Boones Mill Apple Festival 64
Botetourt County 28, 445
Botetourt County Historical Society 218
Botetourt Museum 217
Bottle and Pottery Show and Sale 190
Boxwood Inn Bed & Breakfast 503
Braford Antiques 272
Brandon Oaks 461
Breaks Interstate Park 514, 517
BRI Records 251
Briarpatch Antiques 294
Bridge Street Antiques 287
Bridgewater Air Park 473
Bridgewater College 485
Bridgewater Marina and Boat Rentals and Bridgewate 286
Bridgewater Plaza 58, 286
Bridgewater Village 460
Brookfield Christmas Tree Plantation 291
Brookneal-Campbell County Airport Authority 474
Brownsburg Tavern Antiques and Augusta Antiques 272
Brush Mountain Arts and Crafts Fair 179
Bryce Resort 141, 297, 440
Buchanan Carnival 187
Buchanan County 514
Buchanan County Chamber of Commerce 515
Buck Mountain Grille 393
Buddy's 435
Buddy's Restaurant 421
Budget 470
Buena Vista Labor Day Festival 192
Buffalo Springs Herb Farm 274
Bullitt Mine Complex, 521
Burke's Garden Community Association. 510, 511
Burley Tobacco Festival 510
Burnley Vineyards 155
business schools 483
Byrd Visitor Center 104

C

C and O Restaurant 407
C&O Historical Society Archives 77
C&O Railroad Historical Society 258
Cabin on the River 509
Cabins 104, 131
Cafe Albert 428
Cafe France 416
Cafe Sofia 387
Cambria Emporium 289
Cambria Whistlestop Arts Festival 185
Campgrounds 131
Camping 105, 130
Candy Shop 271
Canoe Outfitters 118
Car Rentals: 470
Carol Lee Doughnuts 435
Carol M. Newman Library 253
Carolina Hosiery 286
Carriage House Motel 516
Carroll County 500
Carter Family Fold, 496, 522
Cascades Club Restaurant 429
Cascades Course 308

Cascades Inn 383
Cascades State Park 124
Cascades waterfall 73
Casey's Country Store 289
Casino 429
Cass Scenic Railroad 79
Castle Rock Recreation Area, 73
Cat & Owl Steak and Seafood House 427
Cave House Craft Shop 509
Cedar Bluff 512
Cedar Bluff Heritage Festival 513
Cedar Creek Battlefield Foundation 88
Cedar Creek Battlefield Foundation Reenactment 90
Cedar Creek Relic Shop 90, 264
Center in the Square 35, 225
Centra Health's Courtside Athletic Club 480
Central Hotel and Star Saloon 30
Central Virginia Area Agency on Aging 463
Central Virginia Invitational Tennis Tournament 185
Chalot's Antiques 266
Champagne and Candlelight Tour 178
Champions Italian Eatery and Cafe 435
Charades 433
Charleys 416
Charlottesville 46, 446
Charlottesville and University Symphony Orchestra 231
Charlottesville Area Association of Realtors 448
Charlottesville Gamelan Ensemble 231
Charlottesville Transit Service 475
Charlottesville-Albemarle Airport 469
Chateau Morrisette 291, 425
Chateau Morrisette Winery 159, 499
Chautauqua Festival 502
Cheers 434
Cheese Shop 23, 271
Chermont Winery, Inc. 158
Cherry Tree Playhouse 244
Chessie Nature Trail 26
Chestnut Creek 451
Chihamba 229
Children's Corner 277
Children's Day at the Market 181
Chilhowie Apple Festival 193
Chili Cook-Off & Independence Day Celebration 188
Christendom College 484
Christiansburg 69
Christmas and Flower Show 198
Christmas at Point of Honor 198
Christmas at the Manse 198
Christmas at the Market 196
Christmas Candlelight Tour 197
Christmas Candlelight Tour of Homes 198
Christmas Craft Fair 196
Christmas Gallery 265
Christmas Open House at Stonewall Jackson's Headquarters 197
Church Mouse 279
City Market 276
City of Lynchburg Department of Parks & Recreation 463

City of Seven Hills 449
Civil War, Battle Reenactments 87
Civil War Living History Weekend 90
Civil War Reenactments 185, 193
Civil War Reenactors' Boot
    Camp 177
Civil War Sites in Virginia, a Tour
    Guide 88, 90
Civil War, Statues 97
Civil War Weekend 185, 256
Claiborne House Bed and
    Breakfast 354
Clarkcrest 507
Clarke County, 438
Classic Collections 287
Clayborne's 431
Clayton's 417
Claytor Lake 76, 124, 128
Claytor Lake Arts and Crafts Fair 192
Claytor Lake State Park 138
Clean Valley Council 32
Clifton Forge 77
Clifton--The Country Inn 338, 407
Clinch River 516
Clinch Valley College and Appalachian
    Traditions 521
Clinch Valley Mountain Wildlife
    Area 507
Clore Sons, Inc. 279
Clothes Line 267
Coal Country 514
Cockram Mill 499
Cockram's General
    Store 71, 254, 290, 436
Cocoa Mill Chocolates 274
Coffee Exchange 408
Collector's Corner 292
College Sports 170
Colleges 483
Colonial Art and Craft Shop 264
Colonnades 464
Colony House Motor Lodge 369
Colony of Virginia, Ltd. 293
Comair 470
Comers Rock 501
Comfort
    Inn 366, 377, 380, 382, 383
Comfort Inn - Roanoke/Troutville 367
Comfort Inn Radford 381
Commercial Airports 469
Community Children's Dance
    Festival 230
Community Children's Theatre 233
Community Concerts 244
Community Hospital of Roanoke
    Valley 477
Community Market 286
Confederate Breastworks 83
Confederate Cemetery 243
Confederate Memorial Service 184
Conservation Festival 185
Consignment Shop 285
Consolidated Glass and Mirror
    Corp 500
Consolidated Shoe Store 286
Constitution Day Celebrations 191
Contra Corners 229
Coopers Corner 419
Cooper's Vantage 300
Copper Kettle Lounge 142
Copper Mine 300
Corned Beef & Co. 395
Corner Cupboard 268

Corner Downtown Cafe 507
Corporate Research Center 491
Councils on Community Service 454
Count Pulaski Day 196
Country Christmas House 291
Country Fare 314
Country Garden Antiques 280
Country Goose Gift and Craft
    Shop 267
Country Heritage 277
Country Manor 279
Country Records 291
Country Store Antique Mall 280
Coupe de Ville's 408, 434
Court Days Festival 184
Court Square Antiques and
    Collectibles 294
Court Square Tavern 408
Covered Bridges 161
Covington 77
Crabtree Falls Trail 115
Craddock-Terry Shoe Factory
    Outlet 285
Craft Memorial Library 512
Crafters Fair 186
Crafter's Gallery 282
Craig County 30
Craig County Fall Festival 218
Craig County Historical Society 218
Craig County Museum 218
Craig's Creek 30
Crickett's 421
Crown Sterling 417
Crows 79
Crozet Arts and Crafts Festi-
    val 180, 194
Culture 199
Cumberland Bowl Park 523
Cumberland Gap 522
Cumberland Gap National Historical
    Park 522
Cumberland Museum and Art
    Gallery 517
Curiosity Shop 266
Cycle Systems 32

D

Daddy Rabbit's 499
Daedalus Bookshop 281
Damascus 501
Damascus Appalachian Trail Days
    Festival 510
Dancescape 230
Daniel Boone Heritage Trail, 523
Daniel Harrison House 207
Daniel Monument 97
Daughters of the American
    Revolution 244
Daynell's Delight 426
Days Inn 377
Dayton 19
Dayton Autumn Festival 207
Dayton Farmer's Market 267
Deck the Halls Open House 198
Deer Meadow Vineyard 150
Deer Run 499
DeLoach Antiques 281
Design Accessories 277
Dickens of a Christmas 198
Dickenson Bundy Log House 515
Dickenson County 516

Dickenson County Chamber 518
Dinner At Dusk 185
Discovery Museum 230
Diuguid's 54
Dixie Caverns 169
Dixie Pottery 510
Dock Boggs Memorial Festival 192
Doe Run Lodge Resort and Conference
    Center 108, 306, 496
Dogwood Festival 178
Dolley Madison's Birthday 180
Dominion Valley 499
Donkenny Fashion Outlet 289
Donovan's Framery 206
Dooley's 434
Douthat Park Restaurant 427
Douthat State Park 117
Downriver Canoe Company 119
Downtown Charlottesville Art and
    Antique Center 281
Dr. Douglas Southall Freeman 52
Dr. Jerry Falwell 489
Dramas of Creation, 301
Draper Mercantile 294
Draper Valley Golf Club 505
Dudley Mart & Restaurant 419
Dulwich Manor 349
Dun Roaming Stables 137
Durty Nelly's Pub & Restaurant 409,
    434
Dusty's Antique Market 270

E

E. Jefferson 282
Eagles Nest 473
Eagle's Nest Restaurant 427
Earl Hamner 45
Early Time Antiques and Fine Art 280
East Coast Raw Bar 435
Easterly Park 516
Eastern Mennonite College and
    Seminary 484
Eastern Standard 434
Edgemont 447
Edgewood Farm Bed & Breakfast 280,
    334
Edgewood Farm Nursery 280
Edinburg Mill 92
El Charro 389
El Dorado 386
El Rodeo Mexican Restaurant 395
Elderhostel 454
Elder's Antique and Classic Autos 270
Elephant Walk 433
Eljo's 283
Elks National Home 247
Elkwallow Wayside 106
Elm Park Estates 461
Elmer's Antiques 279
Elmo's Rest 354
Emerson Creek Pottery 277, 287
Emil's 417
Emory & Henry College 492, 508
Emporium 270
Endless Caverns 167
Estouteville 447
Exchange Hotel 45
Executive Motel 381
Explore Project 37

F

Factory Merchants Outlet Mall   503
Fairview Bed & Breakfast   349
Fairystone State Park   498
Faith Mountain Herbs and
    Antiques   279
Fall Festival   195
Fall Foliage Festival   194
Fall Food Festival   192
Falwell Aviation, Inc.   473
Family Craft Weekend   207
Family Service of Roanoke Valley   458
Fantasies   274
Fantasyland   164
Farfelu Vineyard   152
Farm Basket   417
Farm Basket Shop   285
Farmhouse   422
Fassifern   327
Fayerweather Gallery   228
Fellini's   434
Ferrum College   64, 490
Festival Around Town   185
Festival by the James   185
Festival in the Park   36, 181
Fiddler's Convention   186, 190, 500
Fifth Avenue Presbyterian Church
    Window   221
Fincastle   28
Fincastle Festival   192
Fine Arts Center for the New River
    Valley   256, 293
Firmstone Manor Bed & Breakfast   358
First Night Roanoke   198
First Night Virginia   197
First Night Waynesboro   197
First Night Winchester   197
Fishing   59, 126
Flag Rock Recreational Area   518
Flea Market   266
Fletcher Collins Theatre   212
Flossie Martin Gallery   255
Floyd County   71
Floyd Theatre Group   254
Folk Arts and Crafts Festival   180
Foot Hunting   172
For the Birds   277
Fort Harrison   19, 94, 207
Fort Lewis Lodge   139, 359
Foster Grandparents Program   458
Fountain Hall Bed & Breakfast   332
Four & Twenty Blackbirds   401
Four County Players   233
Fourth of July Celebration and
    Carnival   188
Fourth of July Jubilee   187
Fox and Hounds Pub & Restau-
    rant   389
Foxfield Races   172, 178, 191
Foxridge   450
Frances Christian Brand Galleries   229
Franklin County Court Days   179
Franklin County Fall Arts and Crafts
    Festival   196
Franklin County Festival   182
Franklin County Spring Arts and Crafts
    Festival   179
Franklin Memorial Hospital   480
Fred Clifton Park   498
Frederick County   438
Frederick County Fair   186

Frederick House   320
Free Union   448
Freedom Fest at Montpelier   187
Freeman-Victorious Framing   283
Freight Depot Antiques   268
Friendship Inn   369
From the Heart   288
Front Royal   14
Front Royal Canoe Co.   119
Front Royal-Warren County
    Airport   472

G

Galax   500
Galax-Carroll-Grayson Chamber of
    Commerce   501
Gallery 3   276
Gallery Cafe   424, 436
Gallery of Mountain Secrets   296
Garden Club of Virginia   244
Garden Room   302
Garden Terrace   146, 300
Garland Gray Research Center and
    Library   215
Garment District   283
Garth Newel Music Center   80, 258
Gatewood Reservoir Park   76
Gen. Stonewall Jackson's
    Headquarters   90
General Andrew Lewis   38
General Store   272
George C. Marshall Museum and
    Library   25, 214
George Washington   24
George Washington National
    Forest   20, 77, 113, 125
George Washington's Birthday
    Celebration   177
George Wythe   502
Gerontology Center   453
Gibson Girl Antique Mall   294
Gift and Thrift Shop   266
Gift Connection   270
Giles and Mountain Lake Bicycle
    Ride   185
Giles County   72
Giles Little Theatre   255
Giles Memorial Hospital   481
Gill Memorial Eye, Ear, Nose and
    Throat Hospital   478
Gilmore, Hamm and Snyder, Inc.   285
Gish's Mill   39
Glass Slipper   296
Glenmore   447
Go Pal" Bicycle Shop   283
Golden Horseshoe Inn   280
Golden Olympics   454
Golden Tub Bath Shop   270
Golf   130
Goodwill Tinker Mountain
    Industries,   274
Goshen Pass   24
Grady's Antiques   288
Graham Recreational Park   512
Grand Caverns   168
Grandin Movie Theatre   224
Grandma's Bait Clothing Store   270
Grandma's Memories   292
grass skiing   142
Graves Mountain Lodge   373
Grayson County   500

Grayson County Old Time Fiddler's
    Convention   186
Grayson Highlands Fall Festival   193
Grayson Highlands State Park   500,
    501
Great American Duck Race   189
Greater Bluefield Chamber of
    Commerce   514
Greater Lynchburg Transit
    Company   475
Green Valley Book Fair   268
Greenbrier Clinic,   310
Greenbrier Resort   78, 130, 308
Greene House Shops   280
Greenwood Antique Center   281
Grille   429
Grindstone   501
Gristmill   300
Gristmill Square,   81
Groucho's   433
Guest House Bed & Breakfast   313
Guilford Ridge Vineyard   150
Gypsy Hill Park   21
Gypsy Hill Park Pool   122

H

Hale Fishing Lake   504
Hales Ford   286
Hall of Valor   87, 93
Halloween Weekend   194
Hamiltons   287
Hampton Inn   368
Handcraft House   280
Handworks Gallery   264
Happy Birthday U.S.A.   187
Happy Goose   264
Harb's Bistro   214, 391, 432
Hardware Store Restaurant   409
Harrison Museum of African American
    Culture   219
Harrisonburg   19, 441
Harrisonburg-Rockingham Association
    of Realtors   443
Harry Meador Coal Mu-
    seum   496, 520
Harvest Festival   190, 195
Haunted Caverns   195
Haymarket Theatre   252
Heartwood Bookshop   281
Heartwood Used Books   283
Heathwood   450
Heirloom Originals   288
Henry County,   499
Henry Street Heritage Festi-
    val   192, 219
Heritage Day   192
Heritage Festival   193
Heritage Repertory Theatre   233
Hertz   470
Hevener's   295
High Country Restaurant at Doe Run
    Lodge   109, 306, 382
High Meadows   356
High Valley Antiques and
    Collectibles,   295
Highland County   81
Highland County Arts Council   257
Highland County Crafts   296
Highland County Maple Festival   82
Highland Inn   384, 430
Highland Maple Festival   177

Highlands Arts & Crafts Center 295
Hightower 283
Hiking 112
Hillsville Flea Market 499
Hilton - Lynchburg 378
Historic Crab Orchard Museum 512
Historic Downtown Mall and South
    Street Antiques 281, 283
Historic Fincastle Days 29
Historic Fincastle, Inc 28
Historic Garden Week 178, 216
Historic Old Newbern 256
Historic Staunton Foundation 21
Hockey 174
Holiday in Lexington 216
Holiday in Lexington Weekend
    Celebration 198
Holiday Inn 378, 428
Holiday Inn Blacksburg 422
Holiday Inn Charlottesville/
    Monticello 377
Holiday Inn Covington 383
Holiday Inn Harrisonburg 365
Holiday Inn Hotel Tanglewood 369
Holiday Inn Lexington 366
Holiday Inn North-University
    Area 375
Holiday Inn of Blacksburg 380
Holladay House 335
Hollins College 36, 486
Hollins Communications Research
    Institute 486
Holston Mountain Arts and Crafts
    Cooperative 509
Holy Land USA 61
Holy Land USA Nature Sanctuary 247
Home Builders Association of
    Virginia 438
Home sites 437
Homeplace 396
Homestead Club 436
Homestead Dining Room 429
Homestead Resort 79, 136, 146, 307
Honaker Redbud Festival 179, 516
Hopkins Planetarium 220
Horse Shows 173
Hospice 479
Hospice of the Shenandoah, Inc. 457
Hospitals 476
Hotel Strasburg 15, 361, 387
Hottest Fun in the Sun Beach
    Day 188
House Antiques 281
House of Hunan, 507
Howard Johnson 373
Howard Johnson Lodge 379
Howard Johnson Lodge and
    Restaurant 366
Huckleberry 423
Hull's Drive-In, 27
Hull's Drive-In Theatre 217
Hummingbird Inn 328
Humpback Bridge 161
Humpback Rocks 115
Hungry Mother 496, 507
Hungry Mother Arts and Crafts
    Festival 507
Hungry Mother Campground 507
Hungry Mother Lake 129
Hungry Mother State Park 137, 506
Hunter's Raid at Green Hill Park Battle
    Reenactme 87

Hunting 138
Hupp's Hill Battlefield Park & Study
    Center 91
Hurricane 501
Huyard's Country Kitchen 388

I

Ice Cream Cottage 287
Ikenberry 275
Imagine That! 505
Imperial Wok 428
Independence Celebration 187
Independence Day Celebration 187
Ingalls Field 474
Inn at Burwell Place 330
Inn at Little Washington 331, 402
Inn at Meander Plantation 333
Inn at Monticello 342
Inn at Narrow Passage 314
Inn at Union Run 324
Innkeeper Lynchburg 379
Innkeeper Motel 369
International Springtime Celebra-
    tion 181
International Street Festival 190
Irish Gap Inns 322
Ironwood 443
Iroquois Club 433
Ivy Hill 449

J

Jack Tale Players 251
Jack's Creek Covered Bridge 499
Jackson, Gen. Thomas J. "Stone-
    wall" 86
Jackson Statue 95
Jacob's Lantern 422
Jacob's Nightclub 435
James Burke House Eatery 428
James Burke Inn B&B 511
James Madison Museum 45, 230
James Madison University 484
James Madison University
    Basketball 170
James Madison University Dinner
    Theater 207
James Madison University Life Science
    Museum 207
James McHone Antique Jewelry 266
James River Basin Canoe Livery 26,
    120
James River Reeling and Rafting 120
James River Runners Inc. 119
Jazz in the Park 212
Jazz on the Lawn 195
Jefferson Area Board for Aging 462
Jefferson National For-
    est 29, 60, 113, 125, 501, 503, 505
Jefferson National Park 522
Jefferson, Thomas 236, 247
Jeff's Antiques 266
Jeweler's Eye 283
JM's Pub 431
John Fox, Jr. Museum 520
John W. Flannagan Reservoir 517
Johnny Appleseed Restaurant 364
Joker's 431
Jolly Roger Haggle Shop 268

Jones Memorial Library 245
Jordan Hollow Farm Inn 134, 316
Joseph's Backpacking 518
Joshua Wilton House 318, 388
July 4th Celebration 187, 188
June Tolliver House and Craft
    Shop 520
June Tolliver Playhouse. 520

K

Kafkafe 409, 435
Kaleidoscope 54, 192
Katharine Garland Diggs Trust 244
Katie's Country Club 434
Keep Bed and Breakfast 324
Keller & George 284
Keswick 446
Ki Theatre 228
Kids Kastoffs 288
Kilgore Fort House 522
Kimberly's Antiques and Linens 264
King William Regional Arts
    Center 510
King's Daughters' Hospital 477
Kinsinger's Kountry Kitchen 23, 271
KOA campground 503
Krissia 284
Kurtz Cultural Center 204
Kwanzaa Celebration 219

L

La Difference 285
La Maison Du Gourmet 396
La Varenne 310
Labor Day Spectacular 191
Lake Bonaventure Country Club 516
Lake Keokee 523
Lake Laura 298
Lake Moomaw 78, 128
Landing 304
Landmark Steakhouse and
    Lounge 418
Lands End 288
Langhorne Manor 350
Lantern Tours 211
Latimer-Shaeffer Theatre 207
Laurel Lake 515
Lavender Hill Farm 329
Layman's 275
Le Snail 414
League of Older Americans 458, 468
Lee Chapel 25, 215
Lee County 522
Lee, Gen. Robert E. 86
Lee Hi Truck Stop 392
Lee Statue 97
Lenfest Center for the Performing
    Arts 215
Lenglad 499
Levy's 284
Lewis Glaser 282
Lewis Miller Regional Art Center 252
Lewis Mountain Cabins 104, 105
Lewis-Gale Hospital 478
Lewisburg 79
Lexington 24, 444
Lexington Historical Shop 272
Lexington-Buena Vista-Rockbridge

Board of Realtors 444
Liberty University 489
Lily's 397
Lime Kiln Theatre 26, 216, 432
Limeton Pottery 264
Lincoln Homestead 208
Linden Vineyards 152
L'Italia Restaurant and Lounge 389
Little Gallery 286
Little John's 410
Little Sorrel 215
Live Arts 233
Llewellyn Lodge at Lexington 327
Loft Mountain 105
Log Cabin Antiques 266
Log House 503
London Fog 271
Lonesome Pine Arts and Crafts 179, 520
Long Way Home Outdoor Drama 255
Longdale Recreation Area 78
Longwood Cemetery 98
Lord Browne Antiques 280
Lowell's Restaurant and Lounge 433
Lower Cascades Club Restaurant 429
Luigi's 397
Luray Caverns 18, 167
Luray Caverns Airport 472
Luray Caverns Car and Carriage Caravan 206
Luray Reptile Center and Dinosaur Park 18
Lynchburg Association of Realtors 449
Lynchburg College 488
Lynchburg Fine Arts Center 242
Lynchburg Gas Co 54
Lynchburg General Hospital 479
Lynchburg Historical Foundation 244
Lynchburg Historical Foundation Antique Show and Sale 195
Lynchburg Mansion Inn Bed and Breakfast 351
Lynchburg Museum at Old Court House 97, 243
Lynchburg Red Sox 55, 174
Lynchburg Regional Airport 470

M

Mabry Mill 254, 496, 498
Mabry Mill Blue Ridge Parkway 72
Mabry Mill Coffee Shop 109
Macado's 397, 410, 424, 434
Madam Russell House 506
Madison Antiques Center 280
Madison County 41
Madison House Bed & Breakfast 352
Madison, President James 238
Magic City Station 276
Maharaja 411
Maier Museum of Art 243
Main Street Galleries and C&S Galleries 293
Main Street Grill 411
Mallard Point 450
Mama's Treasures 265
Manor at Taylor's Store 355
Maple Hall 392
Maple Museum 82, 257
Maplewood Farm 509

Maps 129
Marion 506
Marion's Cafe 428
Marriott Ranch 134
Martha Jefferson Hospital 479
Martha Washington College for Women. 509
Martha Washington Inn 508
Martha's Cafe 411
Martinsville Speedway 499
Mary Baldwin College 485
Mary Bladon House 329
Mary Draper Ingles 67
Massanutten Board of Realtors 441
Massanutten Mountain Cloggers 203
Massanutten Resort 20, 143, 298
Mathews Arm 105
Maury River Mercantile 272
Max 435
May Fest 181
Mayberry Presbyterian Church 499
Mayberry Trading Post 499
McCormick Farm 217
McCormick's Pub and Restaurant 432
McDowell Battlefield 83
McDowell Presbyterian Church 99
McGuffey Art Center 229, 282
Meadow Lane Lodge 80, 360
Meadow Run Grist Mill 236
Meadows of Dan 499
Meadowwood 449
Meals on Wheels 457, 463
Meander Inn at Penny Lane Farm 348
MECC Home Crafts Days 196
Medical Care, Hospitals 476
Medical Care, Walk-In 480
Meem's Bottom Bridge 18, 161
Memorial Day Celebration 180
Memorial Day Horse Fair and Auction 180
Memorial Day Observance 181
Memories 294
Memory & Company 412
Merrimac 95
Metropolitan Bus Lines 474
Michie Tavern 236, 412
Mid-Atlantic Chamber Orchestra 194, 212
Middle St. Gallery 227
Middletown 14
Miki Liszt Dance Company· 230
Mill Mountain Star 32
Mill Mountain Theatre 225
Mill Mountain Zoo 162, 226
Mill Street Grill 390, 432
Miller Park 123
Miller School of Albemarle 492
Miller's 434
Milton Hall Bed & Breakfast Inn 358
Mincer's 283
Miniature Graceland 27, 226
Mint Spring 268
Mish Mish 277
Miss Virginia Pageant 188
Misty Mountain Vineyards, Inc. 154
Mock Convention 217
Molly Tynes 511
Molly's Knob 506
Monongahela National Forest 125
Monroe, James 235
Montdomaine Cellars 157
Monte Vista Golf Course 523

Montfair Stables 135
Montgomery County Historical Festival 185
Montgomery Museum 252
Montgomery Regional Hospital 480
Monticello 49, 236
Monticello Trio 232
Monticello Wine and Food Festival 194
Montpelier 43, 238
Montpelier Hunt Races 196
Montpelier Wine Festival 180
Mount Rogers National Recreation Area 114, 116, 496, 500, 507
Mount Rogers Naturalist Rally 182
Mount Rogers Ramp Festival 182
Mountain Cove Vineyards 158
Mountain Empire College 520
Mountain Farm Trail 115
Mountain Heritage Arts and Crafts Festival 184
Mountain Inn 144
Mountain Lake Hotel and Resort, 73, 304
Mountain Lake Symposium & Gallery 254
Mountain Mission School 515
Mountain Springs Stables 133
Mountain Store 279
Mountain Top 515
Mountain View Acres 451
Mountaintop Ranch 135
Mum's the Word 284
Municipal Pools 122
Museum 252
Museum of American Frontier Culture 20, 181, 209
Music for Americans 188

N

Naked Creek Pottery 270
Naked Mountain Vineyard 151
Nannie Ruth 514
NASTAR 142
National Business College. 511
National Cemetery 90
National Forests 124
National Park Service 102
National Rescue Hall of Fame 221
Natural Bridge Caverns 168
Natural Bridge of Virginia 300, 367
Natural Bridge Village Restaurants 392
Natural Bridge Wax Museum 301
Natural Bridge Zoo 162
Natural Chimneys 20
Natural Chimneys Joust 184, 189
Natural Chimneys Regional Park 20
Natural Tunnel 496
Natural Tunnel Park 524
Nature by Design 284
Needlecrafter Custom-made Sweaters 287
Neighborhood Partnership 445
Nelson County 42, 45
Nelson County Summer Festival 184
New Castle Mercantile 275
New London Airport 474
New Market 16
New Market Airport 472
New Market Arts & Crafts Show 190

New Market Battlefield Days Inn 364
New Market Battlefield Historical
    Park 87, 93
New Market Battlefield Military
    Museum 94
New Market Battlefield Museum and
    Hall of Valor 24
New Market Day Ceremony 181
New Market Heritage Days 180
New Mountain Mercantile 290
New Mountain Mercantile Here and
    Now Gallery 253
New River Canoe Livery 120
New River Community College 76
New River Cruise Company 425
New River Historical Society 98
New River Trail State Park 500, 501
New River Valley 66
New River Valley Agency on
    Aging 467
New River Valley Airport 473
New River Valley Arts and Crafts
    Guild 254, 292
New River Valley Arts Council 252
New River Valley Fair 189
New River Valley Home Builders
    Association, 451
New River Valley Horse Show 188
New River Valley Mall 289
New River Valley Speedway 174
Newbern Heights 451
Newcomb Hall Arts Space 229
Newport Agricultural Fair 189
Nicholas & Alexandra Gallery 282
Nichol's Apple Barn 275
Night life 431
Norfields Farm Bed & Breakfast 334
North Mountain Vineyard &
    Winery 150
North-South Skirmish 180
North-South Skirmish Association Fall
    Nationals 193
Norton Holiday Inn, 521
Norwood Art Gallery and Encore Gift
    Shop 292

O

Oak Grove Players 212
Oak Manor Farms 135
Oak Ridge 42, 46, 239
Oakencroft Vineyard and Winery 156
Oaks 357
Oasis Vineyard 152
Of Things Past 268
Oktoberfest 194, 195
Old Cabell Hall 232
Old Chessie Trail 117
Old Church Gallery 253
Old City Cemetery 97
Old Country Store and Deli 287
Old Fiddler's Convention 190, 495
Old Fincastle Festival 218
Old Hardware Store 283
Old Michie Theatre 235
Old Mill Room 302
Old Newbern 74
Old Post Office Restaurant &
    Lounge 386
Old Rock House 502
Old South Antiques, 272
Old Town Christmas Parade 196

Old Town Easter Egg Hunt 178
Old Town Hoe Down 189
Old White Club 436
Olde Mill 500
Olde Salem Days 192
Olde Virginia Barbecue 420
Oliver's 387
Omni Charlottesville Hotel 377
Once Upon a Time Clock Shop 270
Opera Roanoke 35, 223
Orange County 41, 43, 445
Oratorio Society of Charlottesville-
    Albemarle 232
Orchard Gap Deli 109
Oregano Joe's 412
Orkney Springs Hotel 206
Orvis Factory Outlet 277
Other Times LTD 288
Otter Creek Restaurant 109
Our Lady of Peace 465
Outdoor Art Show 181
Outpost 423
Overnight Wilderness Camping 133

P

P. Buckley Moss Museum 23, 211
P.J.'s Christmas Carousel 503
Paddle Wheel Cruises 419
Page County 440
Paine Art Gallery and Summit
    Theatre 512
Paint Bank State Trout Hatchery 78
Paint Lick Mountain, 512
Palais Royal 283
Palette Art Gallery 252
Palmer Country Manor 346
Palms 432
Pampered Palate Cafe 270, 391
Panorama Restaurant 106
Paper Treasures 18, 265
Pappagallo 274
Park-Oak Grove 462
Parkhurst 388
Patina 277
Patrick County 498
Patrick County Chamber of
    Commerce 500
Patrick Henry 498
Patrick Henry Hotel 371
Patsy Cline 12
Peaks Antiques 287
Peaks of Otter Lodge 106, 109, 379
Pearisburg 72
Peddlar Antiques 287
Peddler's Shop 282
Peebles Department Store 289
Peking Palace Restaurant 422
Pennington Gap 523
Perspective Art Gallery 251
Pest House Medical Museum 243
Pest House Medical Museum and
    Confederate Cemetery 97
Peter Kramer 277
Pewter Corner 284
Phoenix 282
Piedmont Association of Realtors 446
Piedmont Aviation, 471
Piedmont Chamber Players 232
Piedmont Virginia Community
    College 229
Pig 'N Steak 415

Pine Knoll Gift Shop 265
Pine Tavern 425, 436
Pioneer Day 181
Pioneer Days 517
Pittston 515
PJ Brown & Company 510
PJ's Carousel Collection Christmas
    stores 294
PJ's Carousel Village 257
Plain Dealing 447
Plains Promenaders Square Dance
    Group 203
Plantation Days Festival 187
Plow & Hearth 284
Plum Alley Eatery 509
Plumb Alley Day 182
Pocahontas Exhibition Mine 513
Point of Honor 54, 244
Polo 171
Poor Farmers Market 290
Poplar Forest 42, 247
Poplar Park 60
Pottery 15
Powell Valley 518
Preparatory schools 483
President Woodrow Wilson 20
Primland Hunting Reserve 138, 499
Prince Michel Restaurant 403
Prince Michel Vineyards 153
Prism Coffeehouse 232, 434
Private Swimming Areas 125
Prospect Hill 415
Prospect Hill Cemetery 92
Prospect Hill Inn 343
Pulaski Community Hospital 481
Pulaski County 74
Pulaski County Speedway 76
Pulaski Fine Arts Center 76
Purcell Oriental Rug Co 284

Q

Quality Inn - Roanoke/Salem 373
Quality Inn Shenandoah Valley 364
Quality Inn Skyline Drive 362
Quilts Unlimited 295

R

Raccoon Branch 501
Race Car Driving 174
Radford 73
Radford Community Hospital 481
Radford University 74, 491, 256
Radford's Gallery Underground 436
Ragged Mountain Running Shop 283
Rail Road Days 185
Railroad Festival 97
Rails, 271
Ralph Stanley Blue Grass Festival 182
Ramada Inn 367
Randolph-Macon Woman's
    College 489
Rappahannock County 41, 445
Raven Cliff. 501
Ray's 436
Real Estate Weekly 448
Realty companies 437
Rebec Vineyards 158, 195
Red Hill 245

Red Lobster Restaurant 418
Redcoat Antiques 285
Regional Ballet Theatre 242
Remington's 398
Reminisce 268
Renaissance Gifts 282
Rendezvous 186
Resorts 297
Restaurants 385
Retirement Communities 464
Reuel B. Pritchett Museum 207
Rev. Jerry Falwell 51
Reynolds Homestead 499
Rhododendron Gap 501
Rhododendron Lodge 514
Richard Bland, 504
Richard's Antiques 266
Richlands 511, 513
Richlands Area Chamber of
    Commerce 514
Richlands Festival 513
Ride and Stride Shop 518
Riner 69
River Farm 18
River Garden 509
River Rental & Campstore 119
River Ridge Ranch 136
River Run and Bicycle Ride 179
Riverfest 188
Riverside Park 98
Rivianna Reservoir 128
Roanoke 32
Roanoke Airport Marriott 371
Roanoke Athletic Club 478
Roanoke Christmas Parade 198
Roanoke College 39, 487
Roanoke County 36
Roanoke Memorial Hospitals 478
Roanoke Railway Festival 195
Roanoke Regional Airport 471
Roanoke Regional Home Builders
    Association 445
Roanoke Symphony 35
Roanoke Symphony Orchestra 224
Roanoke Symphony Polo
    Cup 172, 224
Roanoke United Methodist
    Home 461
Roanoke Valley 27, 445
Roanoke Valley Association of
    Realtors 445
Roanoke Valley Historical Society and
    Museum 220
Roanoke Valley Horse
    Show 185, 227
Roanoke Weiner Stand 398
Roanoker Restaurant 398
Roaring Run Recreation Area 78
Robert Morris 61
Robertson, Professor James I. 85
Rock Castle Gorge Trail 116
Rockbridge Community Festival 189
Rockbridge Concert-Theatre
    Series 216
Rockbridge County 24
Rockbridge Regional Fair 187
Rockbridge Restaurant at Ramada
    Inn 391
Rockbridge Vineyard 151
Rockingham County Fair 189
Rockingham County Parks and
    Recreation Department 456
Rocky Knob 499

Rocky Knob Cabins 108
Rocky Mount Independence
    Celebration 188
Rocky's Antique Mart 270
Rococo's 413
Rodes Farm Inn 46, 300
Rodes Farm Stables 135
Ronald McDonald House 478
Roscoe Cox 292
Rose River Vineyards and Trout
    Farm 152
Rose Street Interiors 268
Round Meadow 499
Rowe Pottery 264
Rowe's Family Restaurant 270
Ruffled Grouse Society 81
Rural Retreat Lake and Camp-
    ground 503
Rush River Company 277
Russell County 515
Russell County Chamber of
    Commerce 516
Russell Fork 516
Russell's Yesteryear 276
Ryan's Fruit Market 268

S

S.P. Petites 285
Sackett's 436
Safe and Sane 4th of July
    Celebration 186
Saigon Cafe 413
Salem 38
Salem Buccaneers 174
Salem Civic Center 38
Salem Fair and Exposition 188
Sal's Pizza Restaurants 419
Salt-Making Week 506
Saltville 506
Saltville Historical Foundation, 506
Saltville Labor Day Celebration 193
Saltville Museum 506
Sam Snead's Tavern 308, 430
Sam's On the Market 277
Sandra's Cellar 276
Sani-Mode Barber Shop 293
Sawhill Gallery 206
School House Fabrics 291
Schooners Restaurant 420
Schuyler 56
Science Museum of Western
    Virginia 220
Scooch's 433
Scott County 521
Scott County Chamber of
    Commerce 522
Scott County Park 522
Scottsville on the James 241
Scrooge Day 198
Scrooge's 503
Scruple's 431
Second Story 274
Second Street Gallery 229
Sedalia Center 61, 248
Senior Center, Inc. 463
Senior Corps of Retired Execu-
    tives 457
Septemberfest 192
Services Unlimited 294
Seven Bends Gallery 265
Seven Hills Inn 326

Shadows Bed and Breakfast Inn 337
Shakin' 212
Sharks 432
Shawsville 69
ShenanArts, Inc. 212
Shenandoah 9
Shenandoah Acres Resort 125
Shenandoah Apple Blossom
    Festival 12, 179
Shenandoah Area Agency on
    Aging 454
Shenandoah Caverns 166
Shenandoah Cloggers 209
Shenandoah County 440
Shenandoah County Homebuilders
    Association 441
Shenandoah County Memorial
    Hospital 476
Shenandoah National
    Park 14, 101, 102, 114, 133
Shenandoah River Outfitters 18, 119
Shenandoah Summer Music
    Theatre 202
Shenandoah University 484
Shenandoah Valley 9
Shenandoah Valley Art Cen-
    ter 23, 208
Shenandoah Valley Bed & Breakfast
    Reservations 313
Shenandoah Valley Bicycle
    Festival 186
Shenandoah Valley Builders
    Association 443
Shenandoah Valley Crafts and
    Gifts 265
Shenandoah Valley Farm Craft
    Days 184, 204
Shenandoah Valley Heritage
    Museum 207
Shenandoah Valley Lodging
    Services 313
Shenandoah Valley Music
    Festival 16, 186, 189, 190, 205
Shenandoah Valley Playwrights
    Retreat 213
Shenandoah Valley Regional
    Airport 473
Shenandoah Vineyards 150
Shenanigans 284
Shenvalee Golf Resort 364
Sheraton Hotel 432
Sheraton Inn Charlottesville 375
Sheraton Inn Roanoke Airport 372
Sheraton Inn Staunton 365
Sheraton Red Lion Inn 380
Sheridan, Gen. Philip H. 90
Sherwood Anderson, 506
Sherwood Anderson Short Story
    Competition 506
Shopping 261
Shot Tower Historical Park 504
Showalter's Orchard and
    Greenhouse 268
Silver Dollar Saloon, 513
Silver Linings 270, 271
Silver Thatch Inn 344, 413
Silversmith Inn 509
Simeon Vineyards 51, 156
Skiing 141
Sky Bryce Airport 472
Skyland Lodge 103, 106, 365
Skyline Caverns 166
Skyline Drive 18, 101

Sleepy Hollow Farm   336
Smith Mountain   304
Smith Mountain Cedar Homes   451
Smith Mountain Dam   57
Smith Mountain Flowers   287
Smith Mountain
   Lake   57, 124, 128, 379, 445
Smith Mountain Lake Airport   474
Smith Mountain Lake Fall Festival   195
Smith Mountain Lake Partnership
   Visitors Center   286
Smith Mountain Lake State Park &
   Visitors Center   247
Smith Mountain Visitors Center &
   Dam   245
Smithfield Plantation   253
Smokehouse   414
Smyth County   505
Smyth County Chamber of
   Commerce   507
Snooper's Antique and Craft Mall   503
Sorghum Molasses Festival   194
South Holston Lake,   508
South Main Cafe   435
Southern Area Agency on Aging   464
Southern Culture   414
Southern Drawl Artworks   227
Southern Inn   392
Southern Kitchen   388
Southern Lamp & Shade Show-
   room   288
Southern Soldier Statue   98
Southwest Virginia Community
   College   511
Southwest Virginia Museum   520
Southwestern Virginia   495
Spanish Theater Group   235
Sperryville Emporium   279
Spring Arts and Crafts Fair   180
Spring Balloon Festival   179
Spring Fly-In   179
Spring Garden Show   179
Spring Hill Cemetery   98
Spring Hill Farm Antiques   279
Spring House   387
Spring Wildflower Sympo-
   sium   180, 300
Springhouse Antiques   279
Springs   80
Squires Studio Theatre   252
St. Andrews Catholic Church
   Museum   221
St. Anne's-Belfield School   492
St. Maarten's Cafe   414
"St. Moor" House Bed &
   Breakfast   350
St. Patrick's Day Parade   177
Stanley Furniture   499
Starving Artist Cafe   510
State Council on Education   484
State Parks   124
Statler Brothers Complex   213
Staunton   20
Staunton-Augusta Art Center   209
Staunton-Augusta Board of
   Realtors   444
Steeple Chase Races   172
Stepping Out   189
Stone Face Rock,   523
Stone's Cafeteria   423
Stonewall and National Cemeter-
   ies   90
Stonewall Brigade Band   212

Stonewall Jackson Cemetery   94
Stonewall Jackson Hospital   477
Stonewall Jackson House   25, 95, 215
Stonewall Jackson's Headquarters   204
Stonewall Vineyards   159, 195
Stoney Creek   448
Stony Mountain Fibers   282
Strasburg   15
Strasburg Emporium   15, 264
Strasburg Museum and Gift Shop   15,
   91, 205
Stuart Mansion   515
Stuarts Draft   23
Sugar Tour   82
Sugar Tree Country Store and Sugar
   House   295
Summer Festival of the Arts at Ash
   Lawn-Highland   184
Summerfield Inn   509
Sun and Sand Beach Weekend   185
Sun Bow Trading Company   281
Sunnybrook Inn Restaurant   399
Sunnyside Retirement Commu-
   nity   459
Sunrise House Chinese Restau-
   rant   422
Super 8 Motel   381
Suter's   266
Swannanoaa   213
Sweeney's Curious Goods   285
Sweet Adelines   232
Sweet Briar College   56, 488
Sweet Chalybeate   78
Swimming   122

T

T.G.I.F   274
T.S. Eways   284
Tanglewood Mall   37
Tastings   414
Tavern   302
Tavern at the Boar's Head Inn   434
Tazewell Area Chamber of Commerce
   & Visitors Center   514
Tazewell County   510
Tazewell County Fair   513
Texas Steak House   418
Texas Tavern   399
Thanksgiving at Wintergreen   196
The 1817 Antique Inn   341
The Boar's Head Inn & Sports
   Club   172
The Frame Gallery   208
The Roanoke Express
   Hockey Roanoke, Inc.   174
The Rotunda   240
Theater Wagon, Inc.   213
Theatre Arts Dept.   251
Theatre at Washington   228
Theatre B   225
Third St. Coffeehouse   433
Thomas Jefferson Birthday
   Commemoration   178
Thomas Jefferson Center for Historic
   Plants   237
Thomas Jefferson Visitors Center   238
Thomas Jefferson's Tomatoe
   Faire   189
Thornrose House   320
Three O Nine First Street   399
Tingler's Mill   30

To the Rescue   35
To the Rescue National Exhibition   35,
   221
Toms Creek Estates   450
Top of Virginia Building Associa-
   tion   440
Top Rail   434
Totier Creek Vineyard   157
Touch the Earth   268
Town and Country Motor Lodge on
   Highway   516
Town Hall   228
Trading Post   279
Traditional Frontier Festival   191, 211
Traditions of Christmas   197
Transportation   469
Traveller Clinic   479
Travelodge - Roanoke North   368
Trax   435
Trebark Outfitters   276
Troutdale   506
Troutville Antique Mart   29, 274
Troutville Fire Station   274
Trudy's Antiques   276
Tuesday Evening Concert Series   232
Tully's Restaurant & Pub   431
Tultex Mill Outlet   286, 499
Tuskegee Institute   249
Tuttle & Spice General Store
   Museum   205
Twelve O'Clock Knob   36

U

U.S. Army Corps of Engineers   517
Uncle Bill's Treasures   292
United Coal Company   509
United Express   470
universities   483
University Cemetery   97
University of Virginia   240, 487
University of Virginia Department of
   Drama   235
University of Virginia Football,
   Basketball   170
University of Virginia Medical
   Center   479
University Transit Service   475
University Village   465
University-Rockbridge Symphony
   Orchestra   215
Upstairs, Downstairs,   294
USAir   470

V

Valentine Craft Show   177
Valentine's Day Weekend   177
Valley Country   434
Valley Crafters   264
Valley MetroGreater Roanoke Transit
   Company   474
Valley Pike Inn   257, 426
Valley Program for Aging Services,
   Inc.   457, 468
Valley View   467
Vanucci's Italian Cuisine   400
Verandah   300
Verona Flea Market   270
Veterans Affairs Medical Center   478

Victor Huggins Gallery 219
Victoria and Albert Inn 509
Village Accents 287
Village Inn 389
Villager Antiques 266
Vinton 39
Vinton Dogwood Festival 182
Vinton July 4th Celebration 188
Vinton's Folklife Festival 40
Virginia Air Pollution Control
 Board 102
Virginia Apparel Outlet 288
Virginia Association of Realtors 438
Virginia Aviation, 471
Virginia Baptist Hospital 479
Virginia Born & Bred 274
Virginia Building 296
Virginia Center for the Creative
 Arts 242
Virginia Center for the Creative
 Arts, 55
Virginia Chili Cook-off 181
Virginia Commission of Game and
 Inland Fisheries 507
Virginia Creeper Trail 116, 508
Virginia Division of Tourism 474
Virginia Etna Springs 36
Virginia Fall Foliage Festival 194
Virginia Festival of American
 Film 50, 194, 241
Virginia Garlic Festival 195
Virginia Governor's Cup 142
Virginia Handcrafts, Inc 285
Virginia Heritage Weekend 194
Virginia High School Coaches
 Association All-Star 55
Virginia Highland Community
 College 506
Virginia Highland Llamas 505
Virginia Highlands Festival 189, 510
Virginia Highlands Gateway Visitor's
 Center 505
Virginia Horse Center 173
Virginia Horse Festival 178
Virginia Kentucky District Fair 190
Virginia Made Shop 270
Virginia Mennonite Retirement
 Community 460
Virginia Metalcrafters Factory
 Showroom 271
Virginia Military Institute 93, 486
Virginia Military Institute and
 Museum 95
Virginia Mountain Outfitters 26, 136
Virginia Museum of Natural
 History 499
Virginia Museum of Transporta-
 tion 223
Virginia Mushroom Festival 15, 180
Virginia Polo Center 171
Virginia Poultry Festival 180
Virginia School of the Arts 55, 245
Virginia Special Olympics 177
Virginia Tech 68, 490
Virginia Tech Airport 473
Virginia Tech Duck Pond 253
Virginia Tech Hokie Basketball 171
Virginia Tech Hokie Football 171
Virginia Trout Company 83
Virginia Wine Marketing Program 149
Virginia Wine Museum 236
Virginian 415
Virginia's Explore Park 223

Visitor's Center 285
VMI Museum 215
Volunteer Meals on Wheels -
 Harrisonburg 457
Volunteer Programs, Councils on
 Community Service 454

W

Waccamaw Pottery 277
Wades Mill 274
Walton House 436
Waltons Mountain Museum 231
War Between the States 85
War Memorial Pool 122
Ward's Rock Cafe 400
Warm Hearth Village Retirement
 Community 468
Warm Springs Spa 99
Warren County 40
Warren Memorial Hospital 476
Warren Rifles Confederate
 Museum 92
Warren-Sipe Museum 94
Washington & Lee University 95, 485
Washington, Booker T. 249
Washington County 508
Washington County Fair 510
Washington County Fair and Burley
 Festival 193
Washington County Park 509
Washington's Office Museum 204
Waterwheel Restaurant 430
Waynesboro 21
Waynesboro Board of Realtors 444
Waynesboro Community
 Hospital 477
Waynesboro Department of Parks and
 Recreation 456
Waynesboro Players 213
Waynesboro Village Factory
 Outlets 271
Wayside Inn and Restaurant 14, 387
Wayside Theatre 14, 202
Westminster Canterbury 467
Westminster Canterbury of the Blue
 Ridge 466
Westminster Organ Concert
 Series 232
Westminster-Canterbury 458
Westover Hills 450
Westvaco Corporation 138
Westvaco Paper Mill 77
Wharf Gallery 209
Whetstone Ridge 108
Whimsies 284
White Horse Antiques 292
White Oak Run 114
White's Mill 508
Whitetop Mountain Maple
 Festival 177
Whitetop Mountain Sorghum and
 Molasses Festival 196
Whitey Taylor's Franklin County
 Speedway, 65
Widow Kip's Bed and Breakfast and
 Antique Shop 265
Widow/Widowers Support
 Group 463
Wilderness Battlefields 45
Wilderness Road Museum 76, 98
Wilderness Road Regional

Museum 256
Wilderness Trail 69
Wilderness Trail Festival 192, 195
Wildflour Cafe and Catering 401
Wildflower Weekend 180
Willa Cather 12
Williams Corner Bookstore 284, 435
Willow Grove Inn 335, 404
Willson-Walker House 392
Wilson Warehouse 29
Winchester 12, 438
Winchester Medical Center 476
Winchester Regional Airport 472
Wine and Cheese Festival 182
Wine Festival 192
Wineries 149
Winridge Bed & Breakfast 353
Wintergreen Mountain Resort 45,
 144, 299, 377, 448
Winton Country Club 56
Wise County 518
Wise County Chamber of
 Commerce 521
Wise Fall Fling 196
Wittle League Hall of Fame 513
Wolf Creek Golf Club 505
Wolftrap Antiques 265
Women's colleges 484
Woodberry Forest 493
Woodberry Inn 499
Woodland 292
Woodlane Craft Shop 295
Woodrow Wilson Museum and
 Birthplace 211
Woodstock 16
Woodstock Museum 16, 205
Woodstone Meadows Stable 134
Words and Music Irish Cafe 503
Wythe Arts Council 503
Wythe County 503
Wythe County Community
 Hospital 502
Wythe County Gun Show and Flea
 Market 182
Wythe Raceway 504
Wytheville 502
Wytheville Community College 502
Wytheville Convention & Visitors
 Bureau 502
Wytheville State Fish Hatchery 504

X

XYZ Cooperative Gallery 251

Y

Yellow Poplar Splashdam 516
Youth Orchestra of Charlottesville-
 Albemarle 232

Z

Zib's Country Connection 265
Zoos 162

Holiday Inn®

University Area of Charlottesville

$10 off First Night of Occupancy
(not applicable with any other discounts)

(804) 293-9111

COME JOIN US FOR SOME REAL
DOWN HOME COOKIN' & SOUTHERN HOSPITALITY!

Come Stop In...Enjoy Our Delicious Dishes & World Famous
Virginia Diner Gourmet Peanuts, Served Up With Genuine Southern Hospitality!

Buy One Meal With This Coupon & Get A Second Meal
For 1/2 Price

(Second Meal Must Be Of Equal Or Lesser Value - Expires 8/31/94)

One coupon per book order please.

$1.00 Off
Any Insiders' Guide®

Charleston, SC • Charlotte, NC • Civil War Sites In The Eastern Theater (Fall '93)
• Lexington, KY (Spring '94) • Myrtle Beach, SC (Fall '93) • North Carolina's Crystal Coast
and New Bern • Orlando, FL • Richmond, VA • The Outer Banks of NC • The Triangle
(NC) • Virginia Beach/Norfolk, VA • Virginia's Blue Ridge • Washington DC (Fall '93)
• Williamsburg, VA • Wilmington, NC (Spring '94)

Mail this coupon and $11.95 (normally $12.95) plus $2.50
postage & handling to: Insiders' Guides®, Inc.
P.O. Box 2057, Mantco, NC 27954 or call 1-800-765-2665.

THE
INSIDERS'®
→**GUIDE**←

*To Virginia's
Blue Ridge*

Offer subject to modification by supplier without notice.
Unless otherwise stated expires: 2/1/95

THE
INSIDERS'®
→**GUIDE**←

*To Virginia's
Blue Ridge*

Offer subject to modification by supplier without notice.
Unless otherwise stated expires: 2/1/95

THE
INSIDERS'®
→**GUIDE**←

*To Virginia's
Blue Ridge*

Offer subject to modification by supplier without notice.
Unless otherwise stated expires: 2/1/95